D0420005

August 1963

'Four frenzied Little Lord Fauntleroys who are earning £5,000 a week'

Shout! The True Story of the Beatles

One of the greatest stories in the history of popular entertainment came to a brutal end when, in December 1980, a hail of bullets ended the life of John Lennon, founder member and wayward leader of the Beatles.

In *Shout!*, Philip Norman recreates the Beatle phenomenon—recalling how John, Paul, George and Ringo rose to international fame and how the eventual collapse of Apple Corps reduced a billion-dollar empire to squalor, anger and suspicion.

'Fascinating' *Financial Times*

'The definitive Beatles biography' *Publishers Weekly*

'The fullest and sharpest Beatles history so far' *New Society*

'A story that still, no matter how carefully documented, seems unbelievable' *Time*

SHOUT!

The True Story of the Beatles

PHILIP NORMAN

CORGI BOOKS
A DIVISION OF TRANSWORLD PUBLISHERS LTD

SHOUT! THE TRUE STORY OF THE BEATLES

A CORGI BOOK 0 552 11961 X

Originally published in Great Britain by
Hamish Hamilton Ltd.

PRINTING HISTORY
Hamish Hamilton edition published 1981
Corgi edition published 1982

This book is set in 9½ pt. Baskerville

Corgi Books are published by Transworld Publishers Ltd.,
Century House, 61–63 Uxbridge Road,
Ealing, London, W5 5SA

Printed and bound in Great Britain by
Cox & Wyman Ltd, Reading

To Helen

Contents

PART FOUR: WASTING

EPILOGUE

Acknowledgements

The author and publisher would like to acknowledge gratefully all those whose copyright photographs are reproduced in this volume:

Colin Hanton, page 1; Dick Matthews, page 2; Jurgen Vollmer, page 3 (top); Sutcliffe family, page 3 (bottom); Dick Matthews, page 4 (all); Rex Features (photographer Dezo Hoffmann), page 5 (both); Rex Features (photographer Dezo Hoffmann), page 6 (bottom); Rex Features (photographer Dezo Hoffmann), page 8; Rex Features (photographer Dezo Hoffmann), page 9 (top); Keystone Press, page 12 (both); United Press International, page 14 (bottom); Camera Press (photographer Bruce McBroom), page 15 (top); Topix, page 15 (bottom); Topix, page 16.

We would also like to thank Northern Songs Ltd. for the three lines from the LP Abbey Road, 'The love you take, Is equal to the love, You make'; and for the line 'All the lonely people' from Eleanor Rigby.

Every effort has been made to acknowledge all those whose photographs have been used in this volume but, if there have been any omissions in this respect, we apologise and will be pleased to make the appropriate acknowledgement in any future editions.

PROLOGUE

December 1980

'He kept me from dying so many times'

In New York, it was now just after midnight. The assassin and his victim had each been taken into custody. People were already massing, in an atmosphere of stunned quiet, opposite the big, old, neo-Gothic archway into the Dakota building. Britain, five hours ahead over the time zones, still knew nothing. In Britain, only dozing security guards and pre-dawn travellers heard, via the BBC Overseas Service, an announcement which even the clipped, old-fashioned newsreader's voice could barely authenticate. John Lennon had been shot outside his New York apartment. John Lennon was dead.

The shock, when Britain awoke to it, had an eerie quality, as of time cut suddenly from underfoot. It was the dubious achievement of the Seventies to turn sudden, senseless murder into a commonplace, scarcely noticeable event. Yet here was an emotion, vast and simultaneous, felt in one kindred flow of horror by all for whom John Lennon's music, and the Beatles', had become a release—a refuge even—from the brutal recent decade. Strangers talked; old friends broke telephone silence to remind themselves when last they had felt at one like this. Not since Kennedy was killed, they said. Not since the murder of Martin Luther King. Not since a day back in 1967, that summer drenched in heat and acid sparkle, when a million heads swam together at the behest of Sergeant Pepper's Lonely Hearts Club Band.

In TV and radio newsrooms, the tributes began to take hurried shape. Bulging file envelopes were brought up from cuttings libraries, their tattered contents spread and quickly sifted. Errors uncorrected 15 years ago became brand new errors for tonight's bulletin and tomorrow morning's feature page. 'At the age of eight, John Lennon saw his mother knocked down by a car and killed . . .' '. . . he was brought up by his Aunt Mimi in a tough working-class district of Liverpool . . .'

Two hours had elapsed since Mark David Chapman—his full name in use, as with all notable killers—yielded up his signed autograph book, his cassettes of Beatles music and his .38 calibre revolver. Across the time-gap, near Bournemouth, dawn was just breaking over Poole Harbour. The half-tame seagull that Aunt Mimi calls Albert strutted over the patio, waiting to be fed by the lean, practical, occasionally uproarious woman who John resembled in so many ways and from whom he inherited not inconsiderable virtues.

John bought this harbour-side bungalow for Mimi long ago in the Sixties, after fan madness had made Liverpool uninhabitable. He found her one night in tears, crumpled on the front staircase, and told her to choose a new house anywhere in England. Mimi lives alone, untroubled but for the occasional pleasure-launch microphone, announcing 'There's John Lennon's aunt's house', and the regular sudden rings at her front-door bell. Mimi, seeing the shapes through the frosted glass, always knows what to expect. Another group of girls, from America, Australia or Japan, following the well-beaten trail of Beatle monuments and shrines. Brusque and soft-hearted, Mimi scolds them and invites them in, just as she once invited in Paul McCartney and George Harrison. Often she puts them up overnight, in the spare room with the little bed whose significance they do not dream. 'I say quite casually, "That used to be John's bed, you know." Oh, you should *see* their faces!'

The bungalow is not luxurious. It is, like Mimi's house in Liverpool, a comfortable, spotless home where feet do better to be wiped. On the television set, a photograph of John in his Quarry Bank school cap hides the place once occupied by his MBE medal. A bureau drawer still contains the little drawings and verses, written on the blue, ruled paper of childhood, which Mimi kept there even after the world had hailed their erratic brilliance. Near the patio window stands the room's single pretentious object: a cocktail cabinet shaped like an antique globe. Asprey's, the Bond Street silversmiths, supplied several such globes to Beatle households in the era when spending money had no limit and its charm was already dwindling fast.

Mimi awoke on 9 December and switched on her radio to hear someone talking about John on the *Today* show. She was not perturbed, not even surprised. She thought what she used to when he was at Quarry Bank and the headmaster's office would telephone; the same vexed, half-smiling thought as so many times down the years. 'Oh Lord—what's he done *now*?'

The crowds that gathered, the following Sunday, opposite Lime Street station in Liverpool, and in Central Park, New York, held a requiem for more than the thin-nosed, impudent boy whose wayward, soon-fatigued virtuosity jolted, entranced and exasperated his generation. The vigil was for John; the farewell was to all the Beatles. A decade after their partnership officially ended, and the magic entity split into four all-too-human fragments, rumours of a second coming had persisted—even strengthened. In 1980 even more than in 1963, the world seemed to be waiting for the Beatles.

The four had long since become reconciled within themselves. There were partial reunions, as when Ringo made an album with Paul and George playing on different tracks. Each year or so, Sid Bernstein, the new York promoter, placed his familiar full-page newspaper advertisement, offering still more millions for a single concert by the Beatles reborn. It was an entreaty not just from the fans; it came also from international charities and relief organisations, suspecting that in the Beatles lay a power greater than theirs to benefit Mankind. This had its effect at least on Paul McCartney's tender social conscience, with the series of London concerts he organised early in 1980 for the Kampuchean refugees. George Harrison and Ringo Starr were both reportedly willing to appear with Paul on stage. John, in New York, refused to be drawn, even after a personal appeal from the United Nations' Secretary-General. To John, the Beatles had benefited Mankind enough. He said as much, in the voice which so often used to bring Paul's schemes and fancies down to earth. 'We gave everything for 10 years. We gave *ourselves*. If we played now anyway, we'd just be four rusty old men.'

The crowds stood in Central Park, chanting songs that for thousands epitomised their youth, and for equivalent thousands predated consciousness, even birth. Some were here in February 1964, flinging themselves against similar Police barricades, that day of snow and madness when the Beatles came to the Plaza hotel. For some the climax occurred in 1967, when Sergeant Pepper's multi-coloured vaudeville show wove its way into a new American Dream. And there were the Seventies' children, nurtured on Beatles music despite the dynasties of glittering frauds that followed, despite the familiar yardstick of Rock hype that this or that merely successful group were 'bigger than the Beatles'. Even when million sellers became common currency, the Beatles outsold as well as eclipsed all others. Their music, that vast, nonchalant treasury, pours out in undiminished strength on record, on radio, in supermarkets, elevators; is hummed on the unconscious breath; is drummed by the fingertips of two continents. A New Yorker of 21 spoke for his whole insecure generation when he said: 'I came here for John. I can't believe he's dead. He kept me from dying so many times.'

In Liverpool, on that time-warped afternoon, 30,000 people filled the piazza of St. George's Hall, round the equestrian statues commemorating Queen Victoria and Prince Albert. The ruined imperial city, its abandoned river, its tormented suburban plain, knew an anguish greater even than the recession and unemployment which had laid Merseyside waste under bombardments more deadly than Hitler's blitz.

This crowd, too, stood hour after hour, chanting She Loves You in the dialect it was written for; scarcely conscious what a part the soot-blackened colonnade before them played in their heroes' earliest history. Across this same piazza in 1959, John, Paul, George and Stu Sutcliffe staggered with the carnival floats they had built for Allan Williams's Mersey Arts Ball. Downhill from here, a brand-new shopping 'precinct' leads into Whitechapel. What used to be NEMS' shop is a branch of Rumbelows, still selling electrical goods and records, though shrunken by a false ceiling. At the edge, you can see up to the old high ceiling, still covered with Brian Epstein's tasteful collage of album sleeves.

It is just across the road, as Brian discovered, that Mathew Street begins. Some say the Cavern Club is down there even now, intact under the car park that abolished it. Further along in a garage entrance rests a tribute which Liverpool, somehow, never got around to erecting—four bronze-laminated Beatle faces left leaning behind the bumpers of an Austin 1100. There is only Arthur Dooley's inn-sign sculpture overhead, honouring 'Four Lads Who Shook the World'. Underneath, on this Sunday, little love notes were stuck to the wall. Single flowers lay sodden on the unchanging cobblestones.

The Beatles eventually ruled over time itself. Epoch after epoch is personified by a guitar chord they had discovered or a shirt collar with a new fastening; their album covers are the portrait gallery of an age. They could not, on their own, put an end to their existence. That required the strength of pure random lunacy, of a mind perhaps unhinged by worship of them. So now, suddenly, stunningly, in the death of their tetchy, honest, foolish, incorruptible soul, the Beatles were seen to be no more. As dusk fell, in New York and Liverpool, candles flickered and smoked in cupped-together hands.

When the candles blew out, only the music was left. Only myths and rumours, multiplying stronger than ever around this scarcely-imaginable, true story.

PART ONE

Wishing

October 1964

'He was the one I'd waited for'

John Lennon was born on 9 October 1940, during one of the fiercest night raids by Hitler's Luftwaffe on Liverpool. All summer, after tea, people would switch on their wireless sets at low volume, listening, not to the muted dance music but to the sky outside their open back doors. When the music cut off, before the first siren went, you knew that the bombers were returning.

Liverpool paid a heavy price for its Naval shipyards, and for the miles of docks where convoys stood making ready to brave the North Atlantic. The city was Britain's last loophole for overseas food supplies. Night after night, with geometric accuracy, explosions tore along the seaming of wharves and warehouses and black castle walls, and over the tramlines into streets of friendly red back-to-back houses, of pubs and missions and corner dairies with cowsheds behind. During the worst week, so many ships lay sunk along the Mersey, there was not a single berth free for incoming cargo. But in Lime Street, the Empire Theatre carried on performances as usual. Sometimes the whole audience would crowd out into the foyer to look across the black acropolis of St. George's Hall, to a sky flashing white, then dark again as more bombs pummelled the port and the river.

Mimi Stanley had always worried about her younger sister, Julia. She worried about her especially tonight with Liverpool aflame and Julia in labour in the Oxford Street maternity home. When news of the baby came by telephone, Mimi set out on foot from the Stanley house in Newcastle Road. 'I ran two miles. I couldn't stop thinking, "It's a boy, it's a boy. He's the one I've waited for."'

She held John in her arms 20 minutes after he was born. His second name, Julia said—in honour of Great Britain's guardian—would be Winston. Just then a landmine fell directly outside the hospital. 'But my sister stayed in bed,' Mimi says, 'and they put the baby under the bed. They wanted me to go into the basement but I wouldn't. I ran all the way back to Newcastle Road to tell father the news. "Get under shelter," the wardens were shouting. "Oh be quiet," I told them. Father was there, and I said, "It's a boy and he's beautiful, he's the best one of all." Father looked up and said: "Oh heck, he *would* be."'

Mimi's and Julia's father was an official with the Glasgow and Liverpool Salvage Company. He was aboard the salvage tug which tried to raise the submarine *Thetis* from her deathbed in Liverpool Bay. He had five daughters and brought them up strictly, though he was often away from home salvaging ships. 'We loved Father,' Mimi says, 'but we liked it when he went away to sea and we girls could kick over the traces a bit. If ever there was a boy I had my eye on, I used to pray at night, "Please God, let no one be hurt but let there be a wreck."'

Mimi was slender, brisk and dark, with fine cheekbones like a Cherokee. Julia was slim, auburn-haired, more conventionally pretty. Both loved laughter, but Mimi insisted there should be sense in it. 'Oh, Julia,' she would endlessly plead, 'be *serious*.' Julia could never be serious about anything.

Her marriage to Freddy Lennon in 1938 had been the least serious act of her life. She met Freddy one day in Sefton Park, and commented on the silly hat he wore. To please her, Freddy sent it skimming into the lake. She started bringing him home, to her whole family's great dismay. He was only a ship's waiter, erratically employed: he preferred, in the nautical term for malingering, to 'swallow the anchor'. Julia married him on an impulse at Mount Pleasant Register Office, putting down her occupation as 'cinema usherette' because she knew how it would annoy her father. 'I'll never forget that day,' Mimi says. 'Julia came home, threw a piece of paper on the table and said, "There, that's it. I've married him."'

When war broke out in 1939, Freddy was aboard a passenger liner berthed in New York. The next Julia heard, he had been locked away with the internees on Ellis Island. Later still, he turned up in North Africa. He returned home briefly in 1940 and 1942, then disappeared, it seemed, for good. The shipping line felt obliged to terminate the wages they had been paying direct to Julia.

All her four sisters took a hand in caring for the new baby. But one sister cared specially—the one who, having no babies of her own, ran through the air raid to hold him. From the moment John could talk, he would say, 'Where's Mimi? Where's Mimi's house?'

'Julia had met someone else, with whom she had a chance of happiness,' Mimi says. 'And no man wants another man's child. That's when I said I wanted to bring John to Menlove Avenue to live with George and me. I wouldn't even let him risk being hurt or feeling he was in the way. I made up my mind that I'd be the one to give him what every child has the right to—a safe and happy home life.'

The fires ceased falling on Liverpool. The city, though cratered like a Roman ruin, returned to its old majestically confident commercial life. St. George's Hall, badly scarred, still stood within its columns, between equestrian statues of Victoria and Albert. Along the docks, the overhead railway remained intact, passing above the funnels and warehouses and branching masts, the horse-drawn wagons and clanking, shuffling 'Green Goddess' Liverpool trams. Business resumed in the streets lined by statues and colonnades and Moorish arches and huge public clocks. At the Pier Head, that broad river front, congregations of trams drew up between the Mersey and its three grey, soaring waterside temples; to the Cunard Company, the Docks and Harbour Board and the Royal Liver Insurance Company. The 'Liver building' was still there, its twin belfries, higher than the seagulls, crowned with two silhouettes which every Liverpool child learns to look for—the skittish, somehow volatile and questing 'Liver birds'.

Liverpool was still business and banking and insurance, and ships. From the southern headland, under rings of tall cranes, came the rhythmic clout of Cammell Laird's yard where they built the *Alabama*, the *Mauretania*, the *Ark Royal*, the *Thetis*. Across from Birkenhead, brisk river ferries crossed the path of ocean liners, warships, merchantmen and the smaller fry of what was still Europe's busiest shipping pool. Ever and again, from a slipway on the broad river bend, some fresh ungarnished hull would slide backward, and ride there, free of dragchains, while tug whoops mingled with cheers from the bank.

Liverpool was docks and ships and as such indistinguishable in Britain's northern industrial fogs but for one additional, intermittent product. Liverpool was where music-hall comedians, like Tommy Handley, Arthur Askey and Robb Wilton, came from. Some elixir in a population mixed from Welsh and Irish, and also lascar and Chinese, and uttered in the strange glottal dialect that simultaneously seems to raise derisive eyebrows, had always possessed the power to make the rest of the country laugh.

Liverpool 'comics' were always preferred by the London theatrical agents. But there was a proviso. It was better for them to lose their Liverpool accents, and omit all references to the city of their origin. No one in London cared about a place so far to the north-west, so grey and sooty and old fashioned and, above all, so utterly without glamour as Liverpool.

*

Woolton, where John grew up, is a suburb three miles to the northeast, but further in spirit, from the Liverpool of docks and Chinatown and pub signs pasted round every street corner. From Lime Street, you drive uphill, past the grand old Adelphi Hotel, past the smaller back-street hotels with no pretence at grandeur, past the Baptist temples and Irish meeting halls, and grassed-over bomb sites, turned into eternal temporary car parks, lapping against some isolated little waterworks or church. Eventually you come to a traffic roundabout known by the name of its smallest tributary, Penny Lane. Woolton lies beyond, in wide dual carriageways with grass verges, and mock Tudor villas whose gardens adjoin parks, country clubs and golf courses.

Woolton, in fact, is such a respectable, desirable and featureless suburb as grows up close to any British industrial city. Until 1963, it had only one claim on history. A lord of the same name was Britain's wartime Minister of Food and inventor of the 'Woolton Pie', which boasted total, if unappetising, nourishment for only one old shilling a portion.

The country village which Woolton used to be is still distinguishable in narrow lanes winding up to its red sandstone Parish Church, St. Peter's. In 1945, it was still more village-like. It even had its own small dairy farm, to which people would go for fresh milk ladled straight from the churn. The farm and dairy belonged to George Smith, the quiet kind-hearted man whom high-spirited Mimi Stanley had married.

George and Mimi lived at 'Mendips', a semi-detached house in Menlove Avenue, round the corner from the dairy, almost opposite Allerton golf course. It was a solid, respectable 1930s bay-windowed villa with Tudor touches, like the wood panelled front hall where Spode and Royal Worcester dinner plates stood on exhibition. There was a 'morning room' where Mimi and Julia would tie the baby in his armchair with a scarf and bank him up with cushions to get the benefit of the sun in the big rear window. A man who worked for George at the dairy came in twice a week to look after the garden.

Julia had settled only a short bus journey away, at Spring Wood. Her man friend was a waiter in a Liverpool hotel, with children of his own. Every afternoon, she came across to her sister's to see John. He called her 'Mummy'; his aunt he called plain 'Mimi'. 'John said to me once when he was little, "Why don't I call *you* Mummy?" I said, "Well—you couldn't very well have *two* Mummies, could you?" He accepted that.'

From the moment Julia gave him to her, Mimi devoted her life to John. 'Never a day passed when I wasn't with him—just that one time a year when he went up to Scotland to stay with his cousins. And at night, for 10 years, I never crossed the threshold of that house. As I came downstairs, I'd always leave the light on on the landing outside his room. This little voice would come after me, "Mimi! Don't waste light."

'I brought him up strictly. No sweets—just one barley sugar at night—and no sitting around in picturedomes. He never wanted it. He'd play for hours in the garden in summer, in his little swimming trunks. I'd go to the butcher's for pheasants' feathers and I'd make him up like an Indian with gravy browning, and put lipstick for warpaint on his cheeks. And when he said his friends were dead, they *were* dead.

'He never had a day's illness. Only chicken pox. "Chicken pots", he called it. And he loved his Uncle George. I felt quite left out of that. They'd go off together, just leaving me a bar of chocolate and a note saying: "Have a happy day".'

Mimi, for all her briskness, liked nothing better than laughter. Julia had always known how to get her going so that she threw her head back and guffawed, slapping her knee. 'I was very slim in those days. Julia would come in in the afternoon and dance up to me, singing "O dem bones, dem bones—" She'd only got to lift her eyebrow and I'd be off.

'John was the same. I'd be battling with him. I'd send him out of the room, then I'd flop down exhausted in the big armchair next to the morning-room window. He'd crawl round on the path and pull faces at me through the window. He'd come at me like a monster, going "Woooo!" He could get me off just the same way Julia could.'

When John was four, Mimi sent him to Dovedale Primary School, near Penny Lane. She took him there each morning, and each afternoon met him at the bus stop, near Penny Lane roundabout. In his class at Dovedale Primary was a boy named Peter Harrison whose younger brother George sometimes came with their mother to meet the three-thirty outpouring from school.

John did well at Dovedale, learning to read by the age of four-and-a-half. He liked sport, especially running and swimming, but was inept at football. The discovery was made that he had chronically poor eyesight. His teachers thought that must be what made his English compositions so unusual. He changed almost every word into another one like it. Instead of 'funds', he would write 'funs'. He loved reading, especially Richmal Crompton's Just William stories about a lawless eleven-year-old. He loved writing and drawing and crayoning. Each Christmas, when Mimi took him to the pantomime at the Liverpool Empire, he would endlessly re-tell the experience in stories, poems and drawings. At the age of seven, he began writing books of his own. One of them was called *Sport and Speed Illustrated*; it had cartoons and drawings and a serial story ending: 'If you liked this, come again next week. It'll be even better.'

At about the same age, while playing on a rubbish tip, John encountered another seven-year-old with a pale pink and white face and fuzzy blond hair. The boy's name was Peter Shotton; his mother kept a small needlewoman's and grocery shop in Woolton village. The encounter quickly turned to combat. 'I'd found out his name was Winston,' Shotton says. 'I was calling out to him, "Winnie, Winnie . . ." He got me down on the ground with his knees on my shoulders. I said: "OK, go ahead and hit me. Get it over with." But he couldn't. He said: "OK, I'll let you off. Just don't call me that name again." I walked away, then I turned round and shouted, "Winnie, Winnie." He was so angry, he couldn't speak. Then I saw his face break into a smile.'

Pete Shotton and John Lennon became inseparable friends. Pete lived in Vale Road, just round the corner from Menlove Avenue. The addition of another Vale Road boy, a mutual acquaintance, named Nigel Whalley, added a new dimension. Three of them made enough for a gang.

Nigel went to school with Pete Shotton in Mosspits Lane. He also sang in the choir with John at St. Peter's, Woolton. He had often sat in the choirstalls in his white surplice, wriggling with laughter at things which the white-surpliced John dared to do. 'He'd steal the Harvest Festival fruit. And every time the Rector, Old Pricey, climbed into the pulpit, John used to say, "He's getting on his drums now." '

The gang grew to four with the arrival of another Dovedale boy, Ivan Vaughan. Thus constituted, it embarked on its career as the terror of Woolton. One of the earliest games was to climb a tree over the busy main road and dangle a leg down in the front of an approaching double-decker bus, then yank it back to safety in the nick of time. If your foot scraped the bus roof, that counted as extra points.

'John was always the leader,' Nigel Whalley says. 'He was always the one to dare you. He never cared what he said or did. He'd think nothing of putting a brick through the glass in a street lamp. He'd dare us to go with him and play on the Allerton golf course, trying to hit golf balls across Menlove Avenue. Once, the Police came and chased us off. We'd pick up these great clods of earth to chuck at the trains when they went into the tunnel at Garston. Something else was putting stuff on the tram rails to try to derail the trams.

'Shoplifting was another thing. We'd go into a sweetshop run by this little old lady. John'd point to things he said he wanted on the top shelf and, all the time, he'd be filling his pockets from the counter. He did the same at a shop that sold Dinky cars, in Woolton—opposite the Baths. He'd put a tractor or a little car in his pocket while the bloke was looking the other way. We went back to that same shop later on but, this time, John hadn't got his glasses on. He wouldn't understand why his fingers couldn't get at the Dinky cars. He couldn't see that the bloke had covered them over with a sheet of glass.

'We'd go to all the garden fêtes in the summer, get under tents and pinch stuff. People would come in, looking for their trays of cakes and buns that we'd eaten. We went to one fête organised by the nuns, and somehow John got hold of this robe and dressed himself up as a monk. He was sitting with some other monks on a bench, talking in all these funny words while we were rolling about under the tent, in tucks.

'Pete was a bit of a bully, always picking on me, so John used to look after me. Whatever he told me to do, I'd do it. "Whalloggs", he used to call me.'

Aunt Mimi approved of Nigel Whalley. His father was a police sergeant. Mimi thought him a wholesome influence.

At the age of 12, John left Dovedale Primary and started at Quarry Bank Grammar School, in Harthill Road, a mile or so from Menlove Avenue. Mimi, distrusting the school outfitter, got his Uncle George's tailor to make his new black blazer with its red and gold stag's head badge and motto, *Ex Hoc Metallo Virtutem* (From This Rough Metal We Forge Virtue). On his Raleigh 'Lenton' bicycle, he would toil up the long hill to school, past old sandstone quarries, long emptied and overgrown. Woolton sandstone built the Anglican cathedral, as well as the many mock-Elizabethan mansions in which Liverpool merchants indulged themselves at the height of their Victorian prosperity.

It was in a local timber baron's Tudoresque 'folly' that Quarry Bank Grammar School was founded in 1922. Despite its newness it was, by the time John arrived in 1952, as steeped in academic lore as any of Liverpool's ancient grammar schools. There was a house system; there were masters in gowns; there were prefects and canings. In later years, after it had produced two Socialist Cabinet Ministers—William Rodgers and Peter Shore—Quarry Bank came to be nicknamed 'The Eton of the Labour Party'.

John's Dovedale friend, Ivan Vaughan, had gone on to Liverpool Institute High School. Nigel Whalley was now at the Bluecoat School near Penny Lane. Pete Shotton was the only one of the Woolton gang who accompanied him to Quarry Bank. 'We went through it together like Siamese twins,' Pete says. 'We started in our first year at the top and gradually sank together into the sub-basement.

'I remember the first time we both went to be caned. I was really terrified. John wasn't—or if he was, he didn't show it. We were both waiting outside the headmaster's study. John started telling me the cane would be kept in a special case, with a velvet lining and jewels all round it. I was in tucks, even though I was so scared.

'John went in first for the cane. I could hear it—swipe, swipe. Then he came out. What I didn't realise was that there was a little vestibule you had to go through before you got into the head's study. John came out through this little vestibule—though I didn't know it—crawling on all fours and groaning. I was laughing so much when I went in that I got it even worse than he had.'

In John's first year at Quarry Bank, Mimi's husband, Uncle George, died suddenly after a haemorrhage. It was a shock to the whole family to lose the quiet, hard-working dairy farmer who got up every morning without complaint to do the milking and whose only unusual demand of Mimi was his two breakfasts a day. Uncle George had been John's ally when he was in disgrace, smuggling buns upstairs to him behind Mimi's back. Uncle George had bought him the mouth organ John carried in his blazer pocket and tinkered on for hours when he ought to have been doing homework.

Mimi was left alone to cope with a boy whose will was now almost the equal of hers and who, by his thirteenth birthday, seemed to glory in idleness and lawlessness and wasting the opportunities he had been given. From his first moderately virtuous year at Quarry Bank, he gravitated, in Pete Shotton's company, to the bottom of the 'C' stream, and made no attempt to rise again thereafter. The two were perpetually in detention or being sent to the headmaster's study for a caning. Frequently, their exploits were serious enough to be reported to their homes. 'I used to dread the 'phone going at ten in the morning,' Mimi says. 'A voice would come on, "Hello, Mrs. Smith. This is the secretary at Quarry Bank . . ." "Oh Lord." I'd think. "What's he done now?" '

'It was mostly skyving,' Pete Shotton says. 'Not doing the things the others did. We were like wanted men. We were always on the run.'

Rod Davis, a studious boy in the 'A' stream, had watched John and Pete's double act since they were seven-year-olds sitting in a ring at St. Peter's Sunday School and John had managed to put a piece of chewing gum into the teacher's hand so that all her fingers stuck together. 'I'd always known him and Pete as the school thugs, dragging on a cigarette they'd got behind their backs, or running into Marks and Spencers and shouting "Woolworths!" '

'John used to turn Religious Knowledge into chaos,' Pete Shotton says. 'One day he cut out all the shiny white cardboard bits from a lot of Weetabix packets and made dog collars for the whole class. When the teacher, McDermott, came in, he was so angry, he couldn't speak. Then he had to start laughing. He made us wear them for the rest of the class.'

The school punishment book records for what diversity of crime J. Lennon and P. Shotton were beaten: 'failing to report to school office'; 'insolence'; 'throwing blackboard duster out of window'; 'cutting class and going awol'; 'gambling on school field during house match'.

'We were in detention once, clearing up the sports field,' Pete Shotton says. 'I found this big envelope full of dinner tickets. You used to pay a shilling a day for a ticket to have your school dinner. These were the used ones that somebody had accidentally dropped. When John and I counted them, we found we'd got the whole school's dinner tickets—about 1,500 of them. And they were worth a shilling each. We sold them off for sixpence each. We were rich. We even gave up shoplifting while that was going on.'

Even John's talent for writing and drawing failed to earn him any good marks or exam distinctions. Only in the last 40 minutes of every day, in the unsupervised 'prep' period, would he show what ability he was relentlessly wasting. He would fill old exercise books and scraps of paper with his cartoons and word play and verse. His nonsense sagas, 'The Land of the Lunapots', and 'Tales of Hermit Fred', were passed to Pete Shotton first, then enjoyed wide under-the-desk circulation. 'He'd do all these caricatures of the masters,' Pete says. 'We'd stick them on bits of cereal packets and make a stall at the school fête where people could throw darts at them. We handed in more money than any other stall—and we still had five times as much in our pockets.'

Often, they would cut school together. They would go on the bus to Spring Wood to see Julia, John's mother—now married to the nervous waiter the boys called 'Twitchy', and with a young son of her own. 'Julia didn't mind if we'd sagged off school,' Pete Shotton says. 'She used to wear these old woollen knickers on her head while she did the housework. She'd open the door to us with the knicker legs hanging down her back. She didn't care. She was just like John.'

John, as he grew older, grew more and more fascinated by this pretty auburn-haired woman, so much more like an elder sister than a mother. For Julia did not echo the dire warnings given by Aunt Mimi and Quarry Bank. Julia encouraged him to live for the present, as she did, and for laughter and practical jokes. 'She'd do these tricks just to make us laugh,' Pete says. 'She'd put on a pair of glasses with no glass in the frames. She'd stand talking to a neighbour and suddenly stick her finger through where the lens ought to have been, and rub her eye.'

Julia thought as John and Pete did, and told them the things they wanted to hear. She told them not to worry about school or homework or what their lives might have in store.

Jim McCartney was no stranger to female admiration. During the 1920s he led the Jim Mac Jazz Band, dapperly outfitted in dinner jackets, paper shirt fronts and detachable cuffs which could be bought then for a penny per dozen. A photograph taken at the time shows a group of girls in silver shoes and stockings, their hair pertly fringed and bobbed, reclining with formal abandon on a dance floor around the Jim Mac drum kit. Among them sits the bandleader, with his close-cropped ears, his twitchy wing collar, his big, soulful, somehow familiar-looking saucer eyes.

Jim was a cotton salesman working for Hannay's of Chapel Street, Liverpool, an old-established firm of cotton brokers and purveyors to the Manchester mills. His position, for a working-class boy, was a good one; he had risen to it by neatness, diligence and a genuine flair for selling, though he lacked the ruthlessness which might have taken him higher. He had taught himself to play the piano by ear, as any young man did who wished for social grace. The Jim Mac Jazz Band performed at socials and works dances, occasionally even in cinemas. Their biggest engagement was providing incidental music for a silent Hollywood epic, *The Queen of Sheba*. When a chariot race began on the screen, Jim Mac and the boys played Thanks for the Buggy Ride. During the Queen of Sheba's death scene, they played Horsy, Keep Your Tail Up.

Perhaps there were too many of those girls in silver shoes and stockings around the drum kit. At all events, Jim McCartney went through his thirties as a bachelor, working at the Cotton Exchange, playing his spare-time dance music, content for his family to be the hospitable reflection of his married sisters, Millie and Jin.

At the very point where he seemed resigned to bachelorhood, and the impending war seemed to confirm it, Jim McCartney proposed marriage to Mary Mohin. She, like Jim, was of the Liverpool Irish, a slender and gently-spoken woman employed by Liverpool Corporation as a district health visitor. Herself in her early thirties, Mary could override the faint objection that Jim did not share her membership of the Catholic Church. They were married in 1941, shortly before Jim's fortieth birthday.

Exempted from military service by partial deafness, he had been transferred from Hannay's to munitions work with Napier's, the firm which produced the Sabre aircraft engine. On 18 June 1942, while Jim was fire watching, Mary gave birth to a son in Walton General Hospital. She had worked there once as nursing sister in charge of the maternity ward, and so received the luxury of a private room. The baby was perfect, with large, round eyes that darkened in time to the hue of his father's. Such was Mary's love for Jim that the more famous saint's name did not receive precedence. The baby was christened James Paul.

His first home was furnished rooms in Anfield, not far from the mass graves where the dead from the dockland blitz had been buried. Jim, no longer needed for munitions work, had left Napier's and become an inspector in the Corporation's Cleansing Department. His job was to follow the dustmen, seeing that they did not skimp their round. The work was badly paid and, to supplement Jim's earnings, Mary returned to her former job as a health visitor. After her second son, Michael, was born in 1944, she took up full-time midwifery.

The process had already begun which was to gouge out the old, shabby, vibrant heart of Liverpool, flattening its bombed streets and scattering their inhabitants wide across an arid suburban plain. Communities whom Hitler could not displace were now induced, by the hundred thousand, to migrate to new estates, dumped down amid transplanted industry, and isolated by walls of dingy open air.

Mary McCartney became a domiciliary midwife on one of the several estates built around Speke's new motor factory settlement. The rent-free council house in Western Avenue helped to reduce the strain on Jim's tiny wage from the Corporation. The disadvantage was that Mary had to be available 24 hours a day. Her kindness and patience became a legend among people already suspecting they may have been forgotten by the authorities. Little gifts of plaster ornaments or somebody's sweet ration were always being brought to the McCartney's back door, or left shyly outside on the step.

Her own children, despite the constant pressure, received immaculate care. Jim, who had been somewhat unprepared for fatherhood—and somewhat dismayed by Paul's redness as a newborn baby—could only marvel at the ingenuity with which Mary found time, and money enough, to dress the boys beautifully and feed them with imaginative good sense. Her special concern was that they should speak well, not in broad Liverpool like other children on the estate.

Paul came to consciousness in an atmosphere of worship. His aunts and the neighbours loved him for his chubbiness, his large eyes and amiable, undespotic disposition. The arrival of a little brother, and potential rival, showed him the importance of maintaining popularity. He soon discovered that he possessed charm, and learned early how to put it to use. Though the boys did things together, and were together in normal boyish scrapes, it would invariably be Michael, the more impetuous and turbulent one, who received punishment. Jim McCartney, for all his mildness, was of the generation which believed in hitting children. Michael remembers being chastised by Jim while Paul, who had escaped, stood by, shouting, 'Tell him you didn't do it and he'll stop.' Where Michael would shout and cry, Paul, if his father hit him, showed no emotion. Later, he would go into his parents' bedroom and tear their lace curtains imperceptibly at the bottom.

Though Mary was a Catholic, she preferred to entrust the boys' education to Protestant schools. Paul started in Speke, at Stockton Road Primary. Michael joined him there and, when the classes became overcrowded, both were transferred to Joseph Williams Primary, Gateacre. Here the same contrast was revealed between them. Paul was quiet and law-abiding, and Michael, hotly argumentative. Where Michael found it difficult to absorb learning, Paul came top in almost every lesson with ease. He especially good at English composition and Art. His handwriting received praise for its clear regularity.

Money remained a difficulty, though the boys never knew it. Jim McCartney had left his job with the Corporation and gone back to cotton selling. This, however, was not the secure trade it had been in prewar days with Hannay's. After a hard week's travelling, Jim would be lucky to find £6 in his wage packet. Mary took a second domiciliary job on the Speke estate, necessitating a move from Western Avenue to another council house, in Ardwick Road. Her husband, worried at the long hours she worked, was relieved when she decided to give up midwifery and return to regular nursing. She became a school nurse, making rounds with school doctors in the Walton and Allerton district.

Bella Johnson met Mary at the central clinic from which both of them worked. A round, little, jolly woman, Bella, too, was finding it difficult to make ends meet. She had been widowed at the age of 36, with two small daughters to educate. This she had done so spectacularly well that one of them, Olive, now worked for the Law Society in Liverpool. The Law Society's offices were only a street away from the Cotton Exchange. On her way to work, Olive used to pass the time of day with Jim McCartney, not knowing that his wife and her mother were colleagues and friends.

Mrs. Johnson and Olive got to know the McCartneys well. Bella remembers a family contented and normal, irradiated by Mary's gentleness and strength. 'She was a beautiful person: it came from something deep inside her,' Olive says. 'Jim adored her. I remember how he'd sometimes tell us a story he'd picked up from the businessmen at the Cotton Exchange. If it was a bit off-colour, Mary used to look at him and say, "*Husband!*" '

Olive had a small car in which they would all go on weekend trips into the Cheshire countryside. She became a big sister to

Paul and Michael, joining in their games, rowing them in a skiff across the lake at Wilmslow. 'Mary always made us a special treat at tea time,' Mrs. Johnson says. 'I'll never forget them. Apple sandwiches with sugar.'

On Coronation Day, 1953, the Johnsons and McCartneys celebrated together at Ardwick Road. The boys had received their commemorative mugs and spoons, and Paul, in addition, had won a book as a Coronation essay prize. They watched, as people did all over Britain in one another's front parlours, the ceremonial flickering over a tiny, bluish television screen.

Michael McCartney sat at his mother's feet, as ever. 'He was the one you always felt you wanted to love and protect,' Olive says. 'With Paul, you loved him but you knew you'd never have to protect him.'

Paul passed the Eleven Plus examination without difficulty, and with sufficient distinction to receive a place at Liverpool Institute, the city's oldest grammar school. The honour entailed a long bus journey each day from Speke into Liverpool and up, behind the Anglican Cathedral, to Mount Street, where the Insitute's square portico juts out into steeply-plunging pavement. Founded in the 1830s as a Mechanics Institute for deserving artisans, the building had been later divided to form the grammar school and the College of Art. Behind the heavy wrought-iron gates was an interior unchanged since Victorian times, save that the gas lamps, over each classroom door, were no longer lit on winter afternoons. *Non nobis solum*, the school motto runs, *sed toti mundo nati*: 'Not for ourselves only but for the good of all the world.'

Among hundreds of boys, swarming through the green-distempered school thoroughfares, Paul McCartney was not conspicuous, nor wished to be. His black blazer was neat and his hair slicked flat with Brylcreem; he belonged to that co-operative species from which are recruited the collectors of exercise books and operators of window-poles; he was, more or less permanently, head boy in his form. With his classmates he was popular, if a little reserved. They called him, not by his surname or a nickname—just Paul. His close friend Ivan Vaughan was an exception to this attitude of noticeable deference.

He had been put into the 'A' stream, tending as he moved higher to specialise in history and languages. He found most lessons easy, and could get high marks even in Latin if he bothered to apply his mind. He was nonchalant about homework, an embarrassing obligation in a council estate where other boys could do what they pleased at night. On the morning bus into Liverpool, he could churn out an essay still impressive enough to receive commendation from his English master, 'Dusty' Durband. Mr. Durband, even so, was aware of the extent to which Paul relied on facility and bluff to see him through. It sometimes failed him, as when he had been given the task of preparing a talk about the Bodley Head edition of Stephen Leacock's works. Paul delivered an impromptu stream of non-sense about the Bodley Head's Elizabethan logo.

He knew what he wanted and, even then, would be satisfied with nothing less. When the Institute put on Shaw's *St. Joan* as its end-of-term play, Paul auditioned keenly for the part of Warwick. He did not get it, and had to be content with the minor role of an Inquisitor in the trial scene. The disappointment made him unusually fractious: Mr. Durband, the play's producer, remembers shouting in exasperation at the medievally-hooded figure which persisted in disrupting rehearsals.

In 1955, when Paul was 13, the McCartneys left Speke and its pallid factory smog. Jim had managed to get a council house in Allerton, one of Liverpool's nearer and better suburbs. It was a definite step up for the family to move into 20 Forthlin Road, a double show of semi-detached houses small and neat enough to pass for privately-owned villas. Mimi Smith's home in Woolton was only a mile or so away, if you cut across the golf course.

For some time, Mary had been troubled by a slight pain in her breast. She did not like to trouble the doctor for fear he would dismiss it as nurse's hypochondria. As she was now in her mid-forties, she and Jim philosophically concluded that 'the Change' must be to blame for the small lump that had appeared, the pain was not too great but would not seem to go away.

Paul and Michael were camping with the Boy Scouts that summer. The weather was very wet and cold, and Mary told Bella Johnson, her friend at the school clinic, that she was worried about the boys under canvas. So one afternoon, Olive took Mary and Jim in her car to visit them. On the way home, Mary was in such pain that she had to lie down on the back seat.

'When she got home, she went straight to bed,' Olive says. 'I went up later and found her crying. "Oh, Olive," she said to me, "I don't want to leave the boys *just* yet." '

After a few days' rest, she felt so much better, she began to think that, after all, the trouble was simply over-work. Then the pain returned, so severely that, at last, she consulted a specialist. He sent her at once into hospital—not Walton General but the old city 'Northern', so that he could keep a close eye on her. Breast cancer was diagnosed. She underwent an operation for mastectomy, which was not carried out: the cancer had already spread too far. Surgery hastened what had been taking place imperceptibly and, a few hours later, Bella and Olive Johnson received the news that Mary had died.

Jim McCartney's predicament was one calculated to crush a younger as well as wealthier man. At the age of 53, he found himself bereft of a loving, capable wife and faced with the task of caring for two adolescent boys, all on a wage which still had need of the extra Mary had earned. That, indeed, was the first thing 14-year-old Paul blurted out in the shock of his mother's loss. 'What are we going to do without her money?'

Mary was buried as a Catholic—the wish she had expressed to Jim on her deathbed. Paul and Michael were taken to stay with their Auntie Jin at Huyton, to spare them the funeral and the sight of their father's devastation. Mrs. Johnson and Olive moved in to Forthlin Road to be with Jim and to prepare him for the boys' return. Their task, at first, seemed hopeless. All he wanted, he kept saying, was to be with Mary.

July 1957

'Quarry Men, strong before our birth'

1956 was a worrying year for English parents. It seemed that something had gone seriously wrong with the Victorian age. The generation born after 1941, despite exterior differences, lived by much the same rules and values as their parents and their grandparents. It boiled down to a single phrase, the base of Victorianism—they 'had respect'. They had respect for their elders and their betters. They had respect for their country with its Empire, now Commonwealth; its God-given right to be called 'Great' Britain. Having just survived a World War, they had respect for politicians and soldiers. They had respect also for clergymen, policemen, schoolteachers and the Queen. And suddenly, in 1956, they realised that their children did not have respect for them.

The year was one of unparalleled national humiliation. It was the year that the British engaged with France in a ludicrous plan to invade Egypt and were foiled by, of all people, the Egyptians. After Suez, the world would never again function at the behest of British gunboats. We had become overnight a 'second-class power', barely noticed in the new, harsh glare of America and Russia's nuclear cohabitation.

The British language, meanwhile, had been invaded by certain bewildering new words. Of these, the most bewildering was 'teenager'. In Britain before 1956, there were no such things as teenagers. There were only children and grown-ups. Transition took place at 16 when boys put on tweed jackets like their fathers' and girls turned into matrons with 'twinsets' and 'perms'. Conscription, or 'National Service', for two years, completed the male maturing process. The only remission was given to university students, a minority, still largely 'upper class', and thus permitted to behave like hooligans on Boat Race night and other fixed ceremonial occasions.

But there now stalked the streets of Britain young men in clothes as outlandish as they were sinister. The costume, of velvet-trimmed drape jackets, frilled shirts and narrow trousers, was inspired partly by Edwardian fashion—hence the name

'Teddy Boy'—and partly by gunslingers and riverboat gamblers in Hollywood movies. Amid the drab uniformity of postwar Britain, they seemed utterly freakish. Their hair, in a land still Army-cropped, was scarcely believable. A greasy cockade flopped over the forehead, swept back past the ears with constant combing to form two flaps like the posterior of a duck. Their socks were luminous pink or orange. Their shoes had soles three inches thick. They were believed to carry weapons such as flick-knives, razors and bicycle chains. Their other, scarcely less threatening predilection, was for 'coffee bars' and 'Rock and Roll'.

Coffee bars, to the British of 1956, might just as well have been opium dens. They had sprung up all at once out of the country's Italian population, and also the sudden Fifties' craze for 'contemporary' design. They were dark and filled with basket chairs and foliage; they had names like 'La Lanterna' or 'La Fiesta'; they dispensed, from huge silver machines, a frothy fluid barely recognisable as the stuff which the British were accustomed to boil with milk in saucepans. They were the haunt of Teddy Boys and Teddy Girls, and of jukeboxes. Their jukeboxes united the Teddy-Boy contagion with that of Rock and Roll.

Rock and Roll, as every sensible Briton knew, was American madness such as one saw as a novelty item at the end of the weekly cinema newsreel. Sometimes it was pole-squatting, sometimes dance marathons, sometimes pie-eating contests. Now it was a young singer who did not sing but merely writhed about, pretending to play a guitar, and yet who aroused American female audiences to transports of ecstasy greater even than had Valentino, the screen lover, or Frank Sinatra, the crooner. His songs, or lack of them, and his 'suggestive movements', had scandalised America. When he appeared on American television, he was shown only from the waist up. His name was Elvis Presley. That, too, the British thought, could only happen in America.

Yet the madness seemed to be drifting this way. In 1955, a song called Rock Around The Clock had caused riots in several British cinemas during shows of a film called *Blackboard Jungle* —significantly, a study of juvenile crime. The singer, Bill Haley, and his 'group', the Comets, had afterwards visited Britain, arriving in London by boat train amid mob scenes unequalled since VE Night or the Coronation.

That had seemed to be a freak occurrence. The country settled back again to its former dull diet of Anglicised American dance-band music—of 'Light Orchestras', crooners named Dennis Lotis and Dickie Valentine, and 'novelty' songs about Italy or little Dutch dolls. Here, at least, there was a powerful guardian of morality and taste. The British Broadcasting Corporation, with its monopoly of all radio, continued to ensure that nothing was played save that in its own image and of its own cold custard consistency.

In February 1956, an Elvis Presley record called Heartbreak Hotel was released in Britain, on the hitherto respectable HMV label. Within days, it had smashed through the crooners and Light Orchestras and little Dutch dolls to first place in the Top Twenty records chart. It remained there for 18 weeks. Another by the same singer followed it, bearing the ludicrous title Blue Suède Shoes; then another, even surpassing that in ludicrousness, called Houn' Dog.

Britain's parents listened, so far as they were able, to the lyric, so far as it could be understood. The vocalist was exhorting some bystander, endlessly and incoherently, not to tread on his blue suède shoes. He was accusing the same bystander, with equal, mumbling persistence, of being a 'houn' dog'. A few people over 20 enjoyed the music, and even recognised it for what it was: an adaptation of American Blues, sharing the same honourable origins as Jazz. Presley was simply applying Blues intonation and phrasing to songs in the white cowboy, or Country and Western, idiom. He was, in other words, a white man who sang like a black man. The charges of obscenity were ironic. All Presley's Blues songs had been purged of their sexual and social content for the white audience's sensitive ears.

To Britain, as to America, the idea that a white man could sing like a black man was intrinsically lewd. It confirmed the malignant power of Rock and Roll music to incite young people, as jungle drums incited savages, to their newly-evidenced violence, promiscuity, disobedience and disrespect. To Britain, as to America, there was only one consolation. A thing so grotesque as Elvis Presley could not possibly last. They said of Rock and Roll what was said in 1914, when the Great War started. In six months, it would all be over.

The headmaster of Quarry Bank Grammar School, Liverpool, considered John Lennon and Peter Shotton to be the worst Teddy Boys among the pupils in his charge. Detentions, canings, even temporary expulsion seemed to have no effect on the insolent-faced, bespectacled boy and his fuzzy-haired companion, whose clothes conformed less and less to school regulation, and who now overtly gloried in their power to cause disturbance. A typical Lennon-Shotton incident occurred when the whole school went into Liverpool to see the film *Henry V* at the Philharmonic Hall. By ill luck, this had been preceded by a Donald Duck cartoon. One did not have to guess from whom, in the tittering auditorium, had come those cries of, 'There he is! There's old King Henry!'

For John, as for most 15-year-olds, Rock and Roll began as a curiosity manifest among slightly older boys. Pete Shotton and he, on their truant-playing days, would often hang around Liverpool, gaping at the full-dress Teddy Boys—mostly seamen on leave from the big ships—whose disregard for authority was on a scale far more gorgeous than theirs. When *Rock Around the Clock*, the first Bill Haley film, reached Liverpool, John went to see it but, to his disappointment, no riot happened. There was just this fat man in a tartan jacket with a kiss curl on his forehead, and saxophones and double basses just like any dance band.

Then, at the beginning of 1956, a friend played him Heartbreak Hotel. 'From then on,' his Aunt Mimi says, 'I never got a minute's peace. It was Elvis Presley, Elvis Presley, Elvis Presley. In the end I said, "Elvis Presley's all very well, John, but I don't want him for breakfast, dinner *and* tea."'

Mimi had been struggling for months to stop her charge from turning into a Teddy Boy. She still sent John to school in blazers that were tailor-made, and saw no reason why these should not do for all social occasions. 'Drainpipe' trousers and drape jackets were, as Mimi constantly affirmed, no kind of dress for a boy who went to Quarry Bank and whose grandfather had been a deep-sea pilot, one of the shipping world's white-collar dandies.

The trouble was that John now spent more and more time out of Mimi's sight with her sister, Julia, his real mother. Julia, as Mimi knew, was too easy-going to worry what John wore. Julia bought him coloured shirts and gave him money to have school trousers 'taken in'. He would leave Menlove Avenue, a nice Quarry Bank schoolboy and then, at Julia's, turn into a Teddy Boy as bad as any to be seen around the docks.

The stunning music that went with the clothes was available only with equal deviousness. John listened to it, as thousands did, under the bedclothes, late at night. Since the BBC would not broadcast Rock and Roll, the only source was Radio Luxembourg, a commercial station, beamed from the Continent with an English service after 8 p.m. The Elvis records came through, fading and blurred with static, like coded messages to an occupied country. Now there were other names and other songs that split open the consciousness with disbelieving joy. There was Little Richard's Tutti Frutti; Bill Haley's Razzle Dazzle; Freddy Bell and the Bellboys' Giddy-up-a-Ding-Dong. The sound came from beyond comprehension; it played, then died out again. You could not catch it, nor sing it nor write it down.

Then, late at night over the hidden radios, a new message came. A banjo-player with the Chris Barber Jazz Band had formed his own small group to record Rock Island Line, an American folk song dating back to the Depression or earlier. The number was played in what Jazz audiences knew already as 'skiffle', a style originating in the poor Southern states where people would hold 'rent parties' to stave off the landlord, playing music on kazoos, tin cans and other impromptu instruments. The banjoist, Tony—or 'Lonnie'—Donegan, sang in a piercing pseudo-Blues wail, set about by elementary rhythm of which the main component was an ordinary kitchen washboard, scraped and tapped by thimble-capped fingers.

Rock Island Line began a national craze. For anyone could form a 'skiffle group' simply by stealing his mother's washboard and fixing a broom handle to a tea chest, then stringing it with wire to make a rudimentary double bass. The biggest craze of all, thanks to Elvis Presley, was for guitars. A straitlaced instrument long muffled in orchestral rhythm sections found itself suddenly the focus of all adolescent desire.

As boys pestered throughout Britain, so did John Lennon pester his Aunt Mimi to buy him a guitar. Each afternoon, when Julia paid her daily visit to Menlove Avenue, she, too, would be entreated to give—even lend—him the money. For Julia, as it happened, could play the banjo a little. John's father Freddy had taught her before disappearing overseas. And Freddy's father, so he had always said, used to play professionally in America with a group of Kentucky minstrels.

It was, however, not Julia but Mimi who eventually gave in. One Saturday morning, she put on her coat, checked the money in her purse and told John unceremoniously to come along.

Hessy's, the music shop in Whitechapel, central Liverpool, had an abundant stock of guitars. Frank Hessy, the owner, was sending a van regularly down to London to buy up every one to be found in the Soho street markets. Jim Gretty, his showroom manager, was selling roughly one guitar a minute from the hundreds festooned along the narrow shop wall. Jim was himself a guitarist, Western-style, and each week held a beginners' class in an upstairs room, chalking huge elementary chord-shapes on the wall.

It was Jim who sold Aunt Mimi the guitar which John said he wanted—a little Spanish model with steel strings and a label inside: 'Guaranteed not to split.' 'It cost me £17, I think,' Mimi says. 'I know I resented paying that, even though I'd been giving £12 each for his school blazers.'

From that moment, John was—as they say in Liverpool—'lost'. Nigel Whalley, calling round at 'Mendips', would find him up in his bedroom, oblivious to time or the first soreness of finger-ends split by the steel strings. 'He'd sit on his bed, just strumming,' Nigel says. 'Strumming the banjo chords Julia had shown him, and singing any words that came into his head. After about ten minutes, he'd have got a tune going.'

When Mimi could no longer stand the noise, or the foot beating time through her ceiling, she would order John out of the house, into the glassed-over front porch. 'He stood there leaning against the wall so long, I think he wore some of the brickwork away with his behind,' Mimi says. 'To me, it was just so much waste of time. I used to tell him so. "The guitar's all very well, John," I used to tell him, "but you'll never make a *living* out of it." '

The first skiffle group he formed had only two members: himself on guitar and his crony Pete Shotton on kitchen washboard, crashing its glass ridges with thimble-capped fingers as the two of them tried out Cumberland Gap, Rock Island Line, Don't You Rock Me, Daddyo and other skiffle classics. They named themselves, in rough-hewn skiffle style, The Quarry Men, after the sandstone quarries dotted around Woolton, and also in unwilling recognition of the school they both attended. The school song contains a reference to 'Quarry men strong before our birth'—a sentiment chorused lustily by John and Pete since it invariably figured in the final assembly of term.

The Quarry Men grew in the image of the gang which had formerly terrorised St. Peter's Sunday School. Nigel Whalley, now a Bluecoat Grammar School boy, and Ivan Vaughan, from the Liverpool Institute, divided the role of tea-chest bass-player amicably between them. Nigel's first Teddy-Boy clothes had been seized by his policeman father and thrown on the fire, so now he kept all his choicer garments down the road at Ivan's house. Each played bass with the Quarry Men when the other could not be bothered.

Quarry Bank Grammar School supplied a further recruit in Rod Davis, the earnest, bespectacled boy in 4A whose parents had just bought him a banjo. Another Woolton boy called Eric Griffiths came in on the strength of his new guitar, and because he claimed to know someone in King's Drive who owned a full-size set of drums. He took the others to meet Colin Hanton, an apprentice upholsterer who had just begun Hire Purchase payments on a £38 kit from Hessy's. Colin was two years older than the others but, as he was extremely small, it didn't matter. He was so small, he carried his birth certificate in his pocket, to prove to suspicious pub landlords that he was old enough to be served with beer.

In the group, as in the gang, John was the undisputed leader. His plaid shirt collar turned up, Teddy-Boy style, scowling like Elvis, he monopolised the foreground and the microphone, if there chanced to be one. 'He always used to beat hell out of his guitar,' Rod Davis says. 'He'd always be busting a string. Then he'd hand his guitar to me, take my banjo and carry on on that while I knelt down in the background and tried to fix the string.

'We did all the skiffle numbers that Lonnie Donegan recorded.

Right from the start, John wanted to play Rock and Roll as well; I can remember him singing Blue Suède Shoes. I'd got some Burl Ives records, so we did Worried Man Blues. The only way you could learn the words was by listening to the radio—or buying the record. Records were six bob each, and none of us could afford that. So John always used to make up his own words to the songs that were popular. "Long, black train" was one of them. Another one went "Come, go with me, down to the Penitentiar-ee". They weren't any worse than the words you were supposed to sing.'

Skiffle contests were happening all over Liverpool, at big ballrooms like the Rialto and Locarno. In 10 minutes between regular band 'spots' three or four groups would hurry onstage and patter out their brief, invariable repertoire. The Quarry Men entered numerous such competitions, without notable success. One of the groups which continually beat them had as its chief attraction a midget named Nicky Cuff, who actually stood on the tea chest bass while plucking at it.

Rod Davis's father had a big old Austin Hereford car in which he would occasionally chauffeur them to a skiffle contest. For most of the time, they travelled on buses, with tea chest, drum kit and all.

On Saturday afternoons they met to practise at Colin Hanton's house since his father, a Co-op shop manager, was guaranteed to be absent. Least practising of all was done at Mimi's, for the boys were somewhat in awe of her sharp tongue. Instead, they would go to Spring Wood to Julia's house, where they were always certain of a welcome and a laugh. Sometimes Julia would take Rod's banjo and demonstrate chords and little runs for John and Eric Griffiths to copy on their guitars. Both as a result learned to play in banjo style, leaving the two bass strings untuned. 'We used to practise standing in the bath at Julia's,' Rod Davis says. 'You could get more of an echo that way.'

In 1956, a new headmaster, William Edward Pobjoy, took charge of Quarry Bank Grammar School. At 35, he was young for such a post, and seemed younger with his boyish quiff of hair, and quiet, sardonic manner. Since the new head resorted neither to shouting nor sarcasm, the Quarry Bank heavies believed they were in for an easy time.

Among the information passed on by his predecessor to Mr. Pobjoy was that John Lennon and Pete Shotton were the school's leading criminals. 'I was told there was even one master whom they not only used to terrorise, but whom Lennon had actually thumped. The poor man was so ashamed, he begged for the matter not to be reported.'

Mr. Pobjoy, in his unobtrusive way, seems to have got the measure of Lennon and Shotton. The punishment book shows that John was caned by him only once. On another occasion, he and Pete were each suspended for a week.

Mr. Pobjoy, they discovered with some astonishment, did not disapprove of skiffle. Nor did he try, on the strength of their other crimes, to stamp out the Quarry Men. He encouraged them to do anything more positive than smoking and slacking. Now when John entered the headmaster's office—the timber merchant's circular book room, with finely-inlaid shelves, where he had been caned so many times—it would not be defiantly, as before, but to ask Mr. Pobjoy, in all humility, if the Quarry Men could play for 10 minutes during the interval at the Sixth Form dance.

Another source of engagements was St. Peter's Parish Church, Woolton. John had sung in its choir and disrupted its Sunday School, and he and Pete Shotton still belonged to its Youth Club, which met in the hall across the road for badminton and ping pong. The Quarry Men would play at the Youth Club 'hops', unpaid and glad of an opportunity to use a stage, and experience acoustics larger than those of John's mother's bathroom. When John broke a guitar string, he was reimbursed from church funds.

The group existed on the most casual basis, expanding and shrinking according to members available. Already there was some dissent between Rod Davis, who wished to play pure folk music, and John with his passion for Elvis. Pete Shotton was in it only for laughs, as he strove to make clear on all occasions. Little Colin Hanton, drumming irregularly, with his birth certificate in his top pocket, was more interested in pubs and pints of Black Velvet. Fights sometimes broke out between the musicians as they were performing, or with members of the audience whose criticisms were untactfully voiced. Fights broke out also if a spectator believed a Quarry Man to be ogling his girl friend, and clambered up among them to take revenge. John Lennon, for some reason, was always the principal target of such attacks, and was seldom averse to using his fists. 'Except if it was a *really* big bloke,' Nigel Whalley says. 'Then John'd be as meek as a mouse. He'd always manage to talk his way out.'

'There were these two particular big Teds,' Rod Davis says. 'Rod and Willo their names were. They were the terror of Woolton. Rod and Willo were always looking for us and threatening to do us over. One night when we got off the bus—with all our gear, and the tea chest as well—Rod and Willo were there, waiting for us. They came chasing after us in their long coats, and we scattered. I know we left the tea chest behind on the pavement.'

The tea chest, which Colin's Mum had covered with wallpaper, remained a prominent feature of Woolton village for about a week afterwards. Sometimes it would be standing on the pavement; sometimes it would have migrated to the middle of the road.

The role of bass-player was transferred after this to Len Garry, another Liverpool Institute boy whom Ivan Vaughan had introduced into the Lennon circle. Nigel Whalley, whose consuming interest was golf not skiffle, assumed the duties of manager. With his sun-tanned complexion and shining white teeth, 'Whalloggs' was amply suited to a diplomatic role. He took bookings for the Quarry Men and prevailed on local shopkeepers to put advertisements in their windows for no fee. He gave out formal visiting cards which read:

Country. Western. Rock 'n' Roll. Skiffle

The Quarry Men

OPEN FOR ENGAGEMENTS

Summer was just beginning when the Quarry Men played at an open-air party in Rosebery Street. A printer friend of Colin Hanton, who had designed the label on their bass drum, was helping to organise festivities for Rosebery Street's centenary. Though the engagement lay some distance from Woolton—and in a 'rough' district of Liverpool 8—it was welcomed for the beer it promised, and the girls. The Quarry Men played standing on the tailboard of a lorry, which had to be moved because somebody was ill in the bedroom above. They played in the afternoon, then again in the evening, after strings of coloured bulbs had come alight on the hundred-year-old, back-to-back houses.

Colin Hanton had, as usual, preceded the engagement by going to a pub, producing his birth certificate, and downing several pints of Black Velvet. By himself at the end of the trailer, he played his drums in happy disregard for what John and Eric Griffiths were singing. Pete Shotton, cradling his washboard, wore a long 'Ted' jacket, draped in hollows against his bony frame. Rod Davis, on banjo, looked serious, as always.

'I suddenly heard these two blokes talking, next to the trailer,' Colin Hanton says. '"Let's get that Lennon," they said. I told John, and we all jumped off the back of the wagon, and ran into my mate's house: the printer. His Mum sat us down and gave us all salad. These blokes that were after us stayed outside, shouting and thumping on the windows. I'd met a girl at the party, so I took my drums and stayed the night at her house. The other lads had to have a policeman to see them to the bus stop.'

*

In Paul McCartney's home, there had always been music. His father, Jim, never tired of recalling those happy prewar days when, in paper collars you could buy for a penny a dozen, he had led his own little group, the Jim Mac Jazz Band. The McCartneys still had what all families once used to—a piano in the living-room. Jim had bought it long ago, when money was easier, from the North End Music Stores in Walton Road. Whenever he had a spare moment—which was not very often—he would move the piled-up newspapers off a chair, sit down at the piano, open its lid and play. He liked the old tunes, like Charmaine and Ramona and, his favourite of all, Stairway to Paradise.

Jim's recovery had been marvellous to see. It was as if Mary's quiet competence had somehow been handed on to him. From the engulfing anguish following her death, he had suddenly clicked into a calm resolution that, for Paul's sake, and for young Michael's, home life must manage to continue.

Though housekeeping was mysterious to him, he applied himself doggedly to mastering its every department. He taught himself to cook and sew, to wash and to iron. Each day, after finishing work at the Cotton Exchange, he would hasten to the grocer's and the butcher's, then home to Allerton to tidy the house and cook Paul and Michael their evening meal. His sisters, Jin and Millie, each came in one full day a week to give the house a thorough cleaning. Bella Johnson and her daughter Olive also remained close at hand. When Paul and Michael came in from school, even if the house chanced to be empty, there would be notes left for them about where to find things, and sticks and paper laid for a fire in the grate.

Like Mimi Smith, Jim McCartney did his utmost to prevent there being a Teddy Boy in the family. The trouble was that, being at work all day, he had no alternative but to trust Paul and Michael to go to the barber's on their own and choose clothes for themselves with the money he gave them. In genuine perplexity he wondered how Paul, in particular, was able to return from the barber's seemingly with more hair than when he went, piled up in a cascading sheaf. There were battles, too, over trousers, which, Jim insisted, must not be 'drainies' but of conventional and respectable cut. Paul would bring home a satisfactory pair and show them to his father; then he would smuggle them out again to one of the tailors who specialised in 'tapering'. If Jim noticed anything, Paul was ready to swear that the 14-inch 'drainies' clinging to his ankles were the same pair that his father had sanctioned.

In 1956, Lonnie Donegan and his Skiffle Group arrived in Liverpool to appear at the Empire theatre. Paul and some friends from the Institute waited outside during their lunch-hour, hoping to catch a glimpse of the star when he arrived for rehearsal. He was slightly delayed and, with great consideration, wrote out notes for the factory workers who had waited to see him, explaining to their foremen why they were late back on shift. This testament of how nice a star could be always stayed in Paul McCartney's mind.

It was after seeing Lonnie Donegan that Paul began clamouring for a guitar. He was lucky in having a father only too glad to encourage him to take up any musical instrument. Already in the house there was a battered trumpet which Paul had tried to learn, but had discarded on being told it would make a callous on his upper lip. For he had now begun to sing—or, at least, to sing in public—without embarrassment. He had always sung to himself in bed at night, not knowing that Jim and Olive Johnson were often listening to him from the bottom of the stairs.

Despite the money shortage, Jim brought home a £15 'cello guitar with violin holes, 'sunburst' colouring and a white scratch plate. Olive Johnson remembers how eagerly he set about trying to teach Paul to play by giving him chords from the living-room piano. 'He'd sit there for hours, shouting, "Come on, Paul. Now try this one!"'

Paul, strangely, made little progress. His left-hand fingers found it irksome to shape the patterns of black dots shown in the tuition book, and his right hand, somehow, lacked the bounce necessary for strumming. Then he made the discovery that, although right-handed for every other purpose, he was left-handed as a guitar player. He took the guitar back to the shop and had its strings put on in reverse order. The white scratch plate, which carried the strummer's hand down after each chord, could not be moved: it was uselessly upside-down in the way that Paul now held the guitar.

From that moment, he, too, was 'lost'. The guitar became a passion overruling all else in his life. It was the first thing he looked at on waking each morning; at night, after the lights were out, his eyes searched the darkness for the glow of its sunburst face. School lessons; games; bus journeys; the meals his father set in front of him—all were things to be endured and rushed through for the sake of that moment when he could pick up the guitar again, and hear the hollow bump it made, and discover if the chord he had been practising came out clearly this time. He played the guitar in his bath, even while sitting on the lavatory.

From an assortment of 'Play in a Day' tutors, he learned enough chords to play all the skiffle hits. Skiffle bored him after a time: what he really wanted to play were the guitar solos on Rock and Roll records—the interludes so magically shrill and blurred that one could not analyse them, but only listen as they shivered and wailed around the voice of Little Richard, Carl Perkins or

Elvis. All Shook Up was his favourite Elvis record. He played it over and over on the gramophone, his voice in vain pursuit of the wonderful, mumbling incantation; his acoustic guitar strumming in a different key, and universe.

He also bought every new record by the Everly Brothers, a newly-popular American act from whom he made the discovery that Rock and Roll could be performed at a lesser volume, in close, even subtle harmony. For a time, he and another boy, Ian James, modelled their lives on the Everlys: they combed their hair alike, wore matching white jackets and hung around fairgrounds where the fast roundabouts always played the latest American hits. Paul's voice was like Phil Everly's, the higher of the duo, although he would torture it with impersonations of Little Richard, the shrieking exponent of Tutti Frutti, Rip It Up and Good Golly Miss Molly.

He even made one or two desultory attempts to involve his younger brother, Michael, in an Everly-style Rock and Roll act. Michael McCartney, to add to their father's difficulties, currently had an arm in plaster after an accident at Boy Scout camp. It was a serious fracture which paralysed his fingers for several months and forced him to give up learning the banjo Jim had bought him to equal Paul's guitar.

That summer of 1957—the first after Mary's death—Jim took Paul and Michael for a week's holiday at Butlin's holiday camp in Filey, Yorkshire. There, Paul roped Michael into joining him in an amateur talent contest. They sang an Everly Brothers song that was rather spoiled by Michael's plaster-encased arm. They didn't win the talent contest. 'But after that, we had our first fan,' Michael McCartney says. 'I remember because it was me she fancied and not our kid.'

The skiffle craze had by now seeped into the ancient precincts of Liverpool Institute grammar school. Paul, however, joined none of the newly-formed groups, even though his friend Ivan Vaughan repeatedly enthused about one over in Woolton to which Ivan and another Institute boy, Len Garry, belonged. Ivan Vaughan offered to take Paul to meet the leader—a 'great fellow', so Ivan said. But Paul did not commit himself; nor, for that matter, did Ivan. He prided himself on taking only other 'great fellows' to meet John Lennon.

The big event in Woolton each summer was a garden fête organised by St. Peter's Parish Church. They made a proper carnival of it, with fancy dress and a procession of decorated floats, representing all the church organisations, that wound through the streets of the old village, gathering up followers for the subsequent gala in the field at the top of Church Road.

The fête planned for 6 July 1957, was to have a particularly elaborate programme. It included, as well as the customary 'Rose Queen' ceremony, the band of the Cheshire Yeomanry and a team of trained police dogs from the City of Liverpool force. This year, too, for the first time, the 'teenagers' of the parish were to be catered for. That Lennon boy had been asked to bring his group, the Quarry Men, to take part in the procession and to perform afterwards at the fête.

The Quarry Men's fortunes were currently at a low ebb. A few days earlier, in common with dozens of other skiffle groups, they had gone into Liverpool to audition for a Carroll Levis 'Discoveries' show at the Empire theatre. The great starmaker Levis had been there in person, selecting local talent for what was presumed to be instant international fame. The Quarry Men had won their audition heat, and then found themselves matched in the final with the group that featured Nicky Cuff, the midget. This other group had played two numbers to the Quarry Men's one and had, on audience response, been declared the winner. 'They were miles better than we were, anyway,' Rod Davis says. 'They all leapt about all over the place. We were the purists. We stood still and didn't even smile.'

Early the next Saturday afternoon, the Quarry Men climbed aboard the gaily-bedecked coal merchant's wagon that was to carry them through the Woolton streets. It had been decided that their float should bring up the rear of the procession, to allay any clash of rhythms with the band of the Cheshire Yeomanry. In between, on vehicles borrowed from other local tradesmen, were tableaux representing the Boy Scouts, Girl Guides, Wolf Cubs and Brownies, and the motorised throne on which the 13-year-old Rose Queen sat, in white lace and pink velvet, surrounded by miniature soldiers and attendants.

Just as had been hoped, the Quarry Men brought a large influx of teenagers into Woolton to see the parade. Among them was Paul McCartney. Ivan Vaughan, his classmate at the Institute, had asked him over, although Len Garry, not Ivan, was playing the tea-chest bass in the group that afternoon. Another strong inducement to Paul was the possibility of picking up girls. He cycled over from Allerton, balancing his piled-up hair carefully against the wind.

It was a warm, sunny, Saturday garden fête afternoon. Liverpool, its ship towers and grime, seemed remote from the village decked in faded flags, and the little red sandstone church up the hill, in whose square tower the gold clock hands seemed to point to perpetual summer.

Beside the churchyard, a rough track led into the two small parish-owned fields. Of these, the smaller one, on upland near the Boy Scouts' hut, was too uneven for anything but the refreshment marquee. On the lower, larger field were set out stalls purveying handkerchieves, hardware, home-made cakes, fruit and vegetables, and sideshows including bagatelle, egg-hoopla, quoits and shilling-in-the-bucket. Beyond the Scouts' airborne kiddy-ride, a blackened stone wall formed the boundary with another of Woolton's worked-out quarries. A constant patrol of stewards was necessary to ensure that no child climbed over and fell into the deep, overgrown pit.

That Saturday had begun badly for John Lennon. In the morning, coming downstairs at 'Mendips', he had revealed himself to his Aunt Mimi as a full-blown Teddy Boy. His toppling hair, his plaid shirt and 'drainpipes' seemed to Mimi to be a repudiation of all her care, self-sacrifice and sense. There had been a furious row, after which John had stalked out of the house to find Pete Shotton. In between leaving Mimi and climbing aboard the coalman's wagon, he had contrived—in his own estimation at least—to get roaring drunk. The parade, the stalls, the Rose Queen, the opening prayers by the Rev. Maurice Pryce-Jones, all reached John through the gaseous mist of several illicit light ales.

Mimi, before she arrived at the fête, seems not to have known of the Quarry Men's existence. 'I'd just got there, and was having a cup of tea in the refreshment tent. Suddenly, in the midst of everything, came this—this eruption of noise. Everyone had drained away from where I stood, into the next door field. And there on the stage I saw them—John, and that Shotton.

'John saw me standing there with my mouth open. He started to make words up about me in the song he was singing. "Mimi's coming," he sang. "Oh oh, Mimi's coming down the path. . . ." '

The Quarry Men's big numbers that afternoon were Cumberland Gap, Railroad Bill and Maggie May, a Liverpool waterfront song in which the references to a famous tart and her beat along Lime Street were, fortunately, incomprehensible to the ladies of the Church Committee. The whole performance was watched keenly by Paul McCartney, standing with Ivan Vaughan next to the little outdoor stage. Paul noticed the tinny banjo chords which the leading Quarry Man played, and how, while singing, he stared about him, as if sizing up or challenging the rest of the world.

While the Police dogs were performing obedience trials, Ivan Vaughan took Paul across the road to the Church Hall, where the Quarry Men had made a small encampment of chairs and their coats. They were due to perform again, at a dance that evening, in alternation with the George Edwards band.

Introductions were made, Pete Shotton remembers, a little stiffly. ' "This is John." "Hi." "This is Paul," "Oh—hi." Paul seemed quite cocky, sure of himself, but he and John didn't seem to have much to say.' The ice positively splintered when Paul revealed a brilliant accomplishment. 'He actually knew how to *tune* a guitar,' Pete Shotton says. 'Neither John nor Eric Griffiths had learned how to do that yet. Whenever their guitars went out of tune, they'd been taking them round and asking a fellow in King's Drive to do it.'

It impressed John further that Paul knew the lyrics of Rock and Roll songs all the way through. He himself could never remember words, which was partly why he preferred to make up his own. Paul was even prepared, in his neat hand, to write out all the verses of Twenty Flight Rock, which Eddie Cochran had sung in the film *The Girl Can't Help It.* Then, with equal obligingness, he wrote out the words of Gene Vincent's Be Bop a Lula.

As Church Committee ladies washed up in the scullery nearby, Paul borrowed a guitar and launched into his full Little Richard act—Long Tall Sally, Tutti Frutti and the rest. As he played, he became aware of someone getting uncomfortably close to him and breathing a beery smell. The Quarry Men's chronically short-sighted leader was doing him the honour of studying the way his fingers went in the chords.

Paul was not immediately asked to join the Quarry Men. His obvious ability, if anything, weighed against him. He was so good, they reasoned, he would hardly want to throw in with them. John in particular gave the idea what was, for John, prolonged thought. Up to that point, he had been the Quarry Men's undisputed leader. By admitting Paul, he would be creating a potential threat to that leadership. The decision was whether to remain strong himself or make the group stronger. A week after the Woolton fête, Paul was cycling to Allerton across the golf course when he met Pete Shotton. Pete told him that John wanted him in.

Pete's own skiffle career ended soon afterwards at a party when John took away his washboard and smashed it over his head. 'All of us were pissed and larking around. It didn't hurt me. I just sat there, framed by the washboard, with tears of laughter running down my face. I'd known for a long time that I was no good at music—I was only in the group through being a mate of John's. I was finished with playing, but I didn't want to say so, nor did John. This way let me out and it let John out.'

If Pete had not left the Quarry Men at that point, it is doubtful whether Paul and John would have become the close friends they subsequently did. For no two temperaments could have been more unalike. John, dour and blisteringly direct, fought against authority and inhibition in any form. Paul, baby-faced and virtuous, hated to be on anybody's wrong side. Not least of the differences in them was their attitude to the money they earned by playing. Whereas John would—and frequently did—give away his last sixpence, Paul showed noticeable signs of thrift. One of his first suggestions on joining the Quarry Men was that Nigel Whalley should not receive equal shares since, as manager, he did not actually play onstage.

What Paul and John had in common was their passion for guitars. They began to spend hours in each other's company, practising, usually at Paul's. John would even let himself be seen in his hated spectacles, the better to understand the chords which Paul showed him, left-handed. Whole afternoons would pass in the living-room at Forthlin Road, where Jim McCartney had papered the walls with a design of Chinese pagodas. Paul's younger brother Mike would often be there, too, taking photographs of them as they played. One of Mike's pictures records the moment when both were able to play a full six-string chord with the left-hand index finger barring the keyboard. Their faces, as they hold up their two guitars, are rigid with pride and pain.

The other Quarry Men did not take quite so strongly to Paul. 'I always thought he was a bit big-headed,' Nigel Whalley says. 'As soon as we let him into the group, he started complaining about the money I was getting them, and saying I should take less as I didn't do any playing. He was always smiling at you, but he could be catty as well. He used to pick on our drummer, Colin—not to his face; making catty remarks about him behind his back. Paul wanted something from the drums that Colin didn't have it in him to play.'

'Paul was always telling me what to do, Colin Hanton says. "Can't you play it this way?" he'd say, and even try to show me on my own drums. He'd make some remark to me. I'd sulk. John would say "Ah, let him alone, he's all right." But I knew they only wanted me because I'd got a set of drums.'

Even Pete Shotton—still a close friend and ally—noticed a change in John after Paul's arrival. 'There was one time when they played a really dirty trick on me. I knew John would never have been capable of it on his own. It was so bad that he came to me later and apologised. I'd never known him to do that before for *anyone*.'

It was shortly after Paul joined the Quarry Men that they bought proper stage outfits of black trousers, black bootlace ties and white cowboy shirts with fringes along the sleeves. John and Paul, in addition, wore white jackets; the other three played in their shirtsleeves. Eric Griffiths, though also a guitarist, did not have the jacket-wearing privilege. A cheerful boy, he did not recognise this for the augury it was.

Their main engagements were still at church halls like St.

Peter's in Woolton or St. Barnabas, off Penny Lane. A step-up came when a local promoter named Charlie McBain booked them to play at regular dances at the Broadway Conservative Club and at the Wilson Hall in Garston. The latter was in a district renowned for its toughness and the size of its Teddy Boys, among whom the fashion had lately arisen of going to skiffle dances with leather belts wrapped round their hands. At Wilson Hall one night, a gigantic Ted terrified the Quarry Men by clambering on to the stage in the middle of a number. But it was only to request Paul quite politely to do his Little Richard impersonation.

Nigel Whalley had left school and become an apprentice golf professional at the Lee Park course. He continued to act as the Quarry Men's manager and, despite Paul's protests, to draw equal shares: his wallet packed with their visiting cards, he would cycle assiduously with news of a booking from one member's house to the next. Through Nigel, they were even once invited to play at Lee Park golf club. 'They did it for nothing, but they got a slap up meal, and the hat was passed round for them afterwards. They ended up making about twice what they would have done if they'd been getting a fee.'

At the golf course, Nigel got to know a doctor named Sytner whose son, Alan, had recently opened a Jazz club in the centre of Liverpool. Nigel arranged for the Quarry Men to appear there, too, late in 1957. The club was in Mathew Street, under a row of old warehouses, and fully deserved its name, the Cavern. It was strictly for Jazz, it allowed skiffle but absolutely barred Rock and Roll. 'We started doing Elvis numbers when we played there,' Colin Hanton says. 'While we were on stage, someone handed us a note. John thought it was a request. But it was from the Management, saying: "Cut out the bloody Rock." '

July 1958

'If I'd just said a few more words, it might have saved her'

John was to leave Quarry Bank school at the end of July 1957. He had taken his GCE Ordinary-level examination and had failed every subject by one grade—a clear enough sign to Mr. Pobjoy, the headmaster, that with a little exertion he could have passed every one. Art, his outstanding subject, had been squandered with the rest. The question paper asked for a painting to illustrate the theme 'travel'. John, for the amusement of his exam-room neighbours, drew a wart-infested hunchback.

He sat out that last summer term, stubbornly resistant to all ideas of soon having to make his way in the world. The panoramic school photograph shows him, slumped behind his Slim Jim tie, conspicuous among a Fifth Form with faces otherwise expectant and purposeful. Rod Davis, the Quarry Men's banjo-player, was to enter the Sixth to do Advanced-level French and German. Even Pete Shotton, John's old partner in crime, had, to his teachers' and possibly to his own great surprise, been accepted as a cadet at the Police College in Mather Avenue.

Aunt Mimi's great fear was that, like his father Freddy 30 years before, John would just drift away to sea. 'I remember him bringing home this boy with hair in a Tony Curtis, they called it, all smoothed back with grease at the sides. "Mimi," John whispered to me in the kitchen, "this boy's got *pots* of money. He goes away to sea." I said, "Well, he's no captain and he's no engineer —what is he?" "He waits at table," John said. "Ha!" I said. "A fine ambition!" '

Mimi afterwards stumbled on a plot between John and Nigel Whalley to run away to sea as restaurant stewards. Nigel says they had got as far as buying their rail tickets to the Catering College. 'I was rung up by this place at the Pier Head,' Mimi says, '. . . some sort of seaman's employment office. "We've got a young boy named John Lennon here," they said. "He's asking to sign up." "Don't you even *dream* of it," I told them.'

Mimi was called to Quarry Bank to discuss with Mr. Pobjoy what John might do with his life. Reviewing his meagre school achievements, there seemed only one possibility—his talent for painting, design and caricature. 'Mr. Pobjoy said to me, "Mrs. Smith, this boy's an artist, he's a bohemian. If I can get him into the Art College, are you prepared to keep him on for the next twelve months?" ' Mimi said that she was.

Quarry Bank's valediction was, in the circumstances, quite kindly. 'He has been a trouble spot for many years in discipline, but has somewhat mended his ways. Requires the sanction of "losing a job" to keep him on the rails. But I believe he is not beyond redemption and he could really turn out a fairly responsible adult who might go far.'

Aunt Mimi went with him for his interview at the Art College in Hope Street. 'Otherwise,' Mimi says, 'he'd never have been able to find it. He'd only ever been into Liverpool on the one sort of bus, to the shop opposite the bus stop where he used to buy his Dinky cars.'

On that day, John managed to make himself a relatively unalarming figure, submitting to both white shirt and tie and an old tweed suit that had once belonged to his Uncle George. When he presented himself for enrolment, however, it was in his Teddy-Boy jacket and lilac shirt and the drainpipe jeans Aunt Mimi had forbidden him to wear. He put them on under normal trousers which he stripped off directly he was out of Mimi's sight.

Hope Street bisects the old, elegant, upland part of Liverpool where cast-iron letters on street-ends enshrine the great shipping dynasties of Canning, Rodney, Roscoe and Huskisson. In 1957, the whole district round the Art College was a haunt of painters, sculptors, poets and writers, sharing the faded Georgiana in amity with small businesses, guest houses, junk shops and West Indian drinking clubs. The Anglican cathedral being still unfinished, the principal aesthetic attraction was the Philharmonic Dining-Rooms, a pub fashioned by Cunard shipwrights in crystal and mahogany, where even the Gents' urinals were carved of rose-coloured marble.

Whatever hopes John may have had of a wild bohemian existence were confounded in his first week at college. He had been accepted for the Intermediate course of two years' general study, followed by specialisation in the third and fourth year. To his disgust, he found himself in a classroom again, obliged to study a set curriculum including figure drawing, lettering and architecture. It was, in other words, no different from the school he had just left.

His Teddy-Boy clothes estranged him instantly from his fellow students in their duffel coats, suède shoes and chunky Shetland sweaters with sleeves pushed up to the elbow. At Art College in 1957, no one liked Elvis or Rock and Roll: what everyone liked was Traditional Jazz, played in cellars flickering with beer bottle candlelight. Indeed, the most famous Liverpool group of the moment was the Merseysippi Jazz Band, frequently to be heard on radio as well as at the Cavern Club in Mathew Street. John hated the Jazz crowd with their sweaters and their GCE passes.

His tutor on the Intermediate course was Arthur Ballard, a balding, soft-spoken man who had once been a middleweight boxing champion. Himself an abstract painter of some reputation, Ballard had no great love for formal teaching and, in fact, held most of his seminars in a tiny pub called Ye Cracke, in Rice Street, where the back room was dominated by gigantic etchings of Wellington greeting Marshal Blücher, and Nelson's death at Trafalgar.

Ballard noticed John Lennon first merely as an ill-at-ease Teddy Boy whose clothes were officially disapproved of and whose posture was less defiant than dejected. 'The students would pin their work up, and we'd all discuss it. John's effort was always hopeless—or he'd put up nothing at all. He always struck me as the poor relation in the group. The rest used to cover up for him.

'Then one day in the lecture room, I found this notebook full of caricatures—of myself, the other tutors, the students—all done with descriptions and verse, and it was the wittiest thing I'd ever seen in my life. There was no name on it. It took me quite a long time to find out that Lennon had done it.

'The next time student work was being put up and discussed, I brought out this notebook and held it up, and we discussed the work in it. John had never expected anyone to look at it, let alone find it funny and brilliant. Afterwards I told him, "When I talk about Interpretation, boy, *this* is the kind of thing I mean as well. *This* is the kind of thing I want you to be doing." '

Around the windy corner, in Mount Street, Paul McCartney still daily climbed the steps to the Institute Grammar School. That summer, he had taken two 'O' levels, passing in Spanish but failing Latin; in 1958, he was due to take six further subjects and then go into the Sixth Form. The ultimate plan, ardently supported by his father, was that Paul should go on to teacher training college. His English master, 'Dusty' Durband, thought this a feasible course. He could imagine Paul one day appearing in the Institute's own staff room, or driving a modest saloon car to and from some small college of adult education.

But Paul's school career, previously so unexceptionable, now grew unsettled and erratic. The presence of John Lennon, literally beyond the classroom wall, affected both his work and his hitherto blameless conduct. More than ever, Mr. Durband noticed, he relied on charm and facility to compensate for skimped or unfinished preparation. He had even, unknown to Mr. Durband, begun to cut certain classes. There was an internal way from the Institute into the Art College, across a small courtyard beside the school kitchens. John would have told him which lecture room was empty and available for guitar practice. No one in the College thoroughfares looked twice at the big-eyed youth with his black raincoat buttoned up to the neck to hide his Institute tie.

The Quarry Men had been hard hit by the flux of the final school year. Rod Davis was too busy in the Quarry Bank Sixth to have any time for banjo-playing. Nigel Whalley had contracted tuberculosis—the consequence, he thinks, of over-work in the cause of skiffle and his golf pro' job. Soon afterwards, Len Garry, the bass player, fell ill with meningitis and joined Nigel at the sanatorium at Fazakerley. 'The other lads used to come and see us on a Sunday. They'd bring their guitars with them, and we'd have a singsong at the end of the ward.'

The skiffle era was by now definitely over. Last year's big names, The Vipers, Chas McDevitt, Bob Cort, even Lonnie Donegan himself, had all dropped the word 'skiffle' discreetly from their billing. In Liverpool, as all over Britain, broom-handles were being restored to their brushes, thimbles returned to maternal work-baskets and tea chests, decorated with musical notes, left outside for reluctant refuse men. But if thousands of skiffle groups broke up, there were hundreds more with a taste —even a talent—for performing who decided to try their luck with Rock and Roll.

They had the consolation of knowing that, however bad they might sound at the beginning, they did not sound much worse than professional English Rock and Rollers. Tommy Steele, launched in 1956 as Britain's 'answer' to Elvis Presley, had set the pattern of cack-handed mimicry. Since then, there had arisen numerous other 'answers' to Presley as well as to the Everly Brothers, Bill Haley, The Platters and Little Richard. There had been Marty Wilde, the Most Brothers, Russ Hamilton, Tony Crombie and the Rockets. Some found hit records and a large following which, for all that, regarded them much as an earlier generation had regarded British films. They were second features to the real elixir, pumped from its only true source: America.

Liverpool stood closer to America than any other place in Britain. There was still, in 1957, a Transatlantic passenger route, plied by ships returning weekly to tie up behind Dock Road's grim castle walls. With them came young Liverpudlian deck-hands and stewards whom the neighbours called 'Cunard Yanks' because of their flashy New York clothes. As well as Times Square trinkets for their girl friends and panoramic lampshades of the Manhattan skyline for their mothers' front rooms, the Cunard Yanks brought home records not available in Britain. Rhythm and Blues, the genesis of Rock and Roll, sung by still obscure names such as Chuck Berry and Ike Turner, pounded through the terraced back streets each Saturday night as the newly-returned mariners got ready to hit the town.

The Quarry Men knew no friendly Cunard Yank who would bring them American records to copy. They had no money, either, for the new electric guitars and amplifiers now thronging Hessy's shop window. They could not even change their name, as all the other groups were doing. The Alan Caldwell Skiffle Group had become Rory Storm and the Raving Texans. The Gerry Marsden Skiffle Group now called themselves Gerry and the Pacemakers. The Quarry Men stayed the Quarry Men because that was the name lettered on Colin Hanton's drums.

In late 1957, American Rock and Roll gave struggling ex-skiffle groups in Britain their first friend. His name was Buddy Holly, although at the beginning he figured anonymously in a group called the Crickets. Among the new performers thrown up after Presley, Buddy Holly was unique in composing many of the songs he recorded, and also in showing ability on the guitar, rather than using it merely as a prop. He gave hope to British boys because he was not pretty, but thin and bespectacled, and because his songs, though varied and inventive, were written in elementary guitar chords, recognisable to every beginner.

Paul McCartney had always used his guitar to help him make up tunes. His main objective in the Quarry Men, however, was to oust Eric Griffiths from the role of lead guitarist. One night at the Broadway Conservative Club, he prevailed on the others to let him take the solo in a number. He fluffed it and, later, in an attempt to redeem himself, played over to John a song he had written, called I Lost My Little Girl. John, though he had always tinkered with lyrics, had never thought of writing entire songs before. Egged on by Paul—and by Buddy Holly—he felt there could be no harm in trying. Soon he and Paul were each writing songs furiously, as if it were a race.

Sometimes, when the Quarry Men played at Wilson Hall, they would be watched by a boy whose elaborate Teddy-Boy hair stood up around a pale, hollow-cheeked, unsmiling face. The others knew him vaguely as a schoolfriend of Paul's and a would-be guitarist, though he played with no group regularly. His name, so Paul said, was George Harrison, and, in Paul's opinion, he would be extremely useful as a recruit to the Quarry Men. No one, to begin with, took very much notice. For Paul's friend was so silent and solemn and, at 14, so ridiculously young.

Paul had got to know him years before, when the McCartneys

still lived at Speke and George used to catch the same bus to school each morning from the stop near Upton Green. Among the shouting, satchel-swinging, homework-copying crowd, George Harrison was known as the boy whose Dad actually drove one of these pale green Corporation buses. When Paul, one morning, was short of his full fare, George's mother gave him extra pennies enough to travel all the way into Liverpool.

The Harrisons, Harry and Louise, had married in 1929 when she worked in a greengrocer's shop and he was a steward on ships of the White Star line. The thin, dapper, thoughtful young shipboard waiter proved a perfect match with the round, jolly, warm-hearted girl whose mother had been a lamplighter during the Great War. In 1931, a daughter, Louise, was born to them and, in 1934, their first son, Harold junior. Harry quit the sea soon afterwards, braving the worst of the Depression to be nearer his wife and children. After 15 months on the dole, he managed to get a job with the Corporation, initially as a bus conductor. A third child, Peter, was born in 1940, at the height of the Liverpool Blitz.

The family lived then at Wavertree, in the tiny terraced house in Arnold Grove which Harry and Louise had occupied since their marriage. It was here, on 25 February 1943, that Louise gave birth to her fourth child and third son, George. When Harry came upstairs to see the new baby, he was amazed at its likeness to himself. Louise, too, noticed the dark eyes that, even then, cautiously appraised the world.

Though Harry earned little on the buses, he made sure his large family lacked for nothing. Louise was a capable and also a happy mother, whose laughter rang constantly through the house. George, as the baby of the family, was petted by everyone, from his big sister Lou downwards. Accustomed to being the centre of attention, he was, at the same time, independent, solitary and thoughtful. Even as a toddler, he forbade Louise to go with him to school, for fear she would get mixed up with 'all those nosey mothers'. It horrified him to think they might ask her what he did and said at home.

The wartime baby 'bulge' had brought in its wake an acute shortage of space at primary schools. George—like his mother—had been baptised a Catholic, but could be fitted in only at an Anglican infants' school, Dovedale Primary, near Penny Lane. He was there at the same time as John Lennon, two forms below.

In 1954, he went on to Liverpool Institute, where he was put into the form below Paul McCartney. Unlike Paul, however, he soon began to do extremely badly. Alert and perceptive, with an unusually good memory, he developed a hatred of all lessons and school routine. Detentions, even beatings, could not lift the firmly-shut barriers of his indifference, and soon the Institute masters found it less fatiguing to leave him alone.

He attracted further odium in coming to school in clothes which did not conform to the Institute's regulation grey and black. Already, in admiration of the dockland Teds, his hair was piled so high that a school cap could only cling on precariously at the back. He would sit in class, his blazer buttoned over a canary yellow waistcoat borrowed from his brother, Harry; his desk-top hiding trousers secretly tapered on his mother's sewing machine. His shirt collar, socks and shoes growing pointed, all uttered the defiance still hidden in his gaunt face while some master or other, like 'Cissy' Smith, was sarcastically making fun of him.

In 1956, his mother noticed him drawing pictures of guitars on every scrap of paper he could find. He had heard Lonnie Donegan, and seen Donegan's guitar. Soon afterwards, he came to Louise and asked her to give him £3 to buy a guitar from a boy at school. She did so; but when George brought it home, he accidentally unscrewed the neck from the body, then found he couldn't put them back together. The guitar lay in a cupboard for several weeks until his brother Peter took it out and mended it.

Learning to play, even the first simple chords in the tuition book, was an agonising process for George. Unlike Paul, he had no inherited musical ability; nor was he, like John, a born adventurer. All he had was his indomitable will to learn. His mother, Louise, encouraged him, sitting up late with him as he tried and tried. Sometimes he would be near to tears with frustration and the pain of split and dusty fingertips.

His brother Peter had taken up the guitar at about the same time, and together they formed a skiffle group, the Rebels. Their first and only engagement was for 10s each at the Speke British Legion Club. At George's insistence, they left the house one at a time, ducking along under the garden hedge so that 'nosey neighbours' wouldn't see.

The family had moved by now to a new council house, in Upton Green, Speke. It was on his bus journey into Liverpool each morning that George met Paul McCartney. Though Paul was a year older and in a higher form at school, their passion for guitars drew them together. Paul would come across from Allerton to practise in George's bedroom, bringing with him his 'cello guitar with the upside-down scratch plate. George now had a £30 guitar which his mother had helped him buy—a far better one than Paul's, with white piping and a 'cutaway' for reaching the narrow frets at the bottom of the keyboard.

To pay back his mother, George did a Saturday morning delivery round for a local butcher, E. R. Hughes. One of the houses on his round belonged to a family named Bramwell, whose son Tony had met Buddy Holly during the star's recent British tour. Tony Bramwell would lend George his Buddy Holly records to listen to and copy. Confidence came from the songs built of easy chords, like E and B7; the changes he could do now from one chord to the other; the solo bass runs that, painfully, unsmilingly, he was learning to pick out for himself.

Paul introduced him to the other Quarry Men one night late in 1957, in the suburb of Liverpool called Old Roan. 'It was at a club we used to go to, called The Morgue,' Colin Hanton says. 'It was in the cellar of this big old derelict house. No bar or coffee or anything, just a cellar with dark rooms off it, and one big blue light bulb sticking out of the wall.'

The others crowded round George, interested in what they could see of his guitar with its cutaway body. They listened while George played all he had been carefully rehearsing. He played them Raunchy, an eight-note tune on the bass strings; then he played the faster and more tricky Guitar Boogie Shuffle.

George was not asked to join the Quarry Men that night. Indeed, they never asked him formally to join. He would follow them with his guitar around the halls where they played, and in the interval stand and wait for his chance to come across and see Paul. Generally, he would have some newly-mastered chord to show them, or yet another solemn-faced bass string tune. If another guitarist had failed to arrive, George would be allowed to 'sit in'. Occasionally, they would give him his own solo. Biting his lip in agony, he would arrange his fingers at the keyboard fret where it began.

No one other than Paul took him very seriously. John Lennon in particular, from the pinnacle of 17 years, considered him just a funny little eager white-faced lad who delivered the weekend meat. Even George's ability as a guitarist became a reason for John to tease him. 'Come on, George,' he would say. 'Give us Raunchy.' George played Raunchy whenever John asked him to, even sitting on the top deck of the number 500 bus to Speke.

The great benefit of letting George tag along was that it brought the Quarry Men another safe house in which to practise. At weekends or on truant days, they could always find refuge at George's. Mr. Harrison would be out on the buses, but Louise always welcomed them, never minding the noise. She developed a soft spot for John Lennon, in whom she recognised much of her own scatty humour. She used to say that John and she were just a pair of fools.

Aunt Mimi, by contrast, did not like John to associate with someone who was, after all, a butcher's errand boy, and whose accent was so thickly Liverpudlian. George called at 'Mendips' one day to ask John to go to the cinema, but John, still thinking him just a 'bloody kid', pretended to be too busy. 'He's a real whacker, isn't he?' Mimi said bitterly when George had gone. 'You always go for the low types, don't you, John?'

To Mimi, in her innocence, George—and even Paul—were the bad influences: if John had not met *them*, he would still be happy in ordinary clothes. 'Paul used to wear these *great* long winkle-picker things, with buckles on the sides. And as for *George*! Well, of course you couldn't wish for a quieter lad. But one day when I came into the house, there was George with his hair in a crew cut, and wearing this *bright* pink shirt. I told him, "*Never* come into this house with a shirt like that on again." '

With George 'sitting in' more and more, the Quarry Men now found themselves with a glut of guitarists. For, as well as John and Paul, there was still Eric Griffiths, the chubby-faced boy who had been a founder member, and who did not realise his growing superfluousness. At length, the others decided that Eric must be frozen out. Colin Hanton, his best friend in the group, was visited by Nigel Whalley and asked to go along with the plan. They still needed Colin or, rather, his £38-drum kit.

'We didn't tell Eric we were going to Paul's house to practise,' Colin says. 'He rang up while we were there. The others got me to talk to him and explain how things stood. Eric was pretty upset. He couldn't understand why they'd suddenly decided to get rid of him. I told him there wasn't a lot I could do about it. I could tell that if they wanted somebody out, he was out.'

Between John Lennon and his Aunt Mimi, the atmosphere had grown increasingly turbulent. Mimi had to support him at Art College for a full year until he qualified for a local authority grant; she therefore felt doubly entitled to pronounce adversely on his clothes, his silly music and the friends who were, in Mimi's opinion, so very ill-attired and unsuitable. Pete Shotton was only one of John's friends who witnessed memorable fights between him and the aunt who so resembled him in strength of will and volatile spirits. 'One minute,' Pete says, 'they'd be yelling and screaming at each other; the next they'd have their arms round each other, laughing.'

Behind Mimi's briskness and sarcasm lay the real dread of losing John. She was only a substitute, as she well knew, for his real mother, her sister Julia. And John, in his teenage years, had grown adept at playing on that fear. After a row at 'Mendips', he would storm out and go straight to Julia's house at Spring Wood, remaining there for days, sometimes weeks on end. With Julia, life was always pleasant and carefree. Having made no sacrifice for him, she bore no grudge against his indolence: she pampered him, bought him coloured shirts and made him laugh. Her husband, the nervous waiter John called 'Twitchy', would frequently press on him a handful of the evening's restaurant tips.

Mimi, aware that she was being exploited, sometimes took dramatic measures to call John's bluff. 'They used to keep a little dog called Sally,' Pete Shotton says. 'John really thought the world of her. One time, when he'd walked out and gone off to Julia's, Mimi got rid of Sally, saying there'd be no one left in the house to take her for walks. That was the only time I ever saw John really heartbroken and showing it—when he came home to Menlove Avenue and didn't find Sally there.'

On the evening of 15 July 1958, Nigel Whalley left his house in Vale Road and took the short cut over the stile into Menlove Avenue to call for John. At 'Mendips', he found Mimi and Julia talking together by the front garden gate. John was not there, they said—he had gone to Julia's for the whole weekend. Julia, having paid her daily visit to Mimi, was just leaving to catch her bus.

'We'd had a cup of tea together,' Mimi says. 'I said, "I won't walk to the bus stop with you tonight." "All right," Julia said, "don't worry. I'll see you tomorrow." '

Instead, it was Nigel Whalley who walked with John's mother through the warm twilight down Menlove Avenue towards the big road junction. 'Julia was telling me some jokes as we went,' Nigel remembers. 'Every time you saw her, she'd have a new one she'd been saving up to tell you.' About 200 yards from Mimi's house, they parted. Nigel continued down Menlove Avenue and Julia began to cross the road to her bus stop.

Old tram tracks, concealed by a thin hedgerow, ran down the middle of the busy dual carriageway. As Julia stepped through the hedge into the southbound lane, a car came suddenly out of the twilight, swerving inward on the steep camber. Nigel Whalley, across the road, turned at the scream of brakes to see Julia's body tossed into the air.

'I can picture it to this day. I always think to myself, "If only I'd said just one more sentence to her, just a few words more, it might have saved her." '

There was first the moment, parodying every film melodrama John had ever seen, when a policeman came to the back door at Spring Wood and asked if he was Julia's son. The feeling of farce persisted in the taxi ride with 'Twitchy' to Sefton General Hospital; in the sight of the faces waiting to meet them there. For Julia had died the instant the car had struck her. The shock was too much for 'Twitchy', who broke down with grief and dread of what would now become of him and his children by Julia. Even in the moment of her death, it must have seemed to John that his mother was someone else's property.

The anguish was drawn out over several weeks. The car which killed Julia had been driven by an off-duty policeman. Pete Shotton was working on attachment from Police College in the local CID department which investigated the case. The driver stood trial, but was acquitted. 'I went as a witness,' Nigel Whalley says, 'but me being only a boy, they didn't give much weight to what I'd seen. Mimi took it very hard—shouting at the fellow in the dock; she even threatened him with a walking stick.'

John, in the weeks after Julia's death, reminded Pete Shotton of the times they would be caned at Quarry Bank, when John used to fight with all his strength not to let out a single sound of pain. Few people knew the extent of his grief since few understood his feeling for the happy, careless woman who had let her life become separate from his. At College, he would sit for hours alone in the big window at the top of the main staircase. Arthur Ballard saw him there once, and noticed that he was crying.

Elsewhere, if his desolation showed, it would be in manic horseplay with his crony Jeff Mohamed, both in College and at the student pub, Ye Cracke, where John was increasingly to be found. 'They'd come back to College pissed in the afternoon,' Arthur Ballard says. 'I caught John trying to piss into the lift shaft.' Ballard was human enough to understand the reason for such behaviour. But even Pete Shotton was shocked to see how much of the time John now spent anaesthetised by drink. 'I remember getting on a bus once and finding John on the top deck, lying across the back seat, pissed out of his mind. He'd been up there for hours with no idea where he was.'

He had never been short of girl friends, though few were willing to put up for long with the treatment that was John Lennon's idea of romance. His drinking, his sarcasm, his unpunctuality at trysts, his callous humour and, most of all, his erratic temper drove each of them to 'chuck' him, not infrequently with the devastating rejoinder that is the speciality of Liverpool girls. 'Don't take it out on me,' one of them screamed back at him, 'just because your mother's dead.'

It was, indeed, not long after Julia's death that his eye fell on Cynthia Powell, an Intermediate student in a group slightly ahead of his. Cynthia was a timid, quiet, conscientious girl with flawless white skin, the closer investigation of which tended to be discouraged by her thick spectacles and deeply conventional clothes. Hitherto, if John had noticed her at all, it was merely to taunt her for living in Hoylake, on the Cheshire Wirral, where primness and superiority are thought to reign. 'No dirty jokes please—it's Cynthia,' he would say while she blushed, knowing full well that dirty jokes would inevitably follow.

This was the girl who, nevertheless, found herself drawn to John Lennon with a fascination entirely against her neat and cautious nature. She dreaded, yet longed for, the days when John would sit behind her in the lettering class and would pillage the orderly pattern of brushes and rulers she had laid out for the work. She remembers, too, a moment in the lecture hall when she saw another girl stroking John's hair, and felt within herself a confusion which she afterwards realised was jealousy.

They first got talking one day between classes, after some of the students had been testing one another's eyesight and Cynthia discovered John's vision to be as poor as hers, despite his refusal to be seen in glasses. Encouraged by this, she took to loitering about the passages in the hope of meeting him. She grew her 'perm' out, dyed her mousy hair blonde, exchanged her wool 'twinset' for a white duffel coat and black velvet trousers, and left off her own spectacles, with frequently catastrophic results. The bus she caught each day from Central Station regularly carried her past Hope Street and the College stop and on into Liverpool 8.

John approached her formally at an end-of-term dance at lunch time in one of the College lecture rooms. Egged on by Jeff Mohamed, he asked her to dance. When he asked her for a date, Cynthia blurted out that was was engaged—as was true—to a boy back home in Hoylake. 'I didn't ask you to marry me, did I?' John retorted bitterly.

In the autumn term of 1958, amid much local astonishment, they began 'going steady'. Cynthia's friends—especially those who had already passed through the John Lennon experience—warned her strongly against it. Equally, in John's crowd no one could understand his interest in a girl who, although nowadays had somewhat improved in looks, still had nothing in common with John's ideal woman, Brigitte Bardot. Even George Harrison forgot his usual shyness in John's company to declare that Cynthia had teeth 'like a horse'.

Against these defects there was about her a gentleness, a malleability that John, brought up among frolicsome and strong-willed aunts, had not met in a female before. Her heart; her body; even her meagre College allowance was willingly made available to buy cigarettes and one-and-ninepenny strings for his guitar. To please him, she began to dress in short skirts, fishnet stockings and suspender belts which shocked her to her suburban soul as well as giving much anxiety while she waited for him outside Lewis's department store, terrified of being mistaken for a 'totty', or Liverpool tart. For him, each night, she braved the last train out to Hoylake, and its cargo of hooligans and drunks.

She was, even then, terrified of John—of his reckless humour no less than the moods and sudden rages and the ferocity with which he demanded her total obedience. He was so jealous, Cynthia says, he would try to beat up anyone at a party who so much as asked her to dance. He would sit for hours with her in a pub or coffee bar, never letting go her hand. It was as if something stored up in him since Julia's death could be exorcised, or at least quieted, through her.

Elvis was tamed. The gold-suited figure whose lip had curled on behalf of all British adolescence, whose windmill-like limbs had altered the posture of a generation, could now be seen meekly seated in a barber's chair preparatory to serving two years in the United States Army. No one yet quite comprehended how much this repentance was a stroke of incomparable showmanship by his manager, 'Colonel' Tom Parker, a one-time huckster at fairs and carnivals. It mattered less to America than to Britain, which Elvis had not yet visited, although rumours of his coming were continually rife. As the Colonel beamed fatly and Elvis shouldered arms, showing what a decent kid he had been all along, England's rockers vowed that, in their eyes at least, 'The King' would never abdicate.

There was some consolation in an upsurge of British Rock and Roll, and a television show capable of reflecting it. *Oh Boy!* every Saturday night, on the solitary commercial channel, filled a dark stage, as in some Miracle play, with major American performers like Eddie Cochran and Gene Vincent, and their British counterparts, Marty Wilde, Dickie Pride, Duffy Power, Vince Eager, Tony Sheridan. There was also a new young Elvis copy, Cliff Richard, whose lip unfurled at the corner like a faulty window blind, and whose backing group, the Shadows, featured in equal prominence around him, stepping to and fro with their guitars in unison. Their first record, Move It, was the first successful British version of American Rock and Roll with its jungle-like bass rhythm and clangorous lead guitar.

Up in Liverpool, the three guitarists in a group still called the Quarry Men watched *Oh Boy!* every Saturday night, crawling close to the television screen when the Shadows came on, to try to see how they did that stupendous Move It intro. Paul McCartney worked it out first and at once jumped on his bike with his guitar to hurry over to John's.

Of all the original, top-heavy skiffle group, apart from John himself, only one member remained. They still had Colin Hanton, the little upholsterer, and the £38 drum kit he was paying for in instalments. They only kept him on, as Colin well knew, for the sake of those drums. Having a drummer, however unsatisfactory, made the difference between a *real* group and three lads just messing around with guitars.

Without Nigel Whalley to manage them, their playing was on a haphazard basis, at birthday parties, youth club dances or social clubs, where they would perform for a pie and a pint of ale. To

Colin, the ale was consolation for knowing they only wanted him for his drums, and for the increasingly acid remarks made by Paul McCartney about his playing.

Both John and George now owned electric guitars. John's was a fawn-coloured Hofner 'Club 40', semi-solid, with two knobs on it, while George had persuaded his mother to help him raise £30 for a Hofner 'Futurama', externally, at least, like the one played by Buddy Holly. But neither could yet afford to buy an amplifier. At a date, if they could not cadge a loan of someone else's, George would wire both guitars perilously through the microphone system.

Colin Hanton was still playing with them when a second chance arrived to become Carroll Levis 'Discoveries'. Again, with every other local group, they presented themselves at the Empire theatre to be auditioned by the great man—this time for his Granada Televison talent show. They got through the Liverpool heats, and were booked to appear in the semi-finals at the Hippodrome Theatre studios in Manchester. Before they left they changed their name to Johnny and the Moondogs.

The journey to Manchester was overshadowed by their general poverty. 'We hadn't worked out in advance how much it would cost us to get there by train and by bus,' Colin Hanton says. 'When we got on the bus in Manchester, Paul discovered he hadn't got enough money to get home again. He was panicking all over the place. "What am I going to *do*? This is *serious*." A bloke stood up at the front to get off and, as he passed Paul, he stuck a two bob bit into his hand. Paul got up and yelled down the bus stairs after him, "I love you."'

Poverty robbed them of their opportunity to appear on television with Carroll Levis's infant ballerinas and players of musical saws. The final judging, on the strength of the audience applause for each act, did not take place until late evening, after the last bus and train back to Liverpool had gone. Johnny and the Moondogs, with no money to spend on an overnight hotel stay, had to leave before the finale.

Colin Hanton appeared with them as drummer for the last time one Saturday night at the Picton Lane busmen's social club. They had got the engagement through George Harrison's father, who acted as MC there and, with Mrs. Harrison, ran a learners' ballroom dancing class. From George's Dad had come the important news that a local cinema manager would be dropping in to see whether Johnny and the Moondogs were suitable to put on in the interval between his Sunday picture shows.

'At the beginning, that night went really well,' Colin Hanton says. 'We were all in a good mood—pulling George's leg and saying, "There's George's Dad; where's his bus?" It was a real stage they'd put us on, with a curtain that came up and down. The curtain got stuck, so we played six numbers, not five, in our first spot. The busmen and clippies were all cheering, they really dug us.

'In the interval, we were told, "There's a pint for you lads over at the bar." That pint turned into two pints, then three. When we went on for the second spot, we were *terrible*. All pissed. The bloke from the Pavilion never booked us. There was a row about it on the bus going home, and I thought, "Right. That's it. I'll not bother playing with them again." '

For the rest of 1958, Johnny and the Moondogs effectively folded. They would still get together and play, but only at small events like birthday parties, where the lack of a drummer did not count so much; calling themselves any name that came into their heads. One night, when they all arrived in different coloured shirts, they called themselves the Rainbows. John and Paul would sometimes sing and play as a duo, the Nurk Twins. George Harrison played part of the time in a steadier group, the Les Stuart Quartet, which had as its regular venue a club out in West Derby called the Lowlands.

A short distance away, in the quiet thoroughfare of Hayman's Green, stood a large Victorian house belonging to a family named Best. Johnny Best had originally been Liverpool's main promoter of boxing matches in the city's 6,000-seat stadium. His wife, Mona, was a brisk, dark-eyed woman of Anglo-Indian birth. The couple had lately separated, leaving Mona Best in the big old house with her bedridden mother, her two sons, Peter and Rory, a collection of paying guests and assorted Eastern mementoes including the Hindu idol that flexed its many arms in the front hall.

Peter, her elder son, was then 18, and in the Sixth form at Liverpool Collegiate Grammar School. An outstanding scholar and athlete, he was also unusually handsome, in a wry, brooding way, with neat, crisp, wavy hair cut in Jeff Chandler style. If, in addition, he was somewhat modest and slow to push himself, then 'Mo', as he called his mother, would be there to back him with her energy, her quick tongue and dark, rapidly-kindling eyes.

Under the house were extensive cellars, used for storage and the boys' bicycles. Pete and Rory, fatigued by the long summer holiday of 1958, asked Mona Best if they could make a den down there for themselves and their friends. There were so many friends that Mrs. Best suggested making the cellar into a real club, like the Lowlands and city espresso bars. For the rest of that year, she, her two sons and a team of potential members redecorated the cellar, installing bench seats and a counter above which, as a final touch, Mrs. Best painted a dragon on the ceiling. Her favourite film being *Algiers*, with Charles Boyer, she decided to call the new club the Casbah.

There then arose the question of finding a group to play on club nights. One of the girl helpers mentioned Ken Browne, who played at the Lowlands in Les Stuart's quartet. Ken Browne paid the Casbah a visit while redecorations were still in progress, bringing with him another quartet-member, George Harrison. 'George didn't seem to show too much enthusiasm for what we were doing,' Mona Best says, 'but Ken Browne threw himself heart and soul into it. He'd come over and help us with the work at weekends.'

When George came back, he brought with him two other musicians for the Casbah's resident group. 'John Lennon walked in with Paul McCartney, and John's girl friend, Cyn'. We were still painting—trying to get ready for our opening night. John got hold of a paint brush to help us, but he was without his glasses and as blind as a bat. He started putting paint on surfaces which didn't require paint. And all in gloss when I'd told him to use undercoat. On opening night, some of the paint still wasn't quite dry.'

In sedate West Derby, the Casbah Coffee Club caught on with teenagers at once. Mona Best ran it in person, selling coffee, sweets and soft drinks behind the miniature bar. John, Paul, George and Ken Browne played, without a drummer and using Ken Browne's 10-watt amplifier, for £3 a night between four of them. They all grew friendly with the Bests, especially with Pete, the handsome, taciturn elder son who, despite his plan to become a teacher, was keenly interested in Rock and Roll and show business. The group proved such an attraction that, at weekends, Mrs. Best would hire a doorman to keep out the rougher element.

'It all went fine,' Mona Best says, 'until this one night when Ken Browne turned up with a heavy cold. I could see he wasn't well enough to play. I said to him, "Look, you go upstairs and sit with Mother"—he often did that; she was bedridden, you see, and he'd sit and talk to her. I said, "I'll bring a hot drink up to you." But Ken said no, he'd stay down in the club and watch. Just John, Paul and George played, and at the end, I gave them 15s each. There was a bit of murmuring; then they said, "Where's the other 15s?" "I've given it to Ken," I told them.

'They didn't like that. They wanted the full £3. But it was too late. I'd already given Ken his 15s. There was a bit of arguing and Ken said right, that was it, he'd finished with them. The other three walked out of the club there and then.

'Pete, my elder boy, had been getting more and more interested, watching the others play. I remember Ken Browne saying to him, "Right. I'm out of that lot. Come on, Pete: why don't you and I get a group up now?" '

Twice each week, Arthur Ballard would leave the College of Art in Hope Street to conduct a private tutorial with the student he considered the most gifted of all under his charge. The student, a white-faced, tiny boy named Stuart Sutcliffe, refused to work in College; he had his own cramped studio, in the basement of a house in Percy Street, where Ballard would visit him, bringing a half-bottle of Scotch whisky for refreshment. The tutorial was a morning's talk, during which Sutcliffe never stopped painting. 'He worked with large canvases, which wasn't at all fashionable then,' Arthur Ballard says. 'He was so small, he almost had to jump with his brush to reach the top.'

Among the students, Stu Sutcliffe was something of a cult. His pale, haunted face, topped by luxuriously swept-back hair, gave him a more than passing resemblance to James Dean, the Hollywood star who had become legendary to that generation for the hectic fame and shortness of his life. Stu was aware of the resemblance, cultivating it with dark glasses and an air of brooding remoteness far from his true personality.

He was born of Scottish parents in Edinburgh in 1940. His father, Charles, a senior Civil Servant, moved to Liverpool on wartime munitions work and subsequently went to sea as a ship's engineer. The rearing of Stuart and his two younger sisters was left to their mother, Millie, an infants school teacher. Charles Sutcliffe's spells at home were marked by heavy drinking and cruelty to his wife, which Stuart frequently witnessed. From the earliest age, Millie Sutcliffe says, he strove to take on the role of her protector. 'I'd sometimes be sitting in my chair with my head in my hands. Stuart would sit at my feet, looking up at me. "You're tired," he'd say. "Come on, we'll put the little ones to bed, then you and me must have a talk." '

He had entered Art College from Prescot Grammar School, below the normal admittance-age, and had quickly revealed a talent of dazzling diversity. His first terms, in addition to prosaic curriculum work, produced notebooks thronging with evidence of a facility to reproduce any style from Matisse to Michaelangelo. Derivative as his student work was, it had a quality which excited Arthur Ballard—a refusal to accept or transmit anything according to convention. 'Stu was a revolutionary,' Ballard says. 'Everything he did crackled with excitement.'

Early in 1959, the path of Hope Street's most promising student crossed that of its most uninspired and apathetic one. At Ye Cracke, the student pub in Rice Street, beneath the etchings of Wellington greeting Blücher at Waterloo, and Nelson's death at Trafalgar, Stu Sutcliffe fell into conversation with John Lennon.

The intermediary was a friend of Stu's named Bill Harry, a curly-haired boy who had won his way from a poor childhood in Upper Parliament Street to become the College's first student of Commercial Design. Bill was a prolific amateur journalist, a writer and illustrator of science fiction 'fanzines', and, like Stu himself, an omnivorous reader. They would sit for hours in Ye Cracke, discussing Henry Miller and Kerouac and the 'beat' poets, Corso and Ferlinghetti, whose works stirred up in them vague restlessness and yearning for open roads and giant skylines traversed by huge old fin-tailed Chevrolet cars.

In Bill Harry, John found someone, not stand-offish and superior as he had thought all his fellow students to be, but down-to-earth, friendly, humorous and encouraging. Bill knew already of John's interest in writing, and, one lunch-time at Ye Cracke, asked if there was anything of John's that he could read. He remembers with what embarrassment John dragged some scraps of paper from his jeans pocket and handed them over. Instead of the Ginsberg or Corso pastiche he had expected, Bill Harry found himself reading a piece of nonsense about a farmer that made him gurgle with laughter.

Stu Sutcliffe's effect on John was more complex. John was fascinated by Stu's clothes. For Stu, in 1959, resembled neither Teddy Boy nor Jazz cellar habitué. He had evolved his own style of skin-tight jeans, pink shirts with pinned collars and pointed boots with high, elasticated sides. His dress, in fact, was disapproved of by the Art College far more than John's, but was tolerated because of his brilliance as a student.

Stu's passionate commitment to his painting, and to art and literature in all young and vital forms, communicated itself to John in a way that no formal teaching had been able to do. From Stu, he learned of the French Impressionists, whose rebellion against accepted values made that of Rock and Roll seem marginal. Van Gogh, even more than Elvis Presley, now became the hero against whom John Lennon measured the world.

John's sudden enthusiasm for his College studies to some extent benefited Paul McCartney also. Paul, still revising for O-levels at the Institute, was only too glad to join in intellectual discussions, passing himself off as a student from the nearby university. For George Harrison, it was more arduous, since John among his Art College cronies was even more inclined to be witty at George's expense. But he was 15 now, and not such a kid, and learning to answer John back.

This new era revived the group which had been languishing again since the dispute at Mrs. Best's. Stu and Bill Harry both sat on the Student's Union committee, and were thus able to get bookings for John, Paul, and George to play at College dances. The trouble was, although John and George had electric guitars, they no longer had Ken Browne and his 10-watt amplifier. On Stu Sutcliffe's recommendation, the Student's Union agreed to buy an amplifier for them to use, on the understanding, of course, that it should not be taken away from College.

Stu's interest in Rock and Roll was a purely romantic and visual one. He passionately wanted to join a group as an adjunct to the personal image he had created for himself. As John Lennon and he became closer friends, the idea grew that Stu, in some or other capacity, should join John's group. That he possessed no ability on any instrument was not considered a disqualification. If he were to buy a guitar—or, better still, some drums—he surely would be able to learn in the way the other three had. Unfortunately, Stu, with his small grant and his straitened family circumstances, had no money to spend at Hessy's music shop.

In 1959, the biennial John Moores Exhibition took place at Liverpool's illustrious Walker Art Gallery. Mr. Moores was, and remains, the city's commercial patriarch, deriving fortunes from football pools, shops and mail-order, of which a sizeable part is philanthropically devoted to encouraging the Arts on Merseyside. This was the second Moores Exhibition, offering £4,000 in prize money and attracting some 2,000 entries from all over the British Isles. A canvas submitted by Stu Sutcliffe was one of the handful selected for hanging.

John Lennon's Aunt Mimi remembers his unfeigned pleasure in Stu's achievement. 'He came *rushing* in to tell me . . . "You'll never guess; it's the Moores Exhibition. You must come and see it. And look *nice!*"

'We went to the Walker Art Gallery and John took me up to this enormous painting. It seemed to be all khaki and yellow triangles. I looked at it and I said, "What *is* it?" Well! John got hold of my arm and hustled me outside; I wasn't allowed to see another picture in the show. "How could you *say* a thing like that, Mimi?" He gave his chest a big thump, and bellowed, "Art comes from in here!" '

As well as hanging in one of Europe's principal galleries, Stu's painting was bought, by the great John Moores himself, for £65. 'He'd never really had any money before,' Millie Sutcliffe says. 'I knew he'd got one or two little debts he needed to pay. The rest would see him right, I thought, to buy his paints and canvases for a few weeks.

'His father was home, and went up to Stuart's room while he

wasn't there. It was his father who found this thing that Stuart had spent *all* the John Moores prize money on. "That's right, Mother," he said. "It's a bass guitar. I'm going to play with John in his group." '

May 1960

'The bass drum used to roll away across the stage'

In Slater Street, on the edge of Chinatown, there was a little coffee bar, with copper kettles in its window, called the Jacaranda. John Lennon, Stu Sutcliffe and their Art College friends went there almost every day, between classes or in place of them. The coffee was cheap, toast with jam cost only fivepence a slice, nor was the management particular about the time its customers spent wedged behind the little kidney-shaped tables. Whole days could be spent, over one cold coffee cup, looking through the window steam at passing Chinese, West Indians, lascars, dockers and men going to and from the nearby Unemployment office.

To the Jacaranda's black-bearded owner, Allan Williams, John and his friends were 'a right load of layabouts'. Williams had studied them at length while passing coffees and toasted sandwiches through from the back kitchen where his Chinese wife Beryl cooked and kept accounts. He had particularly noticed the slightly-built boy in dark glasses whom the others teased for carrying Art materials round with him in a carrier bag. He could not but notice the one called John, who expertly dredged sixpences from the purse of the blonde girl who sat next to him, and could even cajole free drinks and snacks from the more susceptible waitresses.

'The Jac' was not Allan Williams's sole enterprise. He had, in his time, pursued many trades, among them plumber, artificial jewellery maker and door-to-door salesman. Being a Welshman, naturally he had a voice. Indeed, he had almost trained for the operatic stage. His Welsh tenor was heard, instead, in the Victorian pubs and West Indian shebeens round Liverpool 8, where Allan Williams pursued an energetic, but as yet unspecific, career as a bohemian and entrepreneur.

At intervals, his curly-haired, stocky figure would swagger back along Slater Street to the tumbledown house where, on a capital of £100, he had opened his Jacaranda coffee bar. The 'right load of layabouts' would still be there. Prising their coffee cups away, Allan Williams would remark with heavy sarcasm that *they* were never going to make him his fortune.

*

In the world outside Liverpool, unabated disapproval of Rock and Roll had worn it into a more acceptable shape. The word was 'Rock' no longer, but 'Pop'. The taste—again dictated by America—was for cleancut, collegiate-looking youths whose energy had left their pelvic regions and gone into their ingratiating smiles. The British idol of the hour was a former skiffler named Adam Faith, with the looks of a haunted Cassius and a voice which all the artifice of recording engineers could not rid of its heavy adenoids. A ballad called What Do You Want?—or, as Adam Faith enunciated it, Puwhat Do Yuh Pwant?—went to Number One late in 1959, using an arrangement of pizzicato violins unashamedly copied from the American Buddy Holly. Holly lodged no suit for plagiarism, having died in an air crash eight months earlier.

But while Britain listened to Adam Faith and 'Pop', Liverpool listened to Rhythm and Blues. The Cunard Yanks were bringing over records by a new young black performer still confined by his own country to the low indecent level of negro 'race' music. His name was Chuck Berry; the songs he sang were wry and ragged, vividly pictorial eulogies to girls and cars, the joys and neuroses of big city American life. Those songs broke like anthems on the young of a northern city still gripped by the Victorian age, which had had no truck with black people since the slave hulks set sail from Liverpool Bay.

All over Merseyside each Saturday night, in ballrooms, town halls, Co-op halls, even swimming baths and ice skating rinks, there were amateur R & B groups playing Chuck Berry songs, Little Richard, Fats Domino and B. B. King songs: the hymns to fast cars and flashy women which, filtered through a Scouse accent, did not depart much in spirit from the original. For the two races had more in common than might be supposed. Liverpool, too, felt itself segregated from the privileged Midlands and South. Liverpool, too, had withstood its oppressions by mordant wit and indefatigable stylishness of mind.

Rory Storm and the Hurricanes were the city's most popular group. Rory, a blond, amiable youth known by day as Alan Caldwell, was afflicted by a stammer which, fortunately, vanished when he opened his mouth to sing. He had been an outstanding athlete and swimmer, and would enliven his stage performance by feats of acrobatics and climbing. At the Majestic ballroom in Birkenhead, he would shin up a pillar from the stage to the promenade balcony. At the Tower Ballroom, downriver in New Brighton, he would crawl about inside the 100-foot-high dome. His occasional falls increased his drawing power. His group had lately acquired a new drummer—a slightly-built boy from the Dingle, with mournful eyes, prematurely greying sidewhiskers and a habit of burdening his fingers with cheap rings. This drummer's name was Richard Starkey but he preferred, in emulation of his Wild West heroes, to be known as Ringo Starr.

After Rory Storm in popularity came Cass and the Casanovas, a four-man group whose drummer, Johnny Hutch, was the most powerful on Merseyside. They said of Johnny Hutch—as, indeed, he said of himself—that he could take his brain out and lie it on the table, and his drumsticks would still go on hitting in time.

The Saturday dances over, most of the groups would drive back from the suburbs into Liverpool to congregate at Allan Williams's Jacaranda coffee bar. At night in the basement, there was dancing to a full West Indian steel band. Though no alcohol could legally be served, much was drunk in 'spiked' coffee and soft drinks. Ever and again, some disturbance would summon Allan Williams downstairs, whence he would emerge, a little later, breathing stertorously.

Rory Storm, Brian Casser and Duke Duval were personalities whom John Lennon and his followers held in awe. For John's group, such as it was, figured nowhere in the leagues of local favouritism. No less an authority than Johnny Hutch, the Casanovas' drummer, had given his opinion that they 'weren't worth a carrot'.

To begin with, they still lacked a drummer. Johnny Hutch was especially scornful on that point. It would not have mattered so much with a strong undercurrent of bass guitar. But Stu Sutcliffe had only just begun learning to play the big Hofner 'President' bass he had bought with his John Moores prize. The President hung heavy on Stu's slight frame; his slim fingers found difficulty in stretching to the simplest chord-shapes. Even so, at John's insistence, he was appearing on stage with the others. He would stand turning half-away so the audience could not see how little and how painfully he was playing.

They had had, and lost, one opportunity at the Casanova Club, a Sunday afternoon jive session in a room above the Temple restaurant in Dale Street. The promoter, Sam Leach, agreed to try them out in support of his resident group, Cass and the Casanovas. But the club members had little time for a group with no drummer and only one small tinkling amp—a group which did not go in for suits and step dance routines like Cliff Richard's Shadows, but instead wore strange, scruffy, 'arty' black crewneck sweaters and tennis shoes, and jumped and leapt in wild asymmetry. And when Paul McCartney began to sing in his high, almost feminine voice, there were titters of amusement from some of the girls.

They did little better at Lathom Hall, out at Seaforth where the Mersey broadens against the rim of Albert Dock. The night's main group were the Dominoes, featuring 'Kingsize' Taylor, a vast youth visible by day cutting up meat in a local butcher's shop. Paul, John, George and Stu had been hired merely to play during the interval. They were so bad that the management ordered them offstage after their second song. When the Dominoes came on again, Kingsize Taylor saw John, Paul and George standing near the stage, each scribbling furiously on a piece of paper. 'They were writing down the words of the songs as we sang them. They'd take turns to scribble down a line each of Dizzy Miss Lizzie.'

They still practised for hours on end, at George's or Paul's house, using a tape-recorder of the old-fashioned sort that grew gently warm after a couple of hours' use. They had no idea of the way they wanted to be. They knew only that they wanted to be nothing like Cliff Richard's neat, smiling, step-dancing Shadows. A tape has survived of a long, rambling Blues sequence with George on lead guitar, his fingers stumbling frequently over half-learned phrases; John and Paul strumming in a hollow chorus; Stu Sutcliffe keeping up on bass by playing as few notes as possible. At one point, Paul's voice breaks in impatiently with a kind of impromptu jazz scat-singing. Later there are attempts at various rhythms, first rockabilly, then Latin-American, then a note-for-note copy of the Eddie Cochran song Hallelujah I Love Her So. Suddenly they break into a song which was among the first ever written by John Lennon—The One After 909. The beat lifts; their voices coalesce: for a moment they are recognisable as what they were to become. Then they go back to sitting round while George, painfully, tries to learn the Blues.

From the same period, there is a letter drafted by Paul in his scholarly hand, soliciting a mention in some local newspaper after a chance encounter with one of the journalists. The letter claims group accomplishments as much academic as musical; it makes great play with the fact that John goes to Art College, and confers on Paul himself a fictitious place 'reading English at Liverpool University'. Paul's songwriting partnership with John is said to have produced 'more than 50 numbers', among them Looking Glass, Thinking of Linking, Winston's Walk and The One After 909. To cover every option, the group is credited with a 'Jazz feel' and a repertoire of 'standards' such as Moonglow, Ain't She Sweet and You Are My Sunshine. 'The group's name,' Paul wrote, 'is . . .' They still had not been able to make up their minds.

Stu Sutcliffe had lately been evicted from his basement in Percy Street for painting all the furniture white. He suggested to John that they both move into their friend Rod Murray's flat in Gambier Terrace, a big, windswept Victorian parade overlooking the Anglican cathedral. The flat was principally floorboards, strewn with records, stolen traffic signs and the mattresses used by various semi-nomadic tenants. Bill Harry, a frequent sleeper in the bath, remembers all-night talk sessions in which Stu and he elaborated their plan to write a book that would give Liverpool the same cultural identity that Kerouac and the 'beat' poets had given America. John Lennon's chief contributions were word games and charades of elaborate craziness.

Though John soon left Gambier Terrace, his friendship with Stu continued. The two were together most of the day, when Paul and George could not escape class at the Institute. They would sit for hours in the Jacaranda coffee bar, Stu sketching and crayoning while John, with his wolfish smile, appraised the most pliant of the waitresses. So it came about that Allan Williams, with his talent for using people, discovered a way of using even two penniless Art students.

Williams was currently engaged in his first major venture as an entrepreneur. He had hired St. George's Hall, Liverpool's chief public building, as the venue for an 'Arts Ball', modelled on the Chelsea Arts Ball in London. John and Stu found themselves roped in to design and build the decorated carnival floats whose ritual destruction was the best-known feature of the London event. On the day of the ball, Williams used them as a labouring gang to manhandle the floats across St. George's piazza, under the disapproving eye of Victoria and Albert, and into the Great Hall with its priceless mosaic floor, its marble busts of Peel and George Stephenson and its towering pipe organ.

The 1959 Liverpool Arts Ball was an event prophetic of Allan Williams's career as an impresario. The comedian Bruce Forsyth was among VIP guests who watched, not only the ritual destruction of the carnival floats, but also flour and fire extinguisher fights and intermittent attempts to play Rock and Roll on the Civic organ. At midnight, balloons came down from a web of football goal nets suspended in the ceiling. After that, owing to employee-error, the heavy, greasy nets themselves fell on the heads of the crowd.

Among the promoters of British Pop music in the late 1950s, none had so potent a reputation as Larry Parnes. It was Parnes who, in 1956, metamorphosed Tommy Steele, 'Britain's first Rock 'n' Roller', from a Cockney merchant seaman he had spotted strumming a guitar in a Soho drinking club. Tommy Steele's colossal success with British teenagers was due largely to his youthful manager's intuitive brilliance as an agent and image-builder and the jealous care with which, following Colonel Tom Parker's example, he guarded his money-spinning protégé. Though Tommy Steele had now somewhat diminished as a Pop attraction, the enterprises of Larry Parnes had prospered and multiplied.

By 1959, Parnes controlled what he himself liked to call a 'stable' of the leading British male Pop singers. Most were ingenuous youths from unknown provincial cities who had somehow found their way to London and the 2 I's coffee bar in Old Compton Street, hallowed as the place where Larry Parnes had spotted Tommy Steele. It was Parnes's experience that the right stage name could transform almost any teenage warehouse assistant or welder into the latest blow-waved, knee-trembling demigod. Thus, in a series of inspired rebaptisms, he had given the world a Marty Wilde, a Vince Eager, a Dickie Pride, a Duffy Power, a Billy Fury and a Johnny Gentle.

As well as supplying most of the *Oh Boy!* television series, Parnes used his stable to create self-contained travelling shows which for British fans in places far from London represented the sole chance to see 'live' Rock and Roll music. Larry Parnes shows played at theatres and cinemas, but also at town halls, *palaises-de-danse* and rural Corn Exchanges. No audience, however small or distant, would be overlooked by the dark-haired, deferential, ferociously-alert young man whom the business already knew as 'Mister Parnes Shillings and Pence'.

Early in 1960, Larry Parnes promoted a tour headed by two imported American stars, Eddie Cochran and Gene Vincent. Cochran, whose Summertime Blues sold a million copies in 1958, was a 21-year-old Oklahoman with the hulking pout of an Elvis run to fat. Vincent was a 25-year-old ex-sailor, famous for his wailing voice, his group the Bluecaps and a classic piece of Rock and Roll gibberish called Be Bop a Lula. Partly crippled from a motorcycle accident, he performed anchored to the stage by a leg-iron, and irradiating depravity and ill-health. Nor was this present tour destined to build up his constitution.

In Liverpool, as in every city along its route, the Cochran-Vincent show was a sell-out. Larry Parnes himself was at the Empire theatre to watch the wild welcome his artists received, even in this remote corner of the land. Elsewhere, amid the shouting and stamping, three would-be Rock and Rollers from a group last known as Johnny and the Moondogs strained their eyes to try to see the fingering of Eddie Cochran's guitar solo in Hallelujah I Love Her So. In yet another seat, the proprietor of the Jacaranda coffee bar suddenly perceived that there might be easier ways to a fortune than by attempting to bring the Chelsea Arts Ball to Liverpool. In Allan Williams's own words, 'I could smell money. Lots of it.'

Afterwards, Williams sought out Larry Parnes and, as one impresario to another, invited him back to the Jacaranda. By the end of the night, Parnes had been talked into bringing back

Eddie Cochran and Gene Vincent for a second concert, promoted in partnership with Allan Williams at the city's 6,000-seat boxing stadium. Half the programme would consist of Parnes acts; the other half would be provided by Williams from among local groups like Rory Storm and the Hurricanes, and Cass and the Casanovas. The concert, lasting several hours, was fixed to take place after Eddie Cochran and Gene Vincent had finished their current tour.

At the very last minute, however, there was a hitch. Cochran and Vincent had appeared at the Hippodrome theatre, Bristol, and were returning to London by road. Near Chippenham, Wiltshire, their hire car skidded and struck a tree. Eddie Cochran—who, by one of those bilious musical ironies had just recorded a song called Three Steps To Heaven—suffered fatal injuries. Gene Vincent and another passenger, the songwriter Sharon Seeley, were both seriously hurt.

A telephone call to Larry Parnes confirmed the news that Allan Williams had heard over the radio. Eddie Cochran would not be able to appear at Liverpool boxing stadium. Gene Vincent, despite fresh injuries added to his residual ones, might be fit, Parnes thought; just the same it would be wiser to cancel the promotion. Williams, having sold most of the tickets, and feeling death to be insufficient as an excuse to a Liverpool audience, insisted the show should go ahead, and feverishly went in search of more local groups to pad out the programme.

His search took him, among other places, to Holyoake Hall, near Penny Lane, and one of the better-run local jive dances. The hall, unlike most, had its own regular compère and disc jockey, Bob Wooler. A clerk in the railway dock office at Garston, Wooler possessed an encyclopaedic knowledge of local bands and their personnel. On his earliest recommendation, Allan Williams booked Bob Evans and the Five Shillings, and Gerry and the Pacemakers, an up-and-coming quartet whose leader, Gerry Marsden, worked on the railway also, as a van delivery-boy.

The Gene Vincent boxing stadium show, jointly promoted by Larry Parnes and Allan Williams, thus, inadvertently, became the first major occurence of a brand of teenage music indigenous to Liverpool and the Mersey. By an inscrutable irony, the three individuals destined to carry that music into undreamable galaxies of fame were not then considered competent enough to take part. John Lennon, Paul McCartney and George Harrison had to be content with ringside seats and watching Rory Storm, Cass and the Casanovas—even their old rivals, the group that featured the midget Nicky Cuff.

The concert proceeded on a note of rising pandemonium, at the height of which Rory Storm was sent out with his incapacitating stammer to appeal for calm. The show's best performance was unanimously felt to be that of Gerry and the Pacemakers, singing a sentimental ballad, You'll Never Walk Alone. No more inappropriate introduction could have been given to the infirm, black leather-clad figure of Gene Vincent himself, who was at last propelled through the ropes into the boxing ring. As the ringside spectators made a rush to join him, Larry Parnes and Allan Williams trotted round briskly, stamping on their hands.

It was shortly after this memorable night that John Lennon sidled up to Williams at the Jacaranda's kitchen door, and muttered, 'Hey, Al, why don't you do something for us?' John had been there with George and Stu Sutcliffe after the boxing stadium show when Williams brought the great Larry Parnes back to discuss further co-promotions. Parnes, impressed by the Liverpool music, had hinted at the possibility of using local groups to back solo singers from his stable when touring brought them northward.

Allan Williams, while thinking no more highly of John's group than anyone else did, felt he owed them a favour in return for the Arts Ball floats. Though not prepared to offer them to Larry Parnes, he did agree to help Johnny and the Moondogs become better organised. They, in return, would do such small general jobs as Allan Williams required.

Williams further promised to try to find them the drummer they so chronically lacked. From Cass, of Cass and the Casanovas, he heard of a man named Tommy Moore who sometimes sat in on drums at Sam Leach's club and who, despite owning his own full kit, belonged to no group permanently. Within the week, Tommy Moore had been persuaded by Allan Williams to throw in his lot with Johnny and the Moondogs.

The new recruit was a small, worried-looking individual of 36, whose daytime job was driving a fork lift truck at the Garston Bottle-making Works. For all that, in his audition at Gambier Terrace, he proved to be a better drummer than any who had ever sat behind Johnny and the Moondogs. When he showed himself able to produce the slow, skipping beat of the Everly Brothers' song, Cathy's Clown, even Paul McCartney seemed satisfied.

Tommy Moore began practising with them downstairs at the Jacaranda, in preparation for the work which Allan Williams had promised them when they were good enough. Williams, meantime, used them as odd job men to redecorate the 'Jac's' promitive ladies' lavatory. John and Stu Sutcliffe were also encouraged to cover the brick walls of their rehearsal room with voodoo-ish murals.

Tommy soon noticed what peculiar tensions were at work

within Johnny and the Moondogs. 'John and Paul were always at it, trying to outdo each other. It was them at the front and the rest of us way behind. George used to stand there, not saying a word. And didn't they used to send up that other lad, Stuart! Oh, they never left off teasing him. They said he couldn't play his bass—and he couldn't, though he tried.'

To begin with, Allan Williams would allow them to play to the Jacaranda customers only when his regular attraction, the Royal Caribbean Steel Band, had the night off. Since the cellar had no microphone stands, two girls had to be persuaded to kneel in front of John and Paul, holding up hand mikes attached to a mop-handle and broom. 'I could have retired on what we used to get for playing at the Jac',' Tommy Moore says. 'A bottle of Coke and a plate of beans on toast.'

The great Larry Parnes, meanwhile, had contacted Allan Williams again about the possibility of using Liverpool musicians as backing groups for the solo singers in his 'stable'. It happened that 'Mister Parnes Shillings and Pence' was experiencing difficulty in finding London bands willing to go on tour in the north and Scotland for the rates of pay he offered. When Parnes contacted Allan Williams again, it was with a request that Williams should marshal some local groups for audition as possible sidesmen for Parnes's biggest male Pop star, Billy Fury.

The news caused a particular stir in Liverpool because Billy Fury was himself a Liverpudlian. Born Ronnie Wycherley, in the tough Dingle area, he had been a Mersey tugboat hand until two years earlier when his girl friend had sent Larry Parnes some of the songs he had written. Parnes had worked the usual transformation with a tempestuous stage name, a brooding persona and a series of hit records, sung in an Elvis-like mumble. Billy Fury, it was further announced, would be coming up to Liverpool with his manager to attend the audition in person.

Every group that frequented the Jacaranda was agog for what seemed a Heaven-sent opportunity. Williams, in the end, narrowed the field down to Rory Storm and the Hurricanes, Cass and the Casanovas, Derry Wilkie and the Seniors, and Johnny and the Moondogs. In Allan Williams's opinion, Johnny and the Moondogs were now ready for something more than decorating the ladies' lavatory.

One pressing requirement, before Larry Parnes saw them, was for a change of name. What they needed was something spry and catchy, like Buddy Holly's Crickets. Stu Sutcliffe, half-jokingly, wrote down 'beetles' in his sketch book—such a silly idea that the others said, Why not? John, unable to leave any word alone, changed it to 'beat-les', as a pun on beat music.

At the Jacaranda, the new name was greeted with astringent disfavour. No one, Allan Williams assured them, could *ever* take seriously a group who called themselves that. Cass, of Cass and the Casanovas, agreed it was a terrible idea. In Cass's opinion they should stick to the formula of so-and-so and the such-and-such. Prompted by vague memories of Treasure Island, he suggested Long John and the Silver Beatles. Though John refused to call himself Long John, the Silver Beatles was accepted for want of anything better.

The place fixed for the audition was a small working-men's club, the Wyvern, in Seel Street, just round the corner from the Jacaranda. Allan Williams had recently acquired the premises with the object of turning them into a plushy London-style 'night spot'. Punctual to the minute, in through the half-demolished foyer walked Larry Parnes, silk-suited and affable, accompanied by the tall, elegant, woebegone youth, currently the biggest name in British Pop music, who cared rather less for stardom than for the dog and tortoise he was permitted to keep at his manager's London flat.

Down in the basement, the Silver Beatles viewed the competition with dismay. Every group was locally famous, smartly-suited and luxuriously-equipped. Derry and the Seniors had been well known in Liverpool for years as an authentic Rhythm and Blues group featuring a black singer, Derry Wilkie, an electric keyboard and a real live saxophone. Johnny Hutch of Cass and the Casanovas was already setting up the sequinned drumkit which he was said to be able to play in his sleep. Rory Storm was there, deeply-tanned, with his Italian-suited Hurricanes. Rory's drummer, the little sad-eyed, bearded one, came from the Dingle also, and had been in Billy Fury's class at school. Neither John nor Paul in those days much liked the look of Ringo Starr.

Parnes, sitting with Billy Fury at a small table in the twilight, was impressed by the power and variety of the music. Derry and the Seniors and Rory Storm's Hurricanes were both marked down as strong contenders for the prize. Parnes also favoured Cass and the Casanovas, thanks mainly to their bass-player, Johnny Gustafson, a black-haired, extremely good-looking boy. 'Johnny Gus', in fact, was later called down to London to experience the Parnes star-making process on his own.

The Silver Beatles, when their turn came, made rather less of an impression. 'They weren't a bit smart,' Larry Parnes says. 'They just wore jeans, black sweaters, tennis shoes—and lockets.' There was a delay as well, owing to the non-arrival of Tommy Moore, who had gone in search of some stray pieces of drum equipment at the Casanova Club. At length, when Tommy still had not appeared, Johnny Hutch had to be persuaded to sit in with them.

A snapshot, taken in mid-audition, shows the Silver Beatles exactly as Larry Parnes saw them that day at the Wyvern social club. John and Paul occupy the foreground, back to back madly bucking and crouching over their cheap guitars. To the right stands George, his sole concession to rhythm a slight hanging of the head. Stu Sutcliffe, to the rear with his overburdening bass guitar, turns away as usual to hide his inadequate keyboard work. In the background, Johnny Hutch sits at his magnificent drums, showing a great deal of patterned ankle-sock and, very clearly, bored to death.

As to what Larry Parnes thought of them, there are conflicting eyewitness accounts. Allan Williams's version is that both Parnes and Billy Fury were 'knocked out' by the Silver Beatles, excepting Stu Sutcliffe. Parnes would have signed them at once, at £100 per week, provided they would agree to drop Stu. It was John Lennon's curt refusal to betray his friend, so Williams says, which robbed them of their first big chance.

Parnes himself, unfortunately, has no recollection of finding fault with Stu's bass playing. To Parnes, the eyesore of the group was the worried, rather elderly-looking man who arrived halfway through the audition and took over from Johnny Hutch on drums. Tommy Moore had finally made it across town from Dale Street. 'I thought the boys in front were great,' Parnes says. 'The lead guitar and the bass, so-so. It was the *drummer*, I told them, who was wrong.'

What Larry Parnes really wanted, it transpired, were cut-price musicians to accompany his lesser-known artists on tour into Scotland. Cass and the Casanovas were first to be so engaged, as backing group for a gravel-voiced Parnes singer named Duffy Power.

The next letter from Larry Parnes to Allan Williams concerned the Silver Beatles. In mid-May, Parnes was sending another of his stable, Johnny Gentle, on a two-week tour of Scotland. The Silver Beatles could have the job of backing him, for the same as Cass and the Casanovas had received: £18 each per week.

The offer sent the Silver Beatles into transports of elation. Since the Wyvern social club audition, they had thought they'd lost any chance of finding stardom via Larry Parnes. That Johnny Gentle was the least known of all Parnes's singers did not diminish the excitement of being offered their first work as professionals; of going 'on tour' the way the big names did; of performing in real cinemas and theatres, and staying in hotels the whole night.

All five immediately set about disentangling themselves from their everyday commitments in mid-May. For Stu and John it was simply a matter of cutting College for two weeks. It was less simple for Tommy Moore, whose girl friend set great store by his weekly wage packet from Garston Bottle Works. Tommy pacified her with visions of the wealth he would bring back from across the border.

George Harrison, too, was now a working man. He had left the Institute Grammar School at 16, without O-levels and, for want of anything better, had applied for a job as a window-dresser at Blackler's department store. That vacancy had been filled, but there was another one for an apprentice electrician. To be an apprentice, as both his elder brothers were, represented both a safe and an honourable course. But the only way he could get time off to go to Scotland was to take his summer holiday early.

The greatest ingenuity was shown, as usual, by Paul McCartney. He had to find a method of extricating himself from the Institute Sixth form where, supposedly, he was deep in revision for his forthcoming A-level exams in English and Art. His friend Ivan Vaughan told him he would be mad to risk those A-levels for the sake of the Scottish tour. Somehow he managed to convince his father that two weeks off in term time would aid his revision by giving his brain a rest.

Before they set off, they decided that to be real Pop musicians, they must all adopt stage names. Paul took to calling himself Paul Ramon, thinking it had a hothouse 1920–ish sound. George, whose idol was Carl Perkins, called himself Carl Harrison, and Stu became Stu de Stael, after the painter. John Lennon and Tommy Moore decided not to bother.

They embarked by train from Lime Street, wearing the jeans and black sweaters and tennis shoes that were also their stage outfits, and carrying a selection of borrowed amplifiers which Tommy Moore viewed with deep mistrust. 'The amps got by —just. George was the sparks if anything went wrong. I'd always stand well back while he was fiddling with the plugs. My drums didn't have everything they ought to have had either. I hadn't got a spur to hold the bass drum down. When Paul and John got going in one of their fast Chuck Berry numbers, the bass drum used to go rolling away across the stage.'

The tour struck complications from the start. Duncan McKinnon, Parnes's Scottish intermediary, did not like the look of the Silver Beatles. They liked even less the look of the small van in which they and Johnny Gentle were expected to travel through the Highlands. Nor was there any time to rehearse with Johnny Gentle, a handsome young bruiser who, not long previously, had been a merchant seaman putting into Birkenhead.

Johnny Gentle suffered from stage nerves which he would try to assuage by drinking quantities of lager. Even so, he insisted on taking his turn at the driving because that was the most comfortable seat. On about the second day, somewhat the worse for lager, he drove the vehicle, not at all gently, into the rear of a parked Ford Popular with a couple of old ladies sitting in it. The impact dislodged all the luggage and equipment from the interior suitcase rack and hurled it on top of Tommy Moore.

Tommy was taken away in an ambulance, badly concussed, with his front top and bottom teeth loosened. That night, as he lay in hospital—it was in Banff, he thinks—wearing borrowed night clothes and heavily sedated, the others arrived and hauled him out of bed for the night's performance. He remembers playing the drums, still groggy, with a bandage round his head.

Tommy Moore, with most of his teeth loose, and some pain-killing drugs the hospital had given him, climbed back into the van next morning for the journey onward, to Stirling, Nairn and Inverness. 'I hadn't much idea where we were. I looked out once and saw the big distillery. That's how I knew we'd got to the Highlands.'

According to Larry Parnes, the Silver Beatles went down better than any other backing group he had sent to Scotland. Parnes says that Johnny Gentle admitted they were getting more applause than he was, and urged his manager to sign them up without delay. Parnes, however, found the management of solo singers strenuous enough. 'Maybe it sounds silly but I just didn't want the worry of a five-piece group.'

Johnny Gentle and the Silver Beatles travelled as far north as Inverness, arriving too early in the morning to go to their hotel. 'We had to walk the streets, and all around the harbour next to the fishing boats,' Tommy Moore says. 'That was the finish as far as I was concerned. I'd had enough of them all—especially Lennon. And I was hungry.'

Their money did not get through to them until the very end of the fortnight. Tommy Moore remembers that on the train journey back to Liverpool he had a couple of pounds in his pocket. 'I went and sat with Stuart on the journey. He was the only one of them I could stand by that time.'

At Lime Street, Tommy said goodbye rapidly and went to his flat in Smithdown Lane where his girl friend awaited him. 'She said "How much have you brought back then?" I told her, "A couple of quid." "A couple of *quid*!" she said. "Do you realise how much you could have earned in two weeks at Garston Bottle Works?"'

For the Silver Beatles, the most important consequence of the Scottish tour was that Allan Williams had at last begun to take them seriously as a group. The Welshman, through his company Jacaranda Enterprises, now looked after several bands, booking them out to dance promoters in Liverpool and 'over the water' on the Cheshire Wirral. The Silver Beatles were added to the portfolio Williams hawked around, in Birkenhead, New Brighton and Wallasey, using the big Jaguar that was well known to the Mersey Tunnel Police.

The Grosvenor ballroom in Wallasey was run—as it still is—by Les Dodd, a small, brisk stationery retailer with bright blue eyes and a back as straight as a slow foxtrot. Les Dodd had promoted strict tempo ballroom dancing at the Grosvenor since 1936, resisting the successive contagions of Swing, Bebop, Skiffle and Rock and Roll, but by 1960, even he had begun to realise that his customers wanted something more untamed than his regular musicians, The Ernie Hignett Quartet.

For his first reluctant 'Big Beat' dance, on 6 June 1960, Les Dodd paid Allan Williams £10 for a group whose name—if Mr. Dodd understood aright—was the Silver Beetles. So he advertised them, together with Gerry and the Pacemakers, as 'jive and rock specialists'. The same display advertisement carried a reassurance that on Tuesday the Grosvenor's strict tempo night would take place as usual.

Not long after Les Dodd began booking them, Tommy Moore decided he had had enough. He had continued as drummer after the Scottish tour, despite the loss of most of his front teeth, existing on a weekly share-out which, as his girl friend constantly reminded him, could be bettered by almost any type of labouring work. One evening, when the Silver Beetles met before crossing the river to Wallasey, Tommy Moore was not among them. He had gone back to his former, more lucrative occupation of driving a fork-lift truck at Garston Bottle Works.

The Silver Beetles, knowing too well the disgrace of being drummerless, tried hard to win back their elderly colleague. En route for Wallasey, they called at the Bottle Works, found Tommy in the yard on night shift and pleaded with him not to quit. Tommy Moore's only reply was to swivel his fork lift away in the opposite direction. Another night, when Tommy was at home, they went to his flat in Smithdown Road and shouted up at his window. His girl friend, resentful of what had been done to her loved one's income and molars, requested the Silver Beetles to fuck off.

Though Tommy Moore had gone, his drums remained behind. Each week, when they set out for the Grosvenor or for Neston Institute, the drum kit would be taken along. Before the first number, John Lennon would announce half-facetiously that anyone in the audience who fancied himself as a drummer was welcome to come up and have a try. The joke misfired badly one night at the Grosvenor when a huge Wallasey Ted named Ronnie accepted the invitation, sat in on Tommy's drums and produced a din which would have been no worse if he had thrown the kit from the top of a high building. An SOS call brought Allan Williams to the Grosvenor just in time to dissuade the beaming tough from electing himself to permanent membership.

Williams was now booking them into Liverpool halls where gang warfare—between girls no less than boys—was considered essential to a full night's entertainment. At Hambledon Hall or Aintree Institute, there always came a point in the evening, just after the pubs had closed, when up to 50 Teds would come in at once and pass along the jivers, slit-eyed with beer and hope of 'bother'. Most notorious of all were Garston Swimming Baths, known locally as 'the Blood Baths', so violent and gory the battles fought over the floor that concealed the pool. The gangs, which bore tribal names such as 'The Tiger' or 'The Tank', would sometimes forget their emnities in a common assault on the no less frightening squads of bouncers, equipped with bloodlust and weapons to rival theirs. One legendary bouncer was of such size that he never needed to use his fists. A single jog from his stomach could send an assailant flying. Another, more imaginative promoter employed no stewards other than one little old lady to issue tickets. If a Ted cut up rough, the little old lady would shriek at him, 'You stop that or I'll tell your Mum.' These were words to cow the most ruthless Teddy Boy.

Musicians were not immune from attack, particularly if they hailed from a part of Liverpool held in local disfavour, if they played Chuck Berry when the gang preferred Little Richard, or if one of them, however unwittingly, attracted the attention of a local patron's 'judy'. Guitars and drums were frequently smashed and microphone stands turned into clubs and lances if the stage seemed likely to be carried by storm.

The Silver Beetles witnessed their share of violence. At the Grosvenor in Wallasey, a regular uproar took place as local Teds clashed with invading cohorts from New Brighton or Birkenhead. At Neston Institute, one night, a 16-year-old boy was booted to death during one of their performances. Even John, who fancied himself as a fighter, now cared more for protecting his guitar when the chairs and beer bottles began to fly, or girls rolled into view on the dance floor, scratching and spitting.

Their luck held until one night in June or July, when Allan Williams had sent them to Litherland Town Hall, a low-lying municipal building in the north of Liverpool. During or after their performance, something was said or implied which upset a faction in the audience. An ambush was laid for the Silver Beetles as they made their way through the car park back to their van. In the ensuing scuffle, Stu Sutcliffe went down and received a kick in the head.

Millie Sutcliffe had waited up for Stu that night. She found him in his room, with blood still pouring from the gash in his head. He told her it had happened after the Litherland dance and that John Lennon had rescued him, fighting off Stu's attacker so hard that he sprained his own wrist.

'There was blood all over the rug—everywhere,' Mrs. Sutcliffe says. 'I was going to get the doctor but Stuart wouldn't allow me to do it. He was so terribly adamant. "Mother," he said, "if you touch that 'phone, I go out of this house and you'll never see me again." '

August 1960

The Great Freedom

The Silver Beatles hit their lowest point in the summer of 1960. They still had been unable to persuade any drummer to join them. As a result, no dance promoters would book them. Their only regular engagement was at a strip club, part-owned by Allan Williams, off Liverpool's dreary Upper Parliament Street. Williams paid them 10s each to strum their guitars while a stripper named Janice grimly shed her clothes before an audience of sailors, guilty businessmen and habitués with raincoat-covered laps. At Janice's request, the musicians stuck to 'standards' like Moonglow and the Harry Lime Theme, and even gamely attempted The Gipsy Fire Dance from sheet music.

The New Cabaret Artistes Club was run for Allan Williams by a West Indian named Lord Woodbine. Born in Trinidad, 'Woody' earned a varied living as a builder and decorator, steel band musician and freelance barman in several neighbourhood shebeens. His enoblement—after the fashion of calypso singers—derived from a certain self-possessed grandeur as much as the Woodbine cigarette permanently hinged on his lower lip.

Lord Woodbine ran his own 'club', the New Colony, in the attic and basement of a semi-derelict house in Berkeley Street. The Silver Beatles played there, too, sometimes in the afternoons, while merchant seamen danced against hard-faced whores, and occasional troublemakers were pacified by the sight of the cutlass which Lord Woodbine kept under the bar.

Allan Williams promised he would make something better turn up soon. And Williams, by a sequence of cosmic blunders into thousand-to-one chances, did exactly that.

It all started when Williams returned to his coffee bar, the Jacaranda, one night and heard silence when he expected to hear the Royal Caribbean Steel Band. The entire band, he was told, had been lured away by a West German theatrical agent to appear at a club in Hamburg. Down in the basement, set about by Stu Sutcliffe's voodoo murals, not a single 40-gallon steel drum remained.

To Allan Williams, as to most Englishmen of that era, Hamburg, more than London or even Paris, was a city of breathtaking wickedness. British soldiers stationed in West Germany brought back tales of entertainments purveyed by the Reeperbahn, Hamburg's legendary cabaret district—of women wrestling in mud, and sex displays involving pythons, donkeys and other animal associates. Such things could only be whispered about in a Britain where the two-piece bathing costume was still considered rather daring.

Evidently, along with everything else, there were music clubs along the Reeperbahn. Allan Williams's curiosity was further aroused by letters from various members of the Royal Caribbean Steel Band, showing no remorse at their sudden disappearance but telling Williams guilelessly what a great place Hamburg was and urging him to come across with some of his Liverpool beat groups to share it.

His first idea was to take the Silver Beatles with him to Hamburg on an exploratory trip, but chronic shortage of cash prevented this. Instead, he got them to make a tape recording of their music, in company with Cass and the Casanovas and a local Trad Jazz band, the Noel Lewis Stompers, to be played to the Hamburg impresarios.

The journey which Allan Williams made was in every sense characteristic. Wearing a top hat and accompanied by the noble West Indian, Lord Woodbine, he took a cheap charter flight to Amsterdam, intending to proceed to West Germany by train. In one eventful night in the Dutch capital, he succeeded in drinking champagne from a chorus girl's shoe; passing Lord Woodbine off as a genuine English aristocrat; and being thrown into the street after making matador passes at a Flamenco dancer with his coat.

The next evening found him in a similar state, temporarily parted from Lord Woodbine and dazzled by the overarching lights of the Grosse Freiheit, that small but crowded tributary of the Hamburg Reeperbahn, whose name in English means 'The Great Freedom'.

Halfway down the Grosse Freiheit, opposite a Roman Catholic church, Williams stumbled into a downstairs club called the Kaiserkeller. He found it to be decorated in confusedly nautical style, with booths like lifeboats, barrels for tables and a mural depicting life in the South Sea Isles. On a tiny central space, several hundred people danced while an Indonesian group performed Elvis Presley songs in German.

Allan Williams demanded to speak to the proprietor and, after some delay, was shown into the presence of a short, broad-chested man with a quiff of sandy hair, a turned-up nose and disabled leg which little inhibited his movements. Before the conversation had progressed far, a waiter came in to report a disturbance in the club area. Williams, through the open door, saw a squad of waiters systematically working over a solitary customer. Snatching from his desk drawer a long ebony cosh, the proprietor left the room with an agile, hopping gait, to lend them a hand.

The talk then resumed on amiable lines. Allan Williams introduced himself as the manager of the world's best Rock and Roll groups. The Kaiserkeller's owner, whose name was Bruno Koschmider, inquired if they were as good as Tommy Steele. Williams assured him they were better than Elvis Presley. For proof he brought out the tape he had made of the Silver Beatles and others. But when it was played on Herr Koschmider's tape recorder, nothing could be heard but scrabble and screech. Somebody, back in Liverpool, had blundered.

Having failed, as he thought, to convert Hamburg's Reeperbahn to Liverpool beat music, Allan Williams returned to being a functionary of the great Larry Parnes. The Silver Beatles—or plain Beatles, as they now defiantly called themselves—receded somewhat in Williams's mind. His chief property was the Rhythm and Blues group, Derry and the Seniors, which Parnes had promised work in a summer show at Blackpool. The entire band, in expectation of this, gave up their jobs to turn professional. Then at the last minute, a letter arrived, on heavily-crested Parnes notepaper, cancelling the engagement.

An enraged deputation led by Howie Casey, the Senior's sax-player, confronted Williams at his Blue Angel Club in Seel Street. Casey was a youth of powerful build, and Williams promised hastily to find them some alternative work. In sheer desperation, he packed the entire five-piece group and their equipment into his Jaguar and headed for the only place he could think of where work for a Rock and Roll band might magically exist. He was taking them, he said, to the famous 2 I's coffee bar in London. There, in the home of skiffle, where Tommy Steele had first been discovered, something or other must surely turn up.

Fortune now smiled upon the agitated Welshman to the ludicrous, implausible extent that Fortune sometimes did. Upon entering the 2 I's, whom should he see first but a small, barrel-chested West German gentleman with a quiff of sandy hair, a turned-up nose and a disabled leg not at the moment noticeable. It was Herr Bruno Koschmider, proprietor of the Kaiserkeller Club in Grosse Freiheit, Hamburg.

Koschmider, it transpired, had been deeply impressed by Williams's visit to his establishment, playing unintelligible tapes and boasting of Rock and Roll groups better than Elvis. Not long after Williams's dispirited return to Liverpool, Herr Koschmider had decided to visit England and hear these wonderful groups for himself. Naturally, however, it was not Liverpool he visited, but London, and the famous 2 I's coffee bar.

He had already paid one visit to the 2 I's and had signed up a solo singer, Tony Sheridan, to appear at the Kaiserkeller. Sheridan, in fact was a gifted performer, temporarily down on his luck. At the Kaiserkeller, he had been such a sensation that Bruno Koschmider had decided to sack his Indonesian Elvis-impersonators and go over completely to English Rock and Roll. He was thus at the 2 I's a second time, hoping to hire another English group. He had not yet done so when Derry and the Seniors walked in.

It was the work of a few minutes for Williams to get Derry and the Seniors up and playing on the sacred 2 I's stage. Despite having had nothing to eat but some stale cake, they performed so well that Bruno Koschmider booked them for his Kaiserkeller club on the spot. They would receive 30 marks each per day—about £20 a week—with travel expenses and accommodation found. A contract was drafted with the help of a German waiter from the adjacent Heaven and Hell coffee bar.

Derry and the Seniors set off by train from Liverpool to Hamburg with £5 between them and no work permits. If challenged, Allan Williams said, the four tough-looking Liverpool boys and their black lead singer should pretend to be students on vacation. The story did not convince West German frontier officials and at Osnabruck the entire group was ordered off the train and held in custody until Bruno Koschmider could be contacted to vouch for them.

The next news to reach Allan Williams was a great deal better. Derry and the Seniors, together with Tony Sheridan and his band, were a hit at Herr Koschmider's Kaiserkeller. Together with rapturous postcards from various musicians, a letter arrived from Koschmider himself, asking Williams to send across a third group to play in another of Koschmider's clubs, the Indra.

The group Williams wanted to send was Rory Storm and the Hurricanes. They, however, were already committed to a summer season at Butlin's Skegness holiday camp. Gerry and the Pacemakers, his second choice, did not fancy going abroad. So Allan Williams, rather reluctantly, wrote to Bruno Koschmider, telling him to expect a group called the Beatles.

Shortly afterwards, a letter of protest arrived from the Seniors' lead singer, Derry Wilkie. It would spoil things for everyone, Derry said, if Allan Williams sent over a bum group like the Beatles.

*

The offer came when John Lennon's Art College career was approaching the point of collapse. He had recently sat—or rather half-sat—the exam by which his past three years' work would be assessed. The test paper in Lettering, his weakest subject, was supposed to have been completed in May, while the Beatles were touring Scotland with Johnny Gentle. Cynthia, John's girl friend, had risked her own College career by doing the paper for him, racked by pains from a grumbling appendix, under a single light bulb at the Gambier Terrace flat.

And yet, for all John's inexhaustible laziness, there were still glimpses of brilliance, in his cartoons and poster designs, which made Arthur Ballard, his tutor, think him worth defending. In Ballard's view, the only logical place for John was the newly-open Faculty of Design: unfortunately, however, he could not convince the relevant department head. 'I had a row with the fellow in the end,' Ballard says. 'I told him if he couldn't accept an eccentric like John, he ought to be teaching in Sunday school. Then I heard from Cyn' that it didn't matter because John was going to Hamburg. He'd told everyone he'd be getting £100 a week.'

For Stu Sutcliffe the break with College was more serious, coming as it did at the start of a year's postgraduate teacher-training. Stu at first turned down the Hamburg trip; then John and the others talked him into it. The College subsequently indicated it was willing to accept him on the teaching course as a late entrant.

Paul McCartney obtained his father's consent with typical diplomacy and circuitousness. With A level exams now past, he technically had no further school commitments. His English teacher, 'Dusty' Durband, was in fact one of the first to hear of the Hamburg offer, just before the Institute broke up for the summer. Mr. Durband was sceptical. 'As far as I knew, Paul was going on, as his father wished, to teacher training college. When he told me about Hamburg, I said, "Just who do you want to be, Paul? Tommy Steele?" He just grinned and said, "No, but I feel like giving it a try." '

Jim McCartney, when told the big news at last, faced a united front consisting of Paul, his brother Michael and Allan Williams, who came up to Forthlin Road to assure him the arrangements were all above board. Though full of misgivings, Jim felt that if Paul were allowed this one jaunt, he might the sooner return to his senses, and to college. He let Paul go at the price of only a minimal pep talk about being careful and eating regular meals.

George Harrison, though even now only just 17, encountered the least opposition from his family. With his father and elder brothers he had achieved the status of 'working man', and was as such entitled to command of his own affairs. The quiet, hard-working Harrison family, besides, had produced its share of travellers. As well as Harry and his sea voyages, there was Louise, George's grown up sister, now married to an American and living in St. Louis. Germany, by contrast, seemed not too distant; if the Harrisons knew of the Reeperbahn's reputation, they were prepared to trust in George's level head. His mother made him promise to write, and baked him a tin of home-made scones for the journey.

One big worry spoiled the collective excitement. It was the same old plaguing worry—they still had no drummer. What would do as backing for a stripper in Upper Parliament Street would not do, Allan Williams told them forcefully, for a big-time, luxurious Hamburg night spot like the Indra club. The contract with Herr Koschmider specified a full instrumental complement. If the Beatles could not provide one, the chance must be given to someone else.

They had been searching, in fact, ever since Tommy Moore had deserted them to return to his fork lift truck at Garston Bottle Works. The only replacement they had been able to find was a boy called Norman Chapman whom they had overheard one night, practising in Slater Street in a room above the National Cash Register Company. Norman played a few dates with them, happily enough, but was then claimed for one of the last batches of young Britons obliged to go into the Army.

Lately, for want of anything better, the Beatles had gone back to playing at the Casbah, Mona Best's cellar club in Hayman's Green. They had not been there since they were called the Quarry Men, and had walked out over the docking of 15s from their night's fee.

To their surprise, they found the Casbah thriving. Ken Browne, the bespectacled ex-Quarry Man, now led his own group, the Black Jacks, with Mrs. Best's son, Peter, on drums. The Black Jacks were among the most popular groups in that district, drawing even larger crowds to the Casbah than did big names like Rory Storm and the Hurricanes.

Pete Best had just left Liverpool Collegiate Grammar School with abundant GCE passes and athletic distinctions but not so clearcut a plan as hitherto to go on to teacher training college. The taciturn, good-looking boy, to his mother's surprise, announced instead that he wanted to become a professional drummer. Mrs. Best, ever ready to encourage and invigorate, helped him raise the deposit on a brand new drum kit which he had long been admiring in the music department at Blackler's.

That decision taken, nothing much seemed to happen. The Black Jacks were due to disband because Ken Browne was about to move away from Liverpool. No other group had offered Pete a job as drummer, nor was he one to push himself. For several weeks, he sat around at home all day, and at night went downstairs into the club to watch this other group Mo was now booking. Whenever he came in, a little desperate sigh used to run around the girls on the nearer benches.

The Beatles, too, had noticed Pete Best. More specifically, they had noticed his glittering new drum kit. Five weeks after leaving school, Pete was rung up by Paul McCartney and asked if he would like to join them and go on a two-month booking at a club in Hamburg. The question, really, was superfluous. Pete Best said he would.

They were to travel to Hamburg by road. Allan Williams had offered to drive them there himself, not in his Jaguar but in a battered cream and green Austin 'minibus' which he had acquired for his Liverpool enterprises. Williams, thinking he might as well make a party of it, invited along also his Chinese wife, Beryl, his brother-in-law, Barry Chang, and his West Indian business associate, Lord Woodbine. On their way through London, they were to pick up a tenth passenger, the waiter from the Heaven and Hell coffee bar, who was returning to Hamburg to become Bruno Koschmider's interpreter.

None of the five Beatles had ever been abroad before. John Lennon, indeed, only acquired a passport within a few days of setting off. Their preparations, even so, were not elaborate. Allan Williams advanced them £15 to buy new black crewneck sweaters from Marks and Spencer and some extra pairs of tennis shoes. For a stage uniform, they now had little short high-buttoning jackets of houndstooth check. Their luggage was the family type, hauled out from under spare-room beds. Paul also brought along a new, very cheap solid guitar and a tiny Elpico amplifier to go with the one that, strictly speaking, still belonged to the Art College. George Harrison had the tin of home-made scones his mother had baked for him.

Only one parent was outside the Jacaranda to see them off. Millie Sutcliffe, having said goodbye to Stu at home, followed him down to Slater Street secretly and stood in a shop doorway, watching while the van was loaded and its sides were embellished with a legend, THE BEATLES, in cut-out paper letters stuck on with flour and water paste. For some reason, Mrs. Sutcliffe could not stop herself from crying.

At Newhaven, where they were to embark for the Hook of Holland, the dockers at first refused to load the top-heavy conveyance aboard its appointed cross-Channel steamer. John Lennon talked them into it just a few moments before sailing-time. The English coast receded amid a chorus of Bye Bye

Blackbird from the Anglo-Chinese party clustered at the stern rail.

In Holland next morning, the minibus surfaced among crowds of students on bicycles, some of whom leaned against its tattered sides for support. Allan Williams shared the driving with Lord Woodbine while Beryl, perched on the overheating gearbox, acted as navigator. The five Beatles, Barry Chang and the German waiter, Herr Steiner, occupied the rear, cut off by a wall of luggage and utensils for cooking along the way. As they headed off across Europe, some more fitful singing broke out.

Like Derry and the Seniors before them, the Beatles were without the necessary West German work permits. At the frontier, they, too, planned to pose as students on vacation. They had not proceeded far into Holland before Allan Williams began to doubt if they would get even that far. During a brief stop at Arnhem, John Lennon emerged from a shop with a mouth organ which, in Lord Woodbine's words, 'he'd picked up to look at and forgotten to put back'.

The halt is commemorated by a snapshot that Barry Chang, William's Chinese brother-in-law, took at the Arnhem Memorial to the dead of World War Two. Paul McCartney, in turned-up lumberjack collar, sits with Pete Best and George Harrison in front of a marble plinth inscribed with the epitaph 'Their Names Liveth For Ever More'. John is missing from the group; he had refused to get out of the van.

They expected a city like Liverpool, and this, in a sense, they found. There was the same river, broad like the Mersey but, unlike the Mersey, crowded with ships and with shipyards, beyond, that seemed to grow out of lush forests. There was the same overhead railway that Liverpool had recently lost, although nothing resembling the same tired cityscape beneath. Not the bomb-sites and rubbish, but tree-lined boulevards, seamless with prosperity; chic shops and ships chandlers and cafes filled with well-dressed, unscarred, confident people. There was a glimpse of the dark-spired *Rathaus*; of the Alster lake, set about by glass-walled banks and press buildings, and traversed by elegant swans. What was said inside Allan William's minibus that August evening would be echoed many times afterwards in varying tones of disbelief. Wasn't this the country which had *lost* the war?

The journey from the West German frontier had been rich in incident. At one point, they were almost run down by a tram, in whose rails Lord Woodbine had accidentally engaged the minibus's front wheels. Allan Williams, taking over as driver on the outskirts of Hamburg, had immediately rammed a small saloon car.

They arrived on the Reeperbahn just as neon lights were

beginning to eclipse the fairground palings of the night clubs and their painted, acrobatic nudes. Spotting the narrow road junction, where an *imbiss* belched out fumes of *frikadelli* and *curryurst,* Allan William remembered where he was. They turned left into Grosse Freiheit, welcomed by overarching illuminations and the stare of predatory eyes.

Even John Lennon, with his fondness for human curiosities, had not expected an employer quite like Bruno Koschmider. The figure which hopped out of the Kaiserkeller to greet them had begun life in a circus, working as a clown, fire-eater, acrobat and illusionist with 50 small cage-birds hidden in his coat. His dwarfish stature, his large, elaborately-coiffured head, his turned-up nose and quick, stumping gait, all made even John not quite like to laugh. Bruno, for his part, was unimpressed by the look of his new employees. 'They were dressed in bad clothes —cheap shirts, trousers that were not clean. Their fingernails were dirty.'

If Bruno was somewhat disconcerting, his Kaiserkeller club brought much reassurance. The exterior portico bore, in large letters, the name *Derry and the Seniors von Liverpool.* A glimpse inside, on the way to Koschmider's office, showed what seemed a vast meadow of tables and side booths, shaped like lifeboats, around the stage and miniature dance floor. The Beatles, their spirits reviving, began to laugh and cuff one another, saying *this* was all right, wasn't it? Allan Williams reminded them they were not booked to play here but in Herr Koschmider's other club, the Indra.

Further along the Grosse Freiheit, beyond St. Joseph's Catholic church, the illuminations dwindled into a region of plain-fronted bordellos interspersed with private houses where elderly *hausfraus* still set pot plants on the upper window ledges. Here, under a neon sign shaped like an elephant, was to be found the Indra Club. Bruno Koschmider led the way downstairs into a small cellar cabaret, gloomy, shabby and at that moment occupied by only two customers. Down here for the next eight weeks, the Beatles would be expected to play for four and a half hours each week night and six hours on Saturdays and Sundays.

Koschmider next conducted them to the living quarters provided under the terms of his contract with Allan Williams. Across the road from the Indra, he operated a small cinema, the Bambi Kino, which varied the general diet of flesh by showing corny old gangster movies and Westerns. The Beatles' lodgings were one filthy room and two windowless cubbyholes immediately behind —and in booming earshot of—the cinema screen. The only washing facilities were the cinema toilets, from the communal vestibule of which an old woman stared at them grimly over her saucer of pfennigs.

It was some consolation to meet up with Derry and the Seniors and to learn that, despite munificent billing outside the Kaiserkeller, Liverpool's famous R & B group were also having to sleep rough. 'Bruno gave us one little bed between five of us,' Howie Casey, the sax-player, says. 'I'd been sleeping on that, covered by a flag, and the other lads slept on chairs set two together. The waiters used to lock us inside the club each night.'

The Bambi Kino was not a great deal worse than the cellar of Lord Woodbine's New Colony Club or the Gambier Terrace flat back home in Liverpool. Paul and Pete Best took a cubbyhole each while John, Stu and George flopped down in the larger room. All five were soon asleep, untroubled by sounds of gunfire and police sirens, wafted through the grimy wall from the cinema screen.

Their first night's playing at the Indra was a severe let-down. Half a dozen people sat and watched them indifferently from tables with red-shaded lamps. The clientele, mainly prostitutes and their customers, showed little enthusiasm for Carl Perkins's Honey Don't or Chuck Berry's Too Much Monkey Business. The club also bore a curse in the form of an old woman living upstairs who continually 'phoned Police Headquarters on the Reeperbahn to complain about the noise. Bruno Koschmider, not wishing for that kind of trouble, hissed at them to turn even their feeble amplifiers down.

Allan and Beryl Williams, Barry Chang and Lord Woodbine remained in Hamburg throughout that inaugural week. Williams, himself comfortably ensconced in a small hotel, did what he could to improve the Beatles' living quarters—it was at his urgent insistence that Bruno provided blankets for their beds. Beryl shopped in the city centre with her brother, and Lord Woodbine, as usual, remained worried by nothing. He sang calypsos at the Kaiserkeller and, one night, grew so affected by its libations that he attempted to dive into the South Sea Islands mural.

Allan Williams, in his conscientious moments, worried about the club he had committed his charges to, and about their plainly-evinced hatred of it. On their opening night, they had played the entire four-and-a-half-hour stretch mutinously still and huddled-up. 'Come on, boys!' Williams exhorted them from the bar. 'Make it a show, boys!' Bruno Koschmider took up the phrase, clapping his large, flat hands. 'Mak show, boys,' he would cry. 'Mak show, Beatles! Mak show!'

John Lennon's answer was to launch himself into writhings and shimmyings that were a grotesque parody of Gene Vincent on one crippled leg at the Boxing Stadium show. Down the street at the Kaiserkeller, word began to spread of this other group *von* Liverpool who leapt around the stage like monkeys and stamped their feet deafeningly on the stage. They were stamping out the rhythm to help their new drummer, Pete Best, and also to goad the old woman upstairs.

Before long, the rival groups from the Kaiserkeller had come up to the Indra to see them. Howie Casey was astonished at the improvement since their audition as the Silver Beatles in front of Larry Parnes. 'That day, they'd seemed embarrassed about how bad they were,' Howie says. 'You could tell something had happened to them in the meantime. They'd turned into a good stomping band.'

Derry and the Seniors brought with them a wide-eyed, curly-haired youth whom all the Beatles—George Harrison especially—regarded with awe. Born Anthony Esmond Sheridan McGinnity, he was better known as Tony Sheridan, a singer and inspired solo guitarist with many appearances to his credit on the *Oh Boy!* television show. His talent, however, was accompanied by habits too blithely erratic to suit the Rock and Roll starmakers. When Bruno Koschmider hired him, he had been sacked from *Oh Boy!* and most other engagements, and was playing at the 2 I's coffee bar for £1 a night. Even now, the British police were hard on his trail in respect of various hire-purchase irregularities.

Anthony Esmond steered the Beatles, past beckoning doorway touts, for an insider's tour of the Reeperbahn's peculiar delights. They saw the women who grappled in mud, cheered on by an audience tied into a protective communal bib. They visited the Roxy Bar and met ravishing 'hostesses' with tinkling laughs and undisguisably male biceps and breastbones. Two streets away, where a wooden fence forbade entry to all under 18, their companions steered them through the Herbertstrasse, past red-lit shop windows containing whores in every type of fancy dress, all ages from nymphet to scolding granny, smiling or scowling forth, gossiping with one another, reading, knitting, listlessly examining their own frilly garters or spooning up bowls of soup.

The other initiation was into beer. For beer, damp-gold, foam-piling under thin metal bar taps, had never been more plentiful. Derry and the Seniors, when they first opened at the Kaiserkeller, had been allowed beer ad lib in breaks between performing. Though Koschmider had hastily withdrawn this privilege, the nightly allowance still seemed vast to five boys who, at home in Liverpool, had often been hard put to scrape up the price of a corporate half-pint. Then there were the drinks pressed on them by customers at the Indra; the drinks that would be sent up to them on stage while they played. It became nothing unusual for a whole crate of beer to be shoved at their feet by well-wishers whose size and potential truculence underlined the necessity of finishing every bottle.

Everything was free. Everything was easy. The sex was easy.

Here you did not chase it, as in Liverpool, and clutch at it furtively in cold shop doors. Here it came after you, putting strong arms round you, mincing no words; it was unabashed, expert—indeed, professional. For even the most cynical whores found it piquant to have an innocent boy from Liverpool—to lure and buy as a change from being, eternally, bait and merchandise.

The Freiheit provided an abundance of everything but sleep. Sheridan and the other musicians already knew a way to get by, as the barmaids and whores and bouncers and pickpockets did, without it. Someone in the early days had discovered Preludin, a brand of German slimming tablets which, while removing appetite, also roused the metabolism to goggle-eyed hyperactivity. Soon the Beatles—all but Pete Best—were gobbling 'Prellys' by the tubeful each night. As the pills took effect, they dried up the saliva, increasing the desire for beer.

Now the Beatles needed no exhortation to 'mak show'. John, in particular, began to go berserk on stage, prancing and grovelling in imitation of any Rock and Roller or cripple his dazzled mind could summon up. The fact that their audience could not understand a word they said provoked John into cries of *'Sieg Heil!'* and 'Fucking Nazis!', to which the audience invariably responded by laughing and clapping. Bruno Koschmider, who had fought in a Panzer Division, was not so amused.

At 5 or 6 am—according to subsequent adventures—they would stagger back along the sunny Freiheit, past doorway touts unsleepingly active. Behind the Bambi Kino they would collapse into their squalid beds for the two or three hours' sleep that were possible before the day's first picture show. Sometimes it would be gunfire on the screen that jolted them awake, or the voice of George Raft or Edward G. Robinson.

Hounded into consciousness, they would dash to the cinema toilets while the basins were still clean. Rosa, the female custodian, for all her outward grimness, kept clean towels for them, and odds and ends of soap. 'She thought we were all mad,' Pete Best says. 'She'd shout things at us—*verucht* and *beknaakt*—but she'd be laughing. We called her Mutti.'

There were now five or six hours to be disposed of before they began playing and drinking again. At the Gretel and Alphons or Willi's Bar, the Freiheit's two most tolerant cafes, they would breakfast on cornflakes or chicken soup, the only food which their dehydrated frames could endure. They would then drift round the corner, through the stench of *frikadelli* and last night's vomit, to the shop on the main Reeperbahn which fascinated John Lennon especially with its display of flick knives, bayonets, coshes, swords, brass knuckledusters and teargas pistols.

If not too devastatingly hung over, they might catch a tram

into central Hamburg, and stroll on the elegant boulevards, looking at the clothes and the perfumes, the elaborate bakers' and confectioners', the radios and tape-recorders and occasional displays of imported American guitars, saxophones and drums. Since their wages, paid out by Bruno on a Thursday, seldom lasted more than 24 hours, such expeditions were usually limited to gazing and wishing. John, however, blew every pfennig he had on a new guitar, an American Rickenbacker 'short arm'.

The daylight hours improved considerably after someone, walking on the dockside, discovered Hamburg's long-established branch of the British Sailors Society. Investigation proved this rather imposing four-storey building to be the same 'Mission' as on the docks back home in Liverpool, with the same charitable interest in mariners ashore in a foreign port.

Jim Hawke, the resident manager, was a hefty Londoner who had entered Hamburg with the first invading Allied troops and had subsequently done duty as a warder at the Nuremberg trials. In 1960, he and his German wife, Lilo, had been in charge of the Hamburg 'Mission' only a few months. Already, as it happened, they had met Stu Sutcliffe's father, still then a second engineer with the Booth shipping line.

Hawke, a tender-hearted man under his NCO exterior, granted the same privileges to Liverpool musicians as to sailors far from home. Most attractive from the Beatles' point of view were the English breakfasts, cooked by an elderly German woman, Frau Prill, who knew the secret of frying real English chips. 'They never seemed to have any money,' Hawke says. 'You could see them carefully counting out the coins. They always had what was the cheapest—steak, egg and chips, which I put on for 2 marks 80 (about 25p). And big half-litre tankards of milk. Some days they'd have an Oxo cube beaten up in milk.

'They were never any trouble—I wouldn't have stood for it in any case. Just nice, quiet, well-behaved lads they seemed. They didn't even smoke then. They'd sit and play draughts or go upstairs for a game of ping-pong with my daughter, Monica. In the room through the bar we had an old piano that had come from the British NAAFI. They used that, or John and Paul did, to help them write their songs. We had a library as well. I'd leave a bag of books for them on the table in front of the settee they always used. They liked reading, but they never took any of the books away. They said they couldn't read very easily where they were staying.

'They'd come in about eleven in the morning and stay until three or four in the afternoon. They'd be quite subdued. I'd look over from the bar and see the five of them, always round that same table, not talking—just staring into space. I've seen the same look on men who've been away at sea in tankers for a long time. Not with it if you know what I mean.'

One bleary-eyed morning when they emerged from the Bambi Kino, a piece of good news awaited them. Bruno Koschmider, bowing at last to the complaints of his customers and the old woman upstairs, was moving them out of the Indra and into his larger, better club the Kaiserkeller.

The Kaiserkeller, at first, threatened to eclipse even John Lennon in noise and spectacle. The noise came from an audience several hundred strong, frequently containing entire ships' companies from English and American Naval craft visiting the port. The spectacle was provided by Bruno Koschmider's white-aproned waiters, converging on any outbreak of trouble and quelling it with a high-speed ruthlessness that made Garston 'Blood Baths' look like a game of pat-a-cake. If the troublemaker were alone, he might find himself propelled, not to the Exit but into the office of Willi the under-manager, there to be worked over at leisure with coshes and brass knuckles. Finally, as the victim lay prostrate, Bruno himself would weigh in with the ebony night stick from his desk drawer.

Bruno's chief bouncer, a tiny, swaggering youth named Horst Fascher, epitomised the breed. Horst had started life as a featherweight boxer and had represented both Hamburg and the West German national team before being banned from the ring for accidentally killing a sailor in a street fight. It was shortly after serving a prison sentence for manslaughter that he had entered Bruno Koschmider's employment. His squad, nicknamed locally 'Hoddel's gang', recruited from his friends at the Hamburg Boxing Academy, were held among the Freiheit's other strong-arm gangs in profound respect.

Horst took the Liverpool musicians—fortunately for them—to his heart. It became an unwritten rule at the Kaiserkeller that if a musician hit trouble, 'Hoddel's gang' would swoop unquestioningly to his aid. Horst showed them the Reeperbahn's innermost haunts and its choicest pleasures; he also took them home to Neuestadt to meet his mother and brothers and taste Frau Fascher's bean soup. All he asked in return was the chance, sometimes after midnight, to get up with the group on stage and bellow out an Eddie Cochran song.

'The Beatles were not good musicians at the beginning,' Horst Fascher says. 'John Lennon was a very poor rhythm guitarist. I remember Sheridan telling me in amazement that John played chords with only three fingers. And always they are funny —never serious. But they steal from Sheridan, from the Seniors, all the time with their eyes. And all the time the bass drum is beating like your foot when you stamp.

'That John Lennon—I loved him, he was mad. A fighter. He is *zyniker*. You say to him, "Hey John . . ." He would say, "Ah, so fuckin' what." Paul was *lustig*, the clown. He gets out of trouble by making a laugh. George was *schuchtern*, the baby one. I could never get to know Stu. He was too strange. And Pete—he was *reserviert*. You had to pull words out through his nose.'

Soon after the Beatles reached the Kaiserkeller, Derry and the Seniors finished their engagement there. The replacement group, brought out from Liverpool by Allan Williams, was Rory Storm and the Hurricanes. When Rory, blond and suntanned from Butlin's, saw the Hamburg living quarters, his stammer totally overcame him. Nor did his drummer, the little bearded one with rings on his fingers, show great delight at having to sleep on chairs covered with old flags. Ringo Starr, like all the Hurricanes, was used to a little more finesse. 'You want to see what the Beatles have got to put up with,' Allan Williams retorted.

Rory Storm's flashiness and acrobatic feats increased the wildness of the Kaiserkeller nights. A contest developed between the Beatles and Hurricanes to see which group first could stamp its way through the already old and half-rotten timbers of the stage. Rory did it at last, vanishing from sight in the middle of Blue Suède Shoes. A case of junk champagne was the prize, washed down with more 'Prellys' at their favourite bar, the Gretel and Alphons.

Bruno Koschmider fumed and fulminated—but they got away with it. They got away, somehow, with everything. John Lennon got away with standing out in the Freiheit in a pair of long woollen underpants, reading the *Daily Express*. George got away with it time after time in the *Polizei Stunde*, or midnight curfew hour when all under 18 were supposed to have left the club. For their drinking, swearing, fighting, whoring, even vandalising, Grosse Freiheit pardoned them all forms of retribution but one. Allan Williams, the self-styled 'little pox doctor of Hamburg', received many a worried confidence in a back room at the Gretel and Alphons, and, like a connoisseur, held many a beer glass of urine speculatively up to the light.

Pete Best preferred not to take pills. When the others raced downstairs between spots to Rosa the WC attendant—now transferred from the Bambi Kino—when they clustered round the old woman in ankle socks, thrusting out Deutschmarks for 'Prellys' from the sweet jar under her desk, Pete Best would not be with them. He had usually gone to sit and drink on his own, smiling the quirky smile that was addressed to no one, least of all the girls in surrounding booths who strove desperately to catch his eye.

Horst Fascher was not the only one to whom Pete Best seemed *reserviert*. Though perfectly amiable, and capable of drinking his share, he had showed himself devoid of the others' mad ebullience. He played drums well enough—or so it then seemed—hitting his bass pedal in the hard, stamping 'mak show' beat. He seemed, even so, remote from the prancing frontal contest between John and Paul. He was, and knew it, the most handsome Beatle with his athlete's physique, his dark eyes, wry smile and neat, crisp Jeff Chandler hair. Like the girls back home in West Derby, the Kaiserkeller girls were mad about him. Craning their necks to see past John and George, past even Paul, they would scream at Pete Best in English and German to give them a smile.

Having the most German increased Pete's independence, and he was often away from the Freiheit in the daytime, sunbathing alone or buying new parts for his drums. His fellow Beatles grew accustomed to his absence. They had plenty afoot with Tony Sheridan and Rory Storm and the drummer from Rory's group whom they were growing to like more and more. Ringo Starr, in contrast with Pete Best, was friendly, simple, straightforward and, in his slow, big-eyed way, as funny as even John. They also liked the way he played the drums. They were happy with Pete Best's drumming until they began to notice Ringo's.

When Allan Williams next hit town, Paul and John met him, clamouring for his help to find a studio in which they could record. They wanted to try out some numbers with a member of Rory Storm's group, a boy named Wally, whose prodigious vocal range went from bass to falsetto. Pete Best would not be involved. They had already fixed up to use Rory Storm's drummer, Ringo Starr.

The studio Allan Williams found for them was record-your-voice booth at the rear of Hamburg's main railway station. There, John, Paul, George, with Ringo on drums, backed the talented Wally through two numbers, Fever and Summertime. The man who cut the acetate for their recording mistakenly handed back to Williams first an old-fashioned 78-rpm disc with a commercial message for a local handbag shop on its reverse. Eventually some 45-rpm discs were made, on the booth's 'Arnstik' label, of *The Beatles mit Wally*. Just for a few moments—subtracting Wally—the right four had found each other.

Astrid Kirchherr was born in 1938, into a solid, respectable middle-class Hamburg family. Her grandfather, a manufacturer of fairground slot-machines, still owned the factory he had twice seen wrecked by war, and twice painstakingly built up again. Her father was a senior executive in the West German division of the Ford Motor Company. Three generations of Kirchherrs lived together in Altona, a comfortable Hamburg suburb. To Altona people, the dockyard and St. Pauli, the Reeperbahn and Grosse

Freiheit might as well be on another planet: they are mentioned only to warn children sternly never to stray in that direction.

Astrid Kirchherr was never like other children. At the age of four or five, she would protest when her mother decked her out in the flounces and hair ribbons expected of little German girls. She preferred to wear plain black. She knew that best became her white skin, her large, dark eyes and the blanched-gold hair she would shake free of all encumbrances. Frau Kirchherr visited the infants school to confirm that the child must have her curious wish.

Already, she had a strongly-marked talent for drawing and painting; as she grew older, she would design and make clothes for herself. When the family assembled, as was traditional to decide her future, her grandfather agreed that there was only one sensible course. Astrid should go to college and study dress design. Possibly that would encourage her to forsake her eccentric ideas for styles more widely acceptable.

She went, not to the State Art College but to a private academy, the Meister Schule. There she met an elegant boy of equally good family, a doctor's son named Klaus Voorman. Klaus, a talented illustrator, passionately loved Rock and Roll music and wanted to be a designer of Pop record covers. He became Astrid's boy friend, also moving in as a lodger at the hospitable Kirchherr house. Their friends were a set known as *exis*—from 'existentialist'—intellectual, beautiful, ascetic and avant garde. Astrid and Klaus were the most beautiful, most ascetic and avant garde of them all.

At the Meister Schule, Astrid also struck up a friendship with Rheinhardt Wolf, tutor on the photographic course and a well-known contributor to various Hamburg-based magazines. The perceptiveness with which she commented on his work led Wolf to suggest that Astrid should herself try taking some pictures. These proved so impressive that, at Rheinhardt Wolf's insistence, she changed courses from dress design to photography. After leaving the Meister Schule, she was taken on by Wolf as his assistant.

One late summer evening in 1960, Astrid and Klaus Voorman had quarrelled, and Klaus went off to the cinema on his own. Afterwards, walking about aimlessly, he found himself in Grosse Freiheit. A blast of Rock and Roll music was issuing from the open door into the Kaiserkeller club. Klaus decided, against all the instincts of his upbringing, to go in and have a look.

The group on stage at the time was Rory Storm and the Hurricanes. Klaus sat down nervously in the tough crowd, and was at once swept away with excitement and delight. He had never been into a club before, and certainly never seen Rock and Roll played with such crazy ebullience. At a table next to his, some more English musicians, in houndstooth check jackets, with wondrously piled-up, greased-back hair, were waiting their turn to play. In due course this group was announced as the Beatles. The sound they made, and their attitude while making it, transfixed the genteel German boy at their feet. Klaus stayed on to watch the whole of their four-hour performance.

Astrid, when he told her about it, was a little disgusted to hear that Klaus had been hanging around dives in St. Pauli. He could not persuade her to go back with him to the Kaiserkeller and be shown the amazing music. He went again on his own, determined to get talking to the Beatles if he could. Shy and unsure of his English, he took with him a sleeve he had designed for an American record, Walk Don't Run. In a break between sessions he went over to the leader—so he had already identified John Lennon—and in halting English tried to explain about the design. John only muttered, 'Show it to Stu—he's the artist round here,' indicating the one who had interested Klaus most with his pointed shoes, dark glasses and brooding James Dean face.

By the time Astrid did agree to go to the Kaiserkeller, Stu and Klaus Voorman had become good friends. Klaus brought her in at last one night, dressed in her black leather *exi* coat, white-faced, crop-headed and spectrally cool. When the Beatles began playing, she, too, was instantly won over. 'I fell in love with Stuart that very first night. He was so tiny but perfect, every feature. So pale, but very very beautiful. He was like a character from a story by Edgar Allan Poe.'

The Beatles, in their turn, were flattered by the interest of this gentle, beautiful, ghost-eyed girl, so different from the usual Freiheit scrubber. They were still more flattered when, with her few words of English, Astrid asked if she could take their photograph. She met all five of them on the Reeperbahn next day and took them into Der Dom, the city park, where the twice-yearly funfair was in progress. Astrid posed them with their guitars and Pete Best's snare drum on the side of a fairground wagon, then on the broad bonnet of a traction engine. Since John now had his new Rickenbacker guitar, Paul borrowed the old Club 40 model, holding it once again with the scratch plate upside-down.

As well as expensive cameras and a leather coat, Astrid had a little car of her own. The photographing over, she asked the five Beatles back to Altona for tea at her home. Pete Best declined; he said he had some new drum skins to buy. The other four readily piled in around Astrid. 'They met my Mum—she was as knocked out by them as I was. Directly she saw them, she wanted to start feeding them.'

Astrid took them upstairs to the black and white studio she had designed for herself. Their jaws dropped to see the glass-topped table and black satin bed-sheets. They sat there in the candle-light, drinking tea and eating ham sandwiches. 'I wanted to talk to them, but I knew hardly any English then,' Astrid says. 'John seemed very hard—cynical, sarcastic, but something more than that. Paul smiled—he always smiled and was diplomatic. George was just a baby boy with his piled-up hair and his ears sticking out. He said he didn't know people had ham sarnies in Germany.

'I wanted to talk to Stuart. I tried to ask him if I could take his picture but he didn't understand. I knew I would have to ask Klaus to help me speak better English.'

The flattery of being photographed by a beautiful blonde German girl was nothing to the flattery bestowed by the photographs themselves. These were not the usual little snapshots knocked off by some bystander, usually at the least flattering possible moment. These were big, grainy prints, conjured by the girl herself from the recesses of her black satin room and showing the five Beatles as they had never imagined themselves before. Astrid's lens, in fact, captured the very quality which attracted intellectuals like Klaus and her—the paradox of Teddy Boys with child faces; of would-be toughness and undisguisable, all-protecting innocence. The blunt, heavy fairground machines on which they sat seemed to symbolise their own slight but confident perch on grown-up life. John, with his collar up, hugging his new Rickenbacker; Paul, leaning, discontent with a cast-off guitar; George, so babyish; Pete Best, self-contained, a little apart—each image held its own true prophecy. In one shot, Stu Sutcliffe stands with his back to the others, the long stem of his guitar pointing into the ground.

It was the first of many photographic sessions with Astrid in the weeks that followed. Each time she would pose them, with or without their guitars, against some part of industrial Hamburg —the docks or the railway marshalling yard. She was lavish with the prints she gave them and with invitations to meals at her house. 'I'd cook them all the things they missed from England: scrambled eggs, chips.' All the time, with Klaus Voorman's help, her English was improving.

At the Kaiserkeller, a part of the audience now were *exis* brought in by Astrid and Klaus. It became a fad among them to dress, like the rockers, in leather and skin-tight jeans. The Beatles' music belonged to the same intellectual conversion. Soon the *exis* had their own small preserve of tables next to the stage. And always among them, the girl who followed no style but her own sat with Klaus Voorman, or without him, waiting for the moment, late at night, when John and Paul stood aside and Stu Sutcliffe stepped forward with his heavy bass guitar to sing the Elvis ballad, Love Me Tender.

Astrid made no secret of the pursuit and Stu, for his part, was shyly fascinated. Her elfin beauty, combined with big-breasted voluptuousness, her forthright German ways mingled with a yielding softness, were more than sufficient to captivate any young, inexperienced heterosexual male. Across the barrier of language, they found their beliefs, their passionate artistic and literary beliefs, to be one. The talks by candlelight on Astrid's black coverlet quickly led to other delights unenvisaged by a schoolteacher's son from Sefton Park, Liverpool.

Astrid was the initiator and teacher, and Stu the willing pupil. With the skills of the artist and the practicality of the *hausfrau*, she began to model him into an appearance echoing and complementing her own. She did away first with his Teddy-Boy hairstyle, cutting it short like hers, then shaping it to lie across the forehead in what was called the French cut, although high-class German boys had worn a similar style since the days of Bismarck.

When Stu got to the Kaiserkeller that night, John and Paul laughed so much that he hastily combed his hair back into its old upswept style. Next night, he tried the new way again, ignoring the others' taunts. Strangely enough, it was George, the least adventurous or assertive one, who next allowed Astrid to unpick the high sheaf of black hair which had previously so emphasised his babyish ears. Paul tried it next, but temporarily—he was waiting to see what John would do. John tried it, so Paul tried it again. Only Pete Best's hair stayed as before, a crisp, unflappable cockade.

Astrid also began to design and make clothes for Stu. She made him first a suit of shiny black leather jerkin and sheath-tight trousers like the one she herself wore. The other four Beatles so admired it that they at once ordered copies from a tailor in St. Pauli. Theirs, however, were of less fine workmanship, baggy-waisted and with seams which kept coming apart. At that point, for the moment, Astrid's influence over them stopped. They laughed at Stu for wearing, as she did, a black corduroy jacket without lapels, based on Pierre Cardin's current Paris collections. 'What are you doing in Mum's suit then, Stu?' became the general taunt.

Astrid's mother, horrified to learn of Stu's living conditions, insisted on giving him his own room, as Klaus Voorman had had, at the top of the Kirchherr house. In November 1960, two months after their first meeting, they became engaged. They bought each other rings, in the German fashion, and went in Astrid's car for a drive beside the River Elbe. 'It was a real engagement,' Astrid says. 'We knew from the beginning that it was inevitable we should marry. And so it should have been.'

Stu, despite his quietness and gentleness, was not always an easy person. At times he could be moody, and jealously suspect Astrid of being in love with someone else. His emotion, when angry or passionate, could reach an intensity that was almost like a mild seizure. He suffered, too, from headaches, sudden and violent, that shut his eyes in agony behind the dark glasses which were not, she discovered, entirely for show. Then, with equal suddenness, the fit of pain would pass.

Even Astrid could not affect Stu's life as downtrodden butt of the other Beatles' humour. On stage, they teased and taunted him continually, for his smallness, his outrageous new clothes, above all for the bass-playing that never seemed equal to their needs. John Lennon inflicted the worst treatment of all, even though, as Astrid well knew, a deep friendship still existed between Stu and him. It was in Paul McCartney's more bantering tone that the true arrows came. For Paul wanted Stu's job as bass guitarist. 'When John and Stu had a row,' Astrid says, 'you could still feel the affection that was there. But when Paul and Stu had a row, you could tell Paul hated him.'

A few yards up the Reeperbahn there was a large underground arena called the Hippodrome. In former days, it had been a circus, featuring horses ridden by naked girls. By 1960, such entertainments having grown unfashionable, the Hippodrome stood, behind its heavy iron portcullis, dark and in decay. Its owner, a certain Herr Eckhorn, decided to hand it on to his son, Peter, who had recently come home from the sea and was anxious to start a music club in competition with Bruno Koschmider's Kaiserkeller.

Young Peter Eckhorn wasted no time in hitting at his intended rival. First, he suborned Koschmider's chief bouncer, Horst Fascher. While still employed at the Kaiserkeller, Horst was helping Eckhorn convert the old Hippodrome, putting in a stage and dance floor and makeshift wooden booths painted the cheapest colour, black. Horst Fascher, in addition, began to sow discontent at the Kaiserkeller, telling Bruno's musicians of the better pay and conditions which Eckhorn's club—the Top Ten—would offer. 'I showed Tony Sheridan out of the back door right away,' Horst recalls with pride. 'That Koschmider went crazy, but what could he do to me? He had a too great fear.'

The Top Ten club opened in November 1960, with music by Tony Sheridan and his original Soho-levied group, the Jets. Eckhorn also wanted Derry and the Seniors, but they were by now so poverty stricken that they had applied to the British Consul in Hamburg for an assisted passage home to Liverpool.

The Beatles stayed on at the Kaiserkeller, although in a mood of increasing restlessness. The Top Ten, with its circus-like dimensions and higher rates of pay, was infinitely more attractive than Bruno Koschmider's nautically-inspired basement. Their employer, moreover, stung by Horst Fascher's and Tony Sheridan's defection, grew rabidly proprietorial. With a stubby forefinger, he drew their attention to the clause in their contract which forbade them to play in any other club within a 25-mile radius of the Kaiserkeller. It had reached Bruno's ears that, when visiting the Top Ten, they would sometimes get up and jam with Tony Sheridan on stage.

Before long, Peter Eckhorn had persuaded them to forget the residue of their contract with Koschmider and come across to play for him at the Top Ten. Koschmider, according to Pete Best, hinted that if the Beatles joined Eckhorn, they might not be able to walk with complete safety after dark. Horst Fascher's protection enabled them to disregard this possibility.

Retribution of a different sort overtook them, however, possibly with some help from Bruno Koschmider. They were about to open at the Top Ten when the *Polizei*, conducting a belated examination of George Harrison's passport, discovered that he was only 17, and too young to be in a club after midnight. For plainly flouting this rule, George was ordered to leave West Germany. Stu and Astrid put him on the train, dismayed and lost-looking, with some biscuits and apples for the journey.

The others played a few nights at the Top Ten, with John Lennon taking the lead guitar part, or leaving it out, and Paul doubling on a piano that was there. Astrid, Klaus and the *exis* had followed them from the Kaiserkeller; so had Akim Reichel, a dockside waiter who had discovered them first at the Indra. Akim remembers how tired and dispirited the four survivors seemed. They had been on the Reeperbahn, after all, nearly four months. 'They would play sometimes a whole hour,' Akim says, 'sitting on the edge of their amplifiers.'

Peter Eckhorn, as well as paying 10 marks a day more than Koschmider, provided sleeping accommodation above the club, in an attic fitted with bunk beds. Though far from luxurious, and shared with Tony Sheridan's group, it was still a vast improvement on the Bambi Kino. Rosa, the WC lady—who had also forsaken the Kaiserkeller for the Top Ten—was prevailed on by John Lennon to bring coffee and shaving water up to them when they woke in the early afternoon.

In their haste to desert Koschmider, Paul and Pete Best had left most of their belongings in the rooms behind the Bambi. They nerved themselves to go back a few days later, walking in through the cinema foyer without opposition, and finding their property all intact behind the screen. Coming out again, down the dark corridor from their respective cubbyholes, Paul struck a match in order to see. 'There were some filthy old drapes on the wall, like sacking,' Pete Best says. 'Paul caught a bit of that stuff with the match. It wasn't anything like a fire. It just smouldered a little bit.'

Early the next morning, policemen entered the Top Ten club, pounded upstairs to the attic, hauled Pete Best and Paul McCartney out of bed, hustled them off to the Reeperbahn's Station 15 and placed them under lock and key. Between them, using their O-level German, they elicited the fact that they were being held on suspicion of trying to burn down the Bambi Kino. 'They only kept us there a few hours,' Pete Best says. 'Afterwards they admitted it never should have happened.'

No charges were pressed—according to Bruno Koschmider, a magnanimous gesture on his part. Even so, Paul and Pete were both immediately deported. The next day found them on a flight to England, minus most of their clothes and luggage and Pete Best's drum kit.

For John and Stu there was no alternative but to follow the others home. Stu made the journey by air, with a ticket paid for by the Kirchherrs. John went on the train alone, carrying his guitar and the amplifier he had not yet paid for, and terrified he wouldn't find England where he had left it.

January 1961

'Hi, all you Cavern-dwellers.
Welcome to the best *of cellars'*

He reached home in the early hours of a December morning and threw stones at his Aunt Mimi's bedroom window to wake her. Mimi opened the front door and, as John lurched past, inquired sarcastically what had happened to his £100 a week. And if he thought he was going around Woolton in those cowboy boots, Mimi added, he had better think again. John collapsed into bed, not stirring out of doors for a week afterwards. In a little while, there came a timorous knock at the door of the outer porch. It was his ever-faithful, long-suffering girl friend, Cynthia Powell.

Paul McCartney had arrived home with Pete Best in a little more style, by air. At Forthlin Road he found waiting for him a single GCE A level certificate—in Art—and a father who, luckily, was not the type to crow. Even so, Jim McCartney pointed out, it was time to think about getting a proper job. Paul gave in and registered at the local Labour Exchange. The two weeks before Christmas he spent helping to deliver parcels around the docks on the back of a truck belonging to the Speedy Prompt Delivery Company.

He didn't contact John again until just before Christmas, by which time, to add to the gloom, snow was falling. Snow is never pretty in Liverpool. The two ex-Hamburg desperadoes, with watering eyes and fingers huddled in their pockets, met down in the city for a drink. They could feel through their boot-soles, too, the chill damp of dead end failure.

Together, they sought out their erstwhile manager, Allan Williams. They found him in equally deflated spirits. Returning from Hamburg the last time, Williams had decided to open the first Liverpool version of a Reeperbahn beat music club. He had taken over an old bottle-washing shop in Soho Street, and employed Lord Woodbine to effect a brief renovation. The new club was to be called the Top Ten and run by Bob Wooler, the railway clerk and spare-time disc jockey who had helped Williams recruit attractions for his Boxing Stadium concert. Wooler, on the strength of Williams's offer, had even resigned his steady job with the docks office.

Liverpool's Top Ten club opened on 1 December 1960. Six days later, it burned to the ground. Local opinion suspected a 'torch job'.

There remained, it was true, the Casbah, the cellar club in West Derby run by Pete Best's mother. Derry and the Seniors had played there, following their own Hamburg disaster, and had good-naturedly plugged the Beatles' name. When Mona Best gave them their first return booking, a poster was put on the cellar door loyally proclaiming the 'Fabulous Beatles' had returned. George Harrison was then contacted—lying low in Speke, he had not realised that John and Paul were home. Stu Sutcliffe, however, remained out of touch with the others until well into the following January.

That first night back at the Casbah showed what a transformation had happened in Hamburg. The months of sweated nights at the Kaiserkeller had given their music a prizefighter's muscle and power; each number was stamped through as if against a Reeperbahn brawl, or in one last attempt to break through Bruno Koschmider's stage. They literally rocked the little club, under the Victorian house, where nothing was drunk wickeder than Pepsi Cola, nothing 'popped' more potent than peanuts, and where no fracas arose that could not be quelled by Mrs. Best's vigorous, dark-eyed stare.

That same week, a bizarre out-of-town expedition took place. They had met up again with Sam Leach, the promoter who formerly ran the Sunday afternoon sessions at the Casanova club in Temple Street. They liked Sam Leach, as everyone did, for the scope, if not the invariable success, of his concert enterprises. He now ran many—some said, too many—dances all over Liverpool, apparently relishing the continual uncertainty as to whether his door receipts would cover costs. He was a pleasant, big-eyed, scatterbrained youth, always nudging people and laughing.

Sam, even so, was the first local impresario to look beyond the northwest, to London. Realising that no London agent would ever come up to Liverpool, he was planning to start his own record label, and had already booked Gerry and the Pacemakers to cut some demonstration discs in a studio in Crosby. His plan for the Beatles was no less audacious. He would get them on in a hall 'down south', and lure the big London impresarios to see them.

Sam Leach's choice of a southern venue was Aldershot. That glum military settlement, more adjacent to Stonehenge than London, had a dance hall called the Queen's which Sam Leach hired for five consecutive Saturday nights. It wasn't exactly the West End, as Sam conceded, but it was roughly in that direction.

If the Beatles could hit Aldershot in a big enough way, the word might easily spread.

Sam Leach and a photographer friend of his named Dick Matthews made the nine-hour journey from Liverpool to Hampshire in a hired Ford Classic. Following them down the motorway came a van containing the Beatles—all but Stu Sutcliffe—and driven by one of Sam's bouncers, Terry McCann.

They reached the Queen's Hall, Aldershot, to find four people waiting. 'I'd meant to put an ad in the paper,' Sam Leach says. 'But it hadn't got out. Maybe I forgot. We went round all the local cafes, telling people, "Hey, there's a dance on up the road." We said we'd let them in for nothing if they came.'

Eventually, eighteen customers had been rounded up. The lads said it wasn't worth playing at first, but Paul persuaded them. 'Come on,' he said. 'Let's show we're professionals.'

The Beatles gave those 18 people a two-and-a-half hour all-out non-stop session. When they showed signs of flagging, Paul revived them with his Little Richard act, played to the limit. Dick Matthews, a learned-looking man in a tweed sports jacket, photographed them on the little stage with its wallpapered proscenium, and the half-dozen couples, not all very youthful, jiving under a mirror globe which the management felt it not worthwhile to illuminate. Sam Leach also went among the dancers, pleading with them to look more numerous by spreading out.

Helped by Southern Watney's bottled pale ale and Sam's irrepressible spirits, the evening had its measure of jollity. When the last of the few dancers had gone, John and George, in their thin 'shortie' overcoats, danced a ritual slow foxtrot together. 'Then we had a game of football over the dance floor with ping-pong balls,' Sam Leach says. 'When we finally got outside, there was a great wagon load of bobbies waiting for us. "Get out of town," they said, "and don't come back." The next Saturday, 210 people came to the dance, just to see the Beatles—but they weren't there.'

A few days later, they were, once more, sitting round Allan Williams's Jacaranda coffee bar. So was Bob Wooler, the disc jockey who had quit his railway job in the expectation of running a beat club for Williams. That job having gone up in smoke, Wooler was now working for a promoter named Brian Kelly who ran regular dances at Litherland Town Hall, Lathom Hall and Aintree Institute.

'They were moaning to me about how little was happening,' Wooler says. 'I'd never heard them before, but I said I'd try to get Kelly to put them on. In fact, I rang him up from the Jacaranda. I asked for eight pounds for them. Kelly offered four; we settled on six.'

Brian Kelly, a somewhat melancholy man employed by the Mersey Docks and Harbour Company, had no overwhelming enthusiasm for Rock and Roll music. To Kelly, it was a question of simple mathematics. You hired a hall for £5 and by filling it with jivers at 3s each (2s 6d before 8 pm) you showed a profit. As a dance promoter, he possessed one large advantage—he did not mind clearing up vomit. Much tended to appear midway in the evening as late-comers arrived from the pubs.

At Litherland Town Hall, on 27 December 1960, Brian Kelly stood in his usual place on one side of the dance area, waiting to go forth with mop and disinfectant. A large crowd was there, curious more than anything to see the group which Bob Wooler had billed dramatically as 'Direct from Hamburg'. Because of this, many people thought they must be German. Among the spectators was Pete Best's young brother, Rory, and a friend of his called Neil Aspinall, an accountancy student who lodged with the Bests. Neil, a thin, serious boy with an impressive cache of O-levels, had never been much interested in Rock and Roll. He was here tonight only because Rory had said it would be good.

Brian Kelly did not think so. He had booked the Beatles before, in their pre-Hamburg days, and remembered them as very ordinary. He was astonished, when Bob Wooler announced them and the terrible noise started, to see what effect it had on his customers. 'Everyone—the whole lot—surged forward towards the stage. The dance floor behind was completely empty. "Aye aye," I said to myself, "I could have got twice the numbers in here."'

After their performance, the Beatles emerged into the car park where, a few months earlier, Stu Sutcliffe had been knocked down and kicked in the head. Once again, there was an ambush waiting—but of girls this time, squealing and asking for autographs. Their van had been covered with lipstick messages. Some of the girls who mobbed them still thought they were German and complimented them on speaking such good English.

Amid the general acclaim, they had made two important new friends. One was Bob Wooler, the disc jockey. The other was Neil Aspinall, the accountancy student for whom Fate had ordained a future very different from sitting his Finals.

Wooler became the intermediary for further £6 bookings at Brian Kelly's other weekly dances at Lathom Hall and Aintree Institute. He also became the means of spreading the Beatles' name over wider and wider areas of Liverpool. As a disc jockey, he was an unlikely figure with his round face, his earnest politeness and devotion to word-play and puns. He loved to draft elaborate posters and handbills in which, for example, the initial letters of Litherland Town Hall served additionally to spell

'Lively Time Here', and all the bus routes to the hall would be microscopically detailed. 'Jive Fans!' a Wooler handbill would say, 'This is It!' In neat capital letters, he would draft the evening's running order, murmuring to himself such cautionary slogans as 'Horses for courses. Menus for venues.' Somehow, in the shabby jive halls, he maintained the gravitas of a Roman senator, wagging his large forefinger as he strove to impress on beer-crazed 17-year-olds that punctuality and politeness were the primary virtues of life. Yet his voice, through the microphone, was as rich and relaxed as the best to be heard on Radio Luxembourg.

The Beatles were not interested in punctuality or politeness. But they respected Bob Wooler and recognised that his wagging forefinger often conveyed a valuable point. It was Wooler who advised them to begin playing even before the curtains opened, and who delved among his own record collection for a piece of the William Tell overture to play as their private signature tune.

Their other strong supporter was Mona Best, the dark-eyed, volatile woman who had started the Casbah Club for Pete and his friends. They always met first at the Casbah, setting off on dates in a van driven by Mrs. Best's part-time doorman, and usually accompanied by Neil Aspinall, ever ready to leave his accountancy studies to help unload and set up the drums and amplifiers.

Mona Best made forceful efforts on behalf of 'Pete's group', as she considered them. She took their bookings over the telephone, when Pete was not at home to do it: she became, as much as anyone was, their agent and manager. She wrote on their behalf to the BBC in Manchester, requesting a radio audition. The BBC's answer was not discouraging. The Beatles' name would be kept on file.

In Bob Wooler's eyes, too, Pete Best was their principal asset. At Aintree or Litherland, as the first bars of the William Tell overture whinnied out and the crash of guitars began behind still-closed curtains, that shriek of ecstasy, that rush to the front of the stage, was mainly for Pete Best. At a dance on St. Valentine's Day, 1961, Wooler offered the novel idea of moving Pete's drums forward to rank equally with the other three. That night, the girls all but dragged the handsome young drumming star off his stool and off the stage.

One evening just after Christmas, Mrs. Best rang up the Cavern Club in Mathew Street, and asked to speak to the owner, Ray McFall. It happened to be a big Trad Jazz night at the Cavern, starring Humphrey Lyttleton, and, what with the noise, McFall had to press his ear close to the receiver. 'Look here, Mr. McFall,' insisted the dulcet voice that sounded both a little Indian and a little Scouse, 'there's this group called the Beatles—you should have them at the Cavern, you know.' McFall replied politely that he'd think about it.

When Alan Synter started the Cavern as a Jazz club in 1957, Ray McFall had been the family accountant. In 1959, Synter decided to get out, and McFall took over the lease. It was he, in fact, who had booked John Lennon and the Quarry Men the night they gave offence by playing Chuck Berry numbers. Orders to desist were relayed to them from the man who still looked like an accountant with his light grey suit, his close-shaven cheeks and carefully-manicured hands and the small fur hat he wore during winter.

Mathew Street belongs to the system of cobbled lanes which carry goods traffic up from Liverpool docks into a hinterland of dark Victorian warehouses. By day, the lanes are alive with heavy goods lorries, unstacking and loading in the squeak of airborne hoists. By night, they are empty, but for cartons and cabbage leaves, and the occasional meandering drunk.

Underneath the warehouse at 10 Mathew Street, in 1960, could be found the Cavern Jazz Club. Its entrance was a hatchway, under a single naked light bulb. A flight of 18 stone steps turned at the bottom into three arched, interconnecting brick tunnels. The centre tunnel was the main club area, with a stage against the inner wall and an audience of wooden chairs. In the nearer tunnel, the money was taken; in the further one, beyond obscuring pillars, you danced. The best British Jazz bands had performed down there, in an atmosphere pervaded by damp and mould and the aroma of beer slops and small, decaying mammals and the cheeses that were kept in the cellar adjoining.

Ray McFall, though a passionate Jazz fan, was aware of Rock and Roll's growing popularity. The call from Mona Best only confirmed what he had heard about huge and profitable 'beat' dances in out-of-town halls. The short craze for 'Trad' was now definitely over, and Modern attracted only the earnest, intellectual few. McFall, therefore, decided to let Pop into his Jazz stronghold, gradually at first so as not to enrage the existing clientele. His first regular group, the Blue Genes, occupied a curious middle ground, playing both Rock and Jazz, with banjo and stand-up bass. Tuesdays, the Blue Genes' 'Guest Night', became the first break in the Cavern's all-Jazz programme.

McFall had noticed how many young office workers in central Liverpool spent their lunch-hour hanging round music shops like Hessy's, and the record department in NEMS, the electrical shop in Whitechapel, round the corner from Mathew Street. It suddenly occurred to him that he could just as easily open the Cavern for dancing at midday as at night. So he began to put on lunch-hour sessions, featuring Trad Jazz bands in alternation with a beat group called the Metronomes whose singer, Tommy Love, worked in a city insurance office. Derry and the Seniors also got a lunch-time booking after their return from Hamburg.

Bob Wooler, visiting the Cavern one lunch-time, was persuaded by Johnny Hutch of the Big Three to say something into the stage microphone. 'I did it just as the people were going out. I said, "Remember all you cave-dwellers, the Cavern is the best of cellars." I'd prepared that little pun on Peter Sellers's album The Best of Sellers. Ray McFall came across. I thought I was going to get a lecture; but instead he offered me the job of compering the lunch-time sessions.'

Wooler lost no time in urging McFall to hire the Beatles. Paddy Delaney, the club doorman and an accomplished mimic, remembers to this day the emphasis in Wooler's voice and forefinger as he told McFall they would bring in a following of 60, at least.

Delaney, a huge, straight-backed, kind-hearted Irishman, had seen service both in the Guards and the Liverpool Parks Police. He was equally immaculate in his spare-time profession of helping to dissuade Teddy Boys from entering Liverpool's premier dance halls, the Locarno and the Grafton Rooms. In 1959, to oblige his brother-in-law, he agreed to put in one night on the door of the Cavern Club. 'I thought it was a proper place, like the Grafton Rooms, so I turned up smart. I had three dinner suits in those days. I put one of them on with a maroon bow tie, a matching cummerbund with a watermark in it, and three diamond studs in my shirt. I walked up and down Mathew Street three times before I could even *see* the Cavern.'

Paddy Delaney was still there—still in evening dress complete with studs and cummerbund—when the Beatles first played at the Cavern in January 1961. Ray McFall had booked them, tentatively, to appear on a Tuesday, midway through the Blue Genes' Guest Night.

'I'm standing there under the light and I see this lad coming along in a leather jacket, a black polo-necked jersey. I remember thinking to myself, "That's the youngest tramp *I've* ever seen." "Are you a member, pal?" I said to him. He said "I'm George Harrison. I'm in the Beatles." I let him go in, then Paul McCartney came along; then John. Then a taxi came with Pete Best and the drums and their two amplifiers. Just chipboard, those were, no paint or anything, with the speakers nailed up inside.'

Bob Wooler's prophecy was fulfilled. The Beatles brought in at least 60 extra customers, in contingents from Aintree, Litherland and West Derby. The Blue Genes, supposedly the main event of the evening, were totally eclipsed. Paddy Delaney witnessed the furious row upstairs in Mathew Street between Ray McFall and his outraged regular musicians.

McFall was impressed by the door receipts but shocked to the depths of his Jazz-pure soul by the Beatles' unkempt appearance. He had thought, after seeing the Shadows, that groups wore suits. He told Bob Wooler that if the Beatles wanted to play the Cavern again, they must not wear jeans. To this the Beatles replied that Ray McFall could get stuffed. Wooler interceded on their behalf, pointing out to McFall the advantage of block-booking a group which, being 'professional'—that was to say, unemployed—would be available to play lunch-times on any day of the week. 'The Beatles,' Wooler says with pride, 'were what I called the first rock and *dole* group.'

So it came about that, on three or four days each week, the deliverymen and warehouse checkers in Mathew Street witnessed the unprecedented sight of scores of young girls, from city centre shops and offices, in beehive hair and stiletto heels that shocked the ancient cobbles, picking their way down the alleys through straw and tailboards and cast-off orange crates. By noon, when the session began, a queue would stretch from the corner facing Whitechapel, a hundred yards or more, past the wall with barbed wire along the top, past the gloomy warehouse fronts, up to the doorway, like a ship's hatch, that would be unnoticeable save for the bouncer who stood there, blocking it with his arm. As the city clocks struck noon, that queue would start to move forward, by degrees, into the hatchway and down the 18 narrow steps to the table where Ray McFall sat, surrounded by soup bowls full of money. Admission was a shilling each to members; to non-members, 1s 6d. Past McFall was a microscopic cloakroom, tended by a girl named Priscilla White during her lunch-break from a neighbourhood typing pool.

Under the dark arches, as the first girls danced tentatively around their handbags, Bob Wooler's voice would gravely resound in what had become each session's inaugural catechism. 'Hi, all you Cavern-dwellers—welcome to the *best* of cellars.' Wooler broadcast, not from the stage but behind it, in a tiny recess which served also as a changing-room for the bands. The sole ventilation came from the next-door cellar, via a grille which became gradually blocked by a mounting pile of drum kits. A single cupboard served to accommodate the DJ's amplifier and record-playing deck. Between each 'live' session, Wooler sat in this reeking priest hole, playing records from his own large personal collection.

Ray McFall paid the Beatles 25s each per day. For this they did two 45-minute spots at the end of the centre tunnel, on the tiny stage with dead rats under it, and positively no acoustics. The low-arched brick, and the wall of impacted faces and bodies, so squeezed out all empty air that Pete Best's drumbeats rebounded an inch in front of him, making the sticks jump like pistols in his hand. A single Chuck Berry number, in that heat, caused even tidy Paul to look as if his head had been plunged into a water butt. The bricks sweated with the music, glistening like the streams that coursed from their temples, and sending a steady drip of moisture over equipment in which there were many naked wires. Each breath they took filled their lungs with each other's hot scent, mingling uniquely with an aroma of cheese rinds, damp mould, disinfectant, and the perfume of frantic girls.

For their lunch-time audience, they poured out the vast Hamburg repertoire that could switch crazily from American Blues to maudlin Country and Western; from today's Top Twenty hit to some sentimental prewar dance-band tune. It seemed to Bob Wooler that they took a perverse delight in playing what no rival group would dare to do. 'They had to let you know they were different. If everyone else was playing the A-side of a record, they'd be playing the B-side. If the others jumped around, they'd decide to stand still like zombies.' Wooler himself possessed a number of rare American singles which he would play as surprise items over the Cavern loudspeakers. One of these, Chan Romero's Hippy Hippy Shake, besotted Paul McCartney, who begged to be allowed to borrow it and copy down the words. Hippy Hippy Shake became the climax of their catalogue of sheer stage-stamping Rock. A moment later, they would change to the cocktail-lounge tempo of Till There Was You, from the stage show *Music Man,* sung by Paul poignantly with the sweat drying on him.

Stu Sutcliffe was back with them on bass guitar, although little more proficient than he had been before the Hamburg trip. 'He'd bop around like the others,' Bob Wooler says. 'But he seemed to know that the others were carrying him.' Stu was hardly noticed by John and Paul in their perpetual contest to be the cynosure of all eyes. They in turn failed to notice how often those eyes would pass over their bobbing heads, to settle on Pete Best. George, on the right, took no part in the clowning, but waited solemnly, biting his lower lip, for the moment when his solo arrived. To his mother, Louise, he explained that he had no time to horse around—it was up to him to keep the music together.

In the intervals, they would fight their way through the crowds and upstairs, to glimpse daylight. They would go across Mathew Street to The Grapes, a marine-looking pub with scrubbed wooden tables, much frequented by postmen from the GPO in North John Street. There they would sit as long as possible over a fivepenny half of bitter each. The landlady complained they took up seats which might have been more profitably occupied by postmen drinking pints of draught Guinness.

The Cavern provided lunch of a sort—hot soup with mysterious lumps in it; meat pies and rolls and soft drinks. 'Paul borrowed a halfpenny off me once,' Paddy Delaney, the doorman says. 'He wanted a Coke and a cheese roll; it came to sevenpence halfpenny, and he'd only got sevenpence. "There you are, Paul," I said to him. "Remember me when you're up there, famous." '

Paul's father, Jim McCartney, was the first of their parents to investigate this new folly. He had noticed the state in which Paul came home from the Cavern, with clothes stinking of mould and a shirt so drenched it could be wrung out over the kitchen sink. Jim was still in the cotton business, working at the Cotton Exchange just round the corner from Mathew Street. Venturing into the Cavern in his own lunch-hour, Jim could not get near enough to the stage to speak to Paul. When he came after that, it would usually be to drop in some meat he had bought to cook for Paul and Michael that evening. Above the din in the band room, he would give Paul careful instructions about when, and at what number, to switch on the electric cooker.

John Lennon's Aunt Mimi was less easily placated. Ray McFall, sitting behind his soup-bowl exchequer, was dismayed to be confronted by a lean and angry woman demanding the whereabouts of John Lennon. For Mimi, up to that point, still believed John to be studying at Art College. He was on stage at the time, doing a song whose lyrics suddenly changed—as at Woolton fête—to: 'Oh, oh, Mimi's coming. Mimi's coming down the path.' In the break, when he reeled into the band room, he found waiting for him, as well as faithful Cynthia, an extremely grim-faced aunt. 'I said to him, "This is very nice, John, isn't it? This is *very* nice!" '

George's mother also happened to be at the Cavern that day, but in the audience. She would go along and shout and scream for George as loudly as any girl. She saw Mimi going out one day, and shouted exuberantly, 'Aren't they great?' 'I'm glad somebody thinks so,' was Mimi's tart reply.

Allan Williams, although busy with his Blue Angel club, was still the sole exporter of Liverpool groups to Hamburg. Early in 1961, he booked Gerry and the Pacemakers to play a two-month session for Peter Eckhorn at the Top Ten club. It was a well-deserved chance for Gerry Marsden, the little, wide-grinning postboy from Menzies Street, who had made such a success at the Boxing Stadium show by singing You'll Never Walk Alone.

Gerry and his group were quiet boys, intent on saving their

Hamburg money to buy new equipment. Even so, they brought home enough stories—of Willi's Cafe, the Gretel and Alfons and Jim Hawke's Seaman's Mission—to reawaken the Beatles' addiction to Reeperbahn life. Peter Eckhorn had told them they could go back to the Top Ten any time, subject to police and immigration approval. Pete Best's drums were still there, together with the clothes which he and Paul had been compelled to leave behind in the attic.

Pete, with the approval of the other four, rang up Peter Eckhorn from Mona Best's house in Heyman's Green. Eckhorn instantly gave them a booking, to begin in April, at £40 each per week—exactly twice as much as they had been paid by Bruno Koschmider. Nor would they have to pay Allan Williams his 10 per cent agent's commission, having fixed the engagement without his help. Williams, unaware of this decision, applied for work permits to the German Consulate in Liverpool, explaining the circumstances of the Bambi Kino fire, and rendering heartfelt assurances as to their reliability and good character.

Only Stu Sutcliffe did not share the general excitement. He knew he was no musician—that he played in The Beatles only because he was John Lennon's best friend. He knew that Paul despised him, and wanted to take over on bass guitar. He knew that, as long as John was leader, he would not be displaced. His guilt at trading on John's loyalty was nothing, however, to his guilt over having neglected his Art. He determined to go back to Liverpool Art College, as his mother urged, and take his teacher-training diploma. But the College—despite previous contrary indications—would not accept him. Millie Sutcliffe afterwards learned that he was suspected of stealing the Student's Union amplifier which the Beatles had long ago removed from College precincts.

His disappointment plunged Stu into a state of gloom so intense, he believed he might never paint again. Above all, he wanted to get away from Liverpool, its disappointments and prejudice. He wanted to get back to Astrid, his beautiful German fiancée. When the Hamburg trip came up, he buried his—and his mother's—misgivings and sorted out his Hofner 'President' bass.

The Beatles' Top Ten engagement started in April 1961. They had real work permits this time, and real train tickets, purchased with money sent across by Peter Eckhorn. They got down from the train at Hamburg to be greeted by Astrid in her black leather trouser suit. Even the bashful George did not hesitate to fling his arms around her.

The hours at the Top Ten were, if anything, more arduous than at the Kaiserkeller. They went on at 7 pm each night, playing in alternation with Tony Sheridan's band, until 2 or 3 am. The club's barn-like size meant they must 'mak show' even more obviously and violently to be seen out in the remoter terraces. Now, too, along the front of the stage, there would often be photographers—friends of Astrid and Klaus Voorman—training their long lenses upward and shouting, 'More sveat, boys! More sveat.'

Most of their Kaiserkeller friends had forsaken Bruno Koschmider to work at the new Top Ten. There was Horst Fascher, the Reeperbahn's champion bouncer, just released from another prison sentence and ready, in the Liverpool phrase, to 'worship the bones of their bodies.' There was Rosa the WC attendant, and her big sweet jar of 'Prellys'. There were three bold-eyed, powerful barmaids with whom almost everyone had explored the delights of 'muff-diving', 'finger pie' and 'yodelling up the canyon', and who signified when a song had gone down well by setting all the low lampshades over the bar counter swinging and jogging.

Astrid continued her flattering habit of photographing the Beatles at every opportunity. She produced studies of them, lounging on the docks or in railway sidings, complementing their beardless menace with tugboats, railway wagons or other specimens of German industrial design. She did studio portraits, too, using a technique pioneered by the American, Richard Avedon, which gave drama to the face by halving it between shadow, and light. George and John were photographed in this way, but not Pete Best—who was genuinely unconceited about his appearance—and, strangely, not Paul. Astrid tended to be with George, whom she mothered, and John, because, as well as being Stu's closest friend, he fascinated her.

It was no coincidence, perhaps, that Stu persuaded John to allow his own steady girl friend, Cynthia Powell, to come out to visit him in Hamburg. Paul's 'steady', a girl named Dot who worked in a Liverpool chemist's shop, was also invited. The two girls had become friends in their common purdah, squeezing themselves into photography booths for snapshots to send to their lords and masters, or laboriously transcribing the words of the newest Chuck Berry song.

The visit took place in Cynthia's Easter College vacation, and passed off happily, against all the odds. For most of the fortnight, she stayed with the hospitable Kirchherr family. Astrid was nice to her, lent her stunning clothes and drove her down to the Reeperbahn each evening to see the Beatles play. Some nights, she stayed behind, heroically sharing John's bunk in the Top Ten attic, while George snored in the bunk below. Paul and Dot stayed, with Tony Sheridan and other itinerant lodgers, on a harbour barge lent to them by Rosa, the club's lavatory attendant. Most of the meals, as usual, were provided by Jim and Lilo Hawke at the Seaman's Mission. Rosa, walking through the early morning fish market, would steal extra rations for Paul, slipping bananas or sardines into her coat pockets or up her sleeves.

Relations between Stu Sutcliffe and Paul McCartney, meanwhile, grew steadily worse. Paul made no secret of his contempt for Stu's bass playing, and his own conviction that he could do it better. There were rows on the Top Ten stage, behind John's back; one night, Paul's taunts even goaded Stu to physical violence. 'Paul had made some remark about Astrid,' Tony Sheridan says. 'Stu went for him, but he was only a little guy. Paul started beating the shit out of him.'

Stu admitted that his mind was not on Rock and Roll music. All he wanted to do was paint. Astrid encouraged him to, but his self-confidence had gone. He spent the club intermissions talking wistfully to *exis*, like Peter Markmann and Detlev Birgfeld, who were students at the Hamburg State Art College. They and Astrid urged him to try to enrol there as a student. Things were especially good just now they said, as the College had appointed Edouardo Paolozzi—one of Stu's long-time idols—to run a course of painting and sculpture master classes. Eventually, he was persuaded to go and meet Paolozzi, taking some samples of his Liverpool College work.

A brief glance was enough for Edouardo Paolozzi. He promised to use his influence, not only to admit Stu to the State Art College but also to get him a grant from the Hamburg City Council.

In Paolozzi's class, and in an attic studio which Frau Kirchherr gave him, Stu nerved himself to paint again. And once he had started, he could not stop. His Liverpool work, though accomplished, had always been derivative, slipping in and out of identities that caught his fancy. Hamburg, and the Reeperbahn's colours, gave him his own line. Huge swirling abstracts, like crushed Rio carnivals, like cities crumbling into impacted seas, thronged the canvases that, once again, were almost too tall for him to reach the tops. Each one completed in a day or a night, was impatiently stacked aside. Life now seemed too short for the miles his brush had to travel.

For the first month he led a dual life, both studying under Paolozzi and playing at the Top Ten Club. At 2 or 3 am, he would go into his attic and work there until it was time for class. He existed for days without sleep, borne up by pills and drink and the feverish excitement of his work. The headaches, which had intermittently troubled him, began to increase, in frequency and ferocity. Sometimes the pain would send him into a kind of fit when he would smash his head against the wall or scream at

Astrid for some supposed infidelity—then, equally without warning, the anguish would disappear.

He quit the Beatles gradually, without rancour, glad to see how easily they closed ranks behind him. Paul, as Paul had so long wanted, took over bass guitar, borrowing Stu's Hofner President until he could get one of his own. When it came, it was a bizarre new Hofner model, shaped like a violin. At last, it was a left-handed guitar, its scratch plate in the correct position. Once or twice, for old times' sake, Stu 'sat in' with the Beatles, playing bass alongside Paul. A photograph taken at one such moment shows him half in shadow, his eyes frowning, sightless, as in some study taken a hundred years ago. It was a look that his College tutor, Edouardo Paolozzi, found especially disturbing. 'I felt there was a desperate thing about Stuart. I was afraid of it. I wouldn't go down to that club.'

Though Stu was a Beatle no longer, he allowed himself to be deputed for the job which none of the others fancied. He wrote to Allan Williams in Liverpool, informing Williams of the decision to withold his 10 per cent commission. It was shabby treatment for a man who, for all his shortcomings, had made genuine efforts on their behalf. Williams wrote back a long and aggrieved letter, threatening to have them blacklisted among theatrical agents, if not deported from West Germany all over again. He seems, for once, to have been too hurt to exact retribution. True to his own inadvertent career, any legally binding contract he had with the Beatles disappeared in the fire at his own short-lived Top Ten Club. So Allan Williams let the Beatles go.

In Hamburg, meanwhile, a new Messiah had appeared, in Bert Kaempfert, a well-known West German orchestra leader and producer for the German label Polydor. Kaempfert had been to the Top Ten to see Tony Sheridan and immediately put him under contract to Polydor. As a backing group—largely on Tony Sheridan's recommendation—Bert Kaempfert hired the Beatles.

They had gone to bed as usual, Pete Best remembers, just after dawn. At eight sharp, taxis arrived to take them and Tony Sheridan to the recording studio. This, despite Kaempfert's eminence, proved to be no more than the hall of a local infants' school. They recorded on the stage, with the curtains closed.

Bert Kaempfert's idea of Rock and Roll was to put a drum beat behind tunes familiar to a German audience from their nights of beer and boomps-a-daisy. He had chosen for Sheridan and his backing group material that included two of the world's most boring songs, My Bonnie Lies Over the Ocean, and When The Saints Go Marching In. Tony Sheridan sang them in a voice still wide-eyed with last night's 'Prellys', while the 'Beat Brothers'—as

Kaempfert had renamed them—rattled off two versions of the same non-arrangement.

The 'Beat Brothers', thrilled just to be in the proximity of disc-making equipment, were content with their subordinate role. They did prevail on Kaempfert, however, to listen to a handful of Lennon—McCartney songs. The great man's verdict was one to which John and Paul were growing accustomed —their songs did not sound enough like the hits of the moment. But Kaempfert was impressed enough to let them cut a disc in their own right. They did Ain't She Sweet, one of the standbys from their all-night club act, with John taking the vocal and the old Jazz chords rearranged in a style strongly reminiscent of Paul. Kaempfert also liked an instrumental which George had worked out as a parody of Cliff Richard's group, the Shadows. This, too, was taped under the ironic title Cry For A Shadow.

The tracks chosen by Polydor for release were, as might have been feared, My Bonnie Lies Over the Ocean, coupled with When The Saints Go Marching In. The 'Beat Brothers' had played for a flat fee of 300 marks each (about £26), and so could expect no royalty on the disc's quite healthy German sales. Ain't She Sweet and Cry For A Shadow were still in the Polydor vaults in June 1961, when John, Paul, George and Pete caught the train back to Liverpool.

Stu Sutcliffe did not go with them. He had decided to settle in Hamburg, marry Astrid and continue at the State Art College. His mother shortly afterwards received a photograph of him taken by Astrid in his attic studio, in jeans and gumboots, standing before the easel bearing some new work in headlong progress. The technique was the same that she had used on George and John, splitting the face between light and shadow. In this portrait of Stu, the effect was eerie, his features the palest glimmer against what seemed an encroaching dark.

In Liverpool now, beat music raged like an epidemic. From Mathew Street it had seeped up between the warehouses into Dale Street and through the studded gates of the Iron Door, another long-time Jazz stronghold gone over to evening or all-night Pop sessions in overt rivalry with the Cavern. The same had happened all over the city, in clubs like the Downbeat and the Mardi Gras, in dance halls formerly dedicated to quicksteps and Veletas. The Riverside Ballroom and the Orrel Park Ballroom, the Rialto Ballroom, the Avenue cinema, even the Silver Blades Ice Rink clamoured for beat groups to fill their Saturday nights. New groups sprang up by the dozen, mutating from older ones, then splitting like amoebae into newer groups still. Now, as rivals to the Beatles at the Cavern, there were the Searchers at the Iron Door. There were Ian and the Zodiacs;

Kingsize Taylor and the Dominoes; Faron and the Flamingoes; Earl Preston and the TTs; Lee Curtis and the All-Stars; Dale Roberts and the Jaywalkers; Steve Day and the Drifters; the Remo Four; the Black Cats; the Four Jays. Hessy's music store thronged each day with eager customers for new guitars, new basses and drum kits to be paid far into a future that had no relevance compared with the finger-sliding, tom-tomming excitement of tonight.

Bill Harry knew every group and every place there was to play. The little, curly-haired design student from Upper Parliament Street was always to be seen in the clubs and jive halls, talking to the musicians between numbers and intermittently scribbling on bits of paper. He kept notes on every new group that was formed and every new venue opened. For him, as for John Lennon, beat music disrupted an Art College course, though in Bill's case, poor family circumstances dictated that even a hobby should be a matter of feverish hard work. He earned extra money by designing stationery for a local printer, and by writing and drawing anything, anywhere, for anyone.

Bill, an inveterate compiler of Sci-fi 'Fanzines', had long cherished an ambition to start his own music newspaper. For a time, he planned one called *Storyville and 52nd Street*, to cover Jazz. Then in 1961, with details of 350 beat music venues in his notebook, another idea occurred to him. He had noticed, on his trips around clubs and ballrooms, how parochial each one was; how little each audience knew of the sheer size and variety of the beat craze. The musicians, too, often had no idea where their friends or their rivals were performing. Bill Harry conceived the idea of a fortnightly beat music newspaper that would serve both as a guide to clubs and halls and an insight for the fans into the lives of their favourite groups.

The paper, launched on 6 July 1961, was christened *Mersey Beat*. A local Civil Servant named Jim Anderson provided its £50 starting capital. Bill Harry was editor, designer, chief reporter, sub editor and advertisement and circulation manager, all while ostensibly studying at the Art College. Each lunch-hour, he would sprint out of College, down the hill to the *Mersey Beat* office, a single room above a wine merchant's shop in Renshaw Street. His girl friend, Virginia, who typed and took telephone calls, was the only other member of staff.

John Lennon's former Gambier Terrace flatmate could naturally be counted on to give the Beatles plenty of space in his new paper. When Bill asked them for photographs, they handed over a pile of the ones Astrid had taken in Hamburg, together with some informal snapshots of John in his underwear, standing on the Grosse Freiheit and reading the *Daily Express*. John's was precisely the kind of Goon Show humour Bill Harry wanted to flavour the *Mersey Beat* editorial. He had never forgotten the nonsense verses which John had shown him during student lunch-time sessions at Ye Cracke. For *Mersey Beat*'s first issue, he asked John to write his own personal account of the Beatles' beginnings as a group. This was produced, Billy Harry remembers, on scraps of paper, with a hangdog, half-embarrassed air. John clearly did not expect his words to be suitable for publication.

Issue number one of *Mersey Beat* had a print run of 5,000 copies. Bill Harry, as well as writing the entire paper, delivered bundles of it personally to 28 Liverpool newsagents. Further stocks went on sale at local dances, at Hessy's music shop and on the record counters of major city stores like Blackler's. One of Bill's best contacts had proved to be NEMS, the electrical appliance shop in Whitechapel which had a record department run by the owner's eldest son. His name was Brian Epstein. He showed keen interest in *Mersey Beat*, giving Bill Harry a firm order for a dozen copies.

The first issue carried on its dwarfish front page a picture of Gene Vincent, the American Rock and Roll star who had visited Liverpool, as the caption admitted, 'earlier in the year'. Bill Harry, unable to afford to make photographic blocks, was compelled to borrow what he could from a local weekly newspaper. Underneath, a story headed Swinging Cilla told how Cilla Black, the Cavern Club's part-time cloakroom attendant, better known along Scotland Road as Priscilla White, had begun to gain confidence as a singer by after-hours appearances on stage with Rory Storm's group and the Big Three.

The right-hand column was given over to John Lennon's article. Bill Harry had printed it complete under its author's heading 'a short diversion on the dubious origins of Beatles, translated from the John Lennon'. What followed revealed little of those origins but much about the boy whose fascination with words coexisted with utter disregard of all normal punctuation and spelling. 'Many people ask what are Beatles? Why Beatles? Ugh, Beatles, how did the name arrive? So we will tell you. It came in a vision—a man appeared on a flaming pie and said unto them: "From this day on you are Beatles." "Thank you, Mister Man, they said, thanking him." '

Mersey Beat was an immediate sell-out. At NEMS in Whitechapel, all 12 copies went within minutes of their appearance in the record department, and Brian Epstein telephoned Bill Harry with an order for two dozen more. The next day, he requested a further hundred. For issue two, published on 20 July, Brian Epstein's order was 12 dozen copies.

Prominent in the first issue, and every one that followed, was a large display advertisement for the Cavern Club, giving details of its lunchtime, evening and, occasionally, all-night sessions. Here, the Beatles' name, varying in type-size from the garish to the microscopic, rotated week by week with that of Gerry and the Pacemakers, Rory Storm and the Hurricanes, Kingsize Taylor and the Dominoes, and also the Traditional Jazz bands which Ray McFall stubbornly continued to hire.

Though conscientiously filled with news about all groups and their doings, *Mersey Beat* made no secret of its overriding preference. Issue two, when it reached the counter of NEMS record store in Whitechapel, banner-headlined the retrospective hot news of the 'Beatle's' recording session and contract with Bert Kaempfert in Hamburg. Only now did their Liverpool following learn of the existence of the Beatles' music on disc, albeit a little-known foreign label. The story was illustrated by Astrid's photograph of them, with Stu Sutcliffe, on the traction engine at Der Dom. Paul's surname was given, in one of its several *Mersey Beat* versions, as 'McArtrey'.

The paper soon became known, not merely for news about the Beatles but as an extension of the comedy and clowning in their Cavern Club stage act. John Lennon, at Bill Harry's encouragement, contributed more nonsense verses and an irregular column called 'Beatcomber', called after 'Beachcomber' in the *Daily Express*. He also wrote and paid for comic small ads, filling a section which would otherwise have been empty, and prolonging Beatle in-jokes for weeks at the modest cost of fourpence a word. 'HOT LIPS, missed you Friday—Red Nose.' 'RED NOSE, missed you Friday—Hot Lips.' 'Whistling Jock Lennon wishes to contact HOT NOSE.'

Mersey Beat flourished, thanks to its thorough coverage, its misprints, and the sprinting energy of its editor. Anyone who placed a large ad could expect a large story to be written about them. If the advertiser could write his own copy, so much the better. It was on this principle that *Mersey Beat*, in its early August issue, published a short article by one of its best customers, Brian Epstein of the NEMS electrical shop, reviewing the new records NEMS currently had for sale. Mostly, he recommended ballads from musical shows like *West Side Story* and *The Sound of Music*. A cursory reference was made to Chubby Checker's Let's Twist Again, and the Streamliners' Frankfurter Sandwiches. The closing paragraph was devoted to new John Ogden's piano recitals of works by Liszt and Busoni.

Bob Wooler, the Cavern disc jockey, also wrote regularly for *Mersey Beat*. His debut column on 31 August dealt entirely with the Beatles: they were, said Wooler, 'the biggest thing to hit the Liverpool Rock and Roll set up in years'. Among hundreds of groups playing roughly the same R & B material, Wooler pinpointed accurately the novelty in musicians with equal appeal to both sexes—to the boys through their dress and manner; to girls, in Wooler's view, chiefly through the 'mean, moody magnificence' of their drummer Pete Best. Pete, indeed, was the only Beatle singled out by name. Wooler summed them up, with true alliterative relish, as 'rhythmic revolutionaries . . . seemingly unambitious yet fluctuating between the self-assured and the vulnerable. Truly a phenomenon—and also a predicament to promoters. Such are the fantastic Beatles. I don't think anything like them will happen again.' The only other item on the page was the brief column by 'Brian Epstein of NEMS', recommending new releases by Frank Sinatra, the Shadows and the George Mitchell Singers.

Bob Wooler's endorsement in *Mersey Beat* was backed up by ceaseless plugging of their Polydor record, over the Cavern microphone and in the halls where Wooler ran regular dances for Brian Kelly. Such was their drawing power now that Kelly would post bouncers outside their changing-room to stop rival promoters offering them more than £10 per night.

Between the groups, by contrast, there was little competition, save in the sinking of pints and the attracting of 'judies'. Bob Wooler's strict running-order would frequently be confounded by a hybrid semi-orchestra formed of two, or more, groups who felt like jamming together. At Litherland Town Hall one night, the Beatles merged with Gerry and the Pacemakers to form the 'Beatmakers'. Gerry wore George's leather outfit, George wore a hood, Paul wore a nightdress and Gerry's brother Fred and Pete Best played one drum each.

Three or four nights a week at the Cavern, the queue would move, past Ray McFall's soup bowls, into heat barely describable by those who ever experienced it. 'You could feel it as you went down those 18 steps, climbing up your legs,' Paddy Delaney the doorman, says. 'The lads used to faint as well as the girls.' In the glue of bodies, the only space, apart from the stage, was an area at the opposite end of the centre tunnel where the boys would go and urinate. A girl wishing to get to the Ladies' could often make the journey only by being passed over the heads of the crowd.

For all the 'kicks and kudos', as Bob Wooler alliteratively phrased it, the summer of 1961 ended on a note of anticlimax. The Beatles seemed to have progressed as far as any group outside the mystic sphere of London. Other people, like Rory Storm with his Butlin's holiday camp dates, seemed to be forging ahead.

John Lennon took out his boredom in writing for *Mersey Beat*, and in letters to Stu Sutcliffe in Hamburg—long letters in pencil on exercise book paper, full of scribble and doodles, poems that started seriously but petered out into self-conscious obscenity, and anguished cries about the 'shittiness' of life. The correspondence could not be shown to Aunt Mimi or Millie Sutcliffe, teeming as it did with swear words and a running joke whereby Stu took the character of Christ and John, that of John the Baptist. It seemed that Stu, by staying on in Hamburg, had done the adventurous and enviable thing.

One letter from Stu mentioned that Jurgen Vollmer, a photographer friend of Astrid's, was soon going to be in Paris on holiday. John and Paul decided on the spur of the moment to use some money John's Scottish aunt had given him, to go across to Paris and meet Jurgen. They went without a word to George or Pete Best, and despite the imminence of several important bookings. For almost a week, they lived in Montmartre and hung around the Flea Market, looking for sleeveless jackets like the one Jurgen wore. They also persuaded Jurgen to cut their hair in the 'French' style that Astrid had given Stu and George. They returned to Liverpool to find George and Pete Best disgusted with them; for a time, it seemed that the Beatles were finished. Bob Wooler and Ray McFall persuaded them to continue, each lecturing John and Paul sternly on the need to be reliable.

What did it matter anyway? The Cavern was always there, with another night-long session to trap them under ground. Up in Mathew Street, where Paddy Delaney stood in his evening dress, a cloud of steam, created by the tumult below, drifted out under the solitary light.

PART TWO

Getting

November 1961

'What brings Mr. Epstein here?'

Each Wednesday night in the late 1930s, little Joe Flannery would be dressed in his night clothes and taken to spend the evening at the house of his father's best customer, Mr. Harry Epstein. His father, Chris Flannery, was a cabinet-maker, specialising in the heavy sideboards sold at Epstein's Walton Road shop. 'Mr. Harry' was a stickler for quality, refusing to accept any piece whose drawers did not slide in as easily upside-down. But on Wednesday evenings, formality relaxed. The Flannerys and the Epsteins drove into Liverpool together to attend the weekly wrestling bouts. Seven-year-old Joe would wait for his parents at Mr. Harry's house, playing upstairs in the nursery with the Epstein's own golden-haired boy.

This other boy was not like Joe. He was slender and delicate; he had a nanny to look after him in his own softly-lit upstairs domain. He did not speak like Joe, nor like any Liverpool child. And he had many beautiful toys. Joe, in particular, loved the model coach which the boy had been given to mark the Coronation of George VI. It was the State Coach in miniature, made of tin but magnificently gilded, drawn by a dozen plumed tin horses, spurred on by liveried tin postillions and grooms.

The other boy knew how much Joe loved the Coronation Coach. To grant, or arbitrarily refuse, permission to play with it gave him a sensation he slowly recognised as power over someone older and stronger. Though he himself cared little for the coach, he worried that Joe, because of loving it so much, would somehow gain possession of it. So one night while Joe was there, he stamped on the coach until he had broken it.

In 1933, the wedding took place of 18-year-old Malka Hyman to 29-year-old Harry Epstein. The match was approved of, uniting as it did two highly respectable Jewish families and two comparably-thriving furniture firms. Harry's father, Isaac, owned the Liverpool shop he had founded as a penniless

Lithuanian immigrant at the turn of the century. The Hymans, Malka's people, owned the Sheffield Cabinet Company, mass producing such items as 'The Clarendon', a bedroom suite which, in the twenties and early thirties, graced many a suburban English home.

Malka received a comfortable upbringing and a boarding-school education. In 1933, she was a slender, rather refined and artistic girl whose only serious complaint against the world was the way it had Anglicised her given name. Malka is the Hebrew word for queen. So Queenie was what her family, and her new husband, called her.

Her first child was born on 19 September 1934, at a private nursing home in Rodney Street, Liverpool. It was a boy, and as such a cause for rejoicing to grandparents concerned with the perpetuity of business. To Queenie, the golden-haired boy in her arms was something more beautiful than she had dared to imagine. She called him Brian because she liked the name, and Samuel for the sake of the family and the scriptures.

The new baby was brought home to substance and comfort. Queenie's dowry from her parents was a handsome modern town house in Childwall, one of the smartest Liverpool suburbs. 197 Queens Drive was a five-bedroom residence with bay windows and a sunrise design on the glass over the front door, which a uniformed maid would open to visitors. A nanny was needed when, in 1935, Queenie gave birth to her second son, Clive John.

The Epstein family shop occupied a prominent place in Walton Road. A row of tall display windows, extending round the corner into Royal Street, offered a range of furniture and home requisites, from sideboards to standard lamps, whose appearance was not especially chic but whose quality and durability could always be relied on. Next door stood the North End Road Music Stores, a little double-fronted shop which had been there since the days when young men and women bought sheet music to sing around the parlour piano. Jim McCartney's was one of the many local families which bought pianos from 'NEMS' on the instalment plan. Subsequently, Epstein's had taken over the little shop, extending its stock to gramophones and wireless sets.

Harry Epstein worked hard, but enjoyed his pleasures and the sharing of them with his wife. They were keen bridge-players, fond of films and the theatre, well known, in a hospitable community, for the generosity and style of their entertaining. Once a week, they would drive into Liverpool to dine in the Sefton Restaurant at the Adelphi, an hotel then at its splendid apogee. In Ranelagh Place, next to Lime Street, the polished motor cars slid up the ramp. Commissionaires hastened out to welcome them into the majestic, ship-like interior of the entrance hall.

To their two small sons, Harry and Queenie Epstein gave the security, not only of Jewish family life but also of a middle class untroubled, as yet, by any social comparison. For Merseyside, in that time, was racked by unemployment. A few miles from Childwall, on grey and unknown dockyard streets, the men massed at dawn, like livestock, for the favour of even half a day's work at four and sixpence. Unknown children played barefoot on flinty cobble stones. In Queens Drive, the nursery lights were soft; there was Auntie Muriel or Uncle Mac on the wireless, and thin bread and butter for tea.

Brian left babyhood rapidly, learning to walk by the age of 11 months and to talk soon after that, clearly and interrogatively. In looks he was like his father, dark-eyed and round-faced, with wavy, light brown hair. His temperament was Queenie's, most notably in his love of refinement, and a feeling for style manifest even as a toddler. He would stand in his mother's bedroom while she got ready to go out, and gravely confer with her about which dress and accessories she should wear. Like Queenie he loved the theatre, its world of romance, strange light and make-believe. *The Wizard of Oz*, the first film he ever saw, left him astounded, with its wistful fantasy, for days. At the same time, he seemed normally robust, hammering wooden shapes into a plywood board at his first kindergarten school, Beechanhurst in Calderstones Road.

In 1940, during the bombing of Liverpool, Harry Epstein moved his family to relative safety in Southport on the West Lancashire coast. Brian attended Southport College, but hated it so much that Queenie transferred him to a smaller private school. Despite his obvious intelligence and alertness, he did not seem to do well there either. But now it was 1944, and safe to move back to Liverpool. Ten-year-old Brian was arrayed in a new black blazer and sent to Liverpool College, the most exclusive and expensive of the city's fee-paying academies.

Before he had reached his eleventh birthday, the College asked Harry and Queenie to remove him. It was alleged that he had done a dirty drawing in the mathematics class. According to Brian, this had been a design for a theatre programme, legitimately adorned by the figures of dancing girls. Privately the headmaster told Queenie that in other respects, too, Brian had proved to be a 'problem child'. He himself was never to forget the shame of sitting on a sofa at home and hearing his father say, 'I don't know *what* we're going to do with you.' The words produced one of the furious blushes by which Brian betrayed even the smallest discomfiture.

He had not sat the 11-plus exam, and so could not be sent to any of Liverpool's excellent grammar schools. His parents were forced to settle for another small private academy which Brian, predictably, loathed. Queenie by now had begun to suspect that the fault might not be entirely on his side. Anti-semitism was a habit in which many otherwise agreeable British people still overtly and comfortably indulged. The nation which had recently pitted itself against the Nazi holocaust saw no harm in using words like 'Yid' or 'Jewboy' and in passing such expressions on to its children. Queenie Epstein knew the lengths to which Brian went at school to hide the fact that his middle name was Samuel.

They decided to try a school that actually welcomed Jewish boys. The nearest that could be found was Beaconsfield, near Tunbridge Wells in Kent. There, despite Queenie's forebodings, Brian seemed to do a little better. He took up horseriding and was encouraged to paint and draw. He made a friend of another Liverpool boy, Malcolm Shifrin, also the son of furniture people. The experiment was so successful that his younger brother Clive came to Beaconsfield to join him.

He continued to show a precocious love of luxury and refinement. Even when quite small, his greatest treat was to go with his mother and father for dinner at the Adelphi. Throughout the boys' infancy, Harry and Queenie sacrificed holidays abroad in favour of annual seaside visits to Llandudno in North Wales, or St. Anne's. One wet summer in Llandudno, when Brian was 11, as a change from variety shows, Queenie took him to a concert by the Liverpool Philharmonic Orchestra. From that moment he began to love and learn about classical music. Another year, at St. Anne's, the family struck up acquaintanceship with Geraldo, a bandleader famous for his BBC shows. Brian was invited to go into Blackpool to watch Geraldo make a recording. Queenie remembers how he sat spellbound in the studio when the red light went on for silence.

His formal education had yet again run into squalls. Shortly to leave Beaconsfield, he was busily engaged in failing the entrance exams for major public schools such as Rugby, Repton and Clifton. At last he was able to satisfy the requirements of Clayesmoore, a small public school still further away, in Dorset. 'As soon as he got there, he started to grumble,' Queenie Epstein says. 'Oh, those grumbles of his were enormous.'

Clive, his younger brother, a placid, conscientious, practical boy, had passed through prep school without trouble or complaint. Clive was good at exams, and so easily got into Wrekin College, a public school of the higher echelon in Shropshire. On the strength of Clive's suitability, the Wrekin head agreed to accept Brian also.

Wrekin was his eighth school. He stayed there for two years, in a torpor faithfully described in his school reports. His only aptitudes seemed to be for art and—he discovered—acting. He found that he could face an audience without blushing, and that he enjoyed speaking lines. School dramatics brought him friends, at times even won him official commendation. Some worm of reticence, however, nurtured by all the schools he had failed at, prevented him from telling his parents. Queenie Epstein remembers driving down to Shropshire to see a school play about Christopher Columbus, and failing to spot Brian where she expected to see him, among the supporting cast. He had not told her, so she did not realise that he *was* Christopher Columbus.

He left school at 15, without sitting his School Certificate. He had written home that exams were not needed in the career he had chosen. Throughout his final terms, he had come top of his class in art and design. He wanted to go to London and become a dress designer.

Few enough people in 1950 would have wished to see their sons make such a choice of profession. To a northern Jewish family, with its age-old view of filial duty, no more disturbing or wounding suggestion could have emanated from an elder son. Harry Epstein was outraged and made no secret of it: Queenie, though more sympathetic, could see no means of granting Brian's wish within convention. The great scheme was buried quickly, before it could reach the ears of relations.

Another idea, that he might study art, languished as quickly under his father's remorseless practicality. With no exams behind him, no aptitude save that of upsetting his parents, there was nothing left for Brian but to submit to heredity. In September 1950, shortly after his sixteenth birthday, he started work as a furniture salesman in the family's Walton Road shop.

A woman came in to Epstein's that day to buy a mirror. Brian was allowed to deal with her under the critical eye of his parental superiors. By the time the customer left, he had persuaded her that what she really needed was a £12 dining-table.

He was, he discovered, a born salesman. Walton Road was not a grand thoroughfare, nor were they grand people who shopped for furniture at I. Epstein & Sons. This young man who served them, with his dapper suit, solicitous manner and upper-class voice, was decidedly an asset to the shop. Salesmanship awoke in him what eight costly schools could not—the will to work hard and be organised and efficient. He found he enjoyed arranging things for display, and window-dressing. And he was doing something which did not disappoint, but actually pleased, his father.

To his grandfather, he was less pleasing. Isaac Epstein still directed the firm he founded, arriving on the premises each morning as early as 6 am. Isaac, having dictated matters for half a century, looked askance on a grandson who boldly arranged dining-room chairs in the shop window with their back to the street, claiming it was 'more natural'.

Upsets with his grandfather became so frequent that, in 1952, his father and Uncle Leslie judged it wiser to remove him temporarily from Isaac Epstein's sight. For six months that year, Brian worked as a trainee with Times Furnishing Company at their Lord Street, Liverpool, branch. Reports on his progress were consistently favourable. As a salesman, he was smart and efficient; he dressed windows with flair and taste. When his stay with the Times ended, he received a parting gift of a Parker pen and pencil set.

To outward appearances, his position was an enviable one. The son of wealthy parents, adored by his mother, indulged by a father glad to see this new-found business zeal, he seemed, in 1952, the very acme of provincial young bachelorhood. Ample pocket money supplemented his salesman's pay, enabling him to dress with an elegance beyond his 18 years. His suits came from the best Liverpool tailors; his ties were half-guinea silk foulards; he had his hair cut in the salon at Horne Brothers. He belonged to a sophisticated young set which congregated at tennis clubs and cocktail parties, and in fashionable Liverpool haunts, like the Adelphi Palm Court lounge and the Basnett oyster bar. Among this circle he was popular, witty, generous and charming. Girls found him attractive with his wavy hair, his snub nose and delicate mouth and the large soft eyes which did not always look directly into theirs.

The eyes gave no sign of the mystification with which inner eyes looked at himself, nor the horror of what they eventually saw. Before he was 18, Brian Epstein faced a fact which, if once revealed, would condemn him to the detestation of both his countrymen and his religion, render him liable to prosecution under British Law and, on certain streets in Liverpool, would put his life in imminent danger. He had discovered he was a homosexual.

In 1952, he became eligible for National Service. He was put into the Army—not the RAF as he had wished—and sent south to do his basic training in Aldershot. He had hopes of being picked as officer material, but instead became a clerk in the Royal Army Service Corps. He was posted to London, to the RASC depot at Albany Barracks, Regent's Park.

His Army life was mitigated by plentiful pocket money from home and comparative liberty after 6 pm. His mother's sister, his Aunt Freda, lived in Hampstead, only a mile or so away; he was also within easy reach of the West End. He took to going around like a young Guards officer, with bowler hat, pinstripe suit and rolled umbrella. Driving back into barracks one night, he was mistakenly saluted by the gate sentry, and next morning was put on a charge of impersonating an officer.

It was a trivial misdemeanour, hardly explaining the Army's subsequent treatment of Brian. He was confined to barracks: prolonged medical and psychiatric examinations followed. Finally, after less than half his two-year term, he was discharged on 'medical grounds'. The Army, though it could not be rid of him fast enough, provided a character reference describing him as 'sober, conscientious, at all times utterly trustworthy'.

The experience faded; he became once more a dapper and purposeful young man about Liverpool. In the family business he worked hard, and with some additional enjoyment. Epstein's NEMS music shop annexe had lately extended its stock from pianos and wireless sets to gramophone records. Harry Epstein gave Brian the job of organising and running the new record department.

The success he made of it reflected his passion for classical music as well as his new-found business efficiency. Even as a schoolboy he had had his own impressive record collection, housed in a cabinet made specially for him at his Hyman grandparents' Sheffield factory. With his school-friend Malcolm Shifrin he was an ardent supporter of the 'Liverpool Phil''. 'Brian's knowledge of music really was impressive even then,' Shifrin says. 'So was his knowledge of the related Arts, like ballet. He always *knew* music people—John Pritchard, the Philharmonic's conductor was a friend of his. We drove up twice to the Edinburgh Festival, and Brian introduced me to people there. But I always had the feeling he was a lonely person.'

His second undimmed childhood passion was for the theatre. Liverpool's two main theatres, the Playhouse and the Royal Court were surrounded in those days by half a dozen smaller but flourishing professional repertories. Behind the Royal Court was a genuine stagedoor district of pubs and hotel bars which resounded to extravagant greetings in London accents. Brian haunted both the theatres and their adjacent lounge bars in the hope of getting to know stage people. He himself appeared in one or two local amateur productions and, like an actor, acquired the habit of giving away signed photographs of himself to his friends.

Among the actors who befriended him was Brian Bedford, then, at the start of his career, starring in *Hamlet* at the Liverpool Playhouse. To Bedford, Brian confided one night that he hated shop work and Liverpool, and that he, too, wanted to become an actor. Bedford encouraged him to try for an audition at the Royal College of Dramatic Art in London. RADA's director,

John Fernald, as it happened, had formerly run the Liverpool Playhouse. Brian auditioned with Fernald and, to his vast astonishment, was accepted.

The news filled his parents with dismay. In provincial Jewish business circles, 'going on the stage' was hardly less deplorable than becoming a dress designer. All the stability Brian seemed to have acquired was now put away, with his formal suits and ties. 'He'd made up his mind,' Queenie says, 'he was going to be a duffel-coated student. He wouldn't even take his car. We'd given it to him for his twenty-first birthday. A beautiful little cream and maroon Hillman Californian.'

Under John Fernald at RADA, Brian was a more than adequate pupil, sensitive and gentle. 'He didn't have a spectacular talent,' Fernald says, 'but it was a pleasing one. If you think in terms of typecasting, he would have played the second male lead —the best friend in whom the hero can always confide.'

At RADA he acquired—or seemed to—a steady girl friend. Her name was Joanna Dunham; she wore a fur coat dyed red. 'Brian always seemed older than the rest of us,' Joanna says. 'Even though he was only 21. And he drank. That was something hardly anyone at RADA did then, although everyone smoked. Brian would say, just like an older person would, "I *must* have a drink."

'I never thought he had any particular acting talent. There was one time, though, when he *did* surprise me. We had to do a test together for Fernald—a scene from *The Seagull.* We chose the scene between Konstantin and his mother, where Konstantin is adoring to his mother first, then flies into a terrible rage and tears the bandage off his head. The words must have had some special meaning for Brian. As he spoke the lines, I could feel he was getting out of control. When he started tearing the bandage off, I really felt frightened. It was almost as if he were having a nervous breakdown there on stage.'

Brian seems to have tried to resolve his doubts about himself by having an affair with Joanna. One night at a party, he got drunk and started to confide in her some of the secrets of his schooldays. 'I felt he seriously wanted to have a relationship with me, and that he was trying to tell me something. He was very pissed and threatened to drive me home. I behaved very badly, I'm afraid. I just ran away.'

Joanna never discovered what it was that Brian had tried to tell her. On the eve of his fourth RADA term, over a family dinner at the Adelphi, he told his father he had had enough. He wanted to come back to Liverpool again and be a businessman.

For this apparent sacrifice, he was given even further independence within the family firm. His father had bought a small shop in Hoylake, on the Cheshire Wirral, to be stocked with the more exclusive modern furniture which Brian favoured, and run by him on his own. It was his idea that the opening should be performed by a celebrity, 'Auntie Muriel', his childhood radio favourite from BBC Children's Hour.

There now began Brian's uneasy and painful double life. By day, managing Clarendon Furnishings, he was a smart young executive. By night, he became what his nature dictated, searching the Liverpool darkness for others of his kind. He found they did exist, though secretly and fearfully, in a small, surreptitious district. Behind the Royal Court theatre, there was a pub called The Magic Clock; there was also, a few yards on, an old hotel called The Stork. There, out of their common persecution, congregated other young men who were 'gay'.

Brian had found kinship, but he could not find happiness. The guilt and shame of 'going downtown' were bad enough. It was his further misfortune to be attracted to what homosexuals call 'The Rough Trade'—to the very dockers and labourers and merchant seamen who mock, revile and threaten them the most. Those who sought the Rough Trade in Liverpool in 1957 paid a high price, even in that currency of damnation. Rebuffed or accepted, they still went in fear. If there were not a beating up, then there would, later, be extortion and blackmail.

Some time around 1958, Brian began his first, and probably last, happy emotional affair. One night in the Stork Hotel, he met a tall, quiet, dark-haired young man whose evident nerves were kept in check by a quiet, measured Liverpool voice. With mutual astonishment, Brian and he recognised one another. The tall young man was Joe Flannery, the cabinet-maker's son who used to be left in the nursery with Brian every Wednesday night.

Joe, more than most, went in fear of the 'queer-bashing' gangs who roamed Liverpool after dark. His worst fears were borne out by the 'Rough Trade' experiences Brian described to him. There had even been a Court case in which Brian figured anonymously to give evidence against a blackmailer. 'Brian used to say there was a person in prison with a grudge against him. He used to say his life wouldn't be safe when this person was free again.'

The Epstein electrical retail business continued to expand. In 1958, with the start of the television boom, Harry was ready to move into central Liverpool. His first city shop was in Great Charlotte Street, near the Adelphi, and called NEMS after the North End Road Music Stores. Brian ran the record department and his younger brother, Clive, the household electrical side. Once again, at Brian's prompting, there was a celebrity opening, by Anne Shelton, the Forces Sweetheart.

The next year, an even bigger star, Anthony Newley, opened a second, greatly extended NEMS city centre shop. This one was in Whitechapel, close to Liverpool's banking and insurance district, a narrow street recently developed by a 'parade' of contemporary shops. The Whitechapel NEMS had three sales floors with a fourth for stock rooms and offices.

Brian had worked hard enough and produced profits enough at the Great Charlotte Street NEMS to convince his father that the new shop should have a greatly-extended record department. In the event it had two: the classical on the ground floor, popular in the basement. The Whitechapel street window displayed records with a flair developed in Brian's table and chair arrangements for the Times Furnishing Company. Another of his ideas was to cover the ceiling of the ground floor department with hundreds of LP sleeves.

Before long, NEMS in Whitechapel, rather than Lewis's or Blacker's department stores, advertised 'The Finest Record Selection in the North'. The policy, instituted by Brian, was that no request by a customer must ever be turned away. If the record were not in stock, it must be ordered. An ingenious system of cardboard folders with coloured strings kept Brian constantly abreast of which records were in stock, and which had sold out and needed reordering.

He was now 27, but looked older with his dark suit and his conservative haircut. His staff called him 'Mr. Brian'; behind his back they called him 'Eppy'. They laughed a little at his love of pompous executive gadgets, like memos and intercom systems. But they respected him as a decent and considerate employer, though a niggling perfectionist. If some small things were not right, he could fly into a red-faced tantrum, shouting and stamping his foot. Then in a minute, he would again be his usual, quiet, charming, courteous self.

If there were whispers about him, nothing was definitely known. Few who saw him by day in Whitechapel could visualise him in circumstances other than driving out to some smart Cheshire restaurant, accompanied by an equally smart young woman. He liked female company and had several passing girl friends. Once, to please Queenie, he even got engaged. The young woman involved was evidently mad about him. Somehow, his mother had noticed, that was always the point when Brian would grow nervous and evasive.

His adventures had brought him the benefit of certain good, long-standing male friends. There was Geoffrey Ellis, a recent Oxford graduate, now working in Liverpool for the Royal Insurance Company. There was also Peter Brown, who had originally run the record department at Lewis's department store, and had afterwards taken over from Brian as manager of the Great Charlotte Street NEMS. A slender, sensitive young man, rejected by his Catholic family in Bebington, Peter was to model his whole existence on Brian's.

By the summer of 1961, Brian was again growing restless. The Whitechapel shop, well-established and smooth-running, absorbed less and less of his attention and energy. The one small innovation that summer had been *Mersey Beat*, Bill Harry's new music paper, with its mutually advantageous record review column by 'Brian Epstein of NEMS'. The column lapsed when Brian went away, as he regularly did, for a long holiday in Spain. In October, the experience and his tan had faded; he was conscious of a vague dissatisfaction. He felt as if he were waiting for something to happen.

On Saturday, 28 October, an 18-year-old Huyton boy named Raymond Jones strolled into the Whitechapel branch of NEMS. Brian, that morning, happened to be behind the counter, helping with the weekend rush. He himself stepped forward to serve Raymond Jones, whom he recognised vaguely as one of the crowd of printer's apprentices often to be seen in the shop during their lunch-hour, sorting through the Country and Western stock. Like a good businessman, he even remembered that Carl Perkins was this customer's favourite singing star.

Today, Raymond Jones did not as usual ask for anything new by Carl Perkins. He asked for a single called My Bonnie, by the Beatles.

Brian had never heard of the single or the group whose name, in the busy shop, had to be repeated to him: Beatles, with an 'a'. No group of that name, certainly, appeared in the Top Ten chart currently posted on NEMS's front window. No such single had gone into a stock folder, marked by its appropriate coloured string. Raymond Jones could provide no further details of the disc. He had heard about it, he said, at Hambleton Hall, where he and his mates always went on Friday night. The compere, Bob Wooler, had urged them to be sure and ask their record shop for My Bonnie by the Beatles.

The only clue as to the record label was that it 'sounded foreign'. Brian asked if these Beatles were a foreign group. No, Raymond Jones replied, they were Liverpudlians, working abroad sometimes, but mainly playing at a cellar club not far from this very shop.

The NEMS policy, that any disc could be ordered, held sway no less on a busy Saturday, to an 18-year-old in jeans and leather jacket. Brian promised Raymond Jones he would investigate the mystery and on his executive notepad wrote, 'The Beatles —check on Monday.' His resolution to do so was strengthened by two further requests for My Bonnie, from girls this time, before the shop closed that afternoon.

It was certainly a little odd that Brian had not heard of the Beatles until then. He was, after all, in charge of a shop thronging with their admirers and visited regularly, when at a loose end, by the very Beatles in question. He was contributing to a music paper which mentioned their name about a dozen times in every issue. The Cavern Club itself was only just across Whitechapel and round the corner.

But Brian was 27 and therefore at an age, as well as social background, still untouched by Rock and Roll music. His interest in it, like his *Mersey Beat* column, had been cultivated purely for business, and with some inner distaste by an ardent devotee of Sibelius and the Liverpool Phil'. And none of his journeys, by day or night, in Liverpool would be likely to take him into Mathew Street.

He was, nevertheless, intrigued to learn of a home-grown group not only available on disc but also in demand by so discerning a customer as Raymond Jones. The following Monday, he began telephoning around NEMS's usual record wholesalers. None could find in its catalogues any record called My Bonnie by the Beatles.

By this stage, with so small a potential profit at stake, any record dealer would have been justified in abandoning the search. Brian, however, partly as a result of the boredom he had been feeling, seized on the challenge of tracking down Raymond Jones's request. If these Beatles truly were a Liverpool group, he reasoned, it would be quicker to go out and find them and ask which label had released their record. Jones, on his next visit, remembers Brian asking in all innocence, 'Where *is* this Cavern Club everyone's talking about?' Only then did he discover it was less than 200 yards away.

Brian's first visit to the Cavern, at lunch-time on Thursday, 9 November, was arranged with typical formality and precision. He rang up Bill Harry, the editor of *Mersey Beat*; Bill then rang Ray McFall, the Cavern's owner, who in his turn instructed Paddy Delaney, the doorman, that Brian was to pass through without the required one-shilling membership card. Paddy remembers seeing Brian that day on his way up Mathew Street, picking his way around the fruit crates and squashed cabbage leaves. 'He had a dark suit on, very smart. And a briefcase under his arm.'

A few minutes later, he bitterly regretted his decision. The warehouse cellar with its dank archways, its dripping walls and dungeon-like aroma, bore no resemblance to any club in his understanding of the term. Equally discomfiting was the obvious gulf between him, at 27, and the teenage throng among which, luckily, the darkness hid his intrusion, all but the glimmer of his white business shirt. Bob Wooler's record session was still in progress, with no activity yet down the middle tunnel on what could be seen of the stage. His ears affronted only a little less than his nostrils, Brian Epstein decided to wait just a few minutes longer.

What he saw that day was the Beatles giving a routine lunch-time Cavern performance. The club and its audience had become as much a habit as the wild welcome which they scarcely acknowledged, pitching into song after song as if to use time up as fast as possible; in the intervals, talking to each other; wolfing the Cavern snacks that were part of McFall's payment; laughing at private jokes, pretending to cuff one another; at all times picking up and laying down the draggled cigarettes which smouldered dangerously on chairs and amplifier-rims. Then, through the tomfoolery and indifference, would unexpectedly break the pounding, shining sound; the harmony of their grouped faces; the bass and guitars cutting knife-sharp.

On Brian Epstein, their effect was transfixing, but for quite another reason. It is doubtful whether, in those surroundings and with his conservative taste, he could even have begun to appreciate the freshness of the Beatles' music. Rather, it was the sight of four slim boys in form-fitting leather, sweat-drenched and prancing, which held him fascinated. It was a daydream, encountered at midday; a rearing up in public of his most covert fantasies. Most of all, the eye of his secret life watched the boy who seemed most aggressive and untidy, whose offhand manner and bad language would have affronted the daytime Mr. Epstein, but filled the night-time Brian with a scarcely endurable excitement. Though he did not know it then, the one he could not take his eyes off was John Lennon.

At the interval, he pushed his way, briefcase and all, through the middle tunnel to try to speak to the Beatles as they came off stage. He still had no clear idea of why he wanted to meet them or what he might say. Bob Wooler had already mentioned him over the PA system and given a 'plug' to NEMS as the shop where the Cavern bought its records. George Harrison, to whom Brian spoke first, outside the band room, drily inquired, 'What brings Mr. Epstein here?'

He stayed at the Cavern through the Beatles' second session, until 2.10 pm. When he climbed the stairs into daylight again, he had managed to speak to Paul as well as George, and to discover that the record they had made was only as a backing group, and on the Polydor label. He had done his duty, both to NEMS and to Raymond Jones. But by now, a different idea had begun to germinate in his mind.

*

He might have shown less reticence had he known how bored the Beatles themselves were at this moment, and how desperately they, too, were hoping for something to happen.

November 1961 found them in precisely the same position as after their return from Hamburg three months before. They were undisputed kings of the Cavern, and of *Mersey Beat.* They had had the satisfaction of seeing bands which used to condescend to them now avidly copying their R & B repertoire, their clothes and hair and even the types of instrument they played. They had been abroad; they had even made a record, albeit under an alias, which now, it appeared, was selling for actual money in the shops. These were achievements pleasant to contemplate, so long as they did not put their hands in their pockets, to feel the halfpence there, or look down at their shoes, or listen on Saturday morning to the BBC Light Programme, when the Hit Parade was beamed to Liverpool from places still a million miles away.

The outlook would have been even duller but for the sudden resurgence of Sam Leach on the dance-promoting scene. Sam, as was his way, had enjoyed mixed fortunes in the year following his attempt to launch the Beatles via Aldershot. He had continued to put on dances all over Liverpool, not always with receipts sufficient to cover his costs or pay the band; but somehow, with a laugh and a dig in the ribs, he got away with it. He was now, with his other venues, running the Iron Door club, and had lately emphasised his rivalry with Ray McFall by flinging a handful of stink bombs down the stairway to the Cavern.

Bright ideas still rocketed around inside Sam Leach's tousled head. He despised promoters like Brian Kelly for the meanness of their dances, with one group only on stage and a finish well before midnight. Sam dreamed of marathon jive sessions, like they were in America, with half a dozen groups or more on a bill lasting into the early hours. Groups were there in abundance all around: Sam Leach needed only an outside sporting chance of being able to pay them.

Earlier that year, he had negotiated with Tommy McArdle the winter-time hire of the New Brighton Tower Ballroom. This gargantuan relic of Victorian seaside splendour—and of an actual tower, higher than Blackpool's—was the largest dance venue anywhere on Merseyside. Its use for Rock and Roll was spasmodic, ceasing arbitrarily when violence threatened its gilded fabric, or when Rory Storm, climbing up inside the dome, fell to the stage and almost broke through it to the 1,000 seat theatre underneath.

'Operation Big Beat', as Sam Leach called his inaugural Tower night, took place on 10 November 1961, the day after Brian

Epstein had walked into the Cavern Club. The Beatles shared the bill with Gerry and the Pacemakers, Rory Storm and the Hurricanes, Kingsize Taylor and the Dominoes, and the Remo Four. Special coaches were provided to transport the Liverpool fans through the Tunnel and down-river to New Brighton's bleak, unfrequented sea promenades.

'It was a real foggy night,' Sam Leach says. 'The Beatles were on at another dance as well, at Knotty Ash Village Hall. They went on at half-seven in the Tower, then over to Knotty Ash, then they came back later for their second spot at half-eleven.' Neil Aspinall, Pete Best's friend, drove them and their equipment in a second-hand van he had recently bought. He had forsaken his accountancy studies to become their road manager for a fee of 5s from each of them per night.

Operation Big Beat attracted a crowd of 3,500. 'I was that scared,' Sam Leach says. 'I thought maybe I'd not sell any tickets at all. There were hundreds there, even when the Beatles played first at half-seven. When they came back for the half-eleven spot, the kids went wild.' Tommy McArdle, the Tower's general Manager, was somewhat less entranced. 'I was ready to ban the Beatles there and then. I caught them behind the stage, poking their fingers through the backcloth. All starry it was and beautiful, and Lennon and them just sticking their fingers through it.'

As Operation Big Beat wore on, and the empty pint glasses formed regiments on the two licensed bars, the Birkenhead faction expressed itself in the customary way. 'I was in the big downstairs bar,' Sam Leach says, 'and I see this fellow get hold of a table and pick it up. He threw it straight at the mirror behind the bar. It went within just a few inches of Paul McCartney.'

Sam rose to the Birkenhead challenge by hiring bouncers in quantities outnumbering the biggest gang. When 50 Teds from Birkenhead paid the Tower a visit, Sam Leach and a hundred bouncers were waiting. One of his regular helpers, a barrel-like youth named Eddie Palmer, later grew famous in Liverpool gangland as 'The Toxteth Terror'.

'I got so that I could feel trouble coming,' Sam Leach says. 'There were these four big yobboes in one night that I knew were out to give the Beatles a good thumping. They were up near the stage, all pissed and whispering to each other. I'd got a bouncer behind each one of the four of them. The first moment one of them pulled his arm back, all my four lads pounced at once.'

A few days later at the Cavern Club, word was passed to the Beatles that Brian Epstein had come in again. He watched them play and, as before, spoke to them when they came off stage at the break. They still had no idea what he wanted, and so were as inclined as any other Cavernite to laugh at his dark suit and tie and briefcase, and the blush that spread over his face when any of them, especially John, looked him directly in the eye. Even so, they were vaguely flattered to number among their followers this obviously prosperous businessman whose car, it quickly became known, was a new Ford Zodiac.

His aura grew still more impressive when he took to arriving with a 'personal assistant'. Alistair Taylor, an employee in the Whitechapel record shop, had found himself elevated to this mutually-flattering post.

All through November, in a roundabout way, Brian was inquiring about the Beatles: about where they played, for whom and at what fee. The idea that he should manage them was one he had not yet articulated, even to himself. It was in a purely theoretical way that he questioned the record company reps, and contacts in London at the big HMV Oxford Street store, about groups and managers and the relationship of one to another. And everyone whom he quizzed unconsciously reiterated the same discouraging fact. People of his age and social background played no noticeable part in British Pop music.

Meanwhile, Polydor Records had despatched his order of 200 copies of My Bonnie: an event loyally noted by *Mersey Beat*. The record sold moderately well among the Beatles following, though some—Raymond Jones included—were disappointed to find them only a backing group to Tony Sheridan and billed as 'the Beat Brothers'.

Bob Wooler, the Cavern disc jockey, was one of the first to discover Brian's interest in managing the Beatles, even though his overtures were still muffled by his own embarrassment and uncertainty, and by the Beatles' own elaborate indifference to all outsiders. Wooler, as a close adviser, went with them to the first formal meeting suggested by Brian, early in December. It was to take place on a Wednesday afternoon, directly following their Cavern lunch-time show. Wooler and the Beatles stopped off at the Grapes first, and possibly the White Star, and so did not reach Whitechapel until well after the appointed time. It was early closing day, and they found Brian waiting for them on the darkened ground floor, among displays of home appliances. 'He hated to be kept waiting,' Wooler says. 'That was his first introduction to many hours of being kept waiting by the Beatles. He was quite open by that time about wanting to manage them, but they still wouldn't commit themselves. It was left at, "well, we'll see what happens".'

Equally little encouragement came from those in Brian's own circle to whom he confided his plan. He had already consulted his family's solicitor, E. Rex Makin, hoping for some legal help on the kind of contract he might offer the Beatles. Makin lived next door to the Epsteins in Queens Drive and had known Brian and Clive since their boyhood. He was sceptical of what he termed 'just another Epstein idea'.

The other person Brian sought out was Allan Williams. He had discovered that Williams used to have a contract of some kind with the Beatles, and had been responsible for sending them to work in Hamburg. Visiting the Welshman at his Blue Angel Club, Brian found him still resentful about the commission the Beatles owed him. Williams said he wanted nothing more to do with them, and that Brian was at liberty to take them over. His advice, however, was not to touch the Beatles with a barge-pole.

At another after-hours meeting at the NEMS shop, Brian, blushing furiously, succeeded at last in coming to the point. He told the Beatles that they needed a manager; he was willing to do it; did they want him to? A silence ensued, broken by John Lennon's gruff 'Yes'. Paul then asked if being managed by Brian would make any difference to the music they played. Brian assured him that it would not. There was a second uneasy silence, again broken by John. 'Right then, Brian,' he said. 'Manage us.'

Harry and Queenie Epstein, who had been away to London for a week, returned home to find their elder son in a state of high excitement. He sat them down in the drawing-room and insisted that they listen to My Bonnie, telling them all the time to pay no attention to the voice, only to the backing. From Brian's hectic chatter, and the din on a normally well-mannered radiogram, Harry at last extracted the displeasing news that shop business was about to be let slide again. Brian assured his father this was not so: managing the Beatles would require only two half-days each week.

On the Beatles' side, the news spread as rapidly as news in Liverpool generally does. Sam Leach, the tousle-haired promoter, heard it direct from Paul. 'He said there was this millionaire who wanted to manage them.' Sam, though he had been putting the Beatles on regularly at New Brighton Tower, had no contract with them and did not attempt to manufacture one. Nor did Pete's mother, Mona Best, who had helped to get them on at The Cavern, and pushed them in other ways. She was satisfied Brian knew, as everyone did, that Pete was the Beatles' leader.

Not all the parents were quite so content. Olive Johnson, the McCartney family's close friend, received a call from Paul's father in a state of some anxiety over his son's proposed association with a 'Jew boy'. Since Olive knew the world so well, Jim asked her to be at Forthlin Road on the evening that Brian called to outline his intentions for Paul. 'He turned out to be absolutely charming,' Olive says. 'Beautifully mannered but completely natural. He and Jim got on well at once.'

John Lennon's Aunt Mimi was less easily placated. What worried Mimi about Brian was precisely what impressed the other parents—his charm and position and obvious wealth. 'I used to tackle Brian about that,' Mimi says. ' "It's all right for you," I told him, "if all this group business turns out to be just a flash in the pan, it won't matter. It's just a hobby to you. If it's all over in six months, it won't matter to you, but what happens to *them*?"

'Brian said to me, "It's all right, Mrs. Smith. I promise you, John will never suffer. He's the only important one. The others don't matter, but I'll always take care of John." '

'Elvis's manager calling Brian Epstein in Birkenhead'

Brian, at the outset, foresaw no great difficulty in getting the Beatles a recording contract. As a retailer, he was in regular touch with all the major London companies: Decca, EMI, Phillips and Pye. He had given them all good business in building up 'The Finest Record Selection in the North'. Any of them, surely, would be only too glad to oblige so large and reliable a wholesale customer as NEMS Ltd.

There was a further promising augury. Each week, the big, old-fashioned *Liverpool Evening Echo* published a record review column signed with the pseudonym 'Disker'. Brian, soon after meeting the Beatles, had written to 'Disker', soliciting a mention for them. It transpired that 'Disker' was not based with the *Echo* but was a freelance journalist named Tony Barrow, Liverpool-born but now living in London. As well as his journalism, Barrow worked regularly as a writer of album-sleeve notes for the great and powerful Decca organisation.

Tony Barrow wrote back to Brian, saying that as the Beatles had not made a record yet, he could not mention them in 'Disker's' column. What he could do, as a fellow Merseysider, was to recommend them to Decca's 'Artiste and Repertoire' department. The ensuing conversation, strangely enough, was much as Brian had imagined it. 'When I mentioned Brian Epstein,' Barrow says, 'everybody asked "Who?". But when I mentioned NEMS, it was quite different. "Oh, yes—NEMS of Liverpool. *Very* big retailers for us in the north-west."'

The word reached Decca's Head of A & R, Dick Rowe. A large northern record retailer had a Pop group he wanted auditioned. It would be tactful, for business reasons, to say 'Yes'. Dick Rowe did not demur. The job was given to a new young assistant in the A & R department named Mike Smith. The gesture, in fairness was more than perfunctory. Mike Smith offered to come up to Liverpool to hear the group to best advantage in the club where they usually played. And so, Brian, several weeks before the Beatles had agreed to be managed by him, was able to give them an astounding piece of news. Someone from Decca—from the company that had Tommy Steele, and Buddy Holly, and Little Richard, and the Everly Brothers, and Duane Eddy and Bobby Vee—was coming into town to audition *them.*

Mike Smith arrived and, after an expensive dinner with Brian, was conducted to Mathew Street, past Paddy Delaney and down the 18 cellar steps to witness the Beatles in their stifling habitat. Their playing impressed the A & R man, not enough to sign them there and then but certainly enough to arrange a further audition for them as soon as possible in London, at Decca's West Hampstead studios. This second test was quickly confirmed for New Year's Day, 1962.

On New Year's Eve, in cold snowy weather, the participants made their separate ways south. Brian travelled down by train to stay overnight with his Aunt Freda in Hampstead. The Beatles set off at midday by road, packed with their equipment in the freezing rear of Neil Aspinall's van. Neil had never been to London before and, striking blizzards near Wolverhampton, lost his bearings altogether. Not until 10 hours later did they arrive in Russell Square, near King's Cross, where Brian had booked them into a small hotel, the Royal. For the rest of New Year's Eve, they wandered round, watching the drunks in Trafalgar Square and trying to find a place to eat. In Charing Cross Road, they met two men who offered them something called 'pot' on condition they could 'smoke' it together in Neil's van. The Liverpool boys fled.

At Decca studies the next morning, they had to wait some time for Mike Smith. Brian, as ever, punctual to the second, reddened at this implied slight, just because they were unknown and from Liverpool. The Beatles, already nervous, became more so when Smith rejected the amplifiers they had dragged with them from Liverpool, and made them plug their guitars into a set of studio speakers.

Brian believed that the way to impress Mike Smith was, not by John and Paul's original songs, but by their imaginative, sometimes eccentric, arrangements of 'standards'. Among the 15 numbers heard by Mike Smith—and preserved for posterity on 'Bootleg' singles, stolen later from the master tape—are Paul's versions of Till There Was You and September in the Rain; Sheik of Araby, sung by George with jokey Eastern effects; and chaotic Rock versions of Three Cool Cats and Your Feet's Too Big. From scores of Lennon–McCartney songs, the only three selected were Hello Little Girl, Like Dreamers Do and the recently-written Love of the Loved.

The Beatles were far from happy with their performance. Paul McCartney's voice had cracked with anxiety several times; George Harrison's fingers were stickier than usual; at certain points in Chuck Berry's song, Memphis, John Lennon as lead vocalist seemed to have been thinking of something else. And Pete Best kept up the same drum rhythm, patient rather than cohesive. Only on Love of the Loved had the elements coalesced: Paul's voice at its most appealing within an arrangement both neat and dramatic.

Mike Smith reassured them that the session had gone well. So enthusiastic did the young A & R man seem that, when the Beatles and Brian walked out into the snow that evening, the contract seemed as good as signed. Before their hideous van journey with Neil back to Liverpool, Brian took them to a restaurant in Swiss Cottage and allowed them to order wine.

At Decca, meanwhile, Mike Smith was beginning to have second thoughts. The main reason was another group, Brian Poole and the Tremeloes, which had also auditioned that day and had put up a much better show. Dick Rowe was prepared to let Smith have his head only to the extent of signing one new group.

'I told Mike he'd have to decide between them,' Dick Rowe says. 'It was up to him—the Beatles or Brian Poole and the Tremeloes. He said, "They're both good, but one's a local group, the other comes from Liverpool." We decided it was better to take the local group. We could work with them more easily and stay closer in touch as they came from Dagenham.'

On 4 January, issue number 13 of *Mersey Beat* published the results of a poll among its 5,000 readers to find Liverpool's most popular group. The Beatles came top, followed by Gerry and the Pacemakers, the Remo Four, Rory Storm and the Hurricanes, Kingsize Taylor and the Dominoes, and the Big Three. The whole front page was devoted to a photograph of the winners in their black leather, cropped to conceal their scruffy shoes, and captioned by the hand that always rendered Paul's surname as 'McArtrey'. In all four Beatles' homes lay piles of December *Mersey Beats* minus the voting coupon on which, like everyone involved, they had voted for themselves.

Mersey Beat knew nothing, however, of the test for Decca in London. Brian would not risk announcing it until the contract had been definitely awarded. The only mention was in 'Disker's' *Liverpool Echo* column, filed by Tony Barrow from inside Decca, where the signs still seemed good. 'I said it was only a matter of weeks before they came down to record their first single.'

Barrow then learned to his astonishment from Dick Rowe's office that the Beatles were to be turned down. The reasons given were that they sounded 'too much like the Shadows', and that groups with guitars were 'on the way out'.

Brian refused to accept the Decca decision. He travelled to London alone to reason, unavailingly, with Dick Rowe and another Decca man, Beecher Stevens. He also went back to the sales people, reminding them of his position in the retail world. 'I heard afterwards that he'd guaranteed to buy 3,000 copies of any single we let the Beatles make,' Dick Rowe says. 'I was never told about that at the time. The way economics were in the record business then, if we'd been sure of selling 3,000 copies, we'd have been forced to record them, whatever sort of group they were.'

Someone at Decca suggested to Brian the possibility of hiring a studio and a freelance A & R man to supervise a session for the Beatles. He went so far as to contact Tony Meehan, formerly the Shadows' drummer, and now an independent producer. But Meehan proved offhand; besides, the studio hire would have cost at least £100. Brian was not yet prepared to go that far. He walked out of Decca having made the grand pronouncement that his group would one day be bigger than Elvis. The Decca men smiled. They had heard that one so many times.

On 24 January, seven weeks after first approaching them, Brian was finally able to tie the Beatles down to a formal agreement. He had sent away for a sample management contract, and had modified and rewritten the terms in a praiseworthy attempt to make them fairer. The final document, though portentously worded and stuck with sixpenny postage stamps, had no legal validity. Since Paul and George were still under 21, their signatures ought to have been endorsed by their fathers'. And Brian, in his emotion, forgot to sign his own name.

The four still slightly sceptical and uneasy Liverpool scruffs thus found themselves contracted to a real live 'organisation'. It had been Brian's impressive idea to form a limited company, with his brother Clive, to administer his new charges. He called it NEMS Enterprises, after the family business. Over the Whitechapel branch was a suite of offices which his father allowed him to use, mainly because that would enable him to continue running the record shop downstairs. Harry was determined Brian should keep his promise that managing the Beatles would take only two afternoons each week.

His brisk executive efficiency foundered the moment he first tried to fix the Beatles a booking. Only then did he realise he had no idea how to talk to the rough, tough Liverpool dance promoters on whom they depended for regular work. Tommy McArdle, the ex-middleweight boxer who ran New Brighton Tower ballroom, was one of many puzzled local impresarios whom Brian suggested should 'come across and have lunch'.

The first booking he managed to arrange was at a tiny seaside cafe on the Dee Estuary over in Cheshire. The profit to NEMS Enterprises, after paying for posters and Neil Aspinall's petrol and sundry expenses, and giving each Beatle his share, was slightly over £1.

Nor had Brian yet realised the quality for which the Beatles were notorious up and down the Mersey—their dedicated unreliability and unpunctuality. He realised it one day when Ray McFall rang up to say that only three Beatles had turned up for the Cavern lunch-time session. Freda Kelly, who worked for NEMS Enterprises as wages clerk and fan club organiser, saw Brian go into one of many subsequent transports of fury. 'There's only *three* of them!' he kept saying. 'Gerry Marsden's singing with them, standing on an orange box so they needn't bother to let the microphone down to his height.'

At night he would drive in his Ford Zodiac to wherever the Beatles were playing—to Neston Women's Institute Hall, to Birkenhead, Wallasey or New Brighton. Since everyone wore dark suits and white shirts to dances in those days, he was not too conspicuous as he walked in. Approaching the Beatles still threw him into a ferment of embarrassment—a circumstance which John Lennon was quick to spot. The more John stared at him, the more Brian would blush and stammer his way into some shaming faux pas. Sam Leach, all innocence, advised John to accept Brian's proposal that they should fly together for the weekend to Copenhagen. 'John nudged me in the ribs,' Sam says. ' "Shut up," he went, "can't you see he's after me!" '

All the time, he was regularly travelling to London to try to interest other record companies in the Beatles. He now had a dozen of their songs on tape from the Decca audition—Sheik of Araby, Hello Little Girl, Three Cool Cats, Red Sails in the Sunset, Your Feet's Too Big.

Decca, at least, had given them two auditions. At Pye, at Phillips, at EMI's two prestige labels, Columbia and HMV, interest did not even extend to that. No one saw any future in a group which sounded so unlike the Shadows. Groups other than the Shadows, in any case, were believed to have had their day. The fad now was for solo singers—Helen Shapiro, Jimmy Justice, Frank Ifield. Often the mere mention of Liverpool was sufficient to glaze over the A & R man's eye. 'You've got a good business, Mr. Epstein,' one of them said with a show of kindness. 'Why not stick to it?'

At night, when Brian got off the train at Lime Street, the Beatles would be waiting for him. They would go for coffee at the Punch and Judy cafeteria, or Joe's all night snackbar, and Brian would give them the news. Their disappointment gave them something in common. The Beatles would say: Don't worry, Brian. John would say that there was no alternative: they'd have to sign to Embassy, the Woolworth's record label.

One night, with the Beatles at the Iron Door club, Brian

bumped into a tall, familiar figure. It was Joe Flannery, his companion in the nursery and for a brief later period which Joe, at least, had never forgotten. Having not seen Brian since 1957, or thereabouts, Joe could think of no reason why he should be 'downtown' other than the obvious one.

To Joe Flannery, over a drink at the Beehive, in Paradise Street, Brian poured out the frustration of simultaneously trailing round the London record companies and trying to do business with small-time dance-hall managers in the Wirral. 'He told me he was really cheesed off with everything,' Joe says. 'He was thinking of chucking it all in and going back to learning to act at RADA.'

Joe, as it happened, was managing his younger brother's beat group, Lee Curtis and the All Stars. He offered to work unofficially for NEMS Enterprises, talking to promoters on the Beatles' behalf and negotiating fees. He did it simply out of affection for Brian. 'I liked the way Brian spoke on the telephone. He never said "Hello"—just, "Joe . . ." I always liked hearing that.'

With Joe Flannery in charge of bookings, Brian could turn his attention to matters he did understand. He understood, for example, how to design a poster, tastefully yet with an impact maximising the Beatles' meagre achievements. When they were booked to play at the Institute hall in Barnston, a small Cheshire village, Brian's posters blazed the advent of MERSEY BEAT POLL WINNERS! POLYDOR RECORDING ARTISTS! PRIOR TO EUROPEAN TOUR!

On the Beatles themselves, Brian began to effect the same transformation—against much the same resistance—as on the display windows of the family's Walton Road shop. He rearranged the four, black-leather, draggle-headed, swearing, prancing Hamburg rockers to reflect his own idea of what a successful Pop group ought to be.

To begin with, and most important of all, he told them, they must be punctual. They must not go onstage as a three-piece group, backing Gerry Marsden on an orange box. They must play to a programme, not just as they pleased. They must not shout at their friends, and foes, in the audience. They must not eat or drink beer or wrestle and cuff each other onstage, or make V-signs or belch into the microphone. And if they must smoke, let it not be Woodbines, the working-man's cigarette, but some sophisticated brand like Senior Service.

The black '*exi*' suits they had bought in Hamburg, and worn and slept in for more than a year, were Brian's next concern. Black leather, to most people in 1962, still signified Nazis. He suggested an alternative which John Lennon, at first, doggedly refused to consider. Paul agreed with Brian that they should try it. Paul sided with Brian throughout the whole smartening process. George and Pete Best seemed not to mind, so John reluctantly gave way to the majority. On 24 March, when they arrived for their £25-date at Barnston Institute, each carried a bag from Burton's, the multiple tailor. That night, they took the stage in shiny grey lounge suits with velvet collars, cloth-covered buttons and pencil-thin lapels.

Joe Flannery, having special knowledge, guessed at once what underlay Brian's devotion. He had fallen in love with John Lennon. He was besotted, not by the pretty-faced Paul or Pete but by the boy whose facade of crudeness and toughness touched the nerve of his most secret 'Rough-Trade' fantasies. Joe recognised the look in Brian's eye as he blushed and writhed under John's pitiless sarcasm. 'I've sat for hours with him in the car while he's been crying over the things John's said to him.'

Harry and Queenie Epstein, meanwhile, worried over the time and money Brian was spending, and his neglect of record-shop business in pursuit of his mad idea. To add to their anxiety, he had forsaken his smart lounge suits and white shirts and Horne Brothers ties, and taken to going round Liverpool dressed, like the Beatles, in a leather jacket and black polo-neck sweater. He even came to the Cavern dressed that way, not realising that everyone was laughing at him. 'He was champing a lot, too, that night,' Bob Wooler recalls. 'They'd got him on the pep pills, the ones that dried up the saliva.'

Yet for all his efficiency, his headed notepaper, his expenditure on new lounge suits, his typewritten memoranda to the Beatles concerning punctuality and cleanliness, he still could not move them outside the same old drab hemisphere of Merseyside. No one in London had heard of them, save through a brief mention in the music newspaper *Record Mirror*—and that was through a fan's letter, not through Brian. The *Record Mirror* afterwards sent up a photographer to see them. His name was Dezo Hoffman; he was a middle-aged Hungarian freelance. To the Beatles, he seemed God-like. They all had a bath before they came to Whitechapel to meet him. He shot off rolls of film of them around Sefton Park, and lent them a ciné-camera so that they could film each other, leaping up and down in the spring sunshine, and driving round town in Paul's old green Ford Classic.

The only excitement on their horizon, after Hoffmann had gone, was going back to Hamburg. On 13 April, they were to open a new Reeperbahn attraction, the Star-Club. That was the European Tour grandly billed by Brian outside Barnston Institute. Another very grand thing was that they were to go to Hamburg this time by air. Brian insisted on it, knowing what an effect the news would have on *Mersey Beat*'s readership.

He would go to any lengths to convince them that, despite all appearances, a big, wonderful moment was only just around the corner. In Birkenhead, sitting round the pub next to the Majestic ballroom, he whispered to Joe Flannery to go out of the room, then come back in and say that Colonel Tom Parker, Elvis Presley's manager, was trying to reach him on the telephone. 'They believed it,' Flannery says. 'They really believed that Colonel Parker had been trying to ring up Brian Epstein in Birkenhead.'

That Christmas of 1961, while Brian was still wooing the Beatles, their old bass-player Stu Sutcliffe had come over from Hamburg with his German fiancée, Astrid. Stu's friends at the Cavern, like Bill Harry, were shocked by his thinness and translucent pallor. Allan Williams, with typical forthrightness, told him that he looked 'at death's door'.

Stu admitted to his mother that, since settling in Hamburg, in his studio in the Kirchherr house, he had been suffering severe headaches, even occasional black-outs. He had fainted once at Art College, during Edouardo Paolozzi's Master Class. The news had already reached Mrs. Sutcliffe via worried letters from Astrid to Stu's younger sister, Pauline. Astrid feared he was working too hard. For days at a time, she said, he would not come down from his attic to sleep or eat. And the headaches were sometimes so violent, they seemed more like fits. Millie Sutcliffe had described the symptoms, so far as she understood them, to the Dean of Liverpool University Medical School. He told her that she *did* have grounds for concern.

Stu still refused to believe that the headaches were a consequence of anything more than overwork and his and Astrid's all-night Hamburg life. He did agree, for his mother's sake, to see a specialist in Liverpool. The specialist instantly sent him for an X-Ray. No appointment could be made for three weeks: by that time, Stu and Astrid had returned to Hamburg.

From January to April, the only news Mrs. Sutcliffe received were in Astrid's photographs. One of these showed Stu, seated, stiff as a wax-work, in a bentwood rocking chair next to a marble-topped table crowded with liquor bottles. Another was a close-up of Stu and Astrid together. The face, next to the dark-eyed, ravishing girl, was haunted and brittle. 'When I looked at that,' Millie Sutcliffe says, 'something told me that my son was dying.'

In February, Stu again collapsed during an Art School class. This time, he did not return. Astrid's mother forced him to leave his attic and be properly nursed by her in a bedroom downstairs. The Kirchherr family doctor, suspecting a brain tumour, sent him for X-Rays. No tumour showed itself. Two further doctors who examined Stu were equally baffled. 'We tried everything,' Astrid says. 'One treatment was a kind of special massage under water. When Stu came home in the afternoon from his massage, he told my mother he'd been looking in an undertaker's window and seen a beautiful white coffin. "Oh, Mum," he said, "buy it for me. I'd *love* to be buried in a white coffin." '

By March, the headaches brought with them spells of temporary blindness. The pain grew so intense at times that Astrid and her mother had to hold Stu down to stop him from throwing himself out of the window. Yet on other days, he could appear quite normal. Astrid would come home from work to find him sitting up in bed, reading, sketching or writing another long letter to John in Liverpool. He was looking forward eagerly to the Beatles' arrival and the opening of the Star-Cub on 13 April.

On 10 April, Astrid, at work in her photographic studio, received a call from her mother to say that Stu was much worse, and that she was sending him to hospital. It was the day that three of the Beatles—John, Paul and Pete Best—flew out from Manchester Ringway airport. George had 'flu, and was to follow with Brian Epstein a day later.

Stu died in the ambulance, in Astrid's arms. 'At half-past four,' Millie Sutcliffe says, 'I was in my bedroom at home in Liverpool. I felt as if a great strong cold wind came through that house, lifted me up and laid me across the bed. For 15 or 20 minutes, not a muscle in my body was capable of movement. That was the time, I discovered later, when Stuart was dying.'

The news came in two telegrams from Astrid, out of sequence. The first said he had died, the second that he was seriously ill.

Stu's father was away at sea. Mrs. Sutcliffe faced alone the ordeal of breaking the news to her two daughters, getting leave from the school where she was teaching, and booking herself on the first available flight to Hamburg. By chance, it was the one on which Brian Epstein and George Harrison were travelling to join the other Beatles. Brian gave her a lift to Manchester and sat with her on the 'plane.

At Hamburg airport, Astrid was waiting with John, Paul and Pete Best. Paul and Pete were red-eyed, but John showed no emotion. With unintended harshness then, the Beatles' and Millie Sutcliffe's paths diverged. Theirs lay to the Star-Club, where they were to open in a few hours. Hers lay to the mortuary, the formal identification of Stu, the papers to be signed for his clothes, his watch and signet ring.

Cause of death was given officially as 'cerebral paralysis due to bleeding into the right ventricle of the brain'. 'The doctors told us,' Astrid says, 'that Stu's brain was actually expanding—getting too big for the space it floated in. It's a very rare medical condition, but it can happen. Even if Stuart had lived, he would have been blind and probably paralysed. He wouldn't have been able to paint. He would have preferred to die.'

From the mortuary Millie Sutcliffe was taken to the Kirchherr house, to see the room which had been Stu's last home, and the attic where he had worked. Scores of canvases, stacked against every wall showed with what desperate energy his last months were spent. Mrs. Sutcliffe picked up, and never afterwards let out of her sight, the palette on which Stu had mixed his final brilliant colours.

The shock expressed by such eminent figures as Edouardo Paolozzi bore witness to the tragedy that such a talent should be so brutally extinguished. At 22, Stu left behind a body of work in which mere promise already yielded to virtuosity. Those last visions, torn between agony and exhilaration, the blue and crimson carnivals, now left the city whose squalor and glamour had inspired them. So did a sketch he had made, almost subconsciously, at a time when the attacks were getting worse. A boy holds his head in both hands, his eyes downcast from tumescent swirls of pain.

Millie Sutcliffe bequeathed Stu's brain for scientific research at the hospital which had been treating him. Eighteen months later, a set of German X-Ray plates, taken after Stu's death, were brought across to Liverpool by Astrid. These revealed, for the first time, the presence of a small brain tumour. The Hamburg radiologist had attached a note in English: 'Note the depressed condition of the skull.'

Studying the tumour's small shadow, and the cranial depression which seemed to press down on it, Mrs. Sutcliffe remembered a night, some three years before, when Stu had been playing bass with the Beatles, and she had found him in his room late at night with blood pouring from his head after being kicked in a scuffle outside Litherland Town Hall.

The Beatles were devastated by Stu's death. Neither George nor Pete Best could stop crying. Paul felt especially bad, remembering his fights with Stu in the past. He tried to find words of consolation for Mrs. Sutcliffe but, unfortunately, they did not come out quite right. 'My mother died when I was 14,' he told her, 'and I'd forgotten all about her in six months.'

Only John, who had suffered the greatest blow, showed no outward emotion whatever. His dry eyes, at the airport and afterwards, mystified Mrs. Sutcliffe. She believed—and still believes—that Stu's death left him unmoved. Only in one small particular did he give himself away. He asked for, and was given, the long woollen scarf which Stu used to wear, tied round his neck, in their winters together among the cold Liverpool streets and alleyways.

'It was John who saved me,' Astrid says. 'He convinced me, after Stu was gone, that I couldn't behave as if I were a widow.

He pretended to be heartless, but I knew what he said came from a heart. "Make up your mind," he told me. "You either live or die. You can't be in the middle." '

They could not keep up unqualified misery. They were, after all, the main attraction at the largest and newest of the Reeperbahn beat clubs. It stood in Grosse Freiheit, next door to St. Joseph's Catholic Church, in the bowels of what had formerly been a cinema, the Stern Kino. As the Star-Club, it put Koschmider's Kaiserkeller and Eckhorn's Top Ten in the shade. Not that Koschmider or Eckhorn attempted serious competition. The Star-Club owner, Manfred Weissleder, a huge man with a dusting of golden hair, was the biggest strip-club owner on the Freiheit: he was also, very clearly, a gangster. His sex shows throve owing to the particular predilection Manfred Weissleder had for filming naked girls under water.

Weissleder had hired Horst Fascher and his gang of freelance strong-arm waiters to rule the Star-Club's enormous darkness. From 8 pm to 4 am, as many as 15,000 people could pass through it, staying long enough to hear one favoured group, then moving on to other clubs and returning after midnight for the same group's second 'spot'. After 2 am, the club was packed with Freiheit's own population of whores, pimps, bouncers, strippers and transvestites. There were also the ships' companies —French, American and British—from the port, in consideration of whom Horst Fascher maintained a special star bouncer named Ali who could do wrestler's drop kicks and still land on his feet.

Manfred Weissleder, though a figure of fear, was a conscientious employer. Star-Club musicians were boarded across the Freiheit in flats where Weissleder's strippers and mud-wrestlers could sleep between performances. Each musician wore, in his coat lapel, a small gold Star-Club badge. If they ran into trouble elsewhere on the Reeperbahn, that badge was a potent charm. With a murmur of 'Weissleder', the trouble would back off and retire.

The Beatles, the Big Three, Kingsize Taylor and the Dominoes decorated their accommodation with dirty clothes, graffiti and more unspeakable objects. All were now equipped with tear-gas pistols, and able to pot at each other with weapons capable of inflicting at least third-degree burns. Adrian Barber, the Big Three's guitarist, was as mad as John: a sort of contest of madness arose between them. Barber would walk along the Reeperbahn dragging a hair brush behind him on a dog lead. John would walk onstage at the Star-Club, naked, with a lavatory seat round his neck. Barber bought a pig in the fish market and threw it into bed with a singer named Buddy Britten. John, each Sunday, would stand on the balcony, taunting the churchgoers as they walked up to St. Joseph's. He attached a water-filled Durex to an effigy of Jesus and hung it out for the churchgoers to see. Once, he urinated on the heads of three nuns.

'That was the sort of crazy thing you did, full of drink and pills,' Johnny Hutch says. 'Before we started playing at night, we'd shake Preludin down our throats by the tubeful. I've seen John Lennon foaming at the mouth, he's got so many pills inside him.'

The Beatles were still in Hamburg when, towards the end of April, Brian set off from Liverpool for one last try with the London record companies. As his train rattled south, he could not even be sure with whom that try should be made. Every label he could find in the NEMS stock catalogue had by now turned the Beatles down. The only hope really did seem to be Embassy, the one everyone laughed at because it was stocked by Woolworth's.

Someone had suggested that, instead of offering the Beatles on tape, he should have a proper 'demo' disc to play to the A & R men. That was what brought Brian, in his smart dark overcoat, to the teeming HMV record shop in Oxford Street. The shop had a small department where, for a fee of £1, a tape spool could be processed into an acetate disc.

The engineer who cut the acetate could not help but listen to it. Suddenly he looked up at Brian and said it was 'not at all bad'. He advised Brian to take it to EMI's publishing company, Ardmore and Beechwood, which happened to be on a floor above. There and then the engineer arranged for Brian to go up and see the head of Ardmore and Beechwood, Syd Coleman.

Coleman listened to the acetate and liked it. He not only liked it but instantly offered to publish two of the songs on it, Love of the Loved and Hello Little Girl. He asked if the Beatles had a record contract, and Brian said they hadn't. Coleman offered to ring up a friend of his, George Martin, the Head of A & R at Parlophone Records.

Martin was out of his office, but his secretary, Judy Lockhart-Smith, asked Brian to go straight round and make an appointment. Only then did he realise that Parlophone was a subsidiary label of EMI, whose other subsidiaries Columbia and HMV had already rejected the Beatles. He made an appointment to see George Martin the next day, then checked into the Green Park Hotel and spent a sleepless night.

The man he shook hands with next morning bore no resemblance to any A & R executive Brian had yet met. George Martin was not small, common and condescending. He was tall and elegant with a clipped BBC newsreader's accent and the air, so

Brian himself later said, of 'a stern but fair-minded housemaster'.

Martin listened politely to Brian's claim that the Beatles would one day be bigger than Elvis. Like everyone else in the business, he had heard that many times before. Playing the acetate, he could understand why a group partial to Sheik of Araby and Your Feet's Too Big might not be considered an instantly commercial proposition. But, unlike everyone else, he found things to praise. He said he liked that voice—Paul's—and some of the guitar playing, and the jaunty harmony in Hello Little Girl. He was not excited, merely interested. 'There was an unusual quality—a certain roughness. I thought to myself: "There might *just* be something there."'

George Martin agreed to give the Beatles a recording test in June, after their return from Hamburg. It would only be a test, a studio audition like the one they had failed at Decca, and for a label not much in prestige above Embassy. 'Congratulations, boys,' ran the telegram which Brian at once sent to Hamburg. 'EMI request recording session. Please rehearse new material.'

October 1962

'Somebody had to pay for those 10,000 records Brian bought'

When George Martin joined EMI in 1950, people still played 'gramophones' cranked up by handles, and records were heavy black objects one foot in diameter, which broke if you dropped them. Record studios were drab institutional places supervised by men in white coats, and so rigidly formal that not even a Jazz drummer could take his jacket off during the recording-session.

Young George Martin had joined Parlophone as assistant to the head of A & R, Oscar Preuss. He was, even then, suave, elegant and polite. His superiors, in the trade jargon, said he was 'very 12 inch'. They little realised he came from a humble North London background and that his father had once sold newspapers on a street-corner.

He taught himself to play piano by ear, and at school ran his own little dance band, George Martin and the Four Tune Tellers. In 1943, aged 17, he joined the Fleet Air Arm. It was his Navy service which gave him a large social leg-up and also allowed him later to attend the London Guildhall School of Music, to continue his piano studies and take up the oboe. His first job, before joining Parlophone, was with the BBC Music Library. A little of the BBC manner and accent stuck.

EMI in 1950 was a corporation not much different in size and spirit from the BBC. Founded in 1931 as The Gramophone Company, its name changed, as its field diversified, to Electrical and Mechanical Industries. EMI invented the first practicable British television system: it manufactured television sets, medical equipment and weapons systems under contract to the then War Office.

It also made records on a series of labels ingested mostly during the prewar years. Its pride was HMV, the definitive label of wistful dog staring into gramophone trumpet. An HMV dealership in the retail world was as prized as one in Rolls Royce cars.

No one ever prized the dealership for Parlophone. EMI had bought it in the 1930s as the German Lindstrom label—hence the L label logo which was one day to be mistaken for a £ sterling sign. Within EMI in the fifties, it was known derisively as the 'junk' label. To Oscar Preuss and his assistant George Martin were left the despised 'Light Music' items—Sidney Torch and his Orchestra, Bob and Alf Pearson, Roberto Inglez, 'the Latin American Scot'. A sale of only a few hundred copies made any artist viable; to sell a thousand was spectacular. It happened in 1954 when a crooner named Dick James went to Number Two in the Top Twenty with the theme song from the Robin Hood television show.

That year, as it chanced, EMI was in deep trouble. Its chief product, the heavy wooden cabinet TV set, was fast growing obsolete against the new, light, plastic sets coming from Japan. Decca, EMI's great rival, had just introduced the 'long-playing' record, for which EMI's technicians predicted no future other than passing novelty.

In 1954, the EMI chairmanship passed to Joseph Lockwood —not a showbiz man, like his predecessor, but a successful industrialist, big in engineering and flour milling. Lockwood was appalled by the decay of the organisation he inherited. He also quickly decided where the future lay. He ended the production of cabinet TV sets and ordered 20 of the new LP record presses. A year later, in what was considered a foolhardy enterprise, he paid £3m for an established American record company, Capitol.

It was in the flurry of Lockwood's first year as chairman that Oscar Preuss, Parlophone's Head of A & R, retired. By oversight more than anything, George Martin became, at 29, the youngest boss of an EMI label, at a salary of £1,100 per year.

Parlophone, to EMI's bureaucratic mind, remained the 'junk' label. It was simply junk of a different, not unsuccessful kind. Martin, in the late fifties, went in heavily for comic dialogue records like Peter Ustinov's Mock Mozart and Peter Sellers's Songs for Swinging Sellers. One of his coups was to recognise what potential cult followings lay in the new generation of London comedy stage revues. He produced 'live' album versions of Flanders and Swann's *At The Drop of a Hat,* and of a four-man undergraduate show, destined to influence comedy throughout the next decade, called *Beyond the Fringe.*

When Rock and Roll arrived, George Martin shared in the general detestation felt by all trained musicians. It was his duty, however, as an A & R man, to tour the Soho coffee bars for talent. He auditioned and turned down Tommy Steele, preferring to sign up Steele's backing skiffle group, The Vipers. Significantly, in six years up to 1962, Parlophone's only Top Ten hit was a comedy number, Stop You're Driving Me Crazy, by the Temperance Seven.

On EMI's 'important' label, Columbia, the A & R Head Norrie

Paramour meanwhile enjoyed virtually unbroken success and gigantic sales with his discovery, Cliff Richard and the Shadows. George Martin did not particularly like the echoey guitar sound which the Shadows had made all the rage. But he did envy Norrie Paramour his golden, effortless protégés. Each comedy success for Parlophone was the result of an endless search for new original material. With a Pop group, the product was all the same, so Martin thought: you simply sat back and let it happen.

Such was George Martin's frame of mind that April day in 1962 when Brian Epstein walked in and played the Beatles' demo'. After all their efforts to be otherwise, they would have been enraged by Martin's original idea. Perhaps, he thought, he had found his very own Cliff Richard and the Shadows.

On Wednesday, 6 June 1962, George Martin drove along Abbey Road, the tree-shaded North London boulevard which is the very last place one would expect to find the studios of an international record company. Shortly afterwards, a battered van appeared, making its way, with considerably less assurance, to the same destination. Neil Aspinall had found his way straight to London this time: it was St. John's Wood that unnerved Neil —all mansion flats and turrets and shrubberies. He drove past EMI several times, not believing it could possibly be that plain white town house with its high front porch, like a doctor's or dentist's, and only one or two cars parked around the gravel drive.

The Beatles, pressed knee-to-knee behind him, were in a state of bleary-eyed excitement largely induced by Brian's failure to explain precisely what was to happen today. They believed—as did everyone in Liverpool—that the test was merely routine preamble to recording for Parlophone on the basis of a contract already promised. *Mersey Beat* had said so, even giving July as the month of their first record release and inviting readers to suggest possible titles for issue. They were, in any case, still dazed after Hamburg, the Star-Club and six virtually sleepless weeks.

At Abbey Road that day, something entirely unexpected happened. The elegant A & R man and the four scruffily-shod Liverpool boys took a liking to one another. Early in their conversation, George Martin happened to mention he had worked with Peter Sellers and Spike Milligan, the founder members of the radio Goon Show. 'Goon' humour is dear to most Liverpudlians: in John Lennon's eyes, especially, Martin was instantly raised to near-divinity by his connection with the man who had sung the Ying-Tong Song. He was, besides, agreeably plain-spoken, neither ingratiating nor condescending. John and Paul—and especially George—were soon plying him with questions about the studio and its equipment. Only Pete

Best remained, as usual, silent. George Martin does not remember exchanging a word with him all afternoon.

Brian had already sent down a neatly-typewritten list of songs which the Beatles could play if required. A large portion were 'standards', like Besame Mucho, since these, Brian thought —mistakenly—had impressed Martin most on the demo' tape. There was also the batch of new songs they had written in Hamburg, mostly round the battered piano at Jim Hawke's Seaman's Mission on the docks.

Despite everything else on George Martin's mind, the test he gave the Beatles was exhaustive. Ringed by their puny amps, they stood in the well of the huge studio, attacking song after song, then waiting, in sudden silence, for the verdict of the polite, unexcited voice over the control-room intercom. What they did not realise was that Martin was putting each of them on test individually, to try to see which might be the Cliff Richard he still hoped to find. He could not decide between Paul, whose voice was more melodious, and John, whose personality had greater force. George, and his rather strained, adenoidal voice, figured little in these computations. 'I was thinking that on balance I should make Paul the leader,' Martin says. 'Then I realised that if I did, I'd be changing the whole nature of the group. Why not keep them as they were?'

The question of material remained vexing. Martin still felt that Red Sails in the Sunset, Your Feet's Too Big and Besame Mucho were 'too corny'. Nor did he particularly like the songs they had written for themselves. He listened patiently but without inner animation to the one which, plainly, they hoped he would choose as the 'A' side of their record. It was an odd little dirge-like thing whose limited chords and rhymes were the consequence of having been put together largely around Pete Best's drumming. The song was called Love Me Do. That was its opening line. Its second was 'you know I love you'; its third was 'I'll always be true'. George Martin listened, then asked to hear something else.

He had decided from the outset that Pete Best was not a good enough drummer to record. 'At the end of the test, I took Brian on one side and said, "I don't know what you intend to do with the group as such, but this drumming isn't at all what I want. If we do make a record, I'd prefer to use my own drummer—which won't make any difference to you because no one will know who's on the record anyway." ' Pete Best, packing up his gear with the others, knew nothing of this conversation.

'If we make a record,' was still as far as George Martin would commit himself. He liked the Beatles, and felt there was definitely 'something' there. At the same time, he knew that in signing so offbeat and potentially uncommercial a group, he could well risk his own small position within EMI. Besides, he had a full programme of recording celebrities such as Bernard Cribbins, and a 'live' LP to make at London's first satirical night club, The Establishment.

Not until late July did Brian receive a definite offer. George Martin agreed to record the Beatles on Parlophone, subject to the most niggardly contract that EMI's cheese-paring caution could devise. In an initial one-year period, Parlophone undertook to record four titles at a royalty, to Brian and the Beatles together, of one penny per double-sided record. Four further one-year options were open to George Martin, each bringing a royalty increment per record of one farthing. In 1962, the farthing was already a coin so small as to have passed from general circulation.

A few days after the audition, someone said a curious thing to Pete: 'They're thinking of getting rid of you, you know—but they don't dare do it. They're too worried about losing all your fans.'

At about the same time, Bob Wooler, the Cavern disc jockey, making his rounds of Liverpool after dark, came into Danny English's pub to join a meeting in progress between Brian, Paul McCartney and George Harrison. Wooler, as a long-time confidant, had been specially invited though for what reason, Brian would not say. It quickly became obvious that Paul and George were both urging that Pete Best should be sacked.

Brian himself held out for some time against sacking Pete. At first, he seems to have thought he could appease all sides by keeping Pete on for 'live' dates but using a substitute drummer on record, as George Martin had suggested. Brian had nothing against Pete—indeed, he relied heavily on him as the group's most punctual and businesslike member. Pete's home in West Derby, and the little coffee club downstairs, continued to be the Beatles' main rendezvous and base camp. An added complication existed in Neil Aspinall, their indispensable van-driver and bodyguard, who was Pete's closest friend. There would also, in the event of unpleasantness, be Pete's mother to contend with. Mona Best, as Brian already knew, was a force one did not lightly provoke.

All through June and July, before word came from George Martin at Parlophone, the plots simmered against a still unsuspecting Pete. The Beatles—already billed by Brian as 'Parlophone Recording Artists'—were back at their old ballroom haunts, the Grafton, the Majestic in Birkenhead and the New Brighton Tower. It was after a radio appearance in Manchester, on the BBC Light Programme Northern Dance Orchestra show, where he had been literally mobbed by girls, that someone dropped the first hint to Pete. 'They're thinking of getting rid of you, you know.' The thought amused Pete; he even mentioned it jokingly to Brian, who responded by blushing and spluttering how ridiculous. Just the same, when George Martin wrote to him in late July, and the Parlophone contract became real at last, Brian took care not to let Pete Best know.

John stayed out of the plot, having a far more urgent worry on his mind. His girl friend, Cynthia, in one of her rare utterances, had informed him that her monthly 'friend' had failed to pay her a visit. Since John and she were virtually living together, in equal innocence of birth control methods, this crucial 'friend's' arrival had long been in considerable jeopardy. Now it was certain, confirmed by a woman doctor whose harshness drove the mild, blonde, short-sighted girl to tears. Cyn' was going to have a baby.

John Lennon bowed to the inevitable as fatalistically as any North Country working man. In that case, he told Cynthia, there was nothing else for it; they'd have to get married. With Cyn's mother away in Canada, the only parent to be reckoned with was John's volatile Aunt Mimi. They put off breaking it to Mimi until the eve of their hastily-arranged wedding. Mimi's response was a hollow and heartfelt groan. She had groaned in exactly that way in 1938, when her sister Julia came home and threw a marriage certificate casually on the table. 'I told them,' Mimi remembers, 'I'll say one thing only, then I'll hold my peace. You're *too young*! There now, I've said it. Now I'll hold my peace for ever.'

August began, and still Pete Best knew nothing of the contract with Parlophone. The Beatles, en route for the Grafton in West Derby Road, were all in Mona Best's Oriental sitting-room, waiting for Pete to come downstairs. He did so in high spirits, full of the Ford Capri car he had almost decided to buy. Mrs. Best remembers that Paul, in particular, showed unease over the price Pete intended to pay for the car. 'He went all mysterious, suddenly. He told Pete, "If you take my advice, you won't buy it, that's all. You'd be better saving your money."'

On Wednesday, 15 August, they were on at lunch-time in the Cavern. The next night was the first of four major bookings at the Riverpark ballroom in Chester. Pete had decided to make his own way down, giving John a lift. They both came out of the Cavern and Pete asked John what time he should pick him up tomorrow night. John muttered, 'Don't bother,' and walked away in a hurry. Later, at home, Pete Best got a call from Brian in his Whitechapel office. 'He said he wanted to see me there tomorrow morning at 11.30. That was nothing unusual. He'd often ask me things about halls or bookings that I knew from the time when I'd been handling the dates.'

Pete's friend Neil Aspinall drove him into the city to see Brian the next morning. 'I went bouncing into Brian's office,' Pete says. 'As soon as I saw him, I could tell there was something up. He said: "The boys want you out of the group. They don't think you're a good enough drummer." I said, "It's taken them two years to find out I'm not a good enough drummer." While I was standing there, the 'phone rang on Brian's desk. It was Paul, asking if I'd been told yet. Brian said, "I can't talk now. Peter's here with me in the office."

'I went outside and told Neil. He said, "Right then, that's it. I'm out as well." Brian followed me and asked me if I'd still play the dates in Chester as they wouldn't be able to get a replacement drummer in time. I said OK, I would. We went outside, and Neil went straight away to ring home and tell Mo about it. I just went off and had a few pints—numb. I'd been cut and dried and hung out on the line.'

Luck had very seldom visited the boy who was born Richard Starkey on 7 July 1940, at number 9 Madryn Street, deep in the Liverpool Dingle. The baby was one month late and had to be induced with forceps; as his mother, Elsie, lay upstairs, recovering, the sirens sounded Germany's first aerial visitation. The densely-packed Dingle houses had no bomb shelter other than the coal-hole under the stairs. As Elsie, with Ritchie, and three neighbours crouched there, she could not understand why the baby on her shoulder was screaming. Then she realised she was holding him upside-down.

The sad-eyed child they named Ritchie after his father came to consciousness on the tailboard of a removal van as it carried his mother's few possessions from Madryn Street, around the corner to a new, even smaller terrace house in Admiral Grove. His father, Ritchie senior, a bakery worker, had by now moved away from home, but continued conscientiously to support his wife and child. He could only send 30s a week, so Elsie herself took work as a barmaid in a pub. Young Ritchie thus spent much of his early childhood at the home of his grandfather Starkey, a boilermaker in the Mersey shipyards. He was a solitary boy, but philosophical and happy with the little that he had. His only reproach to Elsie was the lack of any brothers and sisters, 'so there'd be someone to talk to when it's raining'.

His education was dogged from the beginning by recurrent ill-health. At the age of six, after only a year at primary school, he was rushed to hospital with a burst appendix. Surgeons operated in the nick of time to save his life, but he remined in a coma for several weeks. Elsie would come in late, after work at the pub, to peep at the little, still figure in its hospital cot. He recovered, became his old cheerful self and was about to come home when he fell out of bed while showing a toy to someone. This first absence from school eventually dragged out to a full year.

At eight, consequently, he was unable to read or write. A neighbour's daughter, Mary Maguire, did her best to help him catch up by sitting with him and reading out magazines. The operation had left his stomach in a delicate state from which it was never to recover fully. When there was lamb scouse—stew—for dinner, Mary would sit by Ritchie, carefully picking the onions out of his portion.

When he was 11, his mother began to keep company with Harry Graves, a Liverpool Corporation house-painter, originally from London. Ritchie liked Harry, and so encouraged the match. He told Elsie he didn't want her to be like her widowed mother, Grandma Gleave, who had not liked to marry the suitor who used to visit her and play serenades on a mouth organ.

Harry and Elsie married in 1953, when Ritchie was not quite 13. He had begun to attend Dingle Vale Secondary School, but was still greatly handicapped by all the lessons he had missed. That same year, he caught a cold which turned to pleurisy and affected one of his lungs. They took him to the big children's sanitorium at Heswall on the Wirral; he remained there for the next two years.

When eventually discharged he was 15 and of school-leaving age. No one remembered him at Dingle Vale Secondary when he went back there for a reference. He could read and write only with difficulty, and the months in hospital had left him thin, weak and sallow. Patches of premature grey were starting to show in his hair and his left eyebrow. His nature, against all the odds, continued cheerful.

The Youth Employment Officer, well accustomed to such lost causes, eventually found him a job with the railway as a messenger boy. He left after six weeks, because they wouldn't give him a uniform, and took casual work as a barman on the ferryboats plying slantwise over the Mersey between Liverpool and New Brighton. Then, thanks to his stepfather, Harry Graves, he was taken on by Hunt's, a local engineering firm, as apprentice to a joiner. The overalls, the slide-rule, the contract binding for years ahead, all promised security for life.

A fellow Hunt's apprentice was a boy named Eddie Miles who lived near the Starkeys in Admiral Grove. When the skiffle craze began in 1956, Eddie and Ritchie started a group to amuse the other apprentices in the dinner-hour. Ritchie, who had always banged and beaten on things, took the role of drummer. Harry Graves bought him his first full kit, paying £10 for it down in London and carrying it valiantly back to Lime Street on the train.

The Eddie Clayton Skiffle Group, as they called themselves, played around the same Church Hall network as John Lennon's original Quarry Men. Ritchie by now was using brand new drums for which his Grandfather Starkey had lent him the £50 deposit. The kit was his passport, around 1959, into Liverpool's most successful amateur group. He joined the Ravin' Texans, afterwards the Hurricanes, the quartet that played while Rory Storm sang and, occasionally, shinned up ballroom pillars. The others nicknamed him 'Rings', because he wore so many, then Ringo as it sounded more cowboyish. 'Starkey' was first abbreviated to 'Starr' at Butlin's Holiday Camp, so that his solo drumming spot could be billed on a poster as 'Starr Time'.

Until 1961, Ringo belonged to a group far more glamorous and successful than the Beatles. He only got to know them in Hamburg, when Rory Storm came over to play the Kaiserkeller and from then on he got to know them well, in many an uproarious bedroom and bar. The Beatles liked him for his droll, harmless humour; for being, in those unreal neon nights, as homely as a Pier Head pigeon. And he was, undoubtedly, a better drummer than Pete Best. The plot to oust Pete dates right back to 1961, when Ringo joined the Beatles as a backing group for 'Wally' in the record-booth at Hamburg railway station.

After Hamburg, Rory Storm's fortunes became somewhat variable. At one point, he even signed on at his local Labour Exchange as 'Rock and Roll pianist'. Ringo had by now given up his apprenticeship; and he, too, spent several weeks on the dole, sitting out vacant days at the Cavern, the Jacaranda or the *Mersey Beat* office upstairs in Renshaw Street. Late in 1961, while sorting through some records, he noticed an LP by Lightnin' Hopkins which gave the singer's birthplace as Houston, Texas. Ringo, who had always adored the Wild West, conceived the idea of emigrating to America. He even wrote to Houston Chamber of Commerce, inquiring about job prospects in that area. The Chamber wrote back helpfully enough, but Ringo lost heart at the sight of the registration forms.

Early in 1962, Peter Eckhorn appeared in Liverpool to recruit musicians for his Top Ten Club. When Brian Epstein priced the Beatles out of his reach, Eckhorn persuaded Ringo to go back to Hamburg with him and join Tony Sheridan's resident band. Eckhorn thought highly enough of Ringo to offer him a permanent job at £30 per week, with a flat thrown in. He was also the special favourite of Jim and Lilo Hawke at the Seaman's Mission. But Ringo felt homesick for Liverpool, Admiral Grove and his mother.

In August, he had rejoined Rory Storm and the Hurricanes and gone south to Skegness with them for their annual hard-sweating season at Butlin's holiday camp. Back in Liverpool, his mother opened the front door one day, to George Harrison's pale, unsmiling face. Mrs. Graves told him that Ringo wasn't at home. 'Tell him we're trying to get him to join us,' was George's message.

It was John who finally got through to Ringo, ringing up Butlin's and then waiting until Ringo could be found and brought to the camp office 'phone. The pay as a Beatle, John said, would be £25 per week. In return, Ringo would have to comb his hair forward and shave off his beard. His 'sidies', however, could remain.

Rory Storm was magnanimous over the theft of his drummer. The only stipulation Rory made was that, when Ringo left the Hurricanes to join the Beatles, his pink stage suit was passed on to 16-year-old Gibson Kemp, who had not yet left school and who was so small that the jacket had to be pinned at the back with clothes pegs to make it fit him.

Mersey Beat broke the news in its issue of 23 August. Pete Best was out of the Beatles and Ringo Starr had replaced him. According to *Mersey Beat*, the change had been mutually and amicably agreed. The story went on to announce that George Martin was ready at last for the Beatles to go to London and record their first single for Parlophone. They would be flying down with their new drummer for a session on 4 September.

The uproar among Pete Best fans was on a scale far greater than even Bob Wooler had predicted. Petitions signed by hundreds of girls poured in to the *Mersey Beat* office, protesting at their idol's banishment. It soon became clear that everyone knew the real facts. When the Beatles went on next at the Cavern, they were heckled by cries of 'Pete Best for ever—Ringo, never!' A night-long vigil was kept outside Pete's house in West Derby. When Mona Best picked up her morning milk from the front step, there were girls asleep all over the garden.

The following day, in chaos compounded of Pete Best's sacking and several pneumatic road drills, John Lennon married Cynthia Powell at Mount Pleasant Register Office. It was the same place where, in 1938, his mother Julia had married Freddy Lennon, putting her occupation down as 'cinema usherette' for a joke. As on that earlier occasion, no parents were present. Cynthia's mother had come from Canada but gone again; and Aunt Mimi could not bear to see history repeat itself so exactly. Cynthia was given away by her brother, Tony, and Brian Epstein—who had obtained the special marriage licence—acted as John's best man. With insufficient money to buy herself a new wedding outfit, Cynthia went before the Registrar wearing some of Astrid's cast-off clothes. Paul and George were there also, torn between embarrassment and giggles. Much of the service was inaudible, owing to road drills. Afterwards, in pouring rain, they ran across the road for a chicken lunch at Reece's restaurant. Since Reece's had no alcohol licence, the toast to the newlyweds was drunk with water.

On Monday, the Pete Best storm broke with renewed fury. There were scuffles outside the Cavern as the Beatles went in to play; when George Harrison appeared on stage, it was with one eye blackened. Brian, after this, refused to go to the Cavern unless Ray McFall, the owner, provided him with a bodyguard. It truly did feel as if sacking Pete Best had turned him into the most hated man in Liverpool. Being Brian, he did not find all the drama entirely distasteful.

Pete's mother had already paid him the first of many wrathful and accusing visits. Mona Best was—and remains—convinced that Pete's sacking was due simply to the jealousy of John, Paul and George. 'He'd given them so much with his beat and everything. To a lot of the fans, he *was* the Beatles. I knew that Brian hadn't wanted to do it; he respected Peter too much. None of the others was introduced to Brian's parents; now why was that? Why was Peter the only one?'

Neil Aspinall found himself in an unenviable position, torn between his loyalty to the Best family and the Beatles' total reliance on him and his van. Largely at Pete's insistence, Neil kept on his job of road manager and general bodyguard. For a time, the Beatles even carried on using the Casbah as a meeting place before engagements, though they were careful to keep out of Mrs. Best's way. 'Then one day Paul knocked on the door and asked me if he could leave his car in the drive. I managed to keep my peace but Kathy, Pete's girl friend, gave John and him a damned good talking-to.'

Brian tried to soften the blow to Pete by offering to build a new group around him. What he eventually did was to fit Pete into Lee Curtis and the All Stars, the group managed by Brian's friend and helper Joe Flannery. Joe agreed to accept Pete despite his misgivings that his good looks would clash with those of Lee Curtis, Joe's younger brother. The transfer was effected, he remembers, with subtlety typical of Brian. 'First Brian got me to agree to have Pete. Then I had to talk to Pete and say: "I think I can arrange it with Mr. Epstein." '

Pete, very naturally, failed to turn up for the first of the Chester Riverpark ballroom dates. Since Ringo had not yet arrived from Skegness, a substitute drummer had to be found at short notice. Brian solved the difficulty by borrowing Johnny Hutch from the Big Three.

The next big beat show at New Brighton Tower, on 27 July, was presented, not by Sam Leach but by NEMS Enterprises. The star was Joe Brown, a popular Cockney Rock and Roller whose song Picture of You was currently high in the Top Ten. Second on the bill were the Beatles. In this way, Brian implanted the idea that Joe Brown, for all his big name, was only a little way ahead. More big names followed, always with the Beatles second on the bill. 'He'd watch the charts all the time and see who was selling most records,' Joe Flannery says. 'When someone like Joe Brown or Bruce Channel came up, Brian would make a big day of it. There'd be an autograph-signing session at the shop, then the show in the evening. American stars used to think that was wonderful. They weren't used to getting that kind of treatment in England, not even in London.'

On 6 September, Brian took a full page advertisement in *Mersey Beat* to announce a coup which any promoter might have envied. Little Richard, Rock and Roll's baggy-suited and clamorous founding figure, was currently touring Britain. Brian had negotiated with Richard's London promoters to bring him to New Brighton Tower for one night, on 12 October. The Beatles were second on the programme, together with more Liverpool groups than had appeared in one place since Allan Williams's Boxing Stadium show.

George Martin knew nothing of the Pete Best sacking. He expected Pete to be still with the others when, on 11 September, they came back to Abbey Road studios. Accordingly, down on the floor of Number Two studio there waited the experienced session drummer whom Martin had engaged to play on the record in place of Pete. When Ringo was introduced to him as Pete's replacement, he saw no reason to depart from his original plan. He knew nothing about Ringo as a drummer, he said, and preferred not to take any chances. Andy White must play on the recording.

After this rather stern beginning, George Martin tried to make amends by involving the Beatles in every facet of the recording process. He explained that, due to the wonders of EMI science, they could record their voices and instruments as separate tracks, to be 'mixed' afterwards for optimum texture and balance. He let them record a warm-up number, then took them into the control room to play it back. He asked them if there was anything they didn't like. George Harrison said, in his slow, gruff way, 'Well, for a start, I don't like your tie.' 'Everyone fell about with laughter at that,' George Martin says. 'The others were hitting him playfully as schoolboys do when one of them has been cheeky to teacher.'

Martin had decided, after all, to use Lennon-McCartney songs as both the 'A' and 'B' side of the single. For the 'A' side, after much deliberation, he chose Love Me Do. The number had improved since he last heard it, chiefly by the addition of a harmonica riff which John had copied from the Bruce Channel hit Hey Baby. For the 'B' side, to bring Paul to the fore, Martin chose PS I Love You, liking the song for its harmonies, its switch from major to minor chords and the way that John's voice chimed with Paul's on key words through the lyric.

During rehearsals that afternoon, Martin somewhat relented in his attitude to Ringo's drumming. 'He hit good and hard, and used the tom-tom well, even though he couldn't do a roll to save his life.' Ringo himself did not know yet that there was a session drummer waiting to replace him. When it was time to record the Love Me Do instrumental track, Ringo was handed a tambourine and instructed to hit it twice on every third beat. He looked so doleful that George Martin relented a little. They would record two versions, Martin said: one with Andy White on drums and one with Ringo. The vocal track would be mixed with whichever version came out best.

The Andy White and Ringo versions became indistinguishable in the quantity of 'takes' that were needed before George Martin was content with the instrumental track. The fifteenth attempt finally satisfied him, even though John Lennon's mouth had grown numb with sliding along the harmonica bars. There was a short break; then they returned to do the backing track for PS I Love You. Andy White sat at the drums and Ringo, this time, was given maracas to shake. He later said that he thought the others were 'doing a Pete Best' on him.

At EMI's next 'supplement meeting', when each label head outlined his release plans for the coming month, George Martin caused a ripple of amusement by announcing that Parlophone was putting out a single by a group called the Beatles. The general view was that it must be another comedy disc. Somebody even asked: 'Is it Spike Milligan disguised?' 'I told them, "I'm serious. This is a great group, and we're going to hear a lot from them." But nobody took much notice.'

Up in Liverpool, Brian had begun to prepare the Beatles for their impending stardom. Freda Kelly from the NEMS office had to go round to each one with a printed sheet for 'Life Lines'—favourite food, favourite clothes, likes, dislikes and so on—just as it was done in the *New Musical Express*. Next to 'Type of car?' Paul wrote 'Ford Classic (Goodwood green)'; next to 'Dislikes?' he wrote 'False and soft people', and next to 'Ambition?' 'Money etc'. George gave his main dislike, ironically, as 'Black eyes', his 'Greatest musical influences?' as Carl Perkins, his 'Ambition?' 'To retire with a lot of money, thank you'. John, using an italic fountain pen, gave his 'Dislikes?' as 'Thick heads, Trad Jazz', his favourite film director as Ingmar Bergman, his 'Ambition?' as 'Money and everything'. Ringo's favourite food was 'Steak and chips'; his 'Likes?' 'Anyone who likes me'.

On 2 October, a second contract was signed by the Beatles and Brian—a thoroughly legal document this time, and witnessed, as the Law required, by Paul's father and George's. The term of the agreement was five years. Brian's share of the earnings was 25 per cent. A further clause—a slip on Clive Epstein's part, hastily rectified soon afterwards—gave each side power to terminate the agreement at six months' notice.

On 12 October, Little Richard and retinue arrived in Liverpool for his show at the New Brighton Tower. The legendary screamer of Good Golly Miss Molly was revealed as a little lemon-headed creature in a sharkskin suit, his narrow moustache in peril of sliding under his top lip, his former greasy curls refined to a woolly stump, his fingernails painted with varnish, his manner strangely mild and ethereal. With him came a representative of his British tour-promoters, one Don Arden. All communications to the Rock and Roll legend, Mr. Arden made clear, should be addressed through him. But one communication —that of a glance between the legend and Brian Epstein —escaped Don Arden's proprietorial vigilance.

Entrepreneurs who have put on Little Richard shows tell blood-curdling stories of his temperament, his unreliability, his bizarre whims and fancies, his refusal in some cases to do anything for the audience but slowly remove his clothes. But on 12 October 1962, when Little Richard performed at New Brighton Tower Ballroom, something seemed to have happened to put him in a mood of perfect tractability and co-operativeness. 'Brian seemed to be able to do anything with him,' Joe Flannery says. 'When Richard finished his act, something had gone wrong with the mike for the next group, Pete MacLaine and the Dakotas. Brian could even get Little Richard to walk across, nice as you please, and hand his personal microphone on to Pete MacLaine.'

Backstage, too, he was seraphically amiable, letting himself be photographed with the Beatles leaning all over him, his hands emotionally gripping theirs. 'There was a terrible row between Brian and Don Arden in the dressing-room,' Joe Flannery says. 'Don Arden couldn't understand why Richard wouldn't listen to him, only to Brian. Don Arden made some remark, then I heard Brian's voice ring out. "I shall call your office on Monday, Mr. Arden. I don't think you'll be working there very long after that." Don Arden couldn't believe it. "I've been all over the world," he said, "and *nobody's* ever talked to me like that before." '

So powerful was Brian's influence over Little Richard that he was able to bring him back to Liverpool for a second concert, at the Empire theatre on 28 October, to head the existing bill of Craig Douglas, Jet Harris and the Jetblacks, and the Beatles. Brian planned the entire event as a means of giving them their first professional booking at the Empire.

Because it was Sunday, none of the groups was allowed to appear in 'costume', so they all took off their jackets. The Beatles played in pink, round-collared shirts. For a fan like Freda Kelly it was no less a miracle that they had crossed the gulf, from underground clubs to this softly-lit, luxurious realm of concert and Christmas panto. 'I remember when the spotlight went on Paul in his pink shirt, and he started to sing Besame Mucho. I thought, "This is *it*. Now they've *really* made it." '

Love Me Do was released on 4 October 1962, in a week when America's grip on the British Top Twenty had seldom been stronger. Carole King, Tommy Roe, Bobby Vee, Little Eva, Ray Charles and Del Shannon all had new songs making, or about to make, their inevitable ascent. The sensation of the moment was Let's Dance by Chris Montez, prolonging the 'Twist' dance craze which French students had imported into Britain during the summer. Among British artists, the continuing success of Helen Shapiro, Jimmy Justice, Kathy Kirby and Shane Fenton seemed to bear out the Decca prophecy that solo singers were what the teenagers wanted; that guitar groups were 'on the way out'.

EMI themselves seemed to think so. After Love Me Do was released, virtually no effort was made to plug the disc to the trade press or BBC radio, or even EMI's own sponsored Radio Luxembourg show. Newspaper publicity was confined to a single printed handout, copied from the 'Life Lines' which Freda Kelly had drawn up in Liverpool, vouchsafing to indifferent Fleet Street record columnists that Paul McCartney's favourite clothes were leather and suède, that Ringo Starr's favourite dish was steak and chips, that George Harrison's greatest musical influence was Carl Perkins and that John Lennon's 'type of car' was 'bus'.

After his experience with Decca, Brian was taking no chances. He himself had ordered 10,000 copies of Love Me Do from Parlophone. He had been told that was the quantity you had to sell to have a Top Twenty hit.

Though the Liverpool fans loyally bought Love Me Do, and though *Mersey Beat*'s Top Twenty made it instantaneously number one, most of the 10,000 copies remained in unopened cartons in a back room of the Whitechapel NEMS shop. 'Brian took me and showed me them,' Joe Flannery says. 'He even made up a little song about all the copies he hadn't been able to sell. "Here we go gathering dust in May," he'd sing.' A few days later, in London, Flannery bumped into Paul McCartney. 'Paul said he was hungry: he'd only had a cake to eat all day. I was amazed. I said, "Paul—how?" Paul said, "Someone had to pay for those 10,000 records Brian bought." '

The first radio play was on Luxembourg, after hundreds of requests from Liverpool. George Harrison sat waiting for it next to the radio all evening with his mother, Louise. She had given up and was in bed when George ran upstairs, shouting, 'We're on! We're on!' Mr. Harrison was angry at being disturbed: he had to be up early the next morning to drive his bus.

A few scattered plays followed on the BBC Light Programme, where Pop was beginning to creep into 'general' music shows like the early evening *Roundabout*. And gradually, on a small scale, something began to happen. *Record Mirror* showed Love Me Do at 49th place in its Top 100. The *New Musical Express*, shortly afterwards, showed it at Number 27. Finally, on 13 December, it reached number 17.

For a first record, especially on Parlophone, that was not at all a bad performance. If Love Me Do had not taken the country by storm, it had confirmed George Martin's instinct that the Beatles could be successful singing the right song. He reached that conclusion even before Love Me Do made its brief Top Twenty showing. The second single under their first year's contract was due to be recorded on 26 November.

Though bound to EMI on record for five years, Brian had made no such deal with Ardmore and Beechwood, the publishing subsidiary which had issued Love Me Do as sheet music. Brian was dissatisfied with Ardmore and Beechwood's performance as song-pluggers, and confided to a not unsympathetic George Martin that he wanted new publishers for the Beatles' second single. His idea was to go to an American firm, Hill and Range, which held British rights on the Elvis Presley catalogue. Martin's advice was to pick a small firm with a drive to succeed that would match Brian's own. 'In other words, what I told Brian he needed was a hungry music publisher.'

The hungriest music publisher George Martin knew was Dick James, a tubby, amiable, bald-headed man whose office was one first floor room at the corner of Denmark and Old Compton Streets. James had started his career as a crooner in the 1930s, as 'featured vocalist' with Primo Scala's Accordion Band. Such noted orchestra-leaders as Henry Hall, Stanley Black and Cyril Stapleton had all, at various times, made use of his serviceably-dulcet voice. His hair's disappearance in the early 1950s led him to abandon stage work for song-plugging. In November 1962, he had been in business on his own as a music publisher for one year exactly. Everyone knew Dick James, everyone liked him but no one yet mistook him for Tin Pan Alley's next millionaire.

In the early 1950s, as a newcomer to Parlophone, George Martin had produced Dick James on several successful records including Tenderly and the Robin Hood theme. It was natural, therefore, that when EMI's own publishing company proved deficient, he should approach Dick James informally, both as a possible publisher for the Beatles and also in James's old capacity as a plugger of likely recording material. The first approach, when Martin mentioned 'this Liverpool group' was not encouraging. Dick James laughed his cuddly laugh and echoed, 'Liverpool? So what's from Liverpool?'

The answer, by then, was a disc with at least a toe-hold in the *New Musical Express* Top 100. Dick James heard Love Me Do, liked the overall sound but agreed with George Martin that the song was 'just a riff'. He promised to use his Tin Pan Alley contacts to find them a good 'professional' song for their follow-up record. This he produced within days, on a demo' disc which he played to Martin. The song was How Do You Do It? by a young composer named Mitch Murray. 'As soon as Dick played it to me,' George Martin says, 'I started jumping up and down. "This is it," I said. "This is the song that's going to make the Beatles a household name." '

He said the same to the Beatles themselves when Brian brought them back to Abbey Road studios on 26 November. He played them the demo' of How Do You Do It? accompanied by his own carefully thought-out ideas on how the song could be adapted to suit their vocal style. He was surprised, and not a little irritated, when John and Paul said flatly that they didn't like it, and wanted to do another of their own songs. This apparent wilfulness in the face of an almost certain Top Twenty hit brought a stern lecture from George Martin. ' "When you can write material as good as this, I'll record it," I said. "But right now, we're going to record *this*." '

His words sent them, chastened, into the studio, to produce a version of How Do You Do It? in which every note, and nuance of John Lennon's lead voice, made plain their lugubrious distaste. George Harrison, halfway through, produced a guitar solo not far removed in scale and ambition from the twanging of a rubber band. Even so, they could not stop a little charm and originality from creeping in.

The song they wanted to record was one of John and Paul's called Please Please Me, one fairly slow version of which had already been tried on George Martin. Since then, they had worked on it, tidying up the lyric and making it faster. The revised version was now played by Paul and John on their acoustic Gibson guitars while George Martin, perched on a musician's high stool, listened critically. Then, as their voices broke together on the 'Whoa yeah', Martin recognised something. His objection was that the song as it stood lasted barely more than a minute. They could lengthen it with an intro on John's harmonica, and by repeating the first chorus at the end.

With these specifications, they went straight back into Number Two studio to record. Ringo Starr settled behind his drums, untroubled by the spectre of Andy White. The first take of Please Please Me was so belligerently alive that George Martin decided to use it, even though Paul had forgotten the words in the first chorus and John, more obviously, had forgotten them in the finale. 'The whole session was a joy,' Martin says. 'At the end, I pressed the intercom button and said "Gentlemen, you have just made your first Number One." '

He now had to break it to Dick James that the Mitch Murray song would not, after all, be out soon on Parlophone. 'George rang me up,' Dick James says. 'His words were, "You know that song the Beatles *were* going to record . . ." ' James held his head in Tim Pan Alley mock anguish, but agreed to meet Brian Epstein the next day with a view to publishing—and plugging—Please Please Me. It was arranged that Brian would bring an early pressing of the single for James to hear at his Denmark Street office at 11 am.

Brian arrived, instead, at 10.20. He had had an earlier appointment with another music publisher, but the man he was supposed to meet had not been there. Instead, it was suggested that he play his demo' disc to the office boy. He had walked out in fury, and come straight on to Dick James Music. James, to his lasting benefit, was at work already, and able to greet the hot-faced young man in person.

A single hearing of Please Please Me was enough for Dick James. He loved the song, he told Brian; could he publish it? Brian, a little nonplussed by the shabby office, asked what James thought he could do for the Beatles that EMI's publicity department had not already done. Dick James's answer was to pick up the telephone and call a friend of his named Philip Jones, the producer of the Saturday night television Pop show *Thank Your Lucky Stars*. He told Jones to listen, then put Please Please Me on to his record-player and held the telephone receiver near to it. Philip Jones agreed that it was very good. He also agreed, at James's skilful prompting, to put the Beatles into *Thank Your Lucky Stars*. In five minutes, Dick James had guaranteed them exposure on what was—after BBC-TV's *Juke Box Jury*—the show with greatest influence over the record-buying public. 'Now,' he asked ingenuously, 'can I publish the song?'

Another reason why George Martin had sent Brian to Dick James was that he knew James to be 'very straight' in financial matters. As a singer, he had himself frequently been done out of large earnings in the days when English artists received no royalty on American sales of their records. Twice in the early 1950s, he had topped the American charts and yet received only £7 each time—the then standard studio fee. The deal he now offered Brian, while not actuated by pure benevolence, was both fair and imaginative.

Under the usual predatory publisher's contract Dick James would have taken 10 per cent of the *retail* price of sheet music, plus up to half of the royalties from radio play and 'cover' versions. Instead, he proposed that a special company be formed within his own organisation but exclusively publishing Lennon–McCartney songs. The company would be called Northern Songs and its proceeds split 50–50: half to Dick James, 20 per cent each to John and Paul and 10 per cent to Brian. It sounded handsome, and it was, notwithstanding the clause that James's own company would take a percentage of Northern Songs earnings 'off the top'. 'Brian said to me, "Why are you doing this for us?"' Dick James recalls. 'What I said to him then was the truth. I was doing it because I had such faith in the songs.'

Please Please Me was not scheduled for release until January 1963. In the meantime, the Beatles were committed to return to Hamburg for a two-week engagement at Manfred Weissleder's Star-Club. The booking had been made back in the summer, before George Martin's advent, at rates of pay which no longer seemed attractive. All four, besides, felt they had had their fill of the Reeperbahn. Also, for the first time, they would be away from home during both Christmas and New Year's Eve. 'I knew they didn't want to come back,' says Weissleder's aide, Horst Fascher. 'I had to give Brian Epstein a thousand marks under the table to make them do it.'

On 2 December, a severe jolt was sustained by the Beatles' collective ego. Brian, by sheer effrontery, had managed to get them into what was then known as a 'package' show of Pop acts currently enjoying Top Twenty success. He had discovered the private telephone number of Arthur Howes, the country's biggest tour-promoter, and had rung up Howes one Saturday afternoon at home in Peterborough. Arthur Howes, a veteran at the agency game, smiled a bit when he heard the name of the group on offer, but was fair minded enough not to refuse them without a trial. He offered to put them on for one night only at the Embassy cinema, Peterborough, in a show headed by Frank Ifield, the Australian yodeller.

The appearance was an unmitigated flop. The staid East Anglian audience had come to see Frank Ifield, not four unknowns from the north; they had come to worship suntan and upswept hair, not eccentric fringes, and to hear sentimental ballads, not Chuck Berry and Carl Perkins music. Total silence followed every perversely-loud number. But something about them appealed to Arthur Howes; he told Brian that the disaster was not all their fault, even making a small offer for the option of using them in future package shows.

On 18 December, with the worst possible grace, they set off for Hamburg and the Star-Club. Love Me Do had come into the Top Twenty only five days earlier: by going abroad now, it was felt, they were throwing away the chance to push the record any higher. To add to their chagrin, they were not even top of the

Star-Club's Christmas bill. That honour had been given to Johnny and the Hurricanes, an American instrumental group whose biggest hits, Rocking Goose and Beatnik Fly, were back in the late 1950s.

It was some consolation, when they arrived, to meet up with Kingsize Taylor and the Dominoes, the Liverpool R & B group led by the big, genial, throaty-voiced butcher's apprentice. Kingsize and his colleagues had earned Manfred Weissleder's warm approval for their stamina on stage and their general reliability. Just the same, after several tear-gas gun incidents in the flats above Maxim's Club, Weissleder had felt it safer to move all the musicians out to a small local hotel, The Pacific. There, the Beatles and Kingsize celebrated their reunion by pelting one another with grapes.

Those who saw the Beatles at the Star-Club in December 1962 remember that much of the old anarchic excitement was missing from their performance. They resented being in Hamburg, they resented missing Christmas at home; and this they made clear on stage, shovelling out their back catalogue of numbers like Your Feet's Too Big, Red Sails in the Sunset, even Frank Ifield's I Remember You. Kingsize Taylor taped them, on his portable recorder, playing through midnight into 1963. Their playing is ragged and careless; they are evidently drunk, and so tired they can scarcely be bothered to reply to the German hecklers. On two songs, the vocal is not by John or Paul but by Horst Fascher, the bouncer. All that seems to concern them about tomorrow is getting out of Hamburg; getting home.

August 1963

'Four frenzied Little Lord Fauntleroys who are earning £5,000 a week'

The winter of 1962–3 was Britain's worst for almost a hundred years. From December to mid-March, the entire country disappeared and a snow-levelled tundra took its place, stretching from north to south, silent and motionless but for snowploughs trying to locate the buried motorways. With the blizzards came Siberian cold that froze the English Channel, annihilated old people and the Essex oyster beds, wiped out the zebra at Whipsnade Zoo, turned milk into cream-flavoured sorbet and caused beer to explode spontaneously in its bottles. South-west England was completely cut off; indeed, there seemed at one point a sporting chance that Wales would never be seen again. As usual in Britain, winter was the last thing anyone had expected and, as usual, the British responded to chaos with cheerfulness. A year of unprecedented uproar, of unparalleled outrage, thus began with a feeling that everything in Britain was much the way it had always been. Everyone talked, and talked, about the weather.

On 12 January, the nation, still snowed into its homes, provided a bumper audience for ABC-TV's Saturday night Pop show *Thank Your Lucky Stars.* The show was popular for two reasons—its teenage record critic 'Janice', and the imaginative studio sets that were built around singers and groups as they mimed, not always accurately, their latest Top Twenty disc. 'Janice's' peculiar magic was a thick Birmingham accent in which, awarding some new release maximum points, she would invariably say: 'Oi'll give it foive.'

A certain act on *Lucky Stars* that night had caused some perplexity to the show's producer, Philip Jones, and his set designer. Jones had kept his promise to his friend Dick James to book the Beatles in the same week that Please Please Me was released. Jones had not met them until the afternoon they arrived at ATV's Birmingham studios, after driving straight down from a tour of Scottish ballrooms. 'We'd no idea how to present them,' Jones says. 'In the end, we just gave up. We decided to put each one of them inside a big metal heart. It was obvious that the song, not our set, would be the thing that sold them.'

The four metal hearts framed a Pop group such as no British teenager south of Lancashire had ever seen before. Their hair was not blowwaved into a cockade; it fringed their eyes like the busbies of Grenadier guardsmen. Their suits buttoned up to the neck, completely concealing their ties. The front three figures did not, as was usual, step to and fro: they bounced and jigged with their guitar necks out of time. One, unprecedently, played a Spanish guitar; another held a bass guitar like a violin, its neck pointing in completely the wrong direction. All four compounded their eccentricity by refusing to look stern and moody, as Pop stars should, but by grinning broadly at the cameras and each other. The song they performed was largely inaudible, owing to the screams of the studio audience—all but for the moment where, with one extra zesty 'Whoa yeah', their voices toppled into falsetto. Then, six million snowbound British teenagers heard what George Martin, on his musician's stool, had heard; what Dick James in his Tin Pan Alley garret had heard; what Philip Jones had heard even down the telephone. It was the indefinable yet unmistakable sound of a 'Number One'.

The same week brought enthusiastic reviews of Please Please Me in the music trade Press. Keith Fordyce, a leading Radio Luxembourg disc jockey said in *New Musical Express* that Please Please Me was 'a really enjoyable platter, full of vigour and vitality'. The *World's Fair* thought the Beatles had 'every chance of becoming the big star attraction of 1963'. Brian Matthew, compere of *Thank Your Lucky Stars* and BBC radio's *Saturday Club*, and the country's most influential commentator on Pop music delivered the ultimate accolade, calling them 'musically and visually the most accomplished group to emerge since the Shadows'.

The national Press, however, still maintained an attitude of scornful indifference to teenagers and their music. One exception was the London *Evening Standard* which on Saturdays published a full page by its young Pop columnist, Maureen Cleave. A friend of Cleave's, the Liverpool-based journalist, Gillian Reynolds, had been urging her for months to come up and write something about the Beatles and the Cavern Club. Late in January, just as Please Please Me was about to enter the Top Ten, Maureen Cleave travelled to Liverpool to interview them for her *Evening Standard* page. On the train she met Vincent Mulchrone, the *Daily Mail*'s chief feature-writer, bound on the same assignment.

The Beatles were in Liverpool to play a one-nighter at the Grafton Ballroom before leaving on the Helen Shapiro package tour. Mulchrone and Maureen Cleave were taken by Brian to see the queues which, as usual, had formed outside the Grafton two hours in advance of opening-time. Some of the girls told Cleave they hadn't bought Love Me Do when it first appeared, for fear the Beatles would become famous, leave Liverpool and never return.

The interview which followed was like none Maureen Cleave had ever experienced before. 'The Beatles made me laugh immoderately, the way I used to laugh as a child at the *Just William* books. Their wit was just so keen and sharp—John Lennon's especially. They all had this wonderful quality—it wasn't innocence, but everything was new to them. They were like William, finding out about the world and trying to make sense of it.'

'John Lennon,' Maureen Cleave wrote, 'has an upper lip which is brutal in a devastating way. George Harrison is handsome, whimsical and untidy. Paul McCartney has a round baby face while Ringo Starr is ugly but cute. Their physical appearance inspires frenzy. They look beat-up and depraved in the nicest possible way.'

The piece caught the knockabout flavour of their conversation —John's threat, for instance, to lie down on the stage like Al Jolson during the Helen Shapiro tour, and Paul's rejoinder that he was too blind to see the audience anyway. In John Maureen Cleave found a fellow-devotee of the William stories. 'After the piece came out, John said to me, "You write like that woman who did the William books." For me, it was like being told one wrote like Shakespeare.'

They had been hired to tour with Helen Shapiro by Arthur Howes, the promoter who saw them die the death at Peterborough but who had, even so, kept an option with Brian to re-book them. This Howes now did, for a bottom-of-the-bill fee of £80 per week. The tour was to last throughout February, visiting theatres as far south as Taunton, Shrewsbury and, once again, Peterborough.

It was by no means one of Arthur Howe's major package tours. Helen Shapiro, who had enjoyed spectacular success as a 14-year-old schoolgirl, was now considered, at 16, to be somewhat past her best. The Beatles, at any rate, found her awesomely star-like with her chauffeur-driven car, her dressing-room TV set and constant, ferocious chaperonage.

She was, as it happened, a friendly girl who preferred to dodge her chauffeur and chaperone and travel with the Beatles and other small fry on the bus. Her chief memory is of snow, and John Lennon, next to her, pulling his cripple face at passers-by through a clear patch in the frosted window. 'He would never sit still—none of them could. They'd always be writing songs or fooling about or practising their autographs. Paul, I remember, used to practise his a lot. They didn't have any give-away photographs of themselves, so they used to practise signing across pictures of me.

'Paul was the PR. He was the one who came up to me on the tour and said, very nervous, "Er—we've written this song, we wonder if you'd like to do it. It was Misery." '

In Carlisle, after they had returned to their hotel, someone came up to Helen and invited her to a Young Conservatives' dance in progress in the hotel ballroom. Feeling cold and bored, she decided to accept. The Beatles also decided to accept. The Young Conservatives door steward saw them all coming down the corridor, taking long steps and snapping their fingers in chorus like a *West Side Story* 'Jets' routine. They got past the door steward but were then, stiffly, asked to leave. The Beatles' leather jackets had caused offence and outrage.

Next morning, the *Daily Express* reported that the famous schoolgirl Pop star Helen Shapiro had been ejected from a dance in Carlisle. Sympathy was entirely with the hotel, the Young Conservatives, and with the schoolgirl star herself, since the incident had obviously not been her fault. It was the leather jackets worn by her companions that gave the story the whiff of sordidness which was Fleet Street's only interest in printing stories about Pop musicians.

On 16 February, while they were still iced into the tour bus with Helen Shapiro, *Melody Maker*'s Top Twenty showed those reprehensible leather jacket wearers' record Please Please Me, at Number Two. That meant another journey south through the snow, to appear a second time on *Thank Your Lucky Stars*, on BBC radio's *Saturday Club* and EMI's own *Radio Luxembourg Show*. On 2 March, the snows were beginning to melt. *Melody Maker*'s chart showed Please Please Me at Number one. Brian spread the paper out on his desk in Liverpool, and Olive and Freda and everyone crowded round to look. It was true.

Liverpool could not believe it. Letters poured into the NEMS office, written on complete toilet rolls, on cardboard hearts four feet high, on cylinders of wallpaper. The fans treated it as their triumph. They celebrated with offerings of life-size cuddly toys, 'Good Luck' cakes from Sayer's, sacks of charm bracelets, brooches, eternity rings, jelly babies, even—from one fan with dockyard connections—a live tarantula in a specially-ventilated box. 'Luckily, I never opened it,' Freda Kelly says. 'I took one look inside the box and ran. Brian sent me out to find a home for it at the School of Tropical Medicine.'

In his third-floor front office, Brian Epstein sat, amid ringing telephones, with a pretence at coolness that, for once, deceived no one. 'I'd never seen him so excited,' Freda says. 'It was the first thing he said to anyone who rang up. "Have you heard about the boys?" If anyone came to see him, it was the first thing out of his mouth: "Have you heard about the boys?" '

George Martin heard the news with elation, but also deep thought. The Beatles were doing this week what the Kalin Twins had done in 1957, what the Allisons had done in 1960 and what the Brook Brothers had in 1961. Any A & R man could reel off a list of such 'one-hit wonders', raised to freakish fame on a single song, then instantly forgotten. Martin's concern was to capitalise on a success which, according to the statistics of the business, had only the smallest outside chance of happening twice.

The way you capitalised on a Number One single in 1962 was to rush-release an LP record of the same name. It was a simple, shameless catchpenny device to persuade the teenage public to buy the same song again, but at 30s instead of 6s 6d. For few, if any, listened to the supporting tracks, knowing all too well what they would be. They would be 'standards', hastily recorded in an insincere attempt to pass off some perishable, new, blow-waved zombie as an 'all round entertainer'.

Martin's instinct was that he could do something better with the Beatles' first LP. He was, after all, distinguished as a producer of 'live' stage recordings. His aim was to catch both the excitement of their stage performance and the melody, struggling to assert itself especially in Paul's part of the sound. He considered, but abandoned, the idea of 'live' taping at the Cavern. His gamble was that they would be able to pour out the excitement anywhere. 'What you're going to do,' he told them on 11 February at Abbey Road studios, 'is play me this selection of things I've chosen from what you do at the Cavern.'

In one 13-hour session, George Martin pushed them through enough songs to complete the 14-track LP. The numbers were those, like I Saw Her Standing There, which John and Paul had knocked up long ago to get them through a Hamburg night, mixed with American Soul songs like Chains and Baby It's You. Martin, once again, confined himself to editing, shaping, rearranging and dovetailing. He added a piano intro—played by himself—to Misery, and the double-tracking of Paul's voice through A Taste of Honey. George and Ringo, in fairness, were given the lead vocal on one song each. George's was a new Lennon–McCartney composition called Do You Want to Know a Secret? He sang it in thick Liverpudlian, barely managing its falsetto line. Ringo, with even less of a voice, still managed to give an infectious joy to Boys, the old Cavern show-stopper. The finale was Twist and Shout, the Isley Brothers song with which their stage act always closed. 'John absolutely screamed it,' Martin says. 'God knows what it did to his larynx because it made a sound like tearing flesh. That *had* to be right on the first take.'

It was the same performance they were giving each night in a different English town, on tour once again for the Arthur Howes Organisation. Howes had booked them—before Please Please Me reached Number One—for the same £80 per week they had got for the Helen Shapiro tour. By now, any promoter would have paid ten times that fee. Brian Epstein would not renege on his agreement with Arthur Howes.

Two American singers, Chris Montez and Tommy Roe, were supposed to be the tour's joint stars. It soon became obvious to Arthur Howes that neither was getting applause on the same scale as the Beatles. Their wages did not increase but their billing did. The running order was changed so that they, and Twist and Shout, closed the show each night.

On 22 March, the release of their album, Please Please Me, provoked fresh interest from the music papers. Even the Jazz-oriented *Melody Maker* welcomed what every reviewer agreed was not the usual cash-in LP dross but a run of songs each in its own way different and surprising. For the first time it became apparent that the Beatles were songwriters on a scale unknown among performers of Pop music. Record buyers, previously, had cared little about who *wrote* the songs they liked. On the back of the Please Please Me sleeve were helpful notes (by 'Disker', the *Liverpool Echo* columnist) detailing which of the songs were the Beatles' own and also acknowledging their debt to American groups like the Shirelles and songwriters like Goffin and King. The front cover photograph showed four figures in Burgundy-coloured stage suits, grinning cheerfully down from a balcony in what seemed to be a block of Council flats. No one seen in the Top Twenty since Tommy Steele had made so overt a declaration of being working class.

By now their personalities as well as their records were reaching a national public. Two BBC radio Pop shows, *Saturday Club* and *Easy Beat*, brought them to London during the Tommy Roe tour, to play in the studio what they were to play on stage this evening, a hundred miles away through the sleet and slush. In London, their faces were still unknown: they could walk as they pleased, with Dezo Hoffman their *Record Mirror* friend, around Shaftesbury Avenue and Berwick Market, and eat at Hoffman's favourite restaurant, the Budapest in Greek Street. Dezo also showed them how to work the new cameras he persuaded a Soho shop to give them in exchange for a signed photograph. Dezo Hoffman saw the same reaction everywhere that he had felt on his first trip up to Liverpool. The Beatles were something that Pop musicians had never been before. They were witty, lively, intelligent; they charmed and tickled and excited all who met them. Brian Matthew, the *Saturday Club* compere, strove in vain to keep up his usual BBC manner against John Lennon's devastating ad libs. 'I was introducing them on one show, going through the usual thing of asking them about the music. I'd just come back from holiday in Spain. As I was talking, John leaned across and said into the microphone, "Brian's nose is peeling, folks." '

To George Martin, John was like a precocious child, only half-aware of the joltingly funny things he said. 'I remember we were having dinner out one night, and the waiter brought *mange-tout* peas. John had very evidently never seen such a thing before, but I said he ought to try them. "All right then," he said, "but put them over there, not near the food." '

Brian Epstein, too, was spending much of every week in London. His father could hardly object to that now. The Whitechapel record shop ran smoothly under Peter Brown's management, and the office upstairs, in Olive Johnson's charge. Olive was the McCartney family friend whom Paul's father had first consulted about Brian. She had afterwards left her job with the Law Society to join NEMS Enterprises as his 'personal assistant'.

In London he still had no base other than his favourite hotel, the Grosvenor House. 'He'd walk into my office,' Dick James says, 'and tell me he'd been offered this date for the Beatles at £200. I'd say: "Tell 'em to double it." Brian would come back in amazement and say, "It worked." "Next time," I'd say, "tell 'em to double that figure again." '

In early 1963, a South London impresario could still book the Beatles for £30 to play for dancing at Wimbledon Palais. Brian's chief concern seems to have been to ensure them a full summer's work, even if the follow-up record to Please Please Me did not get into the charts. One of his arrangements was with Larry Parnes—still Britain's principal Pop impresario—to put them into a series of Sunday concerts at the end of Great Yarmouth pier. But Parnes would pay only £30 and Brian wanted £75. Parnes says: 'Brian told me that if I'd go to that, I could have an option to do shows with the Beatles and all the other NEMS acts for the next five years. In the end, he came down from £75 to £35. I went up to £32. I wouldn't budge and neither would he.'

NEMS Enterprises, Brian decided, must have solicitors in London as well as Liverpool. Characteristically, he chose the most expensive and fashionable of West End law firms specialising in show business clients. The Beatles were now on the books of M. A. Jacobs of Pall Mall, in company with such illustrious past litigants as Marlene Dietrich and Liberace. The firm's senior partner, David Jacobs, was himself a fashionable figure, to be seen tirelessly ministering to his clients' needs at the Savoy or Dorchester. He was, like Brian, cultivated, immaculate, Jewish and a homosexual.

Already, a spot of bother had arisen which required urgent consultation with David Jacobs. The owner of a Gross Freiheit club was threatening to hold a Beatle responsible for his daughter's current pregnancy. Jacobs referred the matter to counsel, who advised a quick settlement. It was the first of countless such claims, consultations, visits to counsel and recommendations to settle out of Court. With David Jacobs, Brian formed a shield around the Beatles that would not be lifted so long as he or Jacobs remained alive.

Early in March, every national and provincial newspaper in Britain received a publicity handout announcing the record debut of a second group managed by NEMS Enterprises. Journalists who bothered to read the handout learned that the group was called Gerry and the Pacemakers, that it recorded on EMI's Columbia label, that it shared the same management as another successful group, the Beatles, and that it came from the same city, Liverpool. For the first time since its birth in Britain's industrial dawn, Liverpool was deliberately invoked as a source of excitement, glamour and novelty.

Brian Epstein was hardly the first to see potential in Gerry Marsden, the ex-messenger boy from Ringo Starr's neighbourhood who had led a successful group on Merseyside since 1958. But no one before Brian had taken the trouble to harness Gerry's boundless energy, nor to dress him in a suit instead of sweaters and jeans, and stop him smoking Woodbines, and tell him to 'project'.

Gerry's first single was How Do You Do It! the song which the Beatles had rejected in favour of Please Please Me. He and the Pacemakers came across from Hamburg to record it, in blissful unawareness that the mutinous John Lennon version was anything other than a helpful demo'. Gerry Marsden's jaunty treatment confirmed what George Martin had said all along—the number was a natural hit. It reached Number One on 22 March. The music papers realised that two hits from the same source constituted a 'sound'. From now on there was constant reference to the Liverpool or the Mersey Sound.

The Beatles' third Parlophone single, From Me To You, released on 12 April, had a similarly stylish publicity send-off. The smallest local paper in Britain received the NEMS handout, written by Tony Barrow and designed much as Brian used to draw up his posters for dances at New Brighton Tower. Instead of the usual glossy studio pose, the Beatles were shown with their instruments on the deck of a Mersey tugboat. Underneath was Brian Matthew's declaration that they were 'visually and musically the most exciting group since the Shadows.'

The song had been written by John and Paul on the bus

during the Helen Shapiro tour. It was Please Please Me, a little slower, with the falsetto repositioned. It received fairly lukewarm reviews. Most of the music papers thought they had 'gone off' since Please Please Me. Keith Fordyce said the new record was not even as interesting as Love Me Do.

On 27 April, From Me To You was Number One, well on the way to selling half a million copies and earning a Silver Disc. How Do You Do It! by Gerry and the Pacemakers was still at Number Three. Everyone who watched television or listened to radio in Britain had heard of the Mersey Sound.

Four days earlier, in Sefton General Hospital, Liverpool, Cynthia Lennon had given birth to a son. The labour was long and painful; the delivery became complicated when the umbilical cord was found to be wrapped round the baby's neck. His father knew nothing of these anxieties, being still out on tour in the Chris Montez show. Not until a week later did John visit Cynthia, and even then he had to wear a crude disguise to avoid the fans waiting outside. He held his son in his arms, watched by a grinning crowd through the glass cubicle wall.

The baby was called Julian, the nearest John could get to his mother's name, Julia. For Julia had died at Sefton General after the accident outside Mimi's house, that summer day in 1958, when 'Twitchy' the waiter had stood and wept but he himself could feel nothing but mindless curses.

His obvious delight in Julian encouraged Cynthia to visions of happy domesticity in Woolton, where they were to have the whole ground floor of Mimi's house. The visions evaporated when John told her that Brian Epstein had asked him to go away on holiday to Spain. Cynthia, recognising that she had no real say in the matter, assented with a show of cheerfulness.

This holiday, in May 1963, was Brian's first and only public declaration of his feelings towards John. It was made in the euphoria of seeing two of his groups in the Top Twenty, when all other impediment to happiness seemed to have been swept away; why not this last intractable one? Close friends like Olive Johnson advised against it, in vain. The two of them flew off to Brian's holiday haunts, leaving Liverpool to gossip as it pleased and Cynthia to take care of the baby.

Recently, Brian's attention had become focused on another, far more conventionally beautiful young man. Billy Ashton—or Kramer as he was known in the dance halls—led a group of Bootle boys called the Coasters, rated third in *Mersey Beat* newspaper's popularity league. Brian paid £50 to acquire Billy from his original manager, an elderly gentleman named Ted Knibbs who had rehearsed the nervous Adonis by making him sing, standing on a chair.

Billy J. Kramer, with the new suits and initial letter which Brian Epstein had bestowed on him, was then brought to London for a recording test by George Martin at Parlophone. Martin gave his opinion that, for the first time, Brian had made a mistake. Though the youth was undoubtedly good looking, his voice was erratic and his personal magnetism rather slight. Brian, however, insisted that 'my Billy' should be allowed to record.

Billy J. was duly taped, backed by a Manchester group the Dakotas, singing the Lennon—McCartney ballad, Do You Want To Know A Secret? If George Harrison's voice had cracked on the falsetto line, Billy J. Kramer's broke into smithereens. George Martin had the worst of it by double-tracking the vocal and filling in the cracks with his own piano accompaniment. The record was released on 26 April; by mid-May every Top Ten chart showed it at Number Two.

That Brian had no idea of what the Beatles were already becoming is amply shown by his activities with NEMS Enterprises during the summer of 1963. Formerly, his desire had been to become a Beatle; to merge his existence, if only spiritually, with theirs. Now he began to see them merely as brand-leaders in an empire of Liverpool artists, founded and ruled over paternalistically by himself. One of the NEMS handouts, indeed, showed all of them, the Beatles, Gerry and Billy J., the Pacemakers and Dakotas, as disembodied heads encircling Brian's in a schoolmasterly mortar-board.

By June, he had signed up the Big Three and the Four Jays, another popular Cavern group, with 22 O-level passes between them, now renamed the Fourmost. He wanted a ballad singer to complement all the groups: Tommy Quigley, a little freckle-faced boy he had seen at the Queen's Hall, Widnes, was even now being groomed, as Tommy Quickly, to fulfil that destiny. One group he was dissuaded from signing was Lee Curtis and the All Stars, even though their manager was his great friend Joe Flannery. The Beatles vetoed the idea, apparently because Lee Curtis, Joe's brother, was too handsome. When the two groups appeared together, Paul McCartney would never sing any songs that Lee Curtis had in his repertoire.

NEMS Enterprises now had a London office and the services of a full-time publicity man. Tony Barrow, in fact, had been industriously writing handouts for Brian since late 1962, still carrying on his PR work for Decca and his 'Disker' column in the *Liverpool Echo*. Brian's offer of £36 per week was exactly double what Barrow earned as a freelance. Another young publicity man, Andrew Oldham, lent him some newspaper names and addresses to copy out in exchange for a 1s 9d lunch. Barrow used

Oldham's office in Poland Street before moving to his own poky first-floor suite in Monmouth Street, Seven Dials.

One of Tony Barrow's first jobs was to reorganise the Beatles' Fan Club, which Freda Kelly still ran from the NEMS office in Liverpool. Freda could no longer cope with the applications for membership, running into tens of thousands, and the sack of letters, inscribed toilet rolls, soft toys and other Beatle-inspired greetings which poured daily into her office and her home. Tony Barrow divided the Club into a northern region, run by Freda in Liverpool, and a southern region, run from Monmouth Street by a girl named Bettina Rose. It was Barrow's idea to invent a National Secretary, 'Anne Collingham', whose duplicated signature appeared on every newsletter. To girls all over the British Isles, 'Anne Collingham' was real, and revered as an intermediary between their idols and them. To Brian Epstein, it was all a harmless exercise, done for PR purposes and likely to peter out at any moment.

More signs to the contrary could be read on the tour the Beatles were now making, with Gerry and the Pacemakers and the American Country and Western star, Roy Orbison. For the first time, thanks to their record success, they were top of the bill, and deeply uneasy about it. As Orbison performed, chinless and tragic, the Beatles would stand in the wings, wondering how they would dare to follow him. Somehow, they did dare, and the scream arose that was the same in Slough, in Southampton, in Southend, Cardiff and Worcester, the same scream, instantaneous and uncritical, although they did not realise this and continued to play with all their might. Out of the scream came hails of jelly babies, because George had said somewhere that he liked them.

Until now they had been looked after single-handedly by Neil Aspinall, the one-time accountancy student whom they had met through Pete Best. Brian, for the first three tours, placed absolute reliance on Neil. It was he who drove them from town to town; carried in their guitars and amplifiers, and saw that they had food, sleep and stage suits, if necessary tending to the latter with a portable iron. Brusque and hollow-cheeked, with hair already thinning, Neil—or 'Nell' as the Beatles called him—was both friend and servant, their equal, yet their errand boy.

In May 1963, after overwork had reduced Neil's weight by three stone, Brian took on Mal Evans as assistant road manager. Mal was a hefty Liverpudlian, formerly employed as a Post Office engineer and part-time Cavern Club bouncer. Despite his size, he was gentle, amiable and filled with the romance of Rock and Roll. At 28 he was noticeably older than the Beatles and Neil; he was married, with a new-born baby son. 'He had a lot of sleepless nights, wondering if he should go on with them,' his widow, Lil Evans, says. 'I didn't want him to. I told him, "You're a person in your own right—you don't need to follow others." But he was star-struck.'

John's Aunt Mimi, having been a seagoing pilot's daughter, did her best to cope with the growing chaos of life at 'Mendips'. Though Cynthia and the baby were living downstairs, all Mimi had seen of John for weeks were the suitcases of sodden stage shirts he would leave for Cyn' and her to wash. The telephone rang continuously; at the front gate there was a permanent picket of girls. 'And if I left the back door open,' Mimi says, 'there wouldn't be a teacup or a saucer left in the kitchen.'

In Speke, Harry and Louise Harrison faced similar problems in their little Council house. The fans were there when Harry left for work in the morning; they queued at the bus stop, hoping to stop his bus. In the Dingle, little Elsie Gleave was frankly bewildered by what had happened to her Ritchie. One minute he was on the dole; the next, he had so much money, his mother wondered if it was all quite honest. 'I remember her coming to me in a terrible state,' Olive Johnson says, 'because she'd found pound notes left all over Ringo's dressing table. He didn't have a bank account until Brian opened one for him.'

Because of the siege of fans at Forthlin Road, Paul's 21st birthday, on 18 June, had to be celebrated at his Auntie Jin's in Birkenhead. The large family party was swelled by John Lennon and Cynthia, Ringo and his girl friend Maureen, George, Brian, Bob Wooler, and Roger McGough and John Gorman, two would-be poets who formed the Scaffold trio with Paul's younger brother, Michael. It was, as Paul had wanted, a typical Liverpool booze-up, riotous and noisy, with children underfoot and Rock and Roll and Jim McCartney's piano renditions of sentimental evergreen songs. John Lennon got into a fight with another guest, beating him up so severely that a payment for damages followed.

Liverpool was currently undergoing a hectic visitation by London A & R men, all eager to sign up their own Beatles and Pacemakers. In July, the Pye label released Sweets for My Sweet by the Searchers, long resident at the Iron Door Club. When Sweets For My Sweet went to Number One, the A & R invasion of Liverpool became positively desperate. Any group would do so long as it talked Scouse, played Rhythm and Blues, buttoned its jackets high and combed its hair forward. The man from Oriole signed Faron's Flamingoes, Rory Storm and the Hurricanes, Earl Preston and the TT's; the Fontana man took the Merseybeats and Howie Casey and the Seniors; the Decca man took Lee Curtis and Kingsize Taylor; the Pye man took the Undertakers and the Chants.

Brian Epstein, a wavy-haired young man whom wise A & R

men had once advised to stick to his record shop, was the cynosure of hungry, incredulous eyes. In June, Gerry Marsden was again Number One with I Like It. In July, Billy J. Kramer did the same with Bad To Me, another Lennon—McCartney song, skilfully doctored by George Martin. At one point, the first three Top Ten places were occupied by NEMS acts—Gerry, Billy J. Kramer and the Beatles' From Me To You. To this day, no other Pop impresario has matched the achievement.

In August, to lessen disruption at the Whitechapel shop, Brian moved NEMS Enterprises to Moorfields, a couple of streets away, near the old Liverpool Exchange station. The new offices, situated above a joke shop, had a 'reception area' which could be decorated with blow-up photographs of all the NEMS acts. Freda Kelly's friend, a deep-voiced Irish girl named Laurie McCaffery, was taken on as receptionist and switchboard operator. Another new arrival was Tony Bramwell, George Harrison's childhood friend, as office boy.

The Beatles were doing what all Pop groups hoped for in summer. They were at the South Coast resort of Margate, appearing with Gerry and the Pacemakers at the Winter Gardens theatre. Dezo Hoffman came down from London to photograph them in their swimming trunks and socks, sunbathing on the terrace of their modest seafront hotel. They did not look like a group with the country's best-selling single *and* album. Hoffman also filmed them, as he had in Liverpool, this time skylarking on the beach in Victorian bathing suits from which their arms and legs emerged, pure white from their cellar and night-time life. A sequence was taken of Ringo Starr alone, standing on a low stone wall, looking, a little bewildered, into the sun. 'He was not a full Beatle yet; he told me that,' Hoffman says. 'He was still only getting a salary.'

Another visitor was Peter Jones, a *Record Mirror* journalist, accompanied by a man named Sean O'Mahoney, who hoped to do a business deal with Brian. O'Mahoney published *Beat Monthly*, a fan magazine devoted to the new 'beat' groups suddenly all over London and the South. Brian had agreed to let him start a separate publication dealing exclusively with the Beatles and their fan club. 'What are you going to find to write about us every month?' Paul McCartney asked him.

They had already been to Abbey Road studios to record their fourth Parlophone single for George Martin. The song was one that John and Paul had dashed off in a hurry in their hotel room, three nights before. They played it to Martin as usual on their acoustic Gibson guitars; and as usual Martin had an editorial suggestion to make. Instead of beginning with the first verse, he said, they ought to go directly into the chorus—She Loves You, and so on.

He also told them their ending was corny; that Glenn Miller used to end with a Major Sixth, the chord their voices had stumbled on. But that bit could stay. If anything sold She Loves You, George Martin thought, it would be the first five-second chorus—the 'Yeah, yeah, yeah'.

Britain, that wet and windy summer, had been enjoying a sex scandal unrivalled since the reign of Edward VII. A Cabinet Minister, John Profumo, holding no less an office than Conservative Secretary of State for War, had been caught out in a sexual liaison with a 22-year-old 'model' named Christine Keeler. The affair was enriched by Miss Keeler's extremely wide circle of men friends, which included sundry West Indians; a property racketeer; a seedy osteopath named Stephen Ward; and—most piquant of all—the Naval attaché at the Russian Embassy in London. It was the possibility that Britain's War Minister shared the same courtesan as a Russian spy which drew Secret Service attention finally to Profumo's sexual habits. Questioned in Parliament, he at first denied the impropriety; then—faced with imminent Police and Press disclosures—he admitted that he had 'misled' the House of Commons.

The Profumo Affair provided Fleet Street with a saga of almost infinite dimensions. From the unhappy Minister, an avenue of scandal stretched in one direction to the Notting Hill slums, where Keeler's ex-lover, Peter Rachman, would set dogs on his unco-operative tenants; in the other direction, it implicated the cream of British aristocracy, the Astor family, on whose Cliveden estate Profumo had made his fatal acquaintanceship. By midsummer, all Britain seethed with rumours of sexual perversion on every level of public life. It was variously claimed that another Cabinet Minister had been caught receiving fellatio in public; that 'up to eight' High Court judges had been involved in a sex orgy; and that at a fashionable dinner-party, one of the country's most eminent politicians had waited at table, naked and masked, with a placard around his neck reading: 'If my services don't please you, whip me.'

Months passed, the summer worsened, the Profumo Affair ran on, and on. Christine Keeler disappeared, then reappeared. Profumo resigned in disgrace. Stephen Ward was arrested for living off immoral earnings. A friend of Keeler's, a fellow model named Mandy Rice-Davies, became practically as famous. Every newspaper front page, day after day, steamed with the torrid, frequently horrid, doings of Christine Keeler and Mandy Rice-Davies. And gradually the surfeit of sex and scandal passed the limit which even the British public could absorb. Attention moved away from Profumo and on to the Prime Minister who had so indolently accepted the lie of his fellow aristocrat. Harold

Macmillan, after 11 years in office, was re-examined in a new and searching light. What it revealed was scarcely credible as a twentieth-century politician. A dusty old man in a walrus moustache hummed and hawed in the accent which had ruled Britain for a thousand years, but which now signified only complacency, crassness and the natural conspiracy between men who shared the same public school and club.

No newspaper will ever admit to there being too much news. But to Fleet Street, in the summer of 1963, that condition was perilously close. Stephen Ward committed suicide on the eve of his trial; then, five days later, a second colossal story broke. A mail train on its way from Scotland to London was waylaid and robbed of £2½ m, the largest haul in criminal history. The pursuit of the robbers was displaced as front page news only by Macmillan's belated resignation and the strife within the Tory party concerning his successor. By the end of September, every editor in Fleet Street was longing for a diversion from this incessant heavy news—something light; something unconnected with the aristocratic classes; something harmless, blameless and, above all, cheerful.

The *Daily Mirror* found the answer first. The *Mirror*, it so happens, belongs to the same publishing group as *Melody Maker*, Britain's oldest-established music newspaper. On 11 September, *Melody Maker* announced the results of a poll among its readers to find the year's most popular record artists. The Beatles—who had barely scraped into the 1962 poll—came out as top British group. Billy J. Kramer was named in the same poll as 'Brightest Hope for 1964'.

As well as a fraternal story about the poll, the *Mirror* ran a two-page profile of the Beatles by its acerbic show-business columnist, Donald Zec. Under the headline 'Four Frenzied Little Lord Fauntleroys Who Are Earning £5,000 a Week,' Zec described the scenes he had witnessed among young girls at a Beatles concert in Luton, Bedfordshire. He afterwards had the Beatles to tea at his flat, an ordeal which they survived with high spirits enough to drain all vitriol from the columnist's pen. They were, Donald Zec said, 'as nice a group of well-mannered music makers as you'll find perforating the eardrum anywhere'.

Other papers, too, were awakening to the existence of a population whose chief interest was not compromised Cabinet Ministers but a particular 'Pop' record—as sub-editors still rendered it—whose wild 'Yeah yeah yeah' chorus kept piercing the summer static. For She Loves You, having gone straight to Number One on advance orders of half a million copies, was still there, almost two months after its release. Radio disc jockeys like Brian Matthew no longer even bothered to announce it. 'Do you realise,' Matthew frequently inquired of his listeners, 'how many songs in the current Top Ten are written by, if not sung by, the Beatles?'

To Brian Epstein, this was still no more than a facet of success on every front. Brian's big autumn project was the launch of NEMS Enterprises' first female artiste. Priscilla White, the Cavern Club's gawky cloakroom girl, now renamed Cilla Black, was to be, not a discovery like the Beatles and Gerry but a *creation*, wrought by Brian's own feminine taste. For weeks, he had lavished attention on Cilla; on her clothes, her hair, her makeup. He had taken her to George Martin, and Martin—privately thinking her a 'Cavern screamer'—had recorded her singing the Lennon–McCartney song Love of the Loved. Tony Barrow, in Monmouth Street, was producing the usual stylish NEMS Press release, describing Cilla's recherchée taste for wearing men's jeans, and relaying Cavern Club slang like 'gear', 'fab' and 'endsville'.

On 13 October, the Beatles were due to appear on British television's top-rated variety programme, *Sunday Night at the London Palladium.* The show went out 'live' on Sunday nights from the famous old, gilt-crusted theatre, in Argyll Street, just off Oxford Circus. In form it was straight music hall, with jugglers, trampolinists, a 'Beat the Clock' interlude in which members of the audience underwent ritual self-humiliation, and finally a top of the bill act which was quite likely to be the Pop singing sensation of the moment. At the end, the entire cast stood on a revolving platform among chorus girls and giant letters spelling out SUNDAY NIGHT AT THE LONDON PALLADIUM.

News of the engagement had circulated among Beatle fans and there were girls waiting in Argyll Street that Sunday morning when the Beatles arrived at the Palladium to rehearse. Dezo Hoffman, who accompanied them, remembers 'about eight girls. The car drew up—we went inside, no trouble'. Since rehearsals lasted all day, the Beatles were provided with a roast lamb lunch in their dressing-room. While they were eating it, a group of girls ran into the auditorium and had to be ejected.

The show that night broke all precedent by putting on its top-of-the-bill act first, for a few seconds only. Bruce Forsyth, the compere, then appeared and stuck out his long chin. 'If you want to see them again,' Forsyth taunted, 'they'll be back in 42 minutes.' That final, short, inaudible performance, before they hurried aboard the revolving stage, was watched by an audience of 15 million.

Next morning, every mass-circulation British newspaper carried a front-page picture and story of 'riots' by Beatle fans outside the London Palladium. 'Police fought to hold back 1,000 squealing teenagers,' the *Daily Mirror* said, 'as the Beatles made their getaway after their Palladium TV show.' Both the *Daily Mail* and *Daily Express* had pictures of the four Beatles peeping out in supposed dread of a mob this time said to number 500. 'A Police motorcade stood by,' the *Mirror* continued, 'as the four Pop idols dashed for their car. Then the fans went wild, breaking through a cordon of more than 60 Policemen' (20, the *Express* said). 'With engines racing, the cavalcade roared down Argyll Street and turned into Oxford Circus, heading for a celebration party at the Grosvenor House hotel.'

This official outbreak of Beatlemania in Britain has certain puzzling aspects. In every case, the published photograph of that '1,000 squealing teenagers' was cropped in so close that only three or four could be seen. The *Daily Mail* alone published a wide-angle shot—Paul McCartney and Neil Aspinall emerging from the Palladium, watched by one policeman and two girls.

'There were *no* riots,' Dezo Hoffman says. 'I was there. Eight girls we saw—even less than eight. Later on, the road managers were sent out to find the Beatles a girl each, and there were *none*.'

November 1963

'Even the jelly babies are symbolic'

In 1963, the simple fact was, Britain's population had become unbalanced by a vast surplus of people under 18. The decline in infant mortality, together with the mysterious non-appearance of a Third World War, had allowed an entire generation to grow up virtually intact. They were the babies born after 1945 and raised in a Britain struggling to transform itself from postwar drabness to the material wellbeing so long observed and envied in America. Cars, radio sets, washing machines, all the luxuries still cherished by their parents, were, to these young people, simply the mundane furniture of life. Television spread the whole world before them, to be casually viewed and judged. In 1960, the kindly Macmillan Government abolished National Service. For those between 16 and 21, no obligation remained save that of spending their ever-increasing pocket money on the amusements demanded by their ever-quickening glands.

Pop music was the most obvious sign of youth's growing economic power. What had begun in 1956 as a laughable, disreputable adolescent outburst was now an industry turning over £100m each year. The attitude to 'teenagers' remained largely unchanged: they were, as in 1956, a puzzling, fractious element of the population, endlessly deplored and advised by politicians, headmasters and clergymen. They were also a market, undreamed of in size and potential, to be wooed and cajoled by the retail trade at every level.

The British teenage girl of early 1963 faithfully reflected what numerous commercial forces battled for her weekly pay packet. Her hair, teased up into a huge, hollow 'bouffant', represented hours at the salon and in arduous private backcombing and curling. Her face was a deathly white, with Woolworth's 'Minors' makeup, save for her two, huge, coal-black 'Dusty Springfield' eyes. Her dress, tight-bodiced, ballooned with stiff petticoats given extra stiffness by soaking in sugar and water. Her shoes, matching her handbag, were white, with Italian 'winkle-picker' points and stiletto heels banned as a destructive agent from so many ballroom floors.

Her boy friend, with whom she did not yet sleep, still more strongly expressed youth's new visual diversity. He might be a 'Mod', with high-buttoned jacket, pin-collar shirt, small trilby hat and Vespa motor scooter. He might be a 'Rocker', with motorcycle, black leather and tattoos. The two factions had sprung up in 1963, simultaneously and with instant mutual loathing. All that summer, in innocent seaside resorts like Clacton and Margate, their set-piece battles had surged back and forth, trampling daytrippers, deck chairs and children's sand castles.

In autumn, the Mod-Rocker war was eclipsed by a new kind of teenage excess that was not new but was louder and wilder than Britain had ever known it before. Television and cinema newsreels added live pictures to those appearing daily in all the national papers. The sequence showed girls in their hollow-spun bouffants and spectral makeup, their black eyes running in rivulets down their faces. The sound was of incessant screaming.

Girls had screamed for Pop stars before, but never quite like this. Never—as they did at the Beatles' ABC, Cambridge concert—hunched into a foetal position, alternately punching their sides, covering their eyes and stuffing handkerchieves and fists into their mouths. Later, when the curtain had fallen and the last dazed girl had been led through the Exits, a further difference from the screams that greeted Valentino became manifest. Hundreds of the cinema seats were wringing wet. Many had puddles of urine beneath them.

Such scenes had been commonplace for six months already: the difference now was that newspapers reported them. Fleet Street had realised that the Beatles were more than a momentary diversion—they were a running story of guaranteed reader interest. The riots faked in Argyll Street were to be seen, ten times more spectacularly, along the route of their current package tour. On 26 October in Carlisle—the small border town they had last seen as nobodies with Helen Shapiro—600 fans queued for 36 hours to buy tickets. When the box office opened, the queue moved forward with such eagerness that shop windows gave way; nine people had to be taken to hospital.

Fleet Street's initial line was simply reporting on the girls' hysteria. It changed the moment someone took the trouble to visit the Beatles' dressing-room. There, in the tiny space hemmed in by teacups and stage suit bags, the 'Street' men found what every journalist craves and what he will distort the plainest fact to manufacture—good 'quotes'. When John and Paul sat down, strumming their guitars, smoking and half-tinkering song lyrics, no one had to invent the dialogue.

'How long do you think the group will last, John?'

'About five years.'

'Are those wigs you're wearing?'

'If they are, they must be the only wigs with dandruff.'

'What kind of guitar is that, Paul?'

'It's a Hofner violin bass. Here, take a look.' The bass—now widely copied by other groups—would be tossed into the startled questioner's lap.

'Are they expensive?'

'Fifty-six guineas. I could afford a better one but I'm a skinflint.'

Ringo, still unsure of himself, would be coaxed forward to say a mordant word or two. If asked why he wore so many rings on his fingers, he replied it was because he couldn't get them all through his nose. 'I don't like talking. Some people gab all day and some people play it smogo. I haven't got a smiling face or a talking mouth.'

George, unless specially asked for, would remain apart, his hollow face cupped in a high black polo neck, his eyes under the Beatle fringe not happy. He would tune guitars assiduously, John's as well as his own, despite knowing they had not the remotest chance of being heard. Even at this early stage, the fan uproar, the flailing screams and toys and jelly babies were a source of detestation to him.

Certain journalists, on the strength of past favours, were excluded from the brusque moments when Neil Aspinall, at a secret signal, would clear the Beatles' dressing-room of the Press. Maureen Cleave from the *Evening Standard* was one such: John Lennon called her 'the Just William woman'. Another was Ray Coleman, from *Melody Maker*. The Beatles liked 'MM' because it troubled to discuss their musicianship as well as the riots. Coleman, a quiet, clerkly figure, would stand in the wings, telling John the words of songs which, even though John himself had written them, he could barely remember from day to day. Usually, when he ran on stage, the words would be written on the back of his hand.

Peter Jones, of *Record Mirror*, found himself in the most difficult position. Jones had written the first article about the Beatles in a national publication; he was now contributor-in-chief to their fan magazine, *Beatles Monthly*. He was at once privy to their most intimate moments and sworn to secrecy concerning all that might have shown them, not as cuddly toys but ordinary, imperfect human beings.

Such were the values of 1963, the teenage magazines had no objection to publishing pictures of the Beatles smoking and gesturing with cigarettes. But on other matters, Peter Jones had to remain silent. He could say nothing about the hatred they already felt for performing night after night, and how Neil Aspinall sometimes literally chased them from their dressing-room into the wings. Jones could not mention the rows they frequently had with one another, or with Brian. Nor, in all conscience, could he refer to the 'girl scene' which was a constant feature of their progress round Britain and which, owing to the limitations of dressing-room life, was usually carried on in some adjacent washroom or toilet.

'At times,' Peter Jones says, 'they could pick on someone for a kind of corporate cruelty that was absolutely merciless. Down on the South Coast, there was this old journalist who went into the swimming pool with them while some photographs were being taken. All four of them really set on this quite elderly guy —pretending it was all fun, but it wasn't. They were so rough with him, they actually broke one of his toes.'

Such stories, if written, would not have been printed. Fleet Street had settled on its view of the Beatles—the four happy-go-lucky Liverpool lads who looked absurd, but knew it, and whose salty one-line witticisms seemed to epitomise the honesty of the working classes, blowing through the seedy lies of the Profumo upper crust. 'You *had* to write it that way,' an ex-*Daily Mirror* man says. 'You knew that if you didn't, the *Sketch* would and the *Express* would and the *Mail* and the *Standard* would. You were writing in self-defence.'

Within a week of the London Palladium Show, Britain's attitude to the Beatles had completely changed. No longer were they just a silly Pop group which incited teenagers to be even sillier than usual. They were also, unprecedently, endowed with wit and intelligence. Whatever the prejudice engendered by their hair and clothes, it vanished as soon as their voices began to speak, in what was half-remembered, through ages of music hall and radio, as comedy's natural dialect:

'None of us has quite grasped wharrit's all about yet. It's washin' over our 'eads like a yuge tidal wave—'

'—I don't s'pose I think mooch about the future. Though, now we have made it, it would be a pity to get bombed—'

'I get spasms of being intellectual. I read a bit about politics. But I don't think I'd vote for anyone. No message from those phoney politicians is coomin' through to me.'

'—We've always 'ad laughs. Sometimes we find ourselves gettin' hysterical, especially when we're tired. We laugh at soft things that other people don't get—we call it "The Cruelies"—'

'Is it true that you were turned down by Decca?'

'A guy at Decca turned us down.'

'He must be kicking himself now.'

'I 'ope he kicks himself to death.'

On 16 October, an announcement was made which both confirmed their new status beyond any doubt and brought Fleet Street northward in a still more maddened pursuit. The Beatles had been chosen to appear in the Royal Command Variety Performance in London on 4 November. Bernard Delfont, the organiser, told reporters he had picked them on the insistence of his 10-year-old daughter. Buckingham Palace, to which the list went for approval, offered no objection.

Late in October, Brian Epstein moved his entire organisation from Liverpool to London. 'It happened at about a week's notice,' Tony Bramwell says. 'Eppy walked in and said he was going south—were we coming?' Tony, Alistair Taylor, Laurie McCaffery the switchboard girl, immediately went home to pack. Freda Kelly's father refused to let her go, although she pleaded. Almost the entire staff managed to reassemble itself in London to greet Brian when he arrived, looking as if he had expected nothing else.

The new NEMS office was in Argyll Street, only a few doors away from the London Palladium. Brian drew great satisfaction from the imminence of this theatrical monument. He drew equal satisfaction from his new cable address: Nemperor, London. It was Bob Wooler, the Cavern's pun-loving disc jockey, who had once said to him on the telephone, 'Is that the Nemperor?'

Brian now had his own London flat, in a fashionable block in William Mews, Knightsbridge. One of the first people he took there was Brian Sommerville, an old friend of his who had recently left the Royal Navy and was now working in Fleet Street. 'The flat was very Brian,' Sommerville says, 'all white walls and black leather cushions. While I was there, he showed me a proof of the Beatles' new LP cover. He was already starting to suggest that we might work together.'

Once installed in the new flat, Brian began to entertain lavishly. David Jacobs, his solicitor, had introduced him to many of the show-business celebrities for whom Jacob's firm also acted. He developed a particular friendship with Lionel Bart, the East End ex-skiffler who had won, and was rapidly losing, a fortune as a composer of West End musicals. He loved all 'show people' and in their cocktail chatter found a measure of security. Show people did not care who was, or was not 'gay'.

He had, as his success grew more hectic, placed increasing reliance on David Jacobs and on his accountants, Bryce, Hanmer and Isherwood of Albemarle Street, Mayfair. Bryce, Hanmer were, in fact, a Liverpool firm whose London office made a speciality of theatrical clients. Dr. Walter Strach, one of the firm's senior members, a gaunt and melancholy Czech, thus found himself, in late 1963, charged with the responsibility of finding London accommodation for all four of the Beatles. Total secrecy was maintained, to evade the fans and to keep the rents within reason.

For John and Cynthia, Dr. Strach found a flat in Emperor's Gate, Kensington, the top floor of a Georgian house in the rather dismal bedsitter region behind West London Air Terminal. Thanks to the almost psychic powers of detection bestowed on Beatle fans, the hideaway became instantly and universally known. Girls waited all day, as well as most of the night, around the pilastered front porch, even venturing into the hallway, if the front door was left open, to settle down with blankets, sleeping bags and vacuum flasks. Across the road was a student hostel with a balcony that looked directly into the Lennons' flat. Whenever Cyn' looked, she would see figures hanging over the balcony and waving. Six flights up, without a lift, she spent days at a time, with baby Julian, in conscientious isolation, keeping her vow of non-existence even when the nearby Air Terminal caught fire.

George and Ringo moved together into a flat lower down in the William Mews block where Brian lived. Old ladies, carrying Pekinese dogs, looked askance at the girls who instantaneously took up station on the front steps. Brian himself was torn between proprietorial pleasure and a fear that George and Ringo might 'find out' what, in any case, they had known about him for years. Even when he asked them to one of his 'gay' parties, he seems to have hoped they would view the all-male gathering as no more than coincidence. 'Do you think they noticed?' he later anxiously asked a friend.

As to the living arrangements of Paul McCartney, not even the most tenacious journalistic 'doorstepper' could hazard a guess. Whereas George and Ringo's address, like John's would invariably be specified in newspaper reports, Paul, since leaving the President Hotel, could only be said ambiguously to be living at 'an address in Central London'.

Four months earlier, at a Pop concert in the Albert Hall, the Beatles had met a young actress called Jane Asher, herself on the way to becoming a celebrity through her appearances on the BBC TV show *Juke Box Jury*. The Beatles crowded round her in their usual way, all four instantly proposing marriage. The others guessed at once that such a 'classy' girl, red-haired and madonna-like, would appeal strongly to the socially-ambitious Paul. They had asked her back to their hotel for a drink and, after some winking and nudging, had left Paul and her alone in the bedroom. It quickly transpired that Jane, as well as being only 17, was still a virgin. When the others came back, she and Paul were sitting there, deep in discussion about their favourite kinds of food.

Jane's background, as much as her chaste beauty, fascinated Paul. Her father, Sir Richard Asher, was a noted psychiatrist. Her mother, a professional musician, had taught George Martin the oboe. Her brother Peter belonged—as did Jane herself—to a teenage top drawer which played its Rock records in the studies of elegant town houses and formed the earliest clientele of the music clubs and 'boutiques' now springing up in the West End and Chelsea. Since heeding his mother's plea not to talk like other estate children, Paul McCartney had dreamed of worlds like this.

The fans knew that Paul and Jane were often seen together, at parties or the theatre. The Ashers' house in Wimpole Street was plagued by telephone gigglings and breathings which Sir Richard could not shut off because the line belonged to his surgery. What few people knew, even within the Beatles' entourage, was that Paul now spent all his time in London with the Ashers. Returning from the Continent late one night, he had missed his connection to Liverpool, and Jane's mother had offered him the spare-room. That room was now permanently his.

To young men long used to staying out all night, London in 1963 offered many diversions. The old West End 'night spots', with their clientele of debutantes and Guards officers, were giving way to 'with it' clubs like Wips, whose advertisement promised 'pirhanas in the dark above London's skyline . . . black velvet and new faces . . . music, strong, hard and moody'. In Soho, for a brief season, flourished the Establishment Club, named for all the hapless official targets, from Royalty downward, flayed nightly by the satirists in its floor show. After Wips came the Ad Lib, the first club to recognise a new aristocracy, coming from Debrett's no longer but from Pop music.

Newspaper acquaintances, like Ray Coleman, who ran into the Beatles after dark at the Ad Lib could be sure both of an eventful night and of a large bill to be camouflaged among expenses. 'None of them ever seemed to have any money,' Coleman says. Peter Jones, the journalist in closest contact with them, received an impression, not so much of Liverpool thrift as of spasmodic insolvency. 'If I was on my way to see them, I'd ring up first. Often they'd say, "Here, pick up some food for us on the way, will you?" '

The fact is that, although the Beatles were Britain's biggest-selling Pop group, their income was—and for a long time remained—astonishingly small. The records now selling in millions earned them, under their original Parlophone contract, a farthing per double-sided disc. Their concert appearances, richly profitable to promoters and cinema circuits, often realised barely enough to cover their travel and hotel expenses. For Brian was still letting them work at rates agreed to months previously.

At Bryce, Hanmer and Isherwood, Dr. Strach's first act—after sorting out certain small tax difficulties arising from their Hamburg days—was to form the Beatles into a limited company for which the grave Czech gentleman himself acted as both treasurer and secretary. It was to Strach that the bills for their flats and living expenses came. In those days, the Doctor says, his main concern was to amass a reserve of money to pay Income Tax after—as must invariably happen—the Beatles had stopped earning money as Pop stars. The residue of their earnings, therefore, simply lay in bank accounts, expecting that evil day. For meals, drinks, the suits and shirts and boots they wore once and then discarded, they turned to Neil Aspinall, their road manager, and the float Neil always carried. Larger expenditure was discouraged by the black-suited figure whom, without much conviction, the Beatles called 'Uncle Walter'.

Dr. Strach remembers how Brian Epstein strove at every step to make his dealings with the Beatles fair. 'He always worried that he might be taking advantage of them. He came to me once and said he wanted to give them a piece of *his* company, NEMS Enterprises. He gave them 10 per cent of it, so they would get back some of the 25 per cent they paid him. Brian didn't have to do that, but he wanted to. He was a decent, honest, average human being.'

Punctilious in small matters, and small amounts, Brian could not adjust his sights to the bigger and bigger commercial prospects now materialising on every side. At the same time, his pride would not allow him to ask advice from older, more experienced people in the same business. Resolutely he did every deal for the Beatles in person, never doubting a mental tariff still based more on Liverpool's values than London's. And among his pursuers, the word rapidly spread. Brian Epstein—in the American entrepreneurial phrase—was not 'street wise'.

In the autumn of 1963, he received an offer for the Beatles to appear in their first feature film. This was already a recognised way of capitalising on Pop music success—simple 'exploitation' movies in which the thinnest background was given to the miming of Top Twenty hits for a cinema audience. United Artists, the company which approached Brian, were at that stage chiefly interested in sales of a Beatles 'sound-track album'.

UA had already hired Walter Shenson, an independent American producer, based in London, with some reputation for making successful low-budget comedy films. Shenson agreed to meet Brian, together with Bud Orenstein, UA's office head in London, to discuss the terms under which the Beatles would be allowed to appear.

'I knew Bud Orenstein well,' Walter Shenson says. 'So I went over to his flat before Brian arrived to talk over the deal that we'd be prepared to make. I knew nothing about Pop music or managers. I said: "What do you think he's going to ask for?" The film was low budget, with not much to pay in advances. Bud and

Earliest known picture of John Lennon's Quarry Men, playing at the Rosebery Street centenary party, summer 1957. 'I could hear these blokes whispering that they were going to get Lennon...the lads had to have a policeman to see them to the bus stop.'

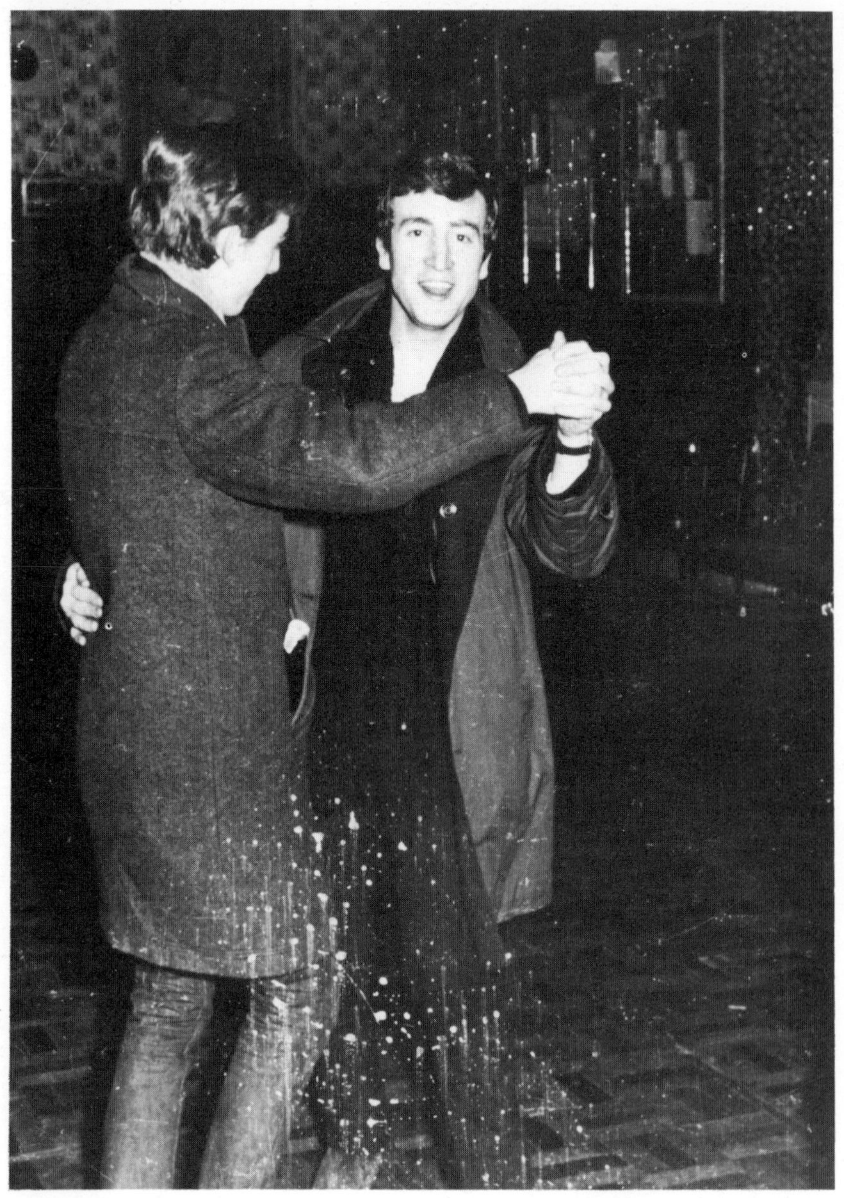

John waltzes with George at the Queen's Hall, Aldershot, December 1960, after playing for two hours to 18 people.

At the Top Ten Club, Hamburg, 1961; Paul still on rhythm guitar, George still using the cheap Hofner he saved for, John still uncertain how to comb his hair.

On the beach near Hamburg, 1961: Stu, the creator and initiator, works on a collage, helped by John, his admirer and disciple.

Paul, John, Pete and George, in the dank days and steamy nights of Cavern Club stardom – a local supremacy chiefly attributed to Pete Best's 'mean, moody magnificence'.

Clowning at the Cavern between sessions; a mock funeral for a still-smoking Paul.

With new hair, and Hamburg leathers, in full flood on the Cavern stage with its heavily autographed and graffiti-ed back wall.

Recording Love Me Do, 4 September 1962, under George Martin's critical eye. George still had the black eye he received in the Pete Best riots. Before taping PS I Love You they broke for tea in the EMI canteen.

The Star-Club, Hamburg, 1962; a postcard view omitting the fights, upturned tables, bludgeoned customers and Ali, the drop-kicking waiter.

Back from Scandinavia, to the astonishing London Airport welcome. 'Is all this meant for someone else?'

Brian Epstein as he most wanted to be: urbane, relaxed, a successful leading man. His giveaway fan picture for 1964 gives no sign of what disquiet already gnawed at his dazzling success.

The first mad rush of Beatle merchandise, from socks and soap to crayons, rugs and Ringo Roll. In America, the bonanza was ten times larger, earning millions of dollars that the Beatles never saw.

Refined by Brian Epstein from a Liverpool Art Student's clothes and a Hamburg girl's hairdessing scissors: the image that at last seized and besotted the world.

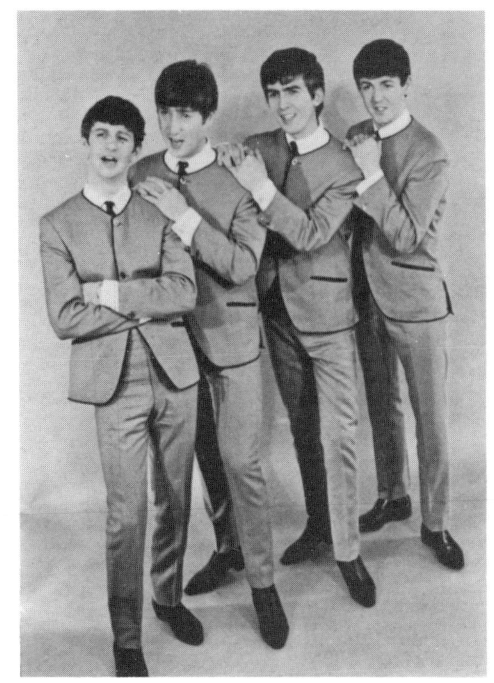

The fans wanted their heroes mapped inch by inch.

THE VITAL BEATLE-ISTICS *yeah! yeah! yeah*

Allan Williams

Bob Wooler

Mal Evans

Bruno Koschmider

Tony Sheridan

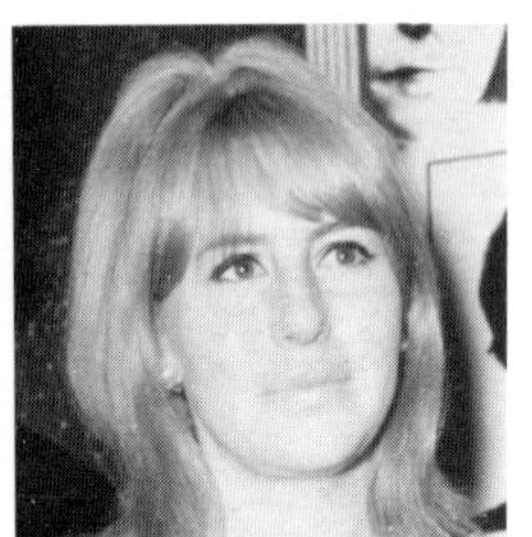
Cynthia Lennon

George Martin

Maureen Starr

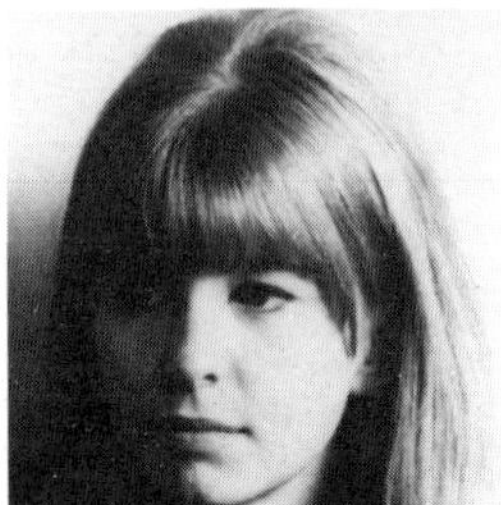
Jane Asher

Pattie Harrison

Maharishi Mahesh Yogi

Derek Taylor

Peter Brown

Linda MaCartney

Allen Klein

Yoko Ono

David Jacobs

Dick James

Neil Aspinall

Bill Harry

Brian at unaccustomed ease, backstage during the '65 American tour that included the Shea Stadium triumph. 'It couldn't have happened that way for anyone else...it only happened because it was Brian Epsteins's fantasy.'

Brian, in an airport lounge, draws up the playing order. 'A fragile bond of memos and lists.

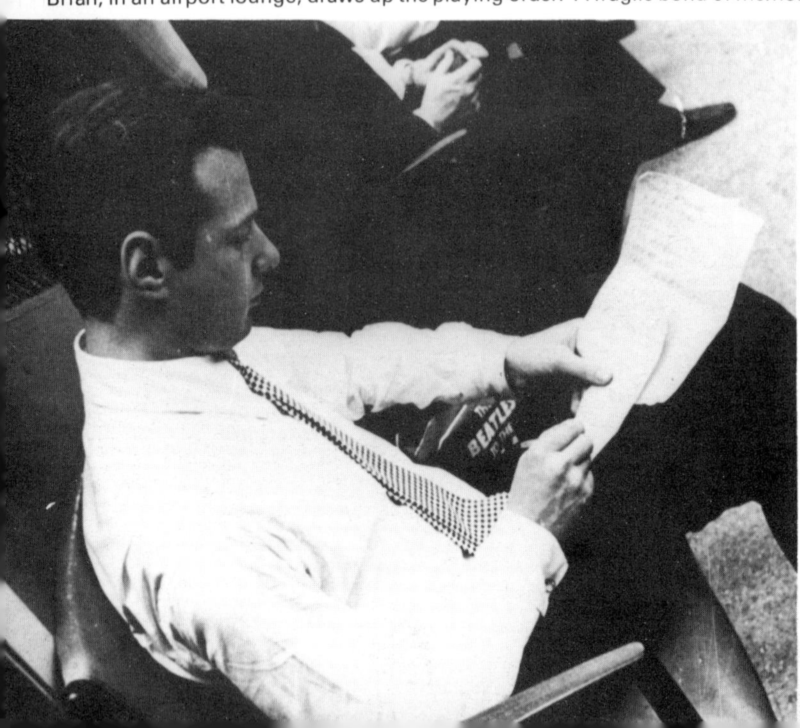

John with George Martin listening to the Sergeant Pepper playback: acid-drenched, sparkling visions from his voyage through LSD.

1968: Pilgrims at Rishikesh with their mirthful guru. The group also includes Mia Farrow and Donovan. Daily competitions were held to see who could meditate longest.

The Georgian town house whe
Apple's empire rose and rotte
The 'vibes' made it first glow
rosily, then turn pale with fear.

April 1969: Pipe-smoking, statesmanlike, Allen Klein tries to reassure the City about his involvement with the Beatles' Northern Songs takeover bid. The Press conference, one paper said, 'must have set some kind of record for unprintable language...'

Linda with Paul, Yoko with John: an infrequent, uneasy quartet. Ringo does his best to keep up the conversation.

969: Paul marries Linda on a leak day for the young women f the western world.

January 1969: The cold, chaotic Apple rooftop session. 'Four musicians playing as no four ever would again.'

I agreed it would be fair to offer Brian and the Beatles 25 per cent of the picture.

'Then Brian came in. He seemed very nice. We put to him the fee we'd thought of—the Beatles would get a salary of £25,000 to work on the picture—and he agreed to that. Then we asked him, "Mr. Epstein, what would you consider a fair percentage of the picture?" Brian thought for a minute, then he said, "I couldn't accept anything less than seven-and-a-half per cent." '

Uproar spilled over into the Beatles' first 'European tour'—a series of concerts in Sweden from 24–29 October. Self-possessed Swedish girls now jigged and shrieked as wildly as any Cavernite, and sensible Swedish boys wore their hair in what Scandinavian newspapers called the 'Hamlet' style. At a concert in Stockholm, these formerly self-possessed and sensible girls and boys rushed the stage, breaking through a 40-strong Police cordon and trampling George Harrison momentarily underfoot. Paul McCartney, between concerts, wore a disguise so effective that not even the other Beatles could recognise him.

Their return to London on 29 October showed them for the first time the full extent of their British following. At Heathrow airport, as their aircraft taxied to a stop, a concerted scream broke out from hundreds of girls massed along the terminal's terraced roof. The invasion had thrown the whole airport into a chaos in which such other celebrities as Britain's Prime Minister, Sir Alec Douglas Home, and the newly-elected Miss World passed by, totally unnoticed.

The 1963 Royal Command Performance, its bill ranging from Latin American zither-players to aged swing orchestras and pig puppets, promised entertainment of the customary standard. The Queen, shortly to give birth to her fourth child, would be unable to attend and the short straw had, metaphorically speaking, been drawn jointly by Queen Elizabeth, the Queen Mother, and Princess Margaret. As usual, the spectacular was to be telerecorded and transmitted a week later over the ATV network.

From the beginning, there was no question as to the night's real attraction. Long before dusk, on that raw afternoon, 500 policemen had been drafted to duty outside the Prince of Wales theatre, off Leicester Square, where the usual crowd, assembled to glimpse the 'Royals', was swollen by several thousand girls, screaming and chanting 'We want the Beatles'. Marlene Dietrich, a legend of 30 years' standing, was able to enter the stage door, unrecognised. But when the Queen Mother herself appeared, waving and smiling, followed by Princess Margaret and Lord Snowdon, a basic British instinct asserted itself: the screaming and chanting changed to applause and cheers.

Brian Epstein, in all the hurry and excitement, very nearly found himself without the evening clothes that are de rigueur at a Royal performance: his dinner jacket, he remembered, too late, was hanging in the wardrobe at home in Liverpool. To add to the tension, he was due to fly to America the next morning. His parents, Harry and Queenie, sitting in the audience, had almost resigned themselves to not seeing him when, just before curtain-up, in his hastily procured tuxedo, he lowered himself into the empty seat next to theirs.

The Beatles, cooped up with Neil and Mal Evans in a dressing-room no more munificent than usual, were also evincing signs of strain. Their spot in the show was brief—four songs near the end, surrounded by carefully-rehearsed bows. What Brian feared more than musical slip-ups was that, despite his entreaties for decorum, some ad lib would be made, offensive to Royal ears. John Lennon had already threatened one ghastly ad lib if the audience proved unresponsive: 'I'll just tell 'em to rattle their fuckin' jewellery.'

Brian's fears proved groundless. The Royal Command audience, stiff-shirted and sycophantic, could hardly have been more vulnerable to the Beatles' insouciant charm and the cheekiness which by instinct they measured out in precisely the right amount. Paul McCartney struck the exact note at once, surveying the dignified dark and saying, 'How are yer—all right?' A joke between songs, about 'Sophie Tucker our favourite American group' produced a ripple of confirming laughter. Then it was John's turn, to announce the final number, Twist and Shout. The line which had jangled Brian's nerves in the dressing-room came out as a perfect mingling of impudence and deference: 'Will people in the cheaper seats clap your hands? All the rest of you, if you'll just rattle your jewellery. . . .'

The next day's papers were unanimous. 'Beatles Rock the Royals', said the *Daily Express*. 'Night of Triumph for Four Young Men', said the *Daily Mail*, roguishly adding 'Yes—the Royal Box was stomping'. It was reported that the Queen Mother had listened to Twist and Shout with every appearance of enjoyment and that Princess Margaret had definitely leaned forward, 'clapping on the off-beat'. John Lennon's little joke was quoted everywhere, as was the banter overheard later when the Beatles stood in the Royal receiving line. Asked by the Queen Mother where they were appearing next, they had together murmured 'Slough'. Her Majesty—whether jokingly or not will never be known—replied, 'Oh, that's near us.'

The *Daily Mirror*'s coverage of scenes outside and inside the Prince of Wales theatre bore the simple headline 'Beatlemania!' The *Mirror* simultaneously gave the epidemic a name and offered its six million readers this deeply-infected diagnosis.

You have to be a real sour square not to love the nutty, noisy, happy, handsome Beatles.

If they don't sweep your blues away—brother, you're a lost cause. If they don't put a beat in your feet—sister, you're not living.

How refreshing to see these rumbustious young Beatles take a middle-aged Royal Variety performance by the scruff of their necks and have them Beatling like teenagers.

Fact is that Beatle People are everywhere. From Wapping to Windsor. Aged seven to seventy. And it's plain to see why these four cheeky, energetic lads from Liverpool go down so big.

They're young, new. They're high-spirited, cheerful. What a change from the self-pitying moaners, crooning their lovelorn tunes from the tortured shallows of lukewarm hearts.

The Beatles are whacky. They wear their hair like a mop —but it's WASHED, it's super clean. So is their fresh young act. They don't have to rely on off-colour jokes about homos for their fun.

To say that Britain, in November 1963, succumbed to an all-excluding obsession with a four-man Pop group—even one which had made Royalty smile—would be palpably absurd. The mania was Fleet Street's; it therefore appeared to blanket the land. In a single week after the Royal Variety Performance, the *Daily Express* ran five front-page stories indicative of Beatlemania at every compass-point. Its chief rival, the *Daily Mail* soon afterwards ceased bothering even to use the name 'Beatles' in headlines. A small cartoon logo of four fringed heads gave all the identification that was needed.

Naturally, the Press soon winkled out the fact which Brian had striven so to conceal—that John Lennon was married, with a baby son. The fans, however, far from resenting Cynthia, seemed to regard her as part of John's inexhaustible originality. She continued, nonetheless, to exist in the deepest hinterland, at the top of the Emperor's Gate flat or some sternly-defined public corral, fenced off by a road manager's shoulder.

The scope of Fleet Street coverage was widening from theatre sieges and screaming and the cheeky things they said. On 10 November, the first school headmaster sent the first teenage boy into public martyrdom for refusing to change a Beatle haircut. On 18 November, the first vicar invoked their name, requesting them to provide a tape of Oh Come All Ye Faithful, Yeah Yeah Yeah for his Christmas congregation. Two days later occurred the first Parliamentary mention. A Labour MP in the House of Commons demanded that Police protection for the Beatles should end. On the *Express* editorial page there appeared a prophetic cartoon. The Prime Minister, Sir Alec Douglas Home, genuflecting before the Beatles, asked: 'Gentlemen—could we persuade you to become Conservative candidates?'

The 'quality' papers, traditionally aloof from such proletarian topics, now weighed in analyses of the Beatles' effect on teenage girls. Since the Lady Chatterley trial, only these papers had dared be explicit about sex. It was, as someone immortally remarked, 'all right if you'd been to university'. The *Observer* published a picture of a Cycladic fertility goddess which, it was maintained, 'dates the potency of the guitar as a sex symbol to about 4,800 years before the Beatle era'. The livelier-minded *Sunday Times* commended the Beatles for enriching the English language with words from their private slang—like 'gear' and 'fab'—which were now in fashionable use. The *Sunday Times* went on to examine Beatlemania in a style and vocabulary that were to be widely imitated. '"You don't have to be a genius," says a consultant at a London hospital, "to see the parallels between sexual excitement and the mounting crescendo of delighted screams through a stimulating number like Twist and Shout, but at the level it is taken, I think it is the bubbling, uninhibited gaiety of the group that generates enthusiasm."'

The habit quickly spread of consulting the medical profession, especially its psychiatric branch, for opinions which would lend scientific weight to the orgies of chortling prose. And doctors and psychiatrists, sensing regular fees, were careful to pronounce nothing unfavourable. Not even the *News of the World* could find anything in Beatlemania against which to caution its credulous readership. Psychologists, the *NoW* said, in its usual comfortably inexplicit way, had been trying to discover why the Beatles send teenage girls into hysteria. One of them had come up with this explanation:

> This is one way of flinging off childhood restraints and letting themselves go . . . the fact that thousands of others are screaming along with her makes the girl feel she is living life to the full with people of her own age . . . this emotional outlook is very necessary at her age. It is also innocent and harmless.
>
> The girls are subconsciously preparing for motherhood. Their frenzied screams are a rehearsal for that moment. Even the jelly babies are symbolic.

EMI hastened to release the second Beatles LP, recorded by George Martin in mid-July and incubated through autumn until sales of the first album, and its spin-off EPs, should finally subside. This second album, With the Beatles, appeared on 22 November. Never before had a Pop LP been released, not to cash in on a Top Ten single but on the strength of its overall content. Advance orders alone totalled 250,000 copies—more than for Elvis Presley's biggest-selling album, Blue Hawaii.

By far the most striking thing about With the Beatles was its cover. Brian Epstein had for months been showing his proof copy to friends and asking anxiously what they thought. Gone was the look of the Please Please Me album—the cheap, cheeky faces, looking down from high-rise flats. A top London fashion photographer, Robert Freeman, had shot the Beatles, heads and shoulders only, in black and white. Faces halved by shadow, hemmed in by their fringes and high polo necks, they could have been a quartet of young actors or art students. It was the same technique Astrid had used to photograph Stu Sutcliffe three years before in Hamburg, in her black and silver room.

A week later came their fifth single, I Want To Hold Your Hand, which advance orders of one million copies placed instantly at Number One in the Top Ten. The pre-Christmas air seemed to transmit little other than that loping, handclapping beat. The album, meanwhile, had its independent existence in the stunning combination of Lennon-McCartney songs like All My Loving and It Won't Be Long, with Chuck Berry's Roll Over Beethoven, Berry Gordy's Money, and other R & B songs so little known to the general Pop audience, it was thought the Beatles must have written those also. 'Disker's' sleeve notes put the matter in perspective.

Never again would Pop music be considered the prerogative only of working-class boys and girls. With the Beatles was played, not only in Council houses but in West London flats, in young ladies' finishing schools and in the blow-heated barns where landowner's daughters held their Christmas dances.

On 5 November, the day after the Royal Command show, Brian Epstein flew to New York, accompanied by Billy J. Kramer, that handsome but awkward young man. Landing at the airport still called Idelwilde, they drove in a yellow cab towards the magic skyline which reveals itself at first in miniature like the crest on a souvenir ash tray. Brian, on the drive, was full of what Broadway plays they would see in between his several very important business meetings. These meetings, Billy J. gathered, were the merest preliminary to the Beatles' instant subjugation of the North American continent. Even if Brian himself ever believed this, he ceased to do so as the cab entered Manhattan and the streets became sheer glass on every side.

America up to now had regarded the Beatles as it regarded

every British Pop performer—an inferior substitute for a product which, having been invented in America, could only be manufactured and marketed by Americans. The view was reinforced by the half-century in which American artists, through every musical epoch, had dominated the English market as against only one or two freakish incursions by English acts travelling the other way. In the same fashion now, American Pop music dwarfed its English counterparts in size and wealth, in the complexity of its chart systems and the corollary role of hundreds of independent radio stations. Even so big a British name as Cliff Richard had attempted only one American tour, half-way down the bill, amid deafening indifference. The British, it was agreed in the boardrooms of Manhattan, should stick to the things they knew best, like whisky, woollen sweaters and Shakespeare.

America in late 1963 had already ordained the new direction of teenage music. Three brothers from California, Brian, Carl and Dennis Wilson, and their cousin Mike Love, known collectively as the Beach Boys, were already internationally famous for their close-harmony songs hymning the West Coast pleasures of surf-riding, drag racing and crewcut, freckled sex. That 'surfing' sound, like previous Pop styles, reflected a nation still jingoistically confident in the perfection of all its values; whose new young President, John F. Kennedy, had precisely the same sun-healthy, college-fresh appeal.

George Martin had found the anti-British barrier impossible to penetrate, even though EMI owned the American Capitol label. When Please Please Me went to Number One in Britain, Martin had immediately sent it to Jay Livingstone, the senior executive at Capitol in New York. Livingstone declined the opportunity in a curt memo: 'We don't think the Beatles will do anything in this market.'

George Martin, to his great irritation, was thus obliged to hawk Please Please Me around other American labels in direct competition with Parlophone's own parent company. It was finally accepted by Vee Jay, a small Chicago-based firm. Released by Vee Jay in February, Please Please Me had instantly vanished without trace. The same happened in May with From Me To You. George Martin offered it to Capitol, who gruffly refused it; issued by Vee Jay, it rose no higher than 116th in *Billboard* magazine's national popularity chart.

In August, when She Loves You began its eight-week blockade of the British charts, George Martin appealed for the third time to Jay Livingstone, and was again told that in Capitol's opinion the Beatles had no prospects in America. Instead, She Loves You was issued by a small New York label, Swan. The sound engulfing the British Isles did not even penetrate the *Billboard* 'Hot 100'.

One American entrepreneur at least—a tubby, sentimental New York agent named Sid Bernstein—disagreed with Capitol's prognosis. Bernstein worked for the General Artists Corporation, America's largest theatrical agency, but, having a thirst for culture, spent his leisure time attending an evening course on the subject of 'Civilisation'. 'Our teacher had told us to study the British way of life as a great democracy comparable with our own. He said the best way to study England was to read the British newspapers. That was how I first heard about what the Beatles were doing over in Europe.'

Quite early in 1963, Bernstein says, he was telling his superiors at GAC that the mania he had read about in the British Press could happen in New York City. 'I could see what they were, and that they were going to be monsters here. I wanted them.'

Brian Epstein arrived in New York, unaware that Sid Bernstein had been trying for several weeks to contact him by transatlantic 'phone. 'I couldn't sell the idea to anyone at GAC,' Berstein says, 'so I decided to make it my own independent promotion. I had already booked Carnegie Hall, the most famous auditorium in New York. You couldn't get Carnegie Hall unless you made the reservation months ahead. I chose 12 February 1964—Lincoln's birthday. The lady I dealt with at Carnegie Hall had a thick Polish accent. "The Beatles?" she said, "Vat are they?" I knew that Carnegie Hall would never allow a Pop concert to happen in its famous auditorium. I said, "They're a phenomenon." "Oh, a *phenomenon*," she said, thinking that was maybe a type of string quartet.'

Brian had only one friend in New York. Geoffrey Ellis, the Liverpool estate agent's son, was still working there for the Royal Insurance Society. Geoffrey had not seen Brian since he was home on holiday in 1962, and Mrs. Epstein confided to him that the family were 'letting Brian get this group thing out of his system'. Geoffrey was astonished to see what a *real* impresario Brian had made himself; how earnestly he dissuaded Billy J. Kramer from buying a cheap shirt, 'because it's not your *image*, Billy'.

Dick James, the music publisher, had recommended him to Walter Hofer, an attorney who already acted for James's company in New York. Hofer, hospitable and an Anglophile, at once invited Brian up to his office on West 57th Street. 'From the beginning he was full of questions,' Hofer says. 'How did American TV work? How did the radio stations work? While he was in town, I gave a cocktail party for him, which was a disaster. No one had ever heard of Brian Epstein. No one came but a few people from Liberty Records, because Billy J. Kramer was signing with them.'

Similarly, no one at Capitol Records Inc. recognised the severely-dapper young Englishman who came in to see their Director of Eastern Operations, Brown Meggs. Brian had called in person to try to persuade Capitol to give the Beatles an American release. With him he had a demo' of the song which John and Paul, working in the basement of Jane Asher's house, had striven to invest with 'a sort of American spiritual sound'. And, indeed, to Capitol's hypersensitive ears, the song did have something which three consecutive British Number Ones had lacked. Brown Meggs, after much corporate deliberation, agreed that Capitol would release I Want To Hold Your Hand. Even so, it was made clear to Brian, the company did not expect a great response. The release date was 13 January 1964.

Brian's other appointment was to meet a little sharkskin-suited, elderly man with heavy jowls, a gruff voice and an air of misanthropy often detectable in those renowned as 'talent spotters' and arbiters of the public taste. At the Delmonico Hotel, Brian Epstein, for the second time, found himself face to face with the great Ed Sullivan.

For 20 years, Sullivan's CBS television show had been famous for 'breaking' new entertainers, not in New York only but across the whole American continent via hundreds of local stations served by the CBS network. Sullivan, a former sports journalist, combined an uncanny instinct for the sensational with an air of bewilderment that his fellow Americans could find such things remotely entertaining. It was Sullivan who had booked Elvis Presley to sing Houn' Dog on condition that the cameras showed him only from the waist up. Sullivan's introduction then was simply a shrug and the words: 'America, judge for yourselves.'

Ed Sullivan had been aware of the Beatles since his recent talent-spotting trip to Europe, when he and Mrs. Sullivan were among many travellers at Heathrow airport inconvenienced by their homecoming from Sweden. He had asked to meet them, and been sufficiently impressed to offer Brian a tentative booking on his show early in 1964.

Sullivan's idea at that stage was to use the Beatles as a minor novelty item in a show constructed around some established American entertainer. Brian, however, insisted they should receive top billing. The Sullivan show's producer, Bob Precht—who happened also to be Ed Sullivan's son-in-law—remembers how surprised both he and the great man were by this unforeseen tactic. Top billing was conceded against a deal otherwise far from munificent. 'I said that if we were going to pay the Beatles' air fares out here,' Bob Precht says, 'we ought to get more than one appearance out of them.' It was agreed that the Beatles should appear in two Ed Sullivan shows, on February 9 and 16, and should record more songs to be used in a subsequent transmission. The fee for each appearance would be $3,500, plus $3,000 more for the taping. 'Even for an unknown act,' Bob Precht admits, 'that was about the least we could pay.'

If America had not fallen, it was at least prepared to listen. Brian had that much to comfort him when, a day or two afterwards, he and Billy J. Kramer flew back to London. He had persuaded Capitol. He had persuaded Ed Sullivan. Short of the fatigue, the 'phoning back, the waiting and the compromise, these would seem dazzling achievements. And halfway over the Atlantic, as he read the British papers, Beatlemania grew audible again.

America, if Brian had only known it, was already his—was moving nearer his unconscious grasp as, far away in Texas, the mechanism of a high velocity rifle was cleaned and checked, and a vantage-point selected. America fell to him on the morning in Dallas that the Presidential motorcade set off on its route, supremely confident and open to the sunshine, and the kerbside ciné-enthusiast turned his camera towards the limousine which carried a young man's unprotected head. This was 22 November, the day the Beatles' second album went on sale in Britain. Late that afternoon, the news began to come through which, for every English person, hardly less than every American, would fix in the memory for ever the exact time, place and circumstances of hearing it.

For their winter tour, through the deepening blizzards of national dementia, Brian entrusted the Beatles to his friend Brian Sommerville, the ex-Naval officer turned Fleet Street journalist. Tony Barrow, NEMS' original Press Officer, now had more work than he could handle alone. It was therefore fixed that Barrow should represent Gerry, Billy J. Kramer, Cilla and the Fourmost while Sommerville—or rather, Sommerville's one-man PR company—acted exclusively for the Beatles. Small, plump, already balding, he had the aspect of a country squire and a quarterdeck brusqueness which did not at once endear him to his new charges.

The tour was the most arduous one yet—six weeks of one-night concerts at Gaumont, ABC or Odeon cinemas in a zigzag course from Cambridge to Sunderland. At the same time, they were rehearsing their pantomime sketches for a special NEMS Christmas show in London, at the Finsbury Park Astoria. In Liverpool in one 24-hour period, as well as their two evening concerts, they taped appearances for two television shows and performed for a convention of the Beatles Northern Area Fan Club. John and Paul were also working on a dozen new songs for the film that Walter Shenson wanted to shoot the following spring.

In university city or Midland industrial town, the procedure was invariable. Mal Evans went in first, driving the van with their equipment through the blue avenues of waiting Police. At dusk, by vainly circuitous routes, would come the Austin Princess limousine containing the Beatles, Neil Aspinall and Brian Sommerville. They would go straight to the theatre, remaining in the dressing-room until the performance while Neil brought in food or pressed their stage clothes and Sommerville stood guard testily outside. As soon as the curtain fell, Sommerville would shoo them, in their damp suits, out through the Police ranks to their beleaguered car. By midnight, they would be trapped inside some provincial hotel which, more often than not, would have stopped serving dinner at 9 pm. On many nights, all they could get to eat were dishes of cornflakes.

In Lincoln, Ringo developed earache and had to be rushed to hospital, disguised in an overcoat, hat and spectacles which, as one reporter noted, 'made him look like Brecht being smuggled out of Germany'. Near Doncaster, their car ran out of petrol and they had to thumb a lift in a lorry. In Sunderland, they escaped from the theatre by running into the adjacent fire station, sliding down the firemen's pole and escaping in a Police car while one of the engines rushed out to create a diversion.

In Liverpool, the Empire theatre had been commandeered by the BBC for a special edition of *Juke Box Jury* featuring all four Beatles as panellists. Disgruntled technicians, faced with this unprecedented journey outside London, were heard muttering that BBC must stand for 'Beatle Broadcasting Corporation'. Before the show, the Beatles mischievously rearranged their name cards so that George Harrison sat behind the one reading 'John Lennon'.

The advantage of Brian Sommerville as publicist was that he spoke in an upper-class voice, in a tone to which policemen, commissionaires and other potential obstacles almost all automatically responded. The Beatles, hemmed-in as tightly by authority figures as by screaming fans, recognised the need for someone, like Sommerville, peppery and abrasive. 'I had a good relationship with John; he called me "old baldy-something-or-other". Paul and I got on well enough, though I always found him rather two-faced. Ringo was just Ringo. I did have one serious fight with George. He never regarded me with anything but muffled dislike.'

Throughout the tour, Sommerville was left totally in charge, to screen the Press seeking interviews, sign the hotel bills and negotiate strategy with theatre managers and the Police. Brian would appear at irregular intervals, in his overcoat and polka-dotted scarf. 'He'd float into the dressing-room, usually with a piece of paper for them to sign,' Sommerville says. 'But if there was any trouble, you could count on Brian to be miles away. He had this wonderful knack of being able to disappear during a crisis.'

Backstage rows were frequent between Brian and Sommerville. It irked Brian to see anyone close to the Beatles but himself. He even suspected Sommerville of trying to usurp his own growing fame as their mentor and mouthpiece. 'Brian already saw himself as a star in his own right,' Sommerville says. '*He* wanted to do the things they did, like appearing on *Juke Box Jury*. He was hurt because he hadn't been asked to chair the special Mersey edition of *Thank Your Lucky Stars*. The worst rows we had were after I'd made some comment, and the Press quoted me instead of Brian. "You had no right to do that!" he'd say.'

And yet, at times, Brian would seem unable to pluck up courage to go into the Beatles' dressing-room, but would stand out in the auditorium, suddenly as distant from them as the furthest screaming girl. 'I saw him once,' Sommerville says, 'in one of those northern ABCs, when the curtains opened and the scream went up. He was standing there with tears streaming down his face.'

It had become clear at an early stage, to various sharp-eyed people, that the Beatles were capable of selling far more than gramophone records by the million. Beatlemania demonstrated as never before to what extent young people in Britain were a 'market', gigantic and ripe for exploitation. From October 1963 onward, Brian Epstein carried in his wake a little trail of businessmen, coaxing, cajoling, sometimes begging to be authorised to produce goods in the Beatles' image.

'Merchandising' as a concept was largely unknown in mid-20th century Britain, even though the Victorians had been adept at it. Walt Disney, that peerless weaver of dreams into plastic, was imitated on a small scale by British toy manufacturers, producing replicas of television puppets. Pop singers until now had lasted too short a time in public esteem to sell any but the most ephemeral goods.

No precedent existed, therefore, to warn Brian that there were billions at stake. He saw the merchandising purely as public relations—a way to increase audience goodwill and keep the Fan Club happy. He worried about the Fan Club, and keeping it happy.

The first Beatle products catered simply for the desire, as strong in girls as in boys, to impersonate their idols. In Bethnal Green, East London, a factory was producing Beatle 'wigs' at the rate of several thousand each week. The hairstyle which Astrid's scissors had shaped for Stu Sutcliffe became a best-selling novelty, a black, fibrous mop, hovering just outside seriousness, 30 shillings apiece. A Midlands clothing firm marketed collarless corduroy 'Beatle jackets' like the one Astrid had made for Stu; the one which the Beatles at the time despised as 'Mum's jacket'. Girls, too, wore the jackets, the tab-collar shirts, even the elastic-sided, Cuban heel 'Beatle boots', obtainable by mail order at '75s 11d, including post and packing'.

Christmas 1963 signalled a fresh avalanche of Beatle products into the shops. There were Beatle guitars, of plastic, authentically 'autographed', and miniature Beatle drums. There were Beatle lockets, each with a tiny quadruple photograph compressed inside. There were red and blue Beatle kitchen aprons, bespeckled with guitar-playing bugs. The four faces and four signatures, engraved, printed or transferred, however indistinctly, appeared on belts, badges, handkerchieves, jigsaw puzzles, rubber airbeds, disc racks, bedspreads, 'ottomans', shoulder bags, pencils, buttons and trays. There was a brand of confectionery known as 'Ringo Roll', and of Beatle chewing gum, each sixpenny packet warranted to contain *seven* photographs. A Northern bakery chain announced guitar-shaped 'Beatle cakes' ('Party priced at 5s') and fivepenny individual Beatle 'fancies'.

Brian, in the beginning, personally examined the products of each prospective licensee. In no case, he ruled, would the Beatles directly endorse any article. Nor would they lend their name to anything distasteful, inappropriate or overtly exploitive of their fans. And, indeed, parents who had scolded their children for buying 'trash' were frequently surprised by the goods' quality and value. The Beatle jacket was smart, durable and well-lined. The 'official' Beatle sweater ('Designed for Beatle people by a leading British manufacturer') was 100 per cent botany wool, hardly extortionate at 35s.

Soon, however, unauthorised Beatle goods began to appear. Though NEMS Enterprises held copyright on the name 'Beatles', infringement could be avoided simply by spelling it 'Beetles'. The vaguest representation of insects, of guitars or little mop-headed men, had the power to sell anything, however cheap, however nasty. Even to spot the culprits, let alone bring lawsuits against them, meant a countrywide invigilation such as no British copyright-holder had ever been obliged to undertake. NEMS Enterprises certainly could not undertake it. And so, after one or two minor prosecutions, the pirates settled down, unhampered, to their bonanza.

By late 1963, the merchandising had got into a tangle which Brian Epstein had not the time nor the will to contemplate. He therefore handed the whole matter over to his solicitor, David Jacobs. It became Jacobs's job, not only to prosecute infringements, where visible, but also, at his independent discretion, to issue new manufacturing licenses. Prospective licensees were referred from NEMS Enterprises to Jacobs's offices in Pall Mall. Since David Jacobs, too, was deeply preoccupied, with social as well as legal matters, the task of appraising designs, production strategy and probable income was delegated to the chief clerk in his chambers, Edward Marke.

This arrangement quickly proved inconvenient. Among the cases currently being handled by M. A. Jacobs Ltd. were several claims for damages by the relatives of passengers lost aboard a cruise ship, the *Lakonia*. The waiting-room where these bereaved litigants sat also served as a dumping ground for cascades of Beatle guitars, plastic windmills and crayoning sets. Mr. Marke, though a conscientious legal functionary, knew little of the manufacturing business. So David Jacobs, in his turn, looked round for someone to take on this tiresome business of making millions.

His choice was Nicky Byrne, a man he had met, and been rather impressed by, at a cocktail party. Byrne, indeed, was rather a celebrated figure at parties, of which he himself gave a great many at his fashionable Chelsea garage-cum-flat. Small, impishly-dapper, formidably persuasive, he had been variously a country squire's son, a Horse Guard trooper and an amateur racing driver. His true avocation, however, was membership of the 'Chelsea Set', that sub-culture of debutantes, bohemians, heiresses and charming cads which, since the mid-Fifties, had flourished along and around the King's Road.

Nicky Byrne was not a totally implausible choice, having in his extremely varied life touched the worlds of show business and popular retailing. In the Fifties, he had run the Condor Club, in Soho, where Tommy Steele was discovered. His wife, Kiki—from whom he had recently parted—was a well-known fashion designer with her own successful Chelsea boutique.

The offer from Jacobs was that Byrne should administer the Beatles' merchandising operation in Europe and throughout the world. He was not, he maintains, very eager to accept. 'Brian Epstein had a very bad name in the business world at that time. Nobody knew who was licensed to make Beatle goods and who wasn't. I got in touch with Kiki, my ex-wife, to see what she thought about it. I mentioned this schmutter firm in Soho that was meant to be turning out Beatle gear. Kiki said, "Hold on a minute." She'd had a letter from a firm in the Midlands, asking her to design exactly the same thing for them.'

Nicky Byrne was eventually persuaded. He agreed to form a company named Stramsact to take over the assigning of Beatle merchandise rights. A subsidiary called Seltaeb—Beatles spelt backwards—would handle American rights, if any, when the

Beatles went to New York in February to appear on the *Ed Sullivan Show.*

Five partners, all much younger than Nicky Byrne, constituted both Stramsact and Seltaeb. One of them, 26-year-old John Fenton, had already been doing some merchandising deals of his own via David Jacobs. Two others, Mark Warman and Simon Miller-Munday, aged 20 and 22 respectively, were simply friends of Nicky's who had been nice to him during his break-up with Kiki.

Nicky Byrne's most picturesque recruit, after himself, was 23-year-old Lord Peregrine Eliot, heir to the Earl of St. Germans and owner of a 6,000 acre estate in Cornwall. Lord Peregrine's qualification was that he had shared a flat with Simon Miller-Munday. Although extremely rich, he was eager to earn funds to recarpet his ancestral home, Port Eliot. For £1,000 cash, His Lordship received 20 per cent of the company.

Only Malcolm Evans, the sixth partner, a junior studio manager with Rediffusion TV, had any definite professional ability of any kind. Evans had met the others at a Nicky Byrne party, the high spot of which was the pushing of a grand piano through the Chelsea streets. 'Nicky had got the entire Count Basie Orchestra to play at his party,' Evans says. 'I remember that they were accompanied on the bagpipes by a full-dress pipe major from the barracks over the road.'

The contract between Stramsact-Seltaeb and NEMS Enterprises was left to David Jacobs to draw up, approve, even sign on Brian's and the Beatles' behalf. 'I was at my solicitor's, just round the corner,' Nicky Byrne says. 'He told me, "Write in what percentage you think you should take on the deal." So I put down the first figure that came into my head—90 per cent.

'To my amazement, David Jacobs didn't even question it. He didn't think of it as 90 per cent to us, but as 10 per cent to the Beatles. He said, "Well, 10 per cent is better than nothing." '

Christmas, far from diverting the mania, actually seemed to increase it. The Beatles *became* Christmas in their fancy dress, playing in the NEMS Christmas Show at Finsbury Park Astoria. One of the sketches was a Victorian melodrama in which George, as 'heroine', was tied on the railway line by 'Sir Jasper' (John) and rescued by 'Fearless Paul the Signalman'. They had acted such plays and farces for years among themselves. Mal Evans, their second road manager, stood by, laughing, as all did, at the good-humoured knockabout fun; Mal had just received a savage tongue-lashing from John for having lost his 12-string 'Jumbo' guitar.

Beatle records made the December Top Twenty literally impassable. As well as I Want to Hold Your Hand at Number

One, it contained six songs from the With the Beatles LP—indeed, the album itself, with almost a million copies sold, qualified for entrance to the *singles* chart at Number 14, the customary seasonal 'gimmick' record was Dora Bryan's All I Want For Christmas is a Beatle.

Two anxiously-awaited messages, that Christmas, went out to the British nation. The first came from Queen Elizabeth, speaking on television from Balmoral Castle. The second came from four young men, unknown a year ago, speaking to their 80,000 Fan Club members in a babble of excited voices. They sang Good King Wenceslas and wished their subjects 'a very happy Chrimble and a gear New Year'.

'An examination of the heart of the nation at this moment,' the London *Evening Standard* said, 'would find the name "Beatles" upon it.' Under the heading 'Why Do We Love Them So Much?' columnist Angus McGill said it was because 'like well-bred children they are seen and not heard'. Maureen Cleave, in another article, could only conclude that 'everybody loves them because they look so happy'.

In marketing terms, the figures they represented were still barely believable. She Loves You had sold 1.3 million copies; I Want to Hold Your Hand had sold 1.25 million. They had transformed the British music industry from complacent torpor to neurotic—though still unavailing—competitiveness. A tiny record label called Parlophone, once noted for Scottish dance bands, towered over the frantic A & R men with a run of success, unequalled to this day. For 37 weeks out of the past 52, George Martin had had a record at Number One. He was currently reading a memo from his EMI superiors explaining that he would not this year qualify for the staff Christmas bonus.

Pop music was legitimised—and not only socially. At the end of December, a ballet, *Mods and Rockers,* was scored with Lennon and McCartney music. *The Times* published an article by its 'serious' music critic, William Mann, who pronounced John and Paul to be 'the outstanding English composers of 1963' for qualities of which they were probably unconscious. In their slow ballad This Boy, Mann detected 'chains of pandiatonic clusters', and in Not a Second Time, 'an Aeolian cadence—the chord progression which ends Mahler's Song of the Earth'. He further noticed their 'autocratic but not by any means ungrammatical attitude to tonality . . . the quasi-instrumental vocal duetting . . . the melismas with altered vowels . . .' That one article raised for all time the mental portcullis between 'classical' and 'Pop'; it also ushered in decades of sillier prose.

No Englishman, however cantankerous, could any longer profess ignorance on the subject. Not even Field Marshal Lord Montgomery, hero of El Alamein, who, speaking from the garden where he still kept Rommel's desert caravan, threatened to invite the Beatles for the weekend 'to see what kind of fellows they are.'

1964 began on a note of post-Christmas acidity. In the Top Twenty, I Want to Hold Your Hand yielded its Number One position to a non-Beatle song, Glad All Over, by the Dave Clark Five. Since the Five all came from the same north London suburb, they were greeted as harbingers of a 'Tottenham Sound'; they had 'crushed' the Beatles, several front page headlines said. The *Daily Mail* published a cartoon in which a group of girls contemptuously regarded one of their number. 'She must be really old,' the caption ran, 'she remembers the Beatles.'

As a prelude to America, they were to visit Paris. Brian had booked them a three-week engagement at the Olympia theatre, beginning on 15 January. The crowd which massed at Heathrow to see them off, described only three Beatles being herded out to the aircraft. Ringo Starr, the newspaper said, was 'fogbound' in Liverpool. Ringo, in fact, most unusually, was having a fit of temperament and had declared he wasn't fookin' coming. Across the Channel, further large and small hitches waited.

The Olympia, a wholly Parisian cross between cinema and music hall, was operated by a wily French promoter named Bruno Coquatrix. For three weeks of nightly Beatles shows, Coquatrix was paying Brian Epstein a fee which did not cover their travel and hotel expenses—particularly since Brian, with typical expansiveness, had booked the entire entourage into Paris's most exclusive hotel, the George Cinq. To offset the loss, Brian Sommerville did a publicity deal with British European Airways. The Beatles were issued with special inflight bags lettered BEAtles. For carrying and prominently displaying these, they and their guardians received three weeks' unlimited air travel between London and Paris.

Brian justified the low fee, once more, against the publicity value. France, until now, had remained noticeably indifferent to Beatlemania. He was determined that the Beatles should conquer Paris, and that Paris should be in no doubt concerning who had engineered that conquest. Before the journey, he asked Dezo Hoffman the photographer to print up 500 giveaway pictures of himself. Hoffman persuaded him this was not a good idea.

A vast contingent of British journalists went to Paris to cover the event. This time, the *Daily Express* led the field, having signed up George Harrison to 'write' a daily column. The writing was actually to be done by Derek Taylor, a Hoylake-born *Express* reporter, formerly the paper's 'northern dramatic critic'. This cultural background, no less than his Italianate good looks, recommended Taylor to Brian for what was a definite attempt to give George a share of the limelight. 'It will be *nice* for George,' Brian told him. 'John and Paul have their songwriting and Ringo is—ah—rather new.'

The George Cinq's mock-Versailles foyer and thoroughfares thronged with expectant photographers, hungrily noting the comings and goings of various important stakeholders in the quartet. George Martin, their record producer, had flown over to supervise a German language recording of She Loves You. Dr. Strach, their accountant, was there; so was Walter Shenson, their prospective film producer, accompanied by Alun Owen, a Liverpool playwright whom the Beatles themselves had requested as scriptwriter. Nicky Byrne, of the Stramsact company, was there to arrange large deals, so he expected, for Beatle merchandise in France and throughout Europe.

As well as variety acts such as jugglers and acrobats, the Beatles shared the Olympia bill with two singers whose French following greatly exceeded theirs. One was Sylvie Vartin, France's own turbulent Pop *chanteuse*. The other, Trini Lopez, was an American with a huge Continental chart success called Lemon Tree.

Lopez's manager, Norman Weiss, instantly sought out Brian Epstein at the George Cinq. Weiss worked with the American General Artists Corporation, whose former associate, Sid Bernstein, had already booked Carnegie Hall in New York in the hope of being able to present the Beatles there. February 12, the date of Bernstein's booking, was only three days after their first *Ed Sullivan Show.* Norman Weiss, therefore, concluded the deal at last on Sid Bernstein's behalf. Brian agreed that the Beatles would give two concerts at Carnegie Hall, each for a flat fee of $3,500.

They themselves were very different now from the four boys in George Martin's studio, earnestly doing everything their producer told them. Martin, waiting at EMI's Paris studio to supervise their recording of Sie Liebt Dich, was coolly informed by telephone that the Beatles had decided not to come. He stormed over to the George Cinq, to find them lounging round their suite while Paul's girl friend, Jane Asher, poured out tea. Such was George Martin's schoolmasterly wrath that all four scattered in terror to hide under cushions and behind the piano.

On the eve of their first concert, while the French and English Press jostled for position outside, John and Paul slept until 3 pm. Dezo Hoffman in the end accepted the hazardous job of waking them. 'I told John, "*Paris-Match* is waiting. They want to do a cover story." "*Paris-Match*?" John said. "Are they as important as the *Musical Express*?" '

Emerging into the Champs Elysées in a circle of retreating

lenses, they found Paris rather less than ecstatic at their arrival. According to Hoffman, very few passers-by even recognised them. The British Press made a valiant attempt to stimulate Beatlemania, posing John and Paul at a pavement cafe and hedging them in among writers and reporters. Vincent Mulchrone remarked on the prevailing apathy in his dispatch to the *Daily Mail*. 'Beatlemania is still, like Britain's entry into the Common Market, a problem the French prefer to put off for a while.'

Backstage at the Olympia the following night, naked violence broke out after the French Press had had the Beatles' dressing-room door slammed in their faces. French photographers, especially those who have served in theatres of war like Algeria and Indochina, are not so easily discouraged. A fierce scuffle followed in which Brian Sommerville received a rabbit punch and Brian Epstein—who tried to interpose himself with outstretched arms and a querulous, 'No—not *my* boys!'—was shoved backwards by the burly Frenchman who had simultaneously trodden on his toes.

The show ran late, as French shows invariably do, and the Beatles did not go on stage until well after midnight. Trini Lopez, who had closed the first half hours before, seemed much more like top of the bill. To add to their unease, a glimpse through the curtains showed the audience to be almost entirely male. 'Where's all the bloody chicks then?' they kept asking in agitation.

During the performance, their usually reliable Vox amplifiers broke down three times. George Harrison, enraged by his fading guitar, began to complain openly of sabotage. Neither John nor Paul made any attempt to speak French, and the audience, for its part, evinced boredom towards Lennon-McCartney songs. All they seemed to want were rock and roll numbers like Twist and Shout, which they greeted with cries of 'un autre, un autre'. At one point, a strange chant became audible. 'Ring-o', it sounded like. 'Ring-o, Ring-o.'

The reviews, next morning, were tepid. *France-Soir* called them *zazous* (delinquents) and *vedettes démodées* (has-beens). According to Nicky Byrne, the effect on merchandising prospects throughout Europe was swift and disastrous. Galaries Lafayette the department store decided, after all, not to fill an entire window with Beatle goods. Nor did Lambretta, the Italian motor scooter corporation, proceed with its plan to market a special model with a Beatle wig for a saddle.

The barbs of *France-Soir*, in common with everything French, had ceased to matter to the *zazous* and their entourage several hours earlier. Dezo Hoffman, eating dinner at a small restaurant with Derek Taylor, received an urgent summons back to the

George Cinq. Both returned, to find the Beatles' suite in a state of eerie quiet.

'Brian was there as well,' Hoffman says. 'He was sitting on a chair and the Beatles were sitting on the floor around him. He said the news had come through that I Want to Hold Your Hand was Number One in the American Top Hundred. The Beatles couldn't even speak—not even John Lennon. They just sat on the floor like kittens at Brian's feet.'

February 1964

'They've got everything over there. What do they want us *for?'*

Early on 7 February 1964, when the New York streets were still empty but for snow and steam and fast-bouncing cabs, a disc jockey on station WMCA sounded the first note of impending madness. 'It is now 6.30 am, Beatle time. They left London 30 minutes ago. They're out over the Atlantic Ocean, headed for New York. The temperature is 32 Beatle degrees.'

America's interest, until the eleventh hour, had remained no more than cursory. The American Press is at the best of times notoriously parochial; and these were the worst of times. Since 22 November, there had been only one newspaper story in America; only one picture, on an amateur's ciné film, endlessly replayed up to that same frozen frame. A young man, next to his wife in an open car, slumped sideways as the bullets struck him.

Just before a Christmas holiday which very few Americans felt disposed to celebrate, Walter Hofer, the New York attorney, sat in his office on West 57th Street. Hofer, like many New Yorkers, had the habit of perpetual work. It was one way, at least, to shut out the dull, slow, directionless feeling that, since President Kennedy's assassination, had shrouded Manhattan like a fog.

'Out of the blue, I got this call from Capitol Records. They wanted to know, was it right that I acted in New York for a British company called NEMS Enterprises? I told them, yes I did. They said they were trying to find out who controlled the publishing on a song called I Want to Hold Your Hand by this British group, the Beatles.'

Capitol, prepared to release that unknown British group's record into the sluggish post-Christmas market, had received some puzzling news from out of town. A disc jockey in Washington, D.C., working on station WWDC, had somehow obtained a copy of I Want to Hold Your Hand, and was playing it on the air amid a commotion of interest from his listeners. The record had come, not from Capitol but direct from London via the disc jockey's girl friend, who was a stewardess with British Overseas Airways.

'Capitol wanted to get clearance on the publishing side, to be able to ship a few hundred copies into the Washington area,' Walter Hofer says. 'In fact, I had to tell them that the publishing rights had been sold to another company, MCA. Sold for almost nothing, it so happened, just to give the song any foothold that was possible over here.'

While Capitol tried to resolve this trifling matter, a second, identical commotion was reported, from Chicago. A radio station was being besieged by inquiries after playing a song called I Want to Hold Your Hand by this British group, the Beatles. Apparently it had been sent on tape from a friend of the disc jockey's at WWDC, Washington. From Chicago, by the same fraternal taping process, it moved west again, to St. Louis. The voices and slow handclap broke now among old office mansions that form the threshold to the highways speeding west.

In New York, as the pavement Santas pessimistically clanged their bells, a drastic change was ordered in the marketing strategy of Capitol Records. A week earlier, Brown Meggs and his colleagues had been uneasy about a prospective pressing for I Want to Hold Your Hand of 200,000 copies. Now three entire production plants—Capitol's own and that of CBS and RCA—were alerted to work through Christmas and New Year, to press one million copies.

By the time the news reached Brian Epstein in Paris, sales were closer to 1.5 million. The night disappeared, after speech had returned, in a wild spree of drinking and piggyback-riding and a restaurant party, joined by George Martin and his wife-to-be Judy Lockhart-Smith, when Brian so far forgot himself as to sit and be photographed with a chamberpot on his head.

Next morning, the American Press were there en masse. *Life* magazine's London bureau chief, having planned to slip over to Paris merely for lunch, found himself, to his dismay, charged with the week's cover story. Equivalent responsibilities had suddenly devolved on representatives of *CBS, Associated Press,* the *New York Times* and *Washington Post.* The Beatles, roused from sleep at 1 pm, were brought in to meet the first deputation, still in their dressing-gowns.

The deputation, crop-haired and collegiate-looking as all good Americans ought to be, saw at once what element in the story their readers would find of consuming but abhorrent fascination.

The *New York Times* tried to put it tactfully.

'Who does your hair while you're in Paris?'

'Nobody does it when we're in *London.*'

'But where did those hair-do's . . .'

'You mean hair-don'ts,' John Lennon said.

'We were coming out of a swimming bath in Liverpool,' George Harrison said, amid earnest note-taking, 'and we liked the way it looked.' So the story went out on the AP and UPI wires.

The most celebrated journalistic visitor was Sheilah Graham, F. Scott Fitzgerald's last love and one of America's most widely-syndicated columnists. She waited an hour and a half while the Beatles underwent medical examinations for their forthcoming film.

At length, only George Harrison put his serious face around the door. 'Why—hello, dear,' Miss Graham said, rising. 'Now tell me quickly—which one are you?'

Nicky Byrne and his Seltaeb partners were already in New York. They had gone ahead of the Beatles to set up merchandising deals according to the 90–10 per cent contract in their favour. Nicky Byrne wore an overcoat with an astrakhan collar. Lord Peregrine Eliot wore a leather jacket belying his ancestral home with its 130 chimney stacks.

New York by this time, late in January, made only one kind of sound. Every radio station every few seconds played a Beatles record. Capitol had now also released the With the Beatles LP —renamed Meet the Beatles—and, to their blank astonishment, had seen it go instantly to the top of the album charts. Nor was the bonanza confined to Capitol. Vee Jay, the Chicago label which had originally released Please Please Me, hastily re-issued it, together with the album of the same name. Please Please Me, the single, was now chasing I Want to Hold Your Hand up a Billboard Hot Hundred chart whose lower reaches were jammed with album tracks on two competing labels. A third company, MGM, had snapped up the rights to My Bonnie and other, formerly uncredited, tracks which the Beatles had made with Tony Sheridan, long ago in Hamburg.

Nicky Byrne and his Seltaeb young men took accommodation at the elegant Drake Hotel and offices on Fifth Avenue. Within hours, they were besieged by manufacturers seeking a part in what the American business world already recognised as the biggest marketing opportunity since Walt Disney had created Mickey Mouse.

The procedure was that Seltaeb, having satisfied themselves as to the suitable nature of the merchandise, issued a licence in exchange for a cash advance against 10 per cent manufacturing royalties. An early licensee, the Reliant Shirt Corporation, paid £25,000 'upfront' for exclusive rights to produce Beatle T-shirts in three factories they had bought for the purpose. Three days after the T-shirts went on sale, a million had been sold.

At Seltaeb's Fifth Avenue office, three or four presidents of major American corporations would obediently wait in line outside Nicky Byrne's door. Byrne, magnificently casual, refused to talk business with anyone below the rank of president. Not the least confusion among these urgent supplicants arose from the knowledge that one Seltaeb director they might deal with was an earl. Lord Peregrine Eliot, more than once, was buttonholed by an anxious, 'Say, listen Earl—'

Within a week of setting up in New York, Nick Byrne received an offer of $½m for Seltaeb from Capitol Records. 'They were willing to pay the money straight into the Bahamas,' Byrne says. '*And* they were willing to let us keep a half-interest in the company. But I turned them down. Part of the deal was that they were going to get me one of the top American merchandising men—a man who'd worked for Disney and who'd since retired. Then I found out that Capitol had no intention of persuading this man to work with us. I turned them down because they'd lied to me.

'Capitol wouldn't take no for an answer. They tried *everything* to get me to sell. They'd check up on me—*all* American big business does that—and found out about my interest in motor racing. At our next meeting, when I said I still wouldn't sell, the Capitol man said, "Just take a look out of the window, Nicky." Down in the street, there was one of the most exclusive Ferraris ever made—the 29. Only one had come into America to be driven by the North American Racing Team. This was it—it had mechanics standing beside it. "That's yours, Nicky," I was told, "if we can do this deal."

'I said, "But it's not as easy as that. I've got five partners." The Capitol man turned round and said, "Joe! Get five more of those." '

At Capitol Records, $50,000 was hastily allocated for a 'crash publicity program' leading up to the Beatles' arrival on 7 February. Five million posters and car windscreen stickers were printed with the cryptic message 'The Beatles Are Coming'. A four-page life story was circulated, with promotional records, to disc jockeys across the continent. Certain stations also received tapes of 'open-end' interviews, pre-recorded by the Beatles, with spaces left for the disc jockey's questions. Capitol executives, like so many repentant Scrooges, were photographed in Beatle wigs.

The *Ed Sullivan Show*, meanwhile, had received 50,000 applications for the 700-odd seats at its transmission on 9 February. Elvis Presley, and his scandalous torso, in 1957, did not attract so big a response. CBS had announced that the Beatles' second appearance for Sullivan, a week later, would be in a special show from the Hotel Deauville, Miami. Not a seat remained for their first American concert, at the Washington Coliseum, nor for Sid Bernstein's two concerts at Carnegie Hall. Mrs. Nelson Rockefeller was one of numerous celebrities whom Bernstein hoped to accommodate by putting extra seats on the stage.

And yet for all this brisk commercial activity, nothing had been done to connect the manifest excitement of American teenagers with the Beatles' physical presence on American soil. A film clip of them, shown on NBC's *Jack Paar Show*, brought confident predictions, notably from the *New York Times*, that, although the Beatles might be coming, Beatlemania definitely was not. 'For all Capitol and CBS cared,' Nicky Byrne says, 'they were just going to walk off the 'plane and go to their hotel. Nobody would even have known they were in America.'

Byrne, as a merchandiser of Beatle goods, had his own reasons for desiring something more. 'I kept ringing London to say, "Look here, Capitol are hopeless, nobody's doing *anything* in the way of publicity." I couldn't get hold of Brian Epstein at all. He'd completely disappeared. So had David Jacobs.'

As 7 February drew near, Nicky Byrne decided to take the initiative. He enlisted the help of a T-shirt manufacturer and of two New York radio stations, WMCA and WINS. 'Every 15 minutes, the same announcement was made over the air. A free T-shirt and a dollar bill for every kid who went out to Kennedy Airport to see the Beatles land.'

The Beatles were seen off from Heathrow Airport by 1,000 banner-waving fans whose screams Cynthia Lennon mistook, in her innocence, for the noise of their waiting Pan Am jet. Cynthia was to accompany the party and, such was the momentousness of the occasion, even received permission to be photographed by the Press corps which packed the VIP lounge. No departure from Britain so mingled national acclamation and hope since Neville Chamberlain's flight to Munich in 1938.

The greater part of Pan Am flight 101 was occupied by the Beatles and their entourage. They themselves sat in the first-class cabin with Brian Epstein, Cynthia and Phil Spector, the American record producer. Certain favoured Press friends travelled first class, such as Maureen Cleave from the *Evening Standard*, and a *Liverpool Echo* journalist, coincidentally blessed with the name George Harrison. George, when he retired from Fleet Street in the 1950s, had thought himself out of the 'rat race'. Now he found himself bound on the world's biggest assignment, with expenses which, for the thrifty *Echo*, was equally phenomenal.

In the Economy cabin sat Dezo Hoffman and the two road managers, Neil and Mal, already deep in their task of forging Beatle signatures on thousands of give-away photographs. Scattered among the other Press, and eyeing each other just as balefully, was a contingent of British manufacturers with ideas for new lines in Beatle merchandise. Unable to contact Brian Epstein on the ground, they hoped he would prove more accessible at 30,000 feet. Notes were passed to Brian throughout the flight, and endorsed with a polite refusal.

The Beatles, though resolutely laughing and larking, all showed signs of fear at what lay ahead. None could be convinced they were any different from previous British entertainers who had taken on America, and lost. The example of Cliff Richard was frequently mentioned. George, on a visit to his elder sister in St. Louis, had seen Cliff's film *Summer Holiday* relegated to a drive-in second feature. Nor did the work permits Brian had obtained seem prophetic of triumphal coming. The H_2 classification allowed them to play, within a strict two-week period, 'so long as unemployed American citizens capable of performing this work cannot be found'.

Paul McCartney strapped himself into his safety belt, not loosening it throughout the flight. To Maureen Cleave and Phil Spector he confided the same disbelief that George Harrison did to his namesake from the *Liverpool Echo*. 'He mentioned all the big American stars who'd come across to Britain,' Harrison says. 'He'd been across, unlike the others; he knew what the place was like. "They've got everything over there," he said. "What do they want *us* for?" '

America, at first, presented only the normal aerial view of coast and long piers and the snow-flecked scrubland up to the runway edge. Even after the wheels struck tarmac, no particular welcome was visible save in the earmuffed men who walked backwards, signalling with their small round bats. Then, as one wing found the terminal buildings, the prospect dramatically changed. Five thousand people waited like a mural beyond the thick window glass. 'The Beatles had no idea it was for them,' Dezo Hoffman says. 'They thought the President must be going to land in a minute.'

The opening of the door let in a sound which made Heathrow and its cataclysms seem merely decorous. Not only were there more fans than the Beatles had ever seen before: they also made twice the noise. Screaming, they hung over balconies and retaining walls; screaming, they buckled against a 100-man Police cordon, oblivious to peril or pain. Blended with the shriek was the shout of photographers, equally possessed, who approached the aircraft clinging to a hydraulic crane. As the Beatles, somnambulistically, began to descend the steps, a girl on the terminal's third outside level flung herself into space and hung there on the arms of two companions, crying: 'Here I am!' Near the bottom step stood the first intelligible New Yorker, a policeman. 'Boy,' he was heard to remark, 'can they use a haircut.'

Brian Sommerville, their Press Officer—who had arrived two days earlier—advanced through the uproar, accompanied by Pan Am officials, not the least of whose concerns was to cover up the Beatles' BEAtle inflight bags. As the remaining passengers descended, each received from Capitol Records a 'Beatle kit' consisting of a 'signed' photograph, an 'I Like the Beatles' badge and a Beatle wig. The Beatles had by now reached the Customs hall, where every item of their luggage was examined. In one direction, several hundred howling girls were chased back by Police and security men; the other way, about 1,000 more flung and flattened themselves like insects against the plate glass wall.

On the first floor of the main terminal, where 200 journalists waited, Brian Sommerville began to show his quarterdeck irascibility. The photographers, massed in front of reporters and TV crews, were making too much noise for any formal question to be heard. Sommerville, after several more or less polite injunctions, grabbed a microphone and snapped: 'Shut up—just shut up.' The Beatles concurred, 'Yeah, shurrup.' This produced spontaneous applause.

The New York Press, with a few exceptions, succumbed as quickly as the fans. Within minutes, one svelte and sarcastic woman journalist was babbling into a telephone: 'They are absolutely too cute for words. America is going to just *love* them.' On another line, an agency reporter began his dispatch: 'Not since McArthur returned from Korea . . .' Meanwhile, in the conference room, their 198 colleagues continued the interrogation which was supposed to have been ironic and discomfiting but which had produced anything but discomfiture. The Beatles were at their flash-quick, knockabout, impudent best.

'Are you going to have a haircut while you're in America?'

'We had one yesterday,' John replied.

'Will you sing something for us?'

'We need money first,' John said.

'What's your secret?'

'If we knew that,' George said, 'we'd each form a group and manage it.'

'Was your family in show business?' John was asked.

'Well me Dad used to say me Mother was a great performer.'

'Are you part of a teenage rebellion against the older generation?'

'It's a dirty lie.'

'What do you think of the campaign in Detroit to stamp out the Beatles?'

'We've got a campaign of our own,' Paul said, 'to stamp out Detroit.'

Outside the terminal, four chauffeur-driven Cadillacs waited. The Beatles, ejected rather than emerging from the rear entrance, were each lifted bodily by two policemen and thrust into a Cadillac. Long after they had returned to England, their arms would still bear the marks of this helpful assistance. Paul, in addition, had a handful of his hair wrenched by a photographer, to see if it was a wig. 'Get out of here, buddy,' a policeman told the leading chauffeur, 'if you want to get out alive.'

Outside the stately Plaza hotel, facing Central Park, the fountains were engulfed by a shrieking mob, against which a squad of mounted policemen bounced ineffectually like corks. Reservations at the Plaza had been made a month earlier in the individual names of Lennon, McCartney, Harrison and Starr, four 'London businessmen'. At the time, the hotel checked only as far as to ascertain their 'good financial status'. Directly the true nature of their business became known, a Plaza representative went on radio, offering them to any other New York hotel that would take them.

As the four Cadillacs sped in from Kennedy, set among their weaving and shouting and grimacing motorcade, the Plaza strove not to capitulate. The Palm Court served tea, as usual, with violin music, though the orchestra leader was vexed to receive requests for Beatles songs. Waiters moved among the pillars and heaped pastries, discreetly requesting the odd errant guest to remove his Beatle wig.

The Beatles and their party had been allocated the hotel's entire twelfth floor. A special force from the Burns Detective Agency was on duty around the clock, to screen all arrivals and conduct periodic searches in the floors above, where some girls had climbed several hundred fire stairs to lie in wait. A bevy of under managers ran around, fearful, as well they might be, for the hotel's cherished fabric. When a photographer asked John Lennon to lie down on a bed and show his boots, a Plaza man interrupted, 'Oh no—*that's* not the image we want to project.' 'Don't worry,' John told him. 'We'll buy the bed.'

Interconnecting suites, 10 rooms in all, had been provided for the Beatles, their solitary wife, their two autograph-manufacturing road managers and their overworked publicist. Only Brian had separate accommodation, on Central Park side, far from everyone else.

Already, visitors were arriving, or trying to arrive. One of the first to get through the security was Geoffrey Ellis, Brian's old Liverpool friend, the Royal Insurance man. 'The whole scene was extremely surrealistic,' Ellis says. 'The Beatles were all sitting round with transistor radios in their ears, listening to their records playing and watching themselves on television at the same time.'

All the evening TV news bulletins carried the Kennedy Airport scenes as top story, though not all expressed unqualified delight. On NBC, Chet Huntley, the celebrated 'front man' quivered with bilious distaste. 'Like a good little news organisation, we sent three cameramen out to Kennedy this afternoon to cover the arrival of a group from England, known as the Beatles. However, after surveying the film our men returned with, and the subject of that film, I feel there is absolutely no need to show any of that film.' A dissident radio station, WNEW, kept saying that I Want to Hold Your Hand made some people want to hold their noses.

On every other Pop frequency, Beatle voices could be heard, conversing in pre-recorded form or as they had spoken a few minutes earlier, 'live' from their hotel suite. Fast-talking disc jockeys found them an easy target, instantly friendly and funny and willing to endorse anything or anyone. The great success in this field was scored by Murray 'The K' Kaufman of station WINS; having first interviewed the Beatles by telephone, he arrived in their suite, accompanied by an entire girl singing group, and was seldom, if ever, got rid of thereafter.

The strain was beginning to tell already on Brian Epstein. First, there was a furious dispute with Brian Sommerville over the room arrangements, and Sommerville threatened to resign. Then Brian came into the Beatles' suite, crimson with anger. Among the products they had obligingly endorsed by telephone were several 'bootleg' recordings of their own music, smuggled out of England and now on sale in the New York shops. 'Brian screamed at them for what they had done,' Dezo Hoffman says. 'They listened to him like naughty children. He still had some authority with them then.'

Shortly after their arrival, George Harrison went to bed, complaining of a sore throat. He had been unwell in Paris, too, dictating his *Daily Express* column—as he was to continue to do—without mention of the disconcerting French habit of administering medicines in suppository form. His elder sister, Louise, who had just arrived from St. Louis, moved into the Plaza to nurse him.

The other three, despite the crowds outside, managed some limited after-dark movement. Paul visited the Playboy Club, leaving subsequently with a bunny girl. The Lennons and Ringo, under Murray the K's garrulous protection, went to the Peppermint Lounge, finding it 'the home of the Twist' no longer; its resident group were imitation Beatles. Later, John and Cynthia scuttled back past the photographers, their two heads covered by a coat. Ringo did not return; it was feared for a time that he might have been kidnapped. He returned in the early hours, unaware of the frenzied unease he had caused.

The next morning, it drizzled. Twelve floors below, the crowds and police horses still struggled together in a muted chant of She Loves You. Brian, in his sequestered drawing-room, made a series of urgent telephone calls. The first was to Walter Hofer, the attorney, on West 57th Street. Hofer, at this time, was not sure if he was still NEMS' New York lawyer. 'Brian told me, "You're our attorney—we need you over here." He gave me the job of dealing with all the Beatles' fanmail. I put my usual messenger service to work on it. Later on, I got this call from the messenger. "Mister—I'm 77 years old! There's 37 sacks of mail here."

'We set up a special department in another hotel to deal with it. One of the letters that was opened had come from Lyndon B. Johnson. Another was from the manager of the Plaza. "When are you guys going to settle your check?" it said.'

Capitol Records received an urgent call for a secretary to work with Brian in New York and Miami. Through their classical music department they found Wendy Hanson, an imposing blonde who had until recently been personal assistant to Leopold Stokowsky. 'I had to fight my way into the Plaza through all this pandemonium,' Wendy says, 'and there, absolutely cut off from it all, was this baby-faced young man, *drenched* in Guerlain. "Hello, my dear," were his first words. "Would you like some tea?" '

The Beatles, meanwhile—minus George Harrison—sat in a limousine packed so close among keening girls, the chauffeur could get in only by crawling across the roof. John Lennon, in dark glasses and Bob Cratchitt cap, was asked if all this bothered him. 'No,' he replied in all innocence, 'it's not our car.'

At the Ed Sullivan Theatre on West 53rd Street, a set had been constructed of half a dozen inward-pointing white arrows. The programme designer explained to a posse of journalists his desire 'to symbolise the fact that the Beatles are *here*'. Even for the rehearsal, with Neil Aspinall standing in for George, three high-ranking CBS executives were turned away at the door. Sullivan himself was all amiability, rebuking his musical director for having told the *New York Times* the Beatles would last no longer than a year, and threatening to put on a Beatle wig himself if George was not well enough for the transmission. He became a little less amiable when Brian Epstein approached him and said grandly: 'I would like to know the exact wording of your introduction.' 'I would like you to get lost,' Ed Sullivan replied.

The *Ed Sullivan Show* on 9 February was watched by an audience of 70 million, or 60 per cent of all American television viewers. At the beginning, a congratulatory telegram was read out from Elvis Presley. Conditioned as they were to hyper-unreality, this event still gave pause to Liverpool boys who had listened to Houn' Dog under the bedclothes, and struggled to learn the words of All Shook Up as it was beamed from its inconceivable Heaven.

The image carried across America bore helpful subtitles giving each Beatle's name. John Lennon's subtitle added: 'Sorry, girls —he's married.'

The *New York Herald-Tribune*, next morning, called them '75 per cent publicity, 20 per cent haircut and 5 per cent lilting lament'. The *Washington Post* called them 'asexual and homely'. The *New York Times* carried reviews by both the television and the music critic. The former judged the Beatles 'a fine mass placebo' while the latter, anxious to out-obfuscate William Mann, discovered in All My Loving 'a false modal frame . . . momentarily suggesting the mixoldyian mode . . .' Earl Wilson, the *New York Post* columnist, was photographed at the head of his afternoon's paragraphs in a bald wig. From UPI came the news that Billy Graham, the evangelist, had broken a lifetime's rule by watching television on the Sabbath.

On that one night, America's crime rate was lower than at any time during the previous half-century. Police precinct houses throughout New York could testify to the sudden drop in juvenile offences. In all the five boroughs, not one single car hubcap was reported stolen.

The nervous plans, the small-scale hopes, the little deals for cut-price fees, all coalesced in a moment that was miraculously right. America, three months earlier, had been struck dumb by a great and terrible event. America now found her voice again through an event which no psychiatrist could have made more therapeutically trivial. That voice was in itself therapeutic, reassuring a suddenly-uncertain people that, at least, they had not lost their old talent for excess.

It was a moment when the potential existed for a madness which nothing indigenously American could unleash. It was a moment when all America's deep envy of Europe, and the eccentricity permitted to older-established nations, crystallised in four figures whose hair and clothes, to American eyes, placed them somewhere near Shakespeare's Hamlet. It was a moment simultaneously gratifying America's need for a new idol, a new toy, a pain-killing drug and a laugh.

On the morning after the *Ed Sullivan Show*, the Beatles were brought to the Plaza hotel's Baroque Room to give a Press conference that was itself record-breaking, both in size and fatuousness. Even superior organs like *Time* magazine and the

New Yorker stiffened themselves to the task of determining whether Beatle hair was correctly described as 'bangs' and their footwear as 'pixie boots'. The *Saturday Evening Post* had sent a photographer with $100,000-worth of equipment to shoot a cover. The *New York Journal-American* had sent Dr. Joyce Brothers, a psychologist with flicked-out blonde hair and her own television show. Dr. Brothers had her pulse humorously taken by the Beatles and afterwards reminded her stunned readership that 'Beatles might look unappetising and inconsequential, but naturalists have long considered them the most successful order of animals on earth'.

The hideous arc-light, the poking, jostling lenses, the questions from people who still had difficulty in telling them apart, all seemed to make no impression on the Beatles' happy obligingness, their impudent deference. It was the stamina bred through Hamburg and Litherland nights, the shared wit sharpened by years of talking their way round trouble. 'Either they're employing the most marvellous concealed gag man,' Maureen Cleave cabled the London *Evening Standard*, 'or Bob Hope should sign them up right away.'

'What do you think of the Playboy Club?' Paul was asked.

'The Playboy and I are just good friends.'

'Why aren't you wearing a tie?' a woman journalist snapped at George.

'Why aren't *you* wearing a hat?'

The inquisition continued all day, without a break for lunch. Instead, some plates of hotel chicken were brought in. 'I'm sorry to interrupt you while you're eating,' a woman reporter said, 'but what do you think you'll be doing in five years time?'

'Still eating,' John replied.

'Have you got a leading lady for your movie?'

'We're trying to get the Queen,' George said. 'She sells.'

'When do you start rehearsing?'

'We don't,' John said.

'—oh yes we do,' Paul put in.

'We don't, Paul does,' John amended. Some papers had already elicited the fact that among the other three, Paul was referred to as 'the star'.

The American Press, in its wild scramble, paid little attention to the other young Englishman, in a polka-dotted foulard scarf, who stood at one side, observing the scene with what the *New York Times* described as 'a look of hauteur'. Even when Jay Livingstone—the same Capitol boss who had said, 'We don't think the Beatles will do anything in this market'—stepped beamingly forward to present them with two million-sale Gold Discs, Brian still did not allow himself the relaxation of a smile.

'He had ice water in his veins before,' another Capitol man remarked. 'Now it's turned to vinegar.'

This was a mistaken diagnosis. What Brian's demeanour in fact betrayed was a fierce desire to seem coolly imperturbable even as, on every side, he could feel important matters slithering from his grasp. The frequent rows he was having with Brian Sommerville provided his only outlet for that great, growing fear.

The record side, to begin with, was in chaos. New York shops already had on sale discs by groups called the 'Beetles' or 'Bugs', in some cases illustrated by a spurious likeness, in one case, at least, innocently advertised on radio by the *true* Beatles. Hardly less abhorrent to Brian was MGM's release of My Bonnie, the same record, from Hamburg days, which had first led him to the Cavern Club. Implicit in his dream for the Beatles was that they should disown all existence before his became entwined with theirs.

Please Please Me, now at number three in the Billboard chart, was bringing vast profits to the hitherto obscure Vee Jay label in Chicago. Vee Jay's president, it so chanced, was also a client of Brian's New York attorney, Walter Hofer. Vee Jay persuaded Brian to sue them as a publicity stunt, with Hofer revealed as lawyer to both parties. Capitol Records pre-empted this wheeze with an injunction to stop Vee Jay issuing further Beatle records. Vee Jay, sure of their ground, retained the law firm of ex-Vice President Adelai Stevenson. Capitol responded by engaging the Chicago law firm of Mayor Richard Daley.

Only now, too, was Brian starting to realise what a catastrophic deal had been made on his behalf with Nicky Byrne's Seltaeb merchandising company. In the aftermath of the *Ed Sullivan Show*, Beatle goods were pouring into the New York shops. REMCO industries had already produced 100,000 Beatle dolls. Beatle wigs were flopping off the production line at the rate of 35,000 a day. The over-indulged American child could choose from a range including Beatle masks, pens, bow ties, 'Flip Your Wig' games, edible discs and 'Beatle nut' ice cream. Agreement was reportedly pending between Seltaeb and a major cola company. Woolworth's and Penney's were negotiating to put 'Beatle counters' in hundreds of their stores, coast to coast. The *Wall Street Journal* estimated that by the end of the year $5m worth of Beatle goods would have been sold in America.

Nor was it reassuring to observe the progress around New York of the man whose company's share of the profits would be 90 per cent. For Nicky Byrne did business on a magnificent scale. His lunches took place at the Four Seasons or the New York Jockey Club. His two chauffeur-driven limousines, on 24-hour standby, would frequently be passed over in favour of a private helicopter. His style quickly communicated itself to the five young men from Chelsea who were his partners. Lord Peregrine Eliot has pleasant memories of dropping into the Seltaeb office, once or twice a week, to draw a $1,000 bill from petty cash.

Nicky Byrne argued—and still argues—that it was the only way to do business with large American corporations. He is equally firm on a point later to be disputed—that as the money in manufacturers' advances poured into Seltaeb, the 10 per cent due to Brian and the Beatles was paid over to them within seven days.

'When Brian arrived in New York, I'd just banked $97,000. So, of course, I handed a cheque to Brian for $9,700. He was delighted at first. "Now," he said, "how much of this do I owe you?" "Nothing, Brian," I said. "That's your 10 per cent." He was amazed and furious all at the same time. "But this is *marvellous*, Nicky," he was saying—because he'd been told I'd fixed the airport business. "How did you *do* it, Nicky—but you had no *right* to do it! But it was marvellous, Nicky . . ."'

Nicky Byrne's claim to have fixed the Kennedy Airport crowd—and thus triggered off America's latent Beatlemania—is not entirely uncorroborated. On the morning after, some newspapers reported that pupils at a girls' school in the Bronx had been bribed to go out to Kennedy and scream. And, Nicky Byrne says, he remained the tour's chief fixer, from pushing Beatles records on radio to buying off a photographer who had obtained some homosexual pictures of Brian.

'He said, "You must work for *me*, Nicky—I'll make you a president, I'll give you a thousand a year." I said, "A thousand a year? Oh come *on*, Brian . . ." Then all of a sudden I realised he was crazy.'

On 11 February, the Beatles were to fly to Washington to give their first American concert, at the Coliseum sports arena. The booking had been made for Brian by Norman Weiss, of the General Artists Corporation, to help offset the loss on the overall trip. Brian had also accepted an invitation from the British Ambassador to a function as yet unclearly defined. 'Is it true,' the Press kept asking them, 'that you're going to a masked ball?' Sir Alec Douglas Home, Prime Minister of England, also due in Washington for talks with President Lyndon Johnson, had wisely put his arrival back by one day.

The morning of their departure, snow began falling thickly on New York. Led by George Harrison, the Beatles flatly refused to fly in a 'fookin' blizzard'. They were, however, amenable to travelling by train. A private carriage was sought, and miraculously appeared in the magnificent shape of an Edwardian sleeping car from the old Richmond, Fredericksburg and Potomac Railroad. This equipage drew out of a shrieking Pennsylvania Station, carrying, with the Beatles and their entourage, dozens of journalists, several TV crews and the egregious Murray the K. Cynthia Lennon, disguised by sunglasses and a brunette wig, was almost left behind on the platform.

At Washington's Union Station, 3,000 teenagers flung themselves against the 20-foot high wrought-iron platform gates. Seven thousand more filled the Coliseum, an arena with the stage in the centre, like a boxing ring. While the Beatles performed, Brian Sommerville had to keep running out to turn them in a different direction. The Washington fans, having read George Harrison's joke about liking jelly babies, resolutely pelted the stage with America's version, the jelly bean—often not troubling to remove them from the packet—as well as buttons, hair rollers and spent flash bulbs. A policeman near the stage philosophically screwed a .38 calibre bullet into each of his ears. And Brian Epstein, once again, was noticed standing and weeping.

The British Embassy visit had been arranged by Brian Sommerville, an old shipmate of the Naval attaché there. The Beatles agreed to go only because Brian thought it would be good for the image. Upon arriving, they were greeted by the Ambassador, Sir David Ormsby-Gore, pleasantly enough. What followed was extremely unpleasant, though not atypical of Foreign Office social life. Men in stiff collars and their gin and tonic wives pushed and struggled for autographs, at the same time exclaiming in patrician amusement, 'Can they actually *write*?' One cawing female produced nail scissors and cut off a piece of Ringo's hair. The purpose of this visit, they discovered, was to announce the prizes in an Embassy raffle. When John Lennon demurred, a group of young F.O. types formed threateningly around him. Ringo, touching his shoulder, said amicably, 'Come on—let's get it over with.'

The story, when given in the British papers, caused a major Parliamentary incident. A Conservative M.P., Joan Quennell, called on the Foreign Secretary, R. A. Butler, to confirm or deny that the Beatles had been manhandled by Embassy personnel. Mr. Butler replied that, on the contrary, the Beatles' manager had written to Lady Ormsby-Gore, 'thanking her for a delightful evening'.

At the White House, meanwhile, Sir Alec Douglas Home had arrived for his talks with President Lyndon Johnson. The big, bewildered Texan, catapulted into charge of the world's richest nation, had one thing at least in common with the tweedy, skeletal English earl. 'I like your advance guard,' LBJ quipped. 'But don't you think they need haircuts?'

And in New York, Sid Bernstein, that portly but quick-witted promoter, sat on the staircase at Carnegie Hall, listening to an uproar which made even the framed portraits of Schubert and Ravel jig slightly on the corridor wall. His 'phenomenon', mistaken by that Polish lady for a string quartet, had in one night recouped Sid Bernstein the losses suffered in promoting the 1960 Newport Jazz Festival. Celebrities like David Niven and Shirley MacLaine had begged for tickets, but had been refused. Mrs. Nelson Rockefeller, with her two daughters, had waited half an hour just for a peep into the dressing-room.

'After the second concert,' Bernstein says, 'I walked with Brian Epstein across to Madison Square Garden. We looked inside the old Garden arena. Seventeen thousand seats. I knew the Garden wanted the Beatles; they could have had tickets printed in 24 hours. I offered Brian $25,000 and a $5,000 donation to the British Cancer Fund. I knew he was tempted. But he gave me that little smile he had. "Sid," he said, "let's save it for next time." '

Next morning, the Police barricades were removed from the front of the Plaza hotel; its elegant lobby grew quiet but for the headlines on the news-stand counter. 'Britain's Boy Beatles Buzz By, Bomb Bobbysoxers.' 'Audience Shrieks, Bays and Ululates.' A large sum of money, which CBS had paid into the hotel for the use of the Beatles' party, was found to be untouched. Nobody even knew it was there.

The Beatles were aboard a National Airlines jet, bound for Miami and their second *Ed Sullivan Show*, their course to the south-west plotted by a flight engineer in a Beatle wig. On landing, they were greeted by four 'bathing beauties', a chimpanzee and a crowd of 7,000 which, in its emotion, smashed 23 windows and glass doors within the terminal precincts. The 'bathing beauties'—from now on a regular but ambiguous fixture of all American journeys—each began furiously to kiss her apportioned Beatle. Police intervention was necessary to stop them being kissed all the way to their limousines and beyond.

At the Hotel Deauville, a dimly-lit Versailles turned end-ways into the sky above Miami Beach, each was decanted into his own lofty, luxurious, three-room prison cell. For the Deauville, like the New York Plaza, was in a state of screaming siege. Two enterprising girls had themselves wrapped in two parcels addressed to the Beatles, but were apprehended on delivery.

George Martin, their record producer, coincidentally in America, came down to Miami to see them, bringing his wife-to-be, Judy Lockhart-Smith. Martin watched the Beatles rehearse in bathing trunks in the hotel ballroom, and later repay Ed Sullivan's $3,500 with a performance destined to break every record in audience ratings for televised entertainment. So far as such things can ever be computed, 75 million Americans watched the *Ed Sullivan Show* that night. During the transmission, from the hotel's Mau Mau Club, a girl next to George Martin broke off sobbing and bouncing to stare at him in surprise. 'Do *you* like them, *too*, sir?' she asked.

Ed Sullivan nearly smiled. Cassius Clay flourished Ringo Starr aloft like a talisman against Sonny Liston, against whom he was shortly to contest the World Heavyweight title. Clay, a peerless siphoner of publicity, had invited the Beatles to visit him at his 5th Street gymnasium. He gave his opinion that they were the greatest but *he* was still the prettiest.

Their only escape from the crowds and Press was a day spent at the beach-side mansion of a Capitol Records executive. Sergeant Buddy Bresner, a Miami cop who had befriended them, arranged for them to escape from the Deauville in the back of a butcher's truck while other policemen brought decoy guitar cases out through the front lobby.

George Martin and Judy joined them for that first real respite since they had sunbathed on the seafront at Margate. Brian was there, too, with his temporary assistant, Wendy Hanson. The householder, though absent, had left an armed bodyguard to look after them. Their protector barbecued steaks for them with a cigarette in his mouth, his shoulder holster clearly visible. 'Brian was complaining about all the bootleg records that were coming out,' George Martin remembers. 'Suddenly, this tough-looking guy who was barbecuing our steaks leaned forward and said: "You want we should take care of them for you, Mr. Epstein?" It was a *very* sinister moment.'

PART THREE

Having

August 1966

'One more stage, one more limo', one more run for your life'

The scene is an oak-panelled room deep in the hallowed precincts of an ancient and illustrious Oxford college. Before the open fire stands the Principal, an elderly gentleman both scholar and diplomat, conversing in mellifluous undertone with his junior dons and one or two of his most favoured students. Close by, a long buffet, covered with smoked salmon and sorbets and the choicest College wines, is attended by white-jacketed scouts. From a distance, through the courts and spires and cloisters, a clock may be heard, civilly striking the hour.

The 15th-century oak door opens, to admit the Beatles. They are wearing, as always, dark suits, deep-collared shirts and boots with elasticated sides. Their manner, as they meet the college Principal, the tutors and undergraduates, is deferential yet impudent. A servant offers Paul McCartney champagne in a silver goblet: Paul says he would rather have milk. George Harrison surveys the exquisite buffet, then beckons to a retainer. 'Have you got any jam butties?' he asks. 'I'll trade you an autograph for a jam butty.'

The scene comes, not from *A Hard Day's Night* but from life. It happened in March 1964, at Brasenose College on the invitation of Principal Sir Noel Hall. It is recorded in the London *Daily Mail*, in a vast picture spread and a story running to three columns. Nothing evokes more powerfully Britain's mood in early 1964 than the *Mail*'s hyperbolic triumph at this coup; its writer's mixture of jocular indulgence and history-witnessing earnestness.

The Beatles were no longer a teenage fad: they had become a national obsession. Their sudden fame, far from exploding as everyone had predicted, somehow fed on its own freakishness, growing vaster still, passing more and still more limits of known celebrity. It was a fame now divorced from their music and personalities. Four Liverpool boys with busby hair and high-buttoned jackets, singing brisk, cheerful songs that went 'Yeah yeah', were somehow coincidental in the huge emotion that blanketed Britain and, even more remarkably, blanketed America. As their fame in America grew, it became almost a point of honour that their British fame should not be allowed to lapse.

In Britain throughout 1964, their doings and sayings ran in all the papers every day like some wildly popular, all-embracing strip cartoon. They had become, like cartoon characters, an elemental silhouette in which all desires and fantasies could be lived and gratified. To most people, the faces under the fringes were still barely distinguishable. There was the funny, sarcastic one, and the pretty, big-eyed one, and the shy-looking one with hollow cheekbones. There was the ugly little one, adored as the runt of the litter. There was also the elegant young manager who sometimes stood with them, looking like a junior Guards officer; a dapper, deferential-voiced reassurance that no one had anything to fear.

The Left-wing *New Statesman* might fulminate on 'The Menace of Beatledom'. Lord Willis might denounce them as 'a cheap candy floss culture-substitute' and Lord Soper wonder audibly, 'In what aspect of the full life of the Kingdom of God can we find a place for the Beatles?' To the British nation, they had received an all-powerful imprimatur. The Royal Family were Beatle fans. Prince Philip, in an address to a youth conference, opined that they were 'good blokes'. Princess Margaret, as was well known, clapped to their music on the off-beat. The Queen herself had received a letter from an American fan, complimenting her on having the Beatles as subjects. A lady-in-waiting wrote back: 'I must explain that it is impossible for the Queen to tell you how to get in touch with them.'

The Variety Club of Great Britain named them, collectively, Show Business Personality of the Year. Their effigies were placed in wax at Madame Tussaud's, their biography summarised in the *Encyclopaedia Britannica*. It was all like a game, played with the roguish connivance of ancient institutions, to see in what unlikely surroundings the Beatles would turn up next, unawed by any grandeur, disarming the pomp of ages with a request for a jam butty.

In April, a literary luncheon, more heavily-subscribed by any that Foyle's bookshop had run since the age of Shaw and H. G. Wells, commemorated John Lennon's entry into authorship. The little drawings and verses he used to doodle under his Quarry Bank desk—and still did at odd moments backstage—appeared as a slim volume entitled *John Lennon In His Own Write*. It was, said *The Times Literary Supplement*, 'worth the study of anyone who fears for the impoverishment of the English language'. Other critics saw, in the book's myopically-mispronounced, punning fragments, the influence of Edward Lear and James Joyce. 'Do you,' a radio interviewer asked John, 'make conscious use of onomatopoeia?' 'Automatic pier?' John echoed. 'I don't know what you're on about, son.'

It was thought shocking, but forgivably so, when the Foyle's luncheon received no speech from the guest of honour. John, who arrived with Cynthia deeply hung-over after a night at the Ad Lib, had not realised he was supposed to say anything. Urged to his feet, he could only mumble, 'Thank you. It's been a pleasure.' An obliging Press translated this into the more Beatle-like: 'You've got a lucky face.'

Musically, they continued far in front of a huge field, inspired by themselves—often supplied with songs they had themselves written. Following Liverpool's glorification, almost every major provincial city now had a 'Sound'. Manchester produced the Hollies, Newcastle the Animals and Birmingham the Applejacks. From West London came a 'Mod' group, The Who; from Kentish suburbs came the Rolling Stones, managed by NEMS' ex-publicist Andrew Oldham, ersatz Beatles then, both in their material (Lennon and McCartney's I Wanna Be Your Man) and in their hairstyles, high-button coats and ingratiating smiles.

The increase was not limited to groups. On Easter Day 1964, 'Radio Caroline', a small merchant ship moored five miles off the East Anglian coast, began broadcasting continuous Pop music in blithe contravention of the BBC monopoly. The public's response to getting what it, rather than the BBC, wanted was instantaneous. Radio Caroline flourished, as did other 'pirate' stations at equally precarious moorings off Essex, on disused Thames Estuary forts and in the mouth of the Clyde.

On pirate wavelengths, as everywhere, the Beatles were pre-eminent. Their new single, Can't Buy Me Love—perhaps the least memorable of all Lennon and McCartney songs—had become the first record ever to go to Number One simultaneously in Britain and America, and that before a note of it had been heard. Advance orders from America alone exceeded three million copies.

The success of their film, *A Hard Day's Night*, seemed part of an inevitable process. It was in fact due to a lucky amalgam of economy, haste and other people's sympathetic talent. The plot, Walter Shenson had decided, would simply show the Beatles being Beatles. Alun Owen's script successfully caught whiffs of the private humour which protected them against the world. Richard Lester's direction, honed on such small Goon classics as *The Running, Jumping, Standing Still Film,* put them into high speed Mack Sennett comedy sequences. The film was shot in six weeks, between their return from America and their departure to tour Europe and the Far East. The budget, held by Shenson at

£200,000—despite the distributor's willingness to double it—was largely spent on evading the crowds which dogged each day's work. The Beatles were filmed in London streets, for the few seconds possible; inside the Scala theatre and on a specially-hired train to the West Country. A unit messenger, returning to Paddington with the day's footage, was chased by girls along the platform, dropping film cans from him as he fled.

The original title, *Beatlemania*, was changed at the last minute to a phrase that Ringo was fond of using. With the film went an album, the first to consist entirely of Lennon–McCartney songs. These had mostly been written months earlier, between *crêpes flambés* at the George Cinq. Yet the album evoked the film, just as the film caught Beatlemania at its maddest and happiest.

The film received a West End premiere in July, attended by Princess Margaret and Lord Snowdon. 'There was a big party afterwards,' Walter Shenson says. 'Nobody thought that Princess Margaret would agree to come to it, so no one invited her. I said we should at least *ask*. It turned out that she and Lord Snowdon had an engagement for dinner but that they'd love to be asked to stop in for a drink first.

'We were all in the ante-room, having drinks before going in to the food. George Harrison gave me a look and whispered: "When do we eat?" I told him, "We can't until Princess Margaret leaves." She and Lord Snowdon had this other engagement but they stayed longer and longer at the Beatles' party, having drinks, chatting. Finally George went across to Princess Margaret and said "Ma'am—we're starved, and Walter says we can't eat until you leave." Princess Margaret just burst out laughing. "Come on, Tony," she called out. "We're in the way." '

A second premiere took place in Liverpool, accompanied by a Civic welcome from the Lord Mayor. 'The Beatles were nervous wrecks about that,' Walter Shenson says. 'Even though they'd just come back from a world tour, they were scared about that appearance in Liverpool. "Ah," they kept saying, "you don't know what people are like up there." '

They drove in from Speke Airport, along the same Woolton avenues where Paul used to cycle with his guitar on his back, and where John would struggle along with the Quarry Men, carrying a tea chest. All the way, between bus stops, crowds stood, waving and cheering. Paul, to his particular pleasure, recognised 'Dusty' Durband, his English teacher from the Institute. And there, beyond what used to be Uncle George's dairy, was the red sandstone tower of St. Peter's, where the annual fête would soon be held.

So the 'four Liverpool scruffs', the black leather, sweat-soaked boys from underground in Mathew Street, came out on to the Town Hall balcony with the beaming Lord Mayor and Aldermen. They did not know how close the old days had come to catching up with them. Earlier that day, leaflets began to circulate yet another paternity allegation. Brian, helped by his brother Clive, had quietly settled the matter.

It was the year they conquered the world, but did not see it. For them the world shrank to a single dressing-room, buried under continents of screaming. More than once, on their zigzag flight down back-alleys between the hemispheres, they would ask which country this was. 'It all looked the same to them,' Tony Bramwell says. 'One more stage, one more limo', one more run for your life.'

In June they toured Scandinavia, Holland, the Far East and Australasia. Ringo Starr was having his tonsils out and missed three-quarters of the journey; in his place sat Jimmy Nicol, a session drummer small and obscure enough to scotch any rumour of permanent change. Nicol drummed with them until Melbourne, where Ringo rejoined: history from then on relates nothing further of Jimmy Nicol.

The entourage for the Far East and Australia included John Lennon's lean and volatile, but now of course proud and smiling, Aunt Mimi. In Hong Kong, the Police cleared a path for her, crying, 'John Mama, John Mama.' The sight of Adelaide and 300,000 fans, the largest Beatle crowd ever, proved too much for Mimi's nerves: after glimpsing New Zealand, she flew home to Menlove Avenue, Woolton. 'I got into trouble,' Mimi says, 'for telling an Australian TV man that John used to be bad at arithmetic when he was at school. So, on TV, this man said to him, "If you're bad at maths, how do you count all that money you're earning?" "I don't count it," John said, "I weigh it."'

In August, they returned to America. This time they did not call on Ed Sullivan to pay their fares. The country which had gone mad over their brief presence had, during their short absence, contrived to go even madder. At one point in April, the first five places in *Billboard* magazine's Top 100 records were Beatles records. *A Hard Day's Night*, opening in 500 cinemas across the country, had earned \$1·3m in its first week. Cinema showings were accompanied by as much screaming as a live concert.

At San Francisco airport, the Beatles were driven from the plane directly into a protective iron cage. Their removal from this by Police, approximately 10 seconds before it crumpled between two ravening mobs, heralded four weeks in which America came as near to orgasm as a continent can and the Beatles were, on innumerable occasions, terrified out of their lives.

The tour had been organised by Norman Weiss of GAC with

one simple objective: to spread Beatlemania like jam over the whole United States. It was Weiss who counselled Brian Epstein to accept bookings only at large arenas, like sports or convention centres, and to ask a standard $25,000 advance against a percentage of gate receipts varying from 40 to 60 per-cent. In special instances, like the Hollywood Bowl, the advance was $50,000.

The Beatles, travelling in their own private aircraft—a none too luxurious Lockheed Electra—performed in 23 cities, crossing and recrossing American airspace on a journey totalling 22,441 miles, or more than 600 miles per day. At times they did not know if they were in Jacksonville, Baltimore, Denver, Cincinnati, Detroit or Atlantic City. Everywhere, there were Mayors and Senators and Senators' wives, and Sheriffs and deputies; there were the town's most exclusive call girls; there were crippled children, lined in wheelchairs near the stage, and later brought into the Beatles' dressing-room as if to see or touch them might work a miracle. From stadium or conference hall, whichever it chanced to be, they would run, in their sodden suits, directly to the aircraft, flying through the night to another sky, another airport, another screaming sea of faces, pressed against Police backs or quilted by steel perimeter wire.

In San Francisco, at the Hilton hotel, a woman guest was robbed and pistol-whipped, her cries unheard in the noise greeting the Beatles' motorcade. At Love Field, Dallas, fans broke through the Police barrier, climbed on to the aircraft wings and belaboured the windows with Coke bottles. Later at the hotel, a chambermaid was kidnapped and threatened with a knife unless she revealed the location of the Beatles' suite; other girls had to be rescued from the air-conditioning shaft. In Los Angeles, the escape from Dodgers Stadium ended in an armoured truck with four flat tyres. In Seattle, as the Beatles left the stage, a girl fell from an overhead beam, landing at Ringo's feet. In Cleveland, they were physically dragged offstage while mounted Police charged the arena, lassooing 200 fans together in a giant net. In New York, the whole of Riverside Drive was cordoned off for their passing; in Toronto, they came in from the airport at 3 am, past seventeen miles of continuous parked cars. Each day the madness differed yet remained the same. It was cops and sweat and jelly beans hailing in dream-like noise; it was faces uglied by shrieking and biting fists; it was huge amphitheatres left littered with flashbulbs and hair rollers and buttons and badges and hundreds of pairs of knickers, wringing wet.

Out of the itinerary of chaos, a single figure came to personify that '64 American tour. His name was Charles O. Finley; he owned a baseball team, the Kansas City Athletics. He first approached Brian Epstein in San Francisco, offering $100,000 if the Beatles would give an additional concert at his baseball stadium in Kansas City. He said he had promised Kansas City they would have the Beatles. Brian replied that the tour could not be extended.

Charles O. Finley did not give up. He reappeared in various other cities, increasing his offer by degrees to $150,000 if the Beatles would let him keep his promise to Kansas City. At length, in Seattle, as it became clear to Brian and Norman Weiss that the tour might not quite cover its gigantic overheads, Charles O. Finley and Kansas City took on a new significance. It was up to the Beatles, Brian said, and whether they were willing to sacrifice one of their few rest days. The Beatles, playing cards with George Harrison of the *Liverpool Echo*, said they would leave it up to Brian. So, at the rate of £1,785 per minute, Charles O. Finley and Kansas City were not disappointed.

In New York, a brisk sale was reported in tinned Beatle's breath. In Denver, the bedlinen they had used at two stopover hotels was bought by a business consortium and placed, unlaundered, in a maximum security bank vault. The sheets were cut into three inch squares and sold at $10 per square, each one mounted on parchment and accompanied by a legal affadavit swearing it to have once formed part of a Beatle's bed.

John Lennon started to put on weight. The face, under the Beatle fringe and the mocking, shortsighted eyes, grew rounder—more contented, so Cynthia hopefully thought. Cyn' did not know what happened on tour, nor did she want to know. When she read the letters John received from girls, she laughed them off as he did, doing her best to mean it. She hoped that between tours he would settle down to his unenforced obligations as husband and father. And for a time, that did seem to please him—just staying in at night after Julian was asleep, smoking, reading, doodling, endlessly playing the same Bob Dylon records.

Paul McCartney was seen with Jane Asher at Belgravia cocktail parties and West End first nights. He was genuinely interested—so far as anything but music and Paul could interest him—in Jane's theatrical career. The sweet-faced, flame-haired, clear-voiced girl both bewitched and stimulated him. But not continually nor exclusively if there chanced to be a more famous celebrity in the room. 'Paul and Jane came out to a dinner party with my wife and me one night,' Walter Shenson says. 'Joan Sutherland the opera singer just happened to be there. Paul zeroed in on her at once as a big star. He left Jane with me and my wife and stayed talking to Joan Sutherland for the rest of the evening.'

George Harrison had been noticed in public with Pattie Boyd, a 19-year-old model who appeared briefly in *A Hard Day's Night*. Long-haired, pale and waif-like, Pattie was the archetype of 1964 high fashion. She now became an object of hatred to George's fans, who booed and jostled her, even once tried to beat her up. A robust girl, despite her looks, Pattie grew accustomed to such treatment. The tolerance shown to Cynthia Lennon was to extend to no other Beatle woman or wife.

Even rougher treatment was being suffered in Liverpool by Maureen Cox, Ringo's 'steady' since Cavern Club days. Maureen worked as a hairdresser: on many occasions, the very head she was shampooing would be uttering threats at her via the mirror. She was herself no mouse, and had become increasingly restive over the stories of Ringo's London girl friends, like the model Vicki Hodge. At last, Maureen, too, became public, visiting the hospital where Ringo was having his tonsils removed. A dark-haired, rather undernourished girl stood on the London pavement in bewilderment, clutching a carrier bag.

The Beatles gave entertainment also for the millions they were presumed to earn; for existing, like boy maharajahs, in clouds of spending money. George, it was reported, had changed his E-Type Jaguar for a white Aston Martin like Paul's. Ringo, fresh from his driving test, now drove an Italian Facel Vega. John, who had not yet learned to drive, owned a Rolls Royce, a Ferrari and a Mini Minor. Their adoption of such consumer status symbols gave vicarious pleasure; their verdict on unattainable luxury was earthily reassuring. An entire newspaper article was based on the revelation that George had tasted his first avocado. 'I've had caviare and I like it,' he told Maureen Cleave, 'but I'd still rather have an egg sandwich.'

All four spent with diminishing pleasure but at increasing speed, in the few seconds possible before the shop became a riot. John, while filming in Bond Street, ran into Asprey's silversmiths through one door and out through another having managed to spend £600. All day, wherever they were, they bought themselves presents, scarcely heeding the accumulation of presents behind them: the suits by the dozen, shirts by the hundred, the ciné-cameras, projectors, watches, gold lighters, the Asprey's silverware and cocktail cabinets shaped like antique globes. Asprey's was as good as Woolworth's, Ringo said—they had everything spread out in the open so you could see it.

The clouds of ready money bought new homes for their families according to Pop star precedent. John's Aunt Mimi left Woolton for a luxury bungalow near Bournemouth, overlooking Poole Harbour. Jim McCartney, now retired from Liverpool Cotton Exchange, moved out on to the Cheshire Wirral to enjoy the house, the wine cellar and the racehorse which Paul had given him. Harry and Louise Harrison gave up their Speke

Council house for a bungalow in the country near Warrington. Only Ringo's mother, Mrs. Graves, said she was happy where she was. She stayed in the Dingle at Admiral's Grove, and her husband, Ringo's step-father, continued to paint Corporation lamp-posts.

The acquisition of country houses and estates for the Beatles themselves took place in late 1964, in the spirit of yet another swift shopping trip. Again, the task devolved chiefly on Dr. Strach, their accountant. Strack lived in Esher, Surrey, and so concentrated his search around that semi-rural haven of accountants and stockbrokers.

For John and Cynthia, Dr. Strach found 'Kenwood', a £30,000 mock-Tudor mansion on the select St. George's Hill estate at Weybridge. 'Sunny Heights', a similar, closely-adjacent property was earmarked for Ringo after his—as yet unannounced—marriage to Maureen Cox. The idea at that stage seems to have been for all four Beatles to live together as in a mock-Tudor, topiary-encircled compound around a fifth property owned by Brian Epstein. It was one of Brian's more impossible dreams to have them in his sight for always; to know that John was literally at the bottom of his garden.

For John, that location could not have been more unfortunate. A mile or so from Weybridge, in the kitchen of an Esher hotel, an elderly dish-washer was even now working up courage to step forward and claim the leading Beatle as his son and heir. It was, indeed, Freddy Lennon, the father John had last seen at the age of four, when Freddy sailed away from Liverpool to North Africa.

Aunt Mimi had always feared that Freddy might turn up again—though not in this terrible way, selling his life story to *Tit Bits* and *Weekend* magazine. 'When they told me who it was,' Mimi says, 'I felt a shock run right through my body to my fingertips and the tips of my toes.'

A meeting was arranged between John and Freddy—only one. When Freddy called at 'Kenwood' later, he had the door slammed in his face. Subsequently, via the Beatles' accounts, he received a flat and a small pension. He resold his life story for diminishing fees and even made a Pop record entitled That's My Life. Julian Lennon did not acquire a long-lost grandfather.

Nor at Weybridge did there materialise Brian's hoped-for village of Beatle mansions. George broke the pattern by buying a bungalow on a different stockbroker estate, at Esher. And Paul, though offered several properties in the district, refused to commit himself yet. The house which Paul bought, and everything in it, was to be the result of minute social calculation. 'He telephoned me one night,' Walter Shenson says, 'but it was my wife he wanted to speak to. They talked for a long time. Paul was asking about a red velvet couch he'd seen at our house. He wanted to know where he could get one made exactly like it and how much it would cost.'

Pattie Boyd was discovering that to be a Beatle's girl friend was like joining a cell of Resistance fighters. Her initiation had been when she and George and the Lennons attempted a weekend at a 'secret' hotel in Southern Ireland, and awoke next morning to find the world's Press loud-hailing them down the telephone. Pattie and Cynthia left the hotel disguised as chambermaids and concealed in two wicker laundry hampers.

That summer, in a bid to go on holiday, they split into two groups. Paul and Jane with Ringo and Maureen flew to the Virgin Isles by way of quick airline changes at Paris, Lisbon and San Juan, Puerto Rico. The Lennons, George and Pattie were sighted variously in Amsterdam, Vancouver—where a radio station incited local teenagers to form 'Beatle posses' to hunt them down—then Honolulu and Papeete, Tahiti. From Papeete they put to sea in a cabin cruiser stinking of diesel oil and largely provisioned with potatoes. The vessel at once ran into heavy seas, causing Cynthia to be sick in the nearest receptacle: her new flowered sun hat.

Drugs occurred, like everything else, in almost wearisome profusion. The need dated from Hamburg and the months without sleep; it remained, amid the dizzying fame, to prop their eyes open through each night's arduous pleasure. Now the pills were bright coloured, like new clothes and cars—French Blues, Purple Hearts, Black Bombers and Yellow Submarines. The reflex grew in their growing boredom with everyday pleasures. More exciting than worship or sex, champagne or new toys, was to swallow a pill, just to see what would happen.

In 1964, in certain fashionable London circles, a curious after-dinner ritual was beginning to take place. A member of the party, upon a certain conspiratorial signal, would take out a small plastic bag, a cigarette-rolling machine such as previously used only by the poorest classes, and a packet of similarly proletarian Rizla cigarette-papers. With much thumb-twisting and paper-licking, a meagre, loosely-packed cigarette would be made. It would be passed round the table for each guest to puff, with a deep inhalation, then handed on to the next as reverently as if it were a portion of the Host.

Marijuana, resin of the Indian hemp or cannabis plant, had been used in England hitherto chiefly by West Indian immigrants to allay, with its languorous fumes, the misery of their Brixton tenements. Now, as 'pot' or 'Hash', the ancient Oriental dream substance became the latest social accessory. That it was also strictly illegal, under laws which had cleansed the drug-crazy

Victorian age, bothered no one very much at first. The Police in those days interfered very little with fashion.

The Beatles had been initiated into pot-smoking in 1964. The tell-tale medicinal fragrance of marijuana 'joints' hung about the set of their second feature film, *Help!* 'They were high all the time we were shooting,' the director, Richard Lester, says. 'But there was no harm in it then. It was a happy high.'

It was a laugh, even better than earning millions, to watch the awkward little cigarette rolled; and to breathe down the sweetish smoke that made laughing even easier. It was a laugh to see what characters began to sidle up, their mouths twitching with the promise of even more sensational pleasures. 'I saw it happen to Paul McCartney once,' Richard Lester says, 'the most beautiful girl I've ever seen, trying to persuade him to take heroin. It was an absolutely chilling exercise in controlled evil.'

Early in 1965, George Harrison took John and Cynthia Lennon and Pattie to a dinner-party given by a friend of his. 'I'll always remember,' Cynthia says, 'that when we walked into this man's drawing-room, there were four lumps of sugar arranged along the mantelpiece. We all had a delicious dinner with lots of wine. When coffee came, one of the four sugar lumps was put into each of our cups.

'It was as if we suddenly found ourselves in the middle of a horror film. The room seemed to get bigger and bigger. Our host seemed to change into a demon. We were all terrified. We knew it was something evil—we had to get out of the house. But this man told us we couldn't leave. We got away somehow, in George's Mini, but he came after us in a taxi. It was like having the Devil following us in a taxi.

'We tried to drive to some club—the Speakeasy, I think it was. Four of us, packed into the Mini. Everybody seemed to be going mad. Pattie wanted to get out and smash all the windows along Regent Street. Then we turned round and started heading for George's place in Esher. God knows how we got there. John was crying and banging his head against the wall. I tried to make myself sick, and couldn't. I tried to go to sleep, and couldn't. It was like a nightmare that wouldn't stop whatever you did. None of us got over it for about three days.'

Their host had playfully dipped their coffee sugar into a substance which, although widely used in mental hospitals and on prisoners of war as a truth serum, was so new as a 'pleasure' drug that it had not yet been declared illegal. It was a man-made substance, odourless and colourless; its chemical name, lysergic acid diethylamide, was usually shortened to LSD.

Britain, meanwhile, had changed Governments and Prime Ministers. The General Election of October 1964 had swept the

Conservatives from power after 13 years and brought back the Labour Party for only the fourth term in its history. Supreme power had passed from an obscure Scottish laird with a voice as strange and remote as his Highland estates. Supreme power now reposed in a plump, white-haired, cherub-faced man who smoked a pipe and holidayed in the Scilly Isles, and about whom little else was known other than that he represented the constituency of Huyton, near Liverpool.

Harold Wilson—Yorkshire-born, a Merseysider only by electoral accident—restored Socialism to office on a tide of stupendously opportune verbal gimmickry. It was opportune in being culled almost entirely from the Pop idiom used by teenagers and would-be teenagers. 'Let's Go With Labour!', the decisive campaign slogan, borrowed Pop music's pre-eminent image—that of being galvanised, as by music, into keen and exhilarating life. Such was the 'New Britain' which Mr. Wilson promised, in language as attuned to the mass mood as any juke-box hit—'a hundred days of dynamic action' . . . 'a dynamic, expanding, confident, above all purposive Britain' . . . 'forged in the white heat of the technological revolution'.

Even Beatlemania was eclipsed by the opening rhythms of Labour's 'hundred days'—the new Ministries and Ministers, one of them not even an MP, another even a woman; above all, the dumpy figure in its tartan-lined raincoat, apotheosis of the ordinary, puffing its pipe and watching for the new, clean, hard, decisive nation to assume tangible shape.

There was, however, another side to Harold Wilson. It had become visible, though not yet diagnosable, the previous April when, as Leader of the Opposition, he had presented the Beatles with their Variety Club award at the Dorchester Hotel. It was perhaps the most astute act of his political career to telephone Sir Joseph Lockwood, Chairman of EMI, and offer to grace the occasion as a 'fellow Merseysider'. Not that the Beatles recognised Mr. Wilson as such—or, indeed, recognised him at all. John Lennon, mistaking him for the Variety Club's 'chief barker', and getting confused with Barker and Dobson toffee, mumbled: 'Thank you, Mr. Dobson.' But Mr. Dobson did not mind. His face, in the double-page newspaper spreads, wore the smile of one who had discovered a great secret.

Britons who had feared the Socialist menace wondered how, for instance, such an apparition could possibly conduct his regular and necessary meetings with the Queen. Yet conduct them the apparition did, with every sign of confidence. And in time, the Menace receded. Despite technology's white heat, the old familiar State apparatus went on functioning as before. Early in 1965, just as last year, the Queen's official birthday was marked by a distribution of honours. Just as last year, the Queen herself merely put a signature to the list drawn up by her Prime Minister.

On 12 June, it was announced that the Beatles were each to receive the MBE—Membership of the Most Excellent Order of the British Empire. One northern newspaper headlined the story: 'She Loves Them! Yeah! Yeah! Yeah!'

The Beatles, recuperating from their second European tour, awoke to find a throng of Press, eager to ascertain how they would feel at being entitled to walk in State processions behind peers of the realm and hereditary knights but in front of baronets' younger sons and 'Gentlemen of Coat Armour'.

They felt confused.

'I thought you had to drive tanks and win wars to get the MBE,' John Lennon said.

'I think it's marvellous,' Paul McCartney said. 'What does that make my Dad?'

'I'll keep it to dust when I'm old,' Ringo Starr said.

'I didn't think you got that sort of thing,' George Harrison said, 'just for playing Rock and Roll music.'

In Harold Wilson's Britain, as would become abundantly clear, you did. The country had elected its first Beatle Prime Minister.

The Wilson Age, which had promised such starkness, such austere purpose, was to produce, instead, an interlude of frivolity unmatched since Charles II sat on the English throne. Newly Socialist Britain in 1965 is remembered, not for 'white heat' or 'driving dynamism' but for short-sighted euphoria and feather-headed extravagance. It is remembered above all, for an hallucination which descended on England's capital city, brilliant at first, but in quickly fading, tawdry colours—the hallucination of 'Swinging London'.

Swinging London was born at a moment when Government debts at home and abroad had brought the country to the edge of economic ruin. Yet the hard times, so earnestly promised by Mr. Wilson, were nowhere visible. All that could be seen was a spending boom registered on the now familiar gauge of teenage fashion. London girls, whey-faced and crop-headed, now tripped along in black and white Op Art dresses terminating scandalously far above the knee. The boys who queued outside the Marquee Club wore 'hipster' trousers and spotted or flowered shirts. Opulence was the rage, and offered to all through Sunday colour supplement ads for 'pure new wool', 'real cream —pour it on thick', the 'unashamed luxury' of sleekly packaged, though inexpensive, after dinner-mints. Magazines like *Town* and *Queen* mirrored the new preoccupation with 'taste' and 'style', publishing extravagant picture stories on emergent arbiters of fashion whose extreme youth and humble backgrounds were invoked, almost unconsciously, as a parallel with the Beatles'. Fame, almost equalling that of Pop stars, descended on the fashion model Jean Shrimpton, the photographer David Bailey, the clothes designers Mary Quant and John Stephen, whose menswear shops were already transforming a West End backwater called Carnaby Street.

Swinging London was a look—of short skirts, floppy hats, white rabbit 'fun' fur—it was also, at the beginning, an attitude. That attitude, to a great extent, came from the Beatles. As they had looked, wide-eyed, around the strange world of their celebrity, so young Londoners now looked round a capital whose ancient sedateness seemed suddenly hilarious. The essence of Swinging London was in happening against a tolerant background of non-Swinging London—of black taxis, red buses, Grenadier Guardsmen, the sacred monuments and statues past which the young, outrageously dandified, zoomed laughingly in open-top Mini Mokes; the Union Jack itself translated to a novelty kitchen apron or carrier bag. The essence was audacity, like the Beatles'; it was certainty that, because they had got away with it, everyone could.

Swinging London was also big business like none before or since. All summer, in the West End around Carnaby Street, in Chelsea around the King's Road, in formerly down-at-heel byways of Fulham and Kensington, there sprang up 'boutiques', as clothes shops were now called; there sprang up hairdressers offering the razor-cut 'Quant look'; bistros, serving newly-fashionable foods, windows jumbled with the latest crazes in Victorian bric-à-brac. A rash of new clubs vied with the Ad Lib to attract those who, in the yearning terminology of that hour, were 'the with it set', the 'new faces', the In crowd.

The innermost In-crowd, the ultimate clique, continued to be the Beatles. Their hair now sculpted and razored, their clothes one jump ahead of Carnaby Street, they were the model, and their songs the background, for boutique shopping, bistro-dining, feather boa-wearing, Swinging London life. They, together with Union Jacks and wooden headed dolls and Great War recruitment posters, were founding effigies in the Pop Art vogue, born of the period's child-like brilliance and bric-à-brac. *Queen* magazine reported in July that Peter Blake, London's leading Pop artist, was employed on a major study of them, while the sculptor David Wynne was casting their heads in bronze for what was predicted to be 'one of the most profound English philosophical portrait sculptures of the 20th century'.

Their film *Help!* is Swinging London personified—part-music, part-colour supplement travelogue, part-Pop Art strip cartoon. Again the producer was Walter Shenson and the director, Richard Lester. Again the theme was the Beatles' private life

—not real life this time but a fantasy one such as their song lyrics and public clowning had led their fans to half-imagine. The opening sequence shows John, Paul, George and Ringo each entering a front door in four identical terrace houses. Within is a communal 'pad' equipped with vending machines, a sunken floor, a grass carpet and a cinema organ.

Various writers, among them the dramatist Charles Wood, had laboured on a plot which, in its final, much-rewritten form, dealt with the efforts of a Hindu murder sect to recover a ring stuck on Ringo's finger. No less appropriate to the moment, the cast included character actors, like Eleanor Bron and Roy Kinnear, well-known from fashionable television 'satire' shows. There being no restraint on budget now, the action moved from London to Salisbury Plain, where the Beatles performed inside a ring of Centurion tanks; then to Austria and—for reasons not entirely cinematic—the Bahamas.

The West End premiere, in Princess Margaret's by now almost inevitable presence, brought reviews hailing the Beatles as 'modern Marx Brothers'. They had, in fact, prepared for their role by studying the Marx Brothers' classic *Duck Soup*. Ringo Starr received special praise for a 'Chaplinesque' performance recognisable to everyone around him as just Ringo being Ringo on camera. On the sleeve of the sound track album, four ski-clad Beatles semaphored a title song which had been Number One in Britain for most of the two preceding months.

Their Investiture as MBEs was performed by the Queen on 26 October. Swinging London was thus united with Buckingham Palace in a spectacle whose solemn pomp and hilarious incongruity spoke prophecies of the Wilsonian honours system. Mr. Wilson's wheeze had not been universally applauded. Several MBE-holders, together with sundry OBEs and BEMs, had returned their decorations in protest that an honour hard won through War or sub-postmastership should be given to what one outraged Naval hero described as 'a gang of nincompoops'. Colonel Frederick Wagg announced his resignation from the Labour Party and cancellation of a £12,000 bequest to party funds. The general delight showed that Mr. Wilson had achieved his object: to reflect the Beatles' popularity upon himself. For that reason—and others possibly less creditable—Brian Epstein was left out of the award.

Crowds, even larger than those which await Royal births and deaths, collected along the Palace railings and around the Victoria Monument's winged chariot to watch the Beatles take their place in the hierarchy of State. Once again, real life had exceeded any scriptwriter's fantasy—in the cries of 'God save the Beatles' as they entered by the Privy Purse Door; in the Lord Chamberlain's official, 6ft 3ins in knee breeches, who instructed them how and when to bow; and, finally, the white and gold State ballroom, and the long red carpet leading to figure destined, on this occasion, to play only a bit-part.

Later at a Press conference, holding up their rose-ribboned silver crosses, they were asked their opinion of Buckingham Palace. Paul McCartney replied that it was a 'keen pad'. They had been to other palaces of course—such as the San Francisco Cow Palace. And the Queen! They liked her, Paul said—she had been 'like a Mum'. The Queen had asked how long they had been together and Ringo had replied 'forty years', at which Her Majesty had laughed. 'Were you scared?' John was asked. 'Not as much as some others in there,' he replied. 'What will you do with your medal?' 'What do people usually do with medals?' Paul replied.

One little Investiture detail they did not think it wise to mention. They had been created Members of the Most Excellent Order of the British Empire in a happy haze of a marijuana joint, quickly puffed by turns in a mahogany-lined Palace washroom.

In Birmingham that same day, Princess Margaret was opening the new offices of the *Birmingham Post and Mail.* The first issue off the new presses had the Beatles' Investiture on its front page. Princess Margaret, glancing at a copy, quipped, 'I think MBE must stand for "Mr. Brian Epstein."'

At the end of 1964, a New York business syndicate had offered Brian £3½m outright for the Beatles. He was also considering —or affecting to—an offer for NEMS Enterprises from the powerful British Delfont Organisation. 'What shall I do? Shall I take it?' he would ask, resting his forefinger along his cheek as the paper millions danced around him.

He was, at the age of barely 30, the world's most envied impresario. Only Colonel Tom Parker, Elvis Presley's manager, could claim equal status as an object of entrepreneurial desire. The two met in 1965, in Parker's Hollywood office, just prior to the Beatles' own encounter with Elvis. So it came about that the figure whom Brian had once fantasised as a telephone call to him in Birkenhead sat across the table from him at a lunch that was also a summit conference. Sitting on chairs made from elephants' feet, they ate patrami sandwiches and drank root beer: the old fairground huckster and the pale young businessman who between them controlled the dreams of two generations.

The Beatles, though the most colossal element in Brian's success, were by no means the only one. Gerry and the Pacemakers had remained consistently popular and were themselves now making a feature film. Even greater had been the impact of Cilla Black, the Cavern Club's metamorphosed cloakroom girl.

Strangely unsuccessful with Lennon-McCartney material, Cilla made her breakthrough with a song which Brian found for her in America: the Burt Bacharach ballad Anyone Who Had a Heart. Hit records continued into 1965 for Cilla Black as they did for Billy J. Kramer, the Dakotas and the Fourmost.

Success beyond exaggeration had brought obvious personal wealth. His suits came from Savile Row, his shirts—of pure monogrammed silk—from Jermyn Street: his presence had the crispness of new banknotes, the cool fragrance of Cologne and triumphant deals. In Chapel Street, Belgravia, he had a Georgian house, furnished with fastidious taste, glittering with ceremonial silver, pale with white gold and quiet with excellent Art. There he maintained a domestic staff befitting a young lord, and entertained with a generosity and thoughtfulness that few of his guests have ever forgotten. He took pains, for instance, to notice which brand of cigarettes each visitor smoked, and to ensure that brand would be next to his or her place at dinner. When George Martin married Judy Lockhart-Smith, each table setting was marked by Brian's gift of 'M' monogrammed silver napkin rings —not the conventional dozen, but 11, commemorating the number present.

It was the same solicitousness that Brian devoted to all his artists at the beginning—the finicking, almost feminine perfectionism which chose Cilla's dresses and worried over Billy J.'s tendency to plumpness; which sent telegrams on first nights, placed flowers and fruit and champagne and portable TV sets in dressing-rooms; which provided hairdressers, tailors, doctors, lawyers; which, in a thousand, almost unnoticed ways, eased gawky Liverpool boys and an even gawkier Liverpool girl into the protective armour of egotism.

The Beatles came first, and everyone knew it: the Beatles were not in Brian's head but his heart. Whatever desire he had once felt for John Lennon had changed, amid the world's worship, into a quadruple infatuation, an affair with an image he had created, yet still doted uneasily on. To be with them, or a few paces behind them, represented his life's only absolute happiness. On their return from America late in 1964, he had gone up to Liverpool; he was in his old office, talking to Joe Flannery, his long-time friend and confidant. 'We made an arrangement to meet for coffee the next morning,' Flannery says. 'That night, the Beatles flew into London Airport. Next day, I was with Brian in his office, the television was on—and there was Brian with the Beatles on the screen. He'd driven all the way down to London to meet them at the airport, then all the way back up to Liverpool to keep his appointment with me. He had to be with them. He could never let go.'

Brian Sommerville discovered as much after that first stormy

American tour, when Brian raged at him for daring to be quoted by name in a news item about the Beatles. Shortly afterwards, he tried to make Sommerville sign a written oath of anonymity in all dealings with journalists. Sommerville refused, dissolved his freelance arrangement with NEMS and went off to read for the Bar.

In his place Brian took on Derek Taylor, the Hoylake-born *Daily Express* reporter who had ghost-written George Harrison's articles from Paris. Among the Fleet Street scrimmage, Taylor had caught Brian's eye with his Italianate good looks and droll, idiosyncratic speech. He joined NEMS in April 1964, initially as Brian's personal assistant. 'I suppose it was because he fancied me that I got the job,' Derek Taylor admits, 'even though, in all the time I knew him, he never so much as laid a finger on my knee.'

Earlier in 1964, Brian had agreed to write his autobiography for a London publisher, the Souvenir Press. Derek Taylor's first NEMS job, even before he had quite left Fleet Street, was to ghost-write Brian's life story on the basis of one weekend with him and a tape recorder at the Imperial Hotel, Torquay. The result was the evasive yet strangely honest self-portrait issued subsequently under the title *A Cellarful of Noise*.

As Beatles' Press Officer, for the first of three terms, Taylor stood in the firing-line of Brian's proprietorial obsession. 'I'd been told he could be cruel. I only realised it when I came to organise a Fab Four Press conference. Brian didn't want it to work. If I made a mess of it, even though the Beatles would be in that mess, he'd be happy—because I'd gained no control over them. He said, "Go ahead—but this is doomed. I look forward to speaking to you about it afterwards." I joined in April; here he was in May, treating me with *massive* cruelty.'

In 1964, during the Beatles' second American tour, Brian met Nat Weiss, a pale, cautious New Yorker who until then had earned his living as a divorce lawyer. Over the next three years, Weiss became to Brian what a few male friends, like Joe Flannery and Peter Brown were—an adviser, a confidant and, with increasing frequency, a means of rescue.

The Brian who revisited Nat Weiss in 1965, however, was still the languid, immaculate young Englishman who loved New York and its arrant luxury, who bought clothes extravagantly up and down Fifth Avenue, who had a weakness for the Waldorf Hotel, French toast and American chef's salads, and whose large intake of alcohol, especially cognac, seemed to produce only greater euphoria. 'When he was high,' Weiss says, 'he'd pile the furniture up. He'd put chairs on top of tables and then more chairs on top, just to see the effect. Moving furniture was always a thing with Brian.

'But however high he was, he'd never talk about the Beatles. I've seen him at parties when people tried to broach the subject. Brian would suddenly change—it was as if an icy shutter had come down.

'Anything he ever told me was in the strictest confidence, over lunch or dinner. To Brian, the relationship with the Beatles was something mystical—he himself used that word. He believed there was a chemistry between the five of them that no one else could understand. They weren't a business to Brian: they were a vocation, a mission in life. They were like a religion to him.'

Nat Weiss came as close as anyone to Brian in those three tumultuous years. His memory is deeply affectionate, admiring and perplexed. For with Weiss, as with even his most intimate companions, Brian Epstein defied understanding. 'He wasn't a Jekyll and Hyde character—he was Jekyll and Hyde and about twenty other people besides.'

He was, on one hand, the ice-cool young tycoon who sat in Walter Hofer's office, saying nothing, only listening, while big brash New York promoters bludgeoned him with their bonhomie, but at the first inconsistency politely interrupting '. . . but I thought you said a minute ago . . .' He was the businessman whose integrity seemed born of an earlier age, whose handshake was as good as a contract, who treated the unknown teenage masses of Denver or Cincinnati with the same scrupulous fairness as customers in his family shop. 'He always insisted that concert promoters should never take advantage of the fans —that tickets always had to be kept as cheap as possible.'

But always there was the other Brian, contradicting each strength with a weakness, each cool-headed triumph with a peevish, destructive temper tantrum, each provident care and precaution with a reckless and fearful risk.

There was the Brian who, with the whole world at his disposal, spent time and energy in buying up *Mersey Beat*, the little Liverpool music paper, simply for the pleasure of firing the incumbent editor's wife. There was the Brian who, unable to adjust his mind from Liverpool shopkeeping values, attempted to woo people like George Martin into his employment by promising them 'a thousand a year'. There was the Brian who, as paper millions whirled around him, hardly realised what tangible millions were slipping through his grasp.

The Beatles' 1964 American tour, though buoyed up on cash advances larger than any in entertainment history, had eventually done little more than cover its gigantic overheads. To make matters worse, the U.S. Internal Revenue had become uneasy about all the dollars which, reputedly, were to be removed from the country. Under a longstanding Anglo-American tax treaty, the Beatles' tour earnings were liable only for British Income

Tax. The U.S. authorities nonetheless obtained a New York court order, freezing $1m in concert proceeds while 'clarification' was sought.

Still worse was the position with Seltaeb, the American merchandising company of whose projected multimillion dollar earnings from Beatle buttons, masks, ice cream and more than 150 other items, NEMS Enterprises' share was fixed at 10 per cent.

In August 1964, the original ludicrous Seltaeb-NEMS contract was renegotiated. The Beatles' royalty from goods in their image rose to 46 per cent. Relations between NEMS and Seltaeb's English president, Nicky Byrne, deteriorated sharply in the process. They deteriorated still further when Byrne's lawyers informed him that some American manufacturers were turning out Beatle merchandise on licences granted, not by Seltaeb in New York but by NEMS direct from London.

As a further complication there was strife within Seltaeb, among Nicky Byrne's young English partners. Lord Peregrine Eliot, after six months of 'good lunacy' as he describes it, received a distinct impression that neither the Beatles nor Uncle Sam had been paid the sums due to them and that, under tax treaty law, Uncle Sam might seek to annexe his Cornish ancestral home, Port Eliot. So, while Nicky Byrne was in London, Lord Peregrine and Malcolm Evans, another Seltaeb partner, instituted court proceedings against him. They claimed that Byrne had failed to pass on Beatle royalties while at the same time spending $150,000 for his own 'comfort and benefit'. The comforts alleged included hotel bills running into thousands of dollars, two Cadillacs and chauffeurs on 24-hour standby and charge accounts for his girl friends at costly Fifth Avenue stores.

At the same time, NEMS began a lawsuit against Seltaeb for alleged non-payment of $55,000 in merchandise royalties. Nick Byrne entered a counter suit claiming breach of contract and damages of $5m.

The NEMS-Seltaeb dispute entered the pre-trial stage of a legal epic destined to last three years, accumulate three tons of documents and dissipate fortunes which no one can ever accurately compute. For the confusion over licences had caused panic among America's litigation-wary retailers. Woolworth's and Penney's instantly cancelled orders together worth $78m. The total of business lost among the lawsuits, in that one year alone, must be closer to $100m.

NEMS Enterprises, meanwhile, had swollen to literally unmanageable size. For Brian, while on the one hand struggling to contain the Beatle phenomenon, continued to sign up any new act which caught his increasingly capricious fancy. Sounds Incorporated, Cliff Bennett and the Rebel Rousers, Paddy, Klaus and Gibson, and the Rustiks—each in turn received the now familiar NEMS treatment of new suits, stylish Press handout and, if fortunate, a Lennon-McCartney song. It did not occur to Brian that his eye could be at fault; that he mistook mere competence for Beatle-size talent; that often his new discoveries only obtained record contracts on the strength of what he had discovered before.

Nor did Brian now have the assiduous energy of 18 months ago. The arrival of Peter Brown from Liverpool in 1965 allowed him to delegate much day-to-day routine to the slim young man who, in so many ways, became his surrogate presence. He had also persuaded his other Liverpool friend Geoffrey Ellis to quit the insurance business and join NEMS, ultimately as a director. The arrival of Vic Lewis, an established London agent, completed the transformation from one-man company to multi-faced, impersonal 'organisation'.

The change was felt most keenly by the Liverpudlians who had followed Brian to London, and now found his attention withdrawn from all but the Beatles and Cilla. Tommy Quickly, his intended solo 'sensation', lost hope of ever seeing the Top 20. Billy J. Kramer put on weight, unreproached. The Fourmost bemoaned their lack of songs to record. The Big Three so hated the prissy image that Brian had given them, they were publicly threatening to 'fill him in'. Gibson Kemp, of Paddy, Klaus and Gibson, supplemented his weekly £15 NEMS salary by working as an office-cleaner.

It was partly this accumulating discontent which led Brian, during 1965, to move away from NEMS' Argyll Street offices to a small command post of his own in Stafford Street, near Piccadilly. There he planned to devote himself only to top-level management—in other words, the Beatles. The move was made with elaborate secrecy: only Peter Brown and Geoffrey were supposed to know his new address. 'Brian spoiled that,' Geoffrey Ellis says, 'by immediately ringing up his 20 closest friends and telling them where he was.'

With him to Stafford Street he took Wendy Hanson, the high-powered, ebullient English girl whom he had wanted as his personal assistant since she had worked for him briefly in America the previous year. Wendy had subsequently come to Europe 'because of a man in Paris'; the man having proved difficult, she found herself able to accept Brian's offer. She remained with him, despite many attempted resignations, until the end of 1966.

Her job in principle was to provide anything a Beatle wanted, from new Asprey's luggage for Ringo to a Coutt's bank account for Paul; from Jane Asher's birthday cake at Maxim's in Paris, to the whole of Harrods kept open after hours for the Beatles as had only been done hitherto for Royalty. There was also the continuing job, for which Wendy's experience among turbulent operatic tenors and prima donnas had only half-prepared her, of trying to organise Brian.

'We were in Nassau while the boys were filming *Help!*; it had all got a bit dull, so Brian decided to go to New York for the weekend. Pan Am couldn't seat us together on the flight, which made Brian *furious*. There and then he wrote a letter to Pan Am, saying "The Beatles will never use this airline again". When we got to New York, there were, I promise you, 20 Pan Am officials, bowing and scraping on the tarmac.

'The next morning we were supposed to leave for London, Pan Am sent their own limo to the airport to fetch us. I was downstairs in the lobby with all my bags—no Brian. I waited and waited. Still no Brian. Eventually, I went up to his room. There he was, still in bed with not one of his 13 suitcases packed.

'All the way to the airport, the limo driver was in radio contact with Pan Am: "We're just crossing the river," I could hear him saying. "We're five miles from Kennedy . . ." They got us on to the flight with literally seconds to spare—in fact, they threw our bags into the compartment after us. Then, as we were taxi-ing along the runway, Brian looked at his watch. "Hm," he said. "Half a minute late in taking off. Typical." '

The move to Stafford Street, far from concentrating Brian's mind, presaged a deterioration which, for the moment, only Wendy Hanson noticed. Wendy, increasingly, found herself left alone with the hot line the Beatles used to communicate their wishes and whims. When they asked for Brian, she would have to admit he had not been in to the office that day.

The trouble was partly insomnia, inherited from his mother and fostered by London's extravagant night haunts. A relentless gambler, he was known to lose up to £12,000 in one roulette or chemin-de-fer session at the Curzon Club. The price was a small one for the company of waiters, croupiers, the rolling ball, the click of cards from the shoe. At dawn or later, dosed with pills on top of the night's brandy, he might, if he was fortunate, fall asleep. The sleep became ever more difficult to penetrate from the office where, at 4 or 5 pm, he would still have not made an appearance.

The trouble, above all, was an emotional life into which fame and money had brought no fulfilment. It was the helpless heart, still lost to any loutish 'rough trade' boy: the beatings-up, the thefts and petty blackmail. It was the pimply young Guardsmen who left Chapel Street at dawn; the steel-hatted construction worker calling to see him at the New York Waldorf at 5 am. It was the fear, reborn each horrified morning, that the Police, the Press—but, most frightful of all, the Beatles—would 'find out'.

That the Beatles had not yet found out remained an hallucination with Brian, despite grins exchanged behind his back, and despite John Lennon's occasional blunt dismissals of the masquerade. 'What shall I call this book of mine?' he had once asked them complacently in a dressing-room. John, fixing him with a merciless eye, said, 'Queer Jew'.

By the time of their European tour, in mid-1965, Brian had stopped trying to keep up appearances. Wendy Hanson was a part of that tour, which confirmed Beatlemania to be as virulent in Lyons as in Genoa; as tearful in Naples as on the Côte d'Azur. Brian vanished in Rome, not reappearing until Madrid, where the performance was to take place in the Plaza de Toros Monumental. And everyone knew by now why he really loved bullfighting, despite his eulogies on the art of the matador.

There was one triumph still to come. It occurred on 23 August, when a helicopter containing the Beatles, Brian and Tony Barrow tilted down through the New York twilight and the pilot pointed out Shea Stadium, though they could already hear the roar of it, and see the flashes of unnumbered cameras pointed hopefully into the sky.

Brian was there at the New York Mets' baseball ground, to witness the concert which, though it grossed $300,000, earned only $7,000 for its promoter, Sid Bernstein. He is there in the film that was made, standing near the stage, nodding his head in time a little jerkily, looking out to the terraces at 55,000 people —in seats kept cheap on his insistence—then back to the four figures for whom 55,000 voices are screaming, with their unbuttoned Army tunics, their hot foreheads, their undaunted, still unwearied smiles.

'If he'd been an ordinary manager, Shea Stadium couldn't have happened,' Nat Weiss says. 'None of it could have happened the way it did. It all only happened that way because it was Brian Epstein's fantasy.'

December 1966

'You stick to your percentages, Brian. We'll look after the music'

At the beginning, two boys in travel-creased shirts would stand in front of George Martin, playing the new song they had scribbled in an old school exercise book. Martin even then saw two personalities at war. A song would be John's aggression held in check by Paul's decorum; it would be Paul's occasionally cloying sentiment cut back by John's unmerciful cynicism. Yet Paul loved all-out Rock and Roll, just as John could be capable of brusque tenderness. Examples of total collaboration were rare. More often, one would write half a song and then come to the other for help with the chorus or 'middle eight'. The formula was established that whoever had written most of the song took the lead vocal, the other providing harmony. That harmony derived its freshness and energy from the contest being waged within it.

Collaboration was dictated, in any case, by close confinement in tour buses, dressing-rooms and, later, aircraft; the pressure of songwriting to order in spaces cleared among newspapers, teacups and the debris of 'the road'. From the early, simple 'yeah yeah' hits up to the Hard Day's Night album, the songs, whether by John or Paul, are chiefly redolent of a common life on the run. Nor was it still absolutely certain that Lennon–McCartney songs were what the public wanted. Their next, and fourth, album, Beatles for Sale, reverted largely to their old Liverpool and Hamburg stage repertoire: Chuck Berry's Rock and Roll Music; Carl Perkins's Honey Don't, Little Richard's Kansas City; Buddy Holly's Words of Love, a track on which their fans first discovered their almost uncanny powers of impersonation.

The importance of George Martin cannot be over-emphasised. First of all, he signed them. Second, he did not cheat them. Third, he did not adulterate them. It would have been easy for him, as all-powerful record producer, to insist that each release should carry a B-side composed by himself. Martin happened to be of the rare breed who are content to use their talents in improving other people's work. To Lennon and McCartney, he was the editor which all creative promise strikes if it is lucky. He took the raw songs; he shaped and pruned and polished them and, with scarcely believable altruism, asked nothing for himself but his EMI salary and the satisfaction of seeing the songs come right. As the songs grew more complex, so did George Martin's unsung, unsinging role.

Paul McCartney was, of the two, the most obviously 'natural' musician. Much came from heredity, and the Jim Mac Jazz Band. He had an instinctive grasp of harmony, a gift of phrasing which raised the bass guitar in his hands to an agile, expressive lead instrument. Already proficient in guitar and drums, he was now taking formal piano lessons. Paul developed by following rules, a notion altogether repugnant to John Lennon. John's music was, like his drawing, bereft of obedience and straight lines, but honest and powerful in a way that Paul's never dared to be.

The *Help!* album brought the two elements for the first time into open contrast. On the one hand, there were unmistakably 'John' songs, like You've Got to Hide Your Love Away, written under Bob Dylan's influence: sardonic and world-weary, idylls of the morning after. On the other hand, there was Paul's solo performance of a song he had been trying out for months under the provisional title Scrambled Eggs; a song now scored, like real music, for accompaniment by a string quartet. The song was Yesterday. It was immediately 'covered' by a leading British ballad-singer Matt Monro, the first of some 2,000 recorded versions.

Rubber Soul, their second album that year, reflected a widening schism belied by the four Carnaby-look Beatles, still barely distinguishable from each other, in its modish fisheye-lens sleeve. Paul and John were by now leading separate—and, as it proved—mutually inimical lives. John's was the dominant presence, through songs that were fragments of current autobiography—the boredom, in Nowhere Man, of sitting at home in his Tudor mansion; the edgy lust of Norwegian Wood, a description of infidelity in some London girl's flat. From Paul came Michelle, a bland love song with words that lapsed into French as a plain act of social climbing.

EMI's Abbey Road studios, whatever other amenities they lacked, were an ideal hideaway. London's northbound traffic sped in total indifference past the plain-fronted white house with its neat gravel driveway and high front steps. Only the commissionaire, eyeing the fan pickets posted respectively at the IN and OUT gateway, hinted at anything discordant with St. John's Wood, acacia bushes, retired publishers and Austrian au pair girls.

In the house's deep lino and rubber-silenced hinterland, Studio Two, that once strictly-apportioned Holy of Holies, was now consecrated almost exclusively to the Beatles' use. George

Martin likewise no longer looked in his diary to see whether or not he could fit in a session. When the source of EMI's current £3m profit felt an urge to record, Martin and his engineer, Norman Smith, obeyed the peremptory summons.

Gone, too, was the producer's old clock-watching authority. Studio Two at Abbey Road became in effect a rehearsal room where new Beatles songs took shape by methods increasingly prodigal of time and expense. Four-track recording, which had replaced two track at Abbey Road in late 1963, altered the entire concept of an album session. Whereas Please Please Me had been blasted off in one 13-hour marathon, Rubber Soul grew over several weeks as a 'layering' of rhythm, vocal and instrumental tracks, any of which could be erased and re-recorded. Both John and Paul, in their different ways, embraced these new technical possibilities. Each built his own private studio where demo' tapes could be produced as a guide to the final Abbey Road version. Both ran through George Martin's domain as through a toyshop, alighting with rapture on this or that novelty of sound. They must have *that* on the track, they would say. Martin, the trained musician, Norman Smith, the trained engineer, would reply that it couldn't work. Then they found it did work. Studio procedure was to be changed for all time by this whim of iron.

At a certain moment in each session, George Martin would leave John and Paul and cross the cable-strewn floor to George Harrison, waiting apart from the others, unsmiling with his Grecht rehearsal guitar. George would then play to George Martin whatever solo he had worked out for the song. If Martin did not like it, he would lead George to the piano, tinker a little phrase and tell him to play that for his solo. Such was the origin of the guitar in Michelle. 'I was,' Martin admits, 'always rather beastly to George.'

In George the world's ecstasy had as yet produced no answering lift of inspiration. He played lead guitar as he always had, earnestly, a little ponderously. He took his turn at lead singing in a voice whose thick Scouse seemed to mask an underlying embarrassment. Latterly, goaded by John and Paul's stupendous output, he, too, had started to write songs. Each new album, in fairness, featured a song by George—just one. He was also learning the Indian sitar, an instrument which Richard Lester had added for comic purposes to a scene in *Help!* Norwegian Wood was the first Beatles song to benefit from the wiry whining and wailing of George's sitar.

As for Ringo, he sat patiently in a corner of the studio, waiting to be called to sing his song or drum as directed; whiling away hours when he was not needed in card games with Neil and Mal.

*

On the night of 5 December, they sat in chintz armchairs in an underground region of Newcastle-on-Tyne City Hall, eating sweltered steak and trifle embroidered with the fancies of some nameless municipal chef. Pushing away the grisly plates, they turned their attention to the TV set in the corner, and an episode of *The Avengers*. Emma Peel, the 'swinging' leather-clad heroine, flung hapless criminals all over the screen while, across the room, elderly waitresses cleared tables, then remained, hovering vehemently with paper napkins to be autographed for granddaughters or little nephews.

It was, although no one realised, the Beatles' last British tour. At that stage, they themselves did not seem to realise it. After the waitresses, reporters were led in and, to their astonishment, welcomed. Paul McCartney handed out bits of Juicy Fruit chewing gum. John and Ringo perched on the chintz chair arms, letting themselves be asked the same old stammeringly banal things.

'Why did you stop doing Twist and Shout in your stage act?'

'We'd been doing it for years,' John said. 'It was starting to sicken us.'

'What's your favourite TV channel, Ringo?'

'Er—what kind of bass guitar is that?'

'It's a Hofner violin bass,' Paul said. 'Here—catch.'

'Are they expensive?'

'Only fifty-two guineas. I'm a skinflint, you see.'

'OK—can you all move out of here,' Neil Aspinall intervened.

'But they said we could stay . . .'

'Well *I* say you've got to go.'

Out on the same City Hall stage, they drove the same four instruments through the same numbing undiscriminating scream. It was an act, simply that, devoid of music or even effort. Ringo now drummed only on the off-beat. John, at his Vox organ, crashed his arm in frustration along the keys.

Liverpool was one more embattled dressing-room. John confided to his old Art School friend Bill Harry that he'd give anything to go into a pub like the Philharmonic or Ye Cracke, and stand under the chandeliers, or the Death of Nelson, just having a quiet pint.

They didn't go to the Cavern Club, although John begged Brian to allow it. 'Couldn't we do a few numbers down there?' he pleaded, 'just for old times sake?' Brian said that if word got out, they would be crushed to death.

The Cavern, in any case, was not the same. Only one fixture remained unchanged. Paddy Delaney, the ex-Irish Guard, still stood watch under the solitary entrance light in full evening dress. So he had through the Cavern's post-Beatles era when every big British Pop group came chasing their mystique, and Rolls Royces would glide up through the cabbage stalks and orange boxes, disgorging the likes of Rex Harrison, Rachel Roberts and Lionel Bart. For such honoured visitors, Paddy would be sent across to The Grapes to fetch half a bottle of gin.

The Beatles' last Liverpool concert was an augury for their first and happiest collective home. Ray McFall, the Cavern's owner, had got into financial difficulties. One night a few weeks later, he came to Paddy Delaney at the door and said that next morning the bailiffs would be in.

Paddy saw the night out in his evening suit, which, as dawn broke, turned a spectral white. The fans' farewell was to set off all the foam fire-extinguishers. At last, bailiffs and Police gained entry, climbing over the wooden Church hall chairs that were piled up the 18 steps to the street. 'The Inspector was a friend of mine,' Paddy says. 'He was as sad to see it all go as anyone. He put his arm round my shoulder. "Knock back that drop of Scotch, Paddy," he told me. "You're going to be the last one to leave." '

So Paddy, too, straightening his back, left the three dripping tunnels, the rough wooden stage that no one could quite stamp through, the forest of names, including the Beatles' own, scribbled over the bandroom wall.

'When I came up into Mathew Street, there were kids sitting down along the warehouses both ways as far as the eye could see. When they saw me, a cry went up, "It's Paddy!" Some of them tried to pull me down to sit with them. I stood there with this Inspector's arm round my shoulders, and all my dinner suit frosty from the extinguishers, and the tears running down my face.'

It did not start out as the Beatles' last tour. It started as their next tour and finished as the one none of them ever wanted to repeat.

It began normally enough, in a ceremonial train—the same used a year earlier to accommodate Queen Elizabeth II—which, on 26 June 1966, arrived at the Central Station, Hamburg. Waiting in the Royal compartment while the riot Police cleared a path, they could see the platform where Stu Sutcliffe and Astrid had put George on the train, alone and bewildered after his deportation. And the concourse to the record booth where, backing the gifted 'Wally', they had cut their very first disc.

There was no more Star-Club. The latter-day Mersey groups had all gone home to settle down as pork butchers and damp course engineers. West Germany now teemed with native groups in the Liverpool image, stiff-backed and tail-coated, solemnly singing lyrics they had learned by watching John Lennon—Shitty

Shitty for Shimmy Shimmy, or I Picked My Nose in Spanish Harlem.

The music once available in eight-hour sessions at the Indra was measured out to Hamburg in 30 inaudible minutes at the Ernst Merck Halle sports arena. 'Don't try to listen to us,' John told the German support group. 'We're really terrible these days.'

Bettina, the Star-Club barmaid, whose friendly nails had raked so many pale young Liverpool backs, was among a large backstage reunion party. So was Bert Kaempfert, the bandleader. They remembered making records for Kaempfert as 'the Beat Brothers' on the stage of that primary school. One old Reeperbahn crony, however, did not make it to the reunion. Horst Fascher, of the cropped head, the merry laugh and the killer punch, was, unhappily, detained elsewhere. They played Roll Over Beethoven in Horst's honour, remembering how he would bellow it out as he flung sailor after sailor from the Kaiserkeller into the street.

Later, in the concealing neon, Paul McCartney walked down Grosse Freiheit, past clubs that were all different, though the fairground painted nudes and doorway touts remained the same. John found his way back to Johannasbollwerk and the Seaman's Mission, to see Jim and Lilo Hawke and stand in the little bar, with its Ludo games and vacant-eyed merchantmen, and eat a nostalgic plate of old Frau Prill's real English chips.

Astrid took time off work to see them. Into the dressing-room walked the delicate, voluptuous girl whose scissors had first shaped the Beatle cut; whose swift German sewing machine had tailored, for Stu Sutcliffe, the first black corduroy Beatle jacket; whose camera lens had first alighted on the image now reproduced on millions of record sleeves. The soft voice spoke English like the Liverpudlian she had almost become. She said she was 'made up' to see them again.

Astrid's photographs of the Beatles had earned her nothing: not even acknowledgement. The famous shot of them sitting on the fairground engine at Der Dom owed its copyright, if at all, to the wire services which had transmitted it across the world. 'It was just one of a bundle of prints I had sent over to Liverpool. Later on, it turned up credited to UPI. I did not try to sue anyone. What would have been the point? To me it was just a photograph of some friends.'

Astrid told the Beatles she had given up photography. She thought she was not good enough. She had taken a job in a female drag bar, dancing as required with the 'men'. In her black-draped room, under a huge blow-up of a fragile-faced boy, candles burned on for the Beatle whom none else but his mother, and those who looked at his pictures, remembered now.

*

The stop after Hamburg was Tokyo, via the Polar route. Because of a typhoon-warning their aircraft was forced to land in Anchorage, Alaska. Nat Weiss in New York was roused from sleep by Brian's voice on the telephone, demanding with some petulance, 'Who *owns* Alaska, Nat? And can you recommend a nice place to stay?'

Their two Tokyo concerts, at the Nippon Budo Kan (Martial Arts Hall) were, not surprisingly, the best-organised of the Beatles' performing career. The promoters explained to Brian that any riot would have brought dishonour upon themselves. Accordingly, the 9,000-strong audience had 3,000 Police to guard them. Backstage, the Beatles were provided with Geisha girls, a perpetual tea ceremony and a Japanese road manager for liaison. Between concerts, in the 24-room Presidential Suite at the Tokyo Hilton, a private bazaar was spread, of radios, cameras, happi coats and painting sets. The Beatles all bought inks and calligraphy brushes and, having nothing intelligible to watch on television, produced a garish mural on one huge sheet of paper that was later given to the Japanese fan club.

They expected something similar in the Philippines. They were charmed, as are all newcomers to Manila, by a miniature Texas set down among tropical islands; by the skyscrapers, specially earthquake proofed, the shanties and juke boxes and brilliant jeep taxis, the jungle foliage reflected in a speed cop's Harley Davidson. After dark, as the bats bounced like shuttle cocks against the rim of Manila Bay, shotgun blasts at random bespoke South East Asia's most uninhibited autocracy.

Imelda Marcos, wife to the President, had herself professed to be a Beatle fan. She had arranged a special garden party at Malacanang, the Presidental fortress, for the express purpose of introducing them to her husband, and 300 specially-selected politicians' and soldiers' children. The invitation delivered to Tony Barrow, however, gave no hint of these elaborate preparations: even Brian saw no particular necessity to attend.

Manila's English Language newspapers next morning carried the banner headline BEATLES SNUB PRESIDENT. When a President happens also to be a military dictator, his wounded feelings naturally evince widespread sympathy. The concert promoters sympathised by refusing to pay Brian Epstein the Beatles' concert fee. Other citizens sympathised by telephoning death threats to the British Embassy.

Brian, horrified by the furore, did his best to make amends. He asked to appear on Manila television the following night to explain that no snub had been intended. The transmission was almost wiped out by heavy static which, coincidentally, vanished as soon as Brian's apology came to an end. So things go in that part of the world, when Presidents become offended.

Departure from Manila Airport on 5 July was accompanied by ugliness unenvisaged even outside Litherland Town Hall. Deprived of all Police protection, the Beatles' party dashed for the aircraft through a concourse of jeering Customs officers; they were jostled, even punched and kicked. The KLM flight for New Delhi took off only after lengthy negotiations between Brian and a Philippines Income Tax official who refused to let them go until they had paid £7,000.

Three weeks later, Nat Weiss telephoned Brian from New York with the news that Beatles records were being ceremonially burned in Nashville, Tennessee.

For some months already, in fact, a large number of Americans had been scratching heads—still resolutely cropped to the scalp bone—and figuring that enough was enough. That vast, God-fearing, Friday night-bowling middle-class majority had watched with rising bewilderment as its children fell under the influence, if not of the Beatles directly then of another British group from the dozens who poured across the Atlantic after them. America, expecting more Liverpool cheek and charm, beheld, instead, the Who, wrecking motel rooms and smashing their instruments on stage; the Animals, sweating and grimacing over uncensored Blues; the Rolling Stones, unrepentantly scruffy and ill-mannered, their lead singer—an embryo Paul no longer—prancing and flaunting a bottom like two collar studs as he pouted a song called Satisfaction which, to chaste American ears, seemed nothing more nor less than an advertisement for playing with yourself.

British groups, playing a Blues repertoire learned in suburban front rooms, had opened the eyes of young Americans at last to their own musical heritage. It was the Animals, from Newcastle-on-Tyne, singing the old New Orleans bordello ballad House of the Rising Sun, who made the most significant conversion. Bob Dylan, hearing it over a car radio, abandoned his folk and 'protest' style to become an infatuated devotee of R & B and Rock. Dylan's new 'electric' songs, Like a Rolling Stone and Subterranean Homesick Blues, gave Pop music a vocabulary it had never had before; a caustic vernacular, teeming with jibes against authority and invitations to join the singer in his drug-assisted flight from all convention. Encouraged by Dylan, young whites were also discovering the black 'soul' performers whom polite society had hitherto kept at a proper, segregated distance. All this was no longer just silly: this was, quite possibly, subversive.

Without the Beatles, as he himself admitted, there would have been no new Dylan. They, in their turn, fell under the spell of the slight, draggled figure they had met several times in hotels or dressing-rooms. The single they put out in early 1966—by now, traditionally, separated from the albums, and a 'double A-side'—frankly echoed Dylan: it echoed everything, in fact, that rival big names were doing. Paperback Writer, by Paul, was the Beatles' first non-love lyric, a vague literary satire—possibly aimed at John—surrounded by heavy guitar chords, such as The Who made their trademark, and intricate four-part Beach Boy harmonies. Rain was by John, in evident homage to the Byrds as they had sounded on Dylan's song Mr. Tambourine Man, yet with the vignette of himself that he could not help but sketch in. The blizzarding sound is rich, drugged and tired. Its final chorus of gibberish was added late at night in his private studio, by drunkenly running the vocal chorus backwards.

As usual, advance orders took Rain/Paperback Writer instantly to Number One in Britain and America. Only after 1½ million copies had been taken home and played did some little uncertainty arise. Paperback Writer, which received most radio play, frankly mystified American fans with its British allusions to Lear and the *Daily Mail*. A suspicion formed, even if no one yet dared to articulate it, that the Beatles were not infallible.

Their fourth American tour, in August 1966, was preceded by an album which was, according to custom, a compilation of existing British ones. Capitol Records, catering to some subtle but evident variation in the taste of the American fans, had combined some songs from *Help!* with some from Rubber Soul, plus a special bonus of three from the new collection not due for British release until late August. The title of this hybrid was The Beatles—Yesterday and Today. Any promise of gentle nostalgia was dispelled by a full-colour sleeve on which the Beatles, wearing white butchers' overalls, nursed dismembered and decapitated toy dolls and brandished bloody joints of meat.

The 'butcher sleeve', as it became known, was the Beatles' own art directing concept. Sean O'Mahony, editor of their fan club magazine, had been present at the photographic session and had covered his eyes in dismay when the properties were brought in. Such was their power by then that Brian's misgivings were overruled. The gruesome tableau appeared first in England, on the cover of *Disc* magazine. Capitol Records, cowed by their former lack of prescience, agreed that it would probably be a winner. 750,000 sleeves had been printed before the first calls came in from disc jockeys almost retching over their advance copies. The sleeve was then axed, together with all promotional material, at a cost of $200,000. A special staff spent one weekend extracting each of the 750,000 discs from its butcher sleeve and inserting it into one hastily improvised round a picture of the

Beatles leaning on a cabin trunk. In many cases, to save trouble, the new sleeve was simply pasted over the old.

As to which Beatle had proposed the bloody joints and limbless dolls, there was never any serious doubt. The banned cover, a bitterly resentful John Lennon said, was 'as relevant as Vietnam'. His tone, people noticed, was neither cheeky nor funny.

The previous February, in one of her regular Beatle reports for the London *Evening Standard*, Maureen Cleave had asked John his views, if any, on organised religion. The response, from an ex-chorister at St. Peter's Church, Woolton, was as might have been predicted. 'Christianity will go. It will vanish and shrink . . . we're more popular than Jesus now. I don't know which will go first—Rock and Roll or Christianity.' He had nothing against Jesus, he went on, but the disciples were 'thick'. 'They're the ones that ruin it for me.'

In Britain, the remark passed unchallenged—indeed, unnoticed. Such was not the case five months later when, on the eve of the Beatles' American tour, Maureen Cleave's interview with John was reprinted by a teenage magazine, *Datebook.* What in the *Evening Standard* piece had been merely an aside was headlined on *Datebook*'s cover: a stray ad lib transformed to vaunting sacrilege. John Lennon was claiming that the Beatles were 'bigger than Jesus Christ'.

The album bonfire in Nashville set off a wave of anti-Beatles demonstrations across the American South. Encouraged by clergymen, Godfearing radio stations and Grand Wizards of the Ku Klux Klan, bonfires of Beatles albums were organised throughout Alabama, Georgia and Texas. One outraged community provided rubbish bins labelled Place Beatle Trash Here; another hired a tree-crushing machine to pulp the idolatrous music. Pastor Thurmond Babbs of Cleveland, Ohio, threatened to excommunicate any of his flock who attended a Beatles concert. Beatles records were banned by thirty-five radio stations from Ogdenburg, New York, to Salt Lake City, Utah.

At Nat Weiss's urgent suggestion, Brian Epstein flew to New York ahead of the main tour party. He was ill with flu'—and more than flu'—and in distress far beyond that of a Pop manager whose image-building has gone wrong. 'He really cared most about the possibility that the Beatles would suffer abuse—that they might even be in danger,' Nat Weiss says. 'The first question he asked me was: "What will it cost to cancel the tour?" I said: "A million dollars." He said: "I'll pay it. I'll pay it out of my own pocket, because if anything were to happen to any one of them, I'd never forgive myself." '

The outrage was not universal. Some newspaper—even some clergymen—admitted that, in terms of audience pulling-power, the Beatles *were* more successful than a personage whose last public appearance had been almost 2,000 years earlier, and who, in a straw poll conducted at the time, had run second in popularity to a robber named Barabbas. What no one questioned was the power of a 26-year-old Pop musician to goad the entire Christian world to furious zealotry; to produce official censure from the governments of South Africa and Spain; to elicit even a Papal response, via the Vatican newspaper *L'Osservatore Romano*, that 'some subjects must not be dealt with profanely, even in the world of beatniks'.

Brian, using all his diplomatic powers, assured the American Press that John had intended no sacrilege, but only wished to express 'deep concern' at the decline in spiritual values. It was announced that when the Beatles arrived on 12 August, John himself would formally apologise. He did so at a Press conference in Chicago, pale and nervous—for the hate mail that he had been receiving had badly shaken him. 'I'm sorry I opened my mouth,' he said. 'I'm not anti-God, anti-Christ or anti-religion. I wouldn't knock it. I didn't mean we were greater or better.'

So began the tour destined to be the worst, if not yet officially last of all. To add to the general unease, a famous American clairvoyant had predicted that three of the four Beatles would die soon in an air crash. Though the prophecy was later retracted, it cast a lingering tremor over the constant shuttle-flights. Mal Evans was convinced he would not survive the tour, and spent one journey between concerts composing a last letter to his wife, Lil, and his new baby daughter, Julie.

All four Beatles became conscious for the first time of a threat which had worried Brian since the American tours began—that, some night, in some huge, open, oval human sea, someone might be hiding with a high-velocity rifle. In each big city stadium, grinding out the numbers they could no longer hear, they felt themselves endangered now by something other than dangerous adoration. At Memphis, their first concert south of the Mason-Dixon Line, the backstage fear was palpable as sweat. Outside, the Ku Klux Klan were holding an 8,000-strong counter demonstration. Instead of jelly beans, rubbish began to land on the stage. Half-way through the performance, a firecracker exploded. Brian, for one hideous moment, thought it was a rifle shot.

Brian was deeply agitated for another reason, known only to his friend Nat Weiss. For the past few months, he had been intermittently persecuted by the most ruthless and predatory of all his ex-boy friends. The youth, who had lived with Brian for a short, violent era was now extorting money from him by threatening to tell the whole story to the Beatles. Through Nat Weiss he had been paid $3,000 to stay away from them on this American tour.

The tour, meanwhile, dragged on over a landscape where ugliness seemed to blossom everywhere. As the Beatles performed in Washington, hundreds of young blacks were on the rampage in their ghetto just beyond the Capitol. At the Los Angeles Dodgers Stadium, Police cleared young girl fans from the arena by means of an heroic baton charge. In Cincinnati, the concert promoter tried to economise by building a stage with no roof or canopy. Just before the Beatles went out to play, a downpour of rain began. They could not have gone ahead without serious risk of electrocution. 'The whole audience —35,000 screaming kids—had to be turned away,' Nat Weiss says. 'They all got passes for a show the next day but, for a while, it really looked ugly out there. All the Beatles were frightened. Paul, I know, was physically sick.'

The final concert of the tour was on 29 August at Candlestick Park, San Francisco. One person, at least, realised there would be no more Beatles concerts after that. 'Brian told me it was the end in San Francisco,' Nat Weiss says. 'He was dejected. "This is it," he told me, "this is the last one ever."'

It was also the moment chosen by Brian's ex-lover to break his $3,000-bond of silence. Returning to their hotel suite, Brian and Nat Weiss found that both their briefcases had been stolen. Brian's, as the thief well knew, contained his pill supply—the 'uppers' and tranquillizers he could not do without—as well as intimate personal correspondence. A blackmail note, in a familiar hand, expressed confidence that the Police would be involved.

So the next evening in Candlestick Park, as the Beatles ran out on to the stage, Brian was detained elsewhere. His remorse was terrible to think he had not been there, on that night of all nights, to watch over the four boys in his charge.

Britain, that summer of 1966, had little cause for either gaiety or optimism. The year, barely half-expended, could already chalk up the varying torments of a General Election and a national shipping strike. The Pound ailed; inflation kept briskly on the ascent. The re-elected Wilson Government stood revealed, not as dynamic or purposeful but merely another set of politicians, with the usual capacity to bungle and vacillate. Rhodesia, having seceded from British rule a year earlier, still thumbed a derisive nose at her fuming mother country across the world. From still farther afield came noises which penetrated even the age-old British indifference to what was still vaguely thought of as The Orient. America began bombing the North Vietnamese cities of Hanoi and Haiphong. A war hitherto faint and far flung ceased to happen comfortably out of earshot.

There was, however, bright sunshine. The British, as they had in the past forgotten pestilence, famine, the Great War, Hitler's bombs and the Suez Crisis, now just as easily forgot Mr. Wilson, Vietnam and the Pay Freeze under the influence of weeks of unbroken summer. So 1966 was to pass into popular remembrance: not for crises, both present and promised, but for blue skies, soft breezes, and for two events—the only two—which fortified that ephemeral happiness.

On 30 July, England won the World Football Cup, audaciously snatching the vital goal in the last seconds of the final against West Germany. Old wartime animosities doubtless assisted the fervour with which, on another hot summer evening, the victorious team was welcomed home to London. Footballers looked like Pop singers now; they grew their hair, wore 'trendy' clothes and received the approbation of great men. For Mr. Wilson, naturally, was there, puffing his pipe as smugly as if England's winning goal had originated in a Cabinet memorandum.

The second, even more insubstantial area of cheerfulness, owed its origin to an article in the 13 April *Time* magazine. *Time*, in characteristic style, had finally noticed the Swinging London phenomenon which, since its apogee in mid-1965, had declined almost to extinction. It was now resuscitated by 12 pages of *Time*-ese, fact and atmosphere being, as usual, processed to meet the expectations of a skyscraper-bound executive in New York. *Time*'s committees wished to see a 'new fashion-capital of Europe'; its editorial armies, by means of many a confused image and relentlessly-applied gimmick word, set about manufacturing one.

The strangest thing of all was—it came true. *Time*'s story, together with still more wishful picture essays in *Life* and the *Saturday Evening Post*, created a tourist boom unprecedented in London's history. These were not the traditional American tourists, with guide books and Alpine hat. They were teenagers, besotted by all British Pop music, who came flooding into Carnaby Street and the King's Road, hopeful of glimpsing their idols, as *Life* and *Esquire* had promised, among the frill-shirted baronets and debutante shopgirls, in the shops, bistros, bric-à-brac markets and artificially-aged pubs. Such was the demand, the product could not help but materialise. London, by some alchemy of hot weather and warm money, burst like a conjurer's bouquet into riotous new fashion, new colours, new furnishings, new restaurants, new daring mini-skirts, new match-thin, long-legged girls, new slow-burning, strange-smelling aromas.

On 5 August, an LP appeared in the record shops which, were it not for the fact that approximately one million copies had been ordered in advance, might have seemed to stand little chance of being noticed on the shelves. Its cover, amid its rivals' Carnaby colours, was plain black and white: a collage of photo-fragments spiralling through what looked like palm fronds but proved on close inspection to be hair, encircling four silhouetted faces so instantly recognisable, it was not thought necessary to print their collective name. Who else in the world would announce themselves in graphics reflecting the smartest magazines? Who would call a record album simply Revolver, investing even that commonplace pun with the sleekness of some new-minted avant garde? Who but the Beatles would have confidence colossal enough to be so chastely downbeat?

Revolver was presented, like no Pop album before it, as a continuous, almost narrative performance. There was, first of all, to underline this, some stagey coughing and throat-clearing. There was then George Harrison singing Taxman, his first wholly original and successful song, a hymn of hate against the Inland Revenue, invoking as a derisive counterpoint the names of real politicians. There was Eleanor Rigby, sung by Paul alone with a string octet: a song more like a short story about a lonely woman, picking up other people's wedding rice. There was John's I'm Only Sleeping, answering back Paul's sentimental conscience with a paean to unrepentant idleness. There was George's Love You To, burdened with Indian sitars, but then the stunning simple charm of Paul's Here There and Everywhere. There was Yellow Submarine, a song for children (as it seemed) perfectly suited to Ringo's happy drone, accompanied by slurpings and gurglings, ringing ships' bells, a sub-aqueous brass band and commands from the bridge in a John Lennon funny voice; and then John's non-funny voice, in She Said She Said, among graffiti-like guitar phrases, actually mentioning death.

On Side Two, to glorify the weather, there was Good Day Sunshine. There was And Your Bird Can Sing, more lucid Lennon nonsense, and Paul's pretty, self-pitying For No One. There was Doctor Robert, a jibe against some medical man or other. There was George's earnest I Want to Tell You, and then Paul's Got To Get You Into My Life, a soul song as brassy, neat and rousing as ever came out of the American South.

In those 14 songs, the LP record ceased to be a catchpenny gimmick and became a creative medium as credible as canvas or print. In that one album, too, a mood and moment are caught as exactly as in the pithiest contemporary journalism. For Revolver *was* London as she flourished in the swinging summer afterglow. It was hot pavements, open windows, King's Road bistros and England soccer stripes. It was the British accent, once again all-conquering.

It was the present, and a portent of things to come. For the Beatles now recognised their power as dictators over era after era. The next era was in the final Revolver track, Tomorrow Never Knows, a song utterly unlike the other 13. John Lennon sang it, in the flat, barely tuneful voice which had replaced his exuberant, mocking grin. Against a background of eerie twangling and squibbled backward-tapes, the voice intoned, not a lyric but an exhortation. 'Turn off your mind, relax and float downsteam . . . Lay down all thought, surrender to the void . . . Listen to the colour of your dreams . . . Or play the game Existence to the end. Of the beginning,' sang the voice as the strange episode faded, leaving its one million listeners baffled, but determined to understand.

The four who stopped running, who stood still at last in 1966, looking curiously about them, were beings such as the modern world had never seen. Only in ancient times, when boy Emperors and Pharaohs were clothed, even fed with pure gold, had very young men commanded an equivalent adoration, fascination and constant, expectant scrutiny. Nor could anyone suppose that to be thus—to have such youth and wealth, such clothes and cars and servants and women, made for any state other than inconceivable happiness. For no one since the boy Pharaohs, since the fatally-pampered boy Caesars, had known, as the Beatles now knew, how it felt to have felt everything, done everything, tasted everything, had a surfeit of everything; to live on that blinding, deadening, numbing surfeit which made each, on bad days, think he was ageing at twice the usual rate.

It was as little comprehensible that to command such fame as Beatles might not be enough: that each, in the stupendous collective adoration, felt himself to be overlooked as an individual: that each on his own should long to test the reality, or otherwise, of his independent existence.

John Lennon seemed the most determined—and best qualified—to make an individual career. That autumn, with Neil Aspinall, he detached himself from the other three to appear in a new film, *How I Won the War*, directed by the now extremely fashionable and financeable Richard Lester. It had been clear to Lester, even in the harmless knockabout of the two Beatles films, that John had serious possibilities as a screen actor. This view was confirmed when *How I Won the War* went on release and John's portrayal of Private Gripweed was singled out for critical praise. 'I told him then he could do anything he wanted in films,' Richard Lester says. 'But he wasn't interested. It came too easily to him. He despised it.'

The Beatle who had vanished into Private Gripweed was never to re-emerge. He kept his hair cropped short—a renunciation already front-page news throughout the world. He took to wearing the glasses he had always hated, perversely choosing little owl-eyed frames like those prescribed for him at Primary school in the 1940s.

Under the cropped hair, the granny glasses, the clothes that tended increasingly towards flowered scarves and loose waist-coats, much of the same old John remained. The same impossible vagueness still caused him to forget the words of his own songs, his ex-directory telephone number, even his Aunt Mimi's Christian name. The same impossible generosity would still press on anyone his last cigarette or whatever was in his pocket, whether sixpence or a thousand pounds. The same blistering sarcasm and silly puns kept those around him suspended between terror of his contempt, and helpless, incredulous laughter.

It was with Tomorrow Never Knows, and songs after it, that the new John emerged. The new John 'dropped' LSD, the 'mind drug', as casually as he had once smoked a cigarette; for the new John, music was to be the means of passing on the visions he had seen. Some of those visions were to be beautiful and brilliant, others grotesque and farcical, others simply and overpoweringly tedious. In time the visions would blur, beauty with grotesqueness, brilliance with affronting stupidity. The pictures would change to riddles, the laughter be swallowed up by causes, the causes grow ever more exhaustingly and exasperatingly hopeless.

In 1966, there seemed so many possibilities. Publishers wanted him to write for them. Print engravers and greeting card companies urged him to draw for them. Art galleries—now springing up in London almost as rapidly as boutiques—begged him to attend their private views. Art seemed to engage his whole attention for a time. He would drive up from Weybridge two or three times a week in the rainbow-daubed Rolls Royce whose Scottish 'chauffeur' also used it as an occasional doss.

Newest of all the new little West End galleries was the Indica in Mason's Yard, run by Marianne Faithful's ex-husband, John Dunbar. In November 1966, the Indica was hanging an exhibition called 'Unfinished Paintings and Objects by Yoko Ono'. The artist, a Japanese-born American, enjoyed minor notoriety in London for having recently exhibited her photographs of various unclothed human bottoms.

The night before the Indica exhibition opened, John Lennon arrived to look at it. He spent quite a long time over the Unfinished Paintings and Objects, particularly a painting attached to the ceiling with a ladder up to it, and an apple unembellished but for a price ticket saying '£200'. Later on, John Dunbar sent Yoko Ono across to speak to him. She proved to be very small and dressed entirely in black, her face—not conventionally beautiful—held in balance by twin clouds of dense black hair. Instead of speaking, she handed John a card on which was written the single word 'Breathe'.

Next day, he was back in the small living-room in one corner of the mansion which had taken nine months to decorate; folded up inside the small sofa he preferred to all his pastel-upholstered acres. He would lie there for hours, watching television or half-watching it, glancing at books and papers, then throwing them aside. He could lie there all day, not speaking to Cynthia, not seeming to notice Julian, his trance penetrable only by some scrap of nonsense from a TV quiz, some stray paragraph from the *Daily Express*, some costly and purposeless toy like his 'nothing box', a black plastic cube in which red lights winked on and off at random. He could spend hours in trying to guess which of the red lights would wink on next.

Late at night, if no excursion was happening, he would unfold himself from the couch and wander away to his studio, the guitars, the Vox organ, the 10 linked-up Brunel tape recorders. Cynthia knew she would not see him again that night. Next day, she would have to keep the house quiet until early afternoon, when she took up his breakfast tray.

Sitting downstairs with her drawing or her needlework, cowed by the feuding between Dot, the housekeeper, and the general factotum's wife, afraid to go outside the grounds in case some photographer saw Julian; thrifty, soft-spoken, eternally hoping for the best, Cyn' was the same person she had always been.

Paul, the most committed performer, the most addicted to worship, the one who had worked the hardest at being a Beatle, now found himself at something of a loss. His first act, after the touring stopped, was to take a long and, for him, extravagant sabbatical. With Mal Evans—whose wife Lil still waited patiently in Sunbury-on-Thames—he set out on a long road safari across Africa.

His future, Paul announced on returning, would be concerned with all-round cultural self-improvement. He felt—as, indeed, both John and George did—that being a Beatle had been a form of missing life. The A-level Institute boy was excited, too, by London's increasing artistic bustle. 'People are saying things and painting things and writing things that are great,' he told the *Evening Standard*. 'I must *know* what people are doing.'

In this endeavour, as in all Paul's private life, his girl friend Jane Asher was the main stimulus. Jane, unlike the other Beatle women, possessed complete independence: now 21, she had her own highly successful stage and film career. With her angelic looks went a strong mind and forthright manner which curtailed Paul's ego, deflated his superstar pomposities and made her a companion altogether preferable to any of the brainless beauties who clustered adoringly round him. He made a point of seeing all Jane's plays, wherever the run happened to start. It was in Bristol, waiting to see Jane in a play, that a shopfront name gave him the idea for Eleanor Rigby. His best love songs had been written for Jane: in Here, There and Everywhere she is an almost tangible presence.

His first project apart from the other Beatles was the composition of theme music for a new British comedy film, *The Family Way*. *Newsweek* magazine—which otherwise would hardly have noticed such a minor piece—considered his score 'neat and resourceful'. He had already begun producing records—for Peter and Gordon, the duo featuring Jane's brother; for a group called The Escourts; and for Cliff Bennett and the Rebel Rousers when they covered his song Got To Get You Into My Life.

He had chosen a house at last: not in stockbroker land with the other Beatles but in Cavendish Avenue, St. John's Wood. The district epitomised his cultural and social ambitions and was also conveniently close to the EMI studios. The house, discreetly large, was enclosed by high walls and protected by electronic security gates. With it, Paul acquired the accessory status-symbols of a married couple, butler and cook. An Old English sheepdog named Martha roamed the extensive garden which, despite his family's protests, he resolutely neglected.

As far as the Press and public were concerned, the most interesting thing about Paul's self-improvement programme was the point in it when he and Jane Asher would announce their engagement. Jane had helped him to decorate and furnish the new house although, with a nicety characteristic of both, she did not officially live with him there.

Each of them had grown adept at fending off the same old, microphone-thrusting question. 'I certainly would be most surprised,' Jane said, 'if I married anyone but Paul.' And Paul himself, caught yet again outside his electronic gates, looked up from his Aston Martin with the geniality that never seemed to falter, listened to the question, considered and replied: 'Just say that when you asked me that, I smiled.'

George, so it seemed, was even more at a loss. He had been a Beatle ever since the age of 15. All his adult life had been spent running or, with his gradually more magnificent guitar, his mop-top framing his pale, wary face, just standing there.

For the final year of touring, if not longer, George had actively hated his Beatle existence. On the outside, it might appear pure gold: on the inside, it bristled with snubs and slights—the heavy patience of George Martin in the studio; the stifling profusion of John and Paul's partnership which allowed him, if he was lucky, one song per album; the realisation that in their eyes he was still what he had been in Liverpool, the kid just tagging along.

His unvented rage he turned upon the adoring world. While Beatlemania was still a laugh to the others, to George it was an affront against the musicianship he had so laboriously taught himself. His fame seemed to have brought him only money and a terrible touchiness—a suspicion, already voiced in one song lyric, of 'people standing round who screw you in the ground'. His wife Pattie—they had married in January 1966—virtually gave up her modelling career lest, in George's eyes, people should try to exploit him through her. Nor was even his wealth a source of perfect pleasure. The words he wrote for Taxman, and the voice in which he sang it, convey bitter personal resentment.

It had been with the idlest curiosity, on the *Help!* film set, that George first heard Indian sitars playing a burlesque version of the Beatles' own song A Hard Day's Night. *Help!* was, of course, a goonish romp about Eastern mystics in pursuit of a sacrificial jewel. The finale was a pitched battle between Beatles and dacoits in the surf along a Bahamas beach while a many-armed Hindu idol lolled in the offshore swell. As Richard Lester remembers, no one quite knew if it was part of the script or not when, in the midst of shooting, an Indian suddenly rode up on a bicycle and handed each Beatle a small religious book.

From the joke film property and the Indian on the bicycle grew the earnest passion which was to make George Harrison the least recognisable Beatle of all. He acquired a sitar of his own and began to play it, initially as if it was a guitar. Clumsy as his first experiments were, they gave him something he had never had before—a definite and distinctive contribution to what the Beatles did in the studio. For not even George Martin could be snooty about sitars. The sound tentatively used on Rubber Soul was one of the prime elements, and praised as such, in Revolver. Henceforward it was recognised that when a group of Indians walked in and squatted down, balancing their strange, giraffe-necked instruments against the ball of one bare brown foot, that was when George took over and gave orders.

In 1966, at a dinner-party, he met Ravi Shankar, the Indian sitar virtuoso. Shankar—not surprisingly, since Indians know better than most the value of a powerful disciple—offered to visit George's bungalow in Esher and give him private tuition.

He had already been to India once, briefly, on the run from the Philippines. In autumn 1966—after what he at least firmly regarded as the Beatles' last appearance—he returned there with Pattie for two months' sitar study under Ravi Shankar. He also met Shankar's spiritual teacher, or guru, who explained to him the Law of Karma—the Buddhist principle of inevitability. He and Pattie travelled to Kashmir, where India comes nearest to unqualified beauty; they witnessed religious festivals and conversed with students and Holy men. They returned to England, filled with India's infinite wisdom and mystery, having perceived nothing of its equally infinite mundaneness.

Just as he had once obsessively applied himself to his £3 guitar, George now devoted his life to sitar practice. In this period, indeed, he rarely touched a guitar outside the recording studio. He practised day and night, sitting on the floor in his Indian smock in his Esher home, holding the sitar under one foot as he had been shown, trying scales as he once had under his mother's encouraging eye, but encouraged now by the perky Indian voice of his master issuing from a tape recorder.

George, too, was now regularly taking LSD. For him, the mental landscape the drug produced was one he had already seen. It was the India of mystic sounds and mystic beings, able to levitate or lie on spikes or bury themselves: the India which, in sight and touch and voice and clamour and calm, was the furthest distance you could go from being a Beatle, wearing a suit and singing 'Yeah, yeah, yeah'. He who had always kept his mind shut tight against all schooling, now began to devour books about Yoga and Meditation. The books promised a state he had so far found unattainable—of perfect pleasure, 'enlightenment' and peace. He need not worry then about the Taxman and who was screwing him; about who recognised him, or failed to recognise him; about the girls who climbed into the garden he cultivated like a Northern working man, and broke the tops off his roses.

Only Ringo seemed to know for certain what he wanted. He wanted to stay at home with Maureen and their new baby, Zak. They called the baby Zak because it was the name Ringo had wished for when small. Life for Ringo was still that simple, even when he stood in the grounds of 'Sunny Heights', looking across his landscaped garden to the wall half-constructed by his own building company; and at his cars, the Facel Vega, the Land Rover, the Mini Cooper; and at the house itself with its miles of soft furnishings, its white carpets, its six TV sets, its ciné equipment, billiard table and one-arm bandit. At odd moments, remembering the Dingle when they walked round to Admiral Grove behind the handcart piled with his mother's few belongings, he would look again at his huge property, and all the toys he had never thought of asking for, and think: 'What's a scruff like me doing with all this lot?'

Even as separate householders and individual millionaires, they could not stop being together. No wife, no girl friend yet had broken the inexplicable bond between four individuals who had not only grown up together but also helped each other through an ordeal none but that four understood. The habit continued of doing things, wearing things, buying things, having crazes for things in unison. When John took to wearing glasses, the others did. Paul and John, during the New Delhi stopover, bought sitars like George's. All took simultaneously to baggy-sleeved flowered shirts, high-buttoning frock coats, wide-brimmed hats and loosely-tied scarves. And early in 1967, on the upper lips of all four, there appeared identical small curved moustaches.

Just as on tour, the people closest to them were the two fellow Liverpudlians who, as road managers, had so long formed their only bulwark against the world. Neil—or, as John called him, 'Nell'—Aspinall, the nervous, clever ex-accountancy student, and Mal Evans, the towering, inoffensive ex-bouncer, continued to fill a role necessary to each Beatle and the four as a unit. Neil and Mal went where the Beatles went, wore what the Beatles wore, smoked what the Beatles smoked: for their not over-large salaries they remained perpetually on call to provide any Beatle with any of life's necessities, from a transcontinental chauffeur to a tray of tea and toast. Mal's wife, Lil, in Sunbury-on-Thames, did not see him for weeks at a time. Neil—paradoxically in the service of such masters—was definitely losing his hair.

Similarly, the close friends each Beatle had tended to be friends acquired collectively, in Liverpool or Hamburg. There was Tony Bramwell, George's childhood acquaintance, who had progressed from NEMS office boy to stage manager of Brian's latest venture, the Savile theatre. There was Terry Doran, another Brian friend, his partner in Brydor Cars, but welcome in every Beatle home for his willingness to go anywhere, fetch anything, and his talent to amuse. There was Klaus Voorman, their Art student friend from Hamburg, the boy whom Astrid forsook for Stu Sutcliffe. Klaus had taught himself to play bass guitar, and now belonged to a successful British group, Manfred Mann. It was Klaus who had designed the Revolver album sleeve. There was also, intermittently, Pete Shotton, John Lennon's old school and skiffle crony, whom John had recompensed for the night he smashed Pete's washboard over his head by buying a supermarket for him to run in Hayling Island.

Their other friends were musicians British and American, whose life like theirs had become increasingly divided between the two countries forming Pop's single hemisphere. The Beatles, with Bob Dylan, the Byrds, the Beach Boys, became the nucleus of an exclusive, mutually-supportive 'superstar' species, not rivals but confederates, fellow-sufferers even, from unabating success. For them had arisen the clubs, like Blase's and Sybilla's —partly financed by George Harrison—which kept out all but the very fashionable and allowed the weary idol to bury his over-photographed face in their high-priced, protecting darkness.

Thus the Beatles knew the Rolling Stones, not as their chief competitor, especially in the American market, not even as their most blatant imitators, but simply as part of the small human minority with whom it was possible to socialise. They had gone around together since 1963, when the Stones were still a pub group, playing authentic Rhythm and Blues. It was George Harrison, in fact, who first recommended them to Dick Rowe of Decca Records. Rowe hastily signed them to Decca, so ridding himself of the stigma of having turned down the Beatles in favour of a group from Dagenham.

There grew up an odd fascination between the Beatles, who owed their success to reassuring the adult world, and the Stones, who got rich by outraging it. 'The Beatles want to hold your hand,' wrote Tom Wolfe, 'but the Stones want to burn your town.' How could Tom Wolfe have known that the Beatles were like that, or worse, in their pre-Brian days? John, in particular, though recognising the Stones' unoriginality, envied Mick Jagger as the epitome of a rebellion from which he himself had been dissuaded.

It had recently come home to Decca, if not yet to EMI, that Pop musicians were ceasing to be innocent, easily-dazzled boys. The Rolling Stones' manager, Brian Epstein's ex-publicist Andrew Oldham, had handed the Stones' financial affairs over to one Allen Klein, a New York accountant who specialised in extracting money from American record companies on behalf of discontented performers. Three years' scandal-ridden success had earned the Stones no more than about £100,000. Allen Klein, by renegotiating their contract with Decca and the London-American label, obtained them almost £3m in advanced royalties.

Mick Jagger, in the dark of Blase's or Sybilla's, enthused about Klein to the Beatles. He could easily do the same for them, Jagger said, with those tight-fisted bastards at EMI.

Nor was this the first time the Beatles had heard of Allen Klein. The same American gentleman also happened to be a large shareholder in the MGM film corporation and, only recently, had been quoted as saying he could turn the Beatles into 'modern Marx Brothers'. Ironically it was Paul McCartney whom this announcement most impressed. Newspaper reports appeared that two of the Beatles—one of them certainly Paul—wanted to hire Allen Klein in an advisory capacity and that, in best espionage style, a 'third man' was to act as intermediary in a deal between Klein's company and NEMS. Brian issued a statement dismissing the reports as 'ridiculous'. Nonetheless, according to music trade gossip, Allen Klein had bet that he would 'have the Beatles by Christmas'.

They never did become modern Marx Brothers. Though committed to make a third film for United Artists, they could not agree with Walter Shenson, their producer, over a script. John, especially, complained that in *Help!* they had been 'extras in our own film'. One idea was that they should make a Western; another was that they should play the Three Musketeers; another—the one that Shenson thought most promising—visualised them as four living facets of the same personality. As with the previous two films, Shenson looked around for a 'quality' writer. A script was commissioned from Joe Orton, the young working-class dramatist whose macabre comedies *Loot* and *Entertaining Mr. Sloane* had each been huge West End successes.

Orton visited Brian Epstein at Chapel Street to discuss the project. Paul McCartney, who had much admired *Loot*, was also there. 'I'd expected Epstein to be florid, Jewish, dark-haired and overbearing,' Orton wrote in his diary. 'Instead, I was face to face with a mousey-haired, slight young man. He had a suburban accent. Rather washed out. Paul was just as in the photographs. Only he'd grown a moustache. "The only thing I get from the theatre," Paul M said, "is a sore arse" . . .'

Orton, typically, produced an outrageous script entitled *Up Against It* in which the Beatles were to be portrayed as anarchists, adulterers and urban guerillas. After a long delay, the script was rejected without comment. 'An amateur and a fool,' wrote Orton angrily of Brian. 'Probably he will never say Yes. Equally he hasn't the courage to say No. A thoroughly weak, flaccid type.'

During November, the Beatles had returned to Abbey Road in what proved an abortive attempt to make an end-of-year follow-up to Revolver. All that appeared that Christmas was a cut-price collection of Beatles Oldies—but Goldies and a fan club record of labyrinthine zaniness.

What with one thing and another nowadays, they seemed to see less of Brian. They heard from various people that he was depressed: in a momentary, inconclusive way, they felt concerned about it. Life was now such, however, that no one thought stayed in their minds very long.

Brian had looked in at Abbey Road late one night while they were recording. Despite their labours with George Martin, the track would still not come right. They looked up to see Brian suddenly there, with one of the boy friends he no longer troubled to hide.

'Brian did something I'd never seen him do before,' George Martin says. 'When John had finished singing, he switched on the studio intercom and said, "I don't think that sounded quite right, John." John looked up at him and said, in his most cutting voice: "You stick to your percentages, Brian. We'll look after the music." '

August 1967

'I don't think there was any hope for him since the day he met the Beatles'

For those who grew up in the 1960s, and who coloured the decade by their growing, 1967 is a year to be remembered above any other. It is not for them, as for objective historians, the moment when Civilisation began its backward lurch towards a new Dark Age. It is, rather, the moment when their own youth reached a dazzling and careless apogee. 1967 may have been the year of Napalm and sudden death: it was also, for an entire generation, the year of 'love', 'peace' and 'flower power'. There are thousands who still wear its relics, still utter its once-powerful phrases, still mourn that burnished epoch when they called themselves Beautiful People.

The year had little inherent beauty. Certainly none existed in Vietnam. John F. Kennedy's dashing 'limited war' had swollen into a catastrophe whose demands grew even greater, even as its purpose grew more obscure, and whose conduct had aroused disgust and condemnation throughout the world. What the world saw were not true-hearted American boys, keeping humanity safe from Communism. The world saw only helicopter gunships attacking straw villages; women of grace and elegance keening over their scorched babies; a child, naked and helpless, wandering down a road between paddy fields towards artillery.

America, for the first time in her history, found herself involved in a war she could not win; a war which, even more bewilderingly, was opposed by many Americans. A wave of pacifist feeling swept the country, not among cranks and beatniks only but among the ordinary teenagers now liable for military service. 'Protest' as a concept left the lunatic fringe, spreading through formerly peaceable universities, spreading also into the black ghettoes whose young men were impartially called on to fight for a system which still oppressed them. Pop music was a reflection—even aggravation—of the new rebellious mood. Bob Dylan's bitter mockery, the sweet reproaches of Joan Baez, became the spur to anti-war demonstrations and marches, and the ever-increasing numbers who fled 'the Draft' to Canada or Europe.

So the American Dream began to dissolve. Yet that bitter awakening, ironically, produced its own short, golden reverie in a city harbouring more American dreams than most. Like the first settlers and the gold-seekers, like the Zen Buddhists of the early Sixties, like Kerouac and his 'beat' poets, America's dissenting youth in 1967 turned their eyes to that side of the republic where the ocean began and in particular, where the ocean's space and freedom seemed reflected in the city of San Francisco.

San Francisco's run-down Haight-Ashbury district had long ago been settled by a homespun and bewhiskered 'hippy' community. That community now swelled with the arrival of draft-dodgers, disaffected students and social 'drop-outs' by the thousand. Fresh hippy colonies sprang up along the North California coast, around Berkeley University and in remote beach hamlets like Big Sur. The environment, with its natural beauty and leisurely policing, was ideally suited to resignation from all conventional American life. More and more came to share the hippy heaven: to grow their hair, put on flowing robes and walk barefoot; to speak softly, behave meekly and hand each other —on every possible pretext—flowers.

They sat round open fires at night, near the booming surf, sharing the small, bedraggled cigarettes which represented their greatest apostasy from decent American ways. Marijuana was the badge of hippy brotherhood, the odour most common in hippy refuges, the initiator of the hippy belief that through drugs lay a path to higher wisdom and humaneness. A middle-aged university physicist, Dr. Timothy Leary, was already their leader—or guru—following his dismissal from Harvard for experiments into the 'psychedelic' (literally, mind-expanding) properties of LSD. Leary and his academic converts led the awakening interest in drug-inspired literature, from Byron to Aldous Huxley, and of drug-sanctioning Eastern religions. Joss sticks were thus tentatively lit in California, and Buddhist prayers phonetically intoned. Astrology became a youth fad to rival the hula hoop. It was through astrology most of all that wisdom became available: an age-old wisdom settling, in the 'pot' smoke, over woolly and impressionable minds. An entire new vocabulary evolved to distinguish the hippy from his persecutor, the 'beautiful' from the short-haired and workaday, the divine souls who 'turned on', 'tuned in', 'freaked out' and 'blew their minds' from the residue of unenlightened humanity.

Musicians, being natural converts, blew the hippy happening like pollen across America. By early 1967, San Francisco groups like Jefferson Airplane and the Grateful Dead were bringing the first rumours to British youth—of Haight-Ashbury and Big Sur and a huge outdoor concert at Monterey; of harsh new metal sounds and flashing lights; of a fresh dream world which they, having no Big Sur, only Margate and Llandudno, supposed they must be content to experience at second-hand.

On 17 February, Parlophone released two new Beatles songs: Penny Lane and Strawberry Fields Forever. The tracks had been recorded late in 1966, for the album that was to surpass Revolver: with a lightweight ditty called When I'm Sixty-Four, they represented the sum of almost three months' work. Since a single was long overdue, George Martin had no choice but to sacrifice the two three-minute productions that, each in its own way, had involved more time and expense than most entire LPs. The 'double A-side' formula was less a boast than a political necessity, since one side was wholly John's and the other entirely Paul's: the weight of creativity packed into each only emphasised what a gulf lay between them.

Strawberry Fields was the name of an old Salvation Army children's home close to where John grew up in Liverpool. The song was, however, explicit only in its title: a mirror only to its author's almost perpetual LSD trip. Yet his feeling for imagery remained strong enough to shine through the scrawl of the drug across his mind. The words are a perverse riddle from which pictures nonetheless struggle, like lazy ectoplasm, to tell a story.

Penny Lane, by contrast—since Paul had not yet succumbed to LSD—recreated with photographic clarity a part of Liverpool known to all the Beatles, on the way to Woolton and Allerton, near the bus depot where Mimi used to see John off to Dovedale Primary, and 'Barney's', the hall where the Quarry Man played; it mentioned the barber's in the little parade, the roundabout and fire station, the 'four of fish' from chip-shop parlance, the 'finger pie' of adolescent bus-shelter naughtiness: it was surrealism from a rational mind, as recognisable yet mysterious as someone else's snapshot album.

As an arranger, George Martin's only guide was Paul's enthusiasm for the piccolo trumpet passage in Bach's Brandenberg Concerto. David Mason of the London Symphony Orchestra stood by in Studio One with his piccolo trumpet while Paul hummed the notes he wanted and Martin inked them into a score.

Strawberry Fields proved an even greater test of the producer's ingenuity. The song, as John first played it on acoustic guitar, was a simple, reflective melody. With the other Beatles added, it changed to the 'heavy' style they were already absorbing from the San Francisco psychedelic groups. John liked it that way at first but then, a few days later, asked George Martin to produce a softer arrangement with trumpets and cellos. In the end, he could not decide between the two versions. He said he liked the beginning of one but preferred the ending of the other. Martin had to find a way of splicing half the 'heavy metal' version with half the orchestral one. To his lasting credit, no one noticed the join.

Self-surpassing talent, given in double measure, resulted in the first Beatles single since 1962 which did not reach Number One in the Top Twenty. It climbed to second place but could not in the end dislodge a mundane cabaret singer, lately renamed Engelbert Humperdinck, singing an oily ballad entitled Release Me.

The fact was, the Beatles now had an influence no longer measurable by the Top Twenty alone. George Melly, the Jazz singer and critic and a fellow Liverpudlian, reviewed Penny Lane as poetry: it was, he said, a true evocation of Liverpool in the 1950s with 'great sandstone churches and the trams rattling past'. The imagery worked with no less power on those who had never seen Liverpool, and barely remembered the Fifties: those for whom Penny Lane's 'blue suburban skies', like Strawberry Fields' acid-swirling bridle-path, became a mirage eclipsing even that of San Francisco. You heard it even better, people said, when you were 'high'.

Late in 1966, at his elegant Belgravia home, Brian Epstein tried to commit suicide with an overdose of sleeping tablets. Fortunately, both his secretary, Joanne Newfield, and his chauffeur, Brian Barratt, were on hand to thwart him. Barratt broke down the double doors to his bedroom while Joanne telephoned for Dr. Norman Cowan, the physician who had been regularly treating him. The three managed to keep Brian conscious until they could get him to his usual clinic.

The attempt was kept secret among those like Joanne, like Peter Brown, who were privy of his homosexual life and so familiar with its *leitmotif* of despair. Doomed love affairs with brutal boys had driven him often to the brink before. But always before he had had the means to recover: to convince himself, as no rational argument could, that his life still held pleasure and purpose.

For Brian Epstein, that pleasure and purpose were extinguished on 29 August 1966, when the Beatles gave their last concert in Candlestick Park, San Francisco; when Brian, terrified and preoccupied as he was that day, would have given anything to unravel the years and the wealth and be back at Barnston Women's Institute, watching four boys arrive with their new stage suits in Burton's carrier bags.

On the homeward flight, he had almost let his unhappiness show. 'What am I going to do now?' he kept saying. 'Shall I go back to school and learn something new?'

The Beatles, for five years, for the centuries contained in each of those years, had been his all-eclipsing passion. He had lived for them, and through them, with intensity granted to few born under his unlucky star. He had loved them, not shamefully, not furtively, but with an idealism which millions found fit to share. That love was as the painter for his canvas, the parent for his children, the lost soul for its salvation. Having been hardly noticed, it was not rejected with any great show of regret.

He remained the Beatles' manager; a celebrity in that due proportion. He was, indeed, rather more often in the papers nowadays since their submersion in private projects and recording. Was it true they had started to break up? Quite untrue, Brian patiently said. They were simply resting. After what they had been through, who could blame them? Just before Christmas 1966, when the Welsh village of Aberfan was engulfed by a coal tip, it was suggested that the Beatles give a concert in aid of the disaster fund. Their refusal to do so aroused widespread criticism. Brian came forward, as of old, to explain and to shield them.

He might convince the Press, but he did not deceive himself. A bond was broken which had, in any case, been so fragile, composed of arrangements, schedules, timetables and notes. Despite the years and miles he had travelled with them, despite a fame and reckless wealth to equal theirs, he had no point of communication with them but a contract. Once their talent outran his efficiency, Brian Epstein had no further part to play. With all else that was to be heard in their brilliant new music, Brian could hear the sound of his own doom.

He was, to outward appearances, still the epitome of that youthful success associated with Swinging London. Not yet 32, he controlled an entertainment organisation which, as well as the Beatles, represented some of the best-known names in show business. His personal wealth was estimated, by the *Financial Times,* at £7m. Outside 13 Chapel Street, his red Rolls Royce or his silver Bentley convertible stood in the lingering Belgravia sun.

NEMS Enterprises, though administered by many hands, still owed its main direction to Brian's personal business judgement, that strange mixture of rashness and prescience. In 1965, he had bought the Savile theatre in Shaftesbury Avenue, impervious to objections that it was just a few yards on the wrong side of the West End. The building appealed to Brian with its Art Deco exterior, its boxes with private ante-rooms in which leopardskin couches stood. At the Savile, he planned to put on straight plays in alternation with Sunday night Pop shows. 'We brought the Four Tops over from America, on the Sunday before their big record, Reach Out, I'll Be There, went to Number One in

Britain,' Tony Bramwell says. 'Brian paid them $32,000 for a £2,000 gross at the Savile. Then, of course, he was able to bring them back to do a seven-week British tour.'

His passion for theatre led Brian to subsidise the Savile through seasons of excellent, barely-profitable productions, both drama and dance. He had his own box there, and his own private bar. At the Savile, he could play theatrical impresario right to the borderline of his true desire, undimmed since his RADA days—that one night on the lit stage, the leading man who entered left, through French windows, would be Brian himself.

The fantasy recurred in various projects with which, after August 1966, he attempted to fill his life. There was, for instance, his plan, in partnership with the disc jockey Brian Matthew, to build a new theatre-cum-record studio in Bromley, Kent. He also dabbled in bullfighting, his other surreptitious passion. He put money into a film about El Cordobes and became a sponsor of the English matador, Henry Higgins.

These ventures were not for profit, since he had more than enough money: they were symptoms of Brian's desperate wish to find some other role than entrepreneur and businessman. He wanted to be creative, as the Beatles were—to establish by any possible means that credential for re-entry into their world. So he tried to produce a record, for the Liverpool singer, Rory Storm. He had always felt guilty at having poached Ringo Starr from Rory's group. He even tried directing a play, *Smashing Day,* at the New Arts theatre. John Fernald, his old RADA teacher, had been supposed to direct it but had fallen ill. 'Brian took over and really threw himself into rehearsals,' Joanne Newfield says. 'He was totally involved, right up to the evening of the dress rehearsal. All the cast were waiting in their costumes—but no Brian. He'd forgotten all about it.'

Joanne had joined NEMS originally as secretary to Brian's assistant, the high-powered Wendy Hanson. She inherited Wendy's job in late 1966, when Brian closed down his Stafford Street office and announced he would be working entirely from Chapel Street. Sitting upstairs, under two life-size David Bailey portraits of him, Joanne was first to see the marked change in Brian's dress and habits. His clothes grew more flamboyant, his gestures more overtly 'camp': it became a struggle for Joanne to keep him to his business engagements. 'I'd find notes for me in the morning, asking me to get him out of appointments—meetings or lunches. I once had to cancel Bernard Delfont four times.'

One business matter had so harried and tormented Brian that he now refused even to think about it. In New York, the lawsuit against Seltaeb, the merchandising company, was about to enter its third year. The huge delay—caused largely by Brian's failure to attend pre-trial examinations—had seen Nicky Byrne's claim for 'lost' revenues rise, as the Beatles grew still more famous, from $5 to $22m. The Beatles themselves even now knew nothing of the millions—perhaps billions—that their name had generated but that Brian had been unable to catch.

His other NEMS artists—apart from Cilla Black: 'my Cilla' —had long ago ceased to absorb his energy. Gerry Marsden was in a West End musical; Billy J. Kramer and the Fourmost had gone to other agencies. The emphasis was now on 'hard Rock', thanks to the addition of Robert Stigwood, a gingery young Australian, to the NEMS high command. The roster of acts brought in by Stigwood included the Bee Gees, the Moody Blues, Cream and the young black American guitarist Jimi Hendrix. Stigwood provided what Brian had been looking for—a chance to be rid of NEMS Enterprises altogether. Larry Parnes had already turned down a controlling interest, since the deal would not include the Beatles. Stigwood became joint managing director, pending his acquisition of a majority shareholding.

Brian himself was now rarely to be seen in the daylight hours. Joanne Newfield, arriving at Chapel Street each morning, would find her day's instructions in the note pushed under his bedroom door—a note written at dawn in amphetamine wakefulness, before the antidote drug plunged him into sleep. Sometimes, pushed under the door, there would be a pile of money, won on his perpetual journey round the Mayfair gambling clubs. 'Jo . . .' one note said, 'Please bank my happiness . . .'

With luck, and a little extra dose, he would not have to open his eyes until mid-afternoon. Joanne knew he had surfaced when the intercom in his bedroom was switched on. 'When he first got up, he always felt terrible—hung over from drink and pills. He'd take some uppers to get over that. At about five o'clock, he'd be full of life. He'd come in and say, "Right. Let's start work."'

The mounting depression, the chemicals warring within him, produced fits of irrational anger which drove Joanne many times to the point of resignation. Like others before her, she could never quite bring herself to do it. 'The smallest thing could send him half-crazy. I got him a wrong number once, and he literally went berserk. He threw a whole tea tray at me. Another time, it was my birthday: he was terrible to me all day. The next day, I found this note. "Jo—good morning. Better late than never. Many happy returns of yesterday. Be a bit tolerant of me at my worst. Really, I don't want to hurt anyone . . ."'

Several times he made a determined attempt to pull himself together. He began seeing a psychiatrist and, on at least two occasions, went into a 'drying-out' clinic in Putney. For one period of several weeks, a doctor and a nurse took up residence at Chapel Street. The nurse went out one afternoon, and Brian escaped. He was missing for two days. No one thought of looking for him where he was more and more to be found—in the dismal trysting alleyways of Piccadilly Underground station.

Life could still return to normal, as when his mother came down from Liverpool for a visit. Paradoxically, spells of conventional illness put him back on the rails. 'I looked after him when he had glandular fever,' Joanne Newfield says. 'He had a bout of jaundice as well, when Queenie came down to stay. Brian got into a good routine then and really seemed to enjoy it. I remember one Saturday afternoon how thrilled he was that he and Peter Brown had been out to Berwick Market to buy fruit. Brian thought this was wonderful. He'd done something normal—something just the same as other people did.'

Early in 1967, he made a second attempt to kill himself with a drug overdose. The Beatles were by then deeply involved in recording their new album. Brian had let an early pressing of Strawberry Fields/Penny Lane be stolen from Chapel Street by one of his boy friends. Shortly afterwards, the words 'Brian Epstein is a queer' were scrawled on the garage door in lipstick. 'He did confide in me how hopeless his private life was,' Joanne says. ' "I'm no good with women and I'm no good with men," he told me. He was in absolute despair that day.

'The doctor told me once that Brian was like a collision course inside himself. He could only be terribly happy or terribly unhappy. If there was any depression or misery, Brian would be drawn helplessly into it. The Beatles caused that happiness, and they caused that unhappiness. I don't think there was any hope for him since the day he met the Beatles.'

He could still rally—entering the room to greet a visitor kept waiting an hour or more while he composed himself, with wake-up pills and an early brandy, into a semblance of that old, smooth, courteous, charming Brian. So he always appeared to Hunter Davies, the *Sunday Times* journalist lately commissioned, with Paul McCartney's support, to write the Beatles' 'authorised biography'. Meticulously, as he had once sent the Beatles out into the Merseyside night, he wrote directions for Hunter Davies to drive to Kingsley Hill, his new country house in Sussex, where they would talk further over dinner.

America still held vestiges of happiness. With his lawyer friend Nat Weiss, he had formed a separate company, Nemperor Artists, to represent NEMS people in New York. Weiss had himself gone over to artist-management, handling groups like Cyrkle, whose song Red Rubber Ball Brian had correctly judged a million-selling U.S. single. Nemperor Artists had another new signing, of talents as yet unrealised—Brian Epstein. He virtually gave the company to Nat Weiss so that Weiss could become *his* agent.

The portly, rather strange New Yorker had become Brian's

most loyal, long-suffering friend. There were difficulties in that city, too, after encounters with predatory boys around Times Square. One day, when Brian was due to be interviewed on radio WORFM, Nat Weiss found him drugged almost insensible with Seconal tablets. Weiss, somehow, revived him and delivered him to the studio.

That interview, with the long-time Beatle adherent Murray the K, has survived on an hour-long tape in Nat Weiss's possession. It is remarkable less for the subjects covered than for the tenacity with which Brian, once on the air, fought his way back from his Seconal coma. At the beginning, he can scarcely even speak. But slowly, his voice frees itself, his thoughts unstick. He can articulate what everyone—what he most of all—has hoped to hear. The Beatles and he remain as close as they have ever been. 'There hasn't been so much as . . . a row.

'At the moment they're doing great things in the studio. They take longer nowadays, of their own volition, to make records. They're hyper-critical of their own work. Paul rang me the other day and said he wanted to make just one small change to a track.

'I hope Penny Lane and Strawberry Fields are going to prove a thing or two. And certainly—*certainly*—the new album is going to prove more than a thing or two.'

'So—there we go,' are Murray the K's sign-off words. 'It's good to know the Beatles are still together. Eppy is still together . . .'

There had been moments at Abbey Road studios during the past four months when George Martin wondered whether the Beatles might have gone too far this time. There was, for instance, the time they asked him to provide farmyard noises, including a pack of foxhounds in full cry. There was the matter of the Victorian steam organs, the 41-piece orchestra with no score to play, and the hours spent searching for a note which only dogs could hear. At such times, the Beatles' record producer feared this new album would end, if it ended at all, merely by baffling its listeners.

The idea all along had been to record something unified and continuous, like a novel or film—a scrapbook, rather, since the theme orginally was the Beatles' own Liverpool childhood. That scheme foundered with the premature release of Penny Lane and Strawberry Fields. They continued recording songs with no theme save the things they were currently doing, the newspapers they chanced to be reading, the London whose language and fashion they continued both to dictate and reflect. The newest London craze was for Victorian militaria, sold in shops with ponderously quaint names like I Was Lord Kitchener's Valet. So one night, the Beatles met to rehearse a new song, in that same vein of moustachioed whimsy, entitled Sergeant Pepper's Lonely Hearts Club Band.

'It was Paul's number,' George Martin says. 'Just an ordinary song, not particularly brilliant as songs go. When we'd finished it, Paul said: "Why don't we make the whole album as though the Pepper band really existed, as though Sergeant Pepper was doing the record. We can dub in effects and things." From that moment, it was as if Pepper had a life of its own.'

That life stemmed at first from simple enjoyment. They relished the idea that the four most famous Pop musicians in the world should create mock bandsmen as their alter ego, and present their music like a non-stop stage show, interspersed with the 'oohs' and 'aaahs' of childhood visits to circus and pantomime. Then, as the sessions progressed, there was born in both musicians and their producer that special life, that sensation comparable only with walking on water, which comes from the certain knowledge that one is making a masterpiece.

Its strength lay in the fact that, to all four Beatles, the vision was the same. All four were now converted to the LSD drug. Paul McCartney, the cautious, the proper, had at last given in. LSD is said to have beneficial effects only if used among close friends. In Sergeant Pepper it did not move the Beatles to brilliant music only: it also restored them to a closeness they had nearly lost in the numbing of the world's adoration. It would be remembered as their best record, and also their very best performance.

George Martin had no idea about the LSD at the time. The Beatles, in deference to their schoolmasterly colleague, kept even innocent 'joints' out of his sight, puffing them furtively in the Abbey Road Gents'. Martin was, in any case, fully occupied with trying to reconcile an infinity of new ideas with Studio One's by now antiquated and inhibiting four-track recording machine. As the kaleidoscope blossomed and expanded, Martin had to cadge extra sound channels by dubbing one four-track machine over another.

Martin had taught the Beatles much: he learned a little, too, in reckless spontaneity. The song which set the circus atmosphere was Being For the Benefit of Mr. Kite, a John Lennon composition suggested by the words of an old theatre bill he had bought in an antique shop. George Martin's instructions as arranger were to provide 'a sort of hurdy gurdy effect'. He did so by means of assorted steam organ sound effect tapes, cut into irregular lengths, thrown on the studio floor, then re-edited at random. The result was a dream-like cacophony, swirling about the Lennonesque big top where 'summersets', rather than somersaults, are executed, and 'tonight Henry the Horse dances the waltz'.

Martin, indeed, found his last reserves melting in admiration of a song like John's Lucy in the Sky with Diamonds, whose images—of 'tangerine trees', 'marmalade skies', 'newspaper taxis' and 'looking-glass ties'—were dazzling enough to a man with his middle-aged senses intact. It did occur to him sometimes that John looked rather strange, if not actually unwell. One night, in the aftermath of an acid trip, he looked so ill that Martin had to take him up on to the studio roof for air. Later, Paul McCartney took charge of him, driving him home to Weybridge and keeping him company in the hoped-for restorative of 'turning on' yet again.

Paul, so thoughtful and considerate on that occasion, could be just as suddenly imperious and petulant. Possibly he knew that John's Sergeant Pepper music was destined to outshine his. Against Lucy in the Sky with Diamonds and A Day in the Life, Paul's chief offering was She's Leaving Home, a song as straightforward as John's were allusive, a miniaturised novel about a girl abandoning her parents to go to London and meet 'a man from the motor trade'. As usual, Paul's 'head arrangement' required George Martin to convert it into a formal orchestral score. Martin, however, could not attend, as Paul wanted, at 24 hours' notice: he therefore found himself summarily dropped in favour of an outside arranger.

In general, the session proceeded with a friendliness that no Beatles album was ever to know again. Whether due to LSD's influence, or Sergeant Pepper's, all ideas synchronised, all four egos remained miraculously in balance. Ringo left his eternal card-school with Neil and Mal to record With A Little Help From My Friends, his only vocal but set in the premium place after the Sergeant Pepper overture. George Harrison's Indian song, Within You Without You, opened the second half—a good old theatrical compromise—to be followed, when the sitars finally ceased, by a burst of derisive laughter in which George himself joined.

Ironically, the song for which the album would be most revered, and damned, was a genuine Lennon-McCartney collaboration. The song was A Day in the Life. John had begun it idly, glancing at newspapers, thinking a little bit of Tara Browne, the Guinness family heir, a friend of both the Beatles and the Rolling Stones, who had died recently in a car accident. Unable to finish the lyric, he asked Paul for anything that might fill its 'middle eight'. Paul gave him some spare McCartney song words, beginning 'Woke up, fell out of bed, dragged a comb across my head . . .' Since the final result clearly had nothing to do with circuses, it was used as an epilogue to the second side.

The finale to A Day in the Life had to be, in John's words, 'a sound building up from nothing to the end of the world'. That was the night George Martin faced the 41-piece symphony orchestra and announced that what they were to perform had no written score. All he would tell them were the highest and lowest notes to play. In between, it was every man for himself.

The song, in its final form, was taped at Abbey Road amid a gala of Pop aristocrats such as Mick Jagger and Marianne Faithfull. The orchestra wore full evening dress and also carnival disguises distributed by the Beatles. One noted violinist played behind a clown's red nose; another held his bow in a joke gorilla's paw. Studio One thronged with peacock clothes, Eastern robes, abundant refreshments and exotically-tinted smoke. The four Beatles sat behind music stands playing trumpets, with Brian Epstein leaning on a chair back among them. Their moustaches had aged them: it was Brian, in this last photograph with them, who suddenly looked like a boy.

As with all masterpieces, the hardest part was stopping. They had filled every track, and every pocket of silence between, up to the final huge chord-echo at the end of A Day in the Life, which slammed the album shut like a sarcophagus lid. They had worked from 7 pm to 3 am simply to produce a chorus of gibberish for the record's play-out groove. As they stood at the microphone, Ringo suddenly remarked, 'I think I'm going to fall over.' He did so, to be caught like a doll in Mal Evans's arms. The final touch was a note at 20,000 hertz frequency, audible only to dogs.

The album sleeve, as much as its music, perfectly evoked the hour of its coming. The Pop artist Peter Blake was commissioned to design a frontispiece as up-to-the-minute as its four subjects were, and as heedless of convention or expense. The Beatles, holding bandsmen's instruments and dressed in satin uniforms, pink, blue, yellow and scarlet, stood mock-solemn behind their own name spelled in flowers, set about by a collage of figures representing their numerous heroes. The group included Bob Dylan, Karl Marx, Laurel and Hardy, Aleister Crowley, Marlon Brando, Diana Dors, W. C. Fields—every fashionable face from the pantheon of Pop Art pseudo-worship. There were also private jokes, such as the Beatles' own ludicrous wax effigies from Madame Tussaud's, a stray Buddha and a doll with a sign reading 'Welcome Rolling Stones'. In one corner, next to Aubrey Beardsley, above Sonny Liston's head, the face of Stu Sutcliffe, the Beatle who was lost, peered out from a snapshot fragment of some long-forgotten Hamburg night.

EMI at first refused to produce the Sergeant Pepper sleeve. It was feared that such of the celebrities who were still alive would institute vast lawsuits against the company. The Beatles, as was their custom, appealed directly to EMI's chairman, Sir Joseph Lockwood. 'Sir Joe' had already seen the cover proof; so had Lord Goodman and Lord Shawcross, Britain's two most foremost legal brains, who happened to be calling on him. 'Both Shawcross and Goodman said the same,' Sir Joseph recalls. ' "Don't touch it," they said. "*Everyone* will sue."

'Paul McCartney talked me into allowing it. "Ah, everyone'll love it," he said. "All right," I said, "but take Gandhi out. We need the Indian market. If we show Gandhi standing around with Sonny Liston and Diana Dors, they'll never forgive us in India. So the Beatles agreed to take Gandhi out." '

EMI further stipulated that the Beatles should indemnify them to the tune of some £20m against possible legal proceedings by Tom Mix or Marlon Brando. In addition, Brian had to undertake to get permission from as many of the 62 celebrities as possible. Wendy Hanson, his former assistant, was brought back specially to undertake this marathon of the transatlantic telephone.

Sergeant Pepper had cost £25,000 to make—twenty times the cost of the first Beatles album in 1963. It was further unique in opening out like a book, and in having the song-lyrics printed in full on the back. Inside with the record was a sheet of cut-out novelties, figments of the Beatles' own comic-book childhood transformed to the last, or next, word in Pop Art—a Sergeant Pepper picture card, a paper moustache, two badges and a set of NCO's stripes.

One other detail from the cover passed unnoticed by EMI's lawyers; nor was it spotted by the keen eye of Lord Goodman or Lord Shawcross. Sir Joseph Lockwood thus remained happily unaware that in the garden where Sergeant Pepper's band stood, there was a neat row of marijuana plants.

Each decade brings but one or two authentically memorable moments. As a rule, only war, or some fearful tragedy, can penetrate the preoccupations of millions in the same moment to produce a single, concerted emotion. And yet, in June 1967, such an emotion arose, not from death or trepidation but from the playing of a gramophone record. There are, to this day, thousands of Britons and Americans who can describe exactly where they were and what they were doing at the moment they first listened to Sergeant Pepper's Lonely Hearts Club Band. That music, as powerfully as Kennedy's assassination or the first moon landing, summons up an exact time and place, an emotion undimmed by time or ageing. The memory is the same to all —how they first drew the shining disc from its gaudy sleeve; how they could not believe it at first and had to play it all through again, over and over.

Musically the conversion was total. It encompassed the most avant garde and most cautious; both fan and foe alike. The wildest acid freak, listening in his mental garret to Lucy in the

Sky with Diamonds, could not doubt that his mind had been blown to undreamed realms of psychedelic fancy. Nervous old ladies, listening to When I'm Sixty-Four in their front parlours, would never be frightened of Pop music again. Sergeant Pepper's cabaret show, with its twangling mystery and workaday humour, its uppercut drive and insinuating charm, invited the elderly as well as young, the innocent no less than the pretentiously wise. On Kenneth Tynan, critic and sage, and on Mark Lewisohn, an eight-year-old in Pinner, Middlesex, the effect was the same. Tynan called Sergeant Pepper a decisive moment in the history of Western Civilisation. Mark Lewisohn stood in the garden as it played, shaking his head wildly while trying not to dislodge the cardboard moustache clenched under his nose.

Tunes that made little boys jig up and down were, at the same moment, receiving praise in *The Times* for their 'sweeping bass figures and hurricane glissandos'. Elsewhere, the practice begun by that paper's music critic, of burying something direct and enjoyable under tormented technical gibberish, was greatly assisted by the provision of the lyrics in full. *The Times Literary Supplement* called them 'a barometer of our times'. The *New Stateman* discerned 'a song cycle cunningly devised by the Beatles to transform old-style camaraderie into a new aloneness'.

In America, where the album was released one day later, critical hyperbole climbed to Gothic heights. The *New York Times Review of Books* announced that Sergeant Pepper heralded 'a new and golden Renaissance of Song'. *Newsweek*'s reviewer Jack Kroll compared the lyrics with T. S. Eliot: A Day in the Life, he said, was 'the Beatles' Waste Land'.

What happened in America, even more than in Britain, was as independent of critical acclaim as of commercial promotion: it was revelation experienced by thousands at once across huge continental distances. Those who recall it most vividly do so in a memory of motion—its first overture bars coming through stations jumbled on car radio; snatches of Lucy wafted from a transistor on a gas-station ledge. The music became a mirage, receding like the horizon, its myriad sounds crystallised in the need to travel, and keep travelling, westward.

Most of all, the divine message came to those whose senses clamoured to receive it, whose minds sought wisdom without learning and their souls a holiness compatible with doing as they pleased. 'I declare,' said Dr. Timothy Leary, high priest of hippydom, 'that the Beatles are mutants. Prototypes of evolutionary agents sent by God with a mysterious power to create a new species—a young race of laughing freemen . . . They are the wisest, holiest, most effective avatars [God incarnations] the human race has ever produced.'

A different view came from the forces of order and social

rectitude. The BBC, true to its tradition of censorship, banned A Day in the Life from all its wavelengths. The strange, tingling elegy, almost an after-thought by John Lennon in private, was accused of 'overt' reference to drugs. Evidence could be cited from the sleeve lyrics—the man who 'blew his mind out in a car'; the needle-marks implied by '4,000 holes in Blackburn, Lancashire'; the ambiguous words 'smoke' and 'dream' in Paul's middle passage; but most of all, the long cry, 'I'd love to turn you on' melting into the orchestral cacophony, itself to be accused of representing an addict's chaotic joy after a 'fix'.

Even greater was the scandal arising from the discovery that Lucy in the Sky with Diamonds was a mnemonic for LSD. In vain did John insist that Lucy in the Sky with Diamonds was the name his son Julian had given to a picture drawn at school. Equally vainly did discerning critics point out that the song was worth more, as music and poetry, than the, undoubtedly intended, coincidence of its title. From here on, the Beatles would be allowed no further private jokes.

Those words, so casually fitted together, so nonchalantly printed on their dark red background, became the object of prolonged and ludicrous study. To the hippy, they were as commandments, endorsing and—once translated—even instructing all hippies everywhere. To moralists, especially fee-earning ones, they were agents and harbingers of subversion and decay.

The motif sought most eagerly by both sides was that of drugs. Paul's Fixing A Hole—a song which, if it referred to anything, probably described his handyman exploits on his Scottish farm —was taken to be an allegory for a heroin needle. Ringo's With A Little Help From My Friends, with its mention of 'getting high' became the subject of a banning crusade in America, led by Senator Spiro T. Agnew. In She's Leaving Home, the 'man from the motor trade'—in reality Brian's car-selling partner, Terry Doran—was interpreted to mean an abortionist. Every right-thinking adult knew that people who smoked drugs practised abortion as casually as they indulged in sex. For many Americans, the songs awakened—as hippies and drugs and long hair did—an old, irrepressible neurosis. The Right-wing ultra-Christian John Birch Society claimed the Beatles were part of a Communist conspiracy and that the Sergeant Pepper music displayed 'an understanding of the principles of brainwashing'.

To its disciples, the album was Holy Writ, to be studied with the naive intensity applied to hippydom's other sacred book, J. R. R. Tolkien's *Lord of the Rings*. Of all the properties imagined in Sergeant Pepper, the most pervasive was that of actual magic. Along with Tarot cards, astrological charts and the *I Ching Book of Changes*, it was believed to hold prophecies, messages and signs. It marked the beginning of a search, among Beatles music past and still to come, for further prophecies, messages and signs. What, for instance, could be the meaning of that streak of gibberish in the Sergeant Pepper play-out groove, whose nearest interpretation seemed to be 'fuck me like a superman'? And why, at a moment of apparent silence, did the dog appear disturbed? The power that had once produced screaming in theatres now drew its clamour silently, in unnumbered cloudy thoughts.

If the Beatles had hated the theatres, they hated the mystery and message-seekers more. John, especially, denied with increasing bitterness that his songs had any motive whatever. 'I just shove a lot of sounds together, then shove some words on,' he told Hunter Davies. 'We know we're conning people, because people want to be conned. They give us the freedom to con them.'

A month earlier in the Beatles' fan magazine, a correspondent had expressed the view of the huge other audience they still had. 'I know that if Paul took drugs, I'd be worried sick,' the letter-writer said. 'But I know he's too sensible.'

It was, however, the most cautious and image-conscious Beatle who, a fortnight after Sergeant Pepper's release and on the eve of his 25th birthday, admitted to *Life* magazine that he had taken LSD. The admission was possible since 'acid' had only recently become illegal. Paul, while stressing the pluperfect tense, spoke nonetheless as an enthusiast. 'It opened my eyes,' he said. 'We only use one-tenth of our brains. Just think what we'd accomplish if we could tap that hidden part.'

The outcry was immediate and violent. The Beatle who had hitherto been looked on as Pop music's best ambassador was denounced, in the *Daily Mail*, as 'an irresponsible idiot'. Intercessionary prayers were offered by Dr. Billy Graham to prevent the world's innocent youth from rushing to emulate him. Paul, protesting he bore no such responsibility, did his best to disarm his attackers with good old Liverpool humour. Taking drugs, he said, was 'like taking aspirin without a headache'. At last, even he could no longer maintain a smile. 'It's you who've got reponsibility not to spread this,' he snapped at a television interviewer. 'If you'll shut up about it, I will.'

He could expect support from only one quarter. The measure of that support was, however, quite unexpected. Brian Epstein joined John and George in admitting that he, too, had taken LSD before it became illegal. He said he had had 'about five trips'. His confession was less astonishing to newspaper readers than to the Beatles themselves. So far as they knew, they had started Brian on drugs—on 'Prellys' back in the Cavern days. They did not know that his drug history far predated theirs, nor did they dream the extent to which his habit now exceeded their own.

The pillorying of one Beatle was forgotten, a week later, in an event which established all four as a literally astral presence. The event was a television programme made up of items from many nations and transmitted to all simultaneously via the new earth-shrinking satellite system. Britain contributed the Beatles, singing a song specially written to express the programme's unironic confidence, a fortnight after the Arab–Israeli Six Day War, in international peace and brotherhood.

So, on 25 June 1967, was registered the ultimate statistic of their career. An audience numbering 200 million saw the Beatles sitting on stools at Abbey Road studios, apparently glimpsed in making their next record, which, by heavy-handed coincidence, happened to be Britain's message to Mankind. 'Love, love, love,' they sang. 'All you need is love, love. Love is all you need.'

The signal arose to the turning orb, to be transmitted across continents of murder and oppression, across deserts where the tanks lay burned, the bodies half-buried, and where prisoners had been freed to walk back a hundred miles without their shoes.

That hot, jangling, joss-scented summer in London, you could buy LSD for less than £1 a trip. You could 'drop' it there and then, on a sugar lump or pellet of blotting paper, then walk off into a crowd that was already half-hallucination. You could nibble a pill for just a 'sparkle', to make the city shimmer as through water or glass. You could take it that way, or buzzing and searing on the warm air, in music played by new California bands whose names—the Strawberry Alarm Clock, the Electric Prunes—were themselves LSD visions, whose distorted guitars, heavy feedback and incomprehensible lyrics both echoed and complemented the drug-bedazzled mind. You could 'trip' almost by reflection—in the lights from the stage at Middle Earth or the UFO club, the colours of clothes boutiques, the whirling flowers, psychedelic pinks, the bright Sergeant Pepper satins, the Buddha bells, the garlands and kaftans and sandals and weird hats. You could shut your eyes and still see colour: you could lie down, it was quite all right. Helplessness, indeed, was all the fashion. Helpless rapture at the music; helpless need for a joint or a 'snort'; helpless—and so, becoming—inability to control that repository of new visions and wisdoms, your 'head'.

Meanwhile in High Street Britain and suburban America, ordinary people in ordinary clothes went about their ordinary, somewhat puzzled affairs. 'Love' and 'Peace', the hippy watchwords, were exhortations possible, it seemed, only to the very young and very rich—to the many elites formed round that ultimate elite whose voices chanted the simple anthem through echo-chambers of impenetrable privilege. For the Beatles, with All You Need Is Love, were, once again, woven into the summer breeze. Ordinary people, meanwhile, stared, a little resentfully. One hot afternoon, near the Sussex village of Heathfield, a Rolls Royce painted in psychedelic colours was forced to stop for mundane traffic lights. A crowd gathered round it, but could see nothing through the black-tinted windows.

Black-windowed cars, secret discotheques and country mansions were ceasing to provide immunity from the non-beautiful, unfreaked out world. In early summer, the British Police began a major offensive against drugs and the drug-inspired cultural 'underground'. Special squads of flat-footed hippy cops were formed to swoop on the offices of underground newspapers, such as the *International Times*, and, on the slenderest pretexts, to plunge with sniffer dogs into homes where marijuana-smoking was rumoured.

The campaign scored an early spectacular success. Mick Jagger of the Rolling Stones, together with the Stones' guitarist Keith Richard, was arrested after a drugs raid on Richard's Sussex estate. Both were removed to prison—a long-cherished Police objective, it seemed. Before their trial began, stories arose concerning what chocolatey cunnilingular perversions the officers had interrupted. It was Profumo and Keeler all over again, just moved down a generation and a class.

The sentencing of Jagger to three months imprisonment set off the debate—which has not yet subsided—concerning the harmlessness or otherwise of 'soft' drugs taken in private. The very debate seemed to merge into a hashish dream featuring Jagger, released on bail, in public discussion with a tribunal of bishops, and prompting *The Times* to criticise his sentence in an editorial headed Who Breaks a Butterfly on a Wheel? *The Times*, on 24 July, carried the first of many full-page advertisements calling for the legalisation of marijuana. Its signatories included Brian Epstein and the Beatles.

Summer reached its unreal climax in the season when, by long British tradition, there is no news whatever. There was only the news that it was hot, it would remain hot, and Joe Orton had been found murdered. The author of *Loot* and other black comedies, once so nearly screenwriter for the Beatles, had been battered to death by his lover Kenneth Halliwell, who afterwards committed suicide, in the bedsitting-room they shared. John Lennon singing A Day in the Life, about 'the lucky man who made the grade', was Joe Orton's funeral music.

Visiting Nat Weiss in New York that Spring, Brian had felt a strong premonition of death. 'He was sure his plane would crash on the journey home,' Weiss says. 'I persuaded him to take the flight—which, in fact, was delayed a long while on the runway at Kennedy.' The jet finally took off, leaving Nat Weiss with Brian's last wish, scribbled in a note at the airport coffee shop. His last wish concerned the packaging of the Beatles' new album: 'Brown paper bags for Sergeant Pepper'.

When Weiss came to London a few weeks later, Brian was back at the 'drying-out' clinic in Putney. The attorney drove to visit him with Robert Stigwood, his Australian heir apparent at NEMS Enterprises. According to Nat Weiss, Brian now regretted his decision to let Stigwood buy control of NEMS. 'Stigwood had the option to buy, but they were still joint managing directors. Brian was telling Stigwood to do things, but it was obvious that Stigwood had no intention of doing them.

'While I was with Brian, a big bouquet of flowers arrived from John Lennon. The card from John said, "You know I love you —I really mean that." When Brian read it, he just broke down.

'He begged me to stay on until he got out of the clinic, but I had to go back to New York. That was the last time I saw him.'

Not even Nat Weiss could comfort Brian in the dread which had begun to torment him—the dread foreshadowed in early summer when Cilla Black announced her intention of leaving NEMS Enterprises. Cilla disliked Robert Stigwood; still more had she been offended by the loss of that feminine solicitude with which Brian had built up her career. The emergency cleared Brian's head. There were meetings with Cilla at Chapel Street: he apologised, was charming—from the haunted, drug-exhausted night-being, enough of the old Brian returned to persuade Cilla, at least, not to leave him.

But the greater, unassuageable dread remained. In October 1967, Brian's five-year management contract with the Beatles ended. He had reason—or thought he had—to believe it would not be renewed.

There had been signs for many months that Paul McCartney, in particular, was discontented with Brian's management. Their relationship, in any case, was never easy. Paul, with his looks, was the one Brian *ought* to have loved: he always felt he owed Paul compensation because he had chosen John. The worst moments of all for Brian, worse even than John's sarcasm, were when Paul decided, in his smiling way to play the prima donna. 'Paul could get to Brian the way none of the other three could,' Joanne Newfield says. 'Whenever I saw him put down the 'phone really upset, he'd always been talking to Paul.'

At the beginning, it was always George, in his dour Liverpool way, who cross-examined Brian closest over business deals. As George absorbed himself in spiritual things, Paul took over, with more unsettling effect, as Brian's chief inquisitor. 'He'd come into Chapel Street, doing his business Beatle bit,' Joanne says. 'That always worried Brian. They never had a row, but you could see he was uneasy when Paul was there.'

Paul had been critical of what might otherwise have seemed a vast improvement in the record royalties paid to the Beatles by EMI and American Capitol. A new agreement, negotiated by Brian in January 1967, abolished EMI's risible 'penny a record' for a 10 per cent royalty on singles and albums, rising to 15 per cent after 100,000 and 30,000 copies respectively. In America, the royalty was 10 per cent, rising to 17½ per cent. The deal, in fact, transformed the economics of the record industry. Never again would the labels be able to reap billions, yet pay out royalties of fractions of a farthing. Paul, however, was unimpressed. He still remembered the $3m deal Allen Klein had done with Decca on behalf of the Rolling Stones.

Paul was the instigator of a feeling within the Beatles that they had now outgrown their need for a manager in the old proprietorial sense. Certainly, Sergeant Pepper, that multi-hued testament to their infallibility, had been made to a large extent against Brian's wishes. By now, too, rumours were beginning to filter out of NEMS, and through each Beatle's personal court, that even as that kind of manager, Brian had made serious long-term mistakes. They were starting to hear about Seltaeb and Nicky Byrne; the 90 per cent merchandising contract given to five strangers; the millions of dollars which had been allowed to blow away.

Brian, on his side, made strenuous efforts to prove that they did still need him as of old. He took special trouble over the arrangements for Paul McCartney's first private trip to America. It was, ironically, the trip which Paul used to formulate much of a future for the Beatles in which there would be small place for anyone named Brian Epstein.

To one person, the imprèsario Larry Parnes, Brian finally confessed what he could still barely articulate in his own mind. 'He told me the Beatles were leaving him,' Parnes says. 'He was losing Cilla and he was losing them. The Beatles were giving him notice.'

His support of Paul in the LSD furore revealed how fervent was Brian's desire to stay at one with the Beatles. And, indeed, it brought him closer to them—certainly, closer to Paul—than for many months. Soon afterwards at Kingsley Hill, he threw a weekend party to which the Beatles and their women drove together, packed into John's psychedelic Rolls. When the Rolls stopped at traffic lights, people crowded round to try to see. It was a day that Cynthia Lennon was to remember with horror. Brian's party, at the house where Churchill used to meet his wartime Chiefs of Staff, was a mass LSD trip. Cynthia took some herself, for only the second time, in her fast-failing attempts to keep up with John. The resultant nightmares drove her seriously to contemplate suicide from a second-storey window.

In July, the Beatles began to think of leaving England and

setting up in hippy commune style on their own private Greek island. The plan went as far as negotiation with the Greek government, whose Fascist complexion cast no shadow on the vision of collective love and peace. The British Treasury indicated consent that the island's purchase price be transferred abroad. John and Cynthia Lennon were even considering the possible education of their son Julian among Greek peasant boys and girls. Brian, who had no part in the scheme, pretended mild amusement. 'I think it's a dotty idea,' he wrote to Nat Weiss, 'but they're no longer children, and must have their own sweet way.'

The fatherly tone is poignant, considering the moment. His own father, Harry Epstein, the hard-working, straight-dealing, uncomplicated Liverpool businessman, had died suddenly of a heart attack, aged 63. It was his second within only a few weeks. When news of the first one reached Brian, at a party, he did not think it sounded serious enough to return home immediately.

The bereavement, paradoxically, had a stabilising effect: it forced him out of his own depression into concern for his family —in particular, his mother, Queenie, widowed after 34 years of marriage. From the age of 18, she had known no existence other than as Harry's wife. After her religion, it was to her elder son that she turned for support. Brian was comforted to realise that someone in the world truly needed him.

He spent several days with Queenie in Liverpool, surprised to discover how a city which had once seemed so dully provincial now soothed and reassured him. After Harry's retirement, his parents had moved from their Queen's Drive house to a more convenient bungalow. Brian visited their old next-door neighbour Rex Makin and sat in Makin's garden, staring at the house with the sunrise over its front door, thinking of the father who had returned from the shop that afternoon to find him sent home from school, and whose angry words were still etched on his son's memory. 'I simply don't know *what* we're going to do with you.'

He wrote to Nat Weiss from Liverpool, mentioning his plan to come to New York on 2 September. Weiss, as his agent, had arranged for him to present a series of chat shows on Canadian television. Brian was excited by this opportunity to test himself as a performer. In comforting his mother, he had himself evidently drawn comfort from the Jewish religion. 'The week of Shiva [mourning] is up tonight,' his letter to Weiss continued, 'and I feel a bit strange. Probably good for me in a way . . .'

His mother came to London to stay with him on 14 August. The idea was that she should move down to London permanently, to be near Brian and her sister, his Aunt Freda. For the 10 days of her visit, Brian forced himself to keep to a normal routine. Queenie would wake him each morning, drawing his bedroom curtains as she used to when he was small, and they would have breakfast together in his room. Brian would then work a conventional office day with Joanne. Each night, he stayed in, watching television with Queenie, rarely going to bed later than 11 pm. Joanne had never seen him so quiet and apparently content.

Mrs. Epstein returned to Liverpool on Thursday, 24 August. That evening, at the Hilton Hotel, sitting on a bedroom floor and staring devoutly upward, the Beatles embarked, three days prematurely, on the era after Brian.

A letter to Nat Weiss was in the post—a cheerful enough letter concerning arrangements Weiss was to make for Brian's American visit, such as the chartering of a yacht and tickets to a Judy Garland concert. There was also mention of Eric Anderson, a folk singer whom Brian wanted to put under contract. '. . . till the 2nd', the letter ended, 'love, flowers, bells, be happy and look forward to the future . . .'

Enclosed was a colour snapshot, taken on the roof at Chapel Street, of a young man—hardly more than a boy—in striped trousers and a frilled shirt open to the waist. His hair was long; it fell in a fringe over his eyes. Four days before his death, Brian at last became what he had striven hardest to be: a Beatle.

The new era took a form already long familiar to London Underground travellers. For it is on tube station walls that advertisements for Indian Holy men and their spiritual crusades in Britain commonly appear. Among this bearded, cross-legged platform-wall fraternity, the most clearly recognisable was the Holy man named Maharishi Mahesh Yogi. In 1967, after a decade of regular visits, the Maharishi—or Great Saint—could claim some 10,000 British converts to his doctrine of Spiritual Regeneration. A still larger number recognised him in the way they recognised chocolate vending machines, posters for Start Rite shoes and illuminated signs to the Central or Bakerloo line.

It was, ironically, not George Harrison but his model wife Pattie who brought the Beatles and the Maharishi together. Pattie had joined the Spiritual Regeneration movement in February after hearing a talk by one of the guru's lieutenants. George, although immersed in Hindu religious study since his Indian expedition, had found no direction as yet. He had been to San Francisco and—accompanied by Derek Taylor, now a fashionable Hollywood publicist—had strolled among the Haight–Ashbury hippies. There he found less love and peace than beggars and souvenir stalls. He had also been in contact with a British-based guru, who persuaded him to go down to Cornwall and climb a hill, with equally disappointing spiritual results.

In the week before August Bank Holiday, Pattie Harrison read that—unheralded, for once, by tube station walls—the Maharishi Mahesh Yogi had come to London, to deliver a single lecture before retiring from his crusade and devoting himself to a 'life of silence' in India. The valedictory lecture was to take place at the mystic's hotel, the Park Lane Hilton, on Thursday, 24 August. Pattie made George contact the other Beatles and persuade them to attend.

The encounter, that Thursday evening next to Hyde Park, did have an air of divine predestination. Amid the small 7s 6d per head audience of the faithful, four Beatles garbed as flower-power aristocrats listened while a little Asian gentleman, wearing robes and a grey-tipped beard, described in his high-pitched voice, interspersed with many mirthful cachinnations, an existence both more inviting and more convenient than mere hippydom. The 'inner peace' which the Maharishi promised, and which seemed so alluring to pleasure-exhausted multi-millionaires—not to mention the 'sublime consciousness' so attractive to inveterate novelty-seekers—could be obtained even within their perilously small span of concentration. To be spiritually regenerated, they were told, they need meditate for only half an hour each day.

Maharishi Mahesh Yogi, despite a highly-developed nose for publicity, did not know the Beatles were in his congregation until after the lecture, when they sent up a request to speak to him in private. There and then, acting as a group, they offered themselves as his disciples. The Holy Man, for whom 'tickled' would be an insufficient adjective, invited them to join him the next day on a course of indoctrination for the Spiritually Regenerated at University College, Bangor, North Wales. The Beatles said they would go.

They did subsequently contact Brian and ask him to join the party. He, too, had been showing some interest in Indian religion. Brian said he had other plans for the Bank Holiday weekend, but that he'd try to get down to Bangor later during the 10-day course.

An incredulous orgy of Press and TV cameras saw them off at Paddington next day, on the Maharishi's special slow stopping train. As well as the Beatles, Pattie and Jane Asher, there was Mick Jagger—whose demon tones could currently be heard in a Beatle-inspired song unconvincingly titled We Love You—and Jagger's girl friend Marianne Faithfull. Cynthia Lennon missed the train, held back by a policeman who thought she was a fan. 'Run, Cindy, run,' called John as she sprinted vainly along the platform.

It was the first journey they had ever made without Brian —without even the two protective road managers. John compared it to 'going somewhere without your trousers'. They all sat rather guiltily wedged into one first class compartment, afraid to venture so much as to the lavatory. They then had a second audience of the Maharishi, who occupied his own first class compartment, squatting on a sheet spread over British Rail's green upholstery. Once again, the Holy Being showed his marked propensity for mirth. He held up a flower—the first of many—and explained that its petals were an illusion, like the physical world. In a telling simile, he compared Spiritual Regeneration to a bank, from which its practitioner could always draw dividends of repose.

If any proof were needed of the sublime state of the Maharishi's mind, it occurred when the train reached Bangor, and a frantic crowd drew into sight on the little seaside platform. The Beatles suggested going on to a further station, then returning to Bangor by taxi. The Maharishi, to whom it had not occurred that the crowd comprised followers other than his own, told them to stay close to him.

That night, the Beatles, the satanic chief Rolling Stone and their female companions found themselves ensconced, with the Maharishi's 300 other conference students, in the spartan bedrooms of a teacher training college. Later, accompanied by Hunter Davies, they went out to the only restaurant open late in Bangor—a Chinese. After a long and noisy meal, it was discovered that no one among the assembled millionaires, had enough money to pay the bill. In London, they were never allowed to pay. Chinese waiters in a North Wales town clearly did not understand this. At last, with the waiters growing restive, George Harrison prised open his sandal sole and produced a wad of £10 notes.

On Saturday, as the Maharishi addressed his followers seated on a couch, the Beatles formed an obedient line to his right. He agreed, with no apparent show of reluctance, to hold a Press conference for the journalists who now swarmed over the college. The questions were hostile and satirical. The Beatles answered with such spirit that the Maharishi's regular disciples broke into spontaneous applause. It was here that the weekend's first major story broke. The Beatles used the Press conference to announce that they had given up taking drugs. 'It was an experience we went through,' Paul McCartney said. 'Now it's over. We don't need it any more. We think we're finding new ways of getting there.'

One of the journalists was George Harrison, their old *Liverpool Echo* acquaintance—for Bangor is just in the *Echo*'s circulation area. Harrison was with them the next afternoon—Sunday—as, fully initiated into Spiritual Regeneration, they strolled around the college grounds.

'There was a 'phone ringing inside,' Harrison says. 'It rang and rang. Eventually, Paul said, "Someone had better answer that." He went in and picked up the 'phone. I could hear him speaking. "Yeah," he said. "Yeah . . ." Then I heard him shout, "Oh, Christ—*no!*"'

That Friday, Brian had suddenly asked Joanne his assistant down to spend the Bank Holiday weekend at his house in Sussex. He also told her to invite a mutual friend of theirs, the Scots singer Lulu. But he had left it too late: both Lulu and Joanne herself had other arrangements. As Brian did not seem too disappointed, Joanne presumed he would be entertaining a large house party. 'He went off on his own on the Friday afternoon. He seemed really bright and happy that day. He'd put the top of the Bentley down. He was waving to me as he drove off.'

At Kingsley Hill, other disappointments waited. A young man whom Brian had hoped to know better that weekend would not, after all, be able to make it. Peter Brown had not arrived yet. He was still in London, trying to get Cynthia Lennon off to Bangor by car. Peter, and Geoffrey Ellis, from the NEMS office, would be the only house guests. They were old friends and familiar companions. Brian, after two quiet weeks, had looked forward to more exciting company.

The three had dinner served to them by Brian's Austrian butler. Afterwards, in an evidently restless mood, Brian began telephoning numbers in London from which male company was available at a price. Again, he seemed to have left it too late. Everyone was already booked. Brian grew more and more restive and finally, at about 10 pm, announced that he was going back to London. Peter and Geoffrey were not offended, nor particularly surprised. Walking out was a habit of Brian's. Peter went with him out to the Bentley and told him he oughtn't to drive after the wine he'd drunk with dinner. 'Brian said I wasn't to worry. He'd be back in the morning before I woke up.'

Some company did eventually arrive. One of the agencies found three boys and sent them the 60-mile journey to Sussex in a London cab. By then, Brian was heading back through the empty Belgravia streets.

Geoffrey Ellis telephoned Chapel Street shortly after midnight to confirm that he had arrived safely. Up to then, Peter and Geoffrey had half-expected him to reappear at Kingsley Hill after a drive round the countryside. The call was taken by Antonio, Brian's Spanish town butler. Antonio said that Mr. Epstein had come in a little time ago and had gone straight upstairs. He tried the intercom to the master bedroom, but got no reply. Peter and Geoffrey were reassured. Brian had managed the car journey safely and had evidently succeeded in falling asleep.

When Peter and Geoffrey got up, late on Saturday morning, Brian had not returned. They thought of ringing Chapel Street, but decided to let him sleep. At about five that afternoon, the telephone rang. It was Brian. He told Peter he had been asleep all day and was still very drowsy. Peter said that if he was returning to Sussex, it would be safer to take the train. Brian agreed to telephone just as he was setting off so that Peter could collect him by car at Lewes station. Peter waited all Saturday evening for his call.

By Sunday morning, Antonio and his wife Maria were beginning to be worried. Brian was still in his room. His Spanish couple had heard nothing from him since breakfast time the previous day. Nor had he gone out, as was his habit, after dark. The Bentley was still as he had left it on Friday night. At the same time, they knew his irregular ways and how angry he could be. A lengthy discussion in Spanish ensued before Antonio decided to take the initiative.

He telephoned Peter Brown in Sussex first, but Peter had gone with Geoffrey Ellis to the village pub. He then telephoned Joanne Newfield, Brian's assistant, at her home in Edgware. Joanne had helped cope with Brian's two suicide attempts: she had also seen several false alarms. She drove at once from Edgware through the Bank Holiday silence to Chapel Street. 'The moment I walked in,' she says, 'I felt uneasy.'

Ceaseless hammering on Brian's door and buzzing of his bedroom intercom brought no reply. Even then, they hesitated to break down his door. They had done so, unnecessarily, once before and Brian had been furious. By this time a doctor had arrived—not Brian's regular Dr. Cowan but another man who understood his case. Peter Brown had rung up again from Sussex and was waiting on the line for news.

Antonio and the doctor broke down the bedroom suite's outer double doors. Beyond the dressing-room lobby, the curtains were drawn. Brian lay on his side amid the litter of documents and correspondence spread over the bed. Joanne approached and shook him. 'Even though I knew he was dead, I pretended to the others that he wasn't. "It's all right," I kept saying, "he's just asleep, he's fine."

'The doctor led me out of the room then. Maria was there, screaming "Why? Why?" Peter Brown was still holding on to the 'phone.

'A little while after that, something really strange happened. We broke into Brian's room at about two o'clock. At three o'clock, the *Daily Express* rang up and said, "We've heard that Brian Epstein's terribly ill. Is there any truth in it?" Only the four of us knew what had happened and none of us had contacted any Press. It was never explained how the story got out to the papers.'

Reporters and photographers were already massed in Chapel Street when Peter Brown and Geoffrey Ellis arrived from Sussex. Alistair Taylor, the NEMS office manager, had been sent for, and also Brian's solicitor, David Jacobs. Peter Brown got through to Bangor and broke the news to Paul McCartney. Then he telephoned Brian's brother Clive in Liverpool. Joanne heard Clive shout: 'You're lying. You're lying.'

Brian's body was taken away in a makeshift Police coffin. Joanne attacked a photographer who pointed his camera at it. 'I just couldn't bear the thought of people seeing Brian in a thing like that.'

By early evening, there were television pictures of the Beatles leaving the Maharishi's conference through forests of microphones and lights. 'How do you feel,' they were asked, 'about Brian Epstein's death?' It emerged that they had been to see the Maharishi again and had been told that Brian's death, being of the physical world, was 'not important'. Their faces, even so, looked ravaged among the garlands and the bells.

The story was told in full on Bank Holiday Monday in newspapers read at the seaside or in back gardens. Brian Epstein Death Riddle: Valet Finds Pop King in Locked Bedroom. It was widely assumed—and still is—that he committed suicide. The story gained weight—not instantly, since Fleet Street still shunned the word—when his homosexuality became public knowledge. To the larger British public in 1967, that was reason enough to want to die.

The inquest, on 8 September at Westminster Coroner's Court, found that Brian had died from an overdose of Carbitrol, a bromide-based drug which he had been taking to help him sleep. That the overdose had not been all at once but cumulative, over two or three days, seemed to rule out the possibility of suicide. The suggestion was that Brian, in a gradually more drowsy state, had not realised he was exceeding the proper dose. The Police inspector, called to Chapel Street, reported having found 17 bottles of various pills and tablets in his bathroom cupboard, in his briefcase and beside his bed.

Nat Weiss travelled from New York to attend the inquest, bringing with him Brian's last letter—the one which seemed so full of confidence in the future. The Coroner, Mr. Gavin Thurston, recorded a verdict of accidental death from 'incautious self-overdoses'.

One person who knew him, and also knew well a particular burden he carried, remains convinced that Brian's death was neither accident nor suicide. According to this, necessarily anonymous, ex-associate, Brian was the victim of a murder 'contract' taken out on him three years earlier in America after the Seltaeb merchandising fiasco.

In 1964, certainly, any number of American businessmen bore him a bitter grudge. The confusion over manufacturing licences, and consequent cancellation by the big stores of $78m worth of Beatle merchandise, brought several manufacturers into serious financial peril. 'One man even had a heart attack and died. I was at a meeting when someone said he was going to kill Brian Epstein. I thought it was just American bullshit. I said, "No—wait until the Courts have finished with him." '

In August 1967, the Courts had finished. The $22m lawsuit between NEMS and Nicky Byrne, Seltaeb's sole survivor, had been settled for a cash payment of $10,000 to Byrne—enough to buy himself a yacht and sail off to find a new life in the Bahamas.

Just before he left New York, Nicky Byrne received a mysterious telephone call. 'This man's voice very low, very polite, said: "Mr. Byrne. I understand that your suit against Brian Epstein is settled, is that right?" I said: "Yes, and what's it got to do with you?" But whoever it was just hung up.

'In August, I was in Florida—actually on my boat—and I got another call. That same very quiet, polite voice. "Mr. Byrne," it said, "you're going to hear soon that Brian Epstein has met with an accident." '

No one has ever explained those two telephone calls to Nicky Byrne, nor explained the curious fact that Brian's death was known in Fleet Street less than an hour after Joanne Newfield burst into his darkened room.

There is one further bizarre coincidence. The signature on the Seltaeb contract—the signature which gave five strangers 90 per cent of Beatle merchandise royalties, and so ensured the back-tracking litigation which followed—was that of Brian's solicitor David Jacobs. A few weeks after Brian's death, David Jacobs was found hanged in his garage. The Coroner's verdict was suicide. But people who knew the urbane lawyer had noticed that, just lately, he seemed frightened.

Brian's funeral, at Long Lane Jewish cemetery in Liverpool, was a private family affair. To his mother's distress, he was not buried next to his father but in a separate avenue of undecorated memorials. The Beatles did not attend. George Harrison sent a sunflower which Nat Weiss threw into the open grave.

Five weeks later, a memorial service was held for Brian at the New London Synagogue, St. John's Wood. It was only a short walk from there to Paul McCartney's house and Abbey Road and the studios where Brian ushered in the Beatles to meet George Martin, on that summer day long ago in 1962.

The Beatles did attend this time, in black suits which the doorstep Press scanned for sartorial novelties. George Martin and Dick James were there, as were scores of people in show business only because of the young man who came down from Liverpool in his dapper overcoat; who blushed easily and never went back on a promise; who could be ecstatic but never happy; who somehow caught the lightning and then somehow let it go. The rabbi's text was chosen from the Book of Proverbs. 'Sayest thou that the man diligent in his business, he shall stand before kings.'

PART FOUR

Wasting

June 1968

'We've got to spend two million or the Taxman will get it'

Since Brian had died without making a will, his entire estate passed automatically to his mother, Queenie. Nor was it anything approaching a fortune of £7m. Lush living had absorbed—even exceeded—a vast yearly income which had never been left to accumulate for one second into capital. What Brian did not spend on himself, or other people or on the roulette table, he invested into offshoot companies and loss-making personal projects, like the Savile theatre. Towards the end, shortage of ready money had led him to borrow heavily from NEMS Enterprises. His debt to his own company was found to be in the region of £150,000. His final cash estate was realised chiefly through the sale of his two houses, his cars, paintings and objets d'art. The residue, after death duties, was a little more than three quarters of a million pounds.

Mrs. Epstein, bereaved within six weeks of both her husband and elder son, was in no state to face the complexities instantly arising from her inheritance. It fell to her younger son, Clive, to try to sort out Brian's tangled business affairs. Clive, as co-founder of NEMS Enterprises, took over the chairmanship, pending discussions on the company's future.

Tony Bramwell, George Harrison's friend, visiting NEMS a few days after Brian's death, found the half-dozen directors in a state of eager consternation. No one at NEMS realised yet that Brian had virtually sold the company to his Australian associate, Robert Stigwood. 'They were all squabbling about who was going to manage the Beatles,' Bramwell says. 'It sickened me. I just walked out.'

Despite Brian's depleted personal wealth, his estate was liable to taxes, based on NEMS' current value, of some half a million pounds. Word quickly leaked on to the London Stock Exchange that, to meet the estate duty, the Epsteins would have no choice but to sell NEMS. It was rumoured that an offer would be made, linking NEMS with Brian's 10 per cent holding in Northern Songs, the Lennon–McCartney publishing company, in a package deal calculated to moisten the lips of the driest, squarest City broker.

The Beatles themselves, meanwhile, sat in a drawing-room in South Kensington at the feet of a little, mirthful Asian gentleman, hearing yet again that little Asian gentleman's teaching that all material things are valueless. Since Brian's death, they had visited the Maharishi constantly and received his wisdom under the equally constant glare of Fleet Street's newly-formed Meditation Corps. They were now full members of the Spiritual Regeneration Movement and, as such, liable to pay a week's earnings per month to support it. They had also undertaken to visit their guru's academy in Rishikesh, North India, to further their studies and ultimately to qualify as 'teachers of Meditation'.

At Buckingham Palace, the Queen held a levée for the Council of Knights Bachelor, whose members include Sir Joseph Lockwood, Chairman of EMI. As Her Majesty entered the room, she called across to Sir Joseph: 'The Beatles are turning awfully *funny*, aren't they?'

A few days after Brian's funeral, the four of them met Clive Epstein at Brian's house in Chapel Street. Queenie, too, had insisted on being there. 'All the boys turned up in suits, out of respect for Queenie,' Joanne Newfield says. 'We all sat around Brian's sitting-room, having tea together. It felt so strange—as though nothing had happened at all. I half-expected Brian to walk in, just the way he used to, and join us.

'It was all too much for me. I just burst into tears. George looked at me very sternly and said, "You're not crying for Brian. You're crying for yourself." '

At that and subsequent meetings, the Beatles agreed to accept Clive as Brian's successor, at least for the two months until their contract with NEMS expired. What they most emphatically did not want was any managerial relationship with Robert Stigwood. Lengthy consultations ensued with Lord Goodman, the country's most eminent lawyer, who had known and acted for Brian. As a result, Stigwood was persuaded to relinquish his option on NEMS. He departed with some £500,000, plus half the NEMS artists roster—among them the Bee Gees, Cream and Jimi Hendrix—to set up, with spectacular success, on his own.

A new company, Nemperor Holdings, was formed to administer NEMS in what Clive Epstein promised would be 'a programme of vigorous expansion'. Vic Lewis, the ex-bandleader, became managing director. Clive, as Chairman, commuted back and forth from Liverpool, though never quite as Brian used to, nor with Brian's assurance. It was the misfortune of a quiet, capable, not insensitive man that people should always remark that.

Peter Brown, at the Epstein family's request, lived on for a time at Brian's Chapel Street house. His resemblance to Brian, and the consequent reliance of Queenie Epstein on him, seemed to guarantee his accession to the role he had so long understudied. He took over Brian's desk and Brian's assistant—even certain of Brian's little executive affectations. 'Brian used to have this habit of dropping all the music papers on the floor and saying, "I've finished with these now," ' Joanne Newfield says. 'A few days after he took over, Peter did exactly the same thing and used exactly the same words.'

It was Peter Brown who now had the direct line to all four Beatles and who, in a voice so very like Brian's, passed along the inter-Beatles messages he received. Paul wanted to have a meeting, just among themselves, to discuss future projects and plans. Could they all meet up on 2 September at Paul's house?

The girls who stood outside Paul's house, watching the cars go in, had never been formally introduced. They knew each other only as syllables, breathlessly gasped out in the running and jumping and climbing and neck-craning of the campaign they pursued in common. There was Big Sue and Little Sue, and Gayleen, and Margo, and 'Willie' and 'Knickers'. Others came and went, or were shooed away, having tried to pre-empt the space allotted by mutual agreement between those half-dozen perennials. Waiting there, day after day, night after night until dawn, as days turned into months, as months lengthened to years, they somehow never did discover one another's surnames.

They waited outside Paul's because he was their favourite Beatle, but also because his house, being in London, and only a short walk from Abbey Road studios, was the recognised listening-post for all Beatle intelligence. Pilgrimages would be made at intervals to John's front gates in Weybridge or to the hedge of George Harrison's Esher bungalow. But always the trail led back to St. John's Wood and Cavendish Avenue and the big black double gates whose electric security lock, as time passed, grew less and less of an impediment.

The Beatles, hardened as they were to the inevitability of pursuit, frequently marvelled at the almost psychic power which enabled these hard-core fans to shadow or waylay them. At Paul's house or Abbey Road, or any ad hoc rehearsal or film-editing rendezvous, Peter Brown's secret call would bring the four together under the scrutiny of those same half-dozen, rather red and breathless faces. 'They used to shout at us, "How did you *know*?" ' Margo says. 'Paul always called us The Eyes and Ears of the World.'

Margo, a brisk, jolly and otherwise deeply rational girl, worked as a children's nanny in Kingsbury, North London. Both job and location had been chosen for their convenience to the greater purpose which brought Margo to London from the Lincolnshire seaside town of Cleethorpes. She arrived in 1968, looked after her two charges conscientiously for 48 hours, then made her way to St. John's Wood. For the next two years, with only the most necessary intervals, Margo stood and waited outside Paul McCartney's house.

The other Beatles had faithful followers, of course, their deviant preference usually indicated by a nickname: 'Sue John' or 'Linda Ringo'. 'We all respected John,' Margo says. 'We were a bit afraid of him really. Ringo would come along and you'd never notice him until someone said "That was Ringo". George always seemed to hate us. He'd push past us and even try to tread on our toes or kick us. He seemed very unhappy in those days.'

Their main objective remained that Beatle who was not only the most irresistibly good looking but also the most patiently amiable and accessible. Margo had first noticed this quality in 1964 while chasing the Beatles' limousine down Monmouth Street, when Paul leaned out of a window and shouted, 'Run girls, run!' There was also a time outside the Scala Theatre, during filming of *A Hard Day's Night,* when he emerged to talk to Margo and her cousin in one of his several disguises. 'This man came up to us with blond hair and a clipboard. He told us where to go if we wanted to see the next day's filming. It was only when he said "Ta-ra" that we realised it was Paul.'

So, in Cavendish Avenue, Margo waited with her Instamatic, and Big Sue and Little Sue and Gayleen and Willie and Knickers waited with their Instamatics. They photographed Paul in the early morning as he came out to walk Martha the sheepdog on Hampstead Heath. They photographed him late at night, returning from holiday, his sunburned nose shining eerily in the flashbulb glow. They photographed him driving out, with Jane or without her, in the Aston Martin or Mini-Cooper; then, hours, even days later, they photographed him driving back in again.

Paul, for his part, presented token discouragement. The front gates would be thrown open suddenly, and the Aston Martin would roar out and away up Cavendish Avenue. The girls were by then so fit, they could beat the car on foot over at least the distance to Abbey Road studios. 'We all got very tough as well,' Margo says, 'through being thrown down the EMI front steps by Mal Evans, the roadie. But we understood that he was only doing his job. At other times he'd be concerned for us, standing out there in all weathers. At heart he was an incredibly gentle person.'

The bulk of the snapshots, however, showed Paul, in his

endlessly-changing suits and shirts and scarves and waistcoats, pausing at an entreaty: turning and smiling. The face—in real life slightly asymmetric—became for the tiniest Kodak what it was in the glossiest magazines. Frequently, too, he would be in a mood for conversation. One snapshot, from the hundreds, shows him playing with a monkey one of the girls had brought. It bit his finger a moment afterwards. 'We told him once we could see him from the back of the house, sitting on the loo,' Margo says. 'We stood him on a flowerpot to show him we were telling the truth.'

Each of the girls by tradition, brought Paul gifts of varying usefulness. 'I gave him three peaches in a bag once,' Margo says. 'He'd eaten one of them by the time he got down the Abbey Road front steps. Another time, we shouted out, "What do you want for your birthday?" He thought for a minute, then he said, "I haven't got any slippers."' The slippers were ceremonially handed over in front of massed Instamatics.

The vigil broadened in scope after someone discovered under which flowerpot Paul was accustomed to hide his back-door key. Selected parties then began letting themselves into the house while he was absent, and moving from room to room in hushed wonder at the opulent chaos mingled with working-class formality: the lace-covered table, the Paolozzi sculpture, and the ranks and ranks of clothes. They would bring away some memento —small at first—a tea towel or a handful of lavatory paper.

'The American girls were worst,' Margo says. 'They started nicking his clothes.' The English girls, though refusing to pilfer, felt their scruples waver when offered a share in the booty. Margo acquired a pair of Paul's underpants and a spotted Mr. Fish shirt. Some Harris tweed trousers were also brought out as a communal prize to be worn reverently, by rota. The hems would be taken up for Little Sue, then lengthened again so that Big Sue could have a turn at wearing them.

Six months earlier, Paul had written a song, or the beginning of one, called Magical Mystery Tour. It was to have been put on the Sergeant Pepper album: it had been arranged, rehearsed, even partially recorded before Paul conceded that it did not quite fit into Sergeant Pepper's cabaret show. The track was held over —indeed, it was forgotten until early September, and the meetings to decide how the Beatles were to begin the era after Brian.

The idea, like the song, was Paul's. He had been thinking in his whimsical way, about little charabanc buses, setting out with coy trepidation on Mystery Tours from British seaside towns. He had been thinking, too, of Ken Kesey's Merry Pranksters, an American hippy troupe which, two years earlier, had journeyed by bus through the California backwoods, buoyed up by LSD diluted into thirst-quenching Kool-Aid. Tom Wolfe's chronicle of their journey, The Electric Kool-Aid Acid Test, recorded, among other things, what mirages the Pranksters saw by taking acid during a Beatles concert in Los Angeles. So, yet again, a vision they had inspired came floating back to them almost unrecognisably as a new idea to copy and adapt.

Paul's plan was to hire a coach and set out on a real life Mystery Tour, as the Pranksters had, to see what adventure—what 'magic'—would be extracted from the unsuspecting English countryside. They would take cameras and film it, Paul said, but this time direct the film for themselves. He showed the others the scenario he had written—or rather, drawn. It was a neatly-inscribed circle, segmented with what were to be the visual high-points. In one segment, Paul had written 'midgets'; in another 'fat lady'; in yet another, 'lunch'.

The prospect, as Paul outlined it, was generally appealing. At last they would be able to make a film unhampered by Walter Shenson, Dick Lester and all the petty restraints which had made *Help!* and *A Hard Day's Night* so ultimately tedious and disappointing. Film-making, as they well knew, was easy enough. All you needed was money and cameras, and someone saying 'Action!'

So exhilarating did the project—and other projects—seem that they decided to postpone their Indian pilgrimage until early 1968. John and George gave their first television interview for two years, appearing on the *David Frost Show* to explain their new found religious beliefs. Even about Transcendental Meditation they were pithy and funny: they seemed calm, cheerful and restored to sanity. Best of all, they no longer incited Britain's gullible youth to experiment with LSD. The *Daily Sketch* spoke for all in noting maternally, 'It's nice to see the roses back in the Beatles' cheeks.'

Certainly, it was simple enough to hire a luxury coach and commission the best graphic artists to design placards reading MAGICAL MYSTERY TOUR, though not quite so easy to make the placards stick to the coach's highly-polished sides. It was easy to hire actors to play the characters specified in Paul's diagram—a fat lady, a midget, a music-hall funny man. It was easy to engage cameras, and three crews to operate them, and to persuade a sprinkling of journalists and NEMS employees to go along as extras. Forty-three people eventually boarded the coach which, early in September 1967, in a secrecy somewhat compromised by its insecurely fixed MAGICAL MYSTERY TOUR placards, headed out of London along the Great West Road towards a still unspecified destination.

Chaos set in from the beginning. The Magical Mystery Tour, far from floating off into a psychedelic sunset, laboured sluggishly and all too materially around Britain's summer holiday routes, hounded by a cavalcade of Press vehicles, surrounded at every random halt by packs of sightseers and fans. Encountering a sign to 'Banbury', they followed it, to see if Banbury had a fair. It didn't, so they turned towards Devon. Traffic accumulating in front of them and behind. The Police of successive counties looked on, watchfully impassive.

The journey, it became quickly evident, held neither magic nor mystery: only poignant reminders of how things used to be when Brian Epstein looked after the travel arrangements. Aboard the coach, becalmed in traffic jams, or trying to register at hotels that were not expecting them, everyone realised at last what a protective shield had been wrenched away. Neil Aspinall realised it, trying to apportion overnight rooms among midgets and fat ladies squabbling over who had to double up with whom. 'When Brian was alive, you never had to worry about any of that. You'd just ask for 15 cars and 20 hotel rooms and they'd be there.'

They reached Devon and started back, still vainly trying to extemporise quicksilver comedy from the all too mundane disorganisation and bad humour. Nothing was explained to the actors or even the cameramen. The script was anything that anyone happened to say.

'We missed the tour ourselves in the end,' Neil Aspinall says. 'We were too busy driving. We drove all the way to Brighton and finished up just filming two cripples on the beach. What we *should* have been filming was the chaos we caused—the bus trying to get over this narrow bridge, with queues of traffic building up behind us, and then having to reverse and go back past all the drivers who'd been cursing us, and John getting off in a fury and ripping all the posters off the sides.'

The plan had been to film on location at first, and then do interior sequences for a week at Shepperton Film Studios. Unfortunately, no one thought of booking time at Shepperton Studios. Instead, they went to a disused airfield in West Malling, Kent. There, under Paul McCartney's direction, a scene was improvised with 40 dwarfs, a military band, a football crowd and a dozen babies in prams. The coach, by now looking decidedly careworn, swerved round the pitted runway with limousines in hot, but unexplained, pursuit. That was the finish of the *Magical Mystery Tour.*

It was the finish, that is to say, but for the editing, which took 11 weeks. A studio was hired in Old Compton Street, Soho, amid the strip clubs and delicatessen stores. 'Paul would come in and edit in the morning,' Tony Bramwell says. 'Then John would come in in the afternoon and re-edit what Paul had edited. Then Ringo would come in . . .' When not editing and re-editing, they would stand in the cutting room, having singsongs with a toothless Soho street busker who carried a Port bottle balanced on his head.

The print eventually passed by all four Beatles was then handed to NEMS Enterprises for distribution. NEMS' response was indecisive. 'It was like giving your film to NBC and CBS and all the networks at once,' Neil Aspinall says. 'Everyone came up with a different comment. "Couldn't you do it this way?" "Couldn't you do it *this* way?"' NEMS eventually sold the British rights to BBC Television, even though the film had been shot in colour and BBC-TV, to all but a select handful, was still black and white. BBC-1 announced, with some little fanfare, that it would be shown on Boxing Day, 1967.

The Beatles had been at Abbey Road since mid-September, recording material for an EP to accompany the film. Their pre-Christmas single, however, was a separate track, Hello, Goodbye, written by Paul, in which a grandstand of overdubbed voices chanted a lyric so simple as to be almost inane and so inane, it appeared subtly ironic. By early December, Hello, Goodbye was Number One in Britain and America. The Beatles continued to walk upon water.

Magical Mystery Tour was launched by a party whose lavishness held no doubt of Sergeant Pepper-like success. The Beatles specified fancy dress. John Lennon came as a Teddy Boy, accompanied by Cynthia in Quality Street crinolines. George Martin came as the Duke of Edinburgh, Lulu as Shirley Temple and Pattie, George's wife, as an Eastern belly dancer. John, that night, made no secret of powerfully desiring Pattie Harrison. He danced with Pattie time after time, leaving Cynthia so disconsolate in her crinolines that Lulu was roused to sisterly indignation. The climax of the party was the moment at which a little ringletted Shirley Temple, clutching an immense lollipop, confronted the chief Beatle in his greaser outfit and roundly berated him for being so mean to his wife.

Fifteen million British viewers, on the dead day after Christmas, tuned their television sets hopefully to BBC-1 and *Magical Mystery Tour*. Expecting a miracle, they beheld only a glorified and progressively irritating home movie. Hand-held cameras wandered among 43 faces, sitting on a bus and, occasionally, disembarking. The Beatles themselves were intermittently glimpsed among the passengers or as four red-robed wizards, messing around in a chemistry lab. Paul, in one of the few professionally-directed sequences, sang Fool on the Hill, against a background of French Riviera mountains and sea. George, squatting Indian style, sang Blue Jay Way, repeating the line 'don't be long' 29 times. The four played I Am the Walrus, John's Lewis-Carrol-inspired sequel to Strawberry Fields through a bewildering compendium of camera effects. A lengthy abstract interlude, devoid of its colour, became merely puzzling cloud-drifts and icebergs. The bus, pursued by cars, dashed round and round what seemed to be a deserted airfield. The finale was one more idea that no one had quite bothered to think through. 'Let's do a Busby Berkeley sequence,' Paul had said. The Beatles, in white tailcoats, descended a staircase, singing Your Mother Should Know, while ballroom dancing teams whirled in aimless formation beneath.

The *Daily Express* TV critic received front-page editorial space next morning to declare that never in all his days of viewing had he beheld such 'blatant rubbish' as *Magical Mystery Tour*. All the papers hated it, none more so than those which had been most adoring through the circulation-fattened years of Beatlemania. Hell hath no fury, indeed, like a British tabloid newspaper obliged to think again.

For the Beatles, it was a shock incalculable to beings other than Beatles: it was the loss of their divinity. Worse, it was the realisation that, all along, that divinity might have been reliant on others. A Walter Shenson, a Richard Lester, a single tedious timetable, might have rescued *Magical Mystery Tour* from disaster. That knowledge came hardest to the one who had conceived it, drawing a clock face and trusting his Pied Piper magic to do the rest. 'Dusty' Durband, at Liverpool Institute High School, could have cited similar mishaps, long ago, when Paul McCartney did not bother to do his homework.

An American TV deal was cancelled on the basis of the British showing and headlines like the *Los Angeles Times*' Beatles Bomb With Yule Film. The BBC, as though in self-absolution, banned I Am the Walrus for 'indecent' references to 'knickers' and 'yellow matter custard'.

For the first time in their existence, the Beatles were unpopular. Nor was there anyone now to stand up for them, intercede for them and stand between them while things were smoothed over. The thought had already occurred to Neil Aspinall as he sorted through hotel bills for midgets, fat ladies, music-hall comics and piles of hangers-on. 'If Brian had been alive, the film would never have gone out. Brian would have said, "OK, we blew £40,000—so what?" Brian would never have let it all happen.'

John Lennon's old schoolfriend, Pete Shotton, had long felt a distinct impression that John was trying to tell him something. Pete still lived in Hayling Island, managing the supermarket John had bought him: on visits to John in London, he could not but notice what larger business preparations were afoot. 'I'd known John so long and had so many laughs with him, he could never come out with anything straight. He'd just grin across the room and say: "When are you coming up here to work then?"

'Eventually he did come out with it. He said he wanted me to come to London and run a boutique the Beatles were opening. He said: "We've got to spend two million or the Taxman will get it." '

Dr. Walter Strach, that dignified financial expert, had many times implored Brian to invest the colossal Beatle earnings simply left on deposit at various British banks. Socialism had as yet closed few of the Tory loopholes for channelling money abroad into tax-exempt trusts and companies. Brian would never do it, partly through a naive respect for capital, partly from a belief that to take money abroad was unpatriotic. 'After the Beatles got their MBEs,' Dr. Strach says, 'Brian always insisted they had to be whiter than white.'

It was therefore on 'Uncle Walter's' advice rather than Brian's that individual Beatles made personal investments, such as John's Hampshire supermarket and Ringo's brief, unsuccessful foray into the building trade. On one occasion, all four came to Strach, eager to put money into a washing-machine company run by a chin-bearded young tycoon named John Bloom. The Doctor takes credit for talking them out of involvement with one of the decade's more spectacular financial crashes.

Strach figured in the single attempt during Brian's lifetime to divert Beatle money from its huge liability under British Income Tax. In 1965, the proceeds from *Help!* were paid directly into a Bahamian company, Cavalcade Productions, formed jointly by the Beatles and the film's producer, Walter Shenson, and administered by Dr. Strach as a temporary resident in Nassau. 'That was why we shot part of *Help!* in the Bahamas,' Shenson admits. 'It was a goodwill exercise to persuade the Bahamian authorities we were an asset to their business community.' Unfortunately, the *Help!* proceeds were banked entirely in sterling. When Harold Wilson devalued the Pound in 1967, Cavalcade Productions lost approximately £80,000.

Towards the end of his life, Brian had been considering more complex measures to protect the Beatles' accumulated fortunes. His concept was not much different in essence from that which would soon spectacularly emerge—a corporation built around the Beatles which would both lighten their Income Tax obligation and allow them to administer their own work at every level, from songwriting to recording, even distribution, marketing and retailing. Brian had also visualised a string of 'Beatle boutiques' or Pop supermarkets, selling records and clothes.

In addition to their original company, Beatles Ltd., the four were now incorporated into a partnership, Beatles & Co. The manoeuvre took place in April 1967 as a means of providing each with some quick personal capital. Beatles Ltd. paid £800,000 for a share in the partnership. By this absolutely legal method of selling themselves a share in themselves, each Beatle received £200,000 and, later on, a tax demand to match.

It therefore came about that, in 1968, they could earn nothing that would not instantly be devoured by Income Tax; they furthermore had to think of a way of dissipating some £2m which they held in common. The process was to prove easier than even they could have imagined.

Simon Posthuma and Marijke Koger were 'beautiful people' from Holland. A dreamy-eyed, lissom boy and girl, they had drifted out of the LSD summer and into the Beatles' innermost coterie, simply for being so beautiful, so softly spoken and so richly and bizarrely dressed. Their clothes, which they themselves designed and made, sparkled with sequins and shone with deep velvet; each ensemble was named for an element, 'Fire' or 'Water'. However vast the Beatles' exhaustion at meeting new people, they could never resist the possibility of acquiring something new to wear.

Simon and Marijke, with another Dutch girl, Josje Leeger, claimed to have founded the avant garde Trend boutique in Amsterdam. When Trend folded—a fact which did not yet appear significant—two of the partners had come to London, hoping to find work as stage designers. They had been taken up by two young theatrical publicists, Barry Finch and Simon Hayes, whose clients included Brian Epstein's Savile Theatre. Their stage designs, like their clothes, were dazzling and fanciful. Together with Barry Finch and Josje Leeger, who had followed Simon and Marijke from Holland, they formed themselves into a design group named—with clairvoyant aptness—The Fool.

Throughout that summer and autumn, The Fool enjoyed the Royal appointment of designers and couturiers to the Beatles. They produced the costumes for the *All You Need Is Love* television sequence. They painted a piano and a gipsy caravan for John and designed a fireplace for George's Esher bungalow. They began to appear in newspaper fashion spreads as heralds of an era to follow wasp stripes, PVC and mini-skirts. 'Simon,' explained *The Sunday Times*, 'is dressed to represent Water. His jacket is glittering Lurex in bluey, greeney colours; his trousers are blue velvet. Marijke is Nature, in blue and green, and has a pastoral scene on her bodice. Josje is Space, her midnight-blue trousers covered with yellow appliqué stars.' To *The Sunday Times*, Simon explained that The Fool was a name with connotations beyond the obvious one. 'It represents Truth, Spiritual Meaning and the circle which expresses the universal circumference in which gravitate all things.'

In September 1967, The Fool received £100,000 to design a boutique on the Beatles' behalf and stock it with their own exotic garments and accessories. It was Paul McCartney, the most dandified Beatle, who announced the imminent unveiling of 'a beautiful place where you can buy beautiful things'. It was Paul who strove to think of a name befitting the new boutique's ideal of chaste elegance, and who found inspiration in a Magritte painting he had recently acquired. The others agreed: they would call their boutique, simply, Apple.

The summer had produced another Beatle friend of similarly pervasive and persuasive charm. His name was Alexis Mardas. He was a young, blond-haired Greek whose father held a high post in the Papadopoulos dictatorship and who had come to Britain knowing only two people: Mick Jagger and the Duke of Edinburgh.

Alexis Mardas was an inventor of electronic gadgets. He invented the 'nothing box' at which John would gaze for hours, trying to guess which of the series of red lights would flash on next. He had other ideas too, which, he explained quietly, needed only a little finance to revolutionise twentieth-century life. There was, for instance, a telephone, programmed to dial its own numbers in obedience to a human voice. There was the transistorised hi-fi; the 'scream' built into a gramophone record to prevent illicit taping; the force field around a house which would keep intruders at bay with a wall of coloured air. Each of Alexis Mardas's inventions played expertly both on the Beatles' thirst for novelty and their endless quest for protection against a cheating, importunate world. John, in particular, having no clue about electronics, believed the murmuring young Greek to be literally magical. For John, no night excursion was complete without 'Magic' Alex and the latest little gadget he would produce from his pocket.

Not everyone succumbed to Magic Alex's charm. Cynthia Lennon, presciently, did not trust him. George Martin surveyed him with folded arms and tight-lipped distaste. The Greek made a habit of visiting Abbey Road studios while the Beatles were recording, and of whispering into John's ear that all the EMI equipment was ridiculously out of date. He claimed that, with a little finance, he could provide them with a 72-track recording machine instead of EMI's 8-track one. Only a little finance, too, was needed to dispense with the acoustic screens around Ringo Starr's drums and replace them with invisible yet impenetrable sonic beams. At this suggestion, ice formed on the upper slopes of George Martin.

Meanwhile, in Baker Street, a respectable 18th-century corner house, not far from Sherlock Holmes's mythical consulting rooms, was being transformed to a condition which might have baffled even Holmes. The Fool hired gangs of Art students to help them cover the side wall along Paddington Street with psychedelic patterns, whizzing and whirling around what seemed to be the face of an enormous Red Indian. 'Magic' Alex was also there, designing floodlights, and mentioning what very little finance was necessary to build a giant artificial sun and suspend it above Baker Street on invisible laser beams.

All the Beatles relished the novelty of setting up a shop. The prettiest, swingingest, girls—among them Pattie Harrison's sister, Jennie—were recruited as staff. Pete Shotton left his supermarket, its detergent and wrapped cheeses, to oversee the arrival of Oriental fabrics and exotic jewellery ordered in profusion by The Fool. 'John would come in every day,' Pete says. ' "You've got to put a partition over here", he'd say. Then Paul would come in and say, "What's that partition here for? Better move it over there." '

The Apple boutique opened on 7 December 1967, with a lavish party and fashion show. 'Come at 7.46,' the invitations said. 'Fashion show at 8.16.' In the elegant, sweating crush, sipping apple juice, only two Beatles were visible: John and George. Ringo was abroad, playing a small part in the film *Candy*, and Paul had decided to go away to his farm in Scotland.

Within a few days, the pattern of trading had been established. Hundreds of people came to Baker Street to look at the Apple boutique, and look inside it. There was no obligation to buy, or to consider buying. Garments began rapidly to leave the premises, though seldom as a result of cash transactions. The musk-scented gloom, with feather boas hanging helpfully from bentwood hat-stands, was a shoplifters' paradise.

It was upstairs from the Apple boutique that the empire named Apple initially took root. On the first floor, in a snow-white office, Terry Doran, 'the man from the motor trade', ran Apple Music, intended nucleus of the Beatles' own independent publishing and recording company. On the second floor, Pete Shotton administered Apple Retail, comprising the boutique, and men's tailoring and mail order subsidiaries. Pete also did much of the hiring for the other Apple provinces springing up almost daily. For the empire, unlike its symbol, did not ripen at leisure. It appeared all at once like a conjuring trick at the imperious clap of four multimillionaires' hands.

Its purpose—to begin with, at least—was clear and concurring in all four multimillionaires' minds. It was to be *theirs*, rather than administered on their behalf. It was liberation from the control of 'men in suits', as John Lennon called the irksome powers at NEMS, Northern Songs and EMI. It was to prove that people of less than middle age, without stiff collars or waistcoats, were capable of building and running an organisation. Apple was to be the first triumphant annexation by youth's living apotheosis of all the power and riches which youth had generated. It was to be free and easy and open-handed; above all, in that poignant Sixties word, it was to be 'fun'.

Magical Mystery Tour, in 1967, was the first production credited to Apple Films. Among future productions, it was announced, would be a film starring Twiggy, the model; possibly a screen version of J. R. R. Tolkein's *Lord of the Rings*. Simultaneously there appeared an Apple Electronics division, run by Magic Alex from a laboratory financed by the Beatles. Alex was to design an entire recording studio for them: meanwhile, his Hellenic wizardry would be applied to such marketable novelties as 'nothing boxes', luminous paint, domestic force fields and plastic apples with miniature transistor radios inside.

In January 1968, Beatles Ltd. changed its name to Apple Corps Ltd. 'It's a pun,' Paul McCartney explained patiently to Fleet Street. 'Apple *Core*—see?' Neil Aspinall was appointed Managing Director and Alistair Taylor, General Manager. The board of directors included Peter Brown and Harry Pinsker, head of Bryce, Hammer, Brian Epstein's old Albemarle Street accountants.

The new divisions, and their newly-appointed directors and managers, quickly spilled over from the Apple shop into a suite of offices in Wigmore Street, a quarter of a mile away. Here was established Apple Records, with Jane Asher's brother, Peter, as A & R man, and Apple Publicity, run by Derek Taylor, the idiosyncratic Press Officer whom the Beatles had wooed home from Hollywood for his second term of serving them. Also at Wigmore Street, Neil Aspinall strove to remember his long-lapsed accountancy lessons in creating an office and filing system despite the fact that, in four years, the Beatles had between them accumulated not one single documentary file.

Even in these formative days, the contrast was evident between friends of the Beatles, working for a moderate salary, and impressive outsiders, recruited to high Apple office at any figure they cared to name. Pete Shotton, whose weekly take-home pay was £37 10s, found himself approving munificent salaries for Denis O'Dell, Head of Apple Films; Ron Kass, Head of Apple Records; and Brian Lewis, lawyer in charge of Apple contracts. 'As soon as they arrived,' Pete says, 'they started going out to lunch. I used to go and fetch a toasted sandwich from the cafe across the road.'

In February, in the midst of Apple's gestation, John and George, with Cynthia and Pattie, flew to India to begin their much-postponed religious studies under the Maharishi Mahesh Yogi.

The advance party also included Pattie's sister, Jennie, and the indispensable Magic Alex. Paul and Jane followed soon afterwards, with Ringo, Maureen and a consignment of baked beans which Ringo had brought as insurance against the curry-eating weeks ahead.

The ashram, to which their pocket-sized guru beamingly welcomed them, was not devoid of fleshy comforts. Situated in verdant foothills above the Ganges at Rishikesh, it accommodated the students of the Maharishi in stone bungalows, equipped with English hotel furniture, telephones and running water. A high perimeter fence and padlocked gate shielded its devotees from sightseers, beggars, *sadhus*, wandering cows and the odour of everyday worship at the *ghats*, or Holy bathing places below, along the river bank. The Maharishi himself occupied an elaborate residence equipped with a launching pad for the private helicopter in which the Holy Man would periodically view his well-appointed domain.

Apart from the Beatles, an impressive netful of personalities had been trawled to sit at the Maharishi's feet. They included Mike Love of the Beach Boys; Donovan, the English folk singer, and his manager, 'Gipsy Dave'; and the film actress Mia Farrow. All put off their Pop hippy finery, the girls to dress in saris, the boys in *kurta* tunics, loose trousers and sandals. At Mike Love's example, both John and George started to grow beards. John even experimented with a turban, though he could not resist the temptation to pull cripple faces when wearing it.

The Maharishi took pains to ensure that ashram life would not be too stringent for his cosseted disciples. The chalets were comfortable—like Butlin's, Ringo said—and the food, though vegetarian, was ample; there were frequent excursions and parties. The Lennons received Indian clothes and toys for their son, Julian, and George Harrison's 25th birthday was celebrated by a seven-pound cake. Obliging houseboys would even smuggle the odd bottle of forbidden wine into the Beatles' cantonment.

Even so, the schedule of fasting, chanting and mass prayer quickly proved too much for Ringo Starr. He left Rishikesh with Maureen after only 10 days, complaining that his stomach couldn't take the highly-spiced food and that he missed his children.

The others showed every sign of sticking out the course for its full three-month duration. Fleet Street journalists who had infiltrated the stockade reported seeing this or that Beatle seated contentedly at a prayer meeting, feeding the monkeys that inhabited the trellises or aimlessly strumming a guitar. It emerged that they were holding a contest among themselves to see who could keep up non-stop Meditation the longest. Paul McCartney led the field with four hours, followed by John and

George with three-and-a-half each. They were also using the unwonted peace and immobility to write songs for their next album.

At regular intervals, Neil Aspinall would fly out from London to report the latest progress in setting up Apple, and the position of Lady Madonna, the single they had left for release in their absence. Neil was also making arrangements for Apple Films to finance a production in which the Maharishi himself would star. 'We had a meeting about it in his bungalow,' Neil says. 'Suddenly, this little guy in a robe who's meant to be a Holy Man starts talking about his two-and-a-half per cent. "Wait a minute," I thought, "he knows more about making deals than I do. He's really into scoring, the Maharishi." '

Paul, who filmed most of his and Jane's nine-week stay, remembered Rishikesh as being like school—mock-serious, with giggles lurking always behind hands. 'We thought we were submerging our personalities, but really we weren't being very truthful then. There's a long shot of you [John] walking beside the Maharishi, saying "Tell me, O Master," and it just isn't you.'

It was in the ninth week, after Paul and Jane had decided to leave, that John himself began showing signs of restiveness. 'John thought there was some sort of secret the Maharishi had to give you, and then you could just go home,' Neil Aspinall says. 'He started to think the Maharishi was holding out on him. "Maybe if I go up with him in the helicopter," John said, "he may slip me the answer on me own." '

By the eleventh week, despite trips above the Ganges in the Maharishi's helicopter, the answer still had not come. Furthermore, it began to be whispered—chiefly by Magic Alex—that the Maharishi was not so divine a being as he had seemed, and that his interest in Mia Farrow might originate in a region somewhat lower than her soul. Even George, the guru's most impassioned disciple, seemed to be having second thoughts. So, to Magic Alex's gratification and Cynthia's dismay, John decided they were going home.

He led the way into the Maharishi's quarters and announced his decision, characteristically mincing no words. The guru, for all his quick-wittedness, seems to have had no idea that the lights had changed. When he asked 'Why?' John would say only, 'You're the cosmic one. You ought to know.' At this, he said later, Maharishi Mahesh Yogi, The Great Soul, gave him a look like 'I'll kill you, you bastard.'

John, in fact, was convinced for a long time afterwards that the Maharishi would wreak some sort of Transcendental vengeance. He told Cyn' it was already starting when, on the way back to Delhi, their taxi broke down, and they both stood panic-stricken, trying to thumb a lift as the Indian dusk and the myriad staring eyes closed in around them.

The Maharishi, his teachings and flowers and Transcendental gurglings were dismissed as utterly as last month's groupie or yesterday's Mr. Fish shirt. 'We made a mistake,' Paul McCartney said. 'We thought there was more to him than there was. He's human. We thought at first that he wasn't.' Into another airport microphone, George concurred: 'We've finished with him.' The Holy Man was left in his mountain fastness to cogitate upon a mystery as profound as any offered by Heaven or Earth. Had the Beatles, or had the Maharishi Mahesh Yogi, been taken for the bigger ride?

Last month's ashram-dwellers were this month's corporate executives, flying to New York with their numerous, highly-paid lieutenants to unveil Apple Corps to the most crucial of its prospective markets. The first board meeting was held symbolically in a Chinese junk, cruising round the Statue of Liberty. There was, indeed, to be a great deal of junk in Apple, and a great many liberties would assuredly be taken.

At Press conferences and on the NBC *Johnny Carson Show*, John and Paul explained the revolutionary but also philanthropic motives which would guide the Beatles' business. 'The aim,' John said, 'isn't just a stack of gold teeth in the bank. We've done that bit. It's more of a trick to see if we can get artistic freedom within a business structure—to see if we can create things and sell them without charging five times our cost.'

Paul said that Apple's aim was 'a controlled weirdness . . . a kind of Western Communism'. It was he who announced the newest sub-division: an Apple Foundation for the Arts. 'We want to help people, but without doing it like a charity. *We* always had to go to the big men on our knees and touch our forelocks and say, "Please can we do so-and-so . . . ?" We're in the happy position of not needing any more money, so for the first time the bosses aren't in it for profit. If you come to me and say, "I've had such and such a dream," I'll say to you, "Go away and do it." '

In other words, the Apple Foundation for the Arts would grant struggling unknown artists in every genre the finance and fulfilment they had been denied by a mercenary, unsympathetic, middle-aged world. Paul designed a proclamation to that effect, issued via full-page advertisements in the British music Press. Alistair Taylor, Apple's general manager, was coerced into posing for a photograph weighed down with the impedimenta of a one-man band. 'This man has talent!' ran Paul's caption. 'One day, he sang his songs into a tape recorder and, remembering to enclose a picture of himself, sent the tape to Apple Music at 94

Baker Street. You could do the same. This man now owns a Bentley.'

The response was as anyone but a Beatle might have predicted. An avalanche of tapes, of novels, of plays and poems and film scripts and synopses and scenaria, of paintings, etchings, sketches, lithographs, sculpture, designs, blueprints, working models and other, less easily classified submissions fell at once, with a huge, soft, slightly deranged thud upon Apple's Wigmore Street office. Many were delivered in person, the artists electing to wait the short time necessary before they received their bursaries from the Apple Foundation for the Arts. The reception area all day thronged with creative, insolvent humanity, from ethnic bards to seaside Punch and Judy men, reminding Richard diLello, a young Californian working for the Press Office, of nothing so much as the VD clinics back home in his native Haight-Ashbury. Brighter even than hope of penicillin shone the belief that the Beatles meant it: that behind those very partition walls even now, they were reading, listening, looking, nodding and saying, 'Yes. Go away and do it.'

They were certainly there, though not engaged precisely as imagined. They had a big corner room in which open house was kept for the fellow Rock stars and friends who dropped in continuously to wish Apple luck and drink, and smoke, its health. John and Paul each kept more or less regular office hours, enjoying the novelty of a fixed destination, a desk and secretaries. John employed an astrologer named Caleb to cast a daily horoscope for senior staff, and guide major policy decisions by consulting the *I Ching Book of Changes.* Paul's concern was that people arrived on time in the mornings and that there was enough lavatory paper in the Ladies'.

It was pleasant, now that they themselves could rise no higher, to act as sponsors of new, young Pop talent to join them on their very own Apple record label. Terry Doran had made the first signing—a teenage group named Grapefruit, and launched to the music Press on a tide of Fortnum and Mason grapefruit in special presentation boxes. A second group, The Iveys, was Mal Evans's discovery. George had his own protégé, a fellow Liverpudlian named Jackie Lomax; in America, Peter Asher had found a raw-boned singer songwriter named James Taylor. Twiggy also kept telling Paul about a sweet little Welsh soprano named Mary Hopkin, the longest consecutive winner of the television *Opportunity Knocks* talent show.

By June 1968, Wigmore Street could no longer contain all this bright, bustling activity and expansion. Neil Aspinall was given half a million pounds and told to find Apple a bigger, nicer place.

Within a few days, Neil found 3 Savile Row, a five-storey

Georgian house standing deep in the heartland of bespoke tailoring, elegant arcades and dealers in hand-made cigarettes. The house knew something of show business: it had previously been owned by Jack Hylton, the theatrical impresario, who in latter days ran it as the Albany Club. On its left, Gieves, the military tailors, guarded the crevice into Regent Street. To its right stretched timbered casements, displaying Royal warrants, in which elderly men with tape measures still toiled round the circumferences of peers and archbishops.

Savile Row was never to be quite the same again.

Derek Taylor, one of the first into the house, annexed the elegant, spacious ground floor front room, with its finely-carved wall panels and ceiling, for Apple's new Press and Publicity department. Unfortunately, the apartment had already been promised to Ron Kass, Head of Apple Records. Taylor, with Richard diLello and accumulating 'Press Office girls', moved into a less well-favoured office on the second floor, overlooking the rearward panorama of Mayfair skylights and fire escapes. Here, between two windows, Taylor established his desk and the big scallop-backed wicker chair he had brought from Hollywood, and girded himself to the task of launching 3 Savile Row upon the world.

Throughout June and July, their new business occupied the Beatles to the exclusion of all else: even music. In six months, they had been to Abbey Road only to record a new single and some reluctant titles for *Yellow Submarine*, the cartoon feature film based on their music. The project had been sanctioned by Brian, chiefly to give United Artists the third Beatle film he still owed them. 'It'll do for the film,' John Lennon would say whenever a studio session did not come up to standard. Even by reissuing the Yellow Submarine song itself, and also resurrecting All You Need Is Love, they could not scrape sufficient titles together for Side One. So George Harrison went away for an hour and wrote It's Only A Northern Song, self-confessed nadir of his ability and their interest. Side Two consisted of Beatles songs scored as orchestral pieces by George Martin. For the first time, the Beatles had given their listeners short weight.

It was all the more surprising therefore that the film should be an artistic triumph. Written by Erich Segal, later a best-selling romantic novelist, it translated Beatle lyrics and Beatle allusions into a genuinely original and appealing fantasy of 'Pepperland', 'Blue Meanies' and 'Nowhere Men'. The Beatles' own voices were supplied by actors bizarrely unlike them in real life. Paul's alter-ego was short and craggy; Ringo's was fat and aggressive. Yellow Submarine opened in London on 17 July. Though poorly reviewed and denied a general release, it brought back much of the goodwill that *Magical Mystery Tour* had lost. The Beatles as little cartoon figures, with big eyes and buttons and neckties, assumed the form in which millions, henceforward, would prefer to remember them.

At Baker Street, meanwhile, the Apple boutique was sliding into chaos. Its psychedelic mural had been scrubbed away, after petitions by local tradespeople, leaving behind what was, after all, just another clothes shop, distinguished only by the chaos of its management. The Fool, despite their personal modishness, had small idea how to run a retail business, nor did they seem interested in any aspect beyond borrowing the better garments in stock. The merchandise was either ludicrously expensive or cheap and shoddy. Shoplifting raged on, barely noticed by assistants, some of whom regularly fiddled up to £50 each week on top of their wages. A new head of Apple Retail, John Lydon, was desperately trying to stop the rot. Stern memos had gone out to The Fool, warning them to take no more garments off the premises and forbidding any further expenditure without direct authorisation.

At the end of July, Pete Shotton was called to a meeting at Paul McCartney's house. 'John told me, "We've decided to close the shop down. We're tired of playing shops." '

The Apple boutique liquidated itself on 30 July by the simple process of giving away its entire stock. A dozen policemen fought to control the mêlée in Baker Street as hundreds grabbed at Afghan coats, Indian beads, Art Deco ashtrays and whatever shop fittings could be detached. The Beatles and their wives had already gone in privately for first pick, gleefully carrying off the choicer spoils with no sense that it was their own property they had got for nothing. To the Press, Paul repeated John's remark, with a grander, almost Napoleonic twist: 'The Beatles are tired of being shopkeepers.'

Bright, fresh, apple green carpet now fragrantly covered all five floors at 3 Savile Row. On 11 August, Apple Records released four inaugural titles on the label that was a pure, simple green Granny Smith apple, halved through for the B-side. Teams of photographers, designers and typographers, not to mention fruiterers, working in London and New York, had laboured for six months, rejecting whole orchards, to produce that stunningly crisp and explicit motif. As a final touch, Alan Aldridge, London's highest-paid Pop illustrator, contributed the 'copyright reserved' message in hand-drawn italic script.

The Beatles' new single, Hey Jude, was accompanied, in a shiny black presentation box, by three of the talents now under their wing: Mary Hopkin, Jackie Lomax and the Black Dyke Mills brass band. Paul McCartney had produced Mary Hopkin's ballad Those Were the Days, and conducted the Black Dyke Mills band's rendering of his own composition, Thingummybob. George Harrison had written and produced Jackie Lomax's song, Sour Milk Sea. Richard diLello, Apple's Afro-haired 'House Hippy', received the job of delivering one boxed set each to the Queen at Buckingham Palace; the Queen Mother at Clarence House; Princess Margaret at Kensington Palace; and the Prime Minister, Harold Wilson, at 10, Downing Street.

By far the greatest augury of Apple was the Beatles' appearance together on television, for the first time in two years, to perform Hey Jude on the *David Frost Show.* The studio audience came and stood round them as Paul, at his piano, sang the wistful wounded ballad that turns, midway, into an anthem seven minutes long. At the Abbey Road session, all the 40-piece symphony orchestra had joined in that final mesmeric la-la chorus. So did the studio audience—and much of the country—join in tonight. It was as though the Beatles were reaffirming their oneness with their audience and with each other, instead of just beginning their drift into chaos and bitter enmity.

October 1968

'Your finances are in a mess. Apple is in a mess'

Cynthia Lennon knew there was no hope left for John and her. The marriage survived only because John could not be bothered to end it. For months, Cyn' had been little more than a prisoner in the mock-Tudor mansion at Weybridge, with its miles of untrodden pastel carpet, its unused gadgets, its antique globe cocktail cabinet from Asprey's, its suits of armour and medieval altar-pieces. Cynthia retreated where the life of the house always had, to the little sun parlour at the back. By day she looked after Julian: at night she watched television, wondering if she would see her husband on it. She did yards of embroidery, and took up drawing and painting again. She slept alone in the huge master bedroom, awakening to find only her half of the bed disturbed. She would then nerve herself to voyage through the house to look for John among the empty bottles, the scattered album sleeves and the groggy, sprawling figures of whatever new strangers he had brought home at dawn.

Sometimes, at her embroidery when the house was quiet, Cyn' would speculate on the type of woman John ought to have married. In this, as in all else about him, she faced impenetrable mystery. She could think only of Brigitte Bardot, his adolescent passion whom Cynthia herself had tried so hard to copy. And Juliette Greco, who was not at all pretty and who played the guitar and sang like a man. Both these images belonged to a past when physical closeness could still shut out the mystery. But for almost a year now, Cynthia and John had lived together 'as brother and sister'.

Cyn' knew he could suffer bouts of depression—desperation even—that were entirely separate from his outward success. One such 'trough' had been in 1965, at the height of Beatlemania, when no one thought to ask why the idol of millions would write a song called *Help!* Another, still deeper trough came in 1967, in the months before he met the Maharishi, when John, under Dr. Timothy Leary's influence, tried to 'destroy' his ego by expanding it to ludicrous proportion. He would arrive at Abbey Road dressed like Sabu the Elephant Boy in a cloak, curly slippers and a turban. At a dinner-party, given by Jane Asher, a guest happened to ask for an ash tray. John crawled under the table and invited her to flick her ash into his open mouth.

Now, in early '68, Cynthia felt another trough beginning. So far as she could divine, it had something to do with student riots —the savage street warfare in Paris, West Germany, even London's own elegant Grosvenor Square. John, in some obscure way, felt himself a part of this world-wide change from lisping hippy Love and Peace to brick-hurling activism. The Underground looked on him as a potential leader, to join Tariq Ali and Daniel Cohn-Bendit and the others whose 'charisma', in the modish word, was akin to that of Rock stars. He had even written a song called Revolution, but then, apparently, lost his nerve. One version said 'You can count me in'; the other said 'You can count me out'. Part of him wanted to be a pamphleteer, a rebel-rouser, a street fighter. The stronger part was still buttoned into his Beatle self, still forged to a corporate smile, still fearful of what his Aunt Mimi might read about him in the Press.

Occasionally, summoning up her courage, Cynthia would ask him if he had found someone else. John always vehemently denied it. He still did not think in remotely that way of the little, unsmiling Japanese woman he had met two years ago at John Dunbar's Indica Gallery, and who, instead of speaking, had handed him a card inscribed 'Breathe'. And yet, as the months passed, as his restlessness grew to match the outside world's, for some unfathomable reason he could not get Yoko Ono off his mind.

It was said of the woman whose name in Japanese means 'Ocean Child' that two experiences in infancy formed the peculiar nature of her ambition. The first occurred when her father, a thwarted concert pianist, examined the three-year-old Yoko's hands to see whether they portended creativity. The second came during World War Two, when her parents sent her out of Tokyo to safety in the care of servants. The servants abandoned her: at nine years old, she was left alone, to forage or starve.

Considering Yoko's own inordinate gift for self-publicity, strangely little is known of her life before 1968. Her parents were wealthy and respectable, with old-fashioned ideas of family pride and female subservience. They emigrated to America when Yoko was in her early teens, settling in the respectable New York suburb of Scarsdale. Yoko attended Sarah Lawrence College, where she studied Art and musical composition. At the age of 18, she rebelled simultaneously against the formality of her home and the tame conventionality of her Sarah Lawrence teachers. She married a Japanese musician and settled with him in an attic in Greenwich Village, New York.

Here she first enjoyed what seemed destined to be a problematical and marginal fame. She belonged to the new wave of artists which sprang up in New York in the early Sixties around the anaemic figure of Andy Warhol. It was a circle which preached that Art's chief virtue lies in its power to shock and its ultimate success in the numbers of people who are, however accidentally, its witnesses. Yoko Ono achieved a reputation for perpetrating what might once have been called hoaxes but were now known as 'events' or 'happenings'. One of her works was an 'eternal time clock', showing only seconds and encased in a sound-proof perspex bubble attached to a doctor's stethoscope. Another was a 'book' called *Grapefruit*, a collection of cards bearing one line 'instructional poems'. The talent in such pieces might be open to question: what was unquestionable was the ruthless success with which Yoko brought them to the public's notice.

She came to England in 1966, to attend a symposium entitled 'The Destruction of Art'. Swinging London was in full bloom, and ripe for events and happenings such as she had staged in New York. She settled in London, with her second husband an American film maker, Tony Cox, and had a daughter by him, Kyoko. She received the mild notoriety the era so freely bestowed by photographing naked human bottoms and, later, wrapping the Trafalgar Square lions in white canvas. She had not, however, heard a single Beatles record until that night at the Indica when John Lennon walked in on her 'Unfinished Paintings and Objects Show', and John Dunbar sent her across to 'chat him up' as a likely sponsor.

Shortly after their first meeting, she asked John to finance her next exhibition, at the Lisson Gallery in North London. This new Yoko Ono event was entitled 'The Half Wind Show', because everything was in halves. There was half a chair, half a table, half a bed, half a pillow, half a washbasin and half a toothbrush. Like the apple with its £200 price ticket, the idea delighted John's sense of the absurd. He put up the money but recoiled in horror when Yoko suggested his name should appear in the catalogue. Instead, the show was credited enigmatically to 'Yoko plus Me'.

She also sent John her book, *Grapefruit*, with its 'instruction poems', written on cards saying 'Bleed' or 'Paint Until You Drop Dead'. John, alternately puzzled and fascinated by these inscrutable suggestions, kept the book at his bedside. While organising yet another happening, entitled 'Dance Event', Yoko sent him further message cards: 'Breathe' or 'Dance' or 'Watch the Light Until Dawn'. At this stage, she was something of a joke between John and Cynthia. They looked at each other rather helplessly, after a Meditation session in London, as the figure, like a little black skittle, climbed into the psychedelic Rolls to sit between them.

John met her again at different galleries and again was unaccountably disturbed. He could not explain the disturbance: it occurred in an unused organ, his mind. It was unrelated to his inbred Northern concept of servile womanhood. It was something he had only ever felt for men—for the tough, mad Liverpool Teds who could make even him defer and keep silent. Yoko Ono, quite simply, did things that John Lennon did not dare.

He began to look out for her across rooms. He would stand with her and simply listen while the little white face, in its clouds of black hair, poured forth ideas bent on only one purpose: to challenge and upset the conventional, complacent Art world. 'As she was talking to me, I'd get high, and the discussion would get to such a level, I'd be getting higher and higher. Then she'd leave, and I'd go back to this sort of suburbia. Then I'd meet her again, and my head would go open, like I was on an acid trip.'

He had considered asking Yoko to join the pilgrimage to Rishikesh, but, at the last minute, lost his nerve. Instead, he wrote to her from India—long, rambling letters like the ones he used to send to Stu Sutcliffe. Yoko replied with further message cards. 'I'm a cloud,' one card said. 'Watch for me in the sky.'

It was at Rishikesh, ironically, that Cynthia felt a small revival of hope for her marriage. She, at least, remained convinced that the Maharishi was a power for good and that only envious whispers, by Magic Alex chiefly, implanted the Beatles' suspicion of him. John, in India, seemed calmer and happier than Cyn' had ever known him. He began writing songs, about childhood and his mother, Julia, that Cyn' could again understand. Then, on the plane back to England—still half-fearful of the Maharishi's revenge—he told Cyn' something which caused her vast astonishment. He told her that, over the years, he had not been completely faithful to her.

Back in Weybridge, their estrangement worsened. Cynthia even suggested, rather wildly, that John would be better off with someone like Yoko Ono than with her. She begged to go with him to New York for the Apple launching, but he refused. In May, he packed her away on holiday to Greece with Jennie Boyd and Magic Alex. His old school crony Pete Shotton came down to Weybridge to keep him company.

'We were just sitting round together one night,' Pete says. 'John suddenly asked me, "Don't you feel like having a woman around again?" Then he said, "I've met this woman called Yoko. She's Japanese." Yoko came over and John took her off to listen to his tapes. I just went to bed.

'When I got up the next morning, John was sitting in the

kitchen, eating boiled eggs. He said he hadn't been to bed. Then he said, "Will you do us a favour? Would you get us a house?" I said "What do you want a house for?" "To live in," he said. "With Yoko. This is it." '

When Cyn' walked in to Kenwood unexpectedly a few days later, she found John and Yoko seated together, with the curtains drawn, in a sea of dirty cups and plates. Both looked nonchalantly up at her and said: 'Oh, hi . . .' A pair of Japanese slippers, standing neatly on an upstairs landing, opened the poor, gentle, shortsighted girl's eyes at long last.

The Beatles first became aware of Yoko at Abbey Road studios. They could hardly do otherwise. She did not stay, as was proper —as was womanly—in the control-room audience. She came down into the arena, settling herself close to John, behind the neck of his guitar. A 20-year-old bond and brotherhood shattered around that small, black, resolute shape.

John was besotted by her. The others had never seen him like this with any woman before; never showing affection, as he did to Yoko, without embarrassment or inhibition. The others exchanged glances, but said nothing. They could not have survived so long as Beatles without a deep tolerance of one another's fancies and blind spots. They expected John to tire of this soon, the way he tired of everything. They tried not to notice Yoko, and referred to her obliquely as 'Flavour of the Month'.

She was still there, however, as Apple grew and its divisions multiplied. She had left her husband now to live with John, at Kenwood first, then in London, at Ringo Starr's Montagu Square flat. Pete Shotton drove them around, glad to have been superseded as John's 'personal assistant'. Such was Yoko's introduction to Sir Joseph Lockwood, the EMI chairman, at a boardroom lunch with all four Beatles, Neil Aspinall and Ron Kass. In the visitor's book after her name, John wrote 'female'. 'This little white figure followed the Beatles in,' Sir Joseph says. 'She sat further down the table with my assistant, but hardly said a word all through the meal. Afterwards, my assistant told me she'd had a tape-recorder running all the time.'

Her first night with John at Kenwood had begun an artistic partnership that was to perplex and enrage the world. When Yoko first arrived John played her all the experimental tapes he had made, knowing they were useless for Beatles albums. After the final tape, Yoko said, 'Let's make one of our own.' It was only as dawn broke that they got around to first making love. As intoxicating to John as that little bird-like body was its instant, audacious challenge: 'Let's do it.'

In June, their first collaboration went on public show. It was a sculpture consisting of two acorns, one labelled 'John by Yoko

Ono', the other 'Yoko by John Lennon, Sometime in May 1968'. The acorns, symbolising peace and simplicity, were to be buried as an 'event' at the National Sculpture Exhibition in the grounds of Coventry Cathedral.

John and Yoko, both dressed in white, drove to Coventry in John's white Rolls, accompanied by their newly-appointed 'Art adviser', Anthony Fawcett. Outside the Cathedral they were met by a Canon, who informed them that objects could not be buried in consecrated ground and that, in any case, acorns were 'not sculpture'. Yoko flew into an impressive rage, demanding that leading British sculptors be instantly telephoned to vouch for her artistic integrity. Someone actually got through to Henry Moore's house, but he was out. As a compromise, the acorns were buried on unhallowed ground, under an iron garden seat. Within a week, they had been dug up and taken by Beatle fans as souvenirs. Two more acorns were buried; a security firm mounted 24-hour guard on the seat that marked the spot.

On 18 July, a stage adaptation of John's book *In His Own Write* opened at the London Old Vic theatre. The play had been heavily censored by the Lord Chamberlain's office, for its blasphemous reference to 'Almighty Griff', and disrespect to such world statesmen as 'Pregnant De Gaulle' and 'Sir Alice Doubtless-Whom'. Fleet Street, by now perceiving a still racier story, were out in force in the summer downpour. When John arrived with Yoko and Neil Aspinall, he was surrounded by Press raincoats and challenging cries of: 'Where's your wife?'

The girls who stood outside Abbey Road studios—and now also outside 3 Savile Row—made no secret of their fierce disapproval. 'Every time we saw Yoko, we shouted awful things,' Margo says. '"Yellow!" "Chink!" Subtle things like that. We all felt so sorry for Cynthia. Once, outside Abbey Road, we'd got this bunch of yellow roses to give Yoko. We handed them to her thorns first. Yoko took them and backed all the way down the stairs, thanking us. She hadn't realised they were meant to be an insult. Nor did John. He turned back and said, "Well, it's about *time* someone did something decent to her."'

In July, John's first Art exhibition opened in London, at the fashionable Robert Fraser Gallery. Its title, inspired by the hackneyed message on British street maps, was 'You Are Here': it acknowledged its motive force with a dedication 'To Yoko from John with love'. It began with the release of 360 white balloons into the sky above Mayfair. Each balloon bore the printed message: 'You are here. Please write to John Lennon, c/o the Robert Fraser Gallery'.

To reach the exhibition, one had to walk through a display of charity street collection boxes in the shapes of pandas, puppets and crippled children. The only other items were a circular piece of white canvas, lettered, 'You are here', and John's hat lying on the floor, its upturned brim inscribed: 'For the artist. Thank You.' When some Art students sarcastically contributed a rusty bicycle, John immediately put that on show also.

The critics were scornful. They said what was to be many times repeated—that if John had not been a Beatle, he would not have dared put such rubbish on show. In this, at least, the critics erred. So long as he was a Beatle, he never dared do anything.

Many people who picked up the white balloons responded to John's invitation to write to him. Their letters, for the most part, combined racial slurs against Yoko with advice concerning the sanctity of wedlock. 'I suppose I've spoiled me image,' John said. 'People want me to stay in their own bag. They want me to be lovable but I was never that. Even at school I was just "Lennon".'

Cynthia, meanwhile, had found herself cauterised from his life with a ruthlessness possible only to one with many competing servants and courtiers. Magic Alex was deputed to travel to Italy, where Cyn', her mother and Julian were staying, and announce that John intended to divorce her. 'Alex was waiting for me one night when I got back to the hotel. He told me John was going to take Julian off me and send me back to my mother in Hoylake.

'When I got back to England, I tried to have a meeting with him and discuss things. The only way I could get in touch with John was to make an appointment with him through Peter Brown at Apple. And when I finally did meet him, Yoko was there. He insisted she should stay while we were talking.'

John, at the outset, intended to divorce Cynthia for adultery supposedly committed in Italy. According to his Aunt Mimi, he was 'mortified' to think that Cyn', after all these years, had decided to be unfaithful. The petition was dropped when it became clear that Yoko had become pregnant. Cynthia sued for adultery, and was granted a decree nisi in November 1968.

A few weeks earlier, as Cyn' was alone and helplessly contemplating the future, Paul McCartney had paid her a surprise visit. With him he brought a song he had written on his way in the car —it was for Julian, he said, although the title was Hey Jude. He gave Cynthia a single red rose, then said, in the old carefree Liverpool way, 'Well, how about it, Cyn'? How about you and me getting married now?' She was moved that Paul should think of her, and grateful for his gesture of friendship and encouragement.

Sometimes, in a surge of ecstasy, the girls on watch outside 7 Cavendish Avenue would approach the black security gates and buzz the Entryphone. As a rule, the voice that answered would belong to Jane Asher, Paul's long-time girl friend. The voice was serious but tolerant and always polite. So Jane was, too, on the hundreds of occasions when she answered the front door. The girls appreciated that civility and patience. Far from resenting Jane, they felt their anger was in deserving hands. They were Jane's admirers in a small way, as well as Paul's. They grew their hair long like hers, washing it only in Breck shampoo, because that was the brand Jane advertised on television; pressing it out straight on their mother's ironing boards.

Everyone close to Paul liked Jane and acknowledged her beneficial influence. For, in her clear-voiced way, she was as down to earth as any Liverpool girl. Alone of the entire female race, she refused to pamper and worship Paul. If Jane disagreed or disapproved, she said so. She could curb his ego, his use of charm as a weapon—rather as John curbed the syrup in his music—and yet do it in a way that commanded respect and a maturing love.

That the relationship had lasted five years was due principally to Jane's skill in avoiding the worst of the Beatle madness, and her insistence on following her own successful film and stage career. When Paul and she met, it was with the freshness and appreciation of new lovers. Paul's farm, near Campbeltown, Argyllshire, was the haven they retreated to. Paul had done the painting and decorating, even knocked up some rudimentary furniture. There, in the uncurious hills, they walked and rode; they talked and read by lamplight and washed in the kitchen sink, and Jane cooked appetising vegetarian dishes. Each time they left, she would pack the remnants thriftily away in plastic bags to await their return.

For Paul, it was the best of two highly pleasurable worlds. His life with Jane provided domesticity, and the refinement and social standing he craved. In her absence, his life reverted to that of Britain's most hotly-pursued bachelor. His casual affairs were conducted with such diplomacy and discretion that Jane never suspected anything. So it might have continued but for a theatre tour that ended prematurely, and a witness who suddenly found herself with a legitimate reason to press Paul's Entryphone.

Margo Stevens, the girl from Cleethorpes, was just beginning her second year of standing outside 7 Cavendish Avenue. She preferred to begin her vigil late at night, when the picket was thinning or absent altogether. She would arrive at about 10 pm, always with some gift for Paul—fruit or a miniature of whisky —on the offchance of handing it to him as he came home late from the studios or a club. She had been standing there so long, Paul vaguely recognised her now. She knew how to open the security gates by kicking them, and had done so once for him when he could not find his key. Latterly, on the recommendation of his housekeeper, Rosie, he had even trusted her to take Martha the sheepdog for walks on Hampstead Heath.

'It was a summer day: we were all standing there as usual,' Margo says. 'Jane was on tour with a play, and Paul brought this American girl home. He waved to us as they drove in. Later on another car turned into Cavendish Avenue—it was Jane. She'd come back to London earlier than she was supposed to. We did our best to warn Paul. Someone went to the Entryphone, buzzed it and yelled, "Look out! Jane's coming!" Paul didn't believe it. "Ah, pull the other one," he said.

'Jane went into the house. A bit later on, she came storming out again and drove away. Later still, a big estate car drew up. It was Jane's mother. She went inside and started bringing out all kinds of things that were obviously Jane's—cooking pots and big cushions and pictures.

'We all thought after that they must have finished with each other for good. But the next day, a whole crowd of us were in Hyde Park. Who did we run into but Paul and Jane. They were walking along, holding hands and eating ice lollies.'

Early in 1967, Jane went on tour in America again with the Bristol Old Vic company. Apart from Paul's visit, to celebrate her 21st birthday, they were separated for almost five months. When Jane returned, she found Paul deeply involved in LSD and the visions that composed Sergeant Pepper. She herself would have nothing to do with acid, and said so bluntly. Paul could not convince her of what she was missing.

Brian Epstein's death was a heavy blow to Jane. She, too, found comfort in the Maharishi: she went with Paul to Rishikesh and felt the experience to have been rewarding. With LSD banished, their understanding returned. Paul, at long last, made ready to commit himself. They announced their engagement at a McCartney family party on Christmas Day, 1967.

The following June, they were back up North for the wedding of Paul's younger brother, Michael. Jane opened in a new play that month and Paul, as usual, attended the opening night. All between them seemed normal until mid-July, when *Yellow Submarine* received its gala premier. Paul arrived alone at the cinema and at the party which followed. Two days later, on a television chat show, Jane was asked a casual question about their wedding plans. She replied that Paul had broken the engagement off and they had parted.

Hey Jude, the song which brought such comfort to Cynthia Lennon, was Paul's expression of his own deep personal unhappiness. The words, for once, were not facile and neat; it was a song written honestly, in pain. It moved even John Lennon as no song of Paul's ever had before. 'Hey Jude, don't be afraid, you were made to/go out and get her', seemed to John to be a message of encouragement for Yoko and him. 'I took it very personally,' he admitted. ' "Ah, it's me!" I said when Paul played it. "No," he said, "it's *me*." I said, "Check. We're both going through the same bit." '

Paul did not lack female company for long. It was as if, among the more brazen young females of the Western Hemisphere, a brisk 'Tally Ho!' had sounded. First in the bold-eyed field came Francie Schwartz, a New Yorker of vaguely cultural leanings who, having talked her way past Apple's outer defences, enjoyed a confident, though brief, stay at Cavendish Avenue. Paul had a weakness for that type of American girl in whom toughness so often coexists with naivetée, and urban thrust with provincial prissiness.

A year or so earlier, another New Yorker, Linda Eastman, had visited Brian Epstein's Stratton Street office to show her photographic portfolio of Rock musicians. Peter Brown, who dealt with her, had already met her in New York: he remembered her, not as a photographer so much as a backstage habituée, at New York concert halls like the Fillmore East. 'She was just an ordinary girl, like so many you saw around then. She'd arrived in London, saying she wanted to photograph the Beatles. I let her in on the Sergeant Pepper session, which was a big thing because only 14 photographers were allowed from the whole world's Press.'

Peter next met Linda one night when he was with Paul McCartney and some other Rock figures at the Bag O' Nails Club. He takes credit for having introduced Paul to the lean, blonde American, not quite a girl, with her wide-set cheekbones and strangely-hooded eyes. 'That was it,' Peter Brown says. 'The two of them just went off together.'

Linda Eastman was not, as generally supposed, and as she herself sometimes hinted a member of the Eastman-Kodak dynasty. Her father Lee, a New York lawyer, had taken the surname to replace one more directly announcing his Jewish immigrant antecedents. Had he not done so, the girl who caught Paul's eye at the Bag O' Nails Club would have been introduced to him by her ancestral name of Epstein.

Lee Eastman ran a successful law practice, specialising in music copyright and also handling certain celebrated American painters. His wife, Louise, was independently wealthy through her family connection with Linders' department stores. Linda and her brother John grew up in the affluent environment of a house in Scarsdale and a Park Avenue apartment. Linda became accustomed to meeting the celebrities who were her father's clients, among them Hoagy Carmichael and—she later claimed —Hopalong Cassidy.

Louise Eastman died in an air crash when Linda was 18. It was in the aftermath of her mother's death that she embarked on the career which was to disturb and displease her elegant, conservative father. She married a geologist named John See, moved with him to Colorado and gave birth to a daughter, Heather. The marriage failed; Linda returned to New York and decided on a career in photography. She worked as an assistant on *Town and Country* magazine. Her real forte, however, was knowing Rock musicians. She became a familiar face, carrying cameras, at the Fillmore East and at photocalls by bands flying in from London. Her ability as a photographer was not highly esteemed. Rather, it seemed a quick route to superstar company. Her subjects included Mick Jagger, Stevie Winwood and Warren Beatty.

She did not see Paul between the Sergeant Pepper session and May 1968, when he came with John to New York to inaugurate Apple. Linda was at the launch party with her journalist friend, Lilian Roxon. On Lilian's advice, she slipped Paul her telephone number. They met at Nat Weiss's New York flat and afterwards in Los Angeles. Paul returned to London but a few weeks later, telephoned Linda and asked her to come and join him.

He brought her home to Cavendish Avenue in his Mini-Cooper, late one summer night. Margo Stevens was on watch by the gates, as always. 'A few of us were there. We had the feeling something was going to happen. Paul didn't take the Mini inside the way he usually did—he parked it on the road and he and Linda walked right past us. They went inside and we stood there, watching different lights in the house go on and off.

'In the end, the light went on in the Mad Room, at the top of the house, where he kept all his music stuff and his toys. Paul opened the window and called out to us, "Are you still down there?" "Yes," we said. He must have been really happy that night. He sat on the windowsill with his acoustic guitar and sang Blackbird to us, standing down there in the dark.'

Linda, at first, did not arouse resentment so much as bewilderment. She seemed so utterly and determinedly unlike Paul's usual taste in girls. The Apple secretaries, back-combed and miniskirted, stared with frank incomprehension at Linda's shapeless dresses, flat-heeled tennis shoes, even ankle socks. She speedily raised the hackles of Margo and the others, both at Cavendish Avenue and on the Savile Row front steps. 'We could tell she viewed us as a threat,' Margo says. 'Every time they both came out, Linda would cling to Paul's arm as much as to say, "*I've* got him now." None of us could understand what he saw in her. She was hairier than he was.'

What Paul saw was initially tinged by his own ever-present social ambition. Linda, for all her outward unkemptness, had the aura of Manhattan's aristocracy—of Saks, Fifth Avenue, imported Shetland and horseriding in Central Park. She was certainly beautiful, though in a cautious, elusive way that no camera would ever quite authenticate. Most of all, she idolised and pampered him in precisely the way Jane had always refused to do. Gripping his arm, she would gaze at him with awe. She would say in his hearing what an honour it would be to bear his children.

Her daughter, Heather, helped to cement the bond between them. Paul had always adored children. His final parting with Jane arose from their disagreement over when to start a family. After meeting Heather, an insecure, rather lonely six-year-old, he insisted she be brought to live at Cavendish Avenue. He delighted in playing with her, reading stories and drawing cartoons for her and singing her to sleep at night.

Linda, meanwhile, was bringing about changes in Paul that Margo and the other girls viewed with deep resentment. They knew, from their illicit journeys round the house, how fastidious he had formerly been. 'He used to shave every day, he always wore fresh clothes and he smelled—delicious. Rosie, the housekeeper, told us he insisted on having clean sheets on his bed every night.

'We heard from Rosie how different Linda was. We hardly recognised Paul once she'd got hold of him. He started to put on weight—and he got so scruffy. I'll swear he didn't wash his hair for three weeks at a time. He never shaved, never wore anything but this old Navy overcoat. He could go on the bus down to Apple, and no one would recognise him. Some of us thought we saw him in Oxford Street one day. We followed this real tramp in a Navy overcoat all the way down Oxford Street, thinking he was Paul.'

In May, the Beatles had met at Abbey Road to begin their first album for release on their own bright, crisp, confident Apple label. The project, at that stage, seemed just as brightly simple and appetising. John and Paul between them had a backlog of some 30 songs, mostly written during their stay in India. George had been earnestly composing; even Ringo had a tune of his own to offer. With so much material at hand, it was decided to use a format common enough in Classical recording but unprecedented in Pop. The collection would appear as two LP discs packed into a single dual-envelope sleeve. Not even Sergeant Pepper started in such an atmosphere of energy and abundance.

Things began to go wrong on the very first day: when John Lennon walked into Studio One, his arm protectively encircling a small, white-clad, frizzy-haired and heart-sinkingly familiar figure. He had not, it seemed, grown tired of Yoko Ono. He was, if anything, more incomprehensibly obsessed by her. As before, Yoko showed no awareness of studio protocol. She settled herself among the Beatles, cutting herself and John off from the other three by the neck of his guitar. His hair centre-parted like hers, his eyes aslant behind pebble glasses, he was even starting to look a little Japanese.

The awkwardness deepened as John and Paul strummed over to each other the finished songs they proposed the Beatles should record. This interchange, so often the flashpoint for brilliance, now produced only non-commital nods. To Paul, John's new music seemed harsh, unmelodious and deliberately provocative. One did not have to look far for the reason why. It sat beside him, huddled close and nodding in an alien irregular way. John, for his part, found Paul's new songs cloyingly sweet and bland. For the first time, Lennon and McCartney saw no bridge between them.

The album that resulted was, therefore, not the work of a group. It was the work of soloists; of separate egos, arguing for prominence. Paul and John each recorded his own songs in his own way, without advice or criticism from the other. George —apart from his own individual sessions—withdrew into a resigned neutrality. Ringo, in his acoustic hutch, bent his drum-sticks as far as possible with the ever-changing currents. Sometimes, Ringo did not even bother to be there.

From John came music that meandered inconclusively among sideshows of resentment and defiance. There was Sexy Sadie, his revenge on the Maharishi—whom at the last minute, possibly still dreading the guru's wrath, he decided not to mention by name. There was Revolution, his half-embarrassed rabble-rouser. Happiness Is A Warm Gun, inspired by an American firearms magazine, swiped in the approximate direction of the Vietnam holocaust. Glass Onion satirised over-earnest Beatle fans with cross-references to earlier lyrics, even a false clue; 'The Walrus was Paul'. The straightforward Rock pieces, like Yer Blues, were one-dimensional and charmless, the playing turgid, the singing harsh and somehow vindictive. Nowhere was his conversion more evident than in the track called Revolution 9, a formless length of electronic noise interspersed with vocal gibberish, which Paul—and everyone else—tried unavailingly to cut from the finished album.

Paul's tracks were neat, polished, tuneful and, in their way, as unbalanced and incomplete—Martha My Dear, a song for his sheepdog; Rocky Raccoon, an unfinished Western doodle; Honey Pie, a glutinous Twenties pastiche. In each, somehow, the most noticeable element was John's missing 'middle eight'. Only in Blackbird, briefly and beautifully, did Paul's gift succeed in editing itself. Back In The USSR, too, was totally successful, a Chuck Berry-style rocker with Beach Boy harmonies which briefly restored the old familiar grin to John's face. In that, as in a few more songs to come, their matchless combination somehow survived in an individual effort. Paul could have written John's song, Julia. It was his memorial, 10 years too late, to the mother whose laughter gave the timbre to his own. But Julia in the song bore another name: 'Ocean Child'.

It was while Lennon fought McCartney, on Ob-la-di, Ob-la-da and Revolution 9, that George Harrison, suddenly and surprisingly gathered strength as a composer and performer. His tally of four songs on the finished 30-track list was the highest John and Paul had ever permitted. As their joint control dwindled, so George's presence increased: his voice, gathering confidence, sounded somehow like John's *and* Paul's. His Savoy Truffle was, after Back In the USSR, the album's best piece of Rock and Roll. Piggies, a black nursery song against meat-eaters was mordantly humorous. Best of all was While My Guitar Gently Weeps, a heavy rock lament, with searing guitar phrases played by George's friend Eric Clapton, of Cream. Clapton could not believe at first that the Beatles needed anyone but themselves.

All this happened amid a constant drip of argument and bad feeling which, strangely enough, took heaviest toll on the Beatle whose placid temper was so often a strength and rallying-point. Ringo, halfway through the sessions, emerged from behind his acoustic screens, looking tired and morose. He was playing badly, he said, and generally 'not getting through'. To John first, then to Paul, he announced he was resigning. The others, tactfully, did not try to stop him. A week at home with Maureen and Zak and his new baby son, Jason, restored him to his old equanimity. When he returned to Abbey Road, Paul and George had covered his drums with Welcome Back messages and flowers.

They had been working on the, still untitled, double album for five months. For all that time, by night as well as day, Margo Stevens and the other girls had waited and watched the Abbey Road front steps. 'We stuck it out through all weathers,' Margo says. 'We were as tough as old boots in the end. When they came in to record, we'd sleep out on the pavement. People who lived in Abbey Road saw us when they came home from work at night. In the morning when they left for work, we were still there. I got so tough, I could sleep in all weathers. When I woke up one morning, there was snow all over me.'

Margo, on these all night watches, shared a sleeping bag with Carole Bedford, a Texan girl to whom George Harrison had once actually said 'Hello'. 'Normally the Beatles would go in to record around midnight,' Carole says. 'They'd finish around 4 am. So we could count on at least four hours sleep. But once they all came out suddenly at about 2.30. Margo and I woke up—we tried to stand up but we couldn't undo the zipper on our sleeping bag. Both of us were hopping round the pavement, shrieking and trying to undo the zipper while the Beatles stood there, laughing at us.'

George Martin had done all he could as adviser and editor. To Martin, the 30 songs, or song fragments, on tape reeked of the argument and self-indulgence that had gone into their making. Vainly he pleaded with John and Paul to drop the double album idea; to lose the scribble, like Goodnight and Revolution 9; to cut out all the linking, meaningless shouts and murmurs and pull the 14 best titles together for a Beatle album like Revolver, packed end-to-end with quality. The answer was no. On that, at least, all four agreed.

'One night, we were all outside—we could tell they'd nearly finished,' Margo says. 'It got to about three in the morning. We could see John through a window, playing with a light cord hanging from the ceiling. "Come *on*, boys," we were all saying, "it *has* been five months." Then they all came out and down the steps. It was all over.'

As a tribute to their five-month wait, Margo and the others were then taken into the empty Studio One, to hear a playback of Back In the USSR, and to pick up and take home as cherished souvenirs the apple cores and crisp packets littering the floor.

The doorman at Apple was a thickset, heavily-genteel young Cockney named Jimmy Clark. He was, so people said, a discovery of Peter Brown's. He wore a stiff City collar, tight-fitting trousers and an exquisitely-cut dove-grey morning coat. On fine days he would bask on the Apple front step, his hands in his coat tails, watching the girls who eternally watched the house. His job was to prevent unauthorised entry via the front door or the area steps to the basement studio. He would block the rush with his broad, dove-grey shoulders and repel it with his large, starch-cuffed, shooing hands. To the resultant boos and insults, Jimmy Clark would grin and bridle delightedly like a cat under the grooming brush.

It was, even so—as hundreds discovered—quite easy to enter the Apple house. Provided that one arrived by taxi and that one carried no banner or other sign of Beatle fanaticism, one was generally assumed to have legitimate business with Apple Corps. The girls fell back, unenviously. Jimmy Clark sardonically stood aside. The white front door yielded to a gentle push.

The front hall was much as in any half-million pound Georgian house. To the right sat a receptionist, instructed, like all Apple staff, to believe in the bona fide of all visitors. Into a telephone, white as the White Album, she would murmur the information that so-and-so was here. She would then smile. 'OK, you can go up. You know the way, don't you?' Everyone knew the way, up the green-carpeted stairs, past the framed Gold

Discs, too numerous to count, and the soft-lit oil painting of two honey-coloured lion cubs.

One did not, if one were scrupulous, try any of the doors of offices on the first floor. One climbed on, past more Gold Discs, to Derek Taylor's second floor Press and Publicity office. This room, in the mornings, was bright with sun and furniture polish. In the late afternoon, it grew dark and bewildering. The only light came under the window blinds and from two projectors which beamed a psychedelic 'light show' of bright-coloured, writhing spermatazoa shapes, travelling in perpetuity across the opposite wall. Though dark and filled with obstructions, the room was exceedingly busy. One crossed the projector beam, conscious of many heads turning, like anxious topiary hedges, in the gloom.

None but the specially important or importunate caller immediately approached Derek Taylor's desk. If one were merely a journalist, one sat initially on a small outlying sofa, behind Taylor's second assistant, Carol Paddon, and next to a tray of water into which several plastic birds endlessly dipped their beaks. Presently, one might move across to the small white button-backed sofa that led directly into Derek Taylor's presence. Already, one would have been offered tea, Scotch and Coke, a cigarette or perhaps something stronger. As each of Taylor's visitors got up and left, one wriggled towards him another few inches. Eventually one would be seated immediately to the right of his huge scallop-backed wicker chair. The slender man with his neat hair and moustache and quiet, discreet voice, would lean over on the wicker arm that was to become split and broken with hours of leaning and listening.

Press Officers by their very nature pursue journalists. It was Derek Taylor's unique accomplishment to be a Press Officer whom journalists pursued. Journalists from every newspaper, magazine, wire service and radio and TV network in the Western world pursued him, as a means of access to the Western world's longest-running headline story. They pursued him also because Derek Taylor, strangely enough, was not a monster. He was amiable, sympathetic, polite to a degree which would ultimately seem miraculous. As an ex-journalist himself, he believed that journalists should get their story. It was simply a matter of time, he always said; and of choosing a moment when one or other 'Fab' would be amenable.

Two side doors connected the Press Office with other Apple departments. On Taylor's right was the door to a downstairs kitchen where two Cordon Bleu-trained debutantes supplied meals to the directors and executive staff, and refreshments to all. On the left was a cupboard, presided over by Taylor's hippy assistant, Richard, and popularly known as the Black Room. Its contents were manifold. It had been used initially as a dumping ground for the entire—and entirely-unread—cache of novels, poems, synopses, plans, blueprints submitted from all over the world as projects deserving support by the Apple Foundation for the Arts. Several thousand manuscripts lay there, forgotten as absolutely as the nearby row of high fashion shoes which Derek Taylor had brought home from Hollywood. What the Black Room principally contained were boxes of LP records by Apple artists; cases of wines, spirits and soft drinks, and cartons of Benson and Hedges cigarettes.

'Press', under Derek Taylor's tolerant regime, was a term of almost infinite elasticity. It described virtually anyone who came to Apple with the ghost of an excuse for sharing in the Beatles' artistic Utopia. It encompassed the sculptress who wanted money to produce 'tactile' figures in leather and oil; and the French Canadian girl, frequently prised from the basement windows, who wanted money to get her teeth capped. It corralled in the same potentially creative ambit, a showman who wanted money to do Punch and Judy shows on Brighton beach, an Irish tramp who wanted money to burn toy dolls with Napalm as an anti-war gesture in the King's Road.

It encompassed, most of all, the hippies, who simply wanted money and who flocked to Savile Row in every type of flowing garment and every degree of dream-eyed incoherence. Several times each week, the call would come to Apple from Heathrow Airport's Immigration department, announcing that yet another Beautiful Person had arrived from California with beads and bells, but without funds or definite accommodation, to look up his four brothers in Karma and Sergeant Pepper. At 3 Savile Row, an entire San Francisco 'family', complete with breast-fed baby, waited to accompany John and Yoko to found an alternative universe in the Fiji Isles. There was also 'Stocky', who said nothing, but perched all day on a Press Office filing cabinet, drawing pictures of genitalia. He was harmless enough, as Derek Taylor always said.

The spirit of Apple in those days is best summed up, perhaps, in a moment when Taylor's desk intercom chirped yet again. 'Derek,' the receptionist's voice said, 'Adolf Hitler is in Reception.'

'Oh, Christ,' Taylor said. 'Not that asshole again. OK, send him up.'

It was a consequence of the hippy age's mingling superstition and vanity that young, fashionable people, in the young, fashionable music industry of the late Sixties, endowed themselves freely with what amounted to psychic powers. Judgement of a person was made according to what vibrations—or 'vibes'—he gave off by his presence and mood. So the people who came to 3 Savile Row were judged not by the legitimacy or sincerity of their purpose but by their 'good' or 'bad' vibes. A person visiting Apple in a beard and sandals, holding a lighted joss stick, portended 'good vibes'. A lawyer, Tax official or policeman portended 'bad vibes'. Colloquys of people, such as board meetings, created vibes proportionately stronger. It was mainly under the influence of these ever-changing, ever-unpredictable vibes that 3 Savile Row, during the next year and a half, alternately glowed with happiness or grew pale with unimagined terror.

To start with, the vibes were nearly all good. Hey Jude, the Beatles' most successful single ever, had sold almost three million copies for their own Apple label. Those Were The Days, by Mary Hopkin, the little Welsh girl Paul McCartney had taken up, was Number One in Britain and Number Two in America. Apple's other new signings, James Taylor, Jackie Lomax, the Iveys—and, a 'prestige' acquisition, the Modern Jazz Quartet—were all receiving an energetic and expensive launch as the Beatles' favoured protégés.

There had been some bad vibes, admittedly, over the Apple boutique, The Fool and their extravagance, and the final, ugly scrimmage for give-away merchandise. Nor were the vibes entirely amiable downwind of the house, among Savile Row's bespoke tailors and outfitters. Dukes and Bishops in their fitting-rooms looked on appalled at the day-long riot, the banners and chanting, the shrieks whenever a white Rolls Royce appeared. But, in general, the West End treated Apple with indulgence. The scene around the front steps made even passersby, with bowler hats and rolled umbrellas, smile.

Best of all were the all-powerful vibes given off by the Beatles' own frequent presence in the Georgian town house, directing their luscious new empire with a zest that infected each member of their ever-multiplying staff. Though largely invisible within Apple, their presence was unmistakable. There would be the commotion on the first floor landing, the tightly-shut door to Neil Aspinall's office, or Peter Brown's. There would be the wakefulness surging suddenly through the Press Office as Derek Taylor answered his intercom. There were the familiar kitchen orders—a one-egg omelette for Ringo; cheese and cucumber sandwiches for George; for John and Yoko, brown rice, steamed vegetables, chocolate cake and caviare.

Bad vibes from the outside made their first major strike on the afternoon of 18 October. Laurie McCaffery, the deep-voiced telephonist who had followed NEMS down from Liverpool, put through a call to Neil Aspinall from someone who declined to give his name. In a moment, John Lennon's voice came on.

'Imagine your worst paranoia,' John said. 'Well—it's here.' He and Yoko were in Police custody, charged with possessing cannabis.

The 'bust' had happened shortly before midday, at Ringo's Montagu Square flat. Six policemen, one policewoman and a 'sniffer dog' had entered by search warrant, and brought to light approximately one-and-a-half ounces of cannabis. Detective Sergeant Norman Pilcher had preferred the additional charge of wilful obstruction of the officers in their search. John and Yoko were now under arrest at Marylebone Police Station.

The Beatles, six months earlier, had announced they were giving up drugs: what they meant was that they were giving up making a fuss about them. The habit continued, not as a key to the Universe—merely a habit. All Rock stars took drugs. It was part of life's endless ritual; a way of using up life's endless money and spare time. Exclusive hybrid substances, compounded into pretty pills and pellets, purveyed by dealers with the very best vibes, were among the natural amenities of the Apple pantry. 'Joints', numerous as teacups, circulated democratically between bosses and office boys. A certain secretary had been drilled to tip the entire stock down the Ladies' lavatory should the Police at Savile Row station, 300 yards away, ever decide to pay Apple a visit. Another girl specialised in 'hash cakes', which she would bake at home and bring to Apple by the batch. She left some out to cool at home one day, and her grandmother accidentally sampled one. The old lady remained unconscious for the next 48 hours.

That John should have cannabis in his possession was no surprise. The surprise was that the Drug Squad should have decided to nail him. Even after the LSD revelations in 1967, no attempt had been made to 'bust' the Beatles. It was even rumoured that, at the famous Mick Jagger arrest, one of the Beatles had also been present but had been quietly ushered from the scene. Detective Sergeant Pilcher's five-man squad was deeply symbolic of what 'vibes' now emanated from the British Establishment. There was to be no more Beatle Lucky Charm.

Paul McCartney at once sought the help of Apple's most powerful ally, Sir Joseph Lockwood, Chairman of EMI. 'As soon as Paul contacted me, I rang Marylebone Police Station,' Sir Joseph says. 'John picked up the 'phone. " 'Ello," he said, "Sergeant Lennon here." "Now stop all that," I said. "You've got to plead guilty. We'll get Lord Goodman on it. Oh no, we can't: he hates drugs. Anyway, you must plead guilty." '

After a preliminary Court appearance, John and Yoko were released on bail. They emerged from Marylebone Magistrates Court into a forest of Press cameras and a 300-strong, palpably gloating crowd. John's slight figure, hemmed in by scowling

Police helmets, hugged Yoko tightly to him. Though his martyrdom was self-inflicted and self-aggravated, there began to be something almost chivalrous in the way his slight body shielded Yoko's even slighter one.

The case was due to be heard in full on 27 November. That date had special irony for a Press Office bracing itself to deal with another John Lennon event whose 'vibes' had already shown themselves practically combustible.

John had been determined from the start that Apple Records should be a medium for his and Yoko's experiments in avant garde electronic music. The first album they had produced together was now ready for release. Entitled Unfinished Music No. 1—Two Virgins, it consisted mostly of the tapes they had made during their first night together at Kenwood. Early in October, John had handed to Jeremy Banks, Apple's 'photographic co-ordinator', the picture he wanted used as the Two Virgins sleeve. Banks immediately shut it in his desk drawer: for some days afterwards, he could be seen surreptitiously peeping at it. The picture had been taken by John himself in the Montagu Square basement, on a delayed action shutter. It showed him with Yoko, their arms entwined, both—as words swiftly circulated—'stark bollock naked'.

The vibes were precisely as expected. EMI flatly refused to distribute Two Virgins unless the sleeve were changed. John appealed direct to Sir Joseph Lockwood, but this time 'Sir Joe' stood firm. 'What on earth do you want to do it for?' I asked them. Yoko said, 'It's Art.' 'In that case,' I said, 'why not show Paul in the nude? He's so much better looking. Or why not use a statue from one of the parks?'

EMI did not, however, disdain the business of manufacturing Two Virgins. British distribution was given to Track Records, a label set up by Rock's earliest and truest anarchists, The Who. A nation growing bored with 'full frontal' nudity in films and on the stage still could not permit two circlets of pubic hair to be depicted on shop merchandise. Each copy of Two Virgins was handed to its purchaser in a brown paper envelope. The same deal was done for America, via a label called Tetragrammation. Thirty thousand copies, awaiting distribution in a Newark warehouse, were confiscated by the New Jersey Police.

From here on, good and bad vibes bombarded Apple Corps with even greater capriciousness than the London weather.

On 22 November, the double album was released whose enmities and unevenness faded in the breathtaking novelty and simplicity of its appearance. The sleeve was pure, plain, shiny, unprecedented white. Its only title appeared on a smallish, slightly crooked diestamp: The Beatles. It was the very ultimate in minimal magnitude. Each copy bore a serial number, making a select limited edition of the first two million pressed. On opening the two-sleeve book, one read only tasteful austerity: on one side the 30 titles, on the other; four separated portraits.

The reviews were of snow-blinded ecstasy. Tony Palmer, in the *Observer*, produced his famous, very foolish statement that Lennon and McCartney stood revealed as 'the greatest songwriters since Schubert'. Palmer's review, more than any other, perpetrated the belief that the White Album (so its public soon renamed it) represented conscious artistic enterprise; that, by going to the opposite extreme of Sergeant Pepper, the Beatles had touched a new, stark, self-surpassing virtuosity. That Sergeant Pepper's abiding quality was disciplined and that the White Album's was disorganisation, quite escaped Tony Palmer's ravished ears. The quality most evident throughout, he wrote, was 'simple happiness'. Even Revolution 9 could not qualify his belief that the Beatles dwelt on 'shores of the imagination others have not yet sighted'.

The day the White Album was released, Yoko lost the baby she had been expecting. Her room at Queen Charlotte's Hospital had a second bed in which John himself lay, propped up with pillows. Throughout the emergency that ended in Yoko's miscarriage, he refused to leave her. When the second bed was wanted, he spent each night in a sleeping bag beside her on the floor.

Their case was heard a week later at Marylebone Magistrates Court. John pleaded guilty, absolving Yoko of all connection with the cannabis. He was fined £150, with 20 guineas costs. On the charge of wilful obstruction, no evidence was offered. His counsel, Martin Polden, entreated leniency for someone who had given pleasure to millions with his music. 'An ounce-and-a-half of compassion,' Mr. Polden said, was not too much to ask.

It was with enforced irony on that same day that Apple released the album which could not be advertised in any music paper and could be bought only like dirty books in a plain brown paper bag. Within each bag, the Two Virgins, their arms entwined, proclaimed their final commitment. The response, if not disgusted, was ribald; if not ribald, mystified. There seemed no good reason why the public should have to look at the genitalia of a 28-year-old man, however famous, and of a small Japanese woman with pointed yet pendulous breasts. To the eyes of 1968, at least, bloodshot with 'porn' and 'streakers' and legitimised smut, there seemed no earthly reason.

The success of Apple Records was unquestionable. But what of the other divisions? Six months had passed since Paul McCartney announced that wide-ranging creative prospectus. Apple Films had yet to make a film. The Apple Press had yet to publish a book. Apple Retail, after the boutique disaster, was virtually moribund. The Apple Foundation for the Arts was something people preferred not to recollect. Occasionally, when Richard diLello went into the Black Room and pulled out another case of wine, the huge, unread pile of manuscripts would totter and slide a little, then once more settle to its eternal rest.

Apple Electronics, run by 'Magic Alex', was perhaps the most striking example of heavily subsidised unproductivity. Alex was still hard at work in his—or rather the Beatles'—laboratory on inventions that were to carry the Apple style into every British home. So far, however, not a single Apple-shaped transistor radio, not a solitary nothing box or domestic force field had appeared on the retail market. Magic Alex possessed the knack of being constantly on the edge of a major breakthrough which needed only a little more finance to bring it to a triumphant conclusion. His other knack, while living in a £20,000 house John had bought, was of appearing totally indifferent to all but his transistors and circuits. Alex was also reputedly hard at work in designing the futuristic studio he had promised the Beatles, complete with 72-track recording machines, down in the Apple basement.

Numerous subsidiary projects had been floated on the seas of Beatle cash. As a rule, these represented the whim of an individual Beatle: they lasted as long, and no longer, than that Beatle's flickering enthusiasm. Paul had at one stage been keen on an offshoot called Zapple, a label which would release 'spoken word' records by modish Underground writers like Ken Kesey and Richard Brautigan. Kesey—the original Merry Prankster, progenitor of the *Magical Mystery Tour*—was brought to London, given an IBM golfball typewriter and invited to write a 'street diary' of his impressions. By then, Paul's enthusiasm had moved elsewhere. There was no one else to read Ken Kesey's street diary. He returned to California, leaving his IBM typewriter at the front desk.

Expenditure ran on at a dizzy rate which was, by Beatle standards, entirely normal. Only now, more people than four were spending and consuming. The tea, the coffee, the Scotch and Coke, the VSOP brandy, the Southern Comfort, the Benson and Hedges Gold dispensed so liberally in Derek Taylor's office were but the visible, obvious part of the largesse poured out by Apple to its visitors and its staff. From a kitchen stocked by Fortnum and Mason, endless relays of food came forth—hot meals, cold meals, cold wine, sandwiches, champagne. Junior staff shared liberally in the beano. A certain brand of vodka favoured by the Apple High Command could be bought only at a restaurant in Knightsbridge. Since the restaurant did no off-sales, two Apple office boys would be sent there to eat an expensive lunch and bring back the vodka. One of the kitchen girls remembers a certain Friday afternoon when a £60-pot of caviare had been ordered from Fortnum's for Yoko, who did not arrive after all. Two girls spread the £60-worth of caviare on a single round of toast, and ate a slice each.

Only after three Apple secretaries had had their pay packets stolen on the same day was it realised that Apple's open-handedness now extended to casual passers-by. 'Security' as a principle barely existed. That 'beautiful people', clad in kaftans and emitting good vibes, could stoop to theft simply did not seem possible. Meanwhile, LPs, hi-fi speakers, television sets, IBM typewriters, any moveable part of the green and white decor, continued to vanish: not through the back door—there wasn't one—but through the front door in broad daylight, before hundreds of staring eyes. Richard diLello unmasked the most imaginative predators: the GPO messenger boys who brought in the sacks of fanmail, and who were methodically stripping off the roof lead and carrying it away in the empty mailbags.

The Beatles' accountants were still, as in Brian Epstein's day, Bryce Hanmer Ltd. of Albemarle Street. Harry Pinsker, the head of the firm, supervised Apple's financial affairs and also sat on the Apple Corps Board. When John and Yoko appeared nude on the Two Virgins album sleeve, Pinsker, and four other directors, resigned. Apple's day-to-day accounting was then delegated to a junior partner, Stephen Maltz. For a few weeks, Maltz worked at 3 Savile Row, attempting to control its vast outgoings. He resigned in late October in a five-page letter to each of the Beatles, warning of dire consequences if they could not find a way to curb Apple's expenditure.

By that time, the company had gobbled up the million pounds set aside to launch it. It had devoured a further £400,000, the second instalment of the £800,000 which the Beatles had realised by selling themselves to their own company. All four had heavily overdrawn their corporate partnership account: John by £64,858, Paul by £66,988, George by £35,850 and Ringo by £32,080.

'As far as you were aware,' wrote Stephen Maltz, 'you only had to sign a bill and pick up a 'phone and payment was made. You were never concerned where the money came from or how it was being spent, and were living under the idea that you had millions at your disposal.

'Each of you has houses and cars . . . you also have Tax cases pending. Your personal finances are in a mess. Apple is in a mess.'

The Beatles by then could see that Apple was in a mess. They could even, however reluctantly, see why. They had all shared Paul McCartney's vision of 'Western Communism'—of young people, freed from turgid conventional business methods, managing their own affairs on the pure, simple dynamo of their own young energy. The lesson of the past six months was that young people were no less greedy, dishonest, avaricious and incompetent than middle-aged ones. Stephen Maltz's letter and horrific warning only confirmed a suspicion, growing even in John Lennon's mind, that turgid, conventional business might have something to recommend it after all. In particular, their thoughts turned towards the very concept which Apple had meant to disown. Someone, they agreed, had better become the boss.

At 3 Savile Row, despite all the high-paid executives in their elegantly-appointed offices, no one was quite the boss. Ron Kass, the Head of Apple Records, probably came the closests. But Kass did not have, as Peter Brown did, the direct hot line to all four Beatle hides. Peter Brown held exquisite managerial lunches. But Neil Aspinall, who never ate lunch, held the post of Managing Director. Neil, their former road manager, was the Beatles' oldest, closest friend; it was his very closeness and trustworthiness which prevented him from seizing full executive power. He simply took on a workload which on several occasions caused him to be physically sick.

If Apple was to have a boss, the Beatles decided, it must be a big boss. It must be the biggest, bossiest boss that the land of business and bosses could provide.

As so often in such matters, they sought guidance from the biggest boss on their horizon: Sir Joseph Lockwood, Chairman of EMI. Sir Joe's advice was to bring in the head of a merchant bank. He himself offered to approach one of the City's most powerful merchant banks, on their behalf. A meeting was arranged between Paul McCartney and the bank's Chairman, Lord Poole, whose expertise was available to no less a property-holder than Queen Elizabeth II.

Sir Joseph accompanied Paul to the Lazard's meeting. 'He'd come along without a tie of course. So Lord Poole took off his tie and jacket and we sat down to lunch. At the end, Lord Poole said, "I'll do it. And what's more, I won't charge you anything." He was offering to sort out Apple—for nothing! But the Beatles didn't bother to follow it up.'

Another highly symbolic approach—by John this time—was to Lord Beeching, the man who 'reorganised' British Railways by shutting down huge lengths of them. The 'Beeching Axe' was not available to be wielded at Apple. Beeching, however, listened sympathetically to the tales of chaos and then offered one wise—and prophetic—recommendation: 'Get back to making records.'

Meanwhile, Christmas was coming. So were the Hell's Angels. The former was to be celebrated with a children's party organised by Derek Taylor in Peter Brown's sumptuous first-floor office. The latter were motorcycling heavies from San Francisco whom George Harrison had invited to drop in on Apple whenever they happened to be passing through London.

The entire San Francisco 'chapter' of Hell's Angels in the end materialised as only two, though sufficiently terrifying, figures, named 'Frisco Pete and Billy Tumbleweed. With them they brought two Harley Davidson bikes—shipped from California at Apple's expense—and a harem a dozen strong. They and their retinue were reportedly en route for Czechoslovakia 'to straighten out the political situation'.

First, 'Frisco Pete and Billy Tumbleweed straightened out Apple, partaking of hospitality made still more liberal by the terror their looks inspired. Carol Paddon, in the Press Office, was one of several Apple girls who mastered the knack, when a Hell's Angel hand went up her skirt, of smiling with ghastly good humour. Naturally, it would have been discourteous, not to say dangerous, to exclude 'Frisco Pete and Billy Tumbleweed from the Apple children's Christmas party.

The party, in Peter Brown's office, featured seas of jellies, blancmange and a conjurer named Ernest Castro. Afterwards there was to be a 'grown-ups' party, with John and Yoko officiating as Father and Mother Christmas. Of the lavish buffet which Apple's Cordon Bleu cooks had prepared, the centrepiece was a 42-lb. turkey, guaranteed by its suppliers to be The Largest Turkey in Great Britain.

The party proved a fitting climax to Apple's Golden Age. John, sitting on the floor with Yoko, a white Santa Claus beard covering his dark one, was bewildered to find himself menaced by both 'Frisco Pete and Billy Tumbleweed. The Hell's Angels resented what they felt was unnecessary delay in starting on The Largest Turkey in Great Britain. When Alan Smith, a music journalist, tried to intervene 'Frisco Pete felled him with a single punch. Smith's toppling body struck John as he was raising a teacup to his lips. Father Christmas sat there, protecting a Mother Christmas of markedly Japanese aspect, with tea dripping down his spectacles.

May 1969

'Am I the way you imagined me?'

Allen Klein knew many ways of bewildering and disconcerting those with whom he did business. His very appearance seemed calculated to bewilder and disconcert. For he looked so utterly unlike his reputation. Instead of a human barracuda, a little dumpy figure in a turtlenecked sweater would amble forward, its hair in a Fifties cowlick, its shamefaced, rather shy grin seeming to savour this moment of deep anticlimax. 'Am I the way you imagined me?' Klein invariably asked. The brown button eyes would dart to and fro as if balance sheets hung invisibly in the air. 'Tell me what you heard about me. Tell me the way you imagined I'd be.'

To imagine Allen Klein, one must imagine the combination of Jewish and New York enterprise at a single, stunning apotheosis. For the child born to a poor New Jersey couple in 1931 possessed few inherited advantages. His mother died when he was a few months old and his father, a hard-up kosher butcher, put him and his two sisters into the care of Newark's austere Hebrew Shelter Orphanage. When his father remarried, Allen was sent to live with an aunt. This coincidence was to prove crucial many years later, in the most important single encounter of Allen Klein's remarkable career.

From early adolescence, his life was devoted to single-minded self-advancement. He worked as a clerk for a New Jersey newspaper distributor, holding down two or three additional part-time jobs to pay for a night-school course in accountancy. At times in class, he would be so exhausted, his head would fall forward on to his arms. When the teacher posed a question in mental arithmetic, Klein would rattle off the answer without so much as opening his eyes.

His career began in earnest in New York in the mid-Fifties, when he worked as a junior in a firm of accountants specialising in show-business clients. He would watch the big stars with absorption as they came and went; he also read their balance-sheets. His was the kind of brain to which balance sheets are as gripping as detective novels, as revealing as a voice in a confessional.

He got to know several of the firm's clients, among them Bobby Darin, a big Pop idol of the time. One day in the late Fifties, Klein and Darin happened to meet at a wedding. Klein took the Pop idol aside and asked him a simple, transfixing question. 'How would you like to make $100,000?'

'What do I have to do?' The startled teen idol asked.

'Nothing,' was Klein's equally devastating answer.

The delivery of a $100,000 cheque to Bobby Darin, for hitherto overlooked fees and recording royalties, established Allen Klein as an accountant such as the entertainment world had not known before. His speciality was ferreting out sums of money owed to performers by their record companies but unpaid, either through negligence or plain dishonesty. High calibre Pop stars, among them Steve Lawrence and Eydie Gorme, swore eternal gratitude to Klein for the huge discrepancies he uncovered between their fame and their bank accounts. The discrepancies were often genuine; in any case, the record companies would invariably pay up rather than lose the artists' goodwill. Frequently, they would pay up rather than undergo further negotiations with Allen Klein, whom to describe as 'tenacious' is rather like calling Attila the Hun 'impolite'.

Klein's other speciality, developed in the early Sixties, was the extraction of huge advances for record stars against future royalties. Sam Cooke, a black Soul singer, became, with Klein's help, the first Pop name to receive a million dollars without singing a note, even though, sadly, he did not live long to enjoy it. In 1965, he was shotgunned to death in a motel room while with a lady other than his wife.

Thus, from two contradictory standpoints, did the legend of Allen Klein evolve. To his clients, he was a hero, a 'Robin Hood' (as was frequently said and written) who won back for poor performers the wealth of which they had been systematically cheated. To the record industry he was a predatory and ruthless contract-buster, bound by no constraints of principle or politeness. He was just 'Klein'. The surname acquired a peculiar resonance, as of some small, sharp-fanged fish.

Klein later admitted he first set his sights on the Beatles in 1964, when I Want to Hold Your Hand burst on the American charts. At that point, even to Allen Klein, they seemed utterly unreachable. Instead, he devoted his ingenuity to annexing their chief rivals, the Rolling Stones. Andrew Oldham, the Stones' original manager, hired him as a business adviser in 1965. Klein's first act was to ease out Oldham's partner, Eric Easton. His second was to fly to London to renegotiate the Stones' contract with the Chairman of Decca, Sir Edward Lewis. A stunned Sir

Edward shortly afterwards found himself agreeing to pay the Rolling Stones $1.25m in advance royalties.

Shortly afterwards, a dispute arose between Klein and Oldham concerning the precise whereabouts and disposal of that $1.25m advance. Oldham sued Allen Klein and Company; in doing so, he found himself merely added to a queue of some 50 other litigants. Writs, to Klein, are as normal a part of life as answering the telephone: he seems to find multimillion dollar lawsuits almost as palatable as the Coca Cola he quaffs so freely throughout the day.

The 'British Invasion' that followed the Beatles to America brought Klein such clients as Herman's Hermits, the Animals, Donovan and the Dave Clark Five. Each in turn enjoyed a vast popularity, though none quite as fantastic and frenetic as the Beatles' own. The Rolling Stones came nearest; they were now entirely Klein's. He had bought off Andrew Oldham's lawsuit for $1m. He publicised Mick Jagger in New York as he had once publicised Sam Cooke: on a Times Square billboard 80-feet high.

The Beatles heard of Klein and his miracles from Mick Jagger after the Rolling Stones' 1966 American tour. They were nettled to think that the Stones, who sold less records than they did, should be making so much more money. In three years of buoying up EMI's profits, it had never occurred to Brian Epstein to demand an advance against royalties. Paul McCartney took the lead in suggesting that Allen Klein be asked to act in some similar hustling capacity for NEMS Enterprises; shortly afterwards, Klein himself was overheard boasting he would 'have the Beatles by Christmas'. Rumours grew of a NEMS-Klein merger, negotiated by a 'Third Man', eventually goading Brian to dismiss the idea angrily as 'rubbish'.

Klein, however, remained a shape on the horizon. The Beatles and Rolling Stones were, after all, close friends and fellow sufferers from superstardom. In 1967, soon after Brian's death, they considered a plan to amalgamate their front offices and jointly finance their own recording studio. Mick Jagger approached Peter Brown to see if he would act for the Stones—as he did for the Beatles—as fixer, social secretary and diplomat. Klein opposed the idea and flew at once from New York to scotch it. There was a meeting, also attended by Clive Epstein, at which Klein struck Peter Brown as 'a rather hysterical, unstable person. Then he calmed down. He realised I wasn't trying to take the Stones over. As he was walking out, he suddenly turned round to Clive and said: "How much do you want for the Beatles?"'

In New York, Klein's notoriety was then at a peak. He had recently taken over Cameo Parkway, a record label once successful with Chubby Checker and the Twist but now on the edge of bankruptcy. At Klein's advent, Cameo Parkway shares rose in value from less than $3 to more than $75 each. Klein was accused of 'talking up' the shares, by creating rumours of takeover bids —of the British music firm Chappell's, for instance—which then did not materialise. He was hit by a further lawsuit: from Cameo Parkway stockholders outraged, among other things, by the $104,000 per year salary their new chief had voted himself. The New York Stock Exchange suspended dealings in Cameo Parkway shares and ordered an investigation into Klein's methods by America's financial 'watchdog' body, the Securities and Exchange Commission.

In the event, Cameo Parkway Records made only one acquisition—the Allen Klein accountancy company. Klein took himself over in reverse, naming the resultant enterprise. ABKCO Industries Inc. The letters stand for Allen and Betty Klein. That Klein should be happily married, to a girl he met soon after graduation from Upsala College, is one further confusingly human aspect of his character.

But the Beatles, his dream—or rather, ultimate caculation —seemed as wide of Klein's grasp as ever. Mick Jagger had repeatedly recommended him to John and Paul as the businessman they needed to make sense of Apple. He himself had tried to telephone John, but John could not be bothered to take the call. They met briefly in December 1968, when John and Yoko went with Eric Clapton to Wembley Stadium, to appear in the Rolling Stones' film *Rock 'n' Roll Circus*. Then John had barely glanced at the little tubby man in a turtlenecked sweater sitting, apparently starstruck, among all the fur-clad super-hippies and freaks.

Not until the following January did Klein's opportunity come, though when it did come, it was as tailored to him as perfectly as a trapdoor to a Demon King. It was a story splashed all over the new 'intelligent' Rock paper, *Rolling Stone*. It was John Lennon's announcement that, if the Beatles carried on losing money at their present rate, John, at least, would be 'broke in six months'.

With Paul McCartney, the need to breathe was scarcely more important than the need to perform. It was a need which transcended mere vanity, and his love of his own bewitching, beguiling, melodic power. He would sing and play for as many, or as few, people who happened to be there when the impulse came that was as natural as breath. Once, on a car journey with Derek Taylor, he stopped in a Bedfordshire village and played the piano in a village pub. He would sing softly through the dark to the girls on watch outside his house. Late in 1968, he and Linda spent a week with Hunter Davies, the Beatles' authorized biographer, in Portugal. The Davieses noticed a phenomenon unchanged since a decade ago in Forthlin Road, Liverpool. Even in the lavatory, Paul could not stop singing and playing his guitar.

Paul had always felt that by giving up road tours and retiring into album work, the Beatles had broken faith with the public to whom, fundamentally, they owed everything. So he began arguing with renewed persistence after the White Album was finished. He had lately—at Linda's encouragement—grown a thick, dark, uncultivated beard. It might have been a keen and determined young schoolmaster who sat in the Apple boardroom, urging the other three that their next project together ought to be a 'live' concert tour.

The chief deterrent, as Paul himself acknowledged, was simple stage fright. It was more than two years since the Beatles had last faced an audience together. In that time, only John had given anything like a live performance, in the *Rock 'n' Roll Circus* film. He had also appeared at the 'Alchemical Wedding', a Christmas rally of Britain's chief hippies and mystics, sitting with Yoko inside a plastic bag on the stage of the Royal Albert Hall.

That was fine, Paul said: at least it was 'live'. He continued chivvying, pushing back his now swept-back hair as he reminded them of stage fright successfully overcome in the past. Wasn't it the same, he said, when they came back from Hamburg and played Leicester de Montfort Hall? John and Ringo seemed ready to be convinced. But George demurred. He could not endure the thought of returning to anything like Beatlemania. Paul agreed: it should be nothing like that. It might perhaps be only a single stage performance. 'But we've got to keep that contact somehow. And it's what we do best.'

Not even Paul could persuade the others to venture back on the road again. Instead, there evolved an elaborate compromise. They would make an album as good as a stage show—an album shorn of all studio artifice, reliant only on their own abilities as singers and musicians, simple and powerful and honest enough to reach back over the years, and the Byzantine sound effects, to their old, punching power in the concert halls. 'Honest' was the word they kept using to George Martin when persuading him to leave his now very successful AIR studios to act, yet again, as their producer. 'They said they wanted to go right back to basics,' Martin says. 'They wouldn't use any overdubbing. They'd do the songs just as they happened.'

The simple resolve of four musicians, however, was now subject to the complexities of Apple Corps, and its still unused subsidiaries, Apple Films and Apple Publishing. It was decided that the making of the album must be made into a film, and that film and record sessions should be described in an illustrated book to accompany each album. The climax of the film would be the 'live' performance Paul wanted, at a location still to be decided.

The arrival of a film crew, led by director Michael Lindsay-Hogg, gave additional scope to Paul's ideas. At one point, with Lindsay-Hogg's encouragement, he proposed giving the concert in a Tunisian amphitheatre; at another, he suggested making the whole album live in Los Angeles. George vetoed both suggestions as 'very expensive and insane'. Another of Paul's schemes was to record at sea, on board an ocean liner. George objected that the acoustics would be impossible. As the argument flew back and forth, John was heard to mutter, 'I'm warming to the idea of doing it in an asylum.'

The project's working title—symbolic of their desire to rediscover their roots—was Get Back. At John's suggestion, they even posed for a photograph looking down from the same balcony as on the cover of their first chirpy, working-class LP. To John, at least, the wheel had come full circle, and stopped.

Rehearsals began on 2 January 1969, at one end of a cavernous sound stage at Twickenham film studios. Michael Lindsay-Hogg's camera crew were already in position to film Mal Evans, the perennial 'roadie', carrying in amplifiers and cymbal-stands, and Paul testing the grand piano, his coat collar turned up, a half-eaten apple before him on the polished lid.

The cameras ran on as Paul, each morning, strove to enthuse the other Beatles to forgetfulness of their dismal surroundings, the unaccustomed daylight playing and the constant, numb-fingered cold. His resemblance to a schoolmaster grew, even as the class grew more plainly recalcitrant. 'OK—right. Er—OK, let's try to move on.' He went and sat with George, as with a backward and also stubborn pupil, tracing with his arm the sequence he wanted George to play. 'You see, it's got to come down like that. There shouldn't be any recognisable jumps. It helps if you sing it. Like this—'

Resentment was not yet in the open. Paul worked conscientiously to provide a falsetto counterpoint to John's still dirge-like and off-key Across The Universe. John played chords as instructed to a pretty little Paul tune that would one day become Maxwell's Silver Hammer. They even, spasmodically, enjoyed themselves. John got up, and Yoko did not follow him: Paul and he sang Two of Us, burlesquing like teenage Quarry Men. When George played over I Me Mine, a new song in turgid waltz time, Paul and Ringo tackled it gamely. John and Yoko, two meagre, white-clad, figures in gym shoes, waltzed to it together across the cable-strewn floor.

As well as the new material, they continually ran through old songs from Liverpool and Hamburg: the Chuck Berry and Elvis and Little Richard songs they had always played to warm up before performing or recording. They even resurrected a Quarry Men song, The One After 909, written by John and Paul on truant afternoons in Jim McCartney's sitting-room with the Chinese pagoda wallpaper and the *Echos* piled under the dresser. 'We always hated the words to that one,' Paul said. ' "Move over once, move over twice. Hey, baby, don't be cold as ice . . ." They're great, really, aren't they?'

Whatever glow these memories awoke soon died again in the chill of the big sound stage. Nor did playing the old songs seem to bring the new songs any nearer to satisfying Paul. 'We've been going round and round for an hour,' he complained wearily at one point. 'I think it's a question of either we do it or we go home.'

As Paul talked to George, a row started. 'I always hear myself—annoying you,' Paul said. 'Look, I'm not trying to *get* you. I'm just saying "Look, lads—the band. Shall we do it like this?" '

'Look, I'll play whatever you want me to play,' George cut in. His voice silting with resentment, he continued: 'Or I won't play at all. Whatever it is that'll please you, I'll do it.'

At lunch time on 10 January, George said he had had enough. He was tired of being 'got at' by Paul. He was quitting the Beatles, he said. He got into his car and drove home to Esher.

It was a temporary flare up, and recognised as such. George knew, and the others did, that he could never resign with an album half-finished. And, sure enough, when a business meeting took place at Ringo's a few days later, George turned up as usual. Work on the album resumed after Paul gave an undertaking not to get at George or try to teach him the guitar. And, they all agreed, they had had enough of Twickenham studios. They decided to move straight into their own studio—the one which Magic Alex had been building in the basement of the Apple house.

George Martin had already visited the basement, to inspect those technological marvels with which Magic Alex had promised to consign Abbey Road studios to instant obsolescence. What Martin had found was something less than miraculous. It was, in fact, something less than even adequate. No 72-track recording console was there—no console of any description. It had not occurred to Magic Alex to provide even such basic amenities as an intercom between studio and control-room. Nor had the Greek wizard noticed that in one corner of the recording area, the air-conditioning plant for the whole house thumped and wheezed and whirred and banged and coughed.

The studio could be made fit for recording only by silencing the air conditioner and by bringing in heavy consignments of sound equipment on hire. This done, the Beatles and their film crew tried again. Now among them, there was an additional, very jovial black face. Billy Preston, a gifted American performer who was George's protégé, joined the sessions as organist. What with the film crew, and this or that friend and acolyte, there was scarcely room in the basement to move. Yoko sat by John, as always, reading or embroidering. When Paul arrived—managing to make an entrance even through that narrow basement doorway—he brought Linda Eastman's little daughter, Heather.

The album that would finally be released, under the final, symbolic title Let It Be, contained only the tiniest fraction of what the Beatles recorded in that crowded basement during January 1969. More than a hundred songs, by every artist they had ever admired or copied, and also from every epoch of their own career, piled up on spools destined never to be released, or even listened to, again. It was as if, to rediscover themselves as musicians, they were putting themselves through the kind of endurance test that Hamburg used to be; seeking to reactivate those old, tight sinews with music that stretched back to their collective birth. They even recorded Maggie May, the Liverpool sailor's shanty which John Lennon sang at the Woolton fete that day in 1957 when Paul McCartney cycled across from Allerton to meet him.

It was after they stopped jamming and returned to today's material that the breakdown always came. Determined to be 'honest', to forsake all artifice, they still wanted from George Martin what he had always given them: a flawless final product. 'We'd do 60 different takes of something,' Martin says. 'On the 61st take, John would say, "How was that one, George?" I'd say, "John—I honestly don't know." "You're no fookin' good then are you," he'd say. That was the general atmosphere.'

Ironically, the best and happiest song on the finished album was one which grew out of random studio ad-libbing. Paul gave it the shorthand name Loretta: only later did it receive the album's original title of Get Back. Several versions of Paul's vocal were taped, among them a sarcastically Powell-ite warning to Pakistani immigrants. Another featured John as lead singer, giving the song a bitter drive and bite that even Paul's best version lacked. Halfway through the John version, both he and Paul suddenly tailed off into silence: it was Ringo, redeeming himself at last in George Martin's eyes, whose quick-witted drum solo forced them back again on target.

The film crew, with 28 hours of footage, finally packed up and left. The Beatles themselves did so a few days later, leaving behind a hundred tracks that not even Paul could face hearing, let alone editing down to 14. John was all for putting out the album as it stood: a confession of their own inner chaos. 'It'll tell people, "This is us with our trousers off, so will you please end the game now?" '

For the benefit of the film cameras, they had given their 'live' performance—not in Tunisia or Los Angeles, but among chimneys and fire escapes, one arbitrarily-chosen afternoon, on the Apple roof. None knew of the concert but their own employees, and passers-by in Savile Row, startled to hear a din suddenly erupting in the sky. To the surrounding tailors and outfitters, it was the final provocation. Police in raincoats appeared, speaking into their lapel-radios and irritably flicking cars and taxis onward. At last, from the conclave of helmets, there emerged a portly sergeant. He crossed the road, mounted the steps of 3 Savile Row and knocked at Apple's white front door.

It was Ray Coleman, the quiet, learned-looking editor of *Disc* magazine, whom John first told that 'if Apple goes on losing money at this rate, we'll all be broke in six months'. Shortly afterwards, on the Apple stairs, Paul berated Coleman furiously for having printed the story. 'This is only a small company and you're trying to wreck it,' Paul shouted. 'You know John shoots his mouth off and doesn't mean it.' Coleman had been close to the Beatles long enough to recognise what was off or on the record.

So it proved when the world's Press poured over the Apple threshold, asking for further and better particulars. John confirmed what he had told Ray Coleman—that Apple was losing some £20,000 a week to its myriad hangers-on, and that he personally calculated he was 'down to my last £50,000'. George, as a rule the closest one in money matters, was equally willing to talk. 'We've been giving away too much to the wrong people—like the deaf and the blind,' George said. 'This place has become a haven for drop-outs. The trouble is, some of our best friends are drop-outs.'

The story that the Beatles were going broke somewhat abated the Apple orgy. It also placed the honest, and rather underpaid, regular staff members under the same stigma as predatory Hell's Angels and larcenous GPO boys. Paul McCartney, in a thoughtful PR gesture, sent round a morale-boosting letter to all Apple artists and employees. 'In case you're worried about anything at Apple, please feel free to write me a letter, telling me about the problem. There's no need to be formal. Just say it. Incidentally, things are going well, so thanks—love, Paul.'

The news that Allen Klein, the Rolling Stones' manager, was in London and wanted to see the Beatles with a view to helping them, did not at first seem vastly portentous. When Klein's first call reached Apple, they were still immured at Twickenham studios, refusing to see anyone. It was simply another message from the hundreds left hanging in the psychedelic twilight of

Derek Taylor's Press Office. 'Allen Klein! What the fuck does he want, man?' 'How the fuck should I know?'

That Klein's message should have reached John Lennon was surprising enough. What was still more surprising was John's instant agreement to meet him, as requested, at Klein's suite in the Dorchester Hotel. John went without telling the other Beatles, accompained only by Yoko, and, as he afterwards admitted, petrified with nerves.

Klein was certainly a shock. For, as usual, he looked nothing like his reputation. A small, tubby man, wearing a sweater and sneakers, met John and Yoko in his hotel room alone; without lawyers or aides. He was evidently just as nervous as John. The other surprising thing about him was his apparent deep enthusiasm for Beatles music. He could quote from every song John had written, right back to earliest Beatlemania. He showed an instinctive grasp of the Beatles' peculiar problems, and had clear and forceful proposals for remedying them. He impressed John with his straightforward manner and the blunt New York wit that put him spiritually not far from a Liverpudlian. The fact that, he, too, had lost his mother in early childhood and been boarded out with an aunt, cemented the bond between them.

By the end of that first meeting, John had made up his mind. There and then he wrote a note to EMI's Chairman, Sir Joseph Lockwood, 'Dear Sir Joe—from now on, Allen Klein handles all my stuff.'

Sir Joseph read the note with a bewilderment shared by others to whom John announced his adoption of Allen Klein. For so far as their closest associates knew, the Beatles had already decided on the man who would rescue them and Apple Corps from chaos.

Late in 1968, Linda Eastman had taken Paul McCartney home to New York to meet her family. He had met her father, the elegant Lee Eastman, and her brother, John, a bright young Ivy Leaguer, already a partner in the family law and management practice. He had tasted the Eastmans' high-caste Manhattan ambiance which formed the highest rung of his social ascent from the little terraced house in Allerton. By that time, he was planning to marry Linda, though with the secrecy required for one whose bachelorhood counted as one of the world's last unsullied treasures.

The Eastmans naturally welcomed someone who was for them an equivalent social and professional asset. Like all lawyers and managers everywhere, they had been watching the Beatles' vain attempt to procure a saviour for Apple. Not that John and Lee Eastman were so unsubtle as to recommend themselves to Paul as such. They simply allowed him to see them, in their cool, quiet Fifth Avenue chambers, poised, efficient, elegant and upper class. Paul returned to London convinced that Eastman & Eastman Inc. were the remedy required at 3 Savile Row.

John Eastman came to London to meet the other Beatles a few weeks later. They were not unequivocally impressed—first because Lee had not bothered to come in person; second because John seemed rather young for the job he was seeking. The Liverpool nose for humbug scented John Eastman's determination to win over John and Yoko with 'arty' talk about Kafka. They also realised by now that John was Paul's intended brother-in-law. Nonetheless, a letter signed by all four Beatles authorised John Eastman to act for them in contractual matters. By the time Allen Klein appeared on the scene, Eastman Junior had begun an ambitious strategy to consolidate Apple's dwindling reserves.

NEMS Enterprises, Brian Epstein's original management company, still hung, ghost-like in the Apple firmament. Under its new name, Nemperor Holdings, it continued to receive the Beatles' earnings and to deduct Brian's 25 per cent before passing on the residue to Apple. Yet NEMS had long since ceased to exercise control over them as agents and managers. The bond was purely technical—and sentimental, since Brian's mother, Queenie, was NEMS' main shareholder and his brother Clive was Chairman. The Beatles themselves still held the 10 per cent share in NEMS allotted to them by Brian's tender conscience.

The Epsteins, on their side, while wishing to retain control of NEMS, still faced the bill for half a million pounds in estate duty which Brian's cash assets had nowhere near covered. Clive Epstein, for all his dutiful efforts to expand NEMS, knew he had no ultimate course but to sell the company. What restrained him was his sense of obligation—to Brian's memory, to his mother, to the remaining Liverpool artists; to everything in fact but his own fervent desire to return to Liverpool's quieter business climes.

Late in 1967, Clive had received an offer for NEMS from the Triumph Investment Trust, a City merchant bank with a reputation for aggressive take-overs. At that stage, however, NEMS, transformed into Nemperor, was committed to a 'programme of vigorous expansion'. The expansion proved less than vigorous, and a year later, preempting a rumoured bid by the British Lion Film Corporation, Triumph's Chairman, Leonard Richenberg, made a second approach to Clive Epstein. This time, Clive was ready to accept Richenberg's offer.

John Eastman's plan was that the Beatles themselves should buy up NEMS, matching Triumph's offer of one million pounds. Sir Joseph Lockwood at EMI had agreed to advance the entire sum against future royalty earnings. Clive Epstein, feeling that the Beatles had a moral right to the company which Brian had launched on their name, notified Leonard Richenberg that the sale to Triumph was off.

It was at this point that John Lennon met, and adopted, Allen Klein. George and Ringo, who met Klein soon afterwards, were struck, as John had been, by Klein's ethnic forthrightness and his thorough grasp of the Apple problem. They did not instantly accept him as their saviour, but they were willing to listen. Paul McCartney was not. He attended only one meeting with Klein, and walked out soon after it had begun.

The plan agreed by the other three was that John Eastman and Klein should *both* work as advisers to Apple. Eastman was to follow up the NEMS deal while Klein looked into their financial position with special regard to EMI's £1m loan.

The Eastmans, father and son, made no secret of the dislike with which they regarded Allen Klein. They were quick to inform Paul—as Leonard Richenberg had independently discovered—that Klein was viewed with suspicion in New York because of the Cameo Parkway affair; that some 50 lawsuits decorated the escutcheon of Klein's company, ABKCO Industries; and that Klein himself currently faced 10 charges by the U.S. Internal Revenue Service of failing to file Income Tax returns.

To George and Ringo that was less important than the stunning promise Klein held out to them. He would go into Apple and clean up the mess. He would also make each of them wealthy in a way that even they, in their clouds of ready cash, had never imagined possible. He had a way of characterising money as some dragon-like entity which had slain Brian Epstein, with his paltry £7m gross, but which Allen Klein, with his ABKCO sword, knew the secret of vanquishing. 'You shouldn't have to worry about money. *You* shouldn't have to think about it. You should be able to say FYM—Fuck You, Money.'

George and Ringo responded, as John had, to Klein's pungent fiscal imagery and down-to-earth manner. They liked him for the brusqueness he did not trouble to moderate, whatever the company. John Eastman, by contrast, wavered between urbane bonhomie and spluttering rage. It was a propensity shared by his father, who had at length flown over from New York to meet the Beatles and Klein together at Claridge's Hotel. A few minutes after the meeting began, Lee Eastman rounded on Klein and began to shout abuse at him. The outburst was, in fact, skilfully engineered by Klein, to reveal Lee Eastman as an hysteric and himself as the stolid underdog. John, George and Ringo naturally sided with the underdog.

Clive Epstein, meanwhile, had begun to suspect that selling NEMS to the Beatles was a process that might drag on for months. He therefore reopened negotiations with Leonard Richenberg and Triumph, though stressing he would still prefer to accept the Beatles' offer. He undertook not to sell for three more weeks, to give them time to conclude their bid.

But the Beatles' advisers were by now bogged down by internecine warfare. Klein claimed that the Eastmans were blocking his access to vital financial details within Apple. John Eastman accused Klein of imperilling the deal by boasts that he could get NEMS 'for nothing' on the strength of sums owed to the Beatles in back payments. Though the deadline had not expired, it clearly would not be met. Clive Epstein sold out to Triumph, for a mixture of cash and stock, on 17 February.

John Eastman flew back to New York. The Beatles continued discussions with Allen Klein—minus Paul McCartney. Instead, Paul would send along his lawyer, a Mr. Charles Corman. The others were amused at first that such a personage was meant to fill Paul's place at the board table. They would ask Mr. Corman why he hadn't brought his bass guitar.

On 11 March, Apple's Press Office issued a brief communiqué confirming the rumour it had for weeks been vigorously denying. Paul McCartney *was* to marry Linda Eastman. The ceremony would take place the following day in London, at Marylebone Register Office.

The bombshell exploded, among other places, in a small house in Redditch, Worcestershire, where Jill Pritchard, a travelling hairdresser, was giving one of her regular customers a shampoo and set. 'Even before I heard it on the radio,' Jill says, 'I had a sort of premonition it had happened. I remember looking at the customer's little girl and wondering how she'd react.

'It was just a short announcement on the BBC News. I finished the shampoo and set, then I drove straight home and packed a little overnight bag. I'd got a bit of money that I'd always kept put by for an emergency. I got a friend to ring up my Mum later and tell her where I'd gone. Then I drove to New Street Station in Birmingham and left my car on a No Waiting sign. I bought myself a ticket to London—first class, so I wouldn't have to sit and cry in a compartment full of people.'

Late that night, wet-eyed and still carrying her suitcase, Jill Pritchard walked up Cavendish Avenue and joined the large, stunned crowd which had gathered there. The first girl she spoke to was Margo Stevens. 'Is *she* in there?' Jill asked. Thousands of girls throughout Europe and America found it similarly impossible to articulate Linda's name.

'We all knew it was going to happen,' Margo says. 'We even knew Linda was pregnant. We'd seen the prescription that Rosie, the housekeeper, collected for her. But we kept hoping Paul would get out of it somehow. He was upset because we were taking it so badly. He'd come out to the gates to talk to us earlier in the day. "Look, girls," he said, "be fair. I had to get married some time." '

Every British newspaper, the day after Paul's wedding, carried pictures of the same desolately weeping girl. It was Jill Pritchard, the travelling hairdresser from Redditch. Photographers whirled her this way and that for most of the afternoon, shouting, 'Go on —cry. You'll be in the papers.' When Paul drove back with Linda after the ceremony, grief began to turn to violence. The security gates were forced apart; the front door was kicked and wads of burning newspaper were pushed through the letterbox. After that, the Police appeared and told everyone to disperse.

Margo, Jill and the other regulars, drained of all emotion, adjourned to the nearest pub. 'We heard later from Rosie that Paul was really upset about us,' Margo says. 'He was standing just inside the front door, saying, "I *must* go out and talk to them again." But when he did come out, none of us was there any more. He couldn't believe we'd all gone away, so Rosie said. When he came back into the house, he was almost in tears.'

That same night, Drugs Squad officers raided George Harrison's Esher bungalow, and discovered a total of 570 grains of cannabis. George was in London, recording his friend Jackie Lomax; when he returned he found the officers sitting with his wife Pattie, watching television and playing Beatles records. By an unkind coincidence, the name of the Police dog which sniffed out the cannabis was 'Yogi'.

Eight days later, at the British Consulate on the Rock of Gibraltar, John and Yoko were secretly married. John wore a crumpled white jacket, an Apostle-length beard and tennis shoes. Yoko wore a white, wide-brimmed hat, sunglasses and an unwisely short, layered mini-dress. The Registrar wore a look of bravely-stifled astonishment. They had decided on marriage suddenly while on holiday in Paris, and chosen Gibraltar as being 'quiet, friendly and British'. Peter Brown made the arrangements from London, and himself flew out to be best man. John and Yoko posed for pictures with the Consulate staff, saw what little of Gibraltar there was to see, then flew back to Paris to own up to the international Press. 'We're going to stage many happenings and events together,' Yoko said. 'This marriage was one of them.'

The Beatles' American Fan Club organiser issued an appeal for tolerance of what the whole world greeted as John's worst aberration yet. 'I know this news is shocking. Please try to understand that we should at least give Yoko the same chance we are giving Linda, and that Maureen and Pattie, got. If it makes John happy, I suppose we should all be enthused too.'

Their honeymoon was the first of Yoko's promised happenings: it also inaugurated their campaign to promote that much desired but fast-fading hippy commodity, Peace. To promote the cause of peace they announced they would spend seven successive days in bed, at the Amsterdam Hilton hotel.

Most of the Press who instantly converged on Amsterdam believed that the newlyweds had actually offered to make love in public. To their disappointment, they found John and Yoko merely sitting up in bed, in a suite decorated with placards reading 'Bed Peace' and 'Hair Peace'. Few papers could understand, any more than could their progressively exasperated readership, how two people cocooned thus in the casual squalor of Rock star hyper-luxury, had any relevance to burned babies in Vietnam or Biafra's living skeletons. Even calling it, with that so-fashionable suffix, a 'Bed-in' could not avert savage criticism of 'the most self-indulgent demonstration of all time'. But the Press was, as always, unable to deliver the ultimate rebuff. It could not stay away. 'Day Two of the Lennon Lie-In', ran a British headline. 'John and Yoko Are Forced Out by Maria the Maid'.

They continued their journey to Vienna for the first television showing of their film, *Rape*—an action they depicted being performed by reporters and TV cameras. Later, in the Sacher Hotel's sumptuous Red Salon, they staged a second 'happening'. This time, the Press found them crouching on a table top inside a bag. It was, so John said, a demonstration of 'bagism' or 'total communication', in which the speaker did not prejudice the listener by his personal appearance. More 'bagism', he suggested, would generate more peace throughout the world. The British *Daily Mirror* spoke for the whole world in mourning 'a not inconsiderable talent who seems to have gone completely off his rocker'.

The loss of NEMS Enterprises had not discountenanced Allen Klein. His countenance remained as set as ever in the belief that the 'Robin Hood of Pop' knew best; that what seemed like defeat would in the long term be advantageous; that, really, he had planned it this way all along. The episode, indeed, had served Klein by revealing shortcomings in John Eastman which even his brother-in-law seemed to acknowledge. For it was with Paul's tacit agreement, or non-disagreement, that Klein began a counter-attack designed to extricate the Beatles from the hold of the Triumph Investment Trust.

A week after Triumph's takeover of NEMS, Klein visited the bank's dapper Chairman, Leonard Richenberg. There followed what Richenberg subsequently described as 'various vague and threatening noises'. According to Klein, the old NEMS company owed the Beatles large sums in unpaid fees from road shows dating back as far as 1966. They would forget these 'arrears' if Triumph agreed to forego the 25 per cent of their earnings Richenberg had bought up with NEMS. Richenberg's response showed him a worthy adversary. He requested Klein in words of one syllable to go away. No more successful was Klein's offer of a million pounds outright from Triumph's stake in the Beatles. Richenberg merely repeated his request to his visitor to depart.

Sir Joseph Lockwood, Chairman of EMI, was Klein's next point of attack. Sir Joseph, a few days later, received a note, signed by all four Beatles, requiring that henceforward their record royalties were not to go to NEMS-Triumph but were to be paid direct to Apple. The letter was timely, since EMI was on the point of disgorging Beatles' record royalties in the region of £1.3m.

Leonard Richenberg had received a similar notification. He wrote back to Neil Aspinall, tersely rejecting the Beatles' claim that their contract with NEMS had expired when the *management* agreement did, in 1967. There remained the nine-year EMI contract, signed in January 1967, under which all record royalties were to be channelled via NEMS. Triumph Investments were thus entitled to collect their 25 per cent for seven more years.

At EMI, Sir Joseph Lockwood faced the uncomfortable alternatives of breaking a manifestly binding legal obligation to NEMS-Triumph or alienating the affections of the four individuals on whom his company's fortunes largely rested. Sir Joseph, with great wisdom, elected to do neither. Triumph then sought a High Court order to 'freeze' the £1.3m pending the obviously protracted legal battle over it.

The application was heard on 2 April in the High Court before Mr. Justice Buckley. Counsel for Triumph, Mr. Jeremiah Harman, QC, said that the Beatles had 'fallen under the influence of Mr. Allen Klein, an American of somewhat dubious reputation'. The Judge, though inclined to agree, refused to freeze the money officially since, he said, EMI themselves would obviously not release it until the dispute was settled.

It was therefore left to Klein and Richenberg—in an atmosphere now tinged by mutual respect—to get down to serious wheeling and dealing. Richenberg agreed to relinquish Triumph's 25 per cent of Beatle earnings in exchange for £800,000 cash, plus a quarter of the suspended £1.3m. Triumph would buy out the Beatles' 10 per cent of NEMS for just under half a million pounds-worth of the bank's own very desirable stock.

Klein could thus go back to the Beatles, claiming to have turned defeat into victory. If they had not managed to acquire NEMS, at least NEMS had no further control over them. He had bought them freedom, in other words, from one cabal of 'men in suits'. The 'Robin Hood of Pop', in his crumpled white polo neck sweater, was one deal up on his rivals in the Apple camp. And if Allen Klein knew anything, he would soon be two deals up.

Dick James was always the first to admit that he was an exceedingly fortunate man. Pure chance had brought Brian Epstein to his office that morning long ago in 1962. Pure chance had ordained that James be there in person, to soothe Brian's ruffled feathers and listen to the demonstration disc he carried in his briefcase. So by pure chance it came about, as the voices pealed round his dusty Denmark Street cubbyhole, that Dick James, the so-so crooner, average song plugger and now struggling music publisher, realised he was on his way to his first million.

He had seized on that luck, of course, with some prescient fair-dealing. As publisher of the early Lennon-McCartney hits, he could have been greedy, and lost them. Instead, he looked to the long term. He saw, not only potential but also sheer quantity. So Heaven whispered in Dick James's ear, prompting him to offer Brian a deal unprecedented in Tin Pan Alley. He would set up a song publishing firm, exclusively for Lennon–McCartney music. It was piquant to remember Brian's disbelieving gratitude when Northern Songs was formed. 'Why are you doing all this for us?'

When the company came into existence in 1963, Dick James and his partner Emannuel Silver between them owned 50 per cent. John and Paul had 20 per cent each and Brian, 10 per cent. James administered the company through his own Dick James Music Ltd. Ironically, he himself only ever published two Lennon–McCartney songs—the first one he ever heard, Please Please Me, and the B-side Ask Me Why. It was as a middleman that he grew wealthy, husbanding a store of hit songs that piled up faster almost than an old time Tin Pan Alley plugger could count.

The Beatles laughed at Dick James for his tubby shape, his bald head, his constant pleas for more nice *tuneful* numbers like Michelle and Yesterday. His knowledge of the music business and its manifold dodges merged into the invisible shield that Brian Epstein built around them. It was Dick James who, on the eve of a new Beatles single, would circulate every American record station with dire legal admonitions not to break the release embargo. It was Dick James who, after the initial chaos, maximised their American impact by ensuring that other singers and groups did not 'cover' Lennon–McCartney material to excess.

The flotation of Northern Songs as a public company in 1965 represented almost the only attempt in Brian's lifetime to harness the Beatles' huge earnings to solid long-term investment. A quarter of the two shilling shares were quoted on the London Stock Exchange at 7s 9d each and bought up: in financial as well as Beatle terms a Number One hit. Three thousand shareholders would henceforward turn to the Top Ten chart as well as the *Financial Times* for their news of their investment.

After the flotation, Dick James and his partner held 23 per cent of Northern Songs. John and Paul held 15 per cent each; NEMS Enterprises held 7.5 per cent, and George and Ringo between them, 1.6 per cent. For two years, Northern's bounding profits were a minor miracle among London's City merchants. No diamond mine in South Africa, no gold or zinc or coffee or sugar cane had quite the same sure fire market certainty as a Lennon–McCartney song. By 1967—the year when two Beatles albums, Revolver and Sergeant Pepper, between them brought profits near the million pound mark—shares in Northern Songs had quintupled their 1965 value.

For any investor, the pièce-de-résistance of Northern were the 159 Lennon–McCartney copyrights, and John and Paul's contractual commitment to carry on composing until 1973. Dick James, however, worked hard to broaden the company's general catalogue. By buying up moribund firms like Lawrence Wright Ltd., Northern Songs acquired such diverse musical properties as Les Parapluies de Cherbourg; Among My Souvenirs; and the theme from television's Coronation Street. James, indeed, worked for Northern somewhat at the expense of Dick James Music Ltd. But he was happy. Everyone in Tin Pan Alley said so. He reminded himself all the time how lucky he was.

Just lately, Dick James had been a little less happy than before. It was not that Lennon–McCartney music had declined in quality. Hey Jude, in 1968, became a publishing success second only in worldwide sales to Yesterday. The trouble was the increasingly erratic behaviour of one half of the publishing credit, and its effects on that sensitive organ the London Stock Exchange. John Lennon's espousal of the Maharishi, his involvement with Yoko, his 'bagism', his nudity—above all, his drug conviction—each produced disquiet among Northern's shareholders and fluctuations in its position on the Stock Exahange. As John's song publisher, Dick James could be tolerant. As managing director of a public company with 3,000 shareholders to consider, he fretted.

Lately, too, his relationship with 'the boys' had grown somewhat strained. The deal which had seemed so miraculous in 1963 had, by 1969, become a source of vague resentment. The Beatles felt, quite simply, that Dick James owned too large a share in their music. Nor was their resentment assuaged by James's habit of sending out inexpensive Christmas gifts such as plastic DJM monogrammed playing cards. A frosty reception had greeted him when he visited Twickenham studios during the Let It Be sessions.

As Northern Songs grew in prosperity, Dick James had received many offers for his 23 per cent. Of these, the most persistent came from Lew Grade, Britain's biggest (and fattest) showbiz mogul, whose ATV network were already minority shareholders, and who, in the dear dead music-hall days, had been James's own theatrical agent. 'He'd been romancing me to sell out to him ever since Brian's death,' Dick James says. 'It was a standing joke between us. "Oh *no*," I'd say, "not *that* again, Lew!" '

It was the addition of Allen Klein to an already unstable Beatle landscape which suddenly changed Dick James's mind. In March 1969, without prior warning, he sold his 23 per cent of Northern Songs to ATV for something over one million pounds.

That the deal went through in secret was, Dick James admits, 'rather unfortunate'. In fairness, both John Lennon and Paul McCartney were out of the country on the respective honeymoons. John read the news in the papers on 28 March, during his Amsterdam Bed-in. Paul found out a few days later in America. The news by then was that ATV, with 35 per cent of Northern Songs under its belt, had bid £9.5m for the rest of the company.

John and Paul contacted one another, united in fury that Dick James had sold them down the river. It would have been fruitless to point out—had anyone dared try—that Northern Songs had long ago ceased to be theirs, but was the legitimate prey of whichever shareholder could get the upper hand. All they knew was that, behind their backs, a major stake in their music had gone to a man who, with his large bulk and still larger Havana cigar, epitomised the hated breed of 'men in suits'. The conciliatory noises which Grade was already making might just as well have been the snarl of an alligator on the banks of the Zambesi.

Allen Klein was recalled from holiday in Puerto Rico to formulate plans for the Beatles themselves to oppose ATV's takeover of Northern Songs. The Eastmans, though still advising Paul McCartney, figured little in the subsequent drama. Paul, once again, was willing to let Klein act for him, in the trouble-shooting capacity that was still unconfirmed by any written contract.

Klein's strategy was that the Beatles, already owning 31 per cent of Northern Songs, should publicly offer £2m for the further 20 per cent which would give them a majority shareholding. The money was to come partly from the Beatles' own coffers, partly from a merchant banker, Henry Ansbacher & Co. Two Beatle companies, Subafilms and Maclen together scraped up almost £1m. Ansbacher's would provide the remaining £1¼m, on collateral furnished by Apple shares and John Lennon's entire stock holding in Northern Songs. Paul—though he had recently increased his own Northern shareholding—refused to pledge any shares as security. Allen Klein completed the bond by guaranteeing £640,000-worth of his own company's MGM stock.

There now began seven weeks of business meetings, long and tortuous enough to surfeit even Allen Klein, in the winding course of which John and Yoko drifted, like rumpled white wraiths, through the grim purlieus of Threadneedle Street. John—to begin with, at least—enjoyed the negotiations. 'It's like playing Monopoly,' he said, 'but with real money.'

A third element in the ATV-Apple struggle had by now shown its hand. This was a consortium of City brokers firms which, over several months, had quietly built up its own stake in Northern Songs to 14 per cent. To capture the company, ATV or the Beatles must buy out—or, at least, win over—the consortium. And from the beginning, it was clear the consortium, which included the Howard and Wyndham theatre chain, was inclined to go along with the Beatles.

The chief drawback in their eyes was Allen Klein. They agreed they wanted no part of a company where Klein might subsequently gain control. The 'Robin Hood of Pop', thanks to various High Court references, was now well-known in London, and was currently suing *The Sunday Times* for a particularly vivid chronicling of his recent career.

Klein did his best to reassure the consortium. At a Press conference in one of Apple's green and white offices—an occasion which, the *Investors Chronicle* suggested, 'must set some sort of a record for unprintable language'—Klein assured the business world that he had no intention of personally muscling in on Northern Songs. And what of the unflattering things said about him by Jeremiah Harmon QC, among others? Klein smiled the tolerant smile of a man whose character had been assassinated more times, and more unavailingly, than Dracula's heart had been pierced by wooden stakes.

His promise was formalised two days later in Henry Ansbacher's proclamation on the Beatles' behalf to Northern's shareholders. If their offer for control were accepted, they said, neither Klein nor any of them would try to meddle with the company's management. The board would be strengthened by the appointment of David Platz, head of the powerful Essex Music Corporation, as Chairman. As a further inducement, John Lennon and Paul McCartney would extend their songwriting contract with Northern beyond its present 1973 expiry-date.

By mid-May, Lew Grade was ready to concede defeat. The Beatles had successfully wooed the consortium, both with assurances of Klein's non-participation and also promises of directorships for the Howard and Wyndham faction. Then, at the very last minute, the pact dissolved. John Lennon had raised objections to the consortium's potential influence over his music. Or, in his own angry words: 'I'm sick of being fucked about by men in suits sitting on their fat arses in the City.'

The consortium melted into Lew Grade's open arms—if not as sellers yet, then as fully-committed allies. On 20 May, ATV achieved effective control of Northern Songs. Grade tempered his victory with earnest hopes that he and the Beatles might still find a basis for co-operation.

That same day's papers announced that Allen Klein had been appointed the Beatles' business manager. Earlier reports that he would receive 20 per cent of their earnings were described as 'exaggerated'.

The agreement had been signed on 8 May. It bore the names of only three Beatles: John, George and Ringo. Paul still had not refused outright: he said he wanted more time—as Klein had repeatedly promised he should have—to go through the management document with John Eastman and his English lawyer. But the others, John especially, had lost patience with Paul's 'stalling'. Klein now told them he needed the signed agreement urgently to take back to New York to present to his ABKCO board. When the four Beatles met at Abbey Road on 9 May, the deed had been done. 'I see you've outvoted me,' Paul said.

So Allen Klein and ABKCO Industries Inc. moved in to 3 Savile Row, W.1. Shortly afterwards within the house, a soft and regular sound became audible. It was the sound of Apple executives perishing under the axe. Ron Kass, Head of Apple Records; Peter Asher, Head of A & R; Brian Lewis, head of the contracts department, all left the Beatles' employment with as much dispatch as if a medieval catapult had propelled them through the white front door. It was the first phase of Klein's promised 'economy drive' to those he condemned as pampered and unproductive management figures. That Ron Kass and Peter Asher between them were responsible for selling some 16 million records on the Apple label did not for one instant stay the hand of their turtlenecked executioner.

After unnecessary management figures on Klein's death list came friends, dependants, now stigmatised as spongers and hangers-on. The scythe swept upward through Apple's subdivisions: through Magic Alex and his electronic workshop; through Zapple, the 'spoken word' label; through Apple Retail, Apple Publishing and the Apple Foundation for the Arts. In vain did the victims appeal to their good friends John, Paul, George or Ringo. The Beatles had suddenly become as remote as Tudor monarchs after signing warrants of execution. So it was even when Klein fired Alistair Taylor, Brian Epstein's original NEMS assistant, and a long time friend and fixer to each of the four. Taylor, when his sentence was pronounced, spent a whole day on the telephone, trying to reach John or Paul, to have his dismissal confirmed first-hand. Neither was available to discuss the matter.

Klein's original intention was that not a single Apple executive should survive to stand between the Beatles and him. He even succeeded, for a short time, in toppling their two closest aides, Neil Aspinall and Peter Brown. Both were on the Apple board of directors; itself a gallows mark. 'I gave Klein the perfect excuse,' Peter Brown says. 'We were just coming up to the annual general meeting. I told him that all the directors had to resign as a formality and then be re-elected. Neil and I both resigned, but we weren't re-elected. We thought the Beatles wouldn't ditch us, but they did.'

Here at least Klein had gone too far. The Beatles could not function without Peter Brown, their immaculate Minister of Court. And Neil Aspinall, their oldest, truest, straightest friend, proved invulnerable to the headsman's axe. For Neil, Klein's coming was ultimately beneficial: it removed the weight of worry he had shouldered as road manager to the whole Apple fiasco. At first, when the burden went, Neil could not believe it had gone. He dreamed strange dreams, that only a road manager to the Beatles could dream: of running in fear from some unknown pursuer, with both arms full of precious silver fish. The more he ran, the more his pursuer gained on him; the more he tried to hold them, the more the silver fish slipped from his grasp.

Those whom Allen Klein did not sack, he filled with a great and quaking dread. The holiday atmosphere, the late morning arrival, the freedom, the free gifts, the long-distance taxi rides, the meals, the drinks, the cigarettes, the joints so freely provided to Apple employees, all were unceremoniously terminated. Swinging, 'laid back', mini-skirted *now* people, to their utter detestation, were obliged to 'clock in' for work each morning. Nothing could be bought without a purchase order signed by Klein or his lieutenant, Peter Howard. Charge accounts that had fed and watered hundreds dried up all over the West End.

It was the New York way of business, sharpened by Allen Klein's own peculiar, unsettling ingenuity. Everyone, from secretaries upwards, felt themselves under the same nervous compulsion: to prove simultaneously that they were essential to Apple and that they posed no obstacle or threat to Klein. Even those he moved upward carried a kind of stigma. Jack Oliver, Ron Kass's young deputy, found himself suddenly in Kass's job as Head of Apple Records, yet with no feeling that he had been promoted. 'I was told: "You're shit, you know that don't you, but this and this needs doing so get on with it." '

Klein had annexed Peter Asher's old office on the second floor, opposite Derek Taylor's Press department. It only added to the terror felt throughout 3 Savile Row that this office remained empty for several days each week, while Klein was in New York dealing with ABKCO Industries business. Then at some unguarded moment in the late afternoon of a day when he appeared to be absent, he would return. Jimmy Clark, on the front doorstep, would hurriedly straighten a dove grey back. The limousine, never quite a Rolls, would disgorge the squat figure which, even in a few steps to the front door, could not bear to break off its study of *Billboard* magazine. Margo and the doorstep brigade had already reached their own unequivocal conclusions. As the door closed on Allen Klein, one of the girls would dart forward and shout 'Mafia!' through the letterbox.

Klein, in fact, despite the 8 May agreement, was still not absolutely sure of his position. How could he be until all four Beatles recognised him as their saviour? John Eastman remained on the scene, representing Paul McCartney and supposedly co-operating with ABKCO Industries in what had been described to the Press as a 'warm, workable relationship'. Riven as he was with contempt for Eastman, Klein recognised that the relationship, if never warm, if barely workable, must at least be maintained. Sooner or later, he hoped to do a deal stunning enough to impress even John Eastman, and so bring Paul into line to complete the equation of his heart's desire. Accordingly, he moderated his opinion of Paul's brother-in-law to a tone of Runyonesque badinage. 'Dear John,' one letter to Eastman began, 'I am on a diet, so stop putting words into my mouth . . .'

A still greater incentive to Klein existed in the three-year contract which John, George and Ringo had signed with ABKCO Industries. This, indeed, gave Klein 20 per cent of their income—but only such income as was generated after his management began. Benefits gained through the NEMS and Northern Songs deal did not fall within the scope of the contract. To earn his 20 per cent, as well as prove himself to the Eastmans and Paul, he must make a major killing in the field where he had strewn so many, earlier corpses. Klein's next target, in other words, were the Beatles' English and American record companies.

Sir Joseph Lockwood was surprised, shortly afterwards, to be visited at his EMI office by Klein and all four Beatles. They had come, Klein announced, to 're-negotiate' the nine-year contract which Brian Epstein had signed with EMI in 1967. 'I said: "All right, we can talk about it," Sir Joseph recalls. "Provided both sides get some benefit, there's no harm in re-negotiating." Klein said: "No, you don't understand. *You* don't get anything. *We* get more."'

'I told them to get out. They went, looking very sheepish. Paul was pulling faces behind the others' backs, as if to say, "Sorry, it was nothing to do with me."

'My assistant was very worried. "You shouldn't have sent them off like this," he said. I said, "It's all right. I recognise the sort of man Klein is. He'll be back in half an hour." And sure enough, half an hour later he rang me to apologise.'

At 3 Saville Row, Klein and the Beatles—excepting Paul—went into conference again. Margo and the other girls were beginning to recognise those conferences by the lights burning late in the big top floor window. In the Press Office, Derek Taylor's light projector cast its wriggling coloured shapes over the wall. Journalists, still waiting for interviews, strained to catch scraps of gossip among insiders who were now all far on the outside.

'—they're just puppets now. I took something in to John and he just said: "Give it to Klein." '

'—they've calmed down a bit. They're eating scrambled eggs.'

'—you know what happened to that note you sent in? Screwed up into a ball and thrown across the room.'

On 26 May, in a suite at the Queen Elizabeth Hotel, Montreal, John and Yoko staged a second, even more ambitious Bed-in. They had meant to hold it in the Bahamas but they decided on Canada as being closest to the country at which their Peace Campaign was chiefly aimed (and which John, through his drug conviction, was now prohibited from entering). The Montreal Bed-in lasted ten days: it included a conversation with Dr. Timothy Leary, 'live' broadcasts to Canadian and U.S. radio stations and a direct hook-up with insurgent students at Berkeley University, California. The climax was the recording at John and Yoko's bedside of the newly-written campaign anthem Give Peace a Chance with a chorus that included Timothy Leary, Murray the K, Tommy Smothers, a rabbi and a troupe of bald headed, bell-ringing, chanting Radha Krishna Temple singers.

It was the prelude to two months in which John, with Yoko at his side, consciously set out to 'saturate' the media with their demonstrations, their slogans—above all, with themselves as a living slogan: 'Mr. and Mrs. Peace'. For John, the campaign was tinged with aggressive satisfaction. He was turning the tables on the Press, exploiting them in precisely the way he, as a Beatle, used to be exploited. He said so in a voice that still incised through the curly Apostle beard, the woolly thought, the inherent heart-sinking fatuousness of representing sitting up in bed in a luxury hotel as a political, humanitarian act. 'The Blue Meanies, or whatever they are, still preach violence all the time in every newspaper, every TV show and every magazine. The least Yoko and I can do is hog the headlines and make people laugh.

We're quite willing to be the world's clowns if it will do any good. For reasons known only to themselves, people print what I say. And I say "peace".'

In June, the campaign moved to 3 Savile Row. The front ground floor office formerly occupied by Ron Kass was commandeered by John and Yoko for their own company, Bag Productions, and their continuing saturation of a still-acquiescent Press. In a rooftop ceremony, before a somewhat bemused Commissioner for Oaths, John changed his name, dropping the Winston his mother gave him as a talisman against Hitler's bombs; becoming, instead, John Ono Lennon. Yoko became Yoko Ono Lennon. Their combined names contained nine O's. Nine was always John's lucky number.

Ron Kass's elegant salon, next to the front door, took on the appearance of an hotel bedroom during a Bed-in. Hand-lettered Peace slogans and Lennon drawings papered the panelled walls. Newspapers, dirty plates, Magic Markers and Gauloises packets submerged the chaste white telephones. In the Georgian fireplace, a plastic doll which had somehow escaped the King's Road Napalm holocaust, stood on its head in a mess of cigarette ends. Yoko sat at the large executive desk with John a little to one side of her. The journalists were brought in at 15-minute intervals.

Sooner or later, in each interview, the talk would turn from Peace and Bagism to a question far more deeply significant to Western Civilisation. Was John truly, as he had said, reduced to his 'last £50,000'? Yes, he said. 'All that stuff about us being millionaires is only true on paper, you know. All we've really got is our houses, our cars and this place. In the old days with Northern Songs, you used to get a cheque occasionally. There's a deal now where a certain percentage of our royalties is paid into this place. So I haven't had any income for about two years. It's all been bloody *outcome*.

'Allen's putting it right for us now. We've made a lot of mistakes, but we're still here. The circus has left town, but we still own the site.'

The presence of John and Yoko downstairs gave a new complexity to the already complex 'vibes' gripping 3 Savile Row. Fear of Klein demanded that they look brisk and businesslike, and sit behind their IBM typewriters like stenographic mice. Fear, no less well-founded of the chief and ever-present Beatle demanded their help in collecting acorns to be sent by John and Yoko as a peace gesture to all world leaders from President Nixon to the King of Yemen. Since early summer is not acorn season, a country-wide appeal had to be launched. One elderly spinster sent in two dried up specimens she had kept for 40 years in a silver box. An entrepreneur, well-versed in the principle of Beatle supply and demand, offered a supply at £1 per acorn.

His Peace Campaign, in fact, aroused John to a belligerence frequently vented on this or that awe-struck Apple employee, unable to tell him, for instance, how to 'fly-post' the whole of London with Peace slogans. Ever since the Two Virgins fiasco, he had suspected the whole house of intent to sabotage his and Yoko's personal projects. He suspected it even more now that their second album, Unfinished Music No. 2—Life with the Lions, had gone on release. The sleeve this time showed Yoko in hospital after her miscarriage, with John in his sleeping bag beside her bed. The tracks were screech and electronic scribble, and a few seconds' heartbeat from the baby that had not survived. John bitterly resented the fact that the album was not mentioned in Apple's current advertising jingle.

And yet none of the Beatles, however artfully approached would let slip a word against Yoko. 'People think they're mad, both of them,' Ringo said, 'but that's not Yoko. That's just John being John.'

On 30 May, Apple released a single which at once seemed to show the Beatles reconciled to Yoko, and Yoko herself to be capable of figuring in an art form that was quite intelligible. It was The Ballad of John and Yoko, a wry chronicle of their recent self-inflicted wanderings between Paris, Gibraltar and Vienna. Each verse led to the chorus 'Christ! You know it ain't easy', so guaranteeing further torment in radio bans. As a gesture of apparent unity, the song was credited to Lennon–McCartney and its performance to the Beatles.

In fact, The Ballad of John and Yoko had been recorded by John virtually single-handed. George and Ringo were both out of the country. The drumming, overdubbed later, was Paul's.

It had been a typical gesture by a personality which, though out-manoeuvred, outvoted and furiously affronted by the events of the past months, still followed its old vocation of presenting the Beatles as a united and invulnerable front. It was no less symbolic of Paul's belief that the Klein era must pass and that, meantime, there was one safe refuge from him. Not even Allen Klein could harm the Beatles in any sphere where they made music together.

Early in July, Paul asked Ringo to drive up and have dinner with him and Linda at Cavendish Avenue. He had by then given up trying to dissuade John or George from appointing Klein. Ringo was, perhaps, a different story. Ringo had gone along with the others, saying that Apple needed 'a hustler'. But Paul evidently still had hopes of the solid common sense which, in so many ways, had given the Beatles their inner strength and balance.

The evening, however, did not turn Ringo against Klein so

much as against Linda McCartney. 'It seemed that as soon as I started saying, well maybe Klein wasn't so bad and we should give him a chance, Linda would start crying. In a few minutes, I'd be saying the same—well, maybe he *isn't* so bad—and Linda would start crying again. "Oh, they've got you, *too*," she kept saying.'

Apple, Paul's brainchild, his living Magritte, his 'Western Communism', was now repugnant to him. London was becoming almost as bad. The girls outside his gates showed increasing hatred of Linda: they broke into the house not just to look now but to steal the new Mrs. McCartney's clothes and photographic prints. When money began to vanish, even Paul's tolerance became exhausted. One day, he and Linda pretended to go out, then kept watch on the house from a garden across the street. Unfortunately, it was the moment chosen by Margo Stevens, his longest-suffering admirer, to leave a bunch of flowers on the front step. 'Suddenly, Paul ran up and started shaking me. "It's *you* all the time, isn't it?" he kept shouting. I was terrified. I said, "No—I only wanted to leave some flowers." I think he could see how much he'd frightened me. He stopped shaking me and started stroking my hair.'

Late in July, Paul got in touch with George Martin. It was now five months since Martin had worked on the Let It Be album. According to Paul, no one had yet been able to face editing the hours of ramshackle playing. The book that was to have accompanied the disc had been written, but then heavily censored in proof by EMI. The film, originally intended for television, was now to be a full-length cinema feature, and so impossible to release before early 1970. The album, when edited, must therefore be held over to accompany the film.

Then Paul made a surprising request. The Beatles, he said, wanted George Martin to produce an album for them 'the way we used to do it'. Martin, remembering his latter experience, responded cautiously. 'I said: "If the album's going to be the way it used to be, then all of you have got to be the way you used to be." Paul said: "Yeah, we will. We promise. Only please let's do the album."'

So it happened, in July and August 1969, as the decade began to wear out, its chief creators agreed to turn back the clock a little way. John Lennon suspended his Peace Campaign. George Harrison broke off from recording the chants of the London Radha Krishna Temple. Ringo interrupted his burgeoning film career. Paul steeled himself to remain in London a little longer. The four Beatles met, for the last time, at Abbey Road.

May 1970

'Everybody had a hard year'

On 22 July 1969, the first men walked on the Moon. It was an oddly disappointing moment. The fascination of centuries had begun to wane several years earlier, when satellite pictures first revealed humanity's ultimate objective in its true lifeless, colourless desolation. One felt disappointed, too, that the explorers did not communicate, as in Hollywood films, by tannoy: they were visible on the entire world's television screens at every ponderous second of their mission. By the time Neil Armstrong took his 'first great step for Mankind', he had become a bore literally larger than the Universe. So the Sixties made it, only just, across the finish-line into the future. Little balloon men bobbed, weightless, on an unlit beach. Humanity yawned, switched off and went to bed.

For millions of the young, that moonshot summer was devoted, perversely, to getting closer to Earth. In early June, on an obscure meadow in upstate New York, 450,000 camped in the open air, watching a four-day pageant of American and British Rock bands: a mighty mass of impacted blue denim, harmlessly rejoicing in its youth and its music; announcing its identity with one vast outbreak of sunny humour; addressing its Government with one gigantic, sardonic voice. If the Sixties ever triumphed, it was not when astronauts bounced up and down on the poor, dead Moon. It was when the Woodstock masses sang, 'There ain't no time to wonder why, hey whoopee, we're gonna die.'

A smaller but sufficient miracle followed later that month in London when Blind Faith, the 'supergroup' formed by Eric Clapton from personnel in already famous bands, gave a performance free of charge in Hyde Park before an audience numbering 150,000. That, too, passed off peacefully and happily, and was followed by an announcement which seemed to confirm the new movement among Rock demigods to use their huge power to benevolent, unselfish ends. The Rolling Stones would give a free concert, also in Hyde Park, on 5 July.

A crowd larger than Woodstock's, some half a million young people, blotted out central London's breathing space to see the group which, by default only—by absence of its obviously pre-eminent rival—now billed itself without contradiction as 'the world's greatest Rock and Roll band'. Before the performance came a moment of bad taste conceivable only to the superstar ego. Three days earlier, Brian Jones, the group's lead guitarist, and only musician of consequence, had accidentally drowned in a swimming pool. Jones, in fact, had been deeply depressed and drug-ridden as a consequence of his ostracism by the other Stones, Mick Jagger in particular. There was thus a schizophrenic element in the rites of mourning performed by Jagger in Hyde Park. Wearing cosmetics and a little girl's party dress, and flanked by Hell's Angel bodyguards, he read out a passage of Shelley that seemed less a memorial to his dead companion than one further medium for his own primping narcissism. The climax was the moment when hundreds of white butterflies were to be released over the Hyde Park throng. The butterflies, unfortunately, were in boxes which Jagger's entourage had neglected to supply with air-holes. Those which had not already suffocated managed only the shortest flight before dropping dead.

With a corpse, a man in makeup and hundreds of dead butterflies, the Hyde Park concert held all too many prophecies for the decade at its turning-point. There was also that metaphor implicit in a short, fat, turtlenecked man who sat amid Jagger's entourage, wearing an expression of innocent wonder. For as well as managing the Beatles, Allen Klein still managed the Rolling Stones.

In August, only the 'Apple Scruffs', as George Harrison nicknamed the doorstep girls, had any reason to be in London. If you were young, you headed south to the Isle of Wight, to green chalk downs where Keats and Tennyson once walked, and where half a million now pitched their tents to hear a poet comparable in stature, though barely believable as a presence under any such small-time seaside sky. Bob Dylan had agreed to appear, and truly did so, emerging from long seclusion in America to play on the grassy slopes above a British holiday camp, and then vanish by helicopter to a destination rumoured somewhere near London. It was in fact John Lennon's new mansion, Tittenhurst Park. As Dylan and he met on the new ancestral lawns, it was hard to say which had changed most out of all recognition.

Each decade ends in the same, hurried, worried search to spot the keynotes of the succeeding one. As the Seventies approached, these open-air concerts and festivals seemed a hopeful sign. It truly appeared that young people, in the decade of their first power and pampering, had learned a secret withheld from earlier generations. They had learned to like each other, and to congregate in huge quantities without trying to do each other harm. Thinking back, one could see where that process had begun. It had begun at the de Montfort Hall, Leicester; at the Odeon, Hammersmith; at Carnegie Hall, Shea Stadium and the Hollywood Bowl. It had begun—and somehow it still ended—with the Beatles.

Also that summer, in Los Angeles, Police were called to a Bel Air mansion occupied by Sharon Tate, a glamorous young film actress, wife of the director Roman Polansky. The scene at the house surpassed any in Polansky's famous horror story, *Repulsion.* His eight-months-pregnant wife, with three friends had been savagely hacked to death and their blood used to scrawl the words 'Helter Skelter' on walls throughout the house. The killing was later admitted to, with several others, by one Charles Manson, head of a hippy 'family' whom he had converted from Love and Peace to disciples in a mock-religious murder cult. Manson claimed under questioning to have been chiefly inspired by those whom Timothy Leary deified to all hippies as 'Divine God agents'; and that he had found his instructions to murder Sharon Tate in two songs, Helter Skelter and Piggies, on the Beatles' White Album.

Not all Apple creatures had perished under Allen Klein. In the Press Office there were still plastic birds, dipping and dipping their beaks around a shallow water-tray. The Press Office, likewise, continued to function, though at what inscrutable whim of Klein's Derek Taylor could not claim to understand. Sometimes in mid-afternoon, when his department became too crowded and the Scotch and Coke fumes too uproariously thick, Taylor would raise himself in his scallop-backed throne, push the hair off his eyes and shout, 'Clear the room now! I mean it!' After one such dismissal, wandering in the sudden space behind Carol Paddon's desk, he paused by the water tray and studied the nodding birds. 'Those beaks are going mouldy,' he remarked gloomily. 'No one told us they'd do that when we bought them. They cost us £1 each.'

Derek Taylor was a frustrated writer. But, unlike most frustrated writers, he had talent. Often he would have dismissed his court simply for the purpose of fighting his way back the few inches across his desk to the typewriter that stood there. He wrote a great deal during Apple's last year: essays and soliloquies and memoranda to himself, all on a theme as constant as the pressure on him from above, below and sideways. Why do I work for the Beatles? And why, of all the complex emotions produced by working for the Beatles, is the commonest one simple fear?

'Whatever the motivation,' Derek Taylor typed, 'the effect is slavery. Whatever the Beatles ask is done. I mean, whatever the

Beatles ask is tried. A poached egg on the Underground on the Bakerloo Line between Trafalgar Square and Charing Cross? Yes, Paul. A sock full of elephant shit on Otterspool Promenade? Give me 10 minutes, Ringo. Two Turkish dwarfs dancing the Charleston on a sideboard? Male or female, John? Pubic hair from Sonny Liston? It's early closing, George (gulp), but give me until noon tomorrow. The only gig I would do after this is the Queen. Their staff are terrified of them, and not without reason. They have fired more people than any comparable employer unit in the world. They make Lord Beaverbrook look like Jesus.'

Then the music would begin again, and Derek Taylor, and Mavis Smith, and Carol Paddon—who was afraid to go on holiday lest her job should vanish—each remembered why they were sitting here. The stagnant sea of journalists and TV men remembered, or almost did. Taylor said the same thing into the telephone a dozen times each day. 'It's called Abbey Road. Yes—the studios are in Abbey Road. It's an album just like they used to make. They sound the way they sounded in the old days.'

Something had stopped the elements diverging, and restored them to their old unsurpassable balance. Abbey Road was John Lennon at his best, and Paul McCartney at his best, and George Harrison suddenly reaching a best that no one had ever imagined. It was John's anarchy, straight and honed. It was Paul's sentimentality with the brake applied. It was George's new, wholly surprising presence, drawing the best from both sources. It was a suite of new songs, not warring internally, as on the White Album, but rounded and unified and performed with taut simplicity. It was the moment, caught again and crystallised, even in the flux of an expiring decade. It was hot streets, soft porn and hippydom fading into a hard reality. It was London here and now, and Liverpool then, and the Beatles, dateless and timeless in a sudden, capricious illusion of perfect harmony.

It was playing on 11 September, Abbey Road filled the Apple house with the same optimism as the green carpets, vacuumed fresh again, and the clean glasses set out for the day's visitors. A quarter of a mile away at Hyde Park Corner, hippy squatters had barricaded themselves behind the stucco of one of the old Piccadilly mansions. Apple sent a messenger with an armful of new albums to fortify them in their ordeal. All that day, until early evening, there might have been no such person as Allen Klein.

In the ground floor office of Bag Productions, the first visitors were led in to meet John and Yoko. They were not journalists; they were two blind, middle-aged Texan girls in pink and orange taffeta ball gowns. Each was led across to touch John, then Yoko led them to the group of four perspex cabinets blocking the fireplace. It was the hi-fi system which John had ironically christened The Plastic Ono Band, and even credited with the playing of Give Peace a Chance. Each blind girl's hand in Yoko's touched the featureless robots hopefully, like a shrine.

Next came the day-long queue of reporters, primed with questions about Peace; about John's interest in the A6 murder case, but mainly about the two films he and Yoko had shown that week at the Institute of Contemporary Arts. The first was *Rape*; the second, entitled *Self-Portrait*, was a 42-minute study of John's penis both in partial and full erection.

The Press asked why. John said it was a self-portrait, that's why. As usual, when he spoke, he made it almost plausible. 'Anything that gets a reaction is good,' he told the *New Musical Express*. 'People are just frozen jellies. It just needs someone to do something to turn off the 'fridge.' Yoko sat beside him, eating brown rice from a bowl with a long wooden spoon. She interjected only to regret that no serious critical comment had been directed at their film of John's penis. Or, as Yoko innocently said, 'The critics wouldn't touch it.'

George and Ringo were both at Savile Row that day. For Ringo, the errand was straightforward. He had come in to give Peter Brown details of the house he wanted to sell, having bought it from Peter Sellers a few months previously. Now he was tired of its extensive parkland, its private cinema and sauna baths and wide frontage, with fishing rights, on the River Wey. Upstairs, the loudspeakers played Octopus's Garden, Ringo's Abbey Road song, as simple and happy as his nature and his attitude to Apple. 'It's a nice place to come in and watch the others doing nice things. And when I want a new watch or pair of boots, it's a bloke at the office who gets them for me.'

George arrived, accompanied by his 'personal assistant', Terry Doran. On Abbey Road that song began which was by common consent the album's most thrilling rebirth of the Beatles' old quintessence. George had written it months before in Eric Clapton's garden: forgetting his sitars and mantras, he called it Here Comes The Sun, and in that simplicity at long last touched a chord of the mystical. Even his voice was freed; for he sounded like John. And in Something, his first-ever Beatles A-side, he sounded a little like Paul. He had found an identity, by forgetting to be himself.

Nowadays, everyone wanted to photograph and interview George. *Bravo*, the West German magazine, waited upstairs, in a studio set banked high with flowers. An elderly workman staggered in, carrying a cardboard box in which a Buddha lay in pieces. Kneeling, the man attempted to fit the eight golden arms into their correct sockets. Even George seemed impressed by the thoroughness of the preparations. 'If I'd known it was going to be like this, I'd have washed me hair,' he said. He decided that his blue denim overalls were not grand enough. A Press Office girl was sent out to Mr. Fish to bring back a selection of silk shirts to be used for the photograph, then given away to anyone who wanted them.

The Beatles ceased to exist that afternoon, when Anthony Fawcett, John and Yoko's personal assistant, picked up a ringing telephone from the debris of papers and plates. It was a Canadian entrepreneur, asking if John and Yoko would attend a Rock and Roll revival concert in Toronto the following day. John took the telephone from Fawcett: he would go, he said, but only if he were allowed to perform. Within hours, the Plastic Ono Band had metamorphosed from perspex robots into an ad hoc 'supergroup' consisting of John, Yoko, Eric Clapton, Klaus Voorman and Alan White. A charter airliner was booked to carry them, if John did get up in time and did not take fright at the last minute at the thought of appearing with an unrehearsed band before an audience of thousands.

Upstairs, while George was being photographed among his flowers, Ringo strolled in to look at the camera equipment. 'You want to use a zoom lens through that prism,' he advised *Bravo.*

'Do you fancy going to Australia to play?' George said sarcastically.

'When do we get back?'

'Tomorrow.'

The house registered no sign of the schism that had occurred. The house was lulled by Abbey Road, playing again: the heavy bass and hissing prelude to Come Together. The Press Office was, as usual, dark, and speckled with psychedelic light and dense with seated figures. In one corner, Mal Evans's discovery, The Iveys—now renamed Bad finger—sat, like very young pantomime pirates, awaiting news of their first release on the Apple label. Mary Hopkin, a sweet, frail, bewildered girl, passed through with her even more bewildered Welsh parents. Neil Aspinall came in to say that the Plastic Ono Band had got away to Canada on the second charter airliner bidden to stand by after they missed the first one. 'Not *another* beard,' Derek Taylor said, looking at Aspinall's face. 'Yeah, we're all doing it,' the loyal road manager replied. 'John, George—even Yoko's trying.'

Now on Abbey Road, the Apple house heard the voice which had first imagined it, and argued to launch it, and which had now abandoned it, leaving only a song lyric behind as explanation. 'You never give me your money,' sang Paul McCartney to the manager he would not recognise. 'You only give your funny paper . . .' He had contrived to make the album that was an act of reunion serve also as an outlet for his bitter frustration, even though, being Paul, he could only do so in hints, between the smiles of one who still hated to admit any unpleasantness.

Late in the afternoon, all sound withdrew into Abbey Road. Somehow, it was always Side Two that played: the sequence of song fragments, Sun King, Mean Mr. Mustard, Polythene Pam, She Came In Through The Bathroom Window, like sketches for a Liverpool folk opera. The side ended with Paul alone, sweet and lyrical as always, as always starting to say something but never quite reaching the point. Golden Slumbers, paraphrase of an Elizabethan cradle song, melted into the desperate seeming Carry That Weight. 'And in the end', sang Paul, as if he really and truly were coming to a conclusion:

'The love you take
Is equal to the love
You make.'

That September, in the heady aftermath of festivals and free concerts, Paul made one last effort to reunite the others on stage again. His idea now was that they should play at small clubs, unannounced, perhaps even in disguise. Ringo supported the idea and George, though noncommital, did not refuse outright. But John told Paul bluntly he must be daft. 'I might as well tell you,' John continued, 'I'm leaving the group. I've had enough. I want a divorce, like my divorce from Cynthia.'

He had reached his decision while flying back with Yoko, Eric Clapton and Klaus after their tumultuous welcome at the Toronto Rock 'n' Roll Revival. Standing up there with Yoko and the robots, singing any words that came into his head, he had realised that ceasing to be a Beatle need not strike him blind. Cold Turkey, his new song, named for heroin's withdrawal horrors, was written to renounce an even worse addiction. He would never again be hooked by Yesterday or Ob-la-di, Ob-la-da. It only remained, in his own phrase, to 'break out of the Palace'.

What restrained him then was an urgent plea from Allen Klein not to jeopardise the deals Klein still hoped to do on behalf of the Beatles as a unit. For Klein, at that very moment, was on the brink of an unequivocal coup in respect of their record royalties. Having failed to browbeat EMI, he had set about browbeating their American label, Capitol. Bob Gortikov, Capitol's President, under pressure from Klein, was proving less inflexible than Sir Joseph Lockwood. But clearly, for John to announce his resignation would seriously weaken Klein's bargaining position. John, therefore, agreed to keep silent—even to the other Beatles —until the Capitol deal was done.

It was a promise he found impossible to keep when Paul, in another long boardroom wrangle, brought up the subject of 'live' performing again. A furious row developed, with John railing bitterly at Paul for his 'granny' music, especially Ob-la-di and

Maxwell's Silver Hammer, on the Abbey Road album, which John had particularly detested. He told Paul he was sick of 'fighting for time' on their albums, and of always taking the B-sides on singles. Then, rather tactlessly, he pointed at George as perennial victim of the Lennon–McCartney 'carve-up'. Paul replied that only this year had George's songs achieved comparable quality with theirs. George interrupted resentfully that songs he had recorded this year were often those he had written years earlier but not been allowed to release. He added that he had never really felt the Beatles were backing him. As John rounded angrily on George, Paul made a sudden, quiet plea to them to remember how they had always overcome disagreements in the past. 'When we go into a studio, even on a bad day, I'm still playing bass, Ringo's still drumming and we're still *there*, you know.'

Paul could not believe that John's resignation was anything other than a fit of temperament—like George's during the Let It Be sessions. When the white Rolls Royce moved off down Savile Row that afternoon, it had been agreed to dissolve, for the time being. Not long afterwards, a slightly stunned President of Capitol Records agreed to Allen Klein's demand for an unheard-of royalty of 69 cents on each Beatles album sold in America. Derek Taylor spoke to Steve Gortikov shortly after Gortikov ended his last session with Klein. 'We would have done the deal anyway,' Gortikov said, 'but did he have to be so *nasty* about it?'

According to Klein, the deal with Capitol swung Paul McCartney in his favour at last. 'Paul congratulated me on the agreement. He said, "Well, if you *are* screwing us, I can't see that you are."' Paul's version, sworn subsequently in a High Court affadavit, was that, on the contrary, he felt uneasy to think the Beatles had received a massive royalty increase at the very moment when their future together was so uncertain. Also, by that time, he had ceased to believe anything Klein said. The most public and PR-conscious Beatle retreated into complete seclusion, with Linda and their newborn daughter, Mary, on his farm in Argyllshire.

With the Capitol deal, Klein was assured of his 20 per cent. He could now turn his attention back to the five-months stalemate over Northern Songs and Lew Grades ATV network. Grade, having gained effective control of Northern, now hoped to woo the Beatles into accepting him as a sort of supercharged Dick James. His plan was to buy out the Howard and Wyndham consortium's blocking 14 per cent, but to persuade John and Paul to retain their 31 per cent, and extend their songwriting contract beyond the present expiry date in 1973.

Late in October, ATV finally bought out its consortium partner, bringing Lew Grade's share of Northern to slightly more than 50 per cent. Hours afterwards, it was announced that John and Paul, and Ringo, were selling their combined 31 per cent shareholding to ATV. The news, when it reached Apple —by a tip-off from the *Financial Times*—sounded very like defeat. Allen Klein, at his customary afternoon breakfast, claimed it as a victory. A threatened lawsuit against Northern for £5m in 'unpaid' Beatle royalties helped to persuade ATV to pay cash rather than stock for the Beatles' holdings. Klein could thus congratulate himself on having enriched John and Paul by about a million and a half pounds each, and Ringo by £80,000.

The American release of Abbey Road, together with Paul McCartney's disappearance, now produced one of Beatlemania's strangest and sickest by-products. A Detroit disc jockey claimed to have received a mysterious telephone call, telling him that Paul McCartney was, in fact, dead, and that corroboration could be found in the Abbey Road sleeve photograph. This, though it might appear a somewhat unimaginative shot of the four Beatles walking over a St. John's Wood zebra crossing, actually, the mystery caller said, represented Paul's funeral procession. John, in his white suit, was the minister; Ringo, dark-suited, was the undertaker, and George, in his shabby denims, the gravedigger. Still stronger funereal symbols were divined from the fact that Paul himself walked barefoot, out of step with the other three and smoking a cigarette right-handed. The clinching clue alleged was a Volkswagen car parked in the background, plainly showing its numberplate '28 IF'—or Paul's age *if* he had lived.

Picked up by other disc jockeys, elaborated by Beatle fanatics, the rumour swept America, growing ever more earnestly labyrinthine and foolish. One faction claimed that Paul had been murdered by the CIA. Another—the most powerful—claimed he had been decapitated in a car accident and that an actor William Campbell had undergone plastic surgery to become his double. Scores of further 'clues' to support this theory were discovered in earlier Beatle albums—in the scraps of gibberish and backwards tapes; the fictional 'Billy Shears' mentioned in Sergeant Pepper, and various macabre John Lennon lines from A Day In The Life and I Am The Walrus. It was said that by holding the Magical Mystery Tour EP sleeve up to a mirror, a telephone number became visible on which Paul himself could be contacted in the Hereafter. The number, in fact, belonged to a *Guardian* journalist, subsequently driven almost to dementia by hundreds of early morning transatlantic telephone calls.

In America, an industry grew up of 'Paul is Dead' magazines, TV inquests and death discs—Saint Paul, Dear Paul, The Ballad of Paul and Paulbearer. It was all something stranger than a hoax: it was a self-hoax. Even when Paul himself surfaced on the cover of *Life* magazine, the rumours did not abate. Consequently, Beatles record sales in America in October 1969 rose to a level unequalled since February 1964. Abbey Road was to sell five million copies, a million more even than Sergeant Pepper. The Beatles, not Paul, had died; yet how could that be when they seemed bigger and better than ever?

In December, Eric Clapton, the virtuoso guitarist, sometime player with Cream, Blind Faith and the Plastic Ono Band, started a British tour with his newest protégés, the American hillbilly duo Delaney and Bonnie. As the tour moved north, from Birmingham to Sheffield and Newcastle, its stage personnel disclosed an additional guitarist, of whose incalculable fame the strangest part was that scarcely anyone recognised him at first. It was Clapton's friend, co-songwriter and admirer, George Harrison.

That shy, rather sad figure on rhythm guitar, burdened with scarves and hair and buckskin fringes, bore little resemblance to a being which the Sixties had raised higher than Heaven. His marriage, like his Beatle life, was nearing its end. His face, blanched with both luxury and deprivation, impassively bore the weight of the decade piled up behind him. It seemed a kind of therapy for him to stand hidden on a stage in Newcastle-upon-Tyne, being led by Clapton through familiar Rock and Roll numbers until his fingers found the old, comforting E and B7 chords.

John kept his promise to say nothing of the break-up. In a curious way, his and Yoko's continuing notoriety served as camouflage. In November, he renounced his MBE, taking it from the top of his Aunt Mimi's television set and sending it back to the Queen as a protest against Vietnam, the war in Biafra and the failure of Cold Turkey to remain in the British Top Twenty. Though that final flippancy made the gesture futile, it was not without a certain coincidental irony. For the statesman who had bought his own popularity with that same small, pink-ribboned medal, still reigned at 10 Downing Street. What Harold Wilson had started with the Beatles he had continued less and less discerningly, showering MBEs, CBEs, knighthoods and peerages on any cheap entertainer who might cadge him a headline or a vote. But for the Beatle Prime Minister, too, only a few weeks remained.

All politicans had learned something from Harold Wilson. In Canada, Prime Minister Trudeau held talks with John and Yoko to hear their plan to turn 1970 into 'Year One for Peace', commemorated by another vast open-air concert in Toronto. *Rolling Stone* magazine, speaking for the new, sleeker-tailored Underground, named John as 'Man of the Year'. 'A five-hour talk between John Lennon and Richard Nixon,' said *Rolling Stone*, 'would be more significant than any Geneva Summit Conference between the USA and Russia.'

Meanwhile, in a drab motorway cafeteria near Sheffield, George sat before a plate of instant mushroom soup and a trifle in a paper cup while waitresses came and peered suspiciously into his face.

'You *are* one, aren't you?' he was asked accusingly. 'You *are* a group, aren't you?'

'No I'm not,' George said. He pointed to Eric Clapton. 'He is, though. That's the world's greatest guitarist: Bert Weedon.'

In Times Square, New York, and prominent places in half a dozen other American cities, vast billboards carried a cryptic seasonal message. 'War is Over if You Want It. Happy Christmas From John and Yoko'. In London, the *Beatles monthly* ceased publication. Princess Margaret attended the premiere of a new film, *The Magic Christian*, featuring Ringo Starr in a small cameo part. In Campbelltown, Argyllshire, Paul McCartney put the final touches to an album he had tried to make already, with Revolver, Sergeant Pepper and Let It Be—an album with nobody else on it but Paul.

In Altamont, California, at a free concert given by the Rolling Stones, Hell's Angel 'stewards' knifed a young black spectator to death in full view of the stage. This was the note on which the Sixties ended: the decade when things happened turning overnight into one where things only unhappened.

Three Savile Row already felt the 'vibes' of the new decade. A house which had stood elegantly intact for two centuries before the Beatles' coming, seemed to decide deep within itself that the effort was no longer worthwhile. The rear promontory began to subside, throwing an ugly crack slantwise across the Cordon Bleu kitchen wall. The apple green carpets were scuffed and threadbare. The deep leather sofas were cracked and split. The framed Gold Discs up the staircase wall were no longer too numerous to count. On the front stairs, the oil painting of lion cubs was torn at one corner where someone had tried to wrench it from its frame.

Though the front door frequently stood wide open, no invaders seized the chance to stampede through it. The 'Apple Scruffs' in their frontstep purdah, had risen above such immature displays. Now they wore badges, denoting seniority and precedence; they had their own magazine, even their own notepaper, headed *'Steps', 3 Savile Row.* Margo, their leader, had crossed the ultimate threshold on their behalf: she now worked inside Apple as a teamaker. She had served George Harrison with cheese and cucumber sandwiches and Ringo with a one-egg omelette. She had seen how ordinary, how rather pale and pockmarked, were the gods whom she had worshipped for the last three years of her life, in all weathers, out of doors.

The Press Office continued functioning, but in broad daylight and a quiet that grew steadily more ominous. John had unilaterally fired the whole department, transferring his publicity arrangements to the Rolling Stones's Press agent, Les Perrin. Derek Taylor had left, at George Harrison's kindly insistence, to finish the book he had been trying to start since 1968. Carol Paddon was fired for telling the *Daily Sketch* the truth, that Apple was 'just an accounting office now'. Mavis Smith, the ex-Ballet Rambert dancer, and Richard diLello, the 'House Hippy', stayed on for the present. All round the room, on the desk supporting a scarlet torso; on the desk with the light show projector; on the desk next to the nodding birds, one by one the telephones stopped ringing.

It was in such a dismal morning-after spirit that the Beatles' Let It Be project limped, at last, towards a conclusion. Klein had sold the film to United Artists, and expected it to open in London in late spring. The album tapes, recorded a year earlier, had been exhumed from Apple's now sepuchral basement studio. There remained only the job of making an LP record from those uncounted hours of rehearsing, improvising, joking, jamming, and angry argument.

With the Beatles' consent, Klein had brought in the American producer Phil Spector to do that sifting and editing job which they themselves could not face. Spector's girl groups and 'wall of sound' technique had been among their earliest and strongest influences: he was, at the same time, renowned for Gothic over-elaboration and triumphant bad taste. His appointment to doctor what had begun as an 'honest, no nonsense' Beatles album only confirmed the weary indifference they now felt to their music, as well as to each other.

Spector laboured, and an album duly went to EMI for pressing. It was, inevitably, a strange, inconclusive affair. Half of it chronicled the sessions as they had happened, with tuning-up noises and parody announcements by John, amid sycophantic laughter from the film crew. The other half had been remixed and augmented by Phil Spector in his own inimitable way. An acetate went to each Beatle accompanied by a long letter from Spector, justifying what he had done but assuring them he would make whatever changes they wished.

When Paul McCartney played the acetate, he was stunned. His ballad The Long and Winding Road had been remixed by Spector, then dubbed with a violin and horn section and topped with a sickly celestial choir. Paul tried to contact Spector, but could not. He wrote to Allen Klein, demanding the restoration of his original version, but to no avail. It was the final affront of the Klein era that the most tyrannically particular and perfectionist Beatle should find he no longer controlled even the way he sang his own songs. Paul decided at last to stop fighting against fighting.

He had completed his solo album in Scotland, with no editor but Linda and no help but from Linda, that untried musician, on backing vocals. In March he returned to London and rang up John, breaking a silence of almost six months.

'I'm doing what you and Yoko are doing,' Paul said. 'I'm putting out an album and I'm leaving the group, too.'

'Good,' John replied. 'That makes two of us who have accepted it mentally.'

Paul then notified Apple, or what remained of it, that he wanted his solo album, McCartney, to be released on 10 April. The date was vetoed by Klein and all the three other Beatles as clashing with the release of Let It Be, and also Ringo's first solo album, Sentimental Journey. Paul, suspecting Klein of sabotage, appealed directly to Sir Joseph Lockwood at EMI. Sir Joseph said he must accept the majority decision.

Ringo well-meaningly visited Cavendish Avenue to add his personal explanation to letters he had brought from John and George, confirming that Paul's solo debut would have to be postponed. Ringo, in his own subsequent High Court affadavit, described his dismay when Paul 'went completely out of control, prodding his fingers towards my face, saying, "I'll finish you all now," and, "You'll pay!" He told me to put on my coat and get out.'

The outburst showed Ringo, at least, what a gigantic emotional significance the McCartney album had for Paul. It is a testament to his eternal good nature that, after Paul threw him out, Ringo went straight back to John and George and talked them into giving Paul his way. Ringo's Sentimental Journey LP was brought forward and Let It Be put back so that McCartney could appear, as Paul now agreed, on 17 April.

With it came the announcement which John had agreed not to make the previous October and which Paul now presented as his decision alone, in a way that revealed his most ingratiating, least agreeable side. A heavily-contrived 'self-interview', inserted into the McCartney album sleeve, proclaimed the irreconcilable split in the Beatles, in smiling yet sly phrases: a vast conclusion that, even now, never succeeded in coming to the point.

Q: Are all these songs by Paul McCartney alone?
A: Yes, sir.
Q: Did you enjoy working as a solo?

A: Very much. I only had to ask me for a decision and I agreed with me. Remember Linda's on it too, so it's really a double act.

Q: The album was not known about until it was nearly completed. Was this deliberate?

A: Yes because normally an album is old before it comes out. (Aside) Witness 'Get Back'.

Q: Are you able to describe the texture or feel of the album in a few words?

A: Home. Family. Love.

Q: Will Paul and Linda become a John and Yoko?

A: No, they will become Paul and Linda.

Q: Is it true that neither Allen Klein nor ABKCO Industries have been or will be in any way involved with the production, manufacturing, distribution or promotion of the record?

A: Not if I can help it.

Q: What is your relationship with Klein?

A: It isn't. I am not in contact with him and he does not represent me in any way.

Q: What do you feel about John's Peace effort? The Plastic Ono Band? Giving back the MBE? Yoko's influence? Yoko?

A: I love John and respect what he does—it doesn't give me any pleasure.

Q: Are you planning a new album or single with the Beatles?

A: No.

Q: Is this album a rest away from the Beatles or the start of a solo career?

A: Time will tell. Being a solo album means it's the start of a new career and not being done with the Beatles it's a rest. So it's both.

Q: Is your break with the Beatles temporary or permanent, due to personal differences or musical ones?

A: Personal differences, business differences, musical differences but most of all because I have a better time with my family. Temporary or permanent? I don't know.

Q: Do you foresee a time when Lennon–McCartney become an active songwriting partnership again?

A: No.

Q: Did you miss the Beatles and George Martin? Was there a moment, e.g., when you thought: 'Wish Ringo was here for this break'?

A: No.

On 20 May, *Let It Be*, the Beatles' last film and final appearance together, received its British premiere simultaneously in London and Liverpool. A vast hoarding had been erected over the London Pavilion, on which four faces, fenced off from each other, stared out with expressions of faint nausea befitting this one more perfunctory ordeal. In Liverpool, a Civic welcome waited in the cinema foyer; the Lord Mayor, aldermen, dignitaries and old friends. The train supposed to be bringing the Beatles pulled in to Lime Street, but they did not alight from it. Nor did they from the train after that. The Civic welcome waited for the next train, and the next.

The Beatles were gone, but how could they be when the screen showed them as always: together, advancing? It was their last trick to make those tired, year-old scenes, at Twickenham studios and in the Apple basement, as much of the moment as any moment they had caught and personified. *Let It Be* was their sad fading; it was also the desperate sadness that they must fade. It was Paul and John, singing Two of Us. It was Paul when he sang The Long and Winding Road in its proper version, with only Billy Preston's keyboard and himself on piano: his make-believe beard, his make-believe hobo suit, his great, round, regretful eyes. It was Paul again, singing Let It Be, the mollifying phrase of a Liverpool mother to a fractious child, as if he forgave and had been forgiven and everything would get better now.

It was the scene in Savile Row when lights still filled every Apple window, and the big white cars drew up outside. It was the day when clamour split the Mayfair skies; when people came across rooftops and climbed down fire escapes to look, and people in the streets stared upward. It was the old soldier in a pork pie hat whom the film crew stopped and asked for comment. 'Yus—well, the Beatles, what I say is, you can't beat 'em. They're out on their own. They're good people. I say, good luck to 'em.'

It was the rooftop concert with their hair blowing into their eyes, with Ringo in a red plastic mac, George in green trousers, John in a ladies' short fur coat. It was four musicians playing together as no four musicians ever could or ever would again. It was voices singing The One After 909, the way they used to on truant afternoons at Forthlin Road. It was slow guitars in the cold wind as John summed up the era they had given their generation. 'Everybody had a good time. Everybody had a wet dream. Everybody let their hair down. Everybody saw the sun shine.' It was Get Back, sung a second time as the Police came up and stopped them; the turning aside and dispersing, stopped in a freeze frame, when freeze frames were new, and John Lennon's voice floating back derisively, through the years of bereavement that were to come:

'I'd like to say thank you very much on behalf of the group and myself and I hope we passed the audition.'

EPILOGUE

December 1980

'All the lonely people . . .'

So much remains and, in a way, so little.

There is a band called Wings with a clutch of Gold and Platinum Discs that long ago lifted it into the *Guinness Book of Records*. Its leader is a multimillionaire businessman who professes himself a simple, unspoilt lad with all the subtlety at his command; who allows his wife to sing on stage, unmelodiously; whose every lyric betrays what editing it has not had, what sentimentality no one dared mock; whose songs, for all their commercial success, can never lay the ghosts of songs a decade before them, nor extinguish the knowledge of what Paul McCartney would do if only he would try.

There are two ex-Beatles, destined never to be less or more than that. One is a landed gentleman-hippy who—with the shining exception of his Concert for Bangladesh—occupies himself with treadmill albums, a country estate at Henley-on-Thames and the consolidation of his now secure fortunes. That is, or rather used to be George Harrison. His face, in the superstar firmament, had the pitted melancholy of an under-employed working man. Ringo, still indubitably and invulnerably Ringo, lives variously in New York, California and Monaco, content with his girl friends, his Mumm Cordon Rouge, his role as history's best-remembered supporting player.

There is, in Savile Row, London W.1., a white Georgian town house, its ground floor windows masked with tin, its open front door revealing only sacks of builder's cement. There is, entailed with the house, a steadfast man named Neil Aspinall, and a decade-long legal wrangle over sums so vaguely huge, among so many teams of accountants and lawyers, that it, too, may one day make the record books, showing how far a simple, happy idea may be corrupted into miasmas of narrow-eyed, turgid commercial argument.

The argument, however, lacks that short, squat, turtlenecked figure which was formerly its chief ornament. Allen Klein parted from Apple Corps in 1973, with a gratuity of £3m. In 1979 a New York court sentenced him to two months imprisonment on

Income Tax changes arising from the Apple period. The judges ruled that Klein had failed to declare income from the sale of record albums which were supposed to have been given away.

There are three Beatle ex-wives, each with a cocktail cabinet shaped like an antique globe. There is a Beatle widow who, at the very end, had her portrait redrawn by an album called Double Fantasy; who is mocked and vilified no longer; who now, through an 'event' more earth-shaking than any she herself could have devised, has been accorded sympathy, credence and respect.

In Hamburg, there is a ghost-eyed woman, still as beautiful as she was in 1960, her English still sprinkled with Mersey dialect words. She works in a small bar on the city's Esplanade. To this day, people seek her out and ask the eternal question: 'Is it true about you and the Beatles? Is it true you invented the Beatle Cut?' Astrid prefers not to speak about it. She returns to the beer taps, whisking away the mugs beneath to customers at the far end of the room.

There is, in Kent, a woman who has expended her indifferent health in efforts to win recognition for the paintings of her long-dead only son. She sits near an open window, because of asthma, surrounded by the dark, wild blue and crimson carnivals on which the boy who was the fifth Beatle chose to sacrifice himself. Against the wall, constantly in her sight, stands the palette where Stu Sutcliffe mixed the last desperate pigments of his life.

The story left others dead: an uncanny number. There was Stu, and then Brian and, soon afterwards, his lawyer, David Jacobs. There was Rory Storm, the blithe, blond Liverpool Rock 'n' Roller, found dead at his bungalow, 'Stormsville', in a suicide pact with his mother. There was Mal Evans, the big, patient, inoffensive road manager, who could endure no other, easier, better-paid life; shot dead by Police through the door of a Los Angeles motel.

There is, in Pinner, Middlesex, a serious young man of 22 who holds the title 'Beatle Brain of Britain', so labyrinthine his knowledge of their music and history. His name is Mark Lewisohn. He, and millions like him in the next generation, know the Beatles only from their songs, from the books that compound the myth, and the scraps of memorabilia offered for sale at Beatle conventions, or in the salerooms of Messrs Sotheby. But it is the 'bootleg' music, filched from studio tapes down the years, which give Mark Lewisohn his most intimate access. He sits by himself in his room, listening to the Beatles play Love of the Loved at their Decca audition; listening to their chaotic New Year's Eve at the Hamburg Star-Club; listening to a newly-famous, newly-astonished and excited foursome sending a

Christmas message for 1963 to their fan club. 'A Happy Chrimble,' their voices chorus, 'and a gear New Year . . .'

There is, in Liverpool, a dignified, baby-faced man, often to be seen at The Grapes in Mathew Street, who has meticulously filed away the posters he drafted for Beatles nights at Aintree Institute and Litherland Town Hall. If such a thing as a great deejay exists, Bob Wooler is one. His voice is seldom heard these days over a microphone. But that voice, when you hear it, has the same stateliness that the wildest all-night Cavern Club thrash could not startle or discommode.

There is, also in Liverpool, a grave at the Long Lane cemetery which, on one day each year, departs from Jewish custom and displays flowers. By special arrangement with the Rabbi, a tall, quietly-spoken, grey-haired man lays a posy on the grave of Brian Epstein. For 13 years, on Brian's birthday, that is how Joe Flannery has remembered him.

And, near Bournemouth, overlooking Poole Harbour, there is a bungalow whose telephone no longer rings at crazy hours from across the Atlantic. Aunt Mimi is alone now, but for the pleasure launches and the gulls. She remembers John, as always, looking like the boy she reared, in his nice Quarry Bank uniform. He appreciated it, Mimi thinks, when he grew older and wiser. In his last months, he asked her to send him over his striped Quarry Bank tie with some other childhood mementoes—his Uncle George's photograph; a Royal Worcester dinner service which used to be displayed in the hall at Menlove Avenue.

Even by transatlantic telephone, Mimi and John could have memorable rows. There was one, over the bungalow's repainting, which ended with Mimi shouting 'Damn you, Lennon!' and slamming the receiver down.

A moment later, the telephone rang again. John's voice came anxiously from the distant hemisphere. 'You're not still cross with me, Mimi, are you?'

Postscript, 1982

'Maybe you'd like to come over and see where we were living'

One ironic consequence of John Lennon's death was to bring the other ex-Beatles as close as they had ever been to a formal reunion. Early in 1981, Paul McCartney and Ringo Starr were reported to be working together at George Martin's studio in the West Indies. A new George Harrison album was announced, featuring tracks with Paul and Ringo, and a song dedicated to John on which all three were said to have played. Both excitements quickly waned. Paul's new album, it became clear, was not to be the Beatles' reborn. And George's tribute, All Those Years Ago, proved an uninspired doodle, sung at the inappropriately cheerful tempo of a Boy Scouts' campfire chorus.

Throughout the long aftermath, Yoko remained silent. Her only public statement was an appeal that John's death should not be used as an excuse for tasteless memorabilia. That appeal was in vain. Six months afterwards, gutter press 'tribute' books and brochures still littered the newsstands. The honourable exception was *Rolling Stone*, whose editor, Jann Wenner, refused to accept one single advertisement to spoil an issue wholly in honour of his old idol and friend.

Yoko, all this time, seemed walled up beyond the archway where John had died. Her visitors were even fewer than during the five years she and he had spent in the Dakota building, buying up apartments and living their enigmatic life of 'role reversal'. Her behaviour, for so long abnormal, now seemed utterly normal. Her son Sean and her 17-year-old stepson Julian became her solace. She would emerge only to go to the recording studio or her mansion on Long Island or, sometimes in the early morning, to walk alone through Central Park.

In April 1981, I came to New York for the American publication of *Shout!* Two days after my arrival, I was asked to appear on the ABC network show *Good Morning America*, to talk about the Beatles and the impact of John Lennon's death. I said what I say in the book: that Lennon was three-quarters of the Beatles. I also remarked in passing that he was not a working class bruiser, as the myth would have it, but a middle class boy whose good upbringing and heritage of decency and honour could show through at the most unlikely moments.

When I returned to my hotel, I found a message asking me to call an unfamiliar number. 'Studio One,' said the voice that answered. In a moment, another voice said: 'Hello, this is Yoko. I saw you on *Good Morning America*. What you said about John was very nice. Maybe you'd like to come over and see where we were living.'

The following is an account of our two-hour conversation.

It is five months since the shots were fired. The Dakota Building shares in that relief which spring fleetingly gives to New York. Beside the gloomy Gothic archway, red geraniums spill out of the big iron vases. There are tourists now, as well as grief-stricken fans, lingering on West 72nd Street. Dispassionate eyes and cameras search for a glimpse of the guard, still shut futilely in his copper box ten feet from the place where Mark David Chapman stepped forward and John Lennon fell.

Under the arch, it becomes eerily like some shipping or insurance office from the Liverpool of John's early childhood. Narrow steps lead through old-fashioned double doors into a wood-panelled vestibule with a polished counter. Behind the counter, another guard watches over his console of TV monitors and automatic locks. A kick-lock gives access to further stairs, a passage twisting to the door marked 'Studio One.'

Inside, two young men loll over desks in a cluttered, high-ceilinged room. One of them withdraws for a moment, then returns. 'Go right in,' he says. 'Yoko's ready.'

Yoko works alone behind a gold-inlaid desk in an office filled with small trees, white sofas and pastel-coloured art deco lamps. Her clothes are black, as they always have been: sleek trousers, high-heeled boots, an undone shirt and tie. Her hair, drawn back to a single tied mass, reveals a smile that few outside these walls have seen. The broad, taut cheekbones, the fierce, dark eyebrows, have so rarely seemed capable of smiling. Yet she does so often, even when talking about the day after John's murder:

'I couldn't eat anything. Then all I wanted to eat was chocolate. I kept remembering how much John loved chocolate. When I would go out, I'd bring him a little chocolate something home, and he enjoyed it so much. Now it was all I wanted to eat. Elton [John] was so sweet—he sent me a big chocolate cake. My diet went crazy for about a month afterwards—nothing but chocolate and mushrooms.

'A few days before it happened, I remember looking at John. And he looked so good, so beautiful. I said to him, "Hey, you're even better looking than when you were a Beatle!"

'He always wanted so much to be thin, but he never really was. Even when he was a Beatle, there was this little pot belly under the Beatle jacket. When we split up and then got back together in '74, he said he *really* wanted to lose weight. I said, "Okay, how much do you want to lose—20lb?" And he did it. His body had gotten to be just the way he always wanted.

'And he was so happy. Both of us were. A few days before it happened, I remember thinking, "This is so good. I wonder if things can go on being as good as this".'

It was a feeling almost as strange as bereavement for Yoko to realise that people do not hate her any more. For the hatred had seemed as durable as the Beatles' own legend. It followed her even after John and she escaped from London to New York; even after their artistic partnership had ceased to puzzle and exasperate the world. No forgiveness appeared possible for the Japanese woman who sundered the Beatles' magic entity, luring John away from lovableness into avant-garde aggression, from pop music into mystifying 'performance art' escapades—'bed-ins' and 'bagism.' The rumours multiply even now about Yoko's alleged pursuit of John: how she intruded on the Beatles in their secret recording sessions, how she once even followed John into the men's lavatory.

'People said that I ran after him, pursued him. What really happened is, neither of us went after the other. We were both too scared. Each of us was married at the time. John was terrified to make any move because of the Beatle thing. After we first met at that gallery [The Indica, where Yoko had an exhibition in 1966], we were circling around one another for about two years. I wouldn't make a move. I never did. I had left London for Paris and John was in India. At that point, I thought we would probably never get started.

'The one time he did try to make a move, it was so sudden, so clumsy, I just rejected it. John had invited me to the record studios. He suddenly said, "You look tired. Would you like to rest?" I thought he was taking me to another room, but instead we went off to this flat—I think it belonged to Neil, the road manager. When we got there Neil started to fold this sofa down into a bed. Maybe John thought we were two adults: we didn't have to pretend. But it seemed so crude, I rejected it. I slept on the divan, I think, and John went into another room.

'I *never* pursued him. If I had, I would have got nowhere. After we started living together, it was John who wanted me there all the time. *He* made me go into the men's room with him. He was scared that if I stayed out in the studio with a lot of other men, I might run off with one of them.

'Jealous! My God! He wrote a song, Jealous Guy, that should have told people how jealous he was. After we were together, he made me write out a list of all the men I'd slept with before we met. I started to do it quite casually—then I realised how serious it was to John. He didn't even like me knowing the Japanese language because that was a part of my mind that didn't belong to him. After a while, I couldn't even read any books or papers in Japanese.

'I used to say to him, "I think you're a closet fag, you know." Because, when we started to live together, John would say to me, "Do you know why I like you? Because you look like a bloke in drag. You're like a mate."

'He was a genius, but he had this huge inferiority complex. He was brilliant as an artist, but he didn't think he was capable of it. Like when he asked me to do his lithographs—he was just too scared to get started on the drawings. We both took mescalin and then he tried. I told him, "That's brilliant, it's beautiful." John said, "But it's only a circle, like a child would do." I said, "Maybe it's childish, but it is still beautiful."

'It was the same when he was asked to write a sketch in the Oh! Calcutta! show. "What am I going to write?" he kept saying. I said, "Write that thing you told me about when you were a boy, and you used to masturbate." He and his friends all used to masturbate together, shouting out the names of film actresses —and then suddenly John or one of them would shout "Frank Sinatra." So he made that the sketch, and it was marvellous.'

The decision to separate in 1973, was Yoko's. She had given John his escape route from Beatledom, but, in the process, had sacrificed all her own ambitions and identity as an artist. She had two husbands before John: she was used to marriages that ended. So John left New York for California and the confused, drunken year which he later described as his 'lost weekend.'

'He came to New York a few times and asked me to go back to him. I wouldn't. I was going out with other people—several others. One of these young guys persuaded me to go to that big concert of Elton's—and suddenly John walked out on to the stage. I didn't know he was going to be there. The audience gave him a terrific reception. But when he bowed, it was too quickly and too many times. And suddenly I thought, "He looks so lonely up there."

'The young guy I was with wanted to go backstage afterwards. I didn't want to, but I said "Okay." And John, of course, was there with a young chick. He said, "Oh, I'm so *happy* to see you." We sat there, talking, holding hands. His young chick and my young guy were still standing there, getting more and more uptight.

'After that, John asked me out. We went to an art show together. We started dating all over again.'

*

They settled down for good, so it seemed, in the strange, old Manhattan apartment building, decorated with dark turrets and cast iron sea serpents, where John had been gradually buying up leases. Yoko got his weight down: he even stopped smoking his eternal Gauloises for the sake of the baby they both wanted. New York, unlike London, left them alone. They bought houses in Florida and Long Island, and prize Holstein cattle for their Dream Street farms. 'All of it was for our old age,' Yoko says, with a wry smile. 'And eating the right foods to keep ourselves healthy. It's so ironic. Since December I've been telling Sean (their son), "Eat anything you want. It doesn't matter." '

On the seventh floor, a guard sits, nursing a raincoat, outside the apartment where John and Yoko spent their five years of role reversal. Opposite is a second apartment, equally large, which they used only for storage. Two smaller ones, lower in the building, were bought by John for specialised uses, like storing and cataloguing their videotape collection.

We entered the principal apartment. A tiny hall, with a single lamp burning in it, leads to the vista of a dozen white rooms and skyscrapers beyond, set down at random among the Central Park treetops. Far beneath, near the place now renamed Strawberry Fields, a glint comes up from mirrors heliographing messages of sympathy.

It was in a small side room that John spent his long retreat, 'watching the trees change colour.' The room is empty now, but for cardboard cartons and the huge TV set he had specially shipped from Japan. In the passage is a painting he did, aged 11, at Dovedale primary School. There are pictures of Julian, his elder son, of Sean, and Yoko's daughter, Kyoko. His clothes still hang in the corner dressing room: revolving boutique-racks crowded with epochs of brief fashion and their attendant cloaks, caps, hats and shoes. Yoko does not use the dressing room any more.

There is a room devoted to Egyptian art, including a full-size mummy in a case. It averts its golden eyes from the mantle of schoolcaps and straw boaters and the tubular steel sculpture spread on the carpet. Nearby, a thin Perspex column supports four silver spoons. The inscription: 'Three spoons, YO 1967.' What attracted John to Yoko in the first place was the humour in her work—perhaps it was there all along.

The room where Yoko now sleeps is modest, quiet and formal. Along the hall, a seamstress sits bent over her work. Sean, the second baby to be born with that uncanny Lennon face, is away at the Long Island house. Three pedigree cats roam at will down the immense but comfortable kitchen. Next door in the playroom, John and Yoko are painted on the wall as Superman and Superwoman, carrying Sean with them up into the sky.

For three months after John's death, apart from dignified messages to his fans, Yoko remained silent. She then decided to release her song Walking On Thin Ice, which John had been helping her to record on the day of his death. Her voice, once so outlandish, sounds normal by today's standards. With the record came a video sequence of scenes from John's last month—his 40th birthday party, his view from the Dakota, his face and Yoko's in the closeness of making love. The same unclothed frankness that disgusted the world on their Two Virgins album sleeve, more than ten years ago, now seems perfectly natural.

Helped by Phil Spector, the American record producer whom John idolised, Yoko is at work on a full solo album, driving herself and those around her to finish it in a fraction of the usual time. Meanwhile, adulation continues for Double Fantasy, the shared album they had just released last December. Ironically, John's most commercially successful music since the Beatles will probably be Starting Over, Woman, and other calm, simple elegies to his life with Yoko.

Contact with the ex-Beatles is rare. They once called her contemptuously 'Flavour of the Month.' Yoko refers to them drily as 'the in-laws.' After John's death, only Ringo Starr flew to New York to see her. Paul McCartney, John's partner in song-writing history, provokes a bleak and bitter look. 'John said that no one ever hurt him the way Paul hurt him. But it's in the past. It's gone.'

She is talking again in the long, dim salon with its trees and soft lamps and huge, solitary inlaid desk. For Yoko Ono Lennon, as for all who suffer loss, small, silly details give passing comfort. 'He would never swear, you know. At least, not in front of Sean. And if I let out a word, he'd clear his throat and say "Oh oh —Mother's getting agitated." '

'He would never have gone back to England. But he still loved England—that's not a paradox. On Sunday nights we would always watch the TV dramas from England, like "Rebecca."

'John used to say he'd had two great partnerships—one with Paul McCartney, the other with Yoko Ono. "And I discovered both of them," he used to say. "That isn't bad going, is it?" '

Author's Note

I would like to acknowledge the invaluable help given to me during the preparation of this book by the four ex-Beatles, John Lennon, Paul McCartney, George Harrison and Ringo Starr. Unfortunately I cannot do so. Though I have interviewed all four several times since 1965, and though I had a unique opportunity to observe them at their breaking-point in 1969–70, none would agree to a formal interview during the two years I spent researching *Shout!* Up to December 1980, I still hoped John Lennon would see me in the burst of accessibility that followed his Double Fantasy album. That hope, with many others, was dashed by an early morning telephone call on Tuesday, 9 December.

I do not think any of them disapproved of my project. I do not think they even knew about it. Part of the Beatles' legacy to Rock music is the intricate court and protocol system which nowadays surrounds every performer. In each ex-Beatle's case, the web of ministers and secretaries is almost Byzantine. After several months' futile application via John's First Counsellor or Paul's Permanent Under-Secretary, I realised I had a choice. I could either spend two years in waiting to see the ex-Beatles, or else retrace their career, as I have done, using the methods of the investigative reporter, historian and critic.

In any case, it had become clear that, just as the Beatles' legend grew up despite interminable interviews with them, so the true story must seek a perspective far wider than theirs. Until late in their careers, the Beatles simply had no idea what was happening to them. They saw only each other and the dressing-room or hotel suite in which they were penned. They remained blissfully unaware of much of the saga I began to unearth—the Seltaeb merchandising fiasco, say, or Brian Epstein's tormented double life. And, in later years, they did not want to know. The effect on each—even on John—was a kind of shell shock; a shrug or offhand phrase would condense or disregard the whole fantastic era. When I hear Paul McCartney maintain, as he did recently to *Rolling Stone*, that he and Pete Best were deported from Hamburg for 'burning a condom', or that the 1964 assault on America was 'all pre-planned', I know the Beatles were as much victims of the Beatle myth as anyone.

The text will show how many people aided my researches, in London, Liverpool, New York and Los Angeles. I thank them all for their patience, hospitality and readiness to trust me with valuable photographs, documents and souvenirs. I am especially indebted to Mrs. Queenie Epstein and Clive Epstein; to Joe Flannery, Mark Lewisohn, Millie Sutcliffe, Derek Taylor, Allan Williams and Bob Wooler; to Harold Evans, Editor of *The Sunday Times*; to John Fielding for vital information on the Apple period; to Alison Jeffery, who typed the manuscript; to Michael Sissons and Pat Kavanagh of A. D. Peters & Co. for constant encouragement; to Helen Stinson for her picture research and for giving me inspiration.

PHILIP NORMAN
London 1980

ALL ABOUT ELVIS

by Fred L. Worth and Steve D. Tamerius.

You may already know the colour of his eyes, where he was born, and his first record. But there are thousands of things about Elvis that hardly anyone knows. Now they've all been gathered into one book —the source book for Elvis Fans everywhere. DO YOU KNOW: Elvis's original middle name. Where Elvis bought his first guitar. Also included are entries for every record Elvis ever made, complete listings of all his movies, concert tour schedules, television appearances and a bibliography of books about Elvis.

0 553 14129 5 £1.95

'H' AUTOBIOGRAPHY OF A CHILD PROSTITUTE AND HEROIN ADDICT.

by Christiane F.

The harrowing tragic expose of young lives shattered. The most shocking account of young people caught up in the dark world of drug, abuse since GO ASK ALICE (also available from Corgi Books)

NOW FILMED AS CHRISTIANE F.

0 552 11899 0

GO ASK ALICE

by Anonymous

Alice is fifteen, white, middle-class. She diets. She dates. She gets decent grades. She thinks someday she'd like to get married and raise a family.

On July 9, Alice is turned on to acid. She digs it. Acid makes the world a better place. So do all the other ups. They open up the world of sex. They make Alice feel free. Sometimes Alice worries about taking drugs. She thinks maybe she shouldn't. But, she figures life is more bearable with drugs than without.

Alice's parents don't know what's happening. They notice changes. They have no idea she's on drugs. They cannot help her.

The difference between Alice and a lot of other kids on drugs is that Alice kept a diary.

0 552 09332 7 £1.25

HOVEL IN THE HILLS

by Elizabeth West

This is the unsentimental, amusing, and absorbing account of the 'simple life' as practised by Alan and Elizabeth West in their primitive cottage in rural Wales. The Wests—she is a typist, he an engineer—moved from Bristol to North Wales in 1965, determined to leave the rat race for good. But the daunting task of converting a semi-derelict farmhouse and turning the unproductive soil into a viable self-sufficient unit was to prove a full-time job. The author describes the very individual and resourceful ways she and her husband tackled the problems which faced them—from slating the roof, curing a smoking chimney and generating their own electricity, growing a wonderful variety of fruit, herbs and vegetables on impossible soil. With a preface by John Seymour, author of "The Complete Book of Self-Sufficiency", "Hovel in the Hills" is a heartwarming and salutary tale which will either leave you yearning for a chance to get away from it all or convince you that the comfortable security of the nine-to-five is not such a bad thing.

0 552 10907 X 95p